How to Use This Book

Look for the following conventions in this book:

- Code lines, statements, functions, operators, and other special computer terms you should type in appear in monospace font.

- Menu commands are shown as File | Open. This means that you pull down the File menu and select the Open command.

- When a line of code is too long to fit on one line of this book, it is broken at a convenient place, and the code continuation character (➡) appears at the beginning of the next line.

- An underscore at the end of a code line is VBA's line continuation character, and it's used to spread a single VBA statement over multiple lines. This is handy if you have a lengthy statement that would otherwise extend past the right side of the window. When you use the line-continuation character, make sure you insert a space before the underscore.

- Note boxes contain pertinent comments that the author feels should be highlighted. These are areas where the author can add value to basic information about the product or procedure. Here's an example:

NOTE

To avoid confusing variables with the names of objects, properties, or methods, many macro programmers begin their variable names with a lowercase letter.

- Tips highlight information the author has gained over time and hopes will help you in your work with Office. Here's an example of a tip:

TIP

If you use MIME encoding, set the character option to US ASCII. The US ASCII character set eliminates some conversion quirks that happen when MIME translates messages from the default Windows character set.

- Cautions let you know that something is very important to observe or do. Learn from others' experience or mistakes! Here's an example:

CAUTION

The amazing features and flexibility of Exchange come at a price, of course: The application is quite resource intensive. You must have at least 8MB of RAM and at least 20MB of free space on the drive that Windows uses to create its dynamic swap file.

Microsoft Office

UNLEASHED

Microsoft Office

UNLEASHED

Sue Charlesworth,

Paul McFedries, et al

SAMS
PUBLISHING

201 West 103rd Street
Indianapolis, IN 46290

To John, for your support, in so many ways.
To David, for bravely accepting that "Mom's working," more times than you liked.
To Guiness, for uncomplainingly missing so many training sessions.
—Sue Charlesworth

Copyright © 1996 by Sams Publishing

International Standard Book Number: 0-672-30819-3

Library of Congress Catalog Card Number: 95-74777

99 98 97 96   4 3 2

Interpretation of the printing code: the rightmost double-digit number is the year of the book's printing; the rightmost single-digit, the number of the book's printing. For example, a printing code of 96-1 shows that the first printing of the book occurred in 1996.

Composed in AGaramond and MCPdigital by Macmillan Computer Publishing

Printed in the United States of America

Trademarks

Publisher and President	*Richard K. Swadley*
Acquisitions Manager	*Greg Wiegand*
Development Manager	*Dean Miller*
Managing Editor	*Cindy Morrow*
Marketing Manager	*Gregg Bushyeager*

Acquisitions Editor
Rosemarie Graham

Development Editor
Sharon Cox

Software Development Specialist
Steve Straiger

Production Editor
Kitty Wilson

Copy Editors
Jill Bond, Kimberly K. Hannel, Bart Reed, Tonya Simpson

Technical Reviewers
Robert Bogue, Chris Caposella, Thomas Hayes, Karen Jaskolka, Angela Murdock, Jan Norman

Editorial Coordinator
Bill Whitmer

Technical Edit Coordinator
Lynette Quinn

Formatter
Frank Sinclair

Editorial Assistants
Sharon Cox, Andi Richter, Rhonda Tinch-Mize

Cover Designer
Tim Amrhein

Book Designer
Alyssa Yesh

Production Team Supervisor
Brad Chinn

Production
Carol Bowers, Georgiana Briggs, Michael Brumitt, Charlotte Clapp, Michael Dietsch, Jason Hand, Ayanna Lacey, Steph Mineart, Casey Price, Erich Richter, Bobbi Satterfield, Laura A. Smith, Josette Starks, Andy Stone, Susan Van Ness, Colleen Williams

Indexer
Jennifer Eberhardt

Overview

Contents

Part III The Common Office

Part V   The Versatility of Excel

Part VI The Organizaton of Access

Part VIII Making Time with Schedule+

Part X Output

Acknowledgments

I'd like to thank and acknowledge the folks at Sams who made this book possible for me: Rosemarie Graham, acquisitions editor, for taking me on faith; Sharon Cox, development editor, for all her night and weekend work, and for putting up with authors (me!) who take it into their heads to add sections, unauthorized, to chapters; Kitty Wilson, production editor; and especially, Lynette Quinn, technical edit coordinator, who got me started on all this in the first place. Thanks for opening up a whole new world for me.

—Sue Charlesworth

About the Authors

Sue Charlesworth has 12 years of experience in PC software development, holding various roles—from tester to programmer to team leader responsible for developing quality assurance standards and high-performance test teams. Her special skills are communicating and organizing small projects. Using her knowledge of software development and many tools such as Microsoft Office, she has helped complete many projects successfully, both in the United States and in the United Kingdom. She has a master's degree in international management and enjoys meeting people and experiencing new places and old cultures. Over the years, she has found that her most enjoyable work involves writing and helping others as a knowledge resource. This has led to recent work involving teaching, technical editing, technical writing, and, most recently, HTML Web page development. She constantly seeks new opportunities to use her knowledge and skills to help others. She can be reached at `sncharle@usa.net` and on CompuServe at 70372,3662.

Paul McFedries runs his own computer consulting firm, specializing in spreadsheets and database applications. He also is a freelance writer who has authored or coauthored more than 20 books for Sams Publishing as well as other publishers. His books for Sams include *Excel Unleashed, Navigating the Internet, Third Edition*, and *DOS for the Guru Wanna-Be*. He can be reached via e-mail at `paulmcf@hookup.net`.

Ryan Edward Bailey is a Microsoft certified trainer based in Nashville, Tennessee, and a developer of Access applications for small businesses. In addition to developing customized business solutions, he keeps himself actively involved as a contract instructor for the Athena Computer Learning Center in Nashville, where he teaches the Microsoft Access Certification courses. He has found that the rapid application development in Access has made custom software affordable for the small business owner, and he is focusing on this area. Ryan entered the computer profession from a different door than most. The five years of professional juggling and three years as a video producer for JTR Productions gave him the resources to experiment with PCs and the valuable people skills needed for teaching. Currently, Ryan is developing applications full time, along with launching JTR Productions into an Internet project. Because his initials are R.E.B., he is called Rebel by his friends. When not mentally absorbed in Access, constructing multimedia programs, or editing digital video, Rebel can be found juggling in Centennial Park, windsurfing on Percy Preist Lake, or dreaming of the ultimate consulting job near a great windsurfing site. Rebel can be found at `rebelnet@aol.com` or `http://www.jtr.com/rebelnet.html`.

Ricardo Birmele is a widely published author of computer books. Their subjects range from desktop publishing to programming languages to applications. His software and hardware review articles have appeared in such magazines as *BYTE, PC,* and *PC World.* Birmele has also edited a number of computer books on subjects as diverse as multimedia and database programming to simple applications. Birmele divides his free time among his wife and two sons, his church, where he teaches teenagers their Sabbath School lessons, and the U.S. Coast Guard Auxiliary, where he is an aviator and the 13th District Information Systems Officer.

Kevin Chestnut is director of advanced products and technology at Active Voice Corporation, a leading provider of PC-based voice messaging and voice processing systems worldwide. In his work at Active Voice, Kevin is responsible for predicting and understanding future trends in telecommunications and applying emerging technology to potential new products. When he is not furiously busy trying to fathom the future or harness vaporware, Kevin spends his free time writing children's books.

Craig Eddy currently resides in Richmond, Virginia, with his wife Susan and two children. Craig holds a B.S. in electrical engineering from Virginia Tech and is a devoted Hokie football and basketball fan. He is currently employed by Pipestream Technologies, Inc., as senior developer for ContactBuilder, a customer information management and sales force automation tool that runs in either a client/server or desktop environment. Craig has been involved in computer programming for more than 15 years and has concentrated on Visual Basic, Microsoft Access, and SQL Server applications for the past 3 years. When not sitting at a computer desk, Craig is involved in private business development, volunteer work, and spending time on the Outer Banks of North Carolina.

Dwayne R. Gifford (`a-dwayg@microsoft.com`) is presently employed by Excell Data Corporation as a systems analyst for Microsoft. He worked for Labatt Breweries of Canada after graduating from Fanshawe College. He could not be where he is today if it were not for his family, especially his wife, Iris, and children, Kevin, Michelle, and Jason.

Ewan Grantham has been involved with microcomputers since the days of the Apple II and the TRS-80. He now runs an independent consulting firm that specializes in the design and creation of electronic documentation and multimedia presentations. In addition to his programming and writing, he teaches classes on related subjects and publishes an "almost monthly" electronic magazine, *RADIUS*. Ewan can be reached on CompuServe at 74123,2232.

Tom Hayes is a graduate of Purdue University and received his MBA in marketing from Indiana University. For the past five years, he has provided marketing solutions to national clients as the owner and general manager of Fax Daily, an Indianapolis-based fax publishing company. While not at work, Tom enjoys golf, ultimate Frisbee, and spending time with his wife, Michelle, and their weimaraner, Simon.

Matt Kinney is a software engineer with Excell Data Corporation, a consulting and application development company in Bellevue, Washington. He has a B.S. in computer science from Louisiana State University in Shreveport. Matt has been programming computers since 1978, when he started on the original Commodore PET, and specializes in online application development and marketing. Before starting with Excell, Matt developed successful applications on Prodigy, AOL, CompuServe, GEnie, and the Internet.

Carmen Knowles has been working with computers for more than ten years. Her interest in computers developed further into how to "break" the programs, and the machine that went with it: an ideal situation for testing both the programs and the machines. A university graduate in sciences, now pursuing postgraduate studies, her main interest is in the computer world. She is a member of ClubWin, a select group of Windows user support volunteers that is active in various online services. Carmen is interested in helping small businesses and institutions to computerize and run their equipment at a minimum cost.

David Medinets has been programming since 1980, when he started with a Radio Shack Model 1. He still fondly remembers the days when he could cross-wire the keyboard to create funny-looking characters on the display. Since those days, he has spent time debugging emacs on UNIX machines, working on VAXen, and messing around with DOS microcomputers. David works at Prudential Insurance in Roseland, New Jersey, and can be reached at `medined@planet.net`.

Jude G. Mullaney graduated from Belmont Abbey College with a degree in business administration in 1988. She entered the computer industry in 1989, holding positions in administration, hardware and software technical support, sales, and training. Her training includes NCR, AT&T, IBM, and Leading Edge. Her software training includes Microsoft products such as Windows, Windows for Workgroups, Windows NT, Access 1.1 and 2.0, Word, Excel, Project, PowerPoint, Publisher, Mail and Schedule +, as well as Lotus Ami Pro, CorelDRAW, and GeoWorks Ensemble. In 1994 she founded VisualAccess Corporation. VisualAccess is a Microsoft Solutions Provider in the business of providing a service to define the software needs of a company and develop that software for future technologies. Its clients include companies such as NationsBank, WIX Corporation, First Union National Bank, and Michelin North America, Inc. Jude currently sits on the Charlotte Chamber of Commerce's Information Technologies Council. She was also an integral part of their annual Blue Diamond Awards. She also sits on the Advisory Board of the Academy of Electronic Technology for the Charlotte Mecklenburg school system. Jude has been the newsletter editor for the Clarion User Group in Charlotte since 1989. She is currently the vice president and newsletter editor for both the Charlotte Area Access Users' Group and Windows Users' Group in Charlotte. Jude also contributed to *Access Unleashed* from Sams Publishing as well as three other books on Microsoft Office and Access for other publishers.

Daniel B. Silkworth is a principal consultant with A. D. E X P E R T S. Mr. Silkworth has recently been involved in the specification and development of Microsoft Office–based solutions for businesses. These applications have included electronic performance support systems, proposal planning knowledge bases, multimedia-retail kiosks, business infrastructure automation, and graphical information collection systems. Mr. Silkworth contributed two prototype applications and a white paper to Microsoft's international satellite broadcast DevCast 95. Mr. Silkworth previously held the position of methodologist and model administrator for all ADW products at KnowledgeWare, Inc. He was responsible for establishing data model administration functions and developing specifications for a multiuser CASE repository product. With more than 15 years of experience in the industry, Mr. Silkworth has a wealth of experience in developing and applying technology for business. He can be reached via CompuServe at 74167,3564.

Dave Speedie has been a computer support analyst for the past $2^1/2$ years. He is currently working for Labatt Breweries of Canada, Information Technology, Helpdesk. There he is also a trainer who teaches PC fundamentals and advanced Word courses. Dave can be reached via the Internet at `dave.speedie@labatt.com`.

Jeff Steinmetz is currently a consultant with Graphical Technologies Corporation, a Microsoft Solutions Provider. He also heads up the Visual C++ users' group in Minneapolis, Minnesota. This year he became a Microsoft Certified Product Specialist, and has been providing consulting for client/server applications and Win32-based development. He can be reached via e-mail at `JeffSteinmetz@msn.com`, or by web browser at `http://www.umn.edu/nlhome/g259/stein060`.

Jim Townsend is president of Information Strategies, a Microsoft Solutions Provider in Washington, D.C., and is certified in Microsoft Access. He specializes in analysis, systems integration, custom database design and implementation, and training. Jim has written more than 40 books and articles, including *Introduction to Databases* (Que) and *Using Paradox for Windows* (Que), and is a contributor to computer journals including *Data Based Advisor, Smart Access, The Quick Answer,* and *Dialogue.*

Ted Williamson is a senior solutions architect with Redmond Technology Partners. Although new to the authoring thing, Ted has extensive experience in client/server application development and his opinion is highly regarded, even if only in his own mind. While work absorbs his every waking hour, he still finds time to work on his favorite pastime, computer games. Ted lives with his author/artist wife, Kerri, and their four children just outside of Seattle, Washington.

Introduction

Microsoft Office brings together full-featured programs and seamlessly integrates them to allow them to do more so you can do more. Quite simply, it gives you easy access to powerful, user-friendly tools that enable you to focus on getting your job done. This integration is provided via the ability to combine documents from the myriad of Office applications into one "virtual document." This level of integration and ease of use is unparalleled in the office suite environment.

Microsoft Office stands out from the rest of the players in the office suite crowd because of its high level of integration among the applications that make up the suite. Getting the job done is the focus of Microsoft Office, and it's a focus that is the most important for you, the user.

The Knowledge to Maximize Your Productivity

Microsoft Office Unleashed takes you beyond what the individual programs in the suite do to accomplish tasks that can be achieved only within an integrated office suite. This book offers the reader some insight into the Microsoft strategy regarding the integrated suite concepts and shows you how to use the combined products more effectively to increase your daily productivity. Each section in the book shows you how to use the individual product, such as Word, Excel, or Access, and then goes into advanced features and how to integrate a particular product with others in the suite.

This book teaches you how to do the following:

- Understand suite integration
- Use features new to Office
- Combine Word, Access, Excel, and other documents with the Office Binder application
- Use the basics of all the individual products: Word, Excel, Access, PowerPoint, Schedule+, and Exchange
- Integrate applications with OLE
- Use features common to Office: graph tools, drawing tools, and the Office toolbox
- Output documents by printing, mailing, and faxing
- Work in a networked environment
- Communicate through the Internet and with Exchange
- Program with Visual Basic for Applications

Microsoft Office Unleashed provides real-world experience drawn from the authors' own experiences in consulting and developing solutions for their work and clients. *Microsoft Office Unleashed* shows you how to truly unleash the power behind the suite.

Who Should Read This Book?

This book is written for users who have used one or two Microsoft products, such as Word and Excel, in the past and are now using Office to fill all their business or personal needs. The authors do not do a lot of handholding, walking you step by step through each detail. They assume that you are familiar with the basic concepts and want to learn the feature new to Office 95 and then move beyond the basics into intermediate and advanced topics. The authors show you how to use each product efficiently and then teach you how to integrate the products to take full advantage of the Office suite.

IN THIS PART

Introduction

PART

I

An Application Suite

1

*by Matt Kinney
and
Ewan
Grantham*

IN THIS CHAPTER

Microsoft Office brings together full-featured programs and seamlessly integrates them to allow them to do more. Quite simply, it gives you easy access to powerful, user-friendly tools that allow you to focus on getting your job done. This integration is provided via the ability to combine documents from the myriad of Office applications into one "virtual document." This level of integration and ease of use is unparalleled in the office suite environment.

Microsoft Office stands out from the rest of the players in the office suite crowd because of its high level of integration among the applications that make up the suite. The biggest leap forward in Office for Windows 95 is the Office Binder, which enables you to keep tabs on all your Office documents for a particular project. Common interfaces, the ability to link data from one application into another, and shared tools all make the high level of integration in Office for Windows 95 possible. Also, because Office for Windows 95 takes full advantage of Windows 95, Microsoft's newest personal operating system, you can use shortcuts, long filenames, and the taskbar to quickly move between Office applications. Getting the job done is the focus of Microsoft Office, and it's a focus that is the most important for you, the user.

Microsoft Office Unleashed has only one purpose as well—to help you learn how to use all the features of Microsoft Office so you can do your job. The book is comprised of a number of sections that focus on building a single document that uses various features of Microsoft Office. It is through this building that you will become better equipped to use Microsoft Office so that you have the freedom to focus on your job.

What's New

While Office has always been an integrated suite of tools working toward a common goal, Microsoft Office 95 has taken that approach even further. Through the increased use of technologies such as OLE (object linking and embedding), ODBC (open database connectivity), and DDE (dynamic data exchange), Office 95 has been enhanced to make it easier than ever to do your work only once.

Some of these changes include the following:

■ This is the next generation of IntelliSense technology, which gives you unprecedented control over Microsoft Office. It makes complex tasks easy and everyday, mundane tasks automatic. It includes AutoCorrect, which corrects your misspellings automatically, the Answer Wizard, which gathers knowledge for you based on your question, and other application-specific enhancements.

■ OfficeLinks is the heart of the integration in Microsoft Office. It enables you to join various file types in a user-friendly project file via the Office Binder. It also has an integrated shortcut bar, as well as enhanced file-locating system and template capabilities.

■ It is optimized for 32-bit performance in Windows NT and Windows 95. This makes the response of the various tools snappier and makes the entire system more robust.

These are only the tip of the iceberg that enables you to access the applications in Microsoft Office. When you look at how the Office series has evolved since it was introduced in 1988, you can see that these changes have all worked to further the integration of the various pieces of Office into an integrated system. This evolution has continued in Microsoft Office for Windows 95 by giving you access to the full capability of the next generation in integrated tools.

Being integrated is the name of the game when it comes to boosting personal and corporate productivity. The less time you spend trying to figure out how to use your applications, the more time you have to do something with them. In Office 95, more than ever, the basic menus and features are common across the different parts. Figure 1.1 shows how similar they have become with a screen shot of the four main menus.

FIGURE 1.1.

The four main menus are more similar than ever in Office 95.

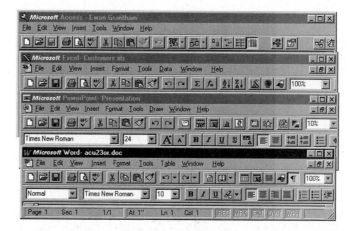

One of the major points Microsoft has been emphasizing about Office 95 is that many of the common features of the programs (such as the File Open dialog box and the spell checker) are now actually shared code. This not only ensures a consistent interface such as similar toolbars and menus, but it also speeds up switching between the programs in the suite since part of the code is already loaded when the first program starts. In addition to the File Open dialog box and spell checker, the Answer Wizard, AutoCorrect, File Starter, Fast Find, Print, and Save functions are part of the shared code in Office 95.

Not only is there code being shared, but there are a number of shared components that ensure that special functions are accomplished in the same way every time. The interface for these components is also open so that you can add third-party utilities that are compatible with the entire suite. Some of these are available in earlier versions of Office and have been updated, and others (such as DataMap) are new to Office 95. The shared components include the following:

■ Clip Art Gallery—Allows you to view all the available Office 95 clip art from a single location. With more than 1000 images included, having a central point to view thumbnail stamps of the images makes finding the right one much easier. Clip Art Gallery also allows you to add your own images.

■ DataMap—Gives you the ability to use geographic location as part of your data analysis. An example is shown in Figure 1.2.

FIGURE 1.2.

A simple map of the United States by population, generated using the DataMap tool from Excel.

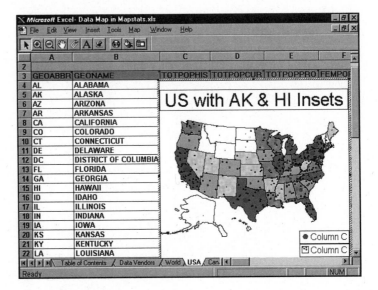

■ Equation Editor—Makes it easy to add fractions, exponents, and other mathematic elements to any Office 95 application.

■ Graph—For the creation, editing, and manipulation of graphs.

■ Imager—Designed to make it easier to import, edit, and manipulate electronic images. It also provides TWAIN, a universal scanning protocol, support to make scanning images into Office 95 easier.

■ Query—Central utility for getting information from a database for use within your Office 95 document or project. If there is an ODBC driver for something, Query can read data from that datasource and bring it in. ODBC is Microsoft's open database connectivity standard, which defines a manner in which to communicate with a database.

■ WordArt—A tool for creating effects using text. You can create different alignments or do 3-D extrusions (make text appear to have depth) and create a number of other effects.

■ Answer Wizard—Allows you to ask in plain language about the features of an application. Answer Wizard will come up with three categories of help: How Do I, Tell Me About, and a Programming and Language Reference category.

Integration is also important to help people work together. Another of the new features in Office for Windows 95 is the Office Binder. The Binder is designed to help you organize documents together into logical groups, even if the documents come from several different Office programs. This also makes it easier to share a project with a co-worker since you can copy the binder for the project and know that he or she will get all the necessary parts. You can even share the binder with your office by putting it in a network location, allowing several people to access and contribute to the project. Not only can you store several different types of documents, but the documents can have different page orientations (in other words, some of the documents can be in landscape while others are in portrait format). Figure 1.3 shows an example of using the Binder for keeping related customer information together.

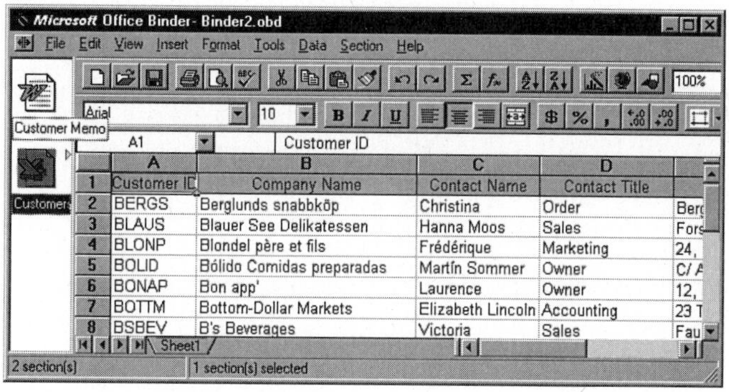

FIGURE 1.3.

A binder with some related customer data from Word and Excel.

Windows 95 and Office 95 Integration

Not only is Office 95 more integrated internally, but it has also been integrated with Windows 95 to take advantage of, and build on, new features of the operating system.

A major component of Office 95 is the new Windows 95–compliant interface. Because this is such a major part of Office 95, it would be wise to examine a few key features of Windows 95 to better understand all the benefits it provides to the Office 95 user. The most immediate changes you will notice are the absence of the Program Manager and an appearance similar to Macintosh and OS/2, which provides a very friendly user interface. One of the main methods of interaction with the operating system is the taskbar, which contains the Start button, where many of your Windows 95 activities begin. (See Figure 1.4.) The Start button reveals a set of cascading menus whose selections represent the programs previously available in program groups. This simple set of menus completely replaces the Program Manager and is very intuitive from the start.

FIGURE 1.4.

The Windows 95 desktop.

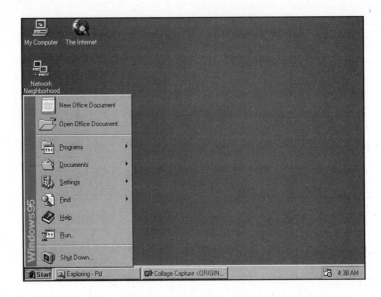

A major change in Windows 95 is the change from the directory to the folder setup. Windows 95 does not use directories; it uses folders. Folders are containers that can hold other folders, files, or applications. Folders can be displayed in different views—large icons, small icons, details, or a list—depending on which option you select. The folder metaphor is also used to represent your system. After installation of Windows 95, three folders are used to represent your system: My Computer, Network Neighborhood, and Microsoft Exchange (if you install it). These folders not only appear on your desktop, but within Explorer, which is Windows 95's replacement for File Manager. You can explore these folders just as you would any other folder. These folders can contain not only other folders, files, and applications, but also represent the devices available on your system, such as CD-ROM drives. The My Computer folder represents all the devices and files that are on your local system. This includes network drives that you have connected to, as well as the Control Panel, Printers folder, and Dial Up Networking if you have it installed. The Network Neighborhood folder includes all of the computers and devices that you can "see" on the network you are connected to, including workgroups and individual computers. Therefore, working with any of the available resources on your computer is a matter of manipulating folders and the icons they contain.

Another way Windows 95 distances itself from the directory concept is through the use of shortcuts. Shortcuts are represented by specialized icons that serve as aliases or shortcuts to files and applications. Shortcuts provide a way to build links to folders, applications, files, and documents. For example, you could create a shortcut to your Office 95 document and have it directly on your desktop, thus enabling you to click the shortcut icon and have the proper Office 95 application automatically start and load your document. The benefit of this approach is that you no longer have to think about which application to open, but only which documents you need to use. Windows 95 takes care of the details of managing the application links to the documents for you.

As you explore further, you will find that the use of the mouse has also changed. You will be double-clicking much less in Windows 95, because the Start menu eliminates most of the need for double-clicking. Anything you used to do with a double-click can now be done with a series of single-clicks in most cases. Another feature that is standardized in Windows 95 is the use of the right mouse button. If you right-click on a screen object such as an icon, a floating menu appears with a list of choices. Not all screen objects have an associated menu, but most icons and shortcuts do. The user can also customize these choices using the Registry Editor; however, I don't recommend that you do so until you're familiar with Windows 95 and the System Registry. In a mail-enabled environment, one of the greatest features of the right-click is the capability to use Send To automatically. This means that you can right-click an icon or shortcut and e-mail it to a colleague or friend, which saves you the trouble of attaching objects to an e-mail message.

Another concept new to Windows 95 is Explorer. Explorer replaces the File Manager from Windows 3.*x*. It provides a tree-style view of your computer, including network paths and drives and the files and resources it can use, as shown in Figure 1.5. This view provides several advantages over the File Manager: It provides access to every file-storage device on your system and it provides access to all icons on the desktop, which is the highest-level folder in the system. Explorer is not only a file-management system but also a complete control center for your computer. Explorer can manipulate and control any resource that is represented by a folder or icon in the Windows 95 system. Explorer is discussed in greater detail later in this chapter.

FIGURE 1.5.

Explorer showing the devices and contents of a system.

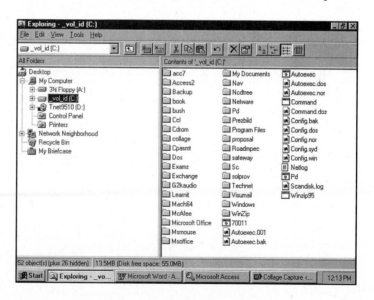

Also included in Windows 95 is Microsoft Exchange. Exchange is the Windows 95 mail, fax, and messaging center component. It can even control all your online mail, from sources such as the Internet, CompuServe, and Microsoft Network. You can directly receive messages in your Microsoft Exchange mailbox from these sources or a standard network e-mail connection from within your company or organization. Exchange provides Inbox, Outbox, Sent Items, and Deleted Items folders, all of which are extensible and can be customized. The Microsoft fax software also resides in Exchange; it keeps track of addresses, phone numbers, and other details that At Work Fax previously did.

Office 95 helps support remote users by working with the Briefcase in Windows 95. Using the Briefcase, you can take files home or share them with remote users and not have to worry about synchronizing your changes when the file returns. Instead, by doing an Update from the Briefcase, all the changes are automatically shared between the two versions of the document, worksheet, or database. This is especially powerful when teamed with Access 95 to create replicated databases that multiple users can work with (for example, a sales team needing order information in the field).

Another feature of Windows 95 that users of Office 95 can take advantage of is the support for long filenames. With filenames up to 255 characters, and the ability to have spaces in those filenames, it's much easier to give files meaningful names. As with Windows 95, files stored with these long filenames are also given 8-character DOS equivalents so that you can still share documents with users of earlier versions of Office.

Also, Word 7 and Excel 7 are backward compatible, which means they use the same file format as they do under Office 4.*x,* which is another step Microsoft took to make it easy for you to exchange documents with people who haven't upgraded yet. It also makes it easier for you to bring your older documents into the new Office 95 environment.

If you tend to get interrupted a lot while you're working, Scrap technology will also make things easier for you. You can now select part of an Excel worksheet, or a couple paragraphs from Word, and drop them directly onto the desktop to pick up later when you're ready to work with them.

Automated Tasks

Office 95 has also increased the use of automated tasks to try to figure out what you're doing while you do it. The idea is to anticipate your needs, and then be ready to fulfill them. Most of these options are specific to a particular program, but they all contribute to your efficiency and effectiveness in using Office 95. While the specifics of all these tasks are discussed later in the book, here's a look at some of the highlights.

One of the ways that automation has been increased is with the new spell checking engine. Word for Windows 95 spell checks your document as you type, running a thread during the time between keystrokes or during typing pauses to find misspellings. Using the default options, the spell checker will highlight words that appear to be misspelled, and if you right-click on them, you'll get a floating spelling menu with suggested changes or the choice to ignore or add the spelling. Even if you decide not to fix the words immediately, the spell checker already knows where the misspellings are, which speeds up a full-document spell check. Figure 1.6 shows a personal example.

FIGURE 1.6.

I think it's spelled right, but at least Word notified me right away...

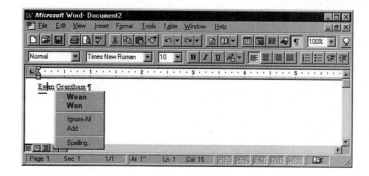

The TipWizard from Excel has been added to Word as well. In both programs, new features are quickly highlighted and explained as they are used. You can then either change the AutoFormat option that activated the tip or click a Show Me button for more information. The tips can appear in the toolbar under the main toolbars in Word and Excel. The tips will automatically appear as a feature is used or activated.

AutoFormat has also been enhanced in Office 95. Additional options make it even easier to format a document, with Word picking up clues from your typing to automatically create lists, convert fractions to the proper format, and so on. Style formatting is pulled from the available lists in Access, Excel, and Word using AutoFormat.

AutoComplete is a new way Excel gets things done faster by completing an entry into a cell for you. Type the first few letters of an entry, and AutoComplete evaluates what you're typing with what you've entered previously to determine what the complete entry should be. If you are entering a lot of repetitive data, this will definitely shave time from your tasks.

Excel has also had an AutoCalculate function added to reduce the need for pulling up Calculator or creating temporary formulas. You can now select a single cell, a whole column, or multiple ranges, and AutoCalculate will automatically perform a sum and show the results on the status bar. You can right-click on the result to have AutoCalculate give you the Average, Count, Max, and Min of the selection.

PowerPoint has added a new Meeting Minder, so that by simply right-clicking on a slide, you can enter notes or action items. Then a new slide that collects these items will be created so that they can be reviewed at the end of the presentation.

Access for Windows 95 hasn't been left out of the automation loop. A new option, Filter By Selection, allows a user to select an entry, click Filter, and have a query run that matches the value of the entry. So, if you had a database of authors and wanted to find books by a particular one, you would simply select the author's name in any datasheet or form for that table and click Filter, and all the matching records would be found.

A feature that used to be available only in Word—AutoCorrect—has now been enhanced to handle problems in any Office 95 application and to handle more common errors and misspellings than before. Here are two examples of this:

- The two initial caps rule is now more intelligent, and won't "fix" items like CDs or MHz.

- If you have CAPS LOCK pressed and type something like also, it will be converted to Also, and CAPS LOCK will be turned off.

Just as it did with Word, you can also define acronyms that will be automatically expanded. This means you can define codes so that entering MN in an Access 95 form will fill the field with Minnesota when you leave it. Once you have entered an entry like this into AutoCorrect, it is available to any of the other Office 95 applications. Therefore, if you type MN in Word, it will be expanded to Minnesota in your Excel documents as well.

Easier Help

Windows 95 includes a major overhaul of the help system. The help system has new features, a new model that makes it easier for users to find help, and more focus on "how" rather than "what" or "why." These major changes and others in the Windows help concept are discussed in the next section.

Windows 95 adopts a much more simple and direct approach to online help. The entire Help system follows a new model that has the following new features:

- Help is always available to the user via the Start menu.

- Cue cards keep a procedure or list of instructions visible until you close it.

- Context sensitivity is better used. Help for an individual field is for that field and not for the entire dialog box.

- Help topics are short and focused on procedures. The text is more direct and focused on the completion of the task for which you need help. Shortcuts can be embedded in help to take you directly to the screen that will complete the task at hand.

- Pop-up topics appear when the user right-clicks a program object.

- More keywords are provided for indexing topics, while cross-referencing is kept to a minimum to reduce complexity.

The help system is now task-centric, which means that the help focuses on how to complete a task or how to get the user to his or her goal rather than giving a broad description of the topic.

The Contents tab of the Help Topics window, shown in Figure 1.7, is very similar to a library. All the major topics are grouped in a "book" that can be opened into further "chapters." These chapters, in turn, can contain other chapters of decreasing generality, but usually for simplicity contain topics related to the chapter. A book can contain merely a single topic and no chapters at all. A topic is generally a document that the user can read or a procedure list used to complete a certain task.

FIGURE 1.7.

The Contents tab of the Help Topics window.

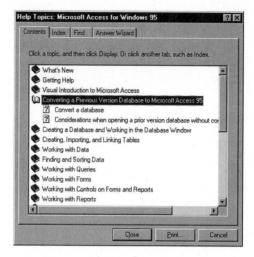

The Index tab of the Help Topics window, shown in Figure 1.8, is a vastly improved version of the Search dialog box from Windows 3.1 help. You can more efficiently scroll through keywords to locate information, and the indexing of topics is more thorough due to the inclusion of more keywords.

FIGURE 1.8.

The Index tab of the Help Topics window.

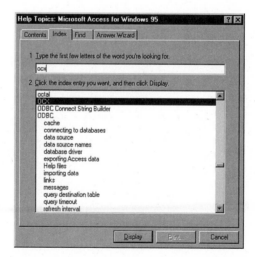

The Find tab of the Help Topics window, shown in Figure 1.9, provides an even better way to search for a help topic. You can enter a word or group of words, and help searches the find database for words that match what you typed. You can then click a word or phrase in the list to narrow your search even further and finally select the topic in the lower window and read it.

FIGURE 1.9.

The Find tab of the Help Topics window.

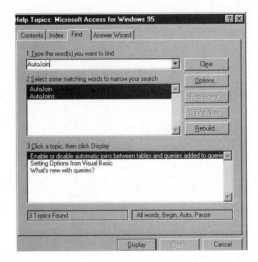

Office 95 goes one better with the addition of the Answer Wizard. Now instead of having to know what phrase or topic you are looking for, when sometimes that is the question you are trying to answer, this Wizard allows you to type in an English sentence, and come out with a list of topics that will likely answer your question. So asking, "How do I send out my sales brochures to a group of clients?" in Word will bring up a list of topics dealing with doing Mail Merge and getting data from Access 95. Asking the same question in Access 95 will bring up a list of topics on sharing data with Word, making sure that you get to the same point no matter where you ask. The Word example is shown in Figure 1.10.

FIGURE 1.10.

Finding help using the Answer Wizard in Word.

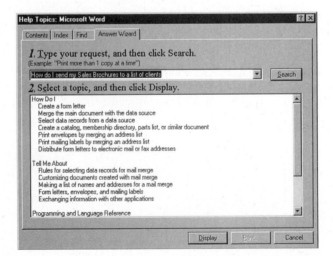

The topics can be presented in a new way using *large cards*, which can show what something would look like on the screen and then let you click on selected areas to find out more. Figure 1.11 shows an example from Access 95 for trying to get more help on how to get help.

FIGURE 1.11.

A large card showing how to get more help in Access 95.

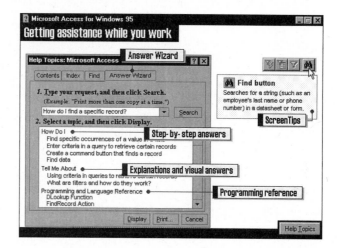

Topics have become more interactive as well, with almost 20% of the Office 95 topics being designed to step you through various processes you want to learn about. Complex actions such as creating a master document or designing a new database are broken down into their component steps, with the options explained along the way. These topics have also been formatted to make it easy to keep them on the screen as you do the work.

Even More Wizards

Office 95 also introduces a number of wizards besides the Answer Wizard as part of making it easier and faster to work with Office. You can find out more about the wizards later in the book, but here are some examples for each product to give you an idea of what is there.

In Access 95 these include a Performance Analyzer Wizard, which is used to examine existing databases and suggest changes to improve performance. This wizard can complete some of the performance enhancements itself, while giving you suggestions for other enhancements to consider.

A Database Wizard in Access 95 essentially provides you with templates for common types of databases (such as inventory control and membership tracking). The name of this wizard is a little misleading since it does more than just create the tables you need for these applications—it also creates default forms and reports. You also are able to do some customization during the process to better tailor the system to your needs.

Excel adds a Template Wizard, which helps you turn an existing worksheet into a template. It also helps you set up an automatic system to track important template fields in a separate database. By using this, you can take something like an expense report, convert it to a template (to be used in another department, for example), and then link it to other worksheets or a database.

PowerPoint weighs in with a new wizard designed to make it easier to take your presentation with you. This PackAndGo Wizard automatically finds all the linked files that are part of a presentation and packs them with the PowerPoint viewer into a complete package. It also compresses the files and can handle spanning multiple floppy disks.

Schedule+ includes a new Meeting Wizard to help you through the process of scheduling a meeting. It covers things like identifying other participants, setting an agenda, and scheduling a location.

Finally, as discussed earlier in the chapter, Word has added the Tip Wizard to make new functions easier to understand, and to make finding those new functions easier, as well.

Summary

Overall, Office 95 has evolved to come ever closer to the goal of creating an integrated suite of tools for being productive and effective. More than ever before you can *do your work only once* and be sure that you can reuse it however you need to.

Not only has Office 95 added new features from the Windows 95 environment, it has also been upgraded with enhanced help, additional automation, and a collection of new and improved add-ons and wizards. In the pages ahead you'll learn more about each of these tools and how they tie together to make it even easier to create custom solutions to your personal and business problems.

Using Microsoft Office 95

2

*by Matt Kinney
and
Ewan
Grantham*

IN THIS CHAPTER

While Office is an integrated suite of applications, each program brings something a little different to the table. In other words, while the programs all work toward a common goal, each contributes something different to getting there. A noncomputerized example of this is an orchestra, where the strings and the woodwinds both play the same song written with the same musical notation, but because of how the instruments are designed, what they play will be different from each other. This chapter introduces you to the various "instruments" that make up Office and how their contributions make the whole thing work.

Office 95, Standard Edition

There are two versions of Microsoft Office: the Standard Edition and the Professional Edition. The idea is that if you don't need a database, you shouldn't have to pay for one. On the other hand, as Access has become easier to use, it's hard to not come up with a reason to use and design your own databases. You can use Access to, among other things, track your wine list or as a contact manager.

Regardless, there are plenty of both versions being sold, and this division works equally well for focusing a discussion on the Office tools as it does for marketing them. This section covers the tools that come in the Standard Edition (and which are also found in the Professional Edition).

Excel

You can think of Excel as the "number crunching" instrument in the Office orchestra. It excels (hence the name) at putting numbers together in a fashion that allows the user to track absolute amounts and analyze trends. To simply classify Excel as a spreadsheet program is inappropriate because its data analysis and presentation capabilities go beyond those of a standard spreadsheet, as well as the fact that is an application development environment. This means that by using only Excel, you can design a complete, customized application that does just what you need. Figure 2.1 shows a blank worksheet in Excel for Windows 95.

Excel for Windows 95 has been greatly enhanced and tuned for speed. It also comes with several new features that allow you to work the way you want while getting your job done easily. Some of these features and enhancements are outlined here:

- Charts—The enhanced Chart Wizard, along with the Drag and Plot and Hands-On Charting make it easy to create impressive charts. From a simple bar graph to an advanced statistical evaluation, Excel for Windows 95 makes it easy.

- Convert to Access Wizard—You use this to convert a spreadsheet into a true relational database for complete integration with Access for Windows 95. You can even generate forms and reports in Access for Windows 95 from within Excel for Windows 95 via the Form and Report Wizards.

■ Template Wizard—You can take an existing spreadsheet and convert it into a template complete with a system to automatically track data. This means you can link worksheet cells to a database effortlessly.

■ Data Map—You can now analyze geographically related data with several kinds of maps to easily create a basic enterprise information system. This is especially useful for sales and marketing forecasts and data analysis.

■ AutoFilter—You can now find the biggest or smallest items in a worksheet by using AutoFilter with its new Top 10 option. AutoFilter also enables you to view any other items with a simple click of your mouse.

FIGURE 2.1.

An empty Excel for Windows 95 worksheet. Note the tabs at the bottom of the screen.

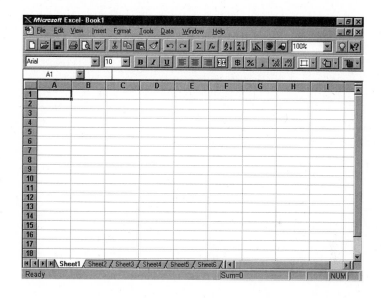

One of the first things you notice about Excel (or any spreadsheet) is all the boxes, or *cells*, on the screen. Each one represents the intersection of a *row* (the space between each two horizontal lines) and a *column* (the space between two vertical lines) and can hold any kind of data. Columns are usually depicted by letters across the top of the worksheet, whereas rows are generally numbered down the left side of the worksheet. At the bottom of the screen are tabs labeled Sheet 1, Sheet 2, and so on. These tabs are designed to allow you to have a collection of worksheets that are related. The collection of worksheets can be thought of as a book (and is called a *workbook*) with many pages, in which case the tabs can be thought of as index tabs to help you find the particular worksheet you are interested in.

You can enter data into each of the cells by clicking in a cell and typing the data directly, or by typing in the formula bar that is located directly above the column headings (the capital letters above the cells) for the worksheet. Not only can you enter data, but also mathematic and logical formulas that determine how to evaluate the contents of one or more cells. To specify that you want a group of cells, you refer to them by their address, which is the column label for the cell followed by the row label. So the first cell in the top-left of the spreadsheet would have the address A1.

It may be a little difficult to get a feel for what you can do with this kind of worksheet, so Figure 2.2 shows a full worksheet that is part of a multipage workbook that has population information for various areas of the world.

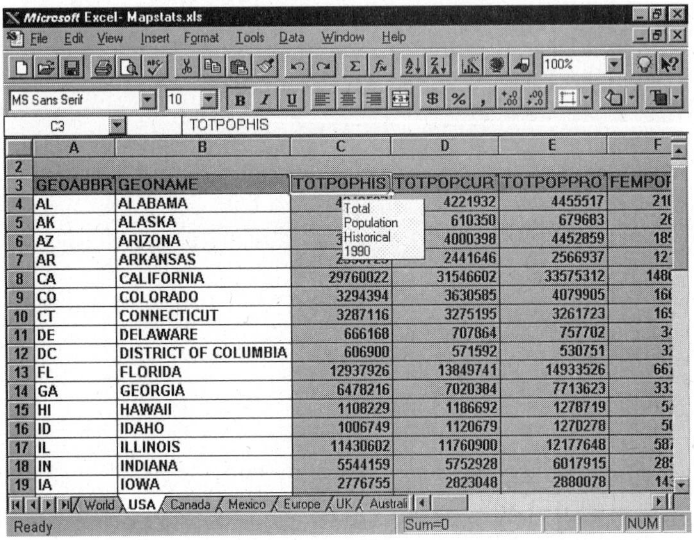

FIGURE 2.2.

An example of an Excel for Windows 95 workbook on world population. Note the tabs at the bottom of the screen, and compare them with those in Figure 2.1.

You'll notice that in Figure 2.2 the tabs have been edited to have meaningful names related to the data on each of the worksheets. You'll also notice a floating title, which is actually a *cell tip* (new to Excel for Windows 95). Cell tips are loaded automatically when you pass the cursor over a cell with a defined tip. This is to help you create context-sensitive help for your worksheet or to annotate someone else's worksheet.

Also notice how the scrollbar at the bottom right and the one along the right side have changed to reflect the size of the currently viewed worksheet. You are not limited to the amount of space that is currently showing on the screen. In fact, each worksheet can have up to 16,384 rows and up to 256 columns. You can also have up to 255 worksheets in the default workbook. One way you can get around this limitation (if it is a limitation for your purposes) is by creating a link between worksheets in separate workbooks (although you can also do this with worksheets in the same book). By doing that, you could tie together several workbooks (for example, to tie together the budgets for several divisions in a company).

Once you've set up your number crunching using various formulas, you can print out the data, create charts using the data, or share it with the other Office applications. In the case of the company budget, you could create links to an Access report that compares the budget for each division with their orders for the same period in the previous year. It is this sort of synergy that makes Office 95 so powerful. For more in-depth discussion of Excel for Windows 95, go to Chapter 16, "Excel Concepts."

PowerPoint

If Excel is the "number crunching" part of the orchestra, PowerPoint is the stage. Just like an orchestral stage, PowerPoint can be used by itself or to show off the results of the other parts of the orchestra. With PowerPoint 95, you can complete an entire conference in a matter of hours instead of days. It can bring your presentations to life with multimedia and sound, eliminating those boring slide-after-slide presentations.

PowerPoint 95 has been enhanced and improved to make the daunting job of preparing presentations easier, as well as to make the actual presentation easier to bear. Some of its new features exploit the graphics capabilities of Windows 95, and others are texture improvements to existing PowerPoint libraries, thus making sure you always have the right tools for your presentation situation. Some of these new and enhanced features are detailed here:

- AutoClipArt—This tool scans your presentation and makes recommendations on the type of digital images you should use to convey your message. This can really make your presentation stand out.

- Presentation Manager—This tool allows you to make your presentations over the network, or review presentations with a remote group of colleagues simultaneously. You can even make a presentation over a wide area network so you can be sitting at your desk in Seattle and doing a presentation in Indianapolis.

- Pack and Go Wizard—This creates a set of disks so you can easily take your presentation on the road with you.

While Excel is number-centric, PowerPoint is presentation-centric. PowerPoint is the program in Office designed to help you make your point to others. Because PowerPoint is so concerned with appearances, it is hard to say what a "default" PowerPoint screen is. Even entering the product you are prompted for the sort of presentation you want to make, and the template, or *slide*, you want to use in creating each screen. A rather bland screen can be designed, and Figure 2.3 shows what that would look like.

Looking at the example, you can already tell how to put together a basic presentation. You literally fill in the blanks with the content you want to present. Of course, simply filling white screens with black text is not going to impress many people. PowerPoint is able to help with that; it has a library of colorful backgrounds, several groups of templates, and access to the Office clip art collection. A better idea of what PowerPoint can do is shown in Figure 2.4, which shows a slide from a more complete presentation.

FIGURE 2.3.

A simple PowerPoint slide.

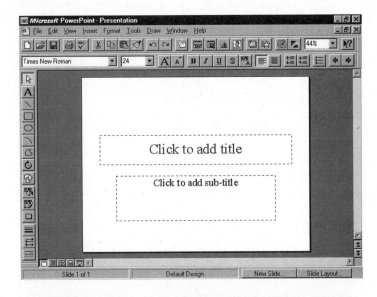

FIGURE 2.4.

A slide from a more fully developed PowerPoint presentation.

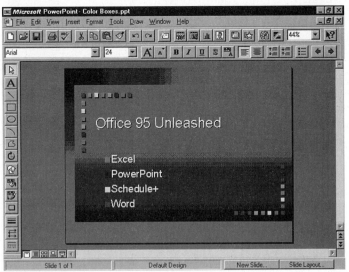

Of course, if you're not very experienced with giving presentations, PowerPoint can help you with that, too. With the AutoContent Wizard, you answer a few questions about the kind of presentation you want to give and the amount of time you want to spend, and a simple presentation along those lines is created for you.

To help make your presentation more effective, PowerPoint also has a style checker that can be run to double-check your spelling as well as look at stylistic issues such as font size and placement. This helps you avoid putting up a slide during a speech at a convention that has your company name misspelled.

As part of the Office 95 suite, PowerPoint can also get accompaniment from the other tools. You can use a Word outline to form the basis of a presentation and bring in Excel graphs to further sell your point.

With PowerPoint and Office 95, your next presentation should be faster to prepare and smoother to deliver. More on how to make that happen can be found in Chapter 37, "Designing an Effective Presentation."

Schedule+

As part of integrating your work with that of others, you need to know when you have time to meet with them and when they can meet with you. Schedule+ can give you that capability (if you have Microsoft Mail on your network) as well as help you organize your time, create To-Do lists, and maintain a personal contacts database. Schedule+ is the time-management system that gives you more of what you need—time.

Schedule+ has been greatly enhanced and improved over previous versions. It even allows workgroup time management and other personal customizations, which assist you in the delicate balance between professional and personal time management. Some of these new features and enhancements are described here:

- Seven Habits Wizard—This enables you to integrate your time management with the principles of the immensely popular book *Seven Habits of Highly Effective People*. This allows you to utilize Schedule+ seamlessly with the Seven Habits system, thus allowing you to keep using the Seven Habits system and make it easier to use.
- Meeting Wizard—This makes it easier than ever to set up meetings with your groups. It is just one of the new features that make workgroup time management a breeze.
- Full contact management—Schedule+ now has features that make it able to act as your contact management software for tracking names, addresses, and phone numbers, as well as setting up meetings.
- Sharing of information—You can now attach documents to a meeting schedule so everyone is fully briefed on the meeting and can thus be more productive.
- Schedule+ Wireless—Schedule+ now works with hand-held devices such as Personal Digital Assistants (PDAs) and the Timex Data-Link Watch. You can effortlessly transfer your Schedule+ data from your PC and take it on the road.

By default, Schedule+ opens to the daily schedule, which for a new user would look like the one in Figure 2.5, which has no entries.

Over time, however, your schedule is sure to be filled with appointments, meetings, anniversaries, birthdays, and so on. Keeping track of them, making it easier for you to plan for them, and setting off alarms to let you know when they are is all part of the package.

FIGURE 2.5.

An empty schedule in Schedule+.

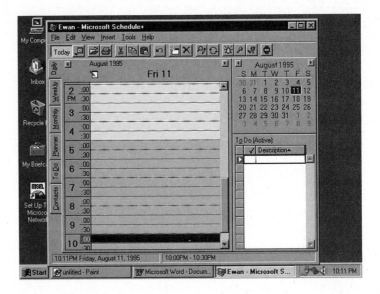

As with Excel, Schedule+ uses tabs (although here they're on the side) to help you to go directly to the part of your information that you need. With choices for Daily, Weekly, and Monthly views of your schedule, you should be able to find a view that you're comfortable working with.

Schedule+ also has wizards to look for times to hold meetings based on the schedules of the other people who need to attend and for helping you to plan a meeting in the first place. By being "group enabled" Schedule+ helps you to integrate your schedule with those of others. Again, these group options require the presence of Microsoft Mail.

To find out more about how Schedule+ can help you plan your day, take a look at Chapter 41, "Schedule+ for Yourself."

Word

The granddaddy of the Office tools, Word has been around long enough that when Microsoft discusses their vision for products, they don't talk about compound databases or compound spreadsheets; they talk about compound documents. Creating documents is what Word is all about. Word for Windows 95 makes complex tasks simpler and everyday tasks automatic.

Word for Windows 95 has several new features and enhancements that make it an even more valuable partner in your office. It even does several things for you automatically so you don't even have to think about them. Some of these new features and enhancements are outlined here:

■ Internet Assistant—Available for free from Microsoft with the coupon in the Office 95 box, Internet Assistant makes it easier than ever to create documents on the World

Wide Web. It integrates seamlessly with Word for Windows 95 and allows even the novice to create Web documents effortlessly.

- AutoFormat—This makes your documents look professional without any effort on your part. Add borders, headers, and other formatting with a few mouse clicks.

- Highlighter—For workgroups, you can use this to emphasize key words or phrases in color while working online.

- Spell It—This automatically underlines misspelled words while you type, and can display alternative spellings on the fly.

- AutoCorrect—AutoCorrect has been greatly enhanced so that it corrects even more errors and typos automatically.

Like any word processor, Word for Windows 95 allows you to enter text, cut it, copy it, format it, and print it. It also allows you to spell and grammar check it, send it as e-mail, and merge it with data from the other Office 95 applications.

Figure 2.6 shows an empty document in Word—the proverbial blank page. The status bar along the bottom tells you where you are in the document, gives some information about the document, and tells which features are (or are not) currently active.

FIGURE 2.6.

A blank page in Word for Windows 95.

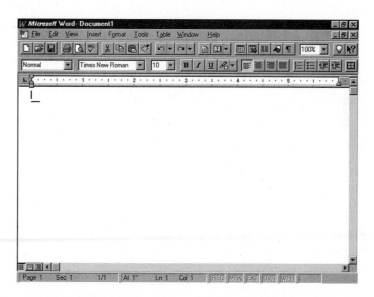

As the figure shows, when Word has a blank page, unlike the other applications, it is *really* blank. There aren't any squares or times or boxes to fill. It's just there, staring you in the face. That is what makes it so flexible. Because it is totally open, you can add your own squares or boxes or graphs. You can even embed sound and video in a Word document.

Figure 2.7 shows a somewhat more complex document that includes an embedded graphic, several fonts, and columns for a newsletter page. It was relatively easy to create this using the Newsletter Wizard, which is one of several wizards in Word for Windows 95 to help you concentrate on your content rather than your format.

FIGURE 2.7.

A sample newsletter created in Word for Windows 95.

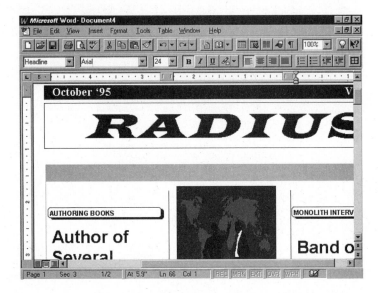

In addition to desktop publishing, Word is also very useful for creating mailings to go to prospective clients or to handle your yearly Christmas card list. The Mail Merge Wizard makes it easy to take a list from databases, spreadsheets, or formatted text files, and build a mailing with names, addresses, and some customization for each recipient.

Word also incorporates a collection of templates designed to make it easy to give your documents a particular look. For an office this can mean a consistent header and style, while for someone writing a film script it can mean making sure that what you type follows the requirements of the studio for placing actions in one section and dialog in another.

When even a template isn't enough, Word allows you to create macros to automate repetitive actions or to handle complex editing. These macros can be created by simply recording how you handle a particular instance, by programming the steps needed using WordBasic, or by using a combination of these techniques. With macros you can do things such as compare fields in two documents with lists, and update one with the information from the other. Or you can designate a keystroke that automatically inserts some special formatting at the current point in the document.

Using the various technologies built into Office 95, it also is simple to create "documents" with links to material from other office applications. Having part of a spreadsheet in the middle of a page reporting on a company's financial status, and having the information updated as the spreadsheet changes is almost as easy as typing a memo. Using Word's ability to do "text crunching" in other applications is also even easier in Word for Windows 95. You can learn more about Word for Windows 95 starting in Chapter 8, "Shared Features."

Office 95, Professional Edition

As mentioned in the last section, the main difference between the two editions is that the Professional Edition has all the software that is in the Standard Edition (Excel, PowerPoint, Schedule+, Word, and the shared components), as well as Microsoft Access. If you get the CD-ROM version of the Professional Edition, you also get a copy of Microsoft Bookshelf '95. Read on to find out more about these programs.

Access

Access for Windows 95 makes it even easier to create a fast, efficient database for home or business use. Not only can it make standalone databases, but it can connect to other databases to give you a consistent front end for your data no matter where it resides. With the introduction of Windows 95, Microsoft provides an unprecedented upgrade to what is arguably the most popular desktop environment ever. In conjunction with this introduction, Microsoft also released an upgrade to its Microsoft Office suite, which includes major enhancements to Access for Windows 95 in its 7.0 release. These major enhancements and features are directed toward end users and developers alike. Some of these features are detailed here:

- Briefcase Replication—One of the most significant new features in Access for Windows 95 is the briefcase replication functionality. Briefcase replication enables the creation of replicas, or "special copies," of a database to distribute to users in different locations so that they can work on their copy of the database independently of other users. Replicas allow for data synchronization so that all the replicas can be put together into a single entity, incorporating all the changes that have been introduced in the individual user's copies.

- Performance Analyzer—The Performance Analyzer assists not only the developer, but the end user as well. Performance Analyzer optimizes any or all of the objects in a database. When the analysis is complete, three kinds of performance suggestions or optimizations, such as query optimizations or form control changes, are displayed: recommendations, suggestions, and ideas.

- Database Splitter Wizard—The Database Splitter Wizard splits a database into two files—one that contains the tables, or the back-end component, and one that contains the queries, reports, forms, and other Access for Windows 95 objects, or the front-end component. This enables an administrator to distribute the front-end files to users while keeping a single source of data on the network.

■ Form and Report AutoFormat—Form and report appearance have been enhanced, as well. If you don't like the way your report or form looks, simply use the AutoFormat function to change the look of your entire report or selected aspects of it. Access for Windows 95 also provides a selection of predefined form and report formats and templates that you can use as is or customize.

Access, like other relational databases, is designed around the concept of having "tables" that hold collections of data of a particular type. So one table might be Patients, another might be Doctors, and another might be Office Visits. Within each of those collections of data is the data itself, which is organized into "records" that contain all the data of a particular type for an individual. So in the case of the Patients table, each record would contain the data for a particular person (such as First and Last Name, Address, and so on), and there would be as many records as there are individuals to track. Each individual piece of information in a record (such as the City in a Patient's record) is called a field and not only tells you something about that record, but serves as a way to group records inside a table. An example is all patients who live in a certain city in a Patients table.

To access the information in the tables, you use forms and reports. Forms are designed for interactive use and can be created for entering new data, modifying old data, and removing data. You can also set up forms for running searches (called *queries*) through the data to answer particular questions you might have (such as in the example of looking for patients in a certain city).

Reports give you a way to display the data on paper and to combine and group data to help analyze it. They are more static than forms, which is good or bad, depending on what you are trying to do.

Figure 2.8 shows the initial Access screen with a blank database. Right now you have what is essentially an empty cupboard that you will be putting containers in as you begin to create your system.

FIGURE 2.8.

An empty database in Access for Windows 95.

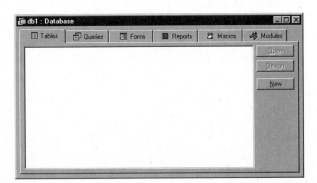

Once again, as so often in Office, you'll notice the use of tabs to show different areas you can work with. While having to build so many different parts of a system (tables and forms and reports, oh my…) may seem a little intimidating, Access for Windows 95 is able to help with the process of setting up a database with the new Database Wizard. With your answers to some questions about what type of data you are trying to track and the general purpose of the database, Access is able to build the basic tables, forms, and reports you'll need. It even gives you a main menu (called the *switchboard*) for jumping to the various parts of this new system.

Regardless of how you create it, you eventually start filling up your cupboard. Figure 2.9 shows an example of a working database.

FIGURE 2.9.

A database in action in Access for Windows 95 showing the tables and a running form.

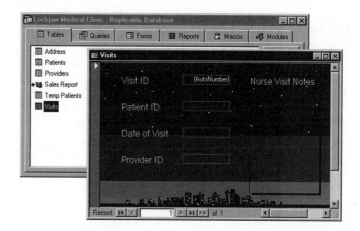

Not only can your data come from tables that are actually in the database, but as this example shows, you can also link to collections of data in other databases or in other applications such as Excel. This allows you to use a single front end to all your database-related work. So even if your company has Oracle or DB2, you can use an ODBC connection to link to tables on those systems and work with them the same way you would a table in Access. You can also import data in various formats into its own table, or update tables you already have, which gives you another way to access large corporate databases. Like the other Office 95 tools, you can also embed data from the other tools. On the sample form shown in Figure 2.9, you'll notice there is a box labeled Nurse Visit Notes. These are used to store Word documents that have information about the Patient's visit.

Access for Windows 95 also makes it easier to share a database. Whether you need to take it home to do some work or make copies for remote users, you can now use the Briefcase Replication feature to distribute your database. More than just creating another copy, however, Briefcase Replication will actually track the changes that are made in both versions of the database and then allow you to run Briefcase's update feature to automatically exchange any changes.

As in Word, Access also has the capability to have macros with which you can automate certain tasks. Rather than using WordBasic, you use a Macro design sheet and associate actions and events. These macros can be used anywhere in the database.

You can also take the information you are working with in Access and export it in various formats to the other Office 95 programs. This is especially helpful for creating and maintaining mailing lists for Word. For more information on creating and working with Access for Windows 95, look at Chapter 27, "Access Concepts."

Bookshelf '95

This application serves as a reference desk for the rest of Office 95, and includes not only a dictionary and thesaurus, but also an atlas, a desktop encyclopedia, a list of U.S. Zip codes, and more. Bookshelf '95 comes with several new features, which are detailed here:

■ Address Builder—Bookshelf '95 now contains the National Five-Digit Zip Code and Post Office Directory so you can get the right address instantly, even if you don't have all the information.

■ One-click access—All the desktop references have been updated to include the 1995 versions. You now have one-click access to volumes of desktop reference material, without ever reaching for a book!

Figure 2.10 shows the opening screen of Bookshelf with All Books selected as the search criteria.

FIGURE 2.10.

Bookshelf '95 open and ready for work.

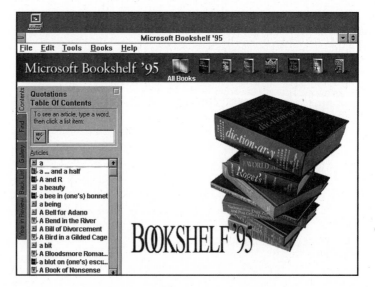

Using this program, you have easy access to several books worth of information in text, audio, and video formats. You can also use the Quick Shelf feature to make it easy to bring material from Bookshelf into your documents.

Figure 2.11 shows the result of a search through the combined books, and also shows how you can select key phrases from one selection to find more information elsewhere.

FIGURE 2.11.

An example of finding a citation in Bookshelf '95.

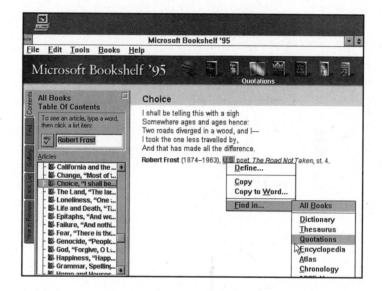

With this selection of eight books at your fingertips, it is even easier to get the basics down when you're working on a project. Whether you need to get the population of Rwanda for a chart in Excel, or a quotation (like the one in Figure 2.11) for a presentation, Bookshelf makes it possible for you to do the work within Office 95.

Summary

This is a high-level introduction to the various parts of Office 95, both the Standard and the Professional Editions. You should now understand what the various parts of the product are and know a little bit more about how they all work together. You can purchase other programs that have been developed to be compatible with the Microsoft Office for Windows 95. These programs will display the Microsoft Office Compatible logo, and only programs that Microsoft certifies can carry it. This allows you to design custom solutions for your home of business and never write a line of code.

Seamless integration is the name of the game with Office 95. With Office 95 you can build an entire solution using the next generation of tools and operating environments and be assured that it will work seamlessly. In Office 95, it's the sum of the parts of Office 95 that makes it the clear winner in office integration. We've already touched on the idea of integration in this chapter, but the next two chapters will focus on what that means and give you a more in-depth look at how it works.

PART

IN THIS PART

Integration Concepts

All About Documents

3

*by Matt Kinney
and Ewan
Grantham*

IN THIS CHAPTER

This chapter is dedicated to the idea that to really understand Microsoft Office 95 you need to understand what a document is. The next several pages explain a concept of documents that may be new to you, but that should become second nature when you see how that concept will help you in creating and using information.

Definition of a Document

Most people think of a document as being like the screen shot of Word for Windows 95 in Figure 3.1—a bunch of somewhat formatted text on a page. But a document is really much more than this. That's not to say that a memo is *not* a document, but that a document can be much more than a memo.

FIGURE 3.1.

An example of what most folks think of when you mention the word document.

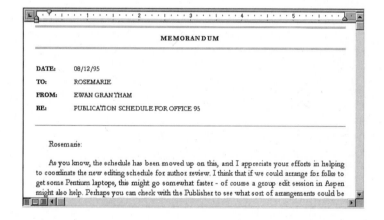

Instead, think of a document as being a container that can hold anything about a subject. It still has a subject and a method of presentation, but it is no longer limited to just what can be printed on a physical page. Now a document is a way to hold data together in a logical manner for review and display. Quite simply, a document is a container that holds a specific object or objects. An object can be anything from a typical Microsoft Word file to a video or animation sequence. In other words, a document can be considered a user interface to a focused set of data.

To see what this means, take a look at Figure 3.2, which shows a document that takes advantage of using text and other objects in order to make a point.

As you can see, an AVI (video for Windows) file has been linked to this document to show a short clip on the coyote with sound and video. The picture that shows in Figure 3.2 is from the first frame of the AVI.

Of course, you can use other types of files besides AVI files. This same page could have been done with the text running down a center column, with rows of photographs on each side. Or it could be a column of photos, a column of text, and then a column of sound samples.

Chapter 3

FIGURE 3.2.

An example of a document using text and other objects.

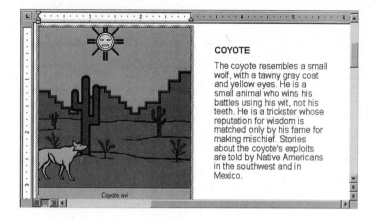

This type of document isn't limited to multimedia education, however. A document that is composed of more than text is also a very important business tool. In Figure 3.3, you see an example of how the various parts of Office can combine to make a document that is both more complete and more persuasive than a more simple memo would be.

FIGURE 3.3.

A business example of using objects and text.

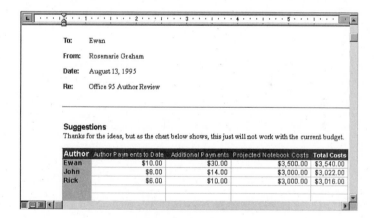

In this example, an Excel spreadsheet has been linked to a Word document to show how and why a particular decision was reached. While the same information could have been conveyed purely with text, it would not have had the same impact. Also, by creating the link, the information that was used for making the decision only had to be entered once, which is part of the *do your work only once* philosophy of Microsoft Office.

So far we have looked at documents as being something created in Word. That is not a requirement for a document, although like the memo, it is often thought of that way. An Access form or report, or an Excel worksheet, is just as much a document as is a Word document. If you think of a document as being a focused collection of data, as discussed earlier, then you can see why that would be the case.

To show this a little more clearly, let's take a look at an Access form that uses multiple objects. Figure 3.4 shows a form that has data and text, as well as a background graphic that contributes to the clinic's sense of place.

FIGURE 3.4.

An Access document with many parts.

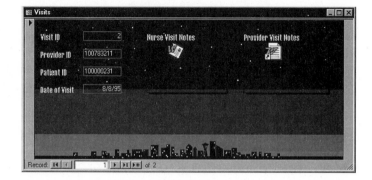

Does all this mean that anything that appears on a computer screen is a document? No. A document is a *collection* of *focused data*. So just having a computer screen, such as the Windows 95 desktop, doesn't create a document. It's only a document when there is defined content.

On the other hand, this does mean that there are a lot more types of documents than you might think, and certainly some documents that aren't as recognizably documents as others.

Things start to blur with the Office Binder. Figure 3.5 shows an example of a binder with data on customers. Take a look at it, and then ask yourself, "Is this a document?" Regardless of your answer, think about why you do or don't consider it a document.

FIGURE 3.5.

An Office binder, which may (or may not) be a document.

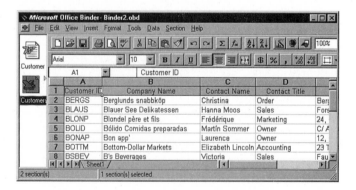

Rethinking what a document is becomes important because of changes in how we work. By using a wider definition of document, it is possible to develop new ways to answer your business and personal questions. Particularly with new methods of presenting information driven by increased use of networked systems (both direct-connect and dial-up), it becomes more important to have information-dense and visually attractive documents. As more content is not only created on computers, but also read on them, the desirability of having as much of the information as possible available in one place increases.

Moreover, when you start to look at a document this way, you can also start to see your applications in a different light. No longer is Word a word processor and Excel a spreadsheet. Rather, each of these products is a type of object that handles data in a different way. These objects can then be combined to build larger objects (documents) to achieve an end result. The process of creating and presenting information then becomes the process of determining what kinds of objects are best suited to each subject.

In other words, if you know that part of the information you want to present is based on an analysis of numbers, then you will think of that part of the document as needing a number-manipulating object. In the case of Office 95, that would probably mean using Excel. On the other hand, perhaps a map is needed to show the relationships of numbers to location. In this case you might use the DataMap object or simply a graphic from a tool such as Paint.

In all of this, the focus is on how you take the data that has been entered or acquired and present it to the user (including yourself) in the best manner.

Document Design

Now that you have a picture in mind of what a document is, it's time to look at how to design those documents. The emphasis will be on documents that have data from more than one source or that are composed of multiple objects.

One consideration that is always confronted with these types of documents is deciding what will be the base for the document. In other words, should I embed an Excel worksheet in an Access form, or should the Access data be embedded in an Excel worksheet? What you have to consider here is where most of the data currently resides and what is the most useful way of working with that data. So if most of the data is already part of an Excel worksheet, and you are just using a couple items from an Access table, it makes more sense for Excel to be the base of the document not only because most of the data is already there, but because it will be easier to work with that data there as well.

You also have to look at how well a particular application can work as the base for a document. Trying to create a document in an image-processing application will generally be frustrating because it is difficult to embed a text-processing object in an image. This is as much a limitation of the current state of software as it is a design problem.

There are two main types of what could be called "composite" documents: master documents and compound documents. Depending on what you are trying to do and how you are trying to do it, one or the other of these should be appropriate. The next two sections tell you more about these types of documents and their uses.

Master Documents

The idea behind a master document, as you might infer from the name, is to be the coordinating document that ties several other documents together. Where master documents really shine is in handling large documents such as books. It is also useful for documents that have large numbers of graphic images and would otherwise be too large to load into memory at once.

A master document is oriented more toward editing and printing than it is toward presentation. Figure 3.6 shows a group of proposals that are linked by a master document.

FIGURE 3.6.

An example of a master document.

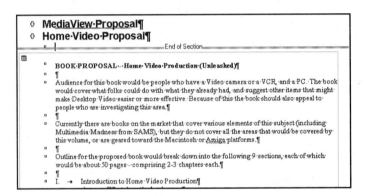

Each of the plus symbols represents a topic that can be clicked on to expand. Each of these topics also represents a subdocument, which is actually a normal document, but is a subsidiary of the master document. While you can create the subdocuments from within the master document, you will generally create the subdocuments separately, and then tie them together with the master document.

One big advantage to a master document is that the subdocuments can be edited separately. This means that if you are working on something like a proposal, the sales staff can work on their part, the technical staff can do their part, and you don't have to worry about who currently has the document. Everything then gets tied together with the master document to produce a single entity.

The problem with a master document is the same problem you have with shortcuts in the Windows 95 shell: If the subdocument moves, the master document doesn't know about it, and you have to set up the new location manually.

When you are considering the use of a master document (and particularly when you are trying to decide between a master document and a compound document), you have to decide what purpose you are trying to achieve by creating a master document. In other words, what is the focus of the end product you are trying to create? From a design standpoint, a master document gives you the ability to enforce a common look on the entire finished product. Since headers, footers, and other style setups on the master document will override what is in the subdocuments, the end result looks like a large, unified document (note that you *can* create section styles to keep the different style of a particular document, but that defeats a lot of the purpose of the master document). If you don't want that commonality, then you might want to give even more consideration to creating a compound document instead.

Compound Documents

This type of document is different from a master document in that it actually merges the various objects. Rather than storing pointers to subdocuments, the objects that are being used (text, graphics, and so on) are stored or linked directly into the compound document. This is both more complex in terms of how the document is created and less complex because everything is right there to be worked with.

Building compound documents requires the use of various technologies, primarily OLE (object linking and embedding) and DDE (dynamic data exchange). With this foundation, Office 95 is able to create documents that consist of parts from within any of its components and programs. Figures 3.2, 3.3, and 3.4 all show how this type of document can help in making more customized, information-dense documents to help answer your questions and explain your answers to others.

From a design standpoint, a compound document can be thought of as a mosaic. You are trying to put together several parts, or objects, to make a unified whole that expresses something in a way that none of the individual parts could do.

In another sense, a compound document begins to bring the power of object-oriented design to your work. By thinking in terms of objects that can be combined, rather than the more traditional notion of having to make everything fit a common mold, you can take advantage of what is best in each package rather than having to export everything to a common format.

Returning to the example in Figure 3.3, it wasn't that long ago that to have this kind of information in a document, you would have had to do an export of the data to a format that a word processor could understand, import the data, and reformat the data to look the way you wanted on the screen. Now, using the object-oriented paradigm of the compound document, you simply choose to have a spreadsheet object in your document container. That object can then reside in the container, or it can exist as a link in the container to another object where the data is actually stored.

In fact, the most common problem with any compound document is deciding whether the component parts should be embedded or linked. Usually this is decided based on how the component data is used in and outside the document. The integration of Office 95 applications into a document-centric format is made possible by OLE. Office 95 provides a new OLE feature, the Binder, which provides a unique method to store objects from multiple applications in a single file by harnessing the power of OLE. OLE, which originally described object linking and embedding technology, has now taken on a much broader scope. The basic elements of OLE are reviewed here, and an example is given of each type of component:

- Linking—Linking is the process by which data from one application is provided to another, while keeping that data updated without user interaction. Say, for example, that you have an employee table for a group of computer consultants. You want to be able to search through your database for the ones who have Access experience. Once you find them, you want to be able to print out their résumés. In this case, the résumés should be linked Word documents so that changes to the résumés will be picked up automatically.

- Embedding—Embedding enables one application to use the objects of another application without running the other application. For example, say you have an Excel for Windows 95 worksheet with salary figures for a group of employees that is totaled as well. You do not want to store this as a separate file because the only place it is used is as a table in Word for Windows 95. Note that embedding simply takes a snapshot of the data or object and is not updated by the master object. You could embed the worksheet into the Word for Windows 95 document and maintain all the functionality of Excel for Windows 95 to work with the salary table.

- Binders—The binder is a container for all your Office 95 objects. A binder allows for single file access to all the objects contained within it, such as Word for Windows 95 documents and Excel for Windows 95 spreadsheets. For example, say you are doing a business plan for a new business. What better way to access all your sales projections in Excel for Windows 95 and your executive summary in Word for Windows 95 than a binder? The binder allows for the creation and maintenance of a true Office document—a heterogeneous collection of Office objects in a single container document.

- Automation—Automation provides the ability to manipulate objects from programming code. This allows the developer to import information from one document or application to another. Say, for example, that you are using Access for Windows 95 as your contact manager that contains all your contacts with their associated addresses. Automation would (and does) allow the user to extract that information and use it in a form letter in Word for Windows 95. This is basically what happens when you do a WordMerge letter.

Now that you have a basic understanding of OLE components, how do you use this technology to your advantage in Office 95? Fortunately, Office 95 applications all have similar methods to accomplish each of these components. The distinct components and methods of accomplishing them are discussed in the following sections.

Linking

As has been previously discussed, you want to link from one application to another when you want to keep updated data from one application available to another. This is transparent to the end user; however, behind the scenes it is another story. When you link data from one application to another, the path of the linked data is actually stored within the application receiving the linked data. You should attempt to make certain that the linked data is not moved from its original folder since it is the path to the data that is stored. If the data is moved, the receiving application will not be able to update the data because it will not know where to look for it. If you must move linked data, remember to update the link with the Links command from the Edit menu of the receiving application's menu bar.

Linking can be accomplished in a couple ways: using the menu bar or using the copy and paste functionality of the Clipboard.

To link using the menu bar, follow these steps:

1. In the application that is going to receive the linked data, select Object from the Insert menu. You should see the Object dialog box. (See Figure 3.7.)

FIGURE 3.7.

The Object dialog box.

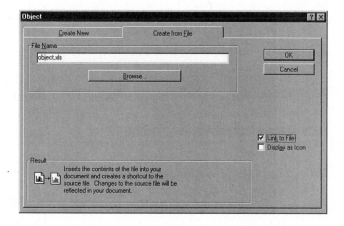

2. Select the Create from File tab in the Object dialog box. Specify the file that you want to link to by either entering the path and filename or clicking on the Browse button and selecting the file from the Browse list.

3. Check the Link to File check box in the Object dialog box, and then click OK.

To link using the copy and paste functionality of the Clipboard, follow these steps:

1. Select the information or data in the original application that you wish to link. This is usually done with the mouse by clicking on an object to select it or dragging the cursor over a block of data to highlight it. Then select Copy from the Edit menu in the menu bar.

2. Go to the application that is going to be receiving the data from the original application.

3. Select Paste Special from the Edit menu in the menu bar. The Paste Special dialog box appears, as shown in Figure 3.8.

4. Select the Paste Link radio button and the object type you are linking and click OK.

FIGURE 3.8.

The Paste Special dialog box.

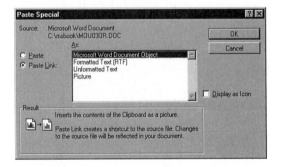

Embedding

You will want to embed data from one application to another when you wish to keep all of your data in a single file. Note that this will increase the size of your document significantly because the entire object for the embedded information is stored in your document. This is potentially a small trade-off, however, because it alleviates the need to keep track of paths (locations of linked data files) to linked data; embedded data is stored in a single file.

Embedding data can be done in much the same manner as linking: You can use the menu bar or the copy and paste functionality of the Clipboard.

To link data using the menu bar, follow these steps:

1. In the application that is going to receive the linked data, select Object from the Insert menu. You should see the Object dialog box, as shown in Figure 3.7.

2. To embed a new object that has not been created in an existing file, select the Create New tab and specify the object type you wish to create. Otherwise, if you want to embed a new object from a previously existing file, select the Create from File tab and specify the filename *without* checking the Link to File check box.

3. Click OK.

To embed data using the copy and paste functionality of the Clipboard, follow these steps:

1. Select the information or data in the original application that you wish to embed. This is usually done with the mouse by clicking on an object to select it or dragging the cursor over a block of data to highlight it. Then select Copy from the Edit menu in the menu bar.

2. Go to the application that is going to be receiving the data from the original application.

3. Select Paste Special from the Edit menu in the menu bar. The Paste Special dialog box appears, as shown in Figure 3.8.

4. Select the Paste radio button and the object type you are embedding and click OK.

The Binder

The binder is essentially a container object that allows you to store all your Office objects in a single file. Each of these object types is represented by a section in the binder. When you have a section selected, you can work in the binder just as if you were in the original application.

The binder, as you can probably guess, is a very handy way to work with Office 95 objects.

To create a new binder, follow these steps:

1. Start Microsoft Binder by selecting Start from the taskbar, and then selecting Programs. You should see a list of programs. Select Microsoft Binder. The binder application will start, and a blank binder will appear, as shown in Figure 3.9.

FIGURE 3.9.

A blank binder.

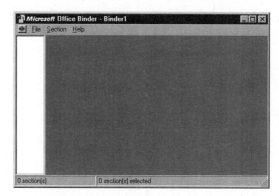

2. Alternatively, once the Binder application has started, you can select New Binder from the File menu to create a new binder.

To add a section to a binder, follow these steps:

1. From the Section menu, select Add. The Add Section dialog box appears, as shown in Figure 3.10.

2. Select the object type from the list in the Add Section dialog box and click OK.

3. Alternatively, you can select Add from File from the Section menu to insert a section from an existing file. The Add from File dialog box appears, as shown in Figure 3.11.

FIGURE 3.10.

*The Add Section
dialog box.*

FIGURE 3.11.

*The Add from File dialog
box showing PowerPoint
objects.*

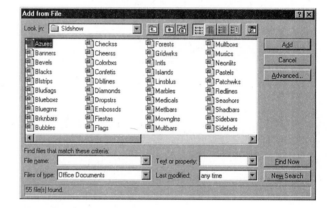

4. Select the file to insert as a section and click on Add.

To work with a section, follow these steps:

1. In the section on the left in your binder, click on the section you wish to modify. The toolbars and menu bars of the Binder will change to reflect the section's application so you can work with the section as if you were in the original application. Alternatively, you may see a screen that looks similar to the one in Figure 3.12.

FIGURE 3.12.

*The binder showing a
section that cannot be
edited in place.*

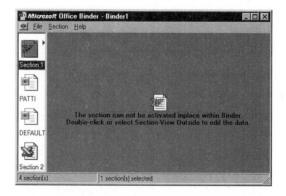

2. If this happens, you can still work with the section, but you have to do it in a different manner. From the Section menu select View Outside from the Binder menu bar. This will start the section's associated application and allow you to edit the object in the section from outside the binder.

Automation

You use OLE automation when you want to integrate features or data from one application with another Office 95 application. Frankly, automation requires programming skills and talent. In-depth coverage of OLE automation programming is beyond the scope of this chapter, but you can get several code examples and a more thorough explanation of automation via the Office 95 help system. You access this via the Help menu in any Office 95 program.

Summary

This chapter introduces you to thinking of your applications as processes that contribute to building an overall document. Each application represents an object, either a data-relation object (in the case of Access for Windows 95) or a text-manipulating object (in the case of Word for Windows 95 and other applications). Much of this is easily accomplished using OLE as well as via the new Office Binder application.

By using this paradigm, it is easier to develop new ways of obtaining and presenting information for your own use or to give to others.

Further, you have seen two of the types of documents that are often created using this paradigm of objects. Master documents can be thought of as collection objects designed for creating a unified image and for correlating information. Compound documents can be thought of as container objects designed to make it easier to bring together other objects for a particular use.

Chapter 4, "Integrating Your Office with OLE," takes this idea even further by exploring the object-oriented nature of developing documents with OLE and DDE and different ways of managing these types of documents.

Integrating Your Office with OLE

4

by
Ricardo Birmele

IN THIS CHAPTER

Because you're reading this book about Microsoft Office, you're probably already familiar with Windows. You know that you can have more than one Windows-based program running at a time, and that you can use the Clipboard to move a Paintbrush picture, say, right into your Word document.

That's pretty convenient; it's certainly a big usability step up from MS-DOS. It would be even more convenient, however, if you didn't have to "start" another program to be able to use it. For example, if you could paint a picture from within your Access database, use Word's spell and grammar checkers while in an Access form, or use Word's wealth of text editing features while in Excel.

That capability is what this chapter is about. The technology involved is called *object linking and embedding* (better known as OLE). In this chapter you'll get an idea of how you can use OLE to easily and automatically work with other programs from within Microsoft Office. (This process is known as *OLE automation.*) Specifically, you'll learn how to use OLE with Microsoft Access.

This chapter begins with a peek at one part of computer history—how OLE came to be—and continues with some definitions and a look at the concepts underlying OLE automation. In addition, it looks at embedding and linking OLE objects and how you can edit them in place. Also, there are two tools you'll learn a bit about. The first of these is the Windows 95 Registration Database—a kind of replacement for the familiar Windows application INI files. The second is the Access Object Browser, which lets you see what objects are available.

> **NOTE**
>
> You might have noticed that Windows 95 displays a number of icons, known as *shortcuts*, on its default desktop. What you might not know is that when you click one of these shortcut icons, you are actually using an OLE link between it and the program itself.

A Bit of History

Back in the good old days of microcomputing—before keyboards and carpal tunnel syndrome—programming was done by flipping switches. You kept track of what you were doing by looking at rows of shining lights. If the power went out just as you set the switches for the last instruction in your program, you were simply out of luck. And, depending on your size and disposition, so were your co-workers.

The people who invented microcomputer technology mostly came from a mainframe computer background. In that world, they used huge tape recording machines on which they stored their data on a long-term basis. Working with that knowledge (and a bit of ingenuity), they came up with a method of using the common cassette tape as a microcomputer storage device. At the same time, they continued the old-fashioned office "file" metaphor to logically represent the physical storage of the data.

Back then—and for a long while—microcomputers and software were single-user and single-task devices. Consequently, they were very inefficient in how they allowed people to share data and work together. The more popular microcomputers became, the more burdensome their limitations became.

Computer scientists followed two roads in trying to make their machines more efficient. The first was to electronically connect computers together in what became known as a *network*. With networks came the capability for people to work together on a common task (using databases, for example). This paralleled the "real world" of the business office, where more than one person at a time can look at a paper file (rudely looking over each others' shoulders, perhaps, but they *can* do it). The advance in usability was much the same—an electronic file stored on one computer could be viewed, and used, by more than one person at a time.

The second road had to do with computers themselves. The scientists created ways in which more than one application at a time could be run on a single computer. As a logical result of that effort, methods were developed by which the components of different applications could share computer resources. Soon it became apparent that the applications should share more than computer resources—they should share pieces of themselves! That led to a standard known as the *component object model*, which makes possible the OLE technology discussed in this chapter.

A Few Definitions

Before we go any further, here are a few definitions to aid in your understanding of the subject. I start with the most important one.

Object

In the physical world, an object is anything you can touch (for example, an apple or your loved one's face—the *object* of your affection, as it were). You know you can touch the object because it exists in space. It has form and characteristics that make it different from other objects. To extend the metaphor, you can differentiate dissimilar apples. An apple might be yellow, red, or green. Yet all apples have a similar size and shape as well as contain seeds and have stems. (See Figure 4.1.)

In the computer world, an object is anything you can figuratively touch. For example, in Access you can touch objects such as forms, fields, and control buttons. You touch each of these objects by using a mouse, through the keyboard, or programmatically through instructions you include in Access macros or code modules.

FIGURE 4.1.

Almost everything in a Windows application is an object.

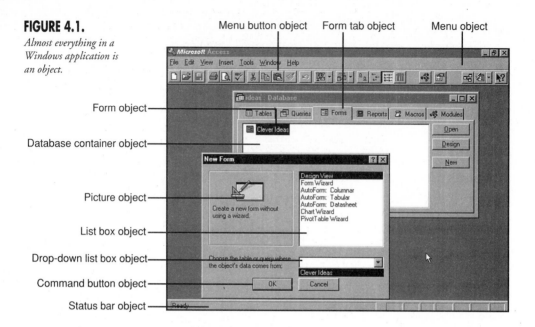

Menu button object   Form tab object   Menu object

Form object

Database container object

Picture object

List box object

Drop-down list box object

Command button object

Status bar object

Like real-world objects, one kind of Access object is roughly similar to every other Access object. Take Access dialog boxes, for example: Each one is similar to every other Access dialog box in that it contains controls; each control is itself an object.

Just as you know what to expect when you pick up and eat an apple, in Access you pretty well know what to expect when you see and manipulate a dialog box. That expectation carries over to when you use a dialog box in another Windows-based application. The controls on a Word for Windows or Excel dialog box behave the same way as the controls in an Access dialog box.

It's this similarity of behavior among controls from different manufactures that makes it possible for OLE, as a technology, to exist.

OLE

OLE is the technology by which different kinds of Windows-compatible applications—spreadsheets, word processors, databases, and so on—can work seamlessly together by exposing certain of their objects to each other. It doesn't matter if the applications come from different manufacturers. What does matter is that the applications and their objects behave in predictable ways, and that they have certain built-in capabilities that comply with the OLE "standard."

> **NOTE**
>
> It's kind of a misnomer to speak of OLE as having or being a "standard" to which applications using that technology have to comply. There's nothing set in stone or yet formally agreed to. Instead, as OLE technology has developed into OLE version 2, more and more software manufacturers are "complying" with the standard.

Exposed Objects

In order to be OLE capable, a software application must be able to expose its objects to other OLE-capable applications. That means that it has the built-in ability to share its objects and their manipulations. The program that is exposing its objects runs in the background—it's hidden. But because it *is* running, that program is what's actually controlling its exposed objects. All you see (or your program sees) are those objects that are being employed by your application.

OLE Clients

There are two participants in an OLE "conversation" between applications. For example, suppose that you are creating an Access database application. In that case, the first participant is Microsoft Access. Because your Access application is going to be served the objects of the other program, much like a client is served by a consultant, the Access database application that you're running as you implement OLE is called the *OLE client*. It is also known as the *container application* because it comes to "contain" the objects of the other software.

OLE Servers

An *OLE server* is the other participant in an OLE conversation. It exposes its objects to the client, thus providing the client with an object to link or embed. If, for example, you are using Word's text-editing capabilities in your Access database, then Word is the OLE server and Access is the OLE client.

Embedded Objects

An *embedded object* is an object that is copied from the OLE server and becomes part of your OLE client. When you activate it in place, a process that is discussed later, it behaves just as if it were still part of the OLE server. Its menus and menu options are the same, it responds to keystrokes and mouse manipulations in the same way, but all the while it is actually a part of the OLE client. Once an object is embedded, a user must be running your same Access database application to be able to modify it. For example, if the object is a Paintbrush picture, then to modify the picture, you would have to call up the picture object from within your Access application.

Linked Objects

A *linked object* is an object that is merely connected to your application. You can use your Access database application to modify it, of course. However, anyone else can also modify that object. They can do so by linking it to their own application or by running its original server application.

With a Paintbrush picture, for example, anyone with access to your computer's hard disk can run PBRUSH.EXE, load your picture into it, and then scribble away with abandon, with no regard for how long it took you to create the picture or how important it is to your project. Of course, this will present you with quite a surprise the next time you open your database. (Only a techie daddy with techie-aspiring children would think up an example like this.)

> **NOTE**
>
> Clearly, the trade-offs between linking and embedding objects have to do with controlling access to the objects. If it's okay (and more efficient) to allow someone to doodle with the object, then link it. On the other hand, it's usually safer to embed it.

Embedding and Linking Objects

Now that you know about objects, it's time to talk about the nature of OLE and compound documents. The bottom line is that OLE is a way that different kinds of software applications can share data between themselves. You may wonder, then, why you can't simply make a single whole piece of software that will do all things for all people. The simple answer is that the resulting software would be huge and cumbersome. Much like the government, it would do a lot of things, but few of them well.

The reason for this is inherent in the nature of different kinds of software applications. When you use a Word processor, for example, you know that it is an application that has been optimized for the manipulation of text. You type your thoughts, the words appear, and when you get to the end of a logical line, the words of the sentence automatically wrap to the next line. That may seem obvious, but think for a moment about all the things the word processing software is doing.

Each time you press a key, if the software recognizes it as an alphabetic character, and because it has kept track of your onscreen position, it places the letter there. Then it increments your onscreen position and prepares to place the next letter you type. If the letter happens to be a space, then it "looks" at the onscreen position to decide whether to place the character there or to start a new line. If the letter is a printable character, the software looks at its onscreen position to see how close to the end of a line it is, looks further at other printable characters falling between it and the preceding space characters to determine if what you are typing is something the software can recognize as being a word, and then decides whether to place this word on the current line or to move all of its letters down to the next line.

Whew! And that's only part of what a word processor does. You can only imagine how complicated things can get if it has to justify your paragraphs—or automatically spell check your document as you type it.

The problems to be solved with spreadsheet software are clearly different. Spreadsheets don't need extensive text editing capability. But they do need to keep very accurate track of the location and value of numbers. And they need to quickly take that data, use it in calculations, and then present the result—the location and value of which must in turn be kept track of.

Before OLE, if you needed to combine the numbers of a spreadsheet with the words of a word processor, you had to do so using two pieces of paper. Now, using OLE, you simply connect the two into what's known as a *compound document*, a single document comprised of objects from different types of software applications.

You have two ways of going about creating a compound document: linking files together or embedding a document from one application into another. Both methods are easy; which you choose, however, can have a tremendous impact on your system's performance. Let's look at each method individually.

Embedding a Spreadsheet Object

Here's a quick scenario: You're employed by a motel and are writing a memo requesting the purchase of replacement bedding. Your boss wants it to be detailed, with all the amounts and costs clearly laid out. Here are the steps you follow:

1. Start Word and create a new document.

2. When you get to the place in the document where you'd like the figures to appear, click the Insert Microsoft Excel Worksheet button on the standard toolbar. Word displays a grid like the one shown in Figure 4.2.

3. The grid represents how big—so many rows by so many columns—your embedded spreadsheet will be. Click one of the grid squares, giving yourself enough rows and columns to hold the figures you'll need. Word calls up Excel, which in turn creates a blank spreadsheet in your document. In this case, we've created an embedded spreadsheet that's five columns wide by four rows deep, as you can see in Figure 4.3.

FIGURE 4.2.

Use this grid to tell Word how big you want your embedded spreadsheet to be.

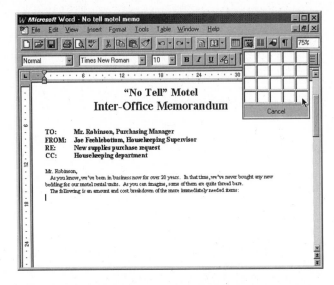

FIGURE 4.3.

The blank embedded spreadsheet, ready to use.

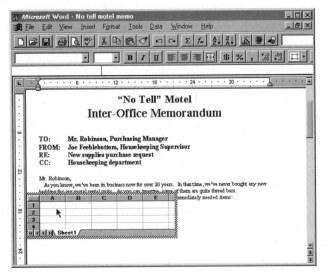

4. Enter data into the blank spreadsheet. As you do so, notice that the toolbars above the document have changed to include an Excel Formula bar, and that Word's Table menu bar has changed to Excel's Data menu bar. Once you're done, click your document somewhere outside the now filled-in spreadsheet. Word closes its link to Excel, brings up its own menu bars, and leaves in your document a table comprising the figures and labels from the spreadsheet, as you can see in Figure 4.4.

FIGURE 4.4.

The embedded spreadsheet after you've used it for figuring data.

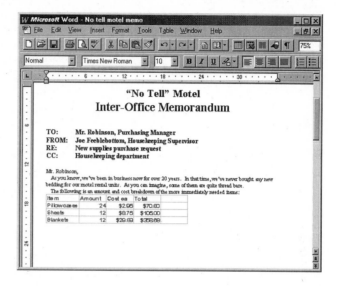

With this process, you have embedded a complete Excel spreadsheet into your Word document. Once you've embedded a spreadsheet—or any other object, for that matter—you can move it just about anyplace you need it to be in your document. Unless you are editing it in place (which is discussed later in this chapter), Word treats the object's placement as if it were a paragraph. To move it up or down, simply adjust its left or right margins or spacing before or after, just as you would any other paragraph.

> **TIP**
>
> There's an even easier way to embed a document: Drag and drop it! In the case of our memo, make sure both Word and Excel are active, drag the spreadsheet to the memo, and—*voila!*—it's embedded.

Linking Objects

Linking an object is as simple as embedding one. As a matter of fact, you as a user may be hard pressed to tell the difference. All that's necessary is for you to show the client application where it can find the data provided by the server application. Once that's done, the client will remember and handle the details for you.

Let's look again at the motel memorandum. This time, however, let's pretend that the bedding spreadsheet exists—we'll call it BEDDING.XLS—separately from our memo. What we'll want to do is to establish a link between the memo and spreadsheet. To do so, perform the following steps:

1. Call up the memo in Word. Word displays it for you as a document.

2. Place your cursor at the point in your document where you want the spreadsheet to appear. Then from the Insert menu, select the Object option. Word displays the Object dialog box. (See Figure 4.5.)

FIGURE 4.5.

The Object dialog box with the spreadsheet's filename entered and link instruction set.

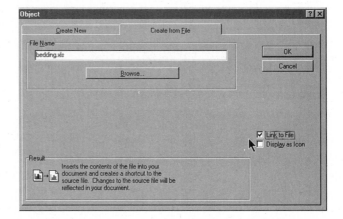

3. We're going to create the link from an already-existing file, so in the Object dialog box, select the Create from File tab.

4. With Create from File active, type the name of the spreadsheet in the File Name text box. If you're not sure of the file's name or location, you can browse for it using the Browse button located just below the text box.

5. Because we're creating a link between this spreadsheet and our memo document, be sure to select the Link to File check box at the dialog box's lower right. Finally, click OK. Word looks for the spreadsheet file on your hard disk (or on the network, of course). Using information contained within it, Word learns that it is Excel data (a fact it will remember), calls up the spreadsheet, and places a copy of it in your memo.

WARNING

If you forget to select Link to File, Word will have no way of knowing that you want to establish a link between the spreadsheet file and the memo document. What it will do instead is make a copy of the spreadsheet and embed it in your memo.

That's all there is to it. The spreadsheet is now part of your memo. As long as it's not moved from its current location, it will be available to your Word memo.

> **TIP**
>
> As you might imagine, there's an easier way to link files. You can do so by copying the server application file, and then selecting Paste, linking it into the client application.

Some Differences Between Embedding and Linking

While they look similar and behave comparably, linking and embedding are two different animals. An embedded document becomes part and parcel of its client document. This can provide you with quite a surprise with graphical files—which can cause your document to multiply in size faster than can rabbit families. A linked file, on the other hand, is more like a distant relative. You can edit it, of course. But so can anyone else with access to the server application. Herein lies another potential surprise, especially if they've ruined your precisely constructed spreadsheet, which you don't have the time/data/inclination to redo.

Table 4.1 delineates for you some of the considerations of linking and embedding.

Table 4.1 Considerations for linking and embedding objects.

Embedding	Consideration	Linking
You'll need one document to contain the object, which is embedded by inserting it from the menu or by dragging and dropping it into the client application.	Creating the object	You'll need two files: one server file and one client file. You create the link by inserting it from the menu or by copying and paste linking.
The client application contains all the information necessary to keep track of the object and its data.	Maintaining the object	Because you can link a single server data file with more than one client application, you will have to keep track of the linked files' locations.

continues

Table 4.1 continued

Embedding	Consideration	Linking
Because the object is completely contained within the client application, only you can update its data.	Updating the object	Anyone with access to the linked file can update it, and so update the object in your client application.
The client grows as the size of the object grows. It also grows with the inclusion of each new embedded object.	Client application file size	There is only a minimal size increase with the linking of each new object into the client application—just enough to keep track of the links themselves.

Activating Your Object in Place

Usually when you want to use some software application, you have to load and run it by clicking an icon. With OLE, that's no longer always necessary. One of the most useful capabilities of OLE objects is that once they're in your client application, you can activate and edit them *in place.*

Let's turn back for a moment to the No Tell Motel memo, shown in Figure 4.5. Notice that you can't tell by looking at it whether the spreadsheet object is embedded or linked. Actually, it doesn't matter.

Let's say you've gotten updated numbers, and you want to modify the figures in the memo. All you have to do is double-click the spreadsheet as it sits there in your client application. Word calls up Excel and displays the spreadsheet object so you can modify it. If the object is linked, then you edit it outside the client, as shown in Figure 4.6. If the object is embedded, then you edit it embedded in the client document, as shown in Figure 4.7.

FIGURE 4.6.

You can edit a linked object from outside the client application.

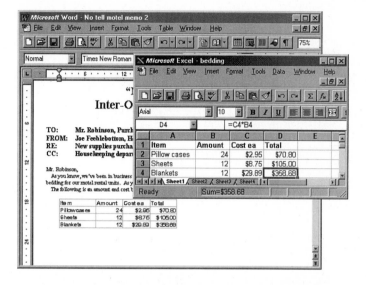

FIGURE 4.7.

Embedded objects are edited in place.

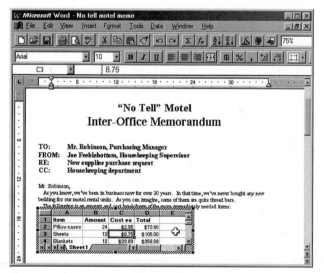

Finding Objects for OLE

It used to be that every Windows application used an initialization file (with an .INI extension) to keep track of various necessary details such as the operating parameters, where data files can be located, and so on. At first it seemed to be a pretty good scheme—until Windows became very popular. Eventually, different applications were using INI files with the same name.

At the same time, more and different kinds of hardware became available to be used with Windows. Each of these often required a place to keep information needed by its driver software. High tech was getting as messy as the average teenager's bedroom.

To solve this problem—one that could only get worse—Microsoft came up with a kind of database called the Windows Registry. Configuration data for hardware and initialization information for software are kept here. It's in this database, also, that the various Microsoft Office applications store the information they need for initialization.

To open the Windows Registry and see its contents, perform the following steps:

1. Click the Start button on the Windows desktop; then select Run. Access displays the Run dialog box.

2. Type regedit in the Open drop-down list box and then click OK. Windows calls up the Registry Editor.

3. In the left-hand pane of the Registry Editor (see Figure 4.8) you can see several keys that begin with HKEY_ listed under the heading My Computer. These are roughly analogous to the bracketed headings in the (now) old-fashioned INI files. Click the plus sign to the left of HKEY_LOCAL_MACHINE. The Registry editor opens the list of local machine parameters.

FIGURE 4.8.

The Registry Editor allows you access to Window initialization and configuration settings.

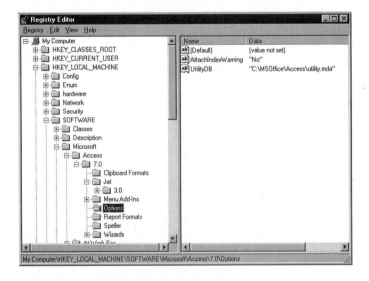

4. Click the plus sign to the left of the SOFTWARE heading. The Registry Editor reveals headings for initialization parameters for the software installed on your computer.

5. In the same way, successively open the Microsoft, Access, and 7.0 lists.

You can change any of the configuration or initialization data by clicking the appropriate field in the right-hand pane of the Registry Editor and then typing in the new data. It becomes active the next time you start Windows.

> **NOTE**
>
> You must be very careful when using the Windows Registry. Any changes you make—inadvertent or not—might be reflected in the behavior of your Windows-based applications. If you're going to do some experimenting, I *strongly* recommend that you first back up the registry.

You'll find this kind of information to be useful the more you get into OLE and its technology. By delving into the system registry, you can divine all of Windows's secrets. You learn things such as what applications can work with which others, what objects they expose, and where the server applications reside.

Browsing Objects

With all the many applications and objects for OLE operations, how can you know which of their properties or methods are available? One easy way is to use the Object Browser available in Access. As an example, let's take a look at the objects the Object Browser exposes to potential Windows clients. (Remember that Access itself can be an OLE server.)

To call up the Object Browser, follow these steps:

1. The Object Browser is available in Access only in a code module window. From the database container window, click the Modules tab.

2. Click the New button. Access opens a code module window.

3. Click the Object Browser button on the Visual Basic toolbar. Access displays the Object Browser window, as you can see in Figure 4.9.

4. In the Libraries/Databases drop-down list box, select Access—Microsoft Access for Windows 95. Access displays its exposable modules in the Modules/Classes list box.

Take a moment to select a module or two. In this example, I've selected the Form class. Notice that its intrinsic methods and properties are displayed to its right in the Methods/Properties list box.

If you select a method or property, its syntax is displayed at the bottom of the Object Browser window. You can then get help on it, specifically, by clicking the Element Help button, located immediately to the left of the syntax example.

FIGURE 4.9.

The Object Browser window shows you what objects and properties can be exposed to client applications.

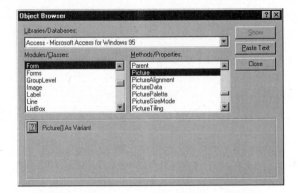

A Few Words About OLE Automation

As you can see, OLE is an easy-to-use manual tool. But if you're a programmer, you can make OLE work for you automatically. You can learn more about this in Chapter 33, "Using OLE and OLE Automation."

When you bring an Excel spreadsheet into Word, you do so because Excel exposes—makes available—its spreadsheet object. And it does so not just to Word, but to any OLE-compliant application. For example, you could just as easily bring a spreadsheet into PowerPoint. As a matter of fact, quite often people bring into PowerPoint charts that they create within Excel from Excel spreadsheet data.

All OLE-compliant applications expose their objects in much the same way. Some, like Word, expose a single object. Others, like Excel, expose almost all their objects. What you as a programmer can do is to access the exposed objects using Visual Basic for Applications, which is included in all the Microsoft Office software to automatically do what we did here manually.

Summary

As you can see, OLE is a powerful tool you can use to make it easier to do your work. With it, you can take the best parts of each kind of software, combine them in new and imaginative ways, and achieve a kind of computerized symbiosis. All it takes is a little daring and a bit of intelligent experimentation. Go for it!

PART

The Common Office

The Microsoft Office Shortcut Bar

5

by David Medinets

IN THIS CHAPTER

Recognizing that users want immediate access to programs, folders, and information, Microsoft has created the Microsoft Office shortcut bar. The shortcut bar gives you the ability to click a button once in order to start programs and open folders.

> **NOTE**
>
> The Office installation program places the shortcut bar in the Startup folder so that it is automatically started whenever your computer is turned on.

The shortcut bar can be displayed as a bar that is attached to the side of the display (this is called *docking*) or a box that can be placed anywhere onscreen (this is called *free-floating*). Figure 5.1 shows how the Office shortcut bar looks when it's docked to the top of the display.

FIGURE 5.1.

The Microsoft Office shortcut bar.

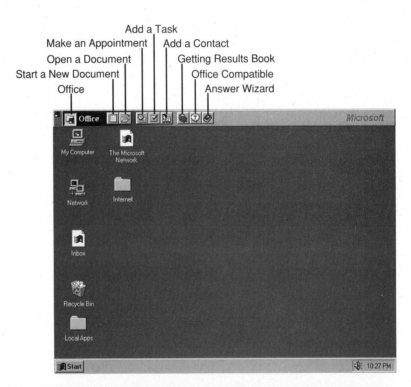

> **TIP**
>
> You can move the shortcut bar by clicking and dragging it. If the cursor is near the side of the display, the drag outline becomes long and narrow to indicate that the shortcut bar can be docked; otherwise, it's a rectangle shape and is free-floating.

Why Is the Office Shortcut Bar Useful?

The Office shortcut bar collects some of the most useful programs and functions of the Office package in one location for easy access. You can think of the shortcut bar as a smorgasbord. Go to the smorgasbord and select your choice with a single click. Contrast this with the taskbar, which requires a minimum of three clicks for you to select a program to run (click Start, click Programs, and then click the options).

You can also think of the shortcut bar as an application that manipulates toolbars. The default toolbar is called Office. However, Microsoft has thoughtfully provided several additional toolbars to make different tasks easier. There are toolbars that duplicate your desktop, display your favorite files, and do many other things. In addition, you can create a new toolbar from scratch, and the shortcut bar will display it in the same manner as the rest.

The ability to dock the shortcut bar to a side of the display makes it easily accessible, no matter what application you are working with. This saves you time: You don't need to close windows in order to start a new task; your options can always be visible. All you need to do is move your cursor to the side of the display and click a button.

What Is a Shortcut?

In order to fully understand the shortcut bar and how it works, you need to know what a shortcut is. A *shortcut* is the way Windows 95 creates a link between a folder and the location of a file. If you have a 5000-byte data file and you want to be able to access it from two folders, you could copy it so that it is in both folders, but this would take up 10,000 bytes. Or you could create a shortcut that links the second folder to the first. The linkage information is held in a file that uses about 350 bytes. Therefore, accessing the data file from two locations only takes about 5350 bytes. This can save a lot of disk space.

Shortcut Bar Options

With the new version of Office, Microsoft has moved toward a more holistic way of working with computers. The Start a New Document and Open a Document features show all of your files, regardless of which application created them. This makes it easier to work with different types of documents. There are also buttons for Schedule+ features, as well as several help files.

NOTE

Microsoft Office uses the term *document* to refer to all data files used by the different applications. A PowerPoint PPT data file and an Excel XLS data file are both considered documents.

The Shortcut Bar Control Menu

You access the shortcut bar Control menu by right-clicking the first button on the toolbar. The "Customize" section of this chapter shows you how to display multiple toolbars. Each toolbar has its own Control menu with the following options:

- ■ Switch to Toolbar—This option displays the toolbar associated with the Control menu you select.

- ■ Hide Toolbar—This option should really be named Disable Toolbar. When selected, it disables the toolbar associated with the Control Menu you select.

- ■ Open—This option opens the folder that holds the shortcut files that make up the toolbar. Unless you are a power user, you won't use this option.

- ■ Properties—This option displays the Properties dialog box. It's not too useful, but you might want to use it to see how much disk space is used by each toolbar.

The Start a New Document Feature

The Start a New Document feature is activated by the first button on the shortcut bar. When you click this button, the New dialog box is displayed. Figure 5.2 shows what the New dialog box looks like.

FIGURE 5.2.

The New dialog box.

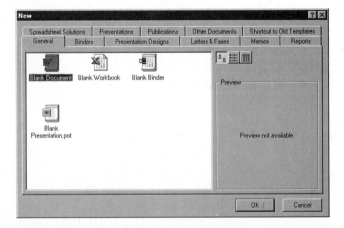

> **NOTE**
>
> The New dialog box does not show up on the taskbar; therefore, if you are using another application while the New dialog box is being displayed, you might need to use the Alt+Tab key combination to select the New dialog box when you want to use it again.

This dialog box contains tabs that organize the application template. A *template* is used as a starting point from which to create a new document. For example, a letter template would have space for the recipient's name and address. A fax cover page template would have space for the sender's name and how many pages are being sent.

There are four types of *blank* or basic templates you can select. Here's a list of them:

- Document—These templates help you to create Microsoft Word documents. Microsoft Word is discussed in Part IV, "The Power of Word."

- Workbook—These templates help you to create Microsoft Excel documents. Microsoft Excel is discussed in Part V, "The Versatility of Excel."

- Binder—These templates help you to create new binders using the Microsoft Binder program. Binders are discussed in Chapter 6, "Binders."

- Presentation—These templates help you to create Microsoft PowerPoint documents. Microsoft PowerPoint is discussed in Part VII, "The Presentation of PowerPoint."

In addition to basic templates, each application has more sophisticated templates. For example, selecting the Publications tab reveals a template called Directory.dot. With this template you can create a directory to show what associate works in each room of a building.

You will also see templates called wizards displayed in the dialog box. A *wizard* is a series of dialog boxes that have been designed to guide you toward a goal. They are fully discussed in Chapter 7, "Wizards."

Each template may have a preview associated with it. A *preview* is the first page of the template and is designed by the creator of the template. Figure 5.3 shows the Elegant Fax template and the preview that is displayed when it is selected. Chapter 10, "Document Patterns and Presentations," shows you how to create your own templates and how to ensure that the preview option is available for your template.

Notice that there are three buttons above the Preview area. These buttons control the way the document list is displayed. The first button displays the document name with a large icon. The second button displays the document name with a small icon, which lets you see more of the document name in the list. The last button displays the details of each document. The details include the name, size, type, and modification date.

The Open a Document Feature

The Open a Document feature is the second button on the shortcut bar. When you click the button, the Open dialog box is displayed as well as a list of all the documents in the My Documents folder. The *My Documents folder* is where all the documents for Office applications are normally saved. Having all your documents in one location makes it easier to find the document you need. It also makes it easier for your family or co-workers to find a letter or document when you are away. Figure 5.4 shows what the Open dialog box looks like.

FIGURE 5.3.

A template with a preview.

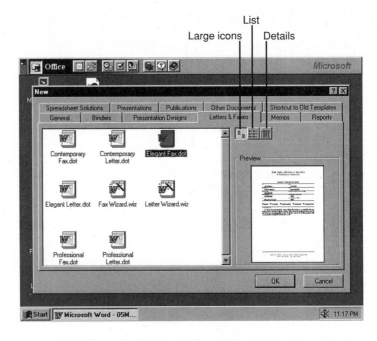

FIGURE 5.4.

The Open dialog box.

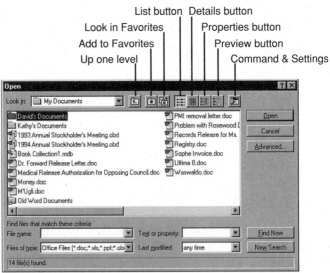

TIP

Files that begin with a tilde (~) are usually temporary documents that Microsoft Word has created. Don't use them; just ignore them.

You can right-click any document displayed in order to see a context menu. A *context menu* contains only options that relate to the object you have clicked. Chapter 8, "Shared Features," discusses context menus.

> **NOTE**
>
> The Open dialog box does not show up on the taskbar; therefore, if you are using another application while the Open dialog box is being displayed, you might need to use the Alt+Tab key combination to select the Open dialog box when you want to use it again.

The Open dialog box is more complicated than the New dialog box. Starting at the top left, here's a brief look at each element:

- Look In drop-down list box—This list box lets you select any of the folders in your system. Once selected, any document that meets the search criteria is displayed.
- Up One Level button—This button moves the current folder up one level in the folder hierarchy. Any documents in the new current folder are displayed.
- Look in Favorites button—This button changes the current folder to Favorites. Any documents in the Favorites folder are displayed.
- Add to Favorites button—This button adds a shortcut, linked to the selected document, to the Favorites folder.
- List button—This button displays the documents in the current folder in simple list format.
- Details button—This button displays the name, size, type, and last modification date of each document. Clicking one of the column titles will sort the documents according to that column.
- Properties button—This button displays the properties of the selected document.
- Preview button—This button displays a preview, if available, of the selected document.
- Commands and Settings button—This button is discussed in detail in the section "The Commands and Settings Button."
- Open button—This button opens the selected document.
- Cancel button—This button closes the dialog box without opening any documents.
- Advanced button—The button lets you use advanced search techniques. It is discussed in detail in the section "The Advanced Button."
- File Name drop-down list box—This list box lets you search for a document by name. You can use wildcards in the filename.
- File of Type drop-down list box —This list box lets you specify the type of document to include in the search.

- Text or Property drop-down list box—This list box lets you enter either some text (such as Presidential or Snowy River) or a property name (such as Authorization Initials). Only documents containing the text or property will be displayed.

- Last Modified—This list box lets you narrow the search drop-down list box to include only those documents modified yesterday, today, last week, this week, last month, or this month. A value of anytime includes all documents.

- Find Now button—This button starts the search after you have filled in the appropriate information.

- New Search button—This button resets the search parameters to include all documents.

The Commands and Settings Button

The Commands and Settings button displays a menu, similar to a context menu, with the following eight options:

- Open Read Only—This option opens the selected document in read-only mode. Changes made to the documents cannot be saved using the original document name.

- Print—This option prints the selected document.

- Properties—This option displays the Properties dialog box of the selected document.

- Sorting—This option displays a dialog box that lets you sort by name, size, type, or modification date.

> **TIP**
>
> Sorting is much easier if you use the detail view and then click the category you would like to sort by.

- Search Subfolders—This option lets you display the documents in the My Documents folder as well as in subfolders.

- Group Files by Folder—This option is only active when you have selected Search Subfolders. When selected, this option displays the subfolders and documents in a hierarchic fashion. This option is highly recommended if you have the Search Subfolders option turned on.

- Map Network Drive—This option lets you link to network drives if you are connected to a local area network.

- Saved Searches—This option lets you select previously saved search criteria. The Advanced Search feature (discussed in the following section) allows you to save search parameters for later use.

The Advanced Button

The Advanced button in the Open dialog box displays the Advanced Find dialog box. This dialog box allows you to set up complicated criteria to guide searches. The set of criteria may be saved and retrieved later so that the same search can be performed repeatedly. Figure 5.5 shows what the Advanced Find dialog box looks like.

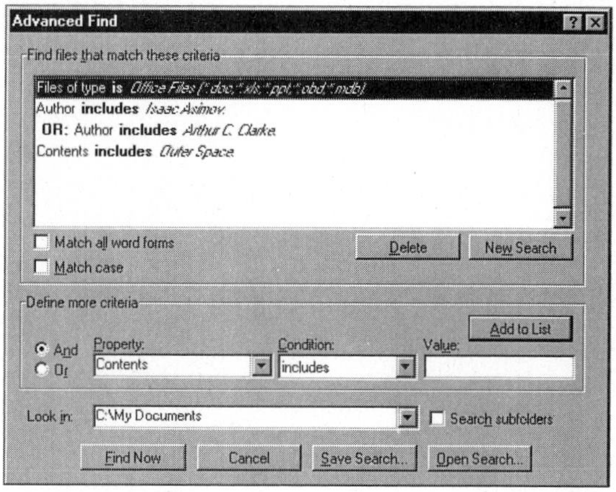

FIGURE 5.5.

The Advanced Find dialog box.

The large area titled Find files that match these criteria holds the different criteria that define a search. You'll also see two mutually exclusive check boxes: Match all word forms and Match case. If you check the Match all word forms check box, then the criteria "Contents includes John is running" will match the phrase "John was running." If you check the Match case check box, the phrase "Joe Smith" will not match "joe smith" because the capitalization is different.

The different ways to specify criteria are controlled by the second area, titled Define more criteria. You can select the logical operand (And or Or), the property, the condition, and the value. Clicking the Add To List button will add the criteria you defined to the criteria list at the top of the dialog box.

The dialog box also lets you specify which folder to start the search in and whether to include subfolders.

After defining a search, you can save the criteria list using the Save Search button. Later, you can recall the criteria list using the Saved Searches option of the Commands and Settings menu.

Schedule+

Schedule+ is one of the new applications included in Office 95. The default button bar contains shortcuts that quickly let you make an appointment, add a task to your to do list, and add a contact to your contact manager. Schedule+ is fully discussed in Part VIII, "Making Time with Schedule+."

The Getting Results Book

The Getting Results book is dedicated to answering questions about how to do *your* work, not what features are available or how each feature works. Here are a few of the topics:

- Get Your Message Across
- Your Numbers Take Shape
- Beyond the Card File
- Budgeting with Microsoft Excel

As you can see from this small sample of topics, Microsoft has focused on how you can be more productive by gently extending your knowledge about how to automate everyday tasks. You don't need to worry about being inundated with trivia about the application; you just get the information that you need *today*!

> **NOTE**
>
> This electronic book is located on the Office CD-ROM. Before clicking the Getting Results Book button, be sure to insert the Office CD-ROM.

The Office Compatible Button

The Office Compatible button starts a catalog of 25 Office Compatible products. A small demonstration of each product can be viewed. The catalog is located on the CD-ROM. Before clicking the Office Compatible button, be sure to insert the Office CD-ROM.

The Answer Wizard

The Answer Wizard is a new help feature of the Office 95 suite. It allows you to ask questions in a natural way and get a response. For example, if you type "How do I create a table?" one of the responses will be "Deciding which Office application to use to create a table." The Answer Wizard is discussed further in Chapter 7.

The Shortcut Bar Context Menu

The shortcut bar options are located on the shortcut bar's context menu. The context menu is displayed by right-clicking anywhere on the shortcut bar (except on a button). Figure 5.6 shows what the context menu looks like.

The top of the context menu lists all the toolbars that the shortcut bar knows about. Toolbars that are currently active have checkmarks next to them. Selecting a toolbar in the menu will toggle its status from enabled to disabled or vice versa.

Chapter 5

FIGURE 5.6.

The Context Menu for the shortcut bar.

In addition to displaying all the available toolbars, the context menu has these three options:

- Auto Hide—This option makes the shortcut bar remove itself from the display while you are working.
- Customize—This option lets you change the features and contents of the toolbars that the shortcut bar manipulates.
- Refresh Icons—If you add programs or delete folders, you can use this option to refresh the toolbars.

These three options are discussed in more detail in the following sections.

Auto Hide

When this option is checked, the shortcut bar will hide itself when the cursor is no longer over it. Watching the shortcut bar sink into the side of the display is kind of fun.

You can retrieve the shortcut bar by moving your cursor to the edge of the display where the shortcut bar was docked. The shortcut bar should instantly appear.

> **NOTE**
>
> This feature is only active when the shortcut bar is docked. If the shortcut bar is free-floating or the option labeled Auto-Fit in Title Bar Area is selected, the shortcut bar will not hide itself.

Customize

The Customize menu option displays a dialog box that has four tabs: View, Buttons, Toolbars, and Settings. You can also display the dialog box by double-clicking the shortcut bar.

View

The View tab has two sections: Color and Options. The Color section lets you select the color of each toolbar. The Options section lets you change the behavior of the shortcut bar. Here is a list of the options:

■ Large Buttons—This option essentially doubles the size of the buttons on the shortcut bar. Larger buttons may make it easier to find the one you need.

■ Show ToolTips—This option displays a small description of a button when the cursor hovers over it. This option is highly recommended.

■ Always on Top—This option keeps the shortcut bar on top of every other window on the display. Most users find that this option becomes annoying after a while because they are constantly moving the shortcut bar to see underneath it.

■ Auto Hide Between Uses—This option is discussed in the "Auto Hide" section of this chapter.

NOTE

If you have Auto-Fit checked, then the Auto Hide option is disabled.

■ Auto-Fit in Title Bar Area—This option positions the shortcut bar at the top of the display in an abbreviated format. The idea is that when an application's window is maximized, the shortcut bar is already positioned to the title bar area. This option is very useful if there is a limited number (about 13 or 14) of choices on the enabled toolbars. Additional choices will start to overwrite the application's title bar information.

TIP

Don't use the Large Button option with Auto-Fit in Title Bar Area because the buttons will display outside the title area.

■ Animate Toolbars—This option causes the toolbars to sweep across the shortcut bar as you select a different toolbar. If your system is slow, turn off this option.

■ Sound—This option plays a short, swishing sound as you select the different toolbars.

■ Show Title Screen at Startup—This option controls the display of the title screen when the shortcut bar first starts.

TIP

Try different combinations of locations and toolbars before making a decision about the style and location you prefer. You might find that you want to use different options depending on the type of work you are doing each day.

The Buttons Tab

The Buttons tab controls which programs or buttons are displayed in each toolbar. Every program that is available for use is displayed in a list box. To the left of each program is a check box that controls whether that program is displayed on the toolbar. There is also an option to add or delete programs (files) and folders to or from the toolbar.

The Toolbars Tab

The Toolbars tab is another way to control which toolbars will be enabled. To enable a toolbar, click the check box next to it.

In addition to the default Office shortcut bar, you can enable shortcut bars that display the following items:

- The desktop
- The Favorites folder
- Microsoft Network programs
- The Programs folder from the Start menu
- The Accessories folder

Figure 5.7 shows the shortcut bar with all the different bars enabled. Notice that the shortcut bar is free-floating. This configuration seems to work best when many toolbars are enabled. You select an alternate toolbar by clicking its title.

FIGURE 5.7.

The shortcut bar with all bars enabled.

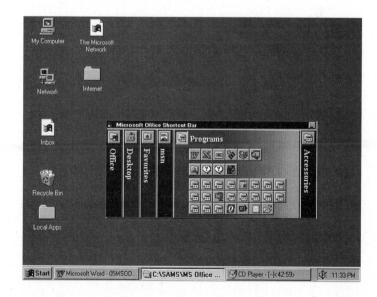

You have total control over which bars are displayed. Therefore, if you want to display only four of the six bars, you can disable the two bars you don't want.

In addition to the predefined shortcut bars, you can create your own bars using the Add Toolbar button. You can make a toolbar that duplicates a folder to allow easy access to the files, or you can create your own toolbar.

> **TIP**
>
> Create a different toolbar for each member of your family. This way, your personal toolbar won't be affected when someone else wants to experiment.

The Settings Tab

The Settings tab lets you change the folder in which the Start a New Document program looks for templates and wizards. You can also tell Office where workgroup templates are located. This is useful in networked offices and homes.

The Refresh Icons Option

The Refresh Icons option is used when the folders that the toolbars are based on have changed. For example, suppose you have enabled the Desktop toolbar. If you then add an icon to your desktop, the Refresh Icons option will synchronize the toolbar to your new desktop.

As an administrator, you can also create and distribute custom toolbars. The toolbars that appear on the shortcut bar are TBB files that are stored in \Office95\Office\ShortCut Bar on the user's computer. The buttons that appear on the Office toolbar by default are shortcut files that are stored in \Office95\Office\ShortCut Bar\Office.

Simply creating the correct files in the directory is not enough; the Registry also needs to be set up correctly. Therefore, you should use the dialog boxes.

Summary

This chapter discusses the Microsoft Office shortcut bar, why it is useful, what the standard buttons do, and how to add new buttons. Using the shortcut bar will help you to become more productive.

Taking the time to think about how you use your computer to perform daily tasks and then changing the toolbar to better fit your needs will make you even more productive. For example, if you find yourself using the Calculator application a lot, then you should place it on the Office toolbar so that you can start it instantly.

Chapter 6, "Binders," discusses another way that Microsoft Office can help you work.

Binders

6

by David Medinets

In Chapter 5, "The Microsoft Office Shortcut Bar," you saw how Microsoft has moved away from looking at applications as separate programs through the implementation of the New and Open dialog boxes, which are used in all Office applications.

With the Office Binder application, Microsoft has gone one step further. Taking a cue from the business office environment, the Office Binder collects documents in an electronic three-ring binder. This application combines Excel, PowerPoint, and Word documents into one file by using extensions to OLE technology. Combining the different application documents into one file lets you open, save, print, or mail them as one unit.

A binder about a business meeting might include an invitation, an address list, an agenda, some presentation slides, the minutes of the meeting, and a wrap-up memo. The binder captures information at and about every stage of the meeting, from scheduling to following up on action items. If you are working with a co-worker to schedule the meeting, having all the information in one location will make collaboration easier. This example is taken from one of the sample templates (Meeting Organizer) that comes with Office Binder. Figure 6.1 shows a blank Meeting Organizer binder. More information about the templates provided with Office Binder can be found in the "Office Binder Templates" section of this chapter.

FIGURE 6.1.

A blank Meeting Organizer binder.

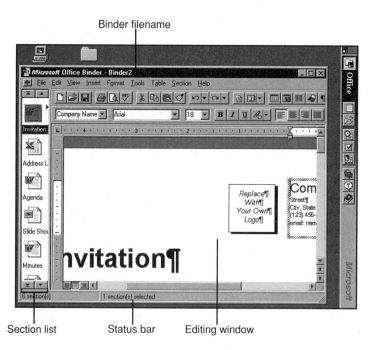

Each document in a binder is called a *section*. Sections can be rearranged, renamed, added, deleted, hidden, and printed. The information in each section is stored inside the binder file. There are no auxiliary files used. For this reason, the binder files can get rather large.

> **NOTE**
>
> When using Windows Explorer to view the file system, you need to know what the file extensions stand for. Here are the three extensions that Office Binder uses:
>
> | Extension | File Type |
> | --- | --- |
> | .OBD | Binder document |
> | .OBT | Binder template |
> | .OBZ | Binder wizard (a binder template that includes macros) |

Office Binder Advantages

The Office Binder has many advantages over simply grouping files together in a window folder. These advantages are discussed in this section.

Consistent Section Order

You can arrange the sections of a binder in any order you like. This order is saved with the binder file. When you group documents in a folder, the operating system controls and limits the ways you can order or sort the documents. For example, if you want to sort documents that begin with numbers, you need to add leading zeros (for example, 001, 050, 400) so that they sort correctly. There is no way to do a reverse sort so that higher numbers appear first.

Consecutive Page Numbers

Using binders lets you print sections with consecutive page numbers. This includes all the different types of applications. An Excel spreadsheet that follows a Word document will start its page number wherever the Word document ends.

E-mail

When using electronic mail to transmit information, it is usually much easier to send one file than many files. In any case, using only one file (the binder) makes it impossible to forget to send one of the needed documents.

More Efficiency

Opening one file (the binder) is more efficient that opening several files; therefore, moving between documents is faster.

Using Briefcase

You can use the Briefcase file synchronization program to allow several people to work on the same binder at once. Each person using the binder copies it to his or her local briefcase from a network file server. Then each user can work on his or her own individual sections. When the original file is updated using Briefcase, only the changed sections are updated.

If the same section has been changed in both the original file and the personal file, you'll be asked how to handle the situation.

Global Spell Checking

With the new Spell It feature (discussed in Chapter 8, "Shared Features"), each section is automatically spell checked as it is created. Therefore, there is no spell check feature for the entire binder.

Office Binder Limitations

There are also some limitations to binders. This section discusses a few of them.

Disabled Features

Some application features are disabled inside the Office Binder program. For example, to reduce possible confusion, the individual application status bars are disabled. Only the Office Binder status bar is visible when a section is being edited.

You also can't create or edit macros inside the sections. In order to do this, you need to save the section to a separate file, add the macro or edit an existing one, and then reattach it to the binder.

> **TIP**
>
> Use the Section | Save As menu option to save a section as a separate document. Then use the Section | Add From File menu option to reattach it.

Large Physical Files

Office Binder files have a tendency to grow quite large. This causes the physical file to sprawl all over your hard disk as the file becomes fragmented. If you notice that a binder takes a long time to load, the following steps will eliminate the fragmentation:

1. Open the binder.
2. Use the File | Save Binder As menu option to save the binder with a new name.

3. Delete the old binder file.

4. Rename the new binder with the old binder name.

Security

Office Binder does not support any type of security. If a password-protected document is added to a binder, the password will be requested when the document is added. However, once added, the password protection is lost.

> **NOTE**
>
> The Protect and Unprotect menu options are still active inside the binder. They just don't protect anything.

You can gain a small measure of security by setting the Read-Only attribute of the binder file using the Windows Explorer. This is done by right-clicking the file, selecting Properties, and then checking the Read-Only check box on the General tab. However, doing so still allows someone to rename the file and save another in its place.

A stronger security measure is to store the binder on a read-only network drive. Talk with your network administrator about this possibility.

The Office Binder Menu Bar

Office Binder is an OLE container application. This means that when editing a document, the menu bar changes to reflect the application that is responsible for that particular document. In addition to the three standard menu commands, each application (Word, Excel, and PowerPoint) adds some of its own menu commands.

> **NOTE**
>
> Each application is subservient to Office Binder. This means, among other things, that the status area is suppressed. For example, Word normally shows the current page and section number in the status area. When you're looking at a Word document in Office Binder, this information is not displayed.

A binder is used to combine the documents of other Microsoft Office applications. Therefore, when Office Binder is started with a blank binder, its menus consist of options that relate to opening a new or existing binder, changing binder properties, adding sections, and accessing some help selections. After the first section is added, more options will become available.

Since Office Binder is a brand-new application, let's take a quick look the basic menu structure. Figure 6.2 shows what the menu structure looks like when no documents have been added to a binder.

FIGURE 6.2.

The basic Office Binder menu structure.

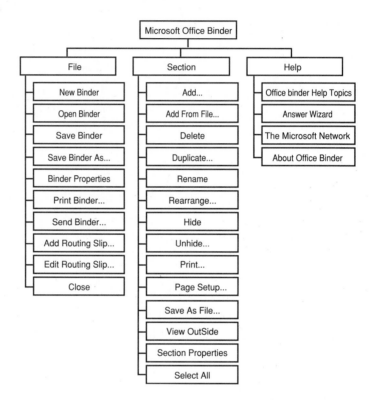

The File Menu

The File menu has options to manipulate the binder as a whole. Each menu option is briefly discussed in the following list:

- New Binder—This option lets you select the type of binder you want to create. The standard types are Blank, Client Billing, Meeting Organizer, Proposal and Marketing, and Report.
- Open Binder—This option lets you select an existing binder to open.
- Save Binder—This option saves the current binder.
- Save Binder As—This option lets you specify a filename for your binder. Remember that you can use long filenames.
- Binder Properties—This option displays the Microsoft Office Binder Properties dialog box, as shown in Figure 6.3.

FIGURE 6.3.

The Microsoft Office Binder Properties dialog box.

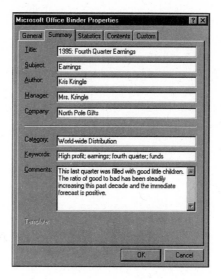

There are five tabs from which to choose:

General—This tab displays the binder name, location, creation date, last modified data, and the size in bytes.

Summary—This tab has input fields for the binder's title, subject, author information, manager information, company information, category names, keywords, and comments.

Statistics—This tab displays the binder creation date, last modification date, last access date, last printed date, who last saved it, and other information such as the number of pages, paragraphs, and lines.

Contents—This tab displays the section names that are in your binder.

Custom—This tab has input fields for adding custom properties to the binder. You can access a drop-down list of 27 properties by clicking the down arrow next to the Name field. You can add as many other properties to the list as you like.

The Summary and Custom tabs both let you set property values. Depending on your point of view, the most important use for the properties might be for documentation. For example, corporations' auditing areas need to know who the last person to modify a document was and when the document was last changed.

Most users, however, will probably use the properties to help them find documents in the future. If you consistently fill in the property information, you can use the new search facilities in the New and Open dialog boxes to find documents quickly. More information about properties can be found in Chapter 8.

■ Print Binder—This option displays a dialog box that lets you select a printer as well as determine the number of copies and collating sequence. In addition, you can request to print only the current section or all sections. This dialog box also controls whether the page numbering is consecutive or restarts for each section.

> **TIP**
>
> To consecutively number pages, you'll need to create headers or footers in each of the sections in the binder. You also need to make sure that the initial page numbers are not reset inside the sections.

■ Send Binder—This option interfaces with your e-mail package to mail the binder.

■ Add Routing Slip—This option lets you add a routing slip to your binder. The routing slip connects to your e-mail system so that you can easily select the names and addresses of future destinations.

■ Edit Routing Slip—After you add a routing slip, the Add Routing Slip menu option changes to Edit Routing Slip.

■ Close—This option closes the Office Binder application. If any sections have been changed, you'll be given the chance to save them.

The Section Menu

The Section menu lets you manipulate each section as an individual element. The menu options are briefly discussed in the following list:

■ Add—This option adds an Excel chart, an Excel worksheet, a PowerPoint presentation, or a Word document to the open binder.

This option does not let you choose a template on which to base your new document. If you need to use a specific template, create the document using the New dialog box (as described in Chapter 5) and then use the Add From File menu option.

You can also add sections by dragging and dropping documents from the file system. If you drop an unknown document type, MS Word will try to convert it automatically to a Word document.

■ Add From File—This option adds an existing document to the binder. It's important to realize that making changes to the new section *does not* change the original document. This is because the section is stored in the binder file along with the other sections.

■ Delete—This option deletes the selected section(s). A confirmation message is displayed to help avoid accidental deleting.

■ Duplicate—This option duplicates the selection. A dialog box will ask you where in the section list the new section should be inserted.

- Rename—This option lets you rename the selected section. You can also rename a section by double-clicking the section name under the icon.

- Rearrange—This option lets you rearrange the order of the sections. You can also rearrange sections by right-clicking a section icon and then dragging it to a new location. A small arrow appears to the right of the section list, indicating where the section will be inserted when you stop dragging.

- Hide—This option hides the active section. A hidden section is not displayed in the section list.

- Unhide—This option displays a dialog box listing the hidden sections. You can select one section to unhide. This section will become the active section.

- Print—This option prints the current sections. The options in the Print dialog box change according to the application that is being used to edit the active section.

- Page Setup—This option lets you modify the page size, margins, and other page settings. The dialog box that is displayed changes according to the application that is being used to edit the active section.

- Save As File—This option lets you save the active section to a separate file. Changes to the new file *will not* be reflected in the binder.

- View Outside—This option moves the editing window out of the Office Binder's window. This way, you can see two sections at once. Also, this makes the application's status area visible and all of the application menu options available.

- Section Properties—This option displays the Section Properties dialog box. This dialog box is exactly like the Binder Properties dialog box, except that the information is pulled from the section instead of the binder as a whole.

- Select All—This option selects all the sections.

The Help Menu

The Help menu options change to reflect which application is being used to edit the active section. The four basic options are briefly discussed in the following list:

- Office Binder Help Topics—This option displays the Office Binder Help dialog box, which has four tabs: Contents, Index, Find, and Answer Wizard.

- Answer Wizard—The Answer Wizard lets you ask a question using everyday English. The Answer Wizard is discussed further in Chapter 7, "Wizards."

- The Microsoft Network—This option connects you to the Microsoft Network.

- About Office Binder—This option displays the Office Binder version number and product ID. There are also buttons for getting system information as well as information about tech support.

Using Unbind

If you right-click a binder (OBD) file, you'll see the Unbind option on the context menu. This option automatically splits a binder into its individual parts using the section names as the filenames. Making changes to the individual files does not change the original binder. The individual files are stored in the same folder as the binder.

Common Problems with Binder

The Office Binder program has its share of problems that may arise. The following are a few of the most common ones:

- The binder is too large to print—If you encounter this problem, simply print the binder in sections, a few at a time. The page numbers will still be consecutive if you have the headers or footers set up correctly.

- The page numbers don't print—The main reason for this problem is that one of the binder sections does not have page numbering enabled.

- Incorrect page numbers—When printing with consecutive page numbers, the initial page number for each section is determined by Office Binder. If you explicitly reset the page numbering inside the section, the page numbers will be incorrect.

   To fix this problem, print each section individually. When the incorrect page numbers appear, edit that section and remove the page number setting. Unfortunately, there is not yet a print preview facility in Office Binder.

- The binder is too large to e-mail—Sending a binder through your e-mail system might be impractical because of its size. If you need to do this often, consider writing a macro to unbind the individual sections, e-mail them, and then recombine them. You might also consider placing the file on a network shared drive.

- External OLE links are unsupported—While it is possible to embed an OLE object in a binder section, you can't link a document to a binder section. Linking between two sections in the same binder is possible.

- Problems opening binders or sections—If you have run into a problem opening a binder or a section, try unbinding the binder; then double-click each separate file to determine which section has the problem. When the section with the problem is found, delete that section from the binder. Alternatively, you can create a new binder and add each section to it.

Office Binder Templates

An Office Binder template is the foundation you use to build your own binders. In the opening paragraphs of this chapter, you read about the Meeting Organizer template. Microsoft has also supplied templates for Proposal and Marketing binders, as well as Report binders. If you use a template to start your binder, remember that you are not limited to those sections already provided. You can add or delete sections as needed. Table 6.1 shows what sections each template provides.

Table 6.1. The Office Binder templates.

Template Name	Section List
Meeting Organizer	Invitation Memo (Word)
	Address List (Excel)
	Slide Show (PowerPoint)
	Minutes (Word)
	Memo (Word)
Proposal and Marketing	Cover Letter (Word)
	Quote (Excel)
	Slide Show (PowerPoint)
	Referrals (Word)
	Details (Word)
	Follow-up (Word)
Report	Cover Letter (Word)
	Executive Summary (Word)
	Slide Show (PowerPoint)
	Analysis (Word)
	Data (Excel)

You can select any of these templates from the Binders tab of the New dialog box. (See Figure 6.4.)

Creating an Office Binder Template

Using templates can save you time: Designing the look of a report or deciding which sections need to be in a presentation can take a significant amount of effort. In order to reduce the effort needed in the future, save your work in template form.

You can create your own Office Binder template by following these steps:

1. Create a binder with the sections you want to save for the future.
2. Select the File | Save Binder As menu option.
3. Change the Save As Type field to Binder Templates.
4. Double-click the Binders folder.

FIGURE 6.4.

The New dialog box showing the Office Binder templates.

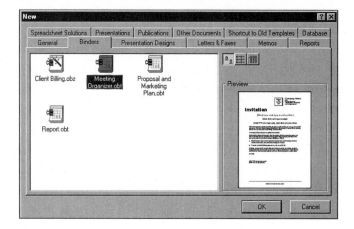

5. Enter a filename for your binder. Remember that you can use long filenames.

6. Click Save.

If you would like to create a preview for your template, make sure to check the Save Preview Picture option on the Summary tab of the Section Properties dialog box in the first section of the binder.

> **TIP**
>
> To save hard disk space, only the first section should have the Save Preview Picture option checked.

The Client Billing Wizard

The Office Binder includes one wizard you can use to help create a binder for client billing.

> **NOTE**
>
> A *wizard* is a series of dialog boxes that automates the creation or formatting of binders, documents, tables, and so on. More information about wizards can be found in Chapter 7.

The Client Billing wizard has six steps. The first step asks you what sections would you like in your binder. You can include any of the following sections in your binder:

Fax Cover (Word)
Cover Letter (Word)

Invoice (Excel)
Timecard (Excel)
Materials Card (Excel)
Attachments (Word)

The rest of the steps customize the binder to your particular needs.

Summary

The Office Binder application will probably prove to be of great use to you. Its advantages are numerous, especially if you take the time to create templates ahead of time.

Anytime you have a recurring document, take a moment to decide if creating a template now will save time in the future.

Microsoft will undoubtedly improve on the Office Binder, so you can look forward to additional functionality as well as more types of documents available to include as sections. For example, wouldn't it be nice to have pictures and sound files independent of Word or PowerPoint? Third-party vendors also will be able to add features to the Office Binder.

Wizards

7

*by David
Medinets*

Most of us would like to be able to answer a few simple questions about the task that we need done, then push a button—and presto!—the task is done. Sounds like magic, right? Well, Microsoft Office has the next best thing—wizards.

A *wizard* is a series of dialog boxes that gather information about a task. When all of the information has been gathered, the task is performed. Wizards operate in a step-by-step fashion. Each dialog box that is displayed is generally considered one step in the process of gathering the information needed to finish the task. However, some steps may be skipped if they do not relate directly to your needs.

There are two wizards that do not follow the norm. They are the Answer Wizard and the Tip Wizard. Both of these are discussed in the next section, "Help Wizards." The section "Application Wizards" discusses the wizards available in each application and how they can help you do your work.

Help Wizards

The new version of Microsoft Office introduces two new wizards used in the help system: the Answer Wizard and the Tip Wizard.

The Answer Wizard

The Answer Wizard lets you type in a phrase like "How do I resize a picture?" in order to get help resizing a picture. Figure 7.1 displays the results of typing in this phrase.

FIGURE 7.1.

The Answer Wizard.

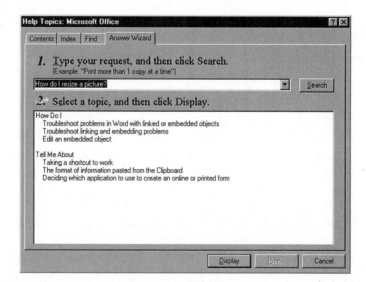

The Answer Wizard works in two steps. The first step asks you to enter a question using plain English into the field at the top of the dialog box. Then, when you press Enter or click the Search button, a list of topics appears in the bottom part of the dialog box. You can elect to view any of the topics. Odds are that one of them will contain the information you seek.

The topics that appear will be in one of three categories:

- How Do I—The help topics listed under this category give you a step-by-step account of *how* to perform a specific task. Figure 7.2 shows you an example of this type of help topic.

FIGURE 7.2.

An example of a How Do I help topic.

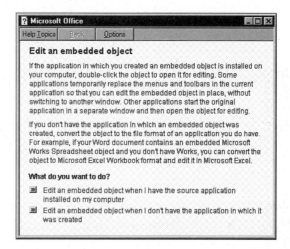

- Tell Me About—The help topics listed under this category are informational in nature, tending to explain why and what things are. Figure 7.3 shows you an example of this type of help topic.

FIGURE 7.3.

An example of a Tell Me About help topic.

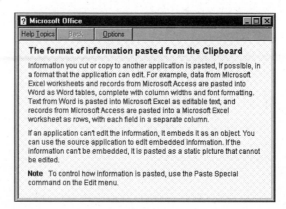

■ Programming and Language Reference—The help topics listed under this category are part of the WordBasic and Visual Basic for Applications online reference material. These help topics assist you when writing macros to automate your work.

The dialog box that displays the Answer Wizard has four tabs. One, of course, is the Answer Wizard. The others—Contents, Index, and Find—let you access the normal help system. If you can't find the information using the Answer Wizard, try the Index or the Find tabs.

The Tip Wizard

The Tip Wizard, when activated, works like a backseat driver. Whenever the Tip Wizard thinks there might be a better way of performing a task, it displays a message. Typical messages relate to alternative ways of formatting or letting you know about shortcut keys.

The View|Toolbars menu option activates the Tip Wizard. Check the box next to the Tip Wizard option.

Application Wizards

Each Microsoft Office application has its own set of wizards to help you with tasks. Microsoft Word has a number of wizards devoted to helping you format documents—from a simple business letter to a complex résumé. Microsoft Excel has wizards to help format charts and to select a function for use in formulas.

Access Wizards

Microsoft Access seems to have the most wizards. It has wizards to help you create forms, tables, queries, and reports. It even has a wizard to guide you in setting up the security constraints for a database.

Database Wizards

Creating a database from scratch can be a daunting task if you do not have experience in database management. In order to help you create some basic databases, Microsoft has developed 22 different Database Wizards, which can all be started with the New dialog box. Figure 7.4 shows the New dialog box with some of the Database Wizards displayed.

Table 7.1 lists the Database Wizards and gives a short description of the databases created by the wizards.

FIGURE 7.4.

The New dialog box showing the Database Wizards.

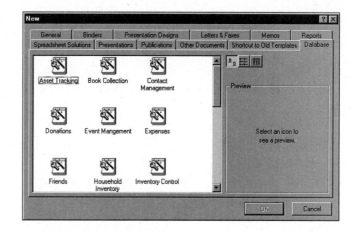

Table 7.1. Descriptions of the 22 Database Wizards.

Wizard Name	Description
Asset Tracking	This database stores asset information, depreciation history, maintenance history, employee information, vendor information, and department information.
Book Collection	This database stores book, author, and quotation information.
Contact Management	This database stores contact and call information.
Donations	This database stores contributor, pledge, and donation campaign information.
Event Management	This database stores event, event attendee, event registration, event type, employee, and event pricing information.
Expenses	This database stores employee, expense report, expense detail, and expense category information.
Friends	This database stores information about your friends such as name, address, e-mail address, birthday, hobbies, and a photograph.
Household Inventory	This database stores information about your household items. The information includes a description, room, purchase price, manufacturer, and a photograph.
Inventory Control	This database stores product, sales, purchasing, purchase order, supplier, and employee information.

continues

Table 7.1. continued

Wizard Name	Description
Ledger	This database stores transaction, account, and classification information.
Membership	This database stores member, membership type, committee, and payment information.
Music Collection	This database tracks album name, format, track information, artist name, and music type (among other things).
Order Processing	This database stores customer, order, order detail, payment, and product information.
Picture Library	This database stores information about rolls of film and photographs.
Recipes	This database stores information about recipes and their ingredients.
Resource Scheduling	This database stores resource, resource schedule, schedule detail, resource type, and customer information.
Service Call Management	This database stores customer, work order, labor, parts, payment, and employee information.
Students and Classes	This database stores department, instructor, class, assignment, student, and student score information.
Time and Billing	This database stores client, project, time card, hours, expense, employee, and payment information.
Video Collection	This database stores videotape, actor, and videotaped program information.
Wine List	This database stores wine and purchase information.
Workout	This database stores workout track record, workout track details, and exercise information.

Each Database Wizard follows the same six steps:

1. The wizard displays information about what is tracked by the database.
2. The wizard lists optional database fields you can add and asks about including sample data.
3. The wizard asks you to choose a style for the screen displays.
4. The wizard asks you to select a style for the printed reports.
5. You choose a title and add a graphic to the main database window and reports.
6. You indicate whether you would like to use the database after creating it.

Form Wizards

The Form Wizards help you to develop forms that display and gather information. Forms can include field names, list boxes, check boxes, graphics, and other ways to display information.

The Form Wizards will only produce forms that include field names and simple input fields (except for the Chart and PivotTable Form Wizards). If you need more complicated forms, you can use a wizard to create a basic form, and then edit it to add the "smarts" you need.

Figure 7.5 shows the New Form dialog box that lists the Form Wizards.

FIGURE 7.5.

The New Form dialog box showing a list of Form Wizards.

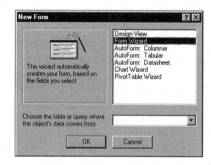

There are four steps to creating a form using the Form Wizards:

1. Select the record source for the form.

> **NOTE**
>
> A *record source* is the table or query from which you pull information.

2. Select a form layout (columnar, tabular, or datasheet).
3. Choose a form style.
4. Enter a title for the form.

If these steps sound familiar, they should. They are identical to Steps 3 through 5 of the Database Wizards. The wizards use the same steps because they need the same information in order to create several behind-the-scenes forms.

AutoForm Wizards

Access has another group of wizards—the AutoForm Wizards—that make it even simpler to create forms. Simply telling Access which record source to use allows these wizards to create columnar, tabular, or datasheet forms. Every field in the table or query will be on the form. These are great wizards to use when you want a basic form to customize.

The Chart Wizard for Forms

The Chart Wizard helps you to create a form that contains 1 of 12 chart types. You can select from area, bar, column, doughnut, line, pie, scatter, 3-D area, 3-D bar, 3-D column, 3-D line, or 3-D pie chart. A sample chart can be displayed during the creation process so that you can be sure you are making it the right way. Figure 7.6 shows the dialog box that lets you choose the chart type for the new form.

FIGURE 7.6.

The 12 chart types.

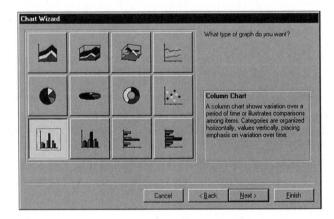

The PivotTable Wizard

The PivotTable Wizard creates a form with a pivot table. This is a powerful way to look at your data. Chapter 23, "Creating and Customizing Pivot Tables," has information about pivot tables and how to use them. The discussion about the Excel PivotTable Wizard in that chapter can be directly applied to this wizard.

Query Wizards

Microsoft Access has the ability to create very powerful and complex queries. A query can involve one or more record sources and can include criteria that records need to meet before being displayed. For example, a query could be this: List all customers whose names begin with *B* and who haven't ordered anything in the last six months.

A temporary table is created to contain the records that fit the guidelines defined by the query. If you change the values in the query table, you will also change these values in the original record source on which the query was based.

You can choose from six different Query Wizards. First, here's a look at the two-step Simple Query Wizard:

1. You select a record source for the query and then determine which fields from the record source will be included.

2. Enter a title for the new query.

If the resultant query is not right, you can rerun the wizard or change the query in design view.

Access has five other Query Wizards. They are discussed in the following sections.

The Crosstab Query Wizard

A crosstab query shows information in spreadsheet fashion. As an example, Figure 7.7 shows a crosstab of Recording Artist plotted against Recording Label using the Music Collection database.

FIGURE 7.7.

A sample crosstab query.

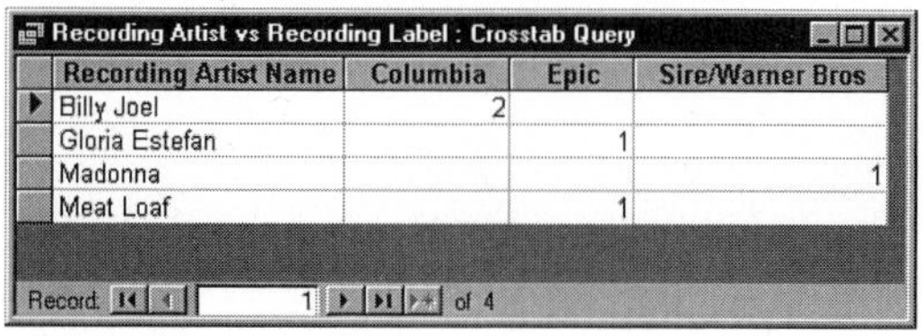

Recording Artist Name	Columbia	Epic	Sire/Warner Bros
Billy Joel	2		
Gloria Estefan		1	
Madonna			1
Meat Loaf		1	

Recording Artist vs Recording Label : Crosstab Query

Record: |◄| ◄ | 1 | ► |►►|►*| of 4

You can see that the database has two albums by Billy Joel, and both were recorded by Columbia. Also, the database has only one album by Meat Loaf; Epic recorded it.

The Find Duplicates Query Wizard

Suppose you need to create a list of recording artists for whom you have more than one album. You can build a query using the Find Duplicates Query Wizard. This works when one field, such as Recording Artist, is common or duplicated in more than one record in a record source. Any value that shows up more than once is displayed.

The Find Unmatched Query Wizard

You might think that finding unmatched records is the opposite of finding duplicate records. However, this is not the case. The Find Unmatched Query Wizard operates on two record sources.

The Find Unmatched Query Wizard creates a query that examines two record sources and finds records in the first record source that have no match in the second record source. For example, if one table holds customers and one table holds orders, you can find customers who have not placed an order. This works because the customers with no orders will have no matching records in the Order table.

In order for the query to work, you need to tell the wizard which field links both tables. For example, OrderID might be a good name for the link field connecting the Customer table with the Order table in this example.

The Archive Query Wizard

The goal of the Archive Query Wizard is to move records from a record source into a new table and then, optionally, delete those records from the original record source.

You can choose to move all the records, or you can choose criteria that must be met before a record can be moved. For example, the order date for an invoice needs to be more than 60 days past due before being moved into the new table.

Report Wizards

Creating a report can be the most complicated task in Microsoft Access because there are many things that need to be defined. The Report Wizard guides you through the process in the following seven steps:

1. Select the record source.
2. Choose the fields to be included in the report.
3. Select the field groupings. For example, do you want the report grouped by customer or transaction type?
4. Select the sort order and summary options for the numeric fields. The options include summation, average, minimum, and maximum.
5. Select the report layout and orientation.
6. Select the report style.
7. Enter the report title.

The Report Wizard is a great help in creating a report, but it still requires some effort to go through all of the steps. If you would like something even easier, the AutoReport Wizards are for you. Access also has a wizard to help in creating a chart in your report and for creating labels.

AutoReport Wizards

These wizards are similar to the AutoForm Wizards in that you only need to specify a record source in order to use them. You can use either the columnar or tabular AutoReport Wizard. Every field in the record source will be in the report when the wizard is done. Then you can edit the report as needed.

The Chart Wizard for Reports

The Chart Wizard guides you through the process of creating a report that contains 1 of 12 chart types. The charts created by this wizard are the same as those created by the Chart Wizard for forms. Refer to Figure 7.6 to see the dialog box that lets you choose the chart type. A sample chart can be displayed during the creation process so that you can be sure you are building it the right way.

The Label Wizard

This wizard helps you create a report geared toward printing labels, especially Avery labels. More than 40 different styles of Avery labels are directly supported by this wizard. You can also use metric sizes and specify custom label sizes, if needed.

Creating labels with your database is extremely easy, and this feature alone might be worth the price of the Office suite if you do mailings for a business or organization. Another idea is to create a database with all the boxes in your basement or attic and use this wizard to create labels to identify the contents.

The Table Analyzer Wizard

The Table Analyzer Wizard looks for duplicate information in a table and suggests ways to make the table more efficient. For example, the name of a supplier might be stored with each product record. The wizard shows a good example of this problem in its initial dialog box. (See Figure 7.8.)

FIGURE 7.8.

The initial dialog box for the Table Analyzer Wizard.

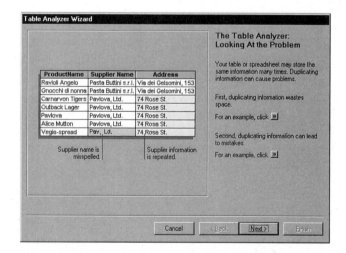

You can see that the supplier Pavlova, Ltd., is repeated in each product record. This duplication wastes space and can lead to typing mistakes. An alternative is to create a separate Supplier table to hold all of the supplier information. Then you can use a link field in the product table to refer to the data in the Supplier table.

The Table Analyzer Wizard examines an existing table for ways to improve it. If you accept its suggestions, it automatically creates any new tables that are needed and inserts the proper link fields. The data in the original table is left unchanged. If you are happy with the new tables, you can delete the original table.

Use the Tools|Analyze|Tables menu option to start this wizard.

Table Wizards

One of the hardest parts about working with databases is getting started. The first question always seems to be, "What data fields will I need?" The answer usually is, "I'm not sure."

Microsoft has tried to help you with this dilemma by programming the wizard with more than 100 sample database tables. These sample tables cover both business and personal needs.

After choosing the sample table on which to base your table, you can choose which of the pre-defined fields to use. Also, you can rename the fields if you want.

If your new table has fields in common with existing tables in the database, Access will automatically create a relationship based on the common field. Otherwise, you'll need to manually set up relationships between the new and old tables.

The Import Table Wizard

This wizard imports objects such as tables, queries, and reports from other databases into the current database. The source database does not need to be a Microsoft Access database—you can import from Microsoft Excel, Lotus 1-2-3, Borland dBASE, Borland Paradox, or any ODBC compliant database.

The Link Table Wizard

The Link Table Wizard helps you create tables that are linked to external files. Changing the data in the Access table also changes the information in the external file. As in the Import Table Wizard, the Link Table Wizard's source database does not need to be a Microsoft Access database.

Linked tables might be useful in a LAN environment if you have a Microsoft Access license and someone else has a Borland Paradox license. You save money by not needing to purchase an additional license just to share information.

The Security Wizard

The Security Wizard creates a secured database from an unsecured database. It does this by copying some or all of the objects into a new, encrypted database. The original database is not changed.

Office Binder Wizards

Chapter 6, "Binders," fully discusses the Microsoft Office Binder application. You can use binders to combine documents from Word, Excel, and PowerPoint inside a single file.

The Client Billing Wizard

The Client Billing Wizard walks you through the process of creating a Client Billing binder. You can choose to include a section with a fax cover sheet, cover letter, invoice, timecard, materials cards, and attachments. Figure 7.9 shows the introduction of this six-step wizard.

FIGURE 7.9.

The introduction to the Client Billing Wizard.

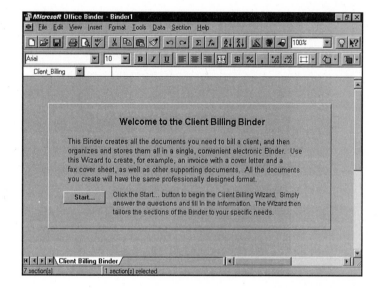

Excel Wizards

Microsoft Excel has several different wizards. A few of them are for interfacing with Microsoft Access so that you can use the form and report capabilities that Microsoft Access provides. Others concentrate on selecting a function or creating a pivot table.

The Access Form Wizard

This wizard helps you to create a Microsoft Access form based on the information in your spreadsheet. You can start it using the Data|Access Form menu option. This wizard converts the spreadsheet cells into an Access database and then starts the Microsoft Access Form Wizard. The Form Wizard is discussed in the "Access Wizards" section. You can create a new database based on the data in the spreadsheet, or you can create a new table inside an existing database. Figure 7.10 shows the Create Microsoft Access Form dialog box, which is used to determine the database where the form will be created.

The Access Report Wizard

This wizard helps you to create a Microsoft Access report based on the information in your spreadsheet. You can start it using the Data|Access Report menu option. This wizard converts the spreadsheet cells into an Access database and then starts the Microsoft Access Report Wizard. The Report Wizard is discussed in the "Access Wizards" section. You can create a new database based on the data in the spreadsheet, or you can create a new table inside an existing database. The dialog box used to determine the database is similar to the dialog box shown in Figure 7.10.

FIGURE 7.10.

The Access Form dialog box

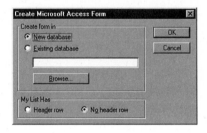

The Chart Wizard for Excel

This wizard helps you to create a chart based on the information in your spreadsheet. You can start this wizard using the Insert | Chart menu option. There are five steps to creating a chart:

1. Select the cells to be charted.
2. Select from the 15 chart types: area, bar, column, line, pie, doughnut, radar, scatter, combination, 3-D area, 3-D bar, 3-D column, 3-D line, 3-D pie, or 3-D surface.
3. Select from up to 10 different chart formats. Each chart type has its own specific formats from which to choose.
4. Determine if your data is in rows or columns.
5. Add a chart legend, if needed, and set the axis labels.

The Convert to Access Wizard

This wizard creates a link between a table in an Access database and your worksheet in Excel. If the data is changed in Access, the change is reflected in Excel and vice versa.

You can start this wizard by selecting the spreadsheet cells to link and then using the Data | Convert to Access menu option. The first dialog box that displays will ask if you want to create a new database or use an existing one. Then the Link Spreadsheet Wizard is started. This wizard guides you through the creation of a new Access table.

The Convert Text to Columns Wizard

This wizard is extremely useful if you need to convert a text file into a spreadsheet. For example, the following three lines show comma-delimited information that includes first name, street address, city, and state:

```
David, 30 Livingstone Pl, Newark, NJ
Janet, 25 Planet Dr, Habor, MA
Joe, 12 Reach Rd, Weston, GA
```

It takes just five steps to convert the data into a spreadsheet:

1. Select a single column of cells to convert.

2. Start the wizard by selecting the Data | Text to Columns menu option.

3. Tell Excel whether the data fields in the text information are fixed width or delimited.

4. Select the delimiter or determine where the fields end in fixed-width mode. A sample of the data is then displayed so that you can see where the column breaks are.

5. Select a formatting option for each column.

The Function Wizard

The Function Wizard helps you to create formulas. When started, this two-step wizard displays a list of all the functions that can be used. Selecting a function shows its arguments and a brief description. The second step guides you in creating the argument list for the function selected. Using the Function Wizard eliminates the problem of misplacing a parenthesis or misspelling a function name. Figure 7.11 shows you the first step in creating a formula.

FIGURE 7.11.

The Function Wizard - Step 1 of 2.

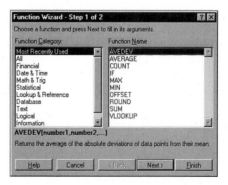

You can even nest formulas using the Function Wizard. When entering a parameter to a function, you can indicate that the parameter should be a function, and the function listing (Step 1) will be redisplayed.

The PivotTable Wizard

This four-step wizard guides you through the task of creating a pivot table. *Pivot tables* are used to summarize data. For example, you can create a table to analyze sales by product on a month-to-month basis.

You can start the PivotTable Wizard by using the Data | PivotTable menu option. Chapter 23 discusses pivot tables and the PivotTable Wizard in detail.

The Template Wizard

This wizard creates an Excel template and a database to hold records created from the template. A separate record is saved each time data is entered into the template. The five-step Template Wizard can be started from the Data | Template menu option. Figure 7.12 shows the first step in the process of creating a template.

FIGURE 7.12.

Step 1 of the Template Wizard.

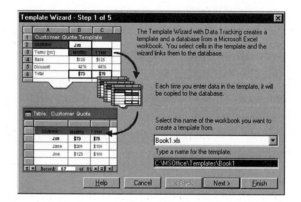

These are the five steps:

1. Select the workbook that will act as the base and the template name.

2. Choose a name and type for the new database.

3. Select the cells that become linked to the database.

4. Add data from another worksheet to the new database.

5. Add a routing slip to the template so that each new worksheet created using this template has the same routing slip.

The Template Wizard is useful when you want to avoid entering information into both an Excel worksheet and an Access database. Making a template ensures that the information is entered the same way into both applications.

The Template Wizard is also good in multiuser environments. Access handles multiple people using the same database at once in a better fashion than Excel. Therefore, using this Wizard allows you to blend the worksheet functionality of Excel with the multiuser capability of Access.

The Text Import Wizard

The Text Import Wizard is very similar to the Convert Text to Columns Wizard. Figure 7.13 shows the first step of the Text Import Wizard.

FIGURE 7.13.

Step 1 of the Text Import Wizard.

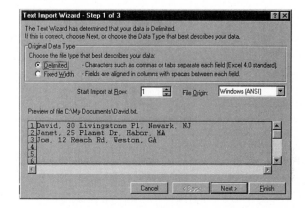

There are three differences between the Text Import Wizard and the Convert Text to Columns Wizard:

- The Text Import Wizard starts automatically when you open a text file from the File | Open dialog box.
- You can choose to start importing at any given line in the text file, bearing in mind that one line of the text file equates to one row in the worksheet.
- You can specify the origin of the file: Macintosh, Windows, DOS, or OS/2.

PowerPoint Wizards

Microsoft PowerPoint has three wizards to guide you in creating a presentation, getting it ready for travel, and creating a network-based presentation.

The AutoContent Wizard

When creating a presentation, you need to focus on the reasons for the presentation. What message or theme do you want to convey to your audience? Are you selling or informing? To help you with this task, PowerPoint provides 12 templates that outline different messages:

Business Plan
Communicating Bad News
Company Meeting
Creativity Session
Employee Orientation

Financial Report
General Marketing Plan
Recommending a Strategy
Reporting Progress
Selling a Product, Service, or Idea
Top Ten List
Training

Each of these templates contains slides that outline the concepts behind the message. The outlines help to stimulate your own ideas as well as give a basic structure to the presentation.

You can create a presentation based on any of these templates by using the New dialog box on the Office shortcut bar. Adding your information to the templates allows you to have a polished presentation very quickly.

The AutoContent Wizard makes getting started even easier by prompting you for some basic information. It can change the style of the presentation to reflect a contemporary or professional look. The wizard also asks you about your presentation hardware (black-and-white overheads, color overheads, onscreen, or 35mm slide) and if you need to print handouts.

Figure 7.14 shows the third step of the AutoContent Wizard. In this step you select one of the 12 messages or themes for your presentation.

FIGURE 7.14.

Choosing the message
for your presentation.

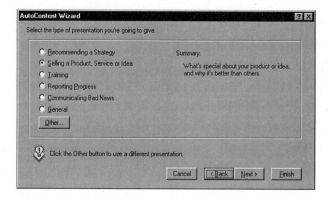

The PackAndGo Wizard

This wizard saves your presentation to disk so that it can be viewed on other computers. It is fully discussed in Chapter 38, "Making the Presentation."

The Presentation Conference Wizard

The Presentation Conference Wizard helps you to either present a presentation over a network or act as a participant in a networked presentation.

As the presenter, you control who can join the conference. You also have access to some tools to help you manage the presentation:

- Meeting Minder—This feature lets you review notes, take meeting minutes, and track action items.
- Slide Navigator—This feature lets you preview and display any slide during the conference.
- Slide Meter—This feature lets you monitor your progress in the presentation according to slide timings that you preset.

TIP

Entering an incorrect computer name in the conference list will cause a delay while PowerPoint looks for a nonexistent computer. Be sure to double-check your typing in order to avoid this problem.

As a participant, all you need to do is start the wizard, check off that you are part of the audience, and then click the Finish button. PowerPoint connects you to the conference, and you can watch the presentation.

Schedule+ Wizards

Schedule+ is the newest application in the Office suite. It has five main wizards. They help you set up meetings, import and export data, and provide inspiration for a better life.

The Meeting Wizard

The Meeting Wizard helps you organize a meeting. It lets you select required and optional attendees, a location, and any audiovisual aids or other resources needed.

You can use Schedule+ to track equipment as well as people. If you have a critical component, such as a color duplex printer or an X-ray machine, you can turn each piece of equipment into a resource. Then, anyone who needs that equipment can indicate the need by scheduling an appointment and including the resource in the list of attendees. Thus, they can indicate that they require access to the equipment for a certain block of time. This is an easy way to ensure that the component is not overcommitted.

When finished, the wizard uses your e-mail system to send notes to the attendees.

The Text Export Wizard

This wizard exports your appointment, to do, event, or contact list to a text file. You can choose which fields to export depending on your needs.

The Text Export Wizard is useful if you need to convert some information to an Excel spreadsheet or Access database.

The Text Import Wizard

The Text Import Wizard does the opposite of the Text Export Wizard. The Text Import Wizard is used to get information into Schedule+ from a text file. You can specify what character delimits fields and if the first record is a list of field names. Then you can set up a correspondence between the fields in the text file and the fields in Schedule+.

The Timex Watch Wizard

This wizard can be used to program a Timex Data Link watch. You can program it with any of the information in Schedule+: appointments, tasks, phone numbers, anniversaries, and alarms. You can even set the current time and the size at which it displays.

You can control exactly which information is transmitted to the watch. For example, exporting phone numbers will display a list of your contacts; you can select any of them from the list. As you select the information to export, the wizard tracks the amount of watch memory used and displays the percentage.

The Seven Habits Wizard

The Seven Habits Tools were designed with the books *The Seven Habits of Highly Effective People* and *First Things First* by Dr. Stephen R. Covey in mind. Schedule+ supports the principles that Dr. Covey teaches in his books in a very integral way. In order to help you develop your own successful habits, the Seven Habits Tools help you to develop a mission statement, find your roles in life, set and achieve goals, and learn wisdom.

There are four wizards that support the Seven Habits Tools. They are discussed in the following sections.

The Overall Seven Habits Wizard

This wizard introduces you to the Seven Habits and the Put First Things First methodology. After answering the questions, you'll begin to understand some of the daily distractions that get in the way of achieving success.

The Connect to Mission Wizard

This wizard helps you to formulate a personal mission statement. This statement articulates what is important to you and serves as a road map for your future. By following it, you'll always be doing something that is important to you. Figure 7.15 shows the third step of the

Connect to Mission Wizard, where you can determine your values and beliefs. These values will become part of your personal mission statement.

FIGURE 7.15.

Step 3 of the Connect to Mission Wizard.

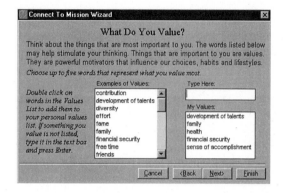

The Review Roles Wizard

People have roles that they assume in society. You might be a volunteer firefighter, a mother, a son, or mayor of a city. There are work roles, personal roles, and social roles. The Review Roles Wizard helps you determine what roles you play and how each one is important.

The Identify Goals Wizard

This wizard lets you set weekly goals that move you toward your long-term goals. A lot of people fall into the trap of saying, "I have a dream," but never doing anything concrete to achieve that dream. By thinking about your dreams and goals each week, you can break the unattainable into small, do-able steps.

The Identify Goals Wizard helps you clarify your thinking about which goal you can work toward *this* week. As you work with this wizard, your weekly goals will align themselves with your personal mission statement. You'll feel a tremendous sense of accomplishment when you look back and find less wasted time and more meaningful tasks being completed.

Word Wizards

Microsoft Word has quite a few wizards. They are covered in the following sections.

Wizards That Preformat Documents

Most Word Wizards are designed to gather information from you and then preformat a certain type of output. For example, there are wizards that create newsletters or memos. These Word wizards can all be found in the New dialog box on the Office shortcut bar. Table 7.2 lists the Word wizards that are available to preformat documents.

Table 7.2. Microsoft wizards that preformat documents.

Wizard Name	Description
Agenda Wizard	This wizard guides you though creating a meeting agenda. You can select from a modern, standard, or boxy style. It also lets you enter your agenda items and rearrange them, if needed.
Award Wizard	This wizard creates an award certificate tailored to your needs.
Calendar Wizard	This wizard creates a monthly calendar. You can choose the starting and ending months. The months print one per page.
Fax Wizard	This wizard creates a fax cover page. It preformats your company information, the orientation of the page, the style, and the recipient's information.
Letter Wizard	This wizard helps you create a business or personal letter. You can also choose from a list of prewritten letters, as shown in Figure 7.16.
Memo Wizard	This wizard helps you create a basic office memo. You are prompted for a memo topic and asked which memo elements you want to include.
Newsletter Wizard	This wizard sets up a new document in a basic newsletter format. You can choose from one to four columns as well as specify the newsletter name, among other things.
Pleading Wizard	Legal documents frequently need to meet exact requirements as defined by the courts. This wizard helps you to format your document correctly.
Résumé Wizard	This wizard guides you in creating a résumé. You can choose an entry-level, a chronological, a functional, or a professional style.

FIGURE 7.16.

The Letter Wizard's list of prewritten business letters.

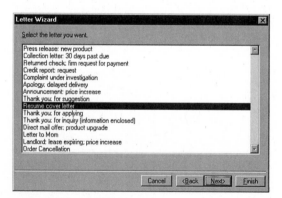

The Table Wizard

The Table Wizard guides you through the steps needed to create a table in your document. It is particularly useful if you need the column or row headings to be numbers, months, or years. The table automatically inserts the headings that you specify. Figure 7.17 shows the dialog box where you specify the column headings for the table.

FIGURE 7.17.

Specifying column headings using the Table Wizard.

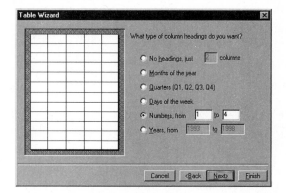

Summary

This chapter covers quite a few wizards in every application of the Office suite. These wizards will help you familiarize yourself with the capabilities of the applications.

Sometimes, features that are hidden in the remote corners of a forgotten dialog box are brought to light during the give-and-take of using a wizard. Other times, it is simply easier to let the wizard do the work. In either case, Microsoft has done a good job of making the wizard an integral part of these applications.

Chapter 8, "Shared Features," discusses some of the capabilities that all of the Microsoft Office applications have in common. The topics include the common menu structure, OLE features, and document properties.

Shared Features

8

by David Medinets

Microsoft Office is more than a bunch of applications thrown together and sold in one box. Hundreds of hours were spent interviewing users. Lists of features were created and prioritized. Then, some of the best minds in the computer industry turned the Microsoft Office into one of the most tightly integrated packages available today.

Many shared features serve to bind the applications closely together. Sharing features between applications saves disk space by storing program code only once on your hard drive and ensures a consistent end-user interface.

This chapter discusses some of the shared features used in Microsoft Office. Some features, such as spell checking and how to use the help system, are common to all Windows applications. Therefore, this chapter does not cover them.

This chapter discusses the following:

- Using the AutoCorrect feature
- Using the common menu options and toolbars
- Creating new documents and using document properties
- Viewing system information
- Using the OLE servers that are part of Microsoft Office

AutoCorrect

The AutoCorrect feature tries to automatically correct or change the text of a document as you are entering it. This ability, while seemingly a small thing, can save time and typing. As you type, little misspellings will be automatically fixed, which reduces the amount of time you'll spend spell checking.

You can also use AutoCorrect to expand abbreviations as you type. For example, let's say that you need to use the word `Phonocardiography` in your documents. You can set up AutoCorrect so that `pcg` will automatically expand to `Phonocardiography`. This makes it faster to type long, complex words. The section "Adding an AutoCorrect Entry" a little later in this chapter discusses how to define the AutoCorrect entries.

All of the Microsoft Office applications, except for Schedule+ and Office Binder, have some AutoCorrect ability. Figure 8.1 shows the AutoCorrect dialog box available with the Microsoft Access, Microsoft Excel, and Microsoft PowerPoint applications. AutoCorrect in Microsoft Word is discussed a little bit later.

The AutoCorrect feature in Access, Excel, and PowerPoint can do three things:

- Correct two initial capitals. For example, if you type `THe`, it will be replaced with `The`.
- Capitalize the names of days. For example, if you type `sunday`, it will be replaced with `Sunday`.

■ Replace text as you type. You can have AutoCorrect replace any sequence of letters with any other sequence. For example, you can have the characters mos be replaced with Microsoft Office Suite.

Access, Excel, and PowerPoint use the same database to store the replacement text. You can add replacement text using the Excel dialog box, and PowerPoint will automatically know about the change.

FIGURE 8.1.

AutoCorrect in Microsoft Access, Microsoft Excel, and Microsoft PowerPoint.

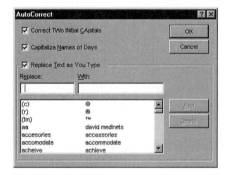

The AutoCorrect feature that comes with Microsoft Word is more advanced. Figure 8.2 shows the AutoCorrect dialog box of Word.

FIGURE 8.2.

AutoCorrect in Microsoft Word.

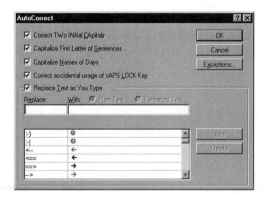

Microsoft Word adds three abilities to AutoCorrect:

■ Capitalize the first letter of a sentence. For example, if you type Jack was here. jill was not., it will be replaced with Jack was here. Jill was not..

■ Correct accidental usage of the cAPS LOCK KEy.

■ Stop automatic capitalization and correction of two initial capital letters with an exception list.

> **NOTE**
>
> The replacement text list has been expanded for Microsoft Word. It will automatically replace more words than will other Office applications.

Creating Replacement Text

You reach the AutoCorrect dialog box by selecting the Tools | AutoCorrect… menu option. Figure 8.1 and Figure 8.2 show the dialog box used by the Office applications.

Adding a new replacement text entry is easy. Enter the abbreviation into the input box underneath the Replace text label. Then enter the full text into the input box to the right. Click the Add button, and the entry is added to the database.

> **NOTE**
>
> Remember that Microsoft Word uses a different database than the other applications to store the replacement text. If you want the replacement text to be available in all applications, you will need to enter it in Microsoft Access, Microsoft Excel, or Microsoft PowerPoint, as well.

While spell checking a document in any of the applications, you can add replacement text to automatically fix common misspelling by entering the correct spelling in the Change To box and then selecting the AutoCorrect button. After doing this a few times your typing will seem to be self-correcting!

Common Menu Structure

One of the key reasons for the popularity of Windows is the consistent look and feel, or user interface, of the applications. An important element of the user interface is the menu structure used to organize the commands and options used inside each application.

Microsoft has done a better job than other software vendors in ensuring that common menu options are found in the same place throughout the five applications in the Office suite. Figure 8.3 shows the menu options that are common to all the applications.

All of these menu options are available in at least three of the five applications. When working with a new application, you can be confident that you know at least part of the menu structure.

Common Toolbars

In addition to having a similar menu structure, the Microsoft Office applications also have toolbars in common. The standard, chart, drawing, formatting, macro, Tip Wizard, Microsoft, and Visual Basic toolbars are all available in two or more applications. Maintaining similar toolbars is another way the Office Suite helps you to shorten your learning curve.

FIGURE 8.3.

A virtual menu for the Microsoft Office Suite.

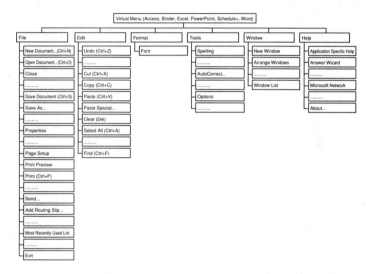

Displaying Toolbars

Every Office application displays toolbars in the same way, inside the *toolbar area*. The toolbar area, which is underneath the menu bar, is shown in Figure 8.4. You can also see the toolbar context menu of Microsoft Word.

You can toggle the display of a toolbar by clicking directly on its name in the context menu. When checked, the toolbar will be displayed. More than one toolbar might be displayed per line. You can tell where the toolbars end by the three-dimensional–looking line that surrounds each toolbar.

FIGURE 8.4.

The toolbar area and context menu in Microsoft Word.

Toolbar area —

Context menu —

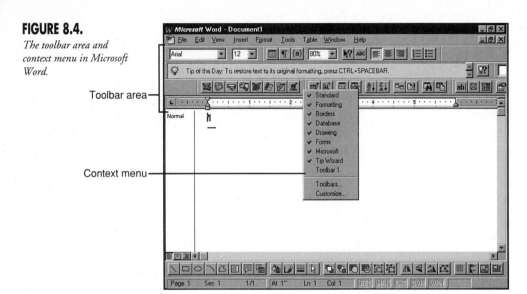

Moving Toolbars

You can choose to make toolbars float on the screen, as shown in Figure 8.5, or you can rearrange them. Both actions are begun by clicking on a toolbar and dragging it. If you drag a toolbar over a document, it turns into a floating window. If you drag a toolbar to the left or right, you will change its starting position on the line. You can also combine two toolbars on one line using drag and drop.

FIGURE 8.5.

Floating toolbars in Microsoft Word.

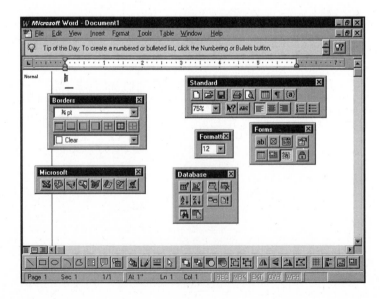

Documents

Microsoft Office uses the term *document* to mean any file that you can create with the Office applications. It can refer to an Excel spreadsheet file as well as a PowerPoint presentation. This section expands on the information covered in Chapter 5, "The Microsoft Office Shortcut Bar," by discussing alternative ways of creating documents. It also mentions document properties—what they are and how to use them.

New Documents

There are three ways to create Microsoft Office documents:

- Using the New dialog box on the Microsoft Office shortcut bar. Chapter 5 discusses this option.
- Using the New option of the Desktop context menu. The "Desktop Document Creation" section discusses this option.
- Using the File | New menu option available in every application. The "Application Document Creation" section discusses this option.

Desktop Document Creation

The Desktop context menu, shown in Figure 8.6, lets you create new Office Binder, Excel, PowerPoint, and Word documents. You can also get to the New dialog box by selecting the Other Office Documents… menu option.

FIGURE 8.6.

The New option of the Desktop Context Menu.

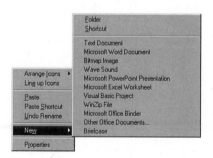

After you select one of the menu options, a blank document is created on the desktop and given a default name. For example, a new Office Binder document would be named New Microsoft Office Binder.obd. You can rename it by double-clicking slowly—wait a moment before each click—on the name section of the icon.

> **TIP**
>
> When renaming newly created documents on the desktop, remember to keep the extension so that the proper application can be automatically started when the document is double-clicked.

Application Document Creation

You can create new documents from inside the Office applications by using the File | New menu option. Every application also has a New icon on the Standard toolbar that you can use. Selecting either option will display the New dialog box. From the dialog box, you can choose the template on which the new document will be based.

Properties

Every Office document has a set of properties associated with it. They range from the document's name and file size to custom properties that you can control. These properties are generally used to help search your My Documents folder. Figure 8.7 shows the Microsoft Office Properties dialog box.

FIGURE 8.7.

The Properties dialog box used by Microsoft Office.

08MOUor.doc Properties		? ☒
General	Summary	Statistics	Contents	Custom		
Created:	Monday, October 16, 1995 12:03:00 AM	
Modified:	Sunday, October 22, 1995 10:07:48 PM	
Accessed:	Sunday, October 22, 1995	
Printed:	Sunday, October 22, 1995 12:01:00 PM	
Last Saved By:	David Medinets	
Revision Number:	69	
Total Editing Time:	3417 Minutes	

Statistics:	Statistic Name	Value
	Pages:	16
	Paragraphs:	228
	Lines:	451
	Words:	4145
	Characters:	20790
	Bytes:	189817

OK   Cancel

The same dialog box is used by all the Office applications. However, some of the applications do not use all the tabs shown. For example, Microsoft Access uses only the General tab.

You might notice that the Properties dialog box used by Microsoft Office is more advanced than the one used by Windows 95. If you would like to see this difference for yourself, follow these steps:

1. Create a blank Microsoft Word document, and then exit Microsoft Word.

2. Using Windows Explorer, right-click on the document in the My Documents folder. Then select the Properties menu option. Look at the Summary tab.

3. Using the Open dialog box from the shortcut bar, right-click on the document, and then select the Properties menu option. Again, look at the Summary tab. You can see that this version of the dialog box has more options.

Property Storage

Properties are stored as part of the document file using OLE structured storage. This means that the properties follow the document no matter where it goes. You can copy it to a disk or mail it through the Internet, and the properties travel with the document.

Because Microsoft is using the OLE standard to store the property information, you will soon see document management software that will be able to read the property information to archive and search your documents. Third-party vendors will be able to create applications not yet thought of that will be able to use your documents.

Property Types

This book discusses the Microsoft Office version of the Properties dialog box, which has five tabs:

- General—This tab shows properties such as the name, type, location, size, and attributes. These properties are usually set by the system. However, you might need to change the read-only, hidden, or archive attributes.

- Summary—This tab shows properties such as the author, keywords, comments, title, subject, and the template on which the document is based.

- Statistics—This tab has properties that indicate who last edited the document and how many pages, paragraphs, and words are in the document. Additional statistical information is also displayed on the page.

- Contents—This tab shows the parts of the document in a hierarchical fashion. Each application shows different information:

  Microsoft Access does not use the Contents tab. In fact, Access uses only the General tab.

  Microsoft Excel shows the worksheet and module names.

Microsoft PowerPoint shows fonts used and the title of each slide, along with other information.

Microsoft Word shows the document title.

■ Custom—This tab shows any custom properties that are part of the document and will let you create, modify, or delete them. Custom properties are discussed in the following section.

Custom Properties

Custom properties are simply properties created by you. You control their names and what type of information they hold. You can create properties that hold text, numbers, dates, or yes/no information.

A custom property might come in handy if you need to quickly find all PowerPoint presentations that your manager has not reviewed. By creating a custom property called Did President Review—using the Yes or No data type—you could search your documents to find the presentations that are candidates for your next review meeting.

Of course, you need to think about and create custom properties before you actually need them. In the example just mentioned, it would have done you little good to create the custom property after 20 presentations were already created. Spend some time thinking about how you work and what additional information could make your work easier in the future.

Figure 8.8 shows the Custom tab of the Properties dialog box where the custom properties are created, modified, and viewed.

FIGURE 8.8.

The Custom tab of the Properties dialog box.

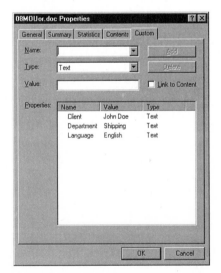

In order to give you some ideas for custom properties, Microsoft has created a list of suggestions. You can see this list by clicking on the arrow to the right of the Name field. Some of the suggestions include Checked by, Date completed, Destination, Mailstop, Status, and Typist.

But you are not limited to Microsoft's suggestions. You can create a property using any name you like. For example, you can add properties called TO and FROM to all your memo documents. Then, when you search through your documents in the Open dialog box, you can search for all documents to a specific person.

You can also link a custom property to the contents of a Word or an Excel document. For example, imagine that you have a series of worksheets that are created each week. The important information in the spreadsheet comes down to weekly profit found inside one cell. You can create a link between a custom property and the cell using the following steps:

1. Create a named range inside Excel that refers to the weekly profit cell. Use the Insert | Name | Define menu option.

> **NOTE**
>
> The name of the range in Excel must consist of only one word with no leading or trailing spaces.

2. Open the Properties dialog box. Use the File | Properties menu option.
3. Click on the Custom tab.
4. Enter `Weekly Profit` as the name of the new custom property.
5. Check the Link to Content check box.
6. Select your named range from the Source drop-down list box.
7. Click on the Add button.

You can create links to bookmarks inside Word documents using essentially the same procedure. Instead of creating a named range in the first step, create a bookmark.

Microsoft System Information

Microsoft has provided an application, called Microsoft System Information, that lets you look at important information about your computer. Figure 8.9 shows what the screen might look like when the application is first started.

FIGURE 8.9.

The Microsoft System Information application.

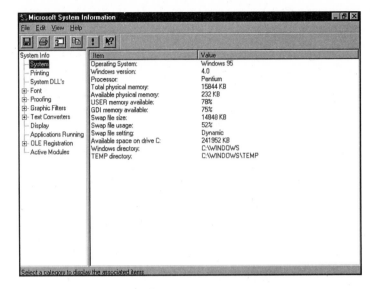

You can access the Microsoft System Information program from any of the Office applications by selecting Help | About, and then clicking on the System Info button.

The left-hand pane of the window shows the different categories of information that is available. The System, Printing, and Applications Running categories have good information. The rest contain information about DLLs and OLE objects that will not make much sense unless you are a programmer.

System Information

This category includes information about how much memory your system has and what percentage of system resources is being used. It also shows how big the swap file is, how much of it is being used, and the location of the temporary directory.

Printing Information

This category is important because it lets you know what version of a print driver is installed on your system. If you ever have flaky behavior from your printer, the technical support team that you contact will probably need to know this information.

You will also see information about the default printer and whether the system is using the print spooler.

Applications Running Information

This category is interesting because you can tell which running applications are 16 bit and which are 32 bit. For example, the MSGSRV32 program, used internally by Windows 95, is 16 bit— despite its name. You might want to check out other software that you run.

Microsoft OLE Servers

Microsoft has several small applets that act as OLE servers. The OLE servers range from a nice front end to help add clip art to your documents to a method to create fancy text.

The OLE servers described in this section can be used from Access, Excel, PowerPoint, and Word. The Insert | Object menu option works identically in each application. After you select a menu option, choose the object that you need from the Create New tab. The OLE server is started after a placeholder is added to your document.

When you're using OLE server, the menu bar will change to reflect the menu options used by that OLE server. The title bar does not change, however. If you step away from the computer for a while, you may not remember which OLE server you were using. You can always look at the first option in the Help menu option to determine which application or OLE server is active.

> **TIP**
>
> If you want to use OLE objects in an Access database, one of the database fields needs to be defined as an OLE object. Then, when data is entered, the Insert | Object option can be used to select the OLE object to add.

Microsoft ClipArt Gallery

The Microsoft ClipArt Gallery is an OLE server that categorizes and previews clip art. You can choose a category from which to view art. You can also change or add categories if you want.

Figure 8.10 displays the Microsoft ClipArt Gallery 2.0 dialog box. Double-click on the clip art that you need and it will be inserted into your document or database.

> **NOTE**
>
> You will need to add clip art to the Office catalog the first time the ClipArt Gallery is used. You can do this by clicking on the Organize button in the ClipArt Gallery dialog box. Then click the Add Pictures button and follow the instructions on the screen.

FIGURE 8.10.

The Microsoft ClipArt Gallery 2.0 dialog box.

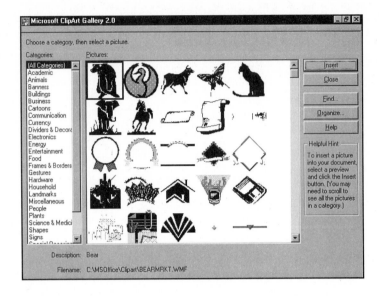

Microsoft Data Map

Microsoft Data Map is an OLE server that is new to Office. It's designed to take information from Access or Excel and place it on a map. For example, the data map in Figure 8.11 was created using the spreadsheet in Figure 8.12.

FIGURE 8.11.

A Data Map showing U.S. state population as well as major airports.

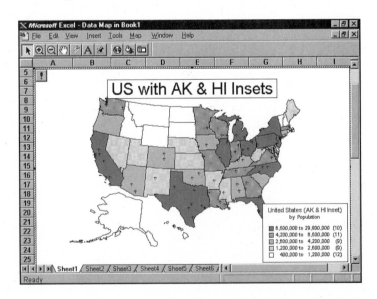

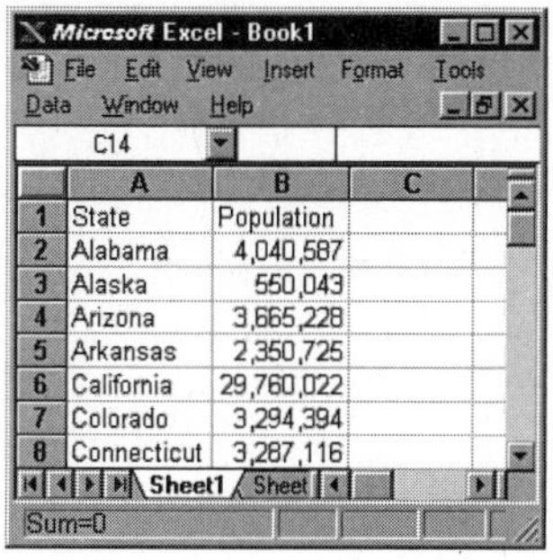

FIGURE 8.12.

Part of the spreadsheet used to create the data map.

This map allows you to correlate the location of airports to population. As you can see, major airports are located in states with large populations.

You can insert a Data Map OLE object into Access, Excel, PowerPoint, or Word using the Insert | Object menu option.

Microsoft has included a document called mapstats.xls that includes geographical names from the world, the USA, Canada, Mexico, Europe, the UK, and Australia. If the geographic names in the source data are incorrect, Data Map will not be able to make a map from them.

> **TIP**
>
> You will probably find the mapstats.xls document in c:\Program Files\Common Files\Microsoft Shared\Datamap\Data. If not, you can use the Tools | Find menu option in Windows Explorer to locate the document.

Microsoft Draw

The Microsoft Draw OLE server lets you use lines, circles, boxes, and text to create an image. Figure 8.13 shows the Microsoft Draw applet.

> **TIP**
>
> For more sophisticated pictures, insert a Paintbrush picture as an OLE object.

FIGURE 8.13.

Microsoft Draw.

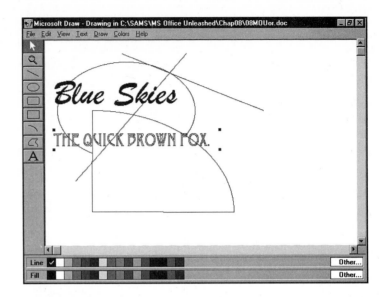

Microsoft Equation Editor

The Microsoft Equation Editor is used to enter mathematical formulas. It lets you display root signs, integral signs, and a host of other mathematic symbols. Figure 8.14 shows an equation designed using the editor.

FIGURE 8.14.

An equation designed using the editor.

$$\sum_{n=2}^{10} 3n + 12 \times \frac{153}{1.3}$$

You can design the equation to be as complicated as needed. You can change the size of the font used by clicking on the equation to display the bounding rectangle, and then dragging one of the corners to make the equation look bigger or smaller.

Microsoft Graph 5.0

Microsoft Graph is designed to let you create a quick graph when you only have a few data items or you simply don't feel like using Microsoft Excel.

Data is entered into a datasheet window, as shown in Figure 8.15. Double-clicking on a label of a given row or column will add or remove it from the graph. For example, row 3 (North) is not displayed in the graph shown in Figure 8.16.

Chapter 8

FIGURE 8.15.

Entering data into a datasheet.

		A	B	C	D	E	F
		1st Qtr	2nd Qtr	3rd Qtr	4th Qtr		
1	East	20.4	27.4	90	20.4		
2	West	30.6	38.6	34.6	31.6		
3	North	45.9	46.9	45	43.9		
4	South	70	23.4	123.2	50		

C:\SAMS\MS Office Unleashe... - Datasheet

FIGURE 8.16.

A Microsoft graph.

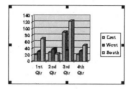

Microsoft Organization Chart 2.0

This OLE server is very useful. Any time you need to display hierarchic information, the Organization Chart OLE server might come in handy. It was used to create the virtual menu structure used earlier in this chapter.

Microsoft Organization Chart lets you depict a hierarchic structure very easily. Figure 8.17 shows the four types of boxes that you can add:

- Manager—The new box is added above the selected box.
- Subordinate—The new box is added below the selected box.
- Coworker—The new box is added beside the selected box. You can choose on which side to add it.
- Assistant—The new box is added below and offset.

The applet lets you move entire subtrees from one location to another. For example, in Figure 8.17, you could take Jackie's whole staff (including Jackie, if you want) and move them under Joan in the hierarchy.

FIGURE 8.17.

An organization chart.

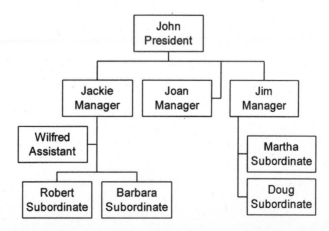

Microsoft WordArt

Microsoft WordArt is an interesting little OLE server. It lets you do fancy things with text. You can outline the text with a second color, add shading and shadows, rotate the text, and even adjust the spacing between characters. Figure 8.18 shows an example of text that is both rotated and shadowed.

FIGURE 8.18.

An example of WordArt.

Summary

This chapter covers only a few of the many shared features of Microsoft Office. As you work with the applications, you will find many more. Don't be afraid to experiment with the software as long as you back up your documents first!

PART

IV

IN THIS PART

The Power of Word

Document Concepts

9

by Ewan Grantham

In many ways Word has been the centerpiece of the Microsoft Office suite—partly because it's the oldest of the applications, and partly because almost anyone who uses a computer has to have a word processor. In this first chapter devoted to Word in this book, you'll be reintroduced to the concept of a document being more than text, as well as given a tour of the new interface. There is also information on creating and formatting a document.

This chapter, as well as the others covering Word for Windows 95, uses plenty of illustrations (to reduce any confusion between what is written and what is meant) and shows multiple ways of completing tasks wherever possible. This will help you adapt Word to fit the way you work.

Document Definition

One of the central ideas in Office 95 is to design business solutions with a *document-centric* viewpoint. The document is not just a collection of text created by a word processor, but instead it's a collection of objects designed to present a central theme. Word fits into this concept as one of the tools for unifying the various elements of a document.

Through various techniques, you can use Word to have information from the other applications tied into a page (or pages) and manage the presentation of that data to the screen or to the printer.

While this chapter mainly shows you how to create text-based documents, later chapters will show you how to add data from the other Office applications, as well as graphics from other sources, to build more complex documents.

Opening Word

There are a number of different ways to start up Word for Windows 95, depending on what you are doing and your personal preferences for doing things. Here are the three most common ways:

- By selecting Start a new document from the shortcut bar and then selecting a Word template.
- By double-clicking a file found in Explorer that is associated with Word (for example, DOC files).
- By choosing Word from the Start menu (Start|Programs|Word).

If you've used Word before, you'll notice several similarities as well as a number of differences. While the menu remains very similar, the default toolbars have changed quite a bit, and if the default option for the Spell-It utility is left on, there is an animated pencil that writes in a little book near the bottom-right corner showing that the utility is running, indicating either that there are spelling errors (with a red × on the side of the book) or that there aren't (a red checkmark). While there are quite a few buttons on the default toolbars, many of them were available under Word 6 but weren't set up by default.

Looking at the menu, you'll notice that each menu selection has a letter underlined (usually the first letter, but sometimes the second). By holding down the Alt key and then pressing the underlined letter, the menu is activated the same as if you used the mouse to click the menu.

In each menu, the choices also have underlined letters. By simply typing that letter after activating the menu, the option is selected (again, the same as if you had used the mouse to click it). Some of these menu choices show other keystrokes that can be used to get to the same function directly (such as Ctrl+C to copy or Ctrl+V to paste). These are referred to as shortcut keys. They allow you to keep your fingers on the keyboard while performing common functions.

The other keyboard item to keep in mind is that once a screen has come up with items to be entered, you can use the Tab key to move from item to item or hold down the Shift key and press the Tab key to move back to an item. This keyboard navigation technique works the same way through most of Windows 95, so learning these keystrokes can shave some time off common chores.

Toolbar Highlights

Without going over *all* the toolbar buttons, there are a couple that you should be aware of. On the top row, the two buttons on the right are the Context-Sensitive Help button (the one on the far right with an arrow and a question mark) and the TipWizard (the one with a light bulb on it, just left of the Context-Sensitive Help button).

Click the Context-Sensitive Help button and then click on the part of the Word window you need help with. Figure 9.1 shows an example where context-sensitive help is used to get more information about the Decrease Indent button.

FIGURE 9.1.

Using context-sensitive help on the Word toolbar.

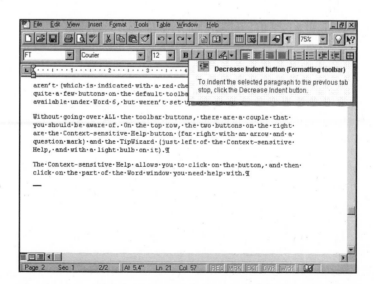

The TipWizard brings up the tip of the day as well as the ShowMe button. Generally you don't use TipWizard this way; instead you wait for it to come up to explain a new function (such as the Spell-It utility the first time it underlines a word). Once that has happened, clicking the TipWizard button closes the tip window. Figure 9.2 shows the TipWizard window with ShowMe activated.

The ShowMe button

FIGURE 9.2.

The TipWizard window with the ShowMe button activated.

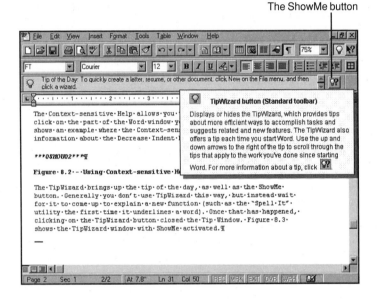

On the second toolbar, most of the items are the same, but a new Highlight button has been added. This is for coloring an area in the same way a highlight pen would. Clicking the area of the button with the pen and colored square allows you to mark an area with that color. Clicking the down arrow to the right of this gives you a choice of colors to use, and it changes the color in the small square according to your choice. Figure 9.3 shows some text in various colors as well as the drop-down list of available colors. In order, left to right, the text is colored yellow, then green, then blue, and then pink.

Finally, below the menu and toolbars is the horizontal ruler. This shows you the current left and right margin (the white area between the markers) and any indents or special tab stops defined for the current section of text.

FIGURE 9.3.

Sections of colored text and a menu of color choices.

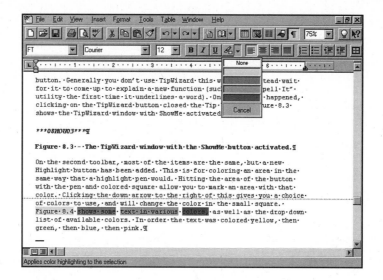

Changing Fonts

One of the first things you are likely to change in a document is the font. While Times New Roman is okay, it may not look that good on your printer, and it certainly is not recommended for documents that are going to be viewed electronically. The easiest way to change this is to go to the Formatting toolbar. The middle list is called the Font box (second from the left). It contains the currently selected font; clicking the arrow drops down a list of fonts available on your system.

The problem with using this method to change the font is that you have to already know what the font will look like. If you don't mind a few additional mouse clicks, you can get a preview of the new font. To do this, you use the Format | Font option. This allows you to not only change the font but also to specify some of the effects you might want. You can also set style and size (which can be done from the toolbar by using some of the other items on the Formatting toolbar). Figure 9.4 shows this Font window and the various options available. Notice that there is also a tab for character formatting, which allows you to define how the spacing should be set with that font.

Again, you can get much of the same effect by using the Font box to set the font, going to the next list over to set the size, and then using the set of buttons after that list to set the font to bold, italic, and/or underlined.

For any of this to work on existing text, you have to make sure you first select the text you're interested in changing, and then select the options you want to use.

FIGURE 9.4.

The Font box and a list of installed fonts.

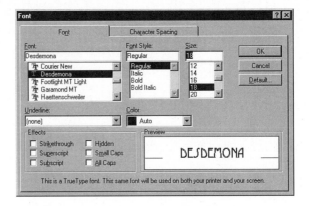

This is a good time to point out a difference between the way Word uses the term *font* and the way most publishers and designers use the term. Normally, a term such as Times New Roman or Arial would be called a *typeface*, whereas a *font* would be Times New Roman, 12-point, bold italic. You can see where the confusion comes in. Knowing the difference is important when it comes time to work with an outside bureau. One other area of confusion when it comes to fonts is the term *points*. This term refers to the size of a font, and it comes from the printing industry, which measures the size in points rather than inches. There are 72 points to an inch, so a 12-point font has six lines of text in a 1-inch section of a printed page. Therefore, larger point numbers result in taller (though not necessarily wider) fonts.

One other consideration to make when working with fonts is whether you will be distributing the electronic version of the document. If all you will be doing is printing it and sending around the printout, you should feel free to use any font on your system. If you think you will be sharing the file, however, you should try to choose from the default Windows fonts. Otherwise, your recipients might not have the font you used. If they don't, your document will end up looking strange because Word will use a substitute font to replace your font.

Working with Margins and Page Setup

Another common change to a document is to adjust the margins. The easiest way to do this for a paragraph (and for the rest of the document from that point on unless you change it back) is to go to the ruler bar and drag the right margin marker to the new point on the ruler. Figure 9.5 gives a rather extreme example of how this works. Notice that the white area of the ruler remains the same. This is because all you have changed is the format from that point on, not for the entire document.

Another way to change margins for the document (or for a particular section), is for you to go to the File menu and select the Page Setup option. Figure 9.6 shows the screen that comes up, with the Margins tab selected.

FIGURE 9.5.

An example of changing the margin with the ruler.

Right margin marker

Text after margin change

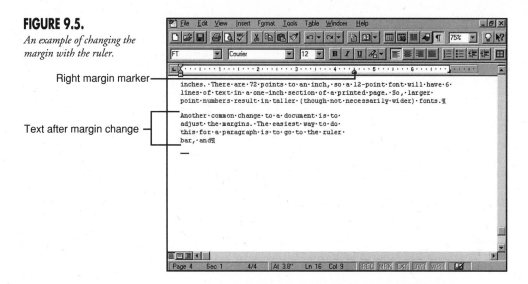

FIGURE 9.6.

The Page Setup dialog box with the Margins tab selected.

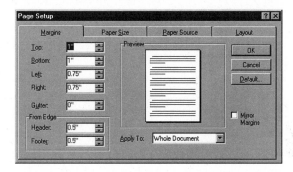

As you'll notice, you can set the top and bottom margins, the left and right margins, and a gutter (which is the extra margin space allowed for binding a document). All of these measurements are based on the distance from the edge of the paper, as defined in the Paper Size tab.

Below these options are the Header and Footer boxes. Remember that these measurements are also based from the edge of the page; your top and bottom margins are not taken into consideration. In other words, make sure you aren't defining your header and footer to print on top of your regular text.

Below the preview page, which shows how your changes affect a page of text, is the Apply To list box, where you can specify if these changes apply to the entire document or just the remaining part of the document from the current point in the text.

There are three buttons along on the right side: OK, Cancel, and Default. OK confirms the changes, Cancel causes Word to ignore your changes, and Default returns the settings to the Word default settings.

Below these buttons is a little check box with the label Mirror Margins. Figure 9.7 shows how the Page Setup screen changes with this option to allow for formatting of facing pages.

FIGURE 9.7.

The Page Setup dialog box after you select Mirror Margins.

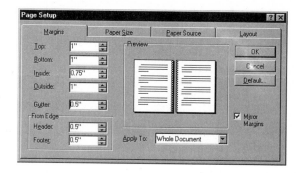

Notice how the left and right margins become inside (next to the binding) and outside. I have also selected a gutter, which is represented by the markings on the inside of the pages. By using this option, reports that will be bound or presented with a cover can be formatted to still look their best.

Selecting the Paper Size tab on the Page Setup screen allows you to define the size of paper used when printing. Because the margin settings are relative to this, you need to be accurate in describing the output. There are several default sizes already defined from which you can choose. One consideration here is to remember that this is the size of paper that you will be printing to. In other words, suppose that you were actually creating a fax. You would want to make sure the paper size matched the options available for the receiving fax.

The next tab is Paper Source; it is mainly used if you have a printer with multiple trays. Even in that case, you'll generally set this once and leave it. If you do need to be able to change your choice, it is supported here. This screen also allows you to specify a separate tray for the first page. Usually this is for using stationery as a first page and bond paper for the rest.

The final tab is the Layout tab, which gives you additional options for applying the setup. The screen in Figure 9.8 is shown after the Line Numbers button has been selected. This screen allows you to set options for sections and vertical alignment. It is most often used to allow special header and footer setups. You can have different headers and footers for the odd and even pages (like in a book where the section is on one side and the chapter is on the other), or you can set up a different header and footer for the first page of the document.

The Line Numbers option is great if you have a document where the line being referenced is important (as with certain legal documents, for example), or if you need to track absolute position in a file. You could also use it for programming, although it would be a rather difficult way to achieve this effect. One other use for this is if you wanted to create a numbered list of items, particularly if its a *long* list.

FIGURE 9.8.

The Layout tab with the Line Numbers dialog box.

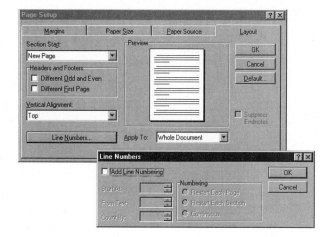

Headers and Footers

Headers and footers are used to present information such as the date and page number at the top (header) or bottom (footer) of each page. Word even gives you the flexibility to *not* put everything on every page.

Interestingly, the command for working with headers and footers is under the View menu. Selecting the Header and Footer option from the View menu brings up the screen shown in Figure 9.9, which is the document in page layout view with the Header and Footer toolbar.

FIGURE 9.9.

The Header and Footer toolbar in Word.

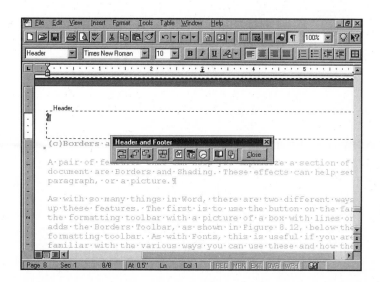

The text for the page you are working on turns gray to indicate that it can't be edited while you are working with a header or footer. Within the Header box that is displayed, you can type in text that you want to display, add graphics, or include fields to automatically add the date or page number. The same is true of the Footer box.

You'll notice by looking at the toolbar that each button has a function that is designed for working with headers and footers. Starting at the far left is the Switch button, used for switching between the Header and Footer box. The next two are the Previous Header/Footer and the Next Header/Footer buttons. If you have multiple headers or footers for different sections of your document, these buttons allow you to move between them. The next button to the right is the Same as Previous button, used for copying a header or footer from one section to the next.

These buttons are followed by the Page Number button, which has a page with a pound sign (#) on it. This adds a field reflecting the current page number and places it at the point in the header or footer where the cursor is. Similarly, the next button inserts a field for the date, which is positioned where the cursor currently is in the header or footer and is filled when the document is printed. Moving farther to the right, the next button is for inserting a field for the time.

Continuing to the right, the next button (the Layout button) takes you to the Page Setup screen with the Layout tab selected. (Refer to Figure 9.8.) This is followed by a button for hiding text displayed in gray on the page. Hiding the text can make it a little easier to tell what is part of the header or footer and what isn't.

The final button, on the far right, is the Close button. This is for returning to the view being used before starting the work on the header and footer. It also makes the text in the main document editable and hides the header and footer.

Borders and Shading

A pair of features that can help you emphasize a section of your document are Borders and Shading. These effects can help set off a paragraph or picture.

As with so many features in Word, there are two different ways to bring them up. The first is to use the button on the far right of the Formatting toolbar (the one with a picture of a box with lines on it). This adds the Borders toolbar below the formatting toolbar. (See Figure 9.10.) As with Fonts, using this toolbar is most useful when you already know how to use it and how it will change the look of your text.

FIGURE 9.10.

The Borders toolbar enabled in Word for Windows 95.

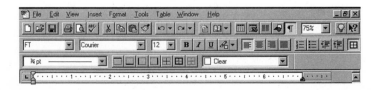

Even though this is called the Borders toolbar, the list box at the right end of the toolbar lets you set shading preferences. If you haven't used these effects much, you'll probably prefer starting with the menu-based version of this by choosing the Format | Borders and Shading option. This brings up the screen shown in Figure 9.11, with the Borders tab selected.

FIGURE 9.11.

The Borders tab of the Borders and Shading dialog box.

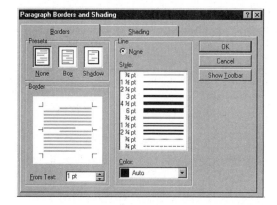

With this option, you get an example of your screen so you can get a feel for how your various choices will actually look once they are applied. To use this, you'll want to select one of the presets on this screen, and then either accept the default spacing from the text or change it to add extra space between the border and your text. Also on this screen, you can select the thickness of the line used to create the border, as well as line and color options. Similarly, clicking the Shading tab (shown in Figure 9.12) gives you a number of options and a preview of what the end result will look like.

FIGURE 9.12.

The Shading tab of the Borders and Shading dialog box.

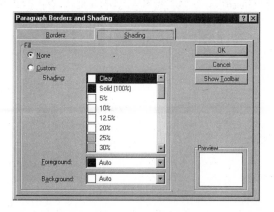

As you can tell by looking at these tabs, there are a number of different options for combining borders and shading to bring out the area you want to show off. One combination that works pretty well is shown in Figure 9.13. The selected paragraph has a $1\frac{1}{2}$–point border with a

Shadow preset and a custom shading of 25 percent. Compared to the rest of the text on the page, this paragraph really stands out, and it is still pretty easy to read. This paragraph should still be legible when printed, as well. You'll not usually want to get much darker than this unless you change the text color to a color like white. This can be done through changing the Foreground and Background options on the Shading tab. Your results when changing these options can be pretty wild, so you want to make sure you have a chunk of time set aside to come up with a good-looking result.

FIGURE 9.13.

The end result of using borders and shading on a section of text.

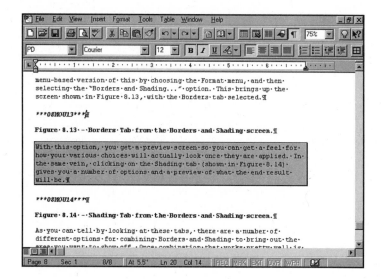

As with any effect, the trick to making it work well in your documents is to use it sparingly. Using this effect to emphasize pictures or sections of text more than once on a page is likely to make these items not stand out much at all.

Columns

Most newspapers, newsletters, and magazines use more than one column of text on a page. Also, if you have a large document and want to break up the text to make it easier to read, you can use Word for Windows 95 to create columns in a couple of ways.

One way is to use the Newsletter Wizard. Even if you don't want to create a newsletter, you can set up your document with this, and then delete the first page that has the logo.

If you want a little more control over the formatting of columns or need some additional effects, choose the Format | Columns option. You'll then get the screen shown in Figure 9.14, where you can set up a number of different column options.

Looking at this screen, you'll see five windows along the top. The first three allow you to choose a simple column setup with one, two, or three even columns. The next two windows allow you to specify an uneven setup, either to the left or to the right. If you select one of these two options, you can change the number of columns with the Number of Columns field, located below these five presets.

FIGURE 9.14.

The Columns dialog box with default settings.

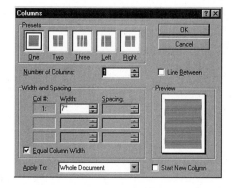

Further down the page is the Width and Spacing section, where you can set up each of the columns if you need that level of control (for example, if you want a small central column and two larger columns on each side). Generally, you'll just leave the Equal Column Width check box selected.

At the bottom of the page on this side you can select to apply these changes to either the whole document or from this point on. On the right side of the screen are the OK and Cancel buttons and the Line Between check box, which draws a line between the columns. At the bottom is the Start New Column check box, which is used to move text after the current cursor point to the next column (note that you must also select the This Point Forward option in the Apply To list).

Tables

One of the most common ways of handling data is to make a list. But when the list starts including three or four details for each item, it can quickly get unwieldy. At that point, creating a table to handle your information makes a lot of sense.

The easiest way to add a table is to go to the Table menu and select Insert Table. This gives you the dialog box shown in Figure 9.15, where you can define a simple table, run the Table Wizard, or use AutoFormat to make your simple table a little more complex.

FIGURE 9.15.

The Insert Table dialog box.

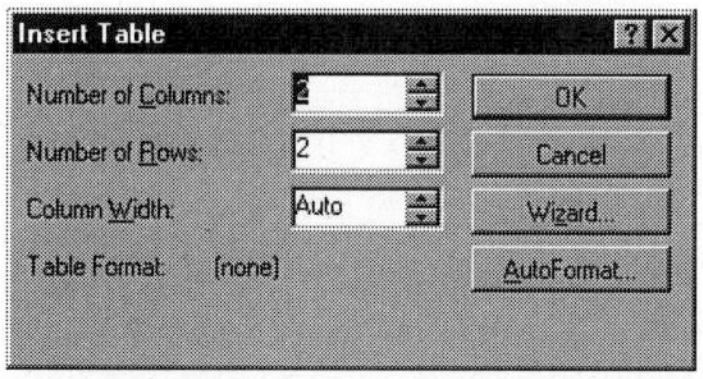

Unless your table is really simple, you'll probably want to select the Table Wizard. It often helps to know what decisions you'll have to make so that you can think about what you want ahead of time. Therefore, I will run through the Table Wizard so that you can see how it works. The first screen you see is the one shown in Figure 9.16, where you begin by choosing one of the basic styles shown on the screen.

FIGURE 9.16.

The first screen of the Table Wizard.

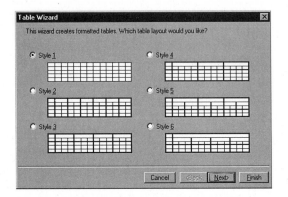

In this example, Style 6 has been chosen to create a table that will be used to track information over the year. This brings up the next screen (see Figure 9.17), which allows you to go with untitled columns or with column titles for the months and quarters of the year. This particular screen in the Wizard is somewhat different depending on which style is chosen in the previous screen. For example, if you choose Style 2, this screen will prompt you for the number of columns you want to use.

FIGURE 9.17.

The second screen of the Table Wizard.

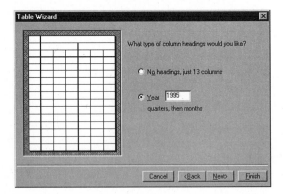

Click the Next button; the third screen, shown in Figure 9.18, comes up to allow you to determine how the column headings are printed on each page as well as how they are formatted in the table. This screen, and the others from this point on, are the same regardless of which type you chose.

FIGURE 9.18.

*The third screen of the
Table Wizard.*

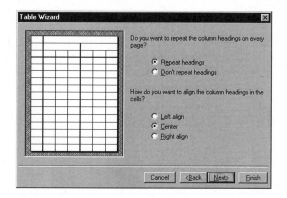

Once you've made your choices on this screen, click Next again for the fourth screen, which handles the row headings for your table. You have a number of options—from simply putting in a number of empty rows to creating rows containing various types of labels. (See Figure 9.19.)

FIGURE 9.19.

*The fourth screen of the
Table Wizard.*

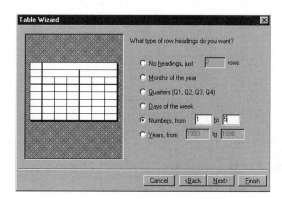

Clicking Next takes you to the fifth screen, which is essentially the same as the one shown in Figure 9.18, only it is for *row* headings instead of *column* headings.

Clicking Next takes you to a screen that allows you to set up the format of the cells (the individual entries) based on the type of data you are entering. Figure 9.20 shows you this screen.

Clicking Next takes you to the Print Orientation screen, used for determining how the table will print out when the document is printed. You can either select the Portrait mode, which is the standard mode you'd normally see in reports, or the Landscape mode, which effectively turns the page on its side. Landscape lets you have longer lines, but fewer of them on a page. Portrait gives you shorter lines, but more lines per page.

Clicking Next takes you to the final screen of the wizard. Clicking the Finish button here will create the table and take you to the AutoFormat screen. This is the last place where you can click the Back button to change your mind about the table's formatting without having to go through the entire process again.

FIGURE 9.20.

The sixth screen of the Table Wizard.

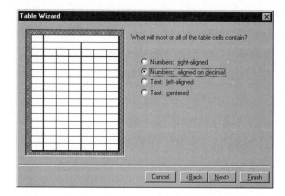

When the AutoFormat Screen comes up, it will look similar to the one shown in Figure 9.21, with a long list of options for formatting your table. When you consider the various options, try to keep in mind how the table will look onscreen as well as how it will look when you print it. This AutoFormat screen is basically the same as the one that is loaded if you don't use the Table Wizard.

FIGURE 9.21.

The AutoFormat screen for Word tables.

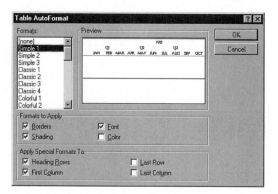

Finally, Figure 9.22 shows the end result of all the choices made in the wizard's screens: a nice table with subdivisions for Quarter and Month and five rows, as well (say, one for each week). To enter data into the table, click the cell you want to put a value in and then use the Tab key to move to the next cell. When you've filled a row, press the Tab key again to take you to the next row.

If you don't like how your table looks, simply click somewhere inside the table; then select the Table | Table AutoFormat option and try one of the other selections. If you already have some text that you think will make a good table (say, a list of items that you have separated with tabs), you can use the Table | Convert Text To Table option to make a table out of the existing text. You get a certain amount of control over how the columns and rows are determined, as the example in Figure 9.23 shows. In this figure, three rows of text (near the bottom of the screen) were selected when this option was chosen. Notice how this feature is able to automatically determine the number of columns and rows as well as the options for changing the delimiting character. Again, you are given the opportunity to use AutoFormat to make your table look the way you want it to.

The Borders and Shading options discussed earlier in the chapter can be used to make your tables easier to read. Select the part of the table you want to change and then use the Borders and Shading selection from the Format menu to add emphasis and impact to your table.

One other way to add a quick table is to click the Insert Table button from the standard toolbar (it's the button with a little table icon right next to a similar icon with the Excel logo). This brings up an empty group of boxes. Selecting a number of rows and columns here, as shown in Figure 9.24, gives you a table of rows and columns. The rest of the formatting is up to you or AutoFormat.

FIGURE 9.22.

The final product—a quarterly/monthly table.

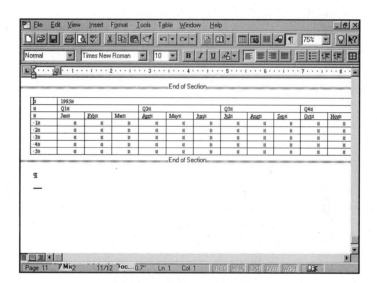

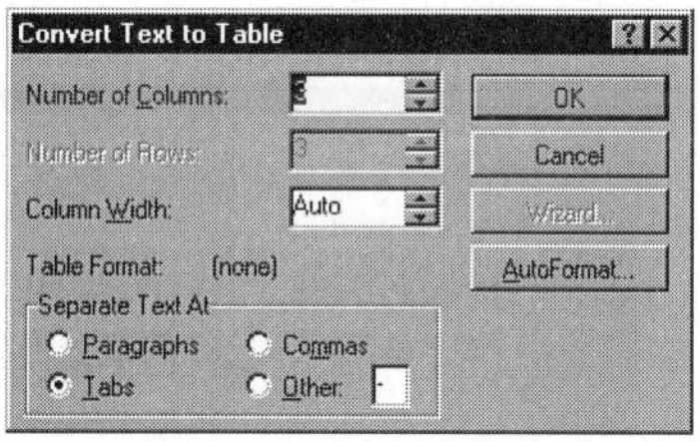

FIGURE 9.23.

Using Convert Text to Table to convert a section.

FIGURE 9.24.

The Insert Table button and a partially selected chart.

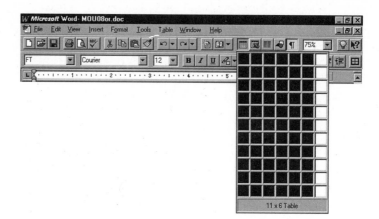

Footnotes and Endnotes

If you're familiar with scientific texts, or if you had to write a thesis when you were in school, you're familiar with using footnotes and endnotes. The idea is that you mark a location in the document with an indicator, and then later in the document you explain what the mark was for. Footnotes are printed at the end of the page, whereas endnotes are printed at the end of the document.

Adding these is relatively easy. Begin by moving to the point in your document where you want to indicate the footnote or endnote. Then, go to the Insert menu and select Footnote for either type of note. You then get the dialog box displayed in Figure 9.25, where you can select whether the note will be a footnote or endnote as well as what type of indicator you want to use. Notice that you can also use a custom symbol if you prefer.

FIGURE 9.25.

The Footnote and Endnote dialog box.

Once you've made your decision, you'll see a marker placed in your text; another window will open where you can type in the information for the footnote or endnote. This is shown in Figure 9.26.

The information you enter here is tied to the marker in your text. When your document is printed, the notes are numbered (assuming you chose that option) and printed at the end of the page or document.

FIGURE 9.26.

The footnote entry screen.

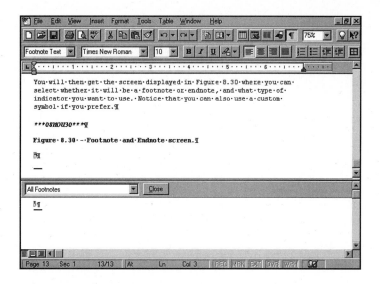

Annotations and Revisions

If you are working on documents with other people, you'll want some way for them to make comments or changes without losing your original work. Using annotations and revisions are the two methods for doing this.

Annotations can be thought of as electronic Post-It notes. These are kept as separate notes that you can view for comments and suggestions. To include an annotation, go to the place in the text where you want to make your comment. Then in the Insert menu select the Annotation option. You get an annotation marker in the text, and an editing area for the annotation is opened, as shown in Figure 9.27. This figure also shows you how to indicate who made the annotation.

One other thing you might notice on the annotation screen is the little cassette tape icon. You can click this icon to record a voice annotation if you have a microphone. Annotations are viewed by either double-clicking the annotation marker or by selecting Annotations from the View menu.

Revisions are designed to allow users to make somewhat more "forceful" suggestions. By turning them on, another person can actually make changes to the document; then the original author or a third-party can decide to accept the changes or return to the original version.

To turn on revisions, go to the Tools menu and select the Revisions option. This brings up the dialog box shown in Figure 9.28.

FIGURE 9.27.

The annotation entry screen, with the list for marking who made the annotation.

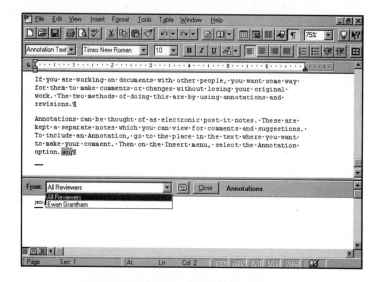

FIGURE 9.28.

The Revisions dialog box.

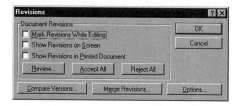

From here, you can choose several options to affect how revisions are shown. You can also choose to use Compare Versions, which enables you compare an open document with another file. The Merge Revisions button lets you take annotations and revisions from one file and merge them with another file.

Summary

In this chapter you have learned the basics of working with Word for Windows 95 and Word documents. You should now feel more comfortable with creating documents, making simple formatting changes, and adding special touches such as borders, shading, and tables.

In Chapter 10, "Document Patterns and Presentations," you'll learn about the templates (and some of the associated wizards) you can use to create various types of documents in Word, as well as how to use different views to see your document in different ways.

Document Patterns and Presentations

10

by Ewan Grantham

IN THIS CHAPTER

Having looked at the basics of creating a word-processing document in Chapter 9, "Document Concepts," we'll now look at some of the tools available in Word for creating more complex documents. This includes using templates (as well as associated wizards for some of them), using the various views in Word to see different things in a document, and other useful tips.

Templates and Template Wizards

There are 27 templates and 10 template wizards that can be accessed from the New Document dialog box in Word for Windows 95. In addition, other templates are available for your special needs in \MSOffice\Winword\Letters. These are all designed to make it easier for you to get a formatted document without having to do all the formatting yourself. In each category you'll find three versions of each template: Contemporary, Elegant, and Professional. These are designed to present similar information with a predefined look. The wizards in each category allow you to enter some of the information that you would enter with a template before the document is created, allowing the wizard to place and format the text properly.

To see the templates and template wizards that are part of the new document setup, you can select either start a new document from the shortcut bar or the New option from the File menu (Ctrl+N is the File|New shortcut).

The File|New screen, whichever way you get to it, looks like the screen shown in Figure 10.1. Because the General tab is somewhat boring, I have selected the Letters & Faxes tab in Figure 10.1.

FIGURE 10.1.

The New File dialog box with the Letters & Faxes tab selected.

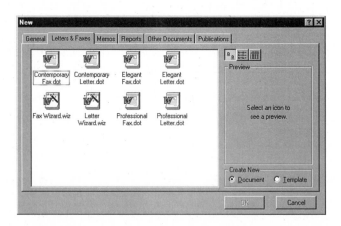

As with the File|Open option, a couple different viewing options can be specified. By default, the templates are shown with large icons. You can also specify the list or details view for showing the available templates and wizards.

To help show the difference between creating a new document with a template versus with a Template Wizard, I will create a newsletter with a template and then create one using a Template Wizard.

Starting with the template, the first step is to select the Publications tab; then double-click the Newsletter.DOT template. This brings up a new newsletter document based on the template.

The document contains a couple pages of information on how to fashion the template and build your newsletter. Some hints on how to create a new template that better reflects your final newsletter are also included. So, although it is initially very quick to set up, there is a lot of time invested in actually getting a product out of it.

For comparison, clicking the Newsletter Wizard brings up the screen shown in Figure 10.2. Because I've run this wizard before, it remembers what I selected the last time and begins with the Modern option as well as the title I used.

FIGURE 10.2.

A newsletter is begun with the Newsletter Wizard.

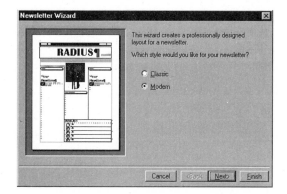

Having made this choice, clicking Next brings up the screen shown in Figure 10.3. Here you choose the number of columns to use in your newsletter. The tip that is given refers to the three-columns option and is designed to help guide someone who is just starting out by providing a quick design lesson.

FIGURE 10.3.

The second screen for the Newsletter Wizard.

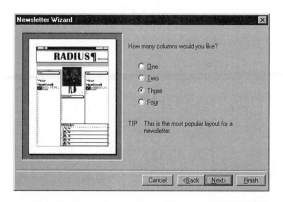

The Next button is again the way to move to the next screen. Here the question concerns the title for the newsletter. The tip in this screen mentions that you can change the title later in the newsletter itself; therefore, if you're not sure of the newsletter's title, just put in a nice place-holder.

Choosing Next takes you to the next screen, which prompts you for the number of pages you think you'll need for your newsletter. If you know approximately how much material you'll use, you should be able to give a fairly accurate number. One thing to keep in mind for this option is how you will be printing out your newsletter. If it will be going on both sides of a folded sheet (this is a newspaper-type format and is most often the format used), then this number should be a multiple of four because there will be a total of four pages printed on each sheet (if you don't see why, pull out a newspaper and look at how pages are printed on the sheets).

Moving to the next screen, you are presented with a number of choices for features to include in your newsletter. Most of these should be familiar. The one choice that might not be is the one labeled Fancy first letters, which creates a large, fancy, first letter at the start of each article. Figure 10.4 shows this screen with a preview of the newsletter when all the options are selected.

FIGURE 10.4.

The fifth screen for the Newsletter Template Wizard. Note the number of choices available here for customizing your newsletter.

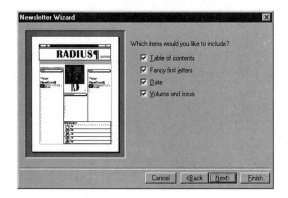

Clicking Next brings you to the final screen in the Newsletter Wizard. This is the last time you can back up through your previous choices and make changes without having to start all over.

Compare the results with those of the basic Newsletter Wizard; notice how much further along you are by creating the newsletter with the wizard. However, you'll also notice that the wizard is more flexible; therefore, if you need to do a lot of customization, you might be better off starting with the template.

The process is the same through most of the templates and Template Wizards in Word. The template is best for items that require a lot of customization, or if you plan on building your own template. Otherwise, you will want to use the Template Wizard.

After having looked at some of the templates available in Word, you might decide you want to create a template for a memo, letter, or some other commonly used document. This is particularly helpful if you want to have a consistent look for your business documents. Using a template ensures that each document maintains a constant style.

A template can contain anything that a document can contain; therefore, if you want to use a graphic as a letterhead, you can store it with the template. Also, any macros you create can be stored.

The two most common ways to create a template involve building from an existing document. The first way is to load an existing template, make your changes, and then save it under a different name. The second way is to set up a document the way you would want it to look, and then under the File menu choose the Save As option, changing the Save As type to Template. By convention, the file extension should be .DOT to indicate that this is a template. If you want the template to be available from the File | New option or from the shortcut bar, you need to make sure the template is saved in the \MSOffice\Templates directory in the appropriate folder (such as Letters & Faxes, if it's a Letter Template).

Creating a wizard requires some heavy-duty macro writing, but you *can* create your own wizards if you want to. As with templates, your best bet is to find a wizard that is close to what you want, edit it to do what you need it to do, and then save it with a new name. The .WIZ extension is traditionally used to indicate a wizard. If you pull up a wizard, you'll notice that many of them are essentially blank documents with a number of macros, two of which (AutoNew and StartWizard) identify a normal wizard. AutoNew is defined to always be the starting macro when creating a new document from a template. You can learn more about macros in Chapter 11, "Word Assistance."

Views

As you might have noticed with both templates and Template Wizards, your document is opened in page layout view. This is one of the three standard views you can work in with your Word documents. To switch between them, you can either click one of the three buttons at the bottom-left of your document (just above the status bar, which shows the page number) or you can use the View menu and pick the appropriate view.

Which view is the best to work in will depend on what you are doing. Normal view is designed for general-purpose typing, editing, formatting, and moving text around. It gives you a basic feel for the text and elements in your document without trying to provide exact WYSIWYG (what you see is what you get) capabilities.

To easily scroll through a long document, move text around, or see the structure of the document, you'll want to use outline view.

Page layout view tries to achieve WYSIWYG (although it is not as accurate as print preview) by showing how elements such as graphics will be positioned on the printed page.

In addition to these standard views, there are two other views you might want to use. If you want to divide a long document into separate files (for example, dividing a book into several chapters), you want to use master document view. Creating master documents is covered in more detail in Chapter 13, "Integrating OLE Objects into Word."

Last but not least, if you want to see your document onscreen without rulers, toolbars, or other screen elements, choose full screen view. In this view, notice the little TV in the bottom-right corner. Clicking it restores the toolbars and other screen elements.

Styles

If you've ever worked for a large company, you probably received a new employee packet on your first day at the job. It probably contained an employee manual, some information on benefits, possibly security information for logging onto the LAN, and other frequently answered questions. Now, imagine if every time someone started working at this large company, someone had to go to several buildings to get the various packets.

The idea behind a style in Word is that if there is a particular format you use often, you shouldn't have to go through the hassle of defining it every time. Like the new employee packet, it stores all the various parts that make up the logical whole as one definition.

Like most features in Word, a style can be defined in several ways. One of these ways is to select the Format | Style option. This brings up the screen shown in Figure 10.5, which allows you to work with current styles or to define a new one.

FIGURE 10.5.

The Style dialog box in Word for Windows 95.

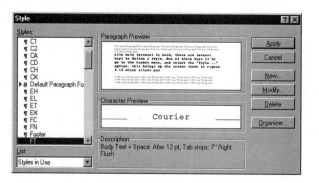

Selecting the New button here takes you to the screen shown in Figure 10.6, where you can set the various options that go into a style definition. Notice all the different settings you have access to within a style. Also, be sure to note that a new style can be based on an old one.

An easier way to do this is to take a section of text that is already defined the way you want for your style. Select the section of text; then select the Style list (it is located to the far-left of the Formatting toolbar, to the left of the Font list) by clicking inside the box. Type the name you want to use for this new style and then press the Enter key. If that name is already being used, you'll get a warning. Otherwise, your new style will become available in the current document, as well as being saved in Normal.DOT (the default template).

FIGURE 10.6.

The New Style definition in Word for Windows 95.

If you want to see what styles are already available, go to the Format menu and select the Style Gallery option. This brings up a screen like the one shown in Figure 10.7, which allows you to preview the various styles available.

FIGURE 10.7.

Using the Style Gallery in Word.

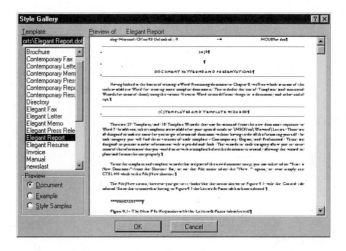

In this example, the Document option has been selected to show how it affects the current document. The example and the style sample options use defined text to show off the various options for each style.

Frames

Frames are used to set aside a section of a page in order to place something in it (often, but not always, a graphics file). Frames allow you to create various effects (for example, setting a graphic in the middle of a page and having the text flow around it). They also make it easier for you to move a graphic around when testing different formatting options.

Once you put something inside a frame, it remains inside the frame, even if you move the frame somewhere else on the page. A frame can be moved outside the normal margins. This allows for some interesting effects.

Not surprisingly, there are a couple different ways to set up frames in your document. The first option is to insert a picture or graphic into the document, select it by clicking it, and then select the Insert | Frame option. The other way is to select the Insert | Frame option and then use the Insert menu again to insert a picture or graphic inside the frame. The end results tend to be similar, although in the first instance you can scale your picture first before you put a frame around it. In the second instance the frame is sized to the default size of the picture, which will likely be too large. Figure 10.8 is an example of how a frame might look in a document with text flowing around it.

FIGURE 10.8.

Using a frame to position a graphic in Word.

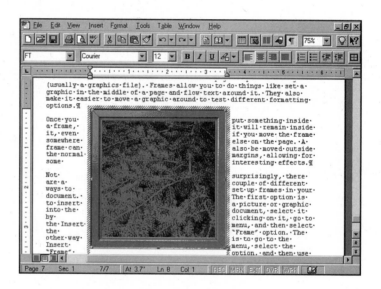

Note the cross-hatched border, which is how Word shows the dimensions of the frame when it has been selected. The small squares around the border are handles for redimensioning the frame. Changing the size of the frame also changes the size of the contents.

Frames aren't only used for graphics. Text and tables can also be put in frames. For example, if you want to position a table in the middle of a page with a headline centered over it, you could use frames for both of these items and still have the main text flow around them.

Print Preview

Particularly when you have a number of frames or other specially formatted objects in a document, it is important to use the Print Preview option from the File menu to see exactly what the end result will look like when printed.

The default view of a document (after you have selected this option) is shown in Figure 10.9. Notice how the image of the page is scaled to fit into the space given. If you want to know how much it was scaled, look at the toolbar above the image where the scale list is shown (34 percent in this case).

FIGURE 10.9.

The print preview of a document.

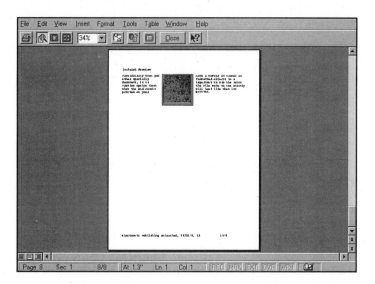

Next to the scale on the toolbar is a button with a picture of a screen with four pages on it. This button is used to preview multiple pages, which are selected from the panel that comes up when you click the button.

Selecting a matrix from this panel determines the number of pages to be shown at once. (The results are shown at the bottom of the dialog box as $N \times N$, where N is the number of pages.) In Figure 10.10, the dialog box was selected once to show the pages, and then selected again to show how the pages were selected. Notice that the scale of each page has dropped to 16 percent. This option tends to be most useful if you have a similar format you are checking across multiple pages.

Another button on the toolbar you'll want to use is the one with a small TV on it (just to the left of the Close button). This is the Full Screen button; it gives you more screen space to display your image. By choosing the Full Screen option, the ratio now jumps to 40 percent, which makes it a little easier to see how your text is affected by different options (in fact, the text is now almost large enough to read).

Just to the left of this button is the Shrink to Fit button. This button alters your document to fit it into a number of full pages, without leaving a partial page at the end. Therefore, instead of having eight full pages and just a couple of paragraphs on the ninth page, your document is changed to make everything fit in eight pages. The trick that Word uses is to scale your font by partial points (for example, changing a 12-point font to an 11.5-point font). Depending on the document, this feature might work well or it might really mess things up.

FIGURE 10.10.

An example of previewing multiple pages.

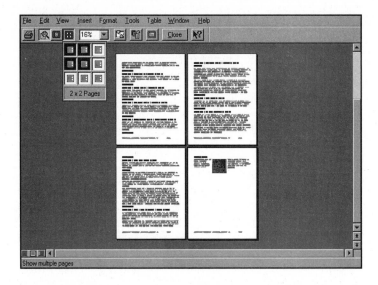

Even though your document appears different in print preview, it can still be edited in this mode. Of course, you'll have a hard time seeing what you are changing; therefore, unless you're moving a graphic, you'll probably want to click the Close button to exit print preview and then edit from the normal view.

Lists

Another useful tool for setting up a document is to create a list using bullets or numbers. Particularly if you're running through a procedure or trying to emphasize the points you're making in a memo, creating a list will mark each point and make it stand out.

The quick way to create a bulleted list is to click the Bullet List button (the one with a picture of three squares in front of three lines) on the Formatting toolbar. Every time you press the Enter key, another bullet point is added. Turning bullet lists off is done by clicking the Bullet List button again.

Similarly, creating a quick numbered list is a matter of clicking the Number List button (the one with the numbers 1, 2, and 3 in front of three lines). Every time you press the Enter key, another numbered point is added. Turning off the numbered list is a matter of clicking the Number List button again.

As is the case with most things in Word, bulleted and numbered lists can be created by using the menu. In this case select the Format | Bullets and Numbering option. This brings up the screen shown in Figure 10.11, with the Bulleted tab enabled.

Looking at this screen, you notice that there are a number of different types of bullet symbols from which to choose. If these symbols are not what you want, select the Modify button to bring up the screen shown in Figure 10.12, which is used to define new symbol characters. In this figure the Bullet button has been selected to illustrate how you can use any character from one of the installed fonts as a bullet character.

FIGURE 10.11.

The Bullets and Numbering dialog box with the Bulleted tab selected.

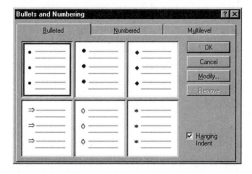

FIGURE 10.12.

The Modify Bulleted List screen and the Symbol requester, used for defining a bullet character.

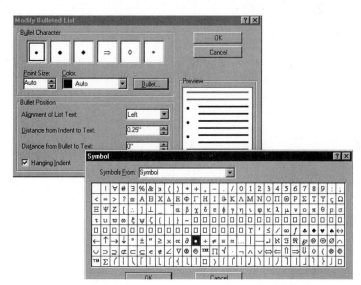

The Numbered tab is similar to the Bulleted tab. (See Figure 10.13.) You'll notice that the definition of a number is stretched somewhat. Perhaps the Fonted tab (indicating that these lists used nongraphic symbols) would have been a better name.

Because the numbered lists use letters and numbers, the modification is different as well. Figure 10.14 shows how the numbered lists can be modified. You'll also notice that you can define text that occurs before and after the number or letter for each point. So instead of having a list with 1 followed by 2 followed by 3, you could have a list with Point 1 followed by Point 2 or Step 1 followed by Step 2.

FIGURE 10.13.

Bullets and Numbering screen with the Numbered tab selected.

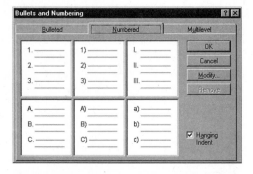

FIGURE 10.14.

The Modify Numbered List screen and the Font dialog box, used to changed the font for characters or numbers.

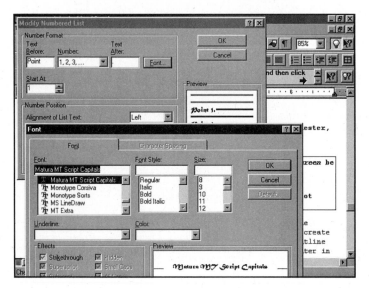

One other option on the Bulleted and Numbered list screen is the Multilevel tab. This tab, shown in Figure 10.15, allows you to create a form of outline, although it is different from the type of outline you create with multilevel headings.

FIGURE 10.15.

The Bullets and Numbering dialog box with the Multilevel tab selected.

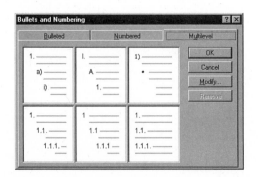

For somewhat obvious reasons, the Modify screen for this option is also different from the other two. Figure 10.16 shows the specifics of this screen; you'll notice how you can define various items for each "level" you expect to use.

FIGURE 10.16.

The Modify Multilevel List dialog box.

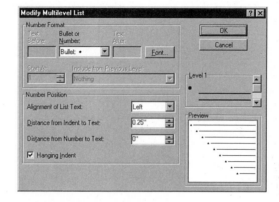

Not only can you use these options to create lists from scratch, but you can also select a section of text to be converted into a list. Simply select the text and then choose one of the options from the toolbar or the Bullets and Numbering dialog box.

Figure 10.17 shows what the end result might look like. In this example, three lists have been set up with different formats to give you an idea for the possibilities of using lists.

FIGURE 10.17.

Several different lists with different formats.

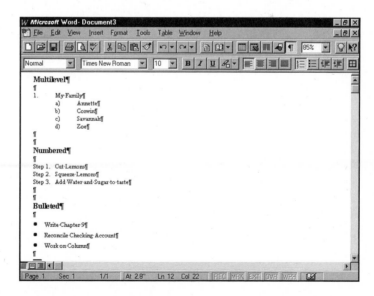

Table of Contents

Another type of specialized list is the table of contents for a report or publication. Word makes it easy to create one for your document by doing a scan for the styles you have specified for the headings. Word uses these styles to determine how things in your document relate to each other. You can use the default heading styles (Heading 1 through Heading 9), or you can specify your own heading styles to use.

To do this, in your document apply the heading styles you want to use to the headings in your table of contents. Then, select the point in the document where you want to insert the table of contents. From the Insert menu select the Index and Tables option; then click the Table of Contents tab. Figure 10.18 shows what this tab looks like. Notice that the Options button has been selected.

FIGURE 10.18.

The Table of Contents tab and the available options.

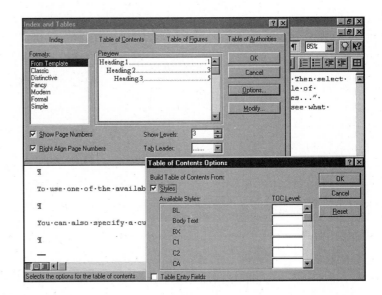

Click one of the available designs under Formats to use it; you can see what this will look like in the preview window.

The table of contents shown in Figure 10.19 is achieved by using these screens and redefining the heading to use the ones for this chapter (notice that the count is somewhat off because the illustrations weren't included in the calculations). The design used in this case is the Modern design.

FIGURE 10.19.

A sample table of contents based on this chapter.

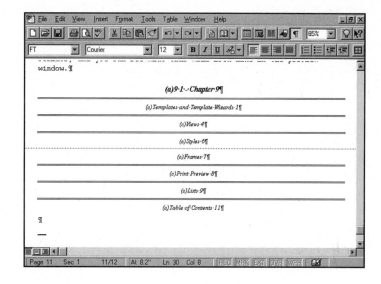

Indexes

Related to the table of contents (and available from the same menu option) is the index. From the Insert menu select the Index and Tables option; then select the Index tab, which gives you the Mark Index Entry box.

From this screen you can choose to mark the entries that will make up your index. Choosing that button will bring up the screen shown in Figure 10.20. From here you can mark multiple entries to be added to your index. In this case, the word *index* itself has been marked.

FIGURE 10.20.

Selecting an entry to be added to the index.

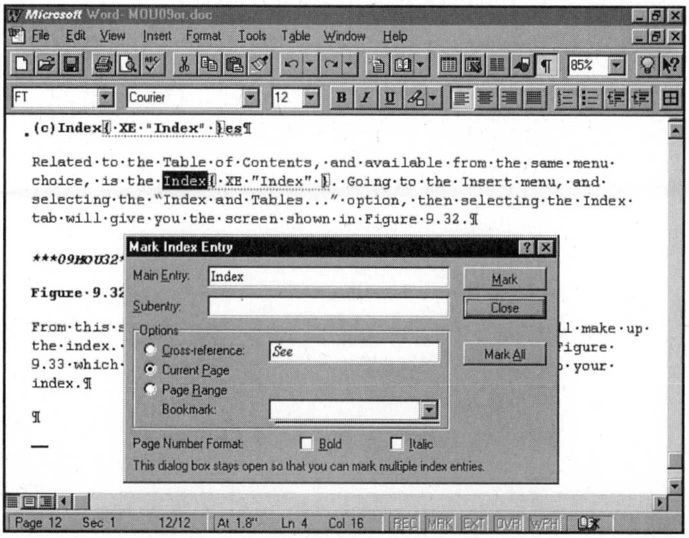

Finally, returning to the index screen, the document will be searched for marked entries, and an index will be created at the current insertion point. With the one entry I marked earlier, the index shown in Figure 10.21 is created (using Mark All it found all the instances of *index*).

FIGURE 10.21.

The final, albeit short, result—an index of index.

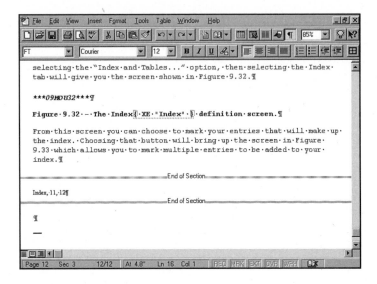

Outlines

Creating an outline using the outline view and setting various levels in your document can be considered an intermediary step between a multilevel list and a master document. You can create an outline of this form by using the outline view to bring up the Outline toolbar; then you use the icons on the toolbar to set the level of the various items in your outline. Figure 10.22 shows a new document created using the outline view with the initial topic entered.

After adding the next line, select it and then set it to the appropriate style (in this case Heading 2). You could also use the second button from the left (the one with an arrow pointing to the right) to demote the item so that it's not the same level as the chapter title. When you add the next line, you can again assign it to a level (such as Heading 3) or demote it. In this particular case, because there will be no lower levels, the third button from the left (the one with a picture of a double-headed arrow pointing left) is used to make the item Body Text, which in this case means it is at the bottom level.

The document in Figure 10.23 is shown with all the levels expanded to reveal all of the current contents of this outline (after a couple more items have been added).

By double-clicking the plus sign located to the left of the topics that have them, you can collapse your outline. Therefore, if you have a number of items, you can keep them all collapsed except for the one you are currently using or examining.

FIGURE 10.22.

Starting to build an outline.

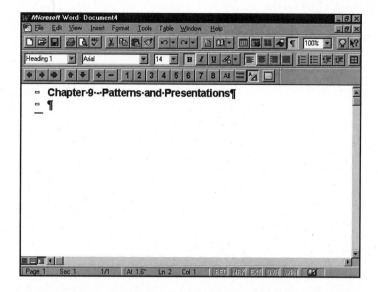

FIGURE 10.23.

An example of an outline in the outline view.

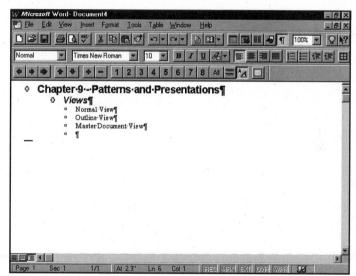

Summary

In this chapter you have learned about a number of different techniques for changing how you look at and organize the information in your document. By using different views you can look an item in different ways, making the item easier to work with and making it easier to figure out how it will print.

With these techniques, you are ready to move on to Chapter 11, where several additional techniques for working with your document are covered.

Word Assistance

11

by Sue Charlesworth

This chapter explores some "little tools" that can help make working with Word a little easier.

Bookmarks

Have you ever wanted to mark a place in a document so you could find it easily, and mark the latest place in the document from which you "jumped" to your marked spot? If you've ever marked places in your document with an odd string of characters like @@@@@ and searched for that string (and had to remember to delete that string before finishing your document), or if you've simply used Page Up and Page Down to move from place to place in your document, bookmarks are for you.

Bookmarks, as the name implies, allow you to place markers in your document, making it easy to return to specific spots in your work. You can mark either a single spot or a block of text. To place a bookmark in your document, move the insertion point to the place where you'd like the bookmark, or select the text you want marked. Select Edit | Bookmark, and the Bookmark dialog box opens. Give your bookmark a name and select Add. (See Figure 11.1.)

FIGURE 11.1.

Adding a bookmark.

NOTE

When you see references to "text" in this chapter, it doesn't actually refer to text only. In these instances, consider text to mean any aspect of your document, including graphics and tables or even a mix of document elements.

The Bookmark dialog box also lists all the bookmarks in your document and allows you to change the order of the list. To see your bookmarks listed alphabetically, select Name as the Sort By condition (Figure 11.2); to see your bookmarks in the order in which they appear in your document, select Location.

To return to the spot or text marked by a bookmark, select Edit | Go To from the menu bar. Select Bookmark from the Go to What list and enter the bookmark's name. (See Figure 11.3.) If you want to see a list of the bookmarks in your document, click on the down arrow next to the bookmark name field and click on the bookmark you want. Once the bookmark's name is in the Enter Bookmark Name field, select the Go To button. Word jumps to the spot or text identified by the chosen bookmark.

FIGURE 11.2.

*Sorting bookmarks
by name.*

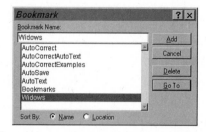

FIGURE 11.3.

Going to a bookmark.

TIP

When you go to a block of text, Word highlights the entire block. This technique can be handy if you know you'll want to repeatedly copy the same block of text and won't be sure it will be in the Clipboard for pasting. Highlight the text, create a bookmark, and go to the marked section when you need it and copy it.

CAUTION

The Sort By button in the Bookmark dialog box does not affect how Word lists bookmarks in the Go To dialog box. Even if you've selected Location as the Sort By criterion in the Bookmark dialog box, the bookmark list in the Go To dialog box is alphabetical.

You can also use the Bookmark dialog box (by selecting Edit | Bookmark from the menu bar) to go to a particular bookmark. In the Bookmark dialog box, select the desired bookmark and then click on Go To.

Bookmarks are invisible in the printed document, but you might want to see their locations in your document. Select Tools | Options from the menu bar, then select the View tab. In the Show box, click on Bookmarks. (See Figure 11.4.) Once Show Bookmarks is turned on, bookmarks of a single point appear as a heavy I-bar in your document and bookmarks of a block of text are marked by heavy square brackets. (See Figure 11.5.) To turn off showing bookmarks, return to Tools | Options | View and click again in Bookmarks to remove the check.

FIGURE 11.4.

Showing bookmarks.

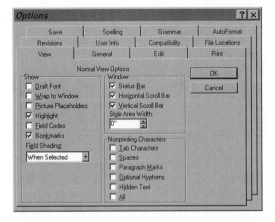

FIGURE 11.5.

Bookmarks marked in text.

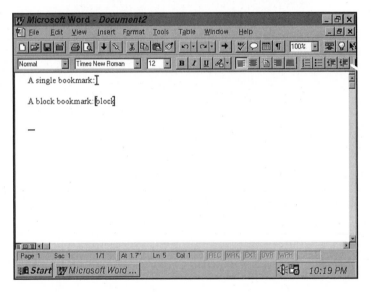

AutoText

Have you ever needed to add the same block of text to different documents, time and again? Are you tired of typing in the exact same stuff, over and over again (making the same mistakes each time)? If you've ever had to dig out an old copy of a document, or type something in for the umpteenth time this week, AutoText is for you.

AutoText provides a way to store blocks of text or graphics, often called "boilerplate" material, and insert the stored blocks elsewhere in the same document or in other documents. To create an AutoText entry, highlight the block, and then select Edit|AutoText from the menu bar. Give your AutoText a name (Word suggests a name by using the first little bit of your text) and click on Add. (See Figure 11.6.) By default, Word places AutoText entries in the Normal template, where all your documents have access to AutoText; if you want to restrict an AutoText entry to a particular template, select that template in the Make AutoText Entry Available To box.

FIGURE 11.6.

Adding AutoText.

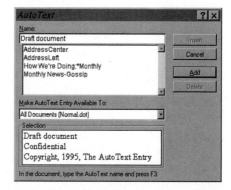

If your AutoText entry has special formatting that you want to preserve, make sure to include the paragraph mark at the end of the text in your AutoText entry.

To change the contents of an AutoText entry, insert the entry into your document, make your changes, select the text, and re-add it as an AutoText entry. Select the entry's original name to save the changes.

When you want to place some AutoText in a document, you can either go through the AutoText dialog box (by selecting Edit | AutoText from the menu bar) or use a keyboard shortcut. From the AutoText dialog box, select the name of the AutoText entry you want to insert and click on Insert.

If you're not sure which AutoText entry you want, look in the Preview box to see a portion of the entry.

To use the keyboard shortcut to insert AutoText, you'll need to know the name of the AutoText entry. Type the AutoText name into your document and then press F3. Word inserts the AutoText entry at the insertion point.

TIP

The "Bookmarks" section mentions how to use a bookmark to make it easy to repeatedly copy and paste a block of text. AutoText does the same thing, making your life easier; when you insert a block of AutoText, you don't lose your place in your document.

AutoText Examples

Let's look at some AutoText examples. A simple one is your company's address. Type it in once, save it as AutoText, and you'll never have to type it in again. What happens if you want the address to appear at the left margin sometimes and centered at the top of a sheet other times? Save the differently formatted addresses as separate AutoText entries, making sure to include the paragraph mark at the end of the text, and insert the appropriate address where needed.

As another example, say you put out your company's news and gossip memo. Rather than construct the heading each time you issue the memo, or copy and paste it from the last issue, or build a template for the memo, simply store the heading as an AutoText entry and insert it each time you create the memo. Note that this AutoText includes both text and a graphic. (See Figure 11.7.)

FIGURE 11.7.

AutoText with a graphic.

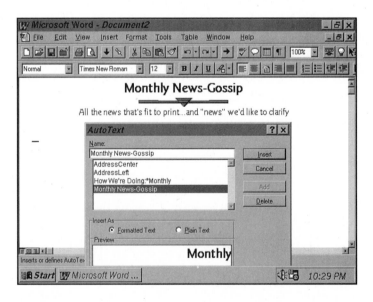

Here's one final example: Each month you publish a summary of the company's sales by type of product and region of the country. You build the table framework, including the format of particular cells, right-justifying the numeric entries, and save it as an AutoText entry. (See

Figure 11.8.) Each month you can insert the AutoText into your document, fill in the appropriate numbers, and you're done.

FIGURE 11.8.

An AutoText table.

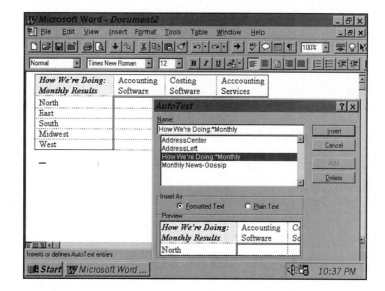

AutoCorrect

Are there words your fingers just won't type in correctly, yet you make the same mistake most times? Do you leave the Shift key down just a little too long and get words beginning with two capital letters? Have you ever left that blasted Caps Lock on and had to go back and retype the whole thing, or play with changing the case to get everything the way it should be? If so, AutoCorrect is for you.

To open AutoCorrect, select Tools | AutoCorrect from the menu bar. The AutoCorrect dialog box opens, allowing you to select a series of common typing corrections (including recovering from that Caps Lock situation) and shortcuts. (See Figure 11.9.) In addition to these corrections, you can also specify if you want AutoCorrect to replace text as you type. Here's where AutoCorrect really comes into its own.

> **NOTE**
>
> In a thoroughly intelligent move, AutoCorrect not only fixes Caps Locked text, it also turns Caps Lock off.

In addition to correcting common typing errors like typing teh for the, AutoCorrect also corrects spelling errors like thier and recieve. If your personal bugaboos aren't included in the list Word provides, add them. Enter your incorrect way of doing things in the Replace field and the correct way in the With field. (See Figure 11.10.) Select Add (if you want to keep the AutoCorrect dialog box open for further entries) or OK (if you want to close AutoCorrect and get on with your document). Then, the next time you type one of the Replace entries, AutoCorrect replaces it with the With entry.

FIGURE 11.9.

The AutoCorrect dialog box.

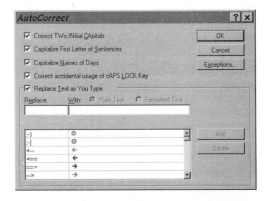

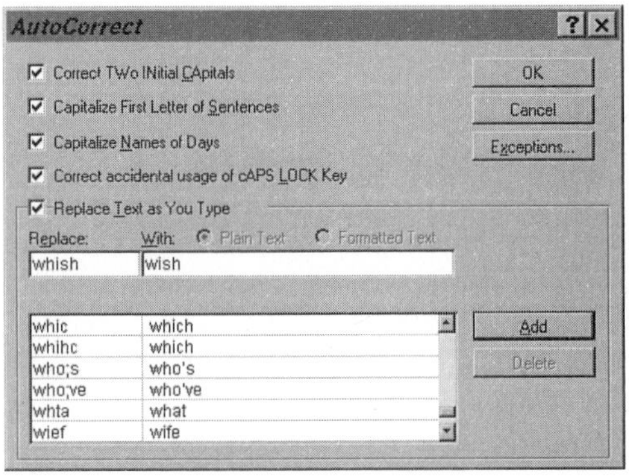

FIGURE 11.10.

Adding an AutoCorrect entry.

If you don't want to type the entry into the With field, select the text in your document and open AutoCorrect. The text appears in the With field, leaving you to enter its "code" word.

> **NOTE**
>
> AutoCorrect doesn't do its replacements until you continue beyond the Replace entry. Once you type a space or a punctuation mark, AutoCorrect goes to work.

Don't be fooled by AutoCorrect's name; it goes far beyond a simple correction mechanism. Did you notice that the With field in the AutoCorrect dialog box is significantly longer than the Replace field? That's so you can replace abbreviations with spelled-out text. Instead of typing out a company name each time you reference it (and Amalgamated Architectural Additions does get trying, doesn't it?), create an AutoCorrect entry to replace aaa with `Amalgamated Architectural Additions`. Then, instead of typing out you-know-what, simply type in aaa and go on your merry way.

You can include symbols or graphics in an AutoCorrect entry. To do so, select the symbol or graphic and any other text you want to accompany it. In the AutoCorrect dialog box, Word places your selection in the With field. Add your shortcut text in Replace, and you're done.

AutoCorrect also includes some nifty formatting changes. Instead of the clunky-looking fraction 1/2, AutoCorrect substitutes the typographically pleasing fraction $^1/_2$. 1st becomes 1st and 3rd, 3rd. The typographically correct em dash is much simplified; type in two hyphens, and Word automatically substitutes the em dash when you begin to type the next word. Simple type arrows —> become arrow symbols →. Keyboard "smileys"—you know, the little smile face made from simple characters—become true smiling faces ☺.

If you want AutoCorrect to stop correcting for any of the checked items in the AutoCorrect dialog box, simply click on the check to turn that feature off. If you want to stop correcting one of your shortcuts or replacements, or one of Word's, go into AutoCorrect, select the item in the Replace Text as You Type list, and click on Delete.

AutoCorrect Examples

The AutoText section talks about storing the Monthly News-Gossip heading as an AutoText entry. You can also store the heading as an AutoCorrect entry, as discussed above, replacing something like mng with the heading. (See Figure 11.11.)

FIGURE 11.11.

AutoCorrect with a graphic.

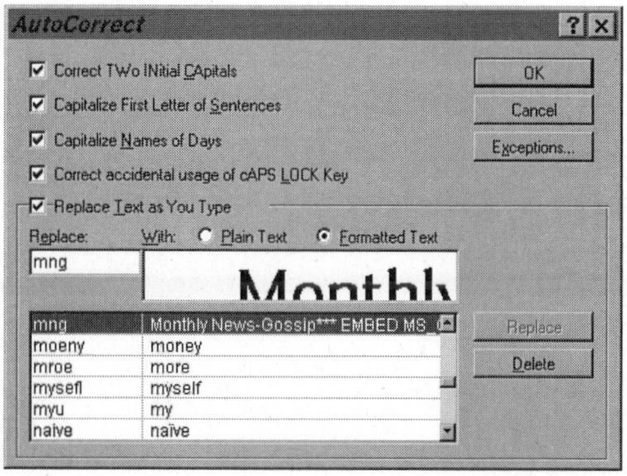

How about replacing your initials with your full name? That could be handy if you type a lot of letters. Create an AutoCorrect entry for your address—or anyone else's—too.

In creating this chapter (and others in this book), I employed a number of AutoCorrect abbreviations. For instance, instead of typing in `AutoText` and `AutoCorrect`, I used att and ac as their respective AutoCorrect entries. For PowerPoint (I hate typing capital letters in the middle of words), I substituted ppt.

> **NOTE**
>
> To intentionally use AutoCorrect entries the "wrong" way, or to use the letter series as I did above, takes some doing. AutoCorrect, of course, replaces the entry when you type it. You'll have to carefully place the code letters in your document without putting a space or punctuation after them. Your best bet is to delete some already-entered text and replace it with your AutoCorrect code.

I have my favorite mistypings, too. For some reason, I have a terrible time with words that end with "ation" and they come out "aiton" instead. When I use an "ation" word a lot—and consistently mistype it—I create an AutoCorrect entry for it.

> **NOTE**
>
> AutoCorrect only deals with whole words; I can't tell it to substitute "ation" for "aiton" wherever my little glitch inserts itself. Similarly, AutoCorrect doesn't handle suffixes: "applicaiton" and "applicaitons" require separate AutoCorrect entries. (See Figure 11.12.)

FIGURE 11.12.
AutoCorrect for suffixes.

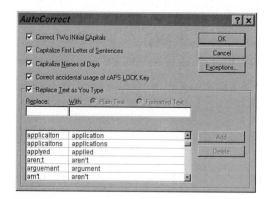

AutoText and AutoCorrect: Which One to Use?

While AutoText doesn't correct misspellings or "expand" abbreviations like AutoCorrect, the two tools both insert text or text and graphics into your document. To add addresses or memo headings or your name, should you use AutoText or AutoCorrect?

Personal preference and working habits determine much of the choice. If you can remember a list of replacement codes and want Word to insert your repeating blocks of text as you go along, use AutoCorrect to insert the text. If you don't want to be bothered with remembering all the codes, or if more than one person shares a computer and can't be expected to know what Auto-Correct items have been added, use AutoText. It's probably easier to scroll the list of AutoText entries and identify the text they replace than it is to scroll through the list of AutoCorrect replacements.

One other difference between AutoText and AutoCorrect is that you can print out a list of your AutoText entries. Select File | Print from the menu bar and then select AutoText Entries from the Print what pull-down list. (See Figure 11.13.) The name and content of each AutoText entry in the current template print.

FIGURE 11.13.

Printing AutoText entries.

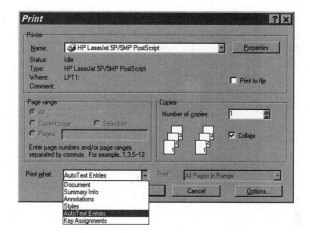

AutoSave

How many times have you heard "You should save your work regularly?" How many times have you gotten so engrossed in your work that you have forgotten to save it—only to have the power fail after you've done extraordinary and unreproducible work for two hours? Activate AutoSave immediately (before you have another power failure).

To activate AutoSave, select Tools | Options from the menu bar and click on the Save tab. Select Automatic Save Every and enter a value for Minutes. (See Figure 11.14.) Word will now automatically save your open documents at the increments you specified. You can also activate AutoSave from File | Save As, and select the Options button. The same Options dialog box opens.

If a power failure or some other problem occurs once you've turned on AutoSave, Word works to recover your documents. After the failure, when you restart Word, it opens all the documents that were active at the time of the failure. Using Save As, save all your documents. You'll lose any work done since the last automatic save, but depending on the AutoSave interval you specified, that could be much better than losing an entire morning's efforts.

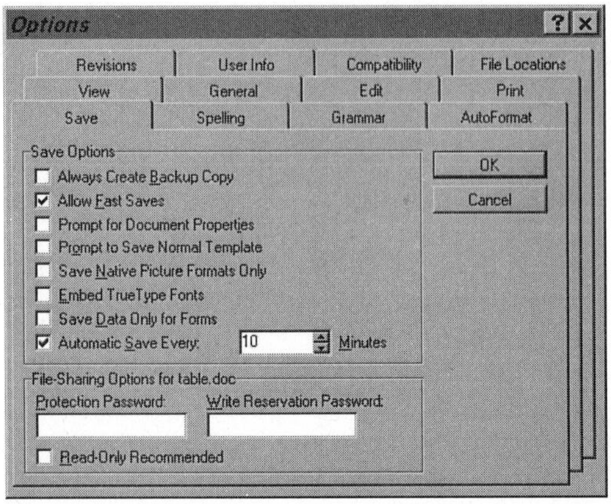

FIGURE 11.14.

Setting AutoSave in the Options dialog box.

TIP

Waiting for Word to AutoSave a document, particularly a long one, can be annoying. Balance your AutoSave interval against the nuisance factor and your memory and other factors. If you can remember (or otherwise have documented) what you've been working on, and you're not under a time crunch, you may want to set AutoSave for a longer interval. If, on the other hand, you can't afford the time to re-enter extensive additions or you can't rely on memory to reconstruct your documents, set the interval to a shorter period. If you've set the AutoSave interval to 10 minutes, that's the most you can lose.

Widows and Orphans

Widows and orphans are those annoying single lines left by themselves at the top or bottom of a page or column of text. For those of you into definitions, a *widow* is a single line at the top of a page or column; an *orphan* is the single line at the bottom. A widow can particularly distract readers by appearing to be a subhead, instead of a line of straggling text. Orphans slow readers down.

Now that you know what widows and orphans are, and that you don't want them in your text, how do you prevent them? Actually, in Word, it's more a case of how do you allow them if you really want them in your text. Select Format | Paragraph from the menu bar, and then select the Text Flow tab. In the pagination box, Widow/Orphan Control defaults to checked (Figure 11.15); Word automatically prevents single lines at the top or bottom of your text. If you want to allow single lines at either the top or bottom of your text, click on the Widow/Orphan Control box to turn widow and orphan prevention off.

FIGURE 11.15.

Widow and orphan control.

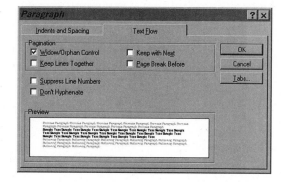

Figure 11.16 shows a section of text with a widow: a single line just beyond the new page marker. Figure 11.17 shows the same section of text, but with Widow/Orphan Control turned on. Note that Word has repaginated the document so that an additional line joins the former widow. Figure 11.18, similarly, has an orphan: a single line just above the new page marker. Figure 11.19 demonstrates the effect of Widow/Orphan Control on that section of text. (Pay no attention to the content of the illustrated text; the text is merely gibberish, repeated until a widow and an orphan appeared.)

FIGURE 11.16.

A widow.

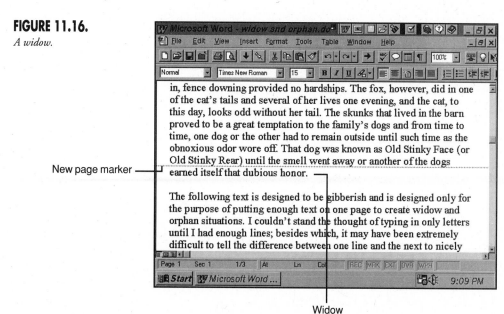

FIGURE 11.17.

The widow controlled.

New page marker

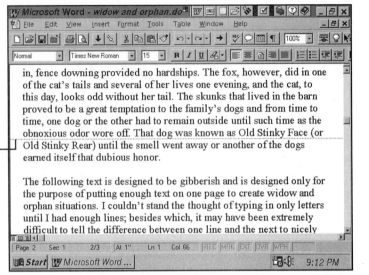

FIGURE 11.18.

An orphan.

Orphan

New page marker

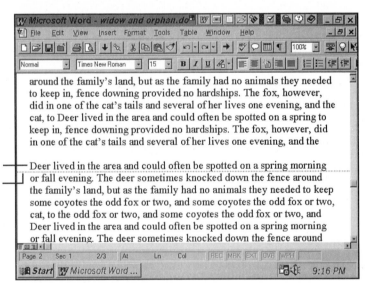

FIGURE 11.19.

The orphan controlled.

New page marker ——

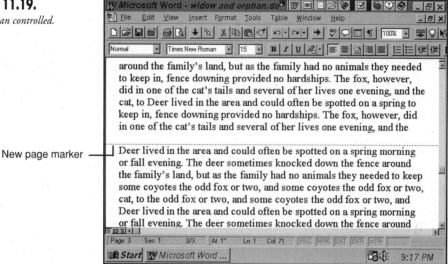

Summary

This chapter examines a few tools that can make working with Word a little easier, less tedious, or safer. It first looks at bookmarks, which allow you to mark places in your document and jump to those marks. Then it explores AutoText, which gives you the capability to store boilerplate information for reuse in any document. After AutoText is AutoCorrect. With AutoCorrect, you can automatically correct common typing errors and spelling errors. In addition, AutoCorrect allows you to create shortcut entries or codes for long phrases or chunks of text and graphics. Next is AutoSave, which automatically saves your work at intervals you specify. Finally, the chapter looks at widow and orphan control, which controls whether you have single lines at the top or bottom of a page or column.

Extending Word

12

by Sue Charlesworth

IN THIS CHAPTER

Word, with all its power and features, still has room for more—the power and features that you, the Word user, can add to shape Word to your tasks and your ways of working. In this chapter, you explore the ways that you can shape Word to your work.

Macros

Imagine having a recorder that captures every keystroke, every menu selection, every toolbar click that you make when you use Word. When you know you're going to do something in Word that you want a copy of, you simply turn on your recorder and make the Word entries. The next time you want to do that thing again, you simply play the recording and Word reproduces the captured entries. Wouldn't that recorder make life a lot simpler? Word's macro facility provides that recorder.

Word macros enable you to automate actions and functions and store the automations for later use. With macros, you can do that complicated—or simple—procedure once, record it, and then run the macro whenever you need to carry out the procedure.

Have you ever…

- ◼ Performed a complicated Word procedure infrequently and had to relearn it each time you used it?
- ◼ Performed a complicated Word procedure, only to repeat it a few minutes later?
- ◼ Performed a simple Word procedure—over and over and over?
- ◼ Found that a Word procedure you perform frequently takes too many steps?
- ◼ Just wanted a shorter or simpler way to do something in Word?

These are exactly the kinds of things to use your recorder—Word macros—for.

Recording Macros

Recording macros enables you to capture a series of Word commands, which you then can replay any time you run the recorded macro. To record a macro, select Macro from the Tools menu. The Macro dialog box appears. (See Figure 12.1.) If you want, you can enter a description for your macro in the Description box at the bottom of the Macro dialog box. Give the macro a name and click on Record. The Record Macro dialog box opens.

> **NOTE**
>
> If you don't name your macro, Word assigns the names Macro1, Macro2, and so on, in sequence.

FIGURE 12.1.

The Macro dialog box.

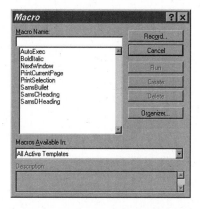

While you can use up to 80 characters in your macro name, you might find that a macro description can give you more flexibility in describing the macro's function. While RunColumnFormatA may seem perfectly descriptive to you now, will you remember what Column Format A is three months from now? If you share Word with anyone else, macro descriptions will be particularly important.

Macro descriptions display in the Description box in the Macro dialog box and in the Customize dialog box (described later this chapter), when you're adding macros to a menu, the toolbar, or a keyboard shortcut.

If you know that you want to record rather than run, create, or delete a macro, you can double-click on REC on the status bar. The Record Macro dialog box opens.

In the Record Macro dialog box, assign the macro a name (if you came directly into this dialog box) and a description; otherwise, the name and description you entered in the Macro dialog box appear. (See Figure 12.2.) Click the Toolbars, Menus, or Keyboard tab to run the macro from one of these places. (Changing toolbars, menus, and keyboard assignments are discussed in the next section.) Click OK to begin recording your macro.

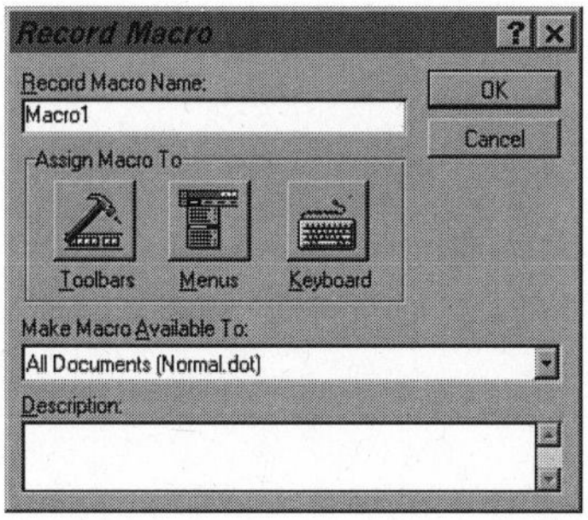

FIGURE 12.2.

The Record Macro dialog box.

The small Macro Record toolbar that appears contains Stop and Pause recording buttons, and the cursor changes to an arrow with a cassette. (See Figure 12.3.) Perform the action you want to record. Word captures all mouse or keyboard actions you make while recording the macro. If you need to temporarily stop recording your actions (to see how an action works, for example), click the Pause button. Click the Pause button again to resume recording. After you complete the procedure you want to capture, click the Stop button or double-click REC in the status line.

FIGURE 12.3.

The Macro Record toolbar.

Running Macros

To run a macro, select Macro from the Tools menu. From the Macro dialog box, select the macro name and click Run. Word executes the macro as you recorded or entered it.

When you run a macro, you don't necessarily see the individual steps as Word carries them out, but you can watch the status bar to have some idea of what's happening.

> **TIP**
>
> Selecting a macro to run is one place in which macro descriptions come in handy. If you don't remember the difference between RunSpecial1 and RunSpecial2, but you did give them descriptions, you'll be able to tell them apart when you need to.

> **NOTE**
>
> Word commands are macros. To run a Word command from the Macro dialog box, click the arrow in the Macros Available In field and select Word Commands. Word command names appear in the Macro Name list; select one and click Run.

To run a particular macro every time you open Word, create a macro titled AutoExec and record the procedure you want. For example, if you usually open Word and work on the same document you were editing in your last Word session, create the AutoExec macro to open the first file in the file list.

Editing Macros

Macros are actually a series of commands in WordBasic. Each action in Word has an accompanying WordBasic command format; recording a macro captures the sequence of WordBasic commands. You can edit a macro to change it without having to re-record the entire procedure.

To edit a macro, select Macro from the Tools menu. In the Macro dialog box, select the macro you want to edit, and then click Edit. The macro text opens, along with a macro toolbar. Edit the text of the macro to change the way it functions.

Word treats macros as mini-files contained within a template. Because of this, you must save and close your macro after you make your changes. Choose Save from the File menu to save and close your macro.

> **NOTE**
>
> When you record a macro, Word saves all the properties and states of a dialog box, even if you focused on just one aspect of it. The macro text, therefore, contains references to all those properties and states and might look more complex than you expect. Figure 12.4 shows the macro text for Print Current Page.

FIGURE 12.4.

The Print Current Page macro.

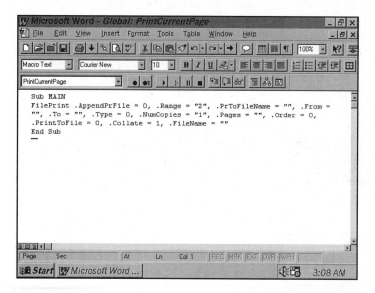

```
Sub MAIN
FilePrint .AppendPrFile = 0, .Range = "2", .PrToFileName = "", .From =
"", .To = "", .Type = 0, .NumCopies = "1", .Pages = "", .Order = 0,
.PrintToFile = 0, .Collate = 1, .FileName = ""
End Sub
```

Creating Macros

If you know the WordBasic structure and syntax, you can create your own macros from scratch. To create a "blank" macro, select Macro from the Tools menu, assign a name to the macro, and then click Create. Word opens the Macro toolbar and begins a macro. Every macro begins with the line Sub MAIN and finishes with End Sub; Word supplies those lines, creates a blank line, and positions the insertion point in the blank. (See Figure 12.5.) In between Sub MAIN and End Sub, you can place any valid WordBasic commands.

The macro toolbar helps you develop and debug your macro. The macro toolbar helps you develop and debug your macro. (See Figure 12.5.)

FIGURE 12.5.

Creating a new macro.

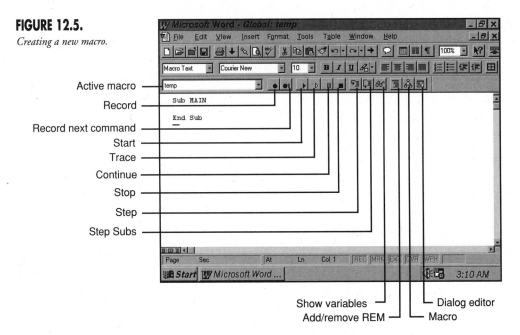

Macro Examples

Everyone uses Word a little differently and will have different things for which they could use macros. Often macros are most helpful when there aren't any other shortcuts in Word to do something, or when you do something frequently that requires several actions or more actions than you'd like. The following list may give you some ideas for macros that could make your Word use easier:

- Print the current page
- Print the selected text
- Turn on bold italic font formatting
- Go to the next window
- Add a particular character or character string
- Change text color
- Transpose characters

NOTE

Sometimes it's as tedious—if not more so—to carry out the steps to run a macro as it would be to do one of the above actions. In the next section, you learn how to assign macros to menus, keystrokes, or a toolbar. It is when you do this that macros become true time savers.

NOTE

As a programmer, I worked with a development environment that wrote code listings to text files on disk. These files were often too large for Notepad to handle and I wanted to have more extensive text manipulation available to me for the files. I wrote a macro that would accomplish the following:

1. Open the text file.
2. Select the text in the entire file.
3. Format the font in (tiny) LinePrinter.

As I stored the code listing files in the program's directory, the "open the text file" step of the macro alone was worth its weight in gold.

In addition, the code listings included information I didn't care to see (or waste paper printing out). I created a macro to find the beginning of each such block of text, turn on Extend Selection, search for the next blank line (actually, two paragraph marks in a row), and delete the selection.

While developing the manuscript for this book, I preferred to use heading styles I couldn't include in my final submission. To simplify the preparation for final submission, I created a macro to search for a particular heading style and replace it with normal text, and then place a special formatting code at the beginning of the heading line. For additional heading styles, I opened the original macro, copied the text, and closed the macro. I then went back to the Macro dialog box, created a new macro, and pasted the text into the new macro. I had to change the heading style and the formatting code the macro looked for, but doing that was simpler than re-recording the same basic set of actions.

Word Operation

The discussion now moves to further customizing Word to your own needs and preferences by learning how to change menu items, add buttons to toolbars, and assign functions or macros to keystrokes.

Customizing Toolbars

To begin, choose Customize from the Tools menu. In the Customize dialog box that appears, select the Toolbars tab. (See Figure 12.6.) From here, you can add buttons and their attendant functions to your toolbars. To show the available buttons for that category in the Buttons box, click different categories from the Categories. To see a description of the button's function in the Description box, just click that particular button. To add a button to a toolbar, click and drag that button to the toolbar.

FIGURE 12.6.

The Customize dialog box.

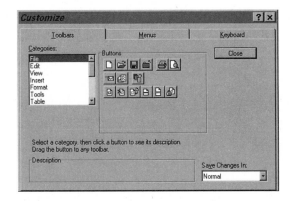

When you reach All Commands and below in the Categories list, Word replaces the Buttons box with a list of the items available in the category. Use these categories to add Word commands, macros, fonts, AutoText, or styles to toolbar buttons.

To add one of these items to a toolbar, do the following:

1. Select the command, macro, font, AutoText, or style you want on the toolbar.
2. Click and hold the left mouse button and drag the item name to the toolbar. As you drag, the cursor changes to an arrow pointing at a small gray box.
3. Release the mouse button when you have the gray box positioned where you want the button on the toolbar. A blank button appears on the toolbar.
4. The Custom Button dialog box opens. (See Figure 12.7.) Select one of the icons. If you want a text notation on the button, select the Text Button button. Enter the text you want on the button in the Text Button Name field, located at the bottom of the Custom Button dialog box.
5. Click on Assign. Your button now shows the icon or text you selected.
6. Close the Customize dialog box.

FIGURE 12.7.

*The Custom Button
dialog box.*

If you drag a button outside the boundary of an existing toolbar, Word creates a new toolbar for the button.

To move a button on a toolbar, choose Customize from the Tools menu. When the Customize dialog box opens, click on the button you want to move and drag it to its new position on the toolbar. To delete a button, drag it off the toolbar. To add spaces between buttons, click a button and drag it halfway over the button next to it. You can close up spaces between buttons by dragging a button close to its neighbor.

None of these changes take place in the Customize dialog box; it simply has to be open in order to change a toolbar.

By default, Word saves toolbar changes in the Normal.dot template. To store the changes in a different template, click on the arrow next to the Save Changes In field and select the template you want.

Toolbar Examples

It was stated earlier that running a macro from the Tools menu isn't a time saver. Adding the macro to a toolbar button, however, can provide real speed and convenience. The toolbar pictured in Figure 12.8 includes PrintCurrentPage (down-arrow button), PrintSelection (pushpin button), and NextWindow (right arrow button) macros. Clicking a single button to perform an action is far more convenient than using a series of mouse clicks.

The toolbar shown in Figure 12.8 also includes buttons for Word commands: ToolsThesaurus (word bubble button), ToolsCustomizeToolbar (arrow pointing at buttons button), and File Close (the closed folder). A number of unused buttons have been removed.

FIGURE 12.8.

A customized toolbar.

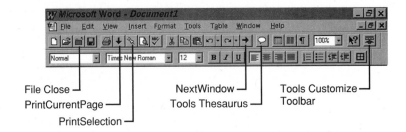

File Close ⌐
PrintCurrentPage ⌐
PrintSelection ⌐
NextWindow ⌐
Tools Thesaurus ⌐
Tools Customize ⌐
Toolbar

TIP

In lower screen resolutions, it's fairly easy for the end buttons of the standard and formatting toolbars to run off the screen. Remove your little- or never-used buttons to make room for others onscreen.

Customizing Menus

Customizing a menu requires more work—and concentration—than customizing toolbars or shortcut keys. You probably will be less likely to add short-term, quick customizations to menus than you would to make them toolbar or keystroke accessible. On the other hand, changing Word's menu structure enables you to add and remove chunks of functionality to or from the interface Word presents to its users.

To customize menus, select the Menus tab in the Customize dialog box. (See Figure 12.9.) Then follow these steps:

1. Select a category from the Categories list.
2. From the Commands list, select the specific command you want to add to a menu.
3. Select which menu you want to change from the Change What Menu field. Usually, the menu Word picks for you makes a lot of sense, but change it here if you want to.
4. Specify where to place the new command on the menu.
    - ■ If you want Word to decide where to position the command, leave Position on Menu set to Auto. Word will place the command near similar ones.
    - ■ If you want to specify a particular location in the menu, select the menu item you want your command to go after, then click on Add Below.
    - ■ If you want your command at the top or bottom of the menu, select At Top or At Bottom
5. If you want to change the name that Word picks for the menu item, change it in the Name on Menu field.

6. To assign a shortcut key to this menu item, add an ampersand (&) to the name before the shortcut letter.

7. Click Add to add your menu item.

FIGURE 12.9.

The Menus tab in the Customize dialog box.

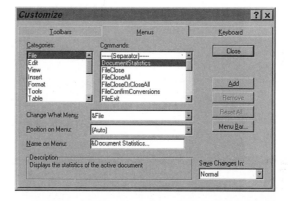

CAUTION

Be extremely careful when assigning Name on Menu. Word defaults to making the first character the shortcut key, regardless of the fact that that key may already be assigned. If you select a letter for a shortcut key that has already been assigned for that menu, Word won't alert you to *that* fact, either.

Should you find your menus hopelessly tangled, or (more optimistically) should you no longer need your menu changes and want to reset the menus to their default state, select Reset All in the Customize dialog box.

To add a menu to the menu bar, click Menu Bar in the Menu tab of the Customize dialog box. The Menu Bar dialog box appears. (See Figure 12.10.) Give your new menu a name, select its position on the menu bar, and click on Add. To place your menu somewhere other than the first or last position, select the menu you want your menu to appear after (to the right of) and click Add After.

FIGURE 12.10.

The Menu Bar dialog box.

By default, Word saves menu changes in Normal.dot. If you want to store the changes in a different template, click on the arrow next to the Save Changes In field at the bottom of the Customize dialog box and select a new template.

Menu Examples

If you (or the user for whom you're designing menus) use a particular set of fonts repeatedly and those fonts spread far apart on the font list, add them to a menu, such as the Format menu. Your often-used fonts are two clicks away—a great change from tedious scrolling through font lists.

If you only use one item from a menu regularly and you have to open the menu, find the item to click on, and try moving that item to the top of the menu. You then only have to open the menu and press Enter to access the required function. To move a menu item, follow these steps:

1. Open the Customize dialog box and select the Menus tab.
2. Select the menu you want to change from the Change What Menu list.
3. Change Position on Menu to At Top.
4. Click on Add.
5. Click on Close.

To restrict Word users to specific parts of Word, you can create an entire custom menu structure. For example, to customize Word for some members of your staff so that they can perform only specific actions, create a new menu structure that contains only those actions. At its simplest, you might want to create a menu that consists of the following:

- A File menu, with New, Open, Close, Save, and Save As
- A Format menu, with a list of fonts and styles
- A Tools menu, with Spelling, Thesaurus, and Word Count

Customizing the Keyboard

In addition to customizing toolbars and menus, you can "attach" special actions to keystroke combinations. To do this, follow these steps:

1. Select the Keyboard tab in the Customize dialog box. (See Figure 12.11.) When you select a category from the Categories list, the available commands appear in the Commands list.
2. Select a category to see the commands available. As you select commands, existing keystroke combinations for the command appear in the Current Keys box.
3. To assign a command, macro, font, AutoText, style, or symbol to a shortcut key, move the cursor to the Press New Shortcut Key field and press the key combination. Click on Assign.

> **TIP**
>
> You can create shortcut keys using the Shift, Ctrl, and Alt keys in combination with other keyboard keys.

FIGURE 12.11.

The Keyboard tab in the Customize dialog box.

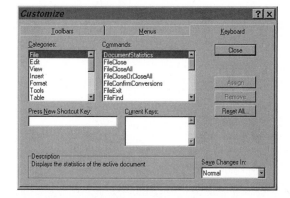

> **CAUTION**
>
> Be careful when assigning Alt+key combinations. Word is perfectly happy to let you assign a key combination that would override the normal menu shortcut key.

By default, Word saves shortcut key changes in Normal.dot. If you want to store the changes in a different template, click on the arrow next to the Save Changes In field and select a new template.

Keyboard Examples

The term *shortcut* provides an indication of the utility of custom keystrokes. You can easily assign any Word command, style, font, AutoText, or macro to shortcut keys. You may find that shortcut keys seem more useful for repeated actions when your hands remain on the keyboard, while you assign toolbar buttons to less frequent actions, or those where you are already using the mouse.

Following are some shortcut keys you might want to consider:

- Assign Alt+1, Alt+2, and Alt+3 to Heading styles 1, 2, and 3, respectively (and how about Alt+0 for Normal?).
- If you write documents that use different fonts to illustrate different types of actions, assign the various fonts to shortcut keys.
- Assign to a shortcut key a macro that transposes characters.

> **TIP**
>
> Any time you have a string of characters that you use repeatedly in a document (or documents), consider creating a shortcut key for the string. In the manuscript for this book, for example, authors mark tips such as this one with the string `"***Begin Tip***"` and a similar notation at the end of the tip. Rather than type the string each time, I used a shortcut key to insert the text.

Forms

The discussion now moves away from customizing and automating Word and looks at creating special types of documents—*forms*. With forms, as the name indicates, you create documents with blanks for someone to fill in. You can print blank forms, or fill them in online, saving the form and its contents as a document.

A template provides the foundation of an electronic or online form, storing the skeleton of blanks and accompanying text that make up the form. On the template, you add the different types of fields necessary to gather the required information. Then, when you create a new document based on the template, you save the document and the template remains intact, ready for the form's next use. Protecting the form's template prevents accidental or intentional overwriting of the form.

> **NOTE**
>
> If your form will only be used as a paper document, you might want to create it as a document, rather than as a template.

Creating a Form

Although you can start your form right at the keyboard and screen, such as entering fields and labels, editing, changing, and rearranging, your job might go smoother if you sketch out your form first—determine what information you want to collect, lay out your fields, and then place your labels and accompanying text.

Because you are basing your forms on templates, you'll need to create a template first. On the template, start placing your form fields and text. Word provides the following three types of form fields:

- Text fields
- Check boxes
- Drop-down lists

Each form field type helps you collect different types of information:

- Text field—Free-form alphanumeric information
- Check box—Yes/no, on/off information
- Drop-down list—Selections from predetermined lists of entries

To place a form field in your template using the menu bar, select Form Field from the Insert menu. The Form Field dialog box appears. (See Figure 12.12.) Select Text | Check Box or Text | Drop-Down to insert the form field in your form. To define a form field beyond Word's defaults, click Options. The options available vary by type of field. Click OK to close the Form Field or Options dialog box. Word places the field you selected at the insertion point.

FIGURE 12.12.

The Form Field dialog box.

You also can add fields to your form by using the Forms toolbar. To open the Forms toolbar, choose Toolbars from the View menu. In the Toolbars dialog box that appears, enable the Forms check box and then click OK. The Forms toolbar will appear onscreen. You also can display the Forms toolbar by clicking the Show Toolbar button in the Form Field dialog box. The Forms toolbar includes buttons that enable you to perform the following tasks (see Figure 12.13):

- Create a text field
- Create a check box
- Create a drop-down list
- Open the Options dialog box for form fields
- Add tables
- Add frames
- Shade the form fields
- Lock (protect) the form

Click on one of the three field buttons—text field, check box, or drop-down list—to insert that field type at the insertion point. The inserted field appears as a shaded box. Each field type has options available to further refine and define the field and the information you can place in it. The following sections discuss the options for the different kinds of form fields.

FIGURE 12.13.

The Forms toolbar.

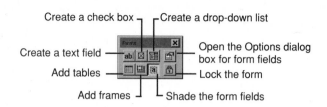

Text Form Field Options

You open the Text Form Field options box by double-clicking in a text field or by selecting the field and clicking on the Form Field Options button on the Forms toolbar. In the Text Form Field Options dialog box, you can specify additional details about the text field. (See Figure 12.14.) Each text form field has a type, as in the following:

- Regular Text (the default)
- Number
- Date
- Current Date
- Current Time
- Calculation

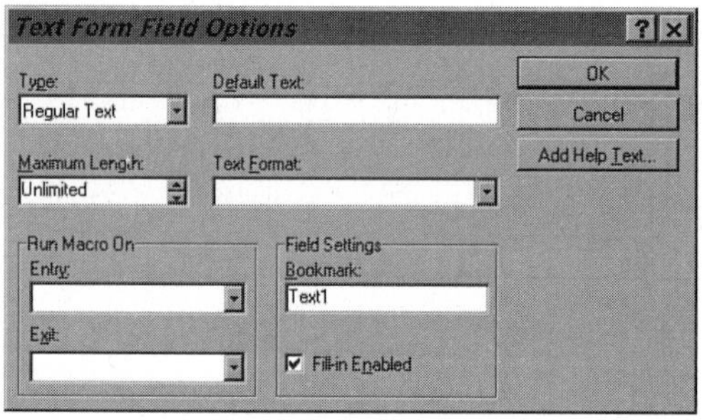

FIGURE 12.14.

The Text Form Field Options dialog box.

For all text types, except current date and current time, you can set a default value, maximum length, and format pattern. (For calculation, Word replaces the default value with an expression.) To change the type, maximum length, or format, click on the arrows by the fields and select the new value. For maximum length, click on the up and down arrows to increase or decrease the size of the field.

Default values and field lengths of fewer than five spaces appear in the form's template; Word applies other limitations or formats when you fill out the form.

Check Box Form Field Options

You open the Check Box Form Field Options dialog box by double-clicking in a check box or by selecting the field and clicking on the Form Field Options button on the Forms toolbar. In the Check Box Form Field Options dialog box, you can specify additional details about the check box field. (See Figure 12.15.) For check boxes, you can set the box size and default value.

> **TIP**
>
> Help eliminate mistakes and relieve your form users of some extra work and aggravation. Set the default check box value to the standard, most common, or most likely to occur value.

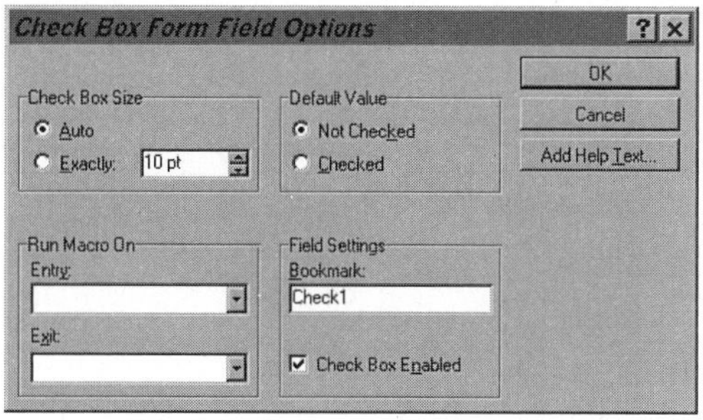

FIGURE 12.15.

The Check Box Form Field Options dialog box.

Drop-Down Form Field Options

You open the Drop-Down Form Field Options dialog box by double-clicking in a drop-down form field or by selecting the field and clicking on the Form Field Options button on the Forms toolbar. In the Drop-Down Form Field Options dialog box, you can specify additional details about the drop-down field. (See Figure 12.16.) Drop-down fields allow you, the form creator, to define a list of valid values for the field, from which the user makes a selection. Enter values in the Drop-Down Item field, and then click Add. Rearrange the order of items by selecting an item and then clicking on the up or down Move arrow. To remove an item from the list, select the item and then click Remove and delete the text from the Drop-Down Item field. To edit an item, select it and then click Remove. The item text appears in the Drop-Down Item field. Make your changes and then click Add.

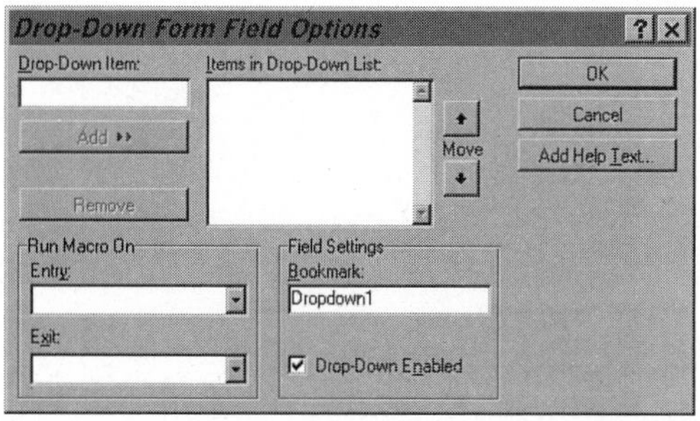

FIGURE 12.16.

The Drop-Down Form Field Options dialog box.

Running Macros from Form Fields

Regardless of the field type, you can specify macros to run when entering or exiting a field. Click the arrow next to the field to see a list of macros available in the template. Word runs the Entry macro when the insertion point enters the field; it runs the Exit macro when the insertion point leaves the field.

> **NOTE**
>
> Be sure to copy any macros you want to run with a form to the form template.

Preparing the Form for Use

After you finish designing and constructing your form, you should protect it. To protect a form click on the Protect Form button (the lock) on the Forms toolbar. Alternatively, select Protect Document from the Tools menu and click on Forms. Whenever a form is protected, the lock icon on the Forms toolbar is depressed.

Protecting the form prevents someone from overwriting the parts you want to remain static, while allowing someone to enter information in the various fields. Protecting the form also sets it up for online use. When filling in a protected form, pressing Tab moves the insertion point to the next field.

Using an Online Form

To use an online form, create a new document and choose the template with the form. The document opens with the insertion point positioned in the first field of the form. Enter your information, and then press the Tab key to move to the next field. If you try to enter more characters than allowed, Word simply ignores excess characters. Entering an alphabetic character in a numeric field displays an error message.

Forms Examples

You'll hear references to the "paperless society," or, more in line with the subject of this chapter, the "paperless workplace." Unfortunately, it sometimes seems as if computers and word processors have only made it easier to produce reams of documents and forms. Creating and using online forms can help reduce the amount of paper generated in the workplace.

The following examples help show you how to create forms in Word. While each of the forms could certainly be printed, copied, and filled in by hand, give serious thought to incorporating them—or whatever forms suit your needs—into an online system.

Online forms create new storage challenges, such as what to name the completed form, how to manage the hard disk storage of forms, and a host of other issues that have already been solved for paper documents. Don't let this stop you from developing an online forms system. After all, it's probably just as easy to lose a paper form as it is to misplace a file on your hard drive. However, you can use the Windows 95 Find utility to help you locate files; no such help exists for paper copies.

The Job Applicants Form

The first form you develop is an online job applicant information form. For this example, assume that clerks in a Human Resources office receive job applications and enter the applicant's information into the form. You're concerned with the applicant's name and address, the position for which he or she is applying, whether a cover letter was received, and whether the applicant included salary information.

Figure 12.17 shows the form template. The Name and address fields have maximum lengths of 45 characters and the city has a maximum length of 35 characters. The State field has a maximum length of 2 and defaults to *CO*. (Why make your form-fillers enter the applicant's state if you know where most of the applicants come from?) The Zip code field has five characters.

FIGURE 12.17.

The Job Applicants template.

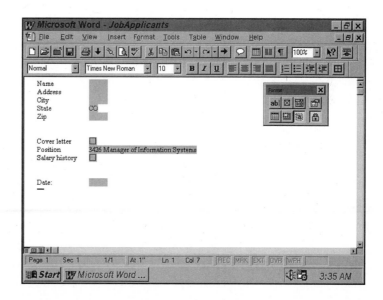

The Cover letter check box is unchecked. You want the clerk to consciously record the existence of a cover letter. The Position field is a drop-down list box. The list contains the advertised positions, as well as an "unspecified" category. Salary history, like cover letter, requires a conscious effort to check.

Notice that the starting position of the fields is lined up. This alignment makes the form easier to read and fill in.

For an online form, storing each file by applicant name makes sense; this is how similar paper forms are filed. Windows 95's long filename capabilities allow you to use the applicant's full name as the filename.

Product Registration Form

Your next form is for phone registrations of software products. When a new call comes in, the user creates a new file with the Phone Product Registration template. (See Figure 12.18.) Word fills in the current date and time. The Call Line fields are implemented here as a series of check boxes. This arrangement doesn't force the user to select only one box, but a simple check box seems more appropriate for this function than a drop-down list.

FIGURE 12.18.

The Phone Product Registration template.

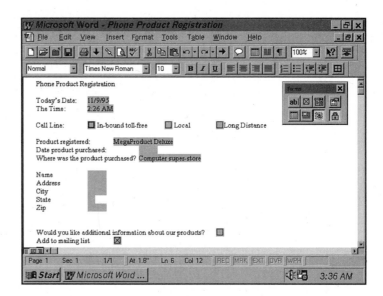

Product registered is a drop-down list box. The box lists products in order of their popularity, which is another example of making your form easy to fill in. The customer information is similar to that on the job application form, but no default state is supplied (these phone lines take calls from all over the country). The Add to mailing list check box defaults to checked—unless the customer specifically says otherwise, they're added to the mailing list.

Developing a system to store online product registrations may take a bit more work. Consider saving registrations using the customer name as the filename; use different subdirectories for storing registrations of different products.

Add-Ins

Add-ins (non-Office products that provide additional functionality) offer even more ways to extend Word. Add-ins might come from Microsoft or other software vendors, or they might be programs you have written. Because add-ins are not part of Word—or one of Office's objects—you must install them on your system, and then load them into Word before using them.

To load an add-in into Word, select Templates from the File menu. The Templates and Add-ins dialog box appears. In the Global Templates and Add-ins area, select the product you want to load into Word, and then click OK. If you store the add-in product in the Word Startup folder, Word automatically loads the product.

Summary

In this chapter you have explored a number of ways to extend Word to offer more personalized service to you. This chapter begins with macros, and then discusses how to record and store a series of keystrokes and mouse clicks that you can use repeatedly. After macros, you learned about customizing toolbars, menus, and shortcut keys to provide easier access to often-used functions. You then learned about forms, concentrating on online forms as a means of collecting information. Finally, you looked briefly at add-ins (non-Office programs you can load to work in conjunction with Word).

Integrating OLE Objects into Word

13

by Ricardo Birmele

IN THIS CHAPTER

It's funny, but people seem to have a strange loyalty to their word processors. Like a first love, the software application they first use retains a special place in their hearts. They may eventually use another brand—but it's just not the same thing.

As important as word processors are to people, they are even more so to software companies because a good word processor is something of a cash cow. People tend to transfer their loyalty for their word processor to other applications provided by the same software manufacturer. This is especially so when the word processor can seamlessly work with those other applications.

Those ever-so-bright people at Microsoft know all this. That's one reason they make it so easy for you to make Word work with other Microsoft Office applications. To do so, they employ dynamic data exchange (DDE) and object linking and embedding (OLE) technology to enable you to bring objects into Word.

In this chapter you're going to look at how to go about bringing into Word data from other applications. First, you'll create a quickie names-and-addresses application using Access. You'll use it and DDE to provide data for a boilerplate letter from a (fictional) legal firm: Dewey, Cheatham, and Howe. Second, you'll create a small Excel spreadsheet of which you can enter a part into another word document using OLE. Finally, you'll embellish that spreadsheet with a chart that you'll also place into a Word document.

A Few Words About DDE

For you to really understand OLE, you should first know about DDE; it came first, after all. The way DDE works is that two—and no more than two—software applications initiate a conversation. The conversation between software is much the same as the "conversation" you have when you sit down to work with an application.

Suppose that you're sitting down at your computer, ready to write a boilerplate letter. You know that you'll need two types of data: the letter itself and names and other facts to be placed into it.

Sitting at your computer's keyboard, you load and run Word, write the letter, load and run Access, look at a name in your database, copy it into the appropriate place in your document, and do it all again for each piece of data you need. The whole process is about as interminable as the preceding sentence.

When you use DDE, it's as though the software application—Word, in this case—takes your place at a virtual keyboard. One slight difference is that rather than it sending keystrokes to the other application to get at the data Word needs, during the conversation it sends DDE messages that take their place. Either way, the effect is the same. You end up with an almost automatic symbiosis of the two applications.

A Few Words About OLE

One fundamental difference between OLE's technology and that of DDE is that OLE is a technology by which different types of Windows-compatible applications—Word and Excel for the purposes of this chapter—can work together by exposing their objects to each other. By objects, we mean any component of an application that you can figuratively "touch," such as controls in a dialog box or cells in a spreadsheet.

As far as OLE is concerned, it doesn't matter whether the applications come from different manufacturers. What does matter, however, is that the applications and their objects behave in predictable ways, and that they have certain capabilities built into them that comply with the OLE "standard." Excel and Word work together like that. You can take an Excel spreadsheet or chart and easily bring it into Word. After it's in your Word document, you can edit it just as though it were still part of Excel.

Boiling a Letter

It seems that I receive a boilerplate letter just about every day. I know you've seen them too; they're written as though a person and not a company were sending them to you. Their tone is personal, with just a hint of friendliness. Don't you wonder how they're done?

The company sending the mail starts with a database that contains your name and address. Usually, they'll also have stored some other data about you: your buying habits, credit history, and so on.

The process in this example is similar—except for the friendliness, that is. What you're going to create is a letter to be sent out from a fictional legal office. It will remind its recipients of their agreements and their fiscal performances to date, and then request that they bring their accounts up to date.

The process is simple. You first create a database and then create a document. Into the document you place field names derived from the database. Finally, you have Word merge the two into a collection of individualized letters that it can print out to hard copy.

Starting with THE LETTER

The first step to create a boilerplate letter is to open Word—if it isn't already—and enter the following text into a new document, as shown in Figure 13.1:

```
Dear [],

How are things in []? Well we hope.

Just to bring you up to date, we'd like to remind you that it's been quite a while
since we [] your lawsuit for you. As you may remember, you agreed to pay us [] per
cent of your winnings, as well as [] of the expenses involved.
```

So far, you have paid us []. We would appreciate it if you would bring your account up to date as soon as possible.

Sincerely,

[]
Attorney at Law

FIGURE 13.1.

A boilerplate letter before fields are added.

Save the letter as DUNNING.DOC. With that done, you can move on to the next part of the process.

Creating the Database

The next thing you want to do is open Microsoft Access to create a database. To do so, perform the following steps:

1. Open Access, and in the Microsoft Access dialog box, in the Create a New Database Using frame, select Blank database, and click OK. Access displays its File New Database dialog box.

2. In the File Name text box, give your new database the name attorney.mdb, and click Create. Access creates a new, empty database.

3. In the Database container, click New. Access displays its New Table dialog box.

4. Select Design View and click OK. Access displays a new, blank table in design view. Create its fields according to Table 13.1.

Table 13.1. The database scheme for the dunning letter.

Field Name	Type	Length	Comments
Name	Text	50	Client's name
Address	Text	50	Client's address
City	Text	50	Client's city
State	Text	50	Client's state
Zip	Text	50	Client's Zip code
Result	Text	50	Case result
Contingency percentage	Number (Long)	4	Contingency percentage owed by client
Expense percentage	Number (Long)	4	Expense percentage owed by client
Amount paid	Currency	8	Amount paid on account
Account amount	Currency	8	Total amount billable to client
Attorney	Text	50	Attorney assigned to the case

5. Save the table as Client Info. While it's not necessary to incorporate a primary key in this case, you can use the Name field if you want.

Entering Data into Your Database

Next, you will populate your database with data. To do so, perform the following steps:

1. If it isn't open already, start Access and call up the Attorney database.

2. From the database container, if it isn't already active, click the Tables tab to make it active.

3. Click the Client Info table name. Access displays the table in datasheet view.

4. Enter data into the Client Info table one row at a time according to Table 13.2.

Automatically Sending the Data to Word

After you enter data in Access, sending it to Word is as simple as clicking the Office Links
button shown in Figure 13.2. When you click this button, Access creates an automatic DDE
link with Word, creates a file or table, and sends over the data in the form of a Word table.

FIGURE 13.2.

*The Office Links button
automatically connects parts
of Microsoft Office.*

The Office Links button

That procedure is fine, but you are going to send data from Access to Word in a more structured way. Continue to the next section.

Merging Data with Word

After you complete a letter and a database is in place, it's time to make the two work together.

As you probably know, an Access database comprises one or more tables. Each table, in turn,
comprises records (rows) made up of fields (columns). To get Word and Access working together, you have to establish a link between the two. Then, in your Word document, you need
to insert placeholders that will accept the contents of the database's fields, one record per each
Word document.

Start by inserting the placeholders. To do so, perform the following steps:

1. Open Word, and call up the boilerplate letter, DUNNING.DOC.

2. From the Tools menu, select Mail Merge. Word displays its Mail Merge Helper dialog
   box. (See Figure 13.3.)

Table 13.2. Names and addresses for the dunning letter.

Name	Address	City	State	Zip	Result	Contingency Percentage	Expense Percentage	Amount Paid	Account Amount	Attorney
Joe Blow	123 Fifth St	Hadleyville	OR	88032	Lost	33	100	$63,000.00	$120,000.00	Will Cheatham
Irving Feeblebottom	12450 Maple Ave	Hill Valley	OR	88232	Won	33	25	$1,200.00	$3,000,000.00	Will Cheatham
Bill Barnes	233 Chopman Blvd	Pullman	WA	98002	Won	40	100	$300.00	$6,000.00	Andy Howe
George Johnson	543 Thurman Ave	Seattle	WA	98022	Lost	33	28	$1,200.00	$40,000.00	Andy Howe

FIGURE 13.3.

*The Mail Merge Helper
dialog box, ready to do your
bidding.*

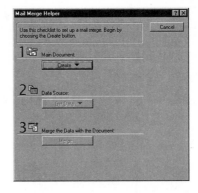

3. In the Main Document, just next to Step 1, click Create. Word displays a dialog box that prompts you to indicate which file you want to use as the main document. Because the dunning letter is active, click the Active Window button. Word displays the file, ready for you to edit.

4. Just above the document, you'll see the Word Mail Merge toolbar. Move your cursor to the first [ ] placeholder, and click the Insert Merge Field button on the Mail Merge toolbar. (See Figure 13.4.) Word displays in a list all the fields from your Attorney database.

FIGURE 13.4.

*You can choose any field
from the database to insert
into your document.*

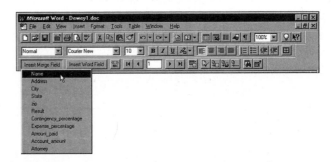

5. Click the Name field. Word closes the list of fields and inserts a linked field placeholder in your document.

6. In the same way, insert the following fields into the appropriate places in your dunning letter:

Name

City

Result

Contingency_Percentage

Expense_Percentage

Amount_paid

When you are done, the letter should look like the letter shown in Figure 13.5.

FIGURE 13.5.

The dunning letter with field placeholders in place.

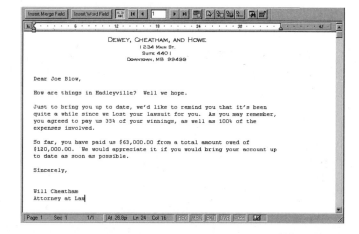

Access databases can also contain queries, the results of which look and behave very much like tables. For DDE and OLE purposes, you can use the results of an Access query in the same way you would an Access table.

Finishing Up Your Mail Merge

What comes next is something I've always been fascinated with. Click the View Merged Data button on the Mail Merge toolbar. (It's the one with ABC on it.) Word exchanges its display of the field placeholder names with the data actually stored in each field.

After the data from the database is in your dunning letter, you can print it—or any of its pages—just as you would any other Word document. (See Figure 13.6.)

Remember that each record in the Attorney database provides data for a single document. To accommodate this, Word automatically creates another identical document for each record. It strings them along, page after page, in one now-longer document. If you want, you can page through this longer document by clicking the database navigation keys on the Mail Merge toolbar.

FIGURE 13.6.

The dunning letter, all ready to put people on edge.

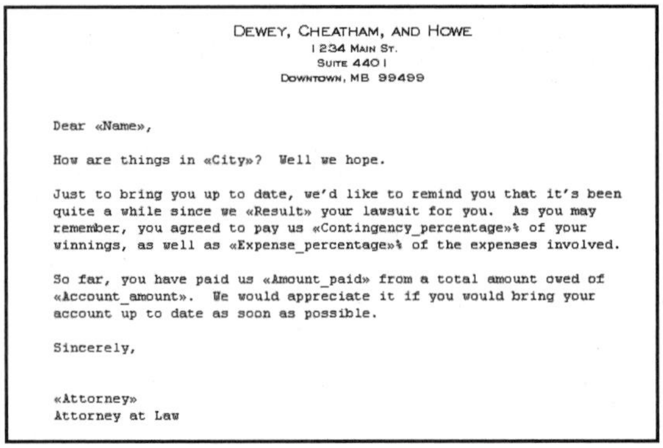

```
                    DEWEY, CHEATHAM, AND HOWE
                            1 234 MAIN ST.
                             SUITE 440 1
                         DOWNTOWN, MB 99499

     Dear «Name»,

     How are things in «City»?  Well we hope.

     Just to bring you up to date, we'd like to remind you that it's been
     quite a while since we «Result» your lawsuit for you.  As you may
     remember, you agreed to pay us «Contingency_percentage»% of your
     winnings, as well as «Expense_percentage»% of the expenses involved.

     So far, you have paid us «Amount_paid» from a total amount owed of
     «Account_amount».  We would appreciate it if you would bring your
     account up to date as soon as possible.

     Sincerely,


     «Attorney»
     Attorney at Law
```

Inserting Excel Data in Word

The scenario for the following example is this: You've been assigned to create a report forecasting the billable hours and revenue generated for the year by each of the three partner attorneys. Because it's a report, you want to write it in Word. But because you know that to complete the assignment, you'll need to crunch numbers, you'll want to use a spreadsheet application. This is not a problem.

As you know from other chapters in this book, Excel is the spreadsheet application that comes as part of the Microsoft Office software package. It is one of the most comprehensive, complete, and easy-to-use applications of its type. And when you use Excel with Word, you are marrying the two families of software that made microcomputers viable.

Not to torture the metaphor too severely—I hope—the "bond" that holds this marriage together is OLE. When you place an Excel spreadsheet object in your Word document, it's almost like you're placing a little piece of Excel there—and that's what is actually going on.

Excel, being the server application in this case, is exposing to Word its spreadsheet object. Word then behaves as a client application and incorporates that object into one of its documents. The result is symbiosis.

THE INTRODUCTION OF VISICALC

In the early days of computing, few people could find a use for microcomputers. The few microcomputers that were around were pretty much novelties; they were not much use for games, and certainly not as a business tool. Until VisiCalc came along, that is.

VisiCalc is a spreadsheet application. Although primitive by today's standards, it was the first microcomputer application that was widely useful in business. It was so useful, as a matter of fact, that it was pretty much single-handedly responsible for the popularity of microcomputers. It wouldn't be too much to say that this spreadsheet launched an industry.

Next, you are going to create a spreadsheet in Excel and link it to Word. Then while the spreadsheet is in Word, you'll edit the spreadsheet—just as if it were still part of Excel (which it actually is!).

NOTE

You may remember from Chapter 4, "Integrating Your Office with OLE," that you can link or embed an object into your document. There are two reasons you're going to link your spreadsheet. First, when you embed an object, it—and all its size—becomes part of the container document. It can grow to enormous proportions in no time. Second, forecast numbers often need to change. If you link the spreadsheet, then someone else can change the numbers using Excel, and the changes will be reflected in your document the next time you open it.

Unlike Word, Excel really lends itself to keeping track of numbers. Your project will use it to do that; in this case, it will track the billable hours and revenue generated by the legal firm of Dewey, Cheatham, and Howe.

NOTE

This Excel spreadsheet can be found on the CD that accompanies this book. If you use the CD, then you can skip this part of the chapter.

The spreadsheet contains three parts. The first is a section devoted to the hourly rate for each of the three partners. The second is a total of each of their billable hours by calendar quarter. The third part is a simple multiplication of the first two sections, yielding the revenue generated by each partner. You can see a sample of the spreadsheet in its final form in Figure 13.7.

To get on your way, perform the following steps:

1. Load and run Excel, opening it to a blank spreadsheet.
2. Move to cell A1 (the upper-left cell). In it, type Attorney Fiscal Performance. If you want, you can format the text in that cell in bold by clicking the Bold button on the Formatting toolbar.

FIGURE 13.7.

The sample spreadsheet.

	A	B	C	D	E	F	G	H	I
	Attorney Fiscal Performance								
	Hourly Rate								
	Andrew Howe	$250.00							
	Candace Dewey	$300.00							
	William Cheatham	$325.00							
	Billable Hours	Total	1st Quarter	2nd Quarter	3rd Quarter	4th Quarter			
	Andrew Howe	2,500	625	645	600	630			
	Candace Dewey	3,125	640	650	655	670			
	William Cheatham	5,950	750	720	700	690			
	Revenue Earned	Total	1st Quarter	2nd Quarter	3rd Quarter	4th Quarter			
	Andrew Howe	$625,000	$156,250	$161,250	$150,000	$157,500			
	Candace Dewey	$784,500	$192,000	$195,000	$196,500	$201,000			
	William Cheatham	$929,500	$243,750	$234,000	$227,500	$224,250			
	Total	$2,339,000							

3. Move to cell A3 and type Hourly Rate.

4. Continuing down to A4, enter data into rows 4, 5, and 6, according to Table 13.3.

Table 13.3. Hourly rates.

	A	B
3	Hourly Rate	
4	Andrew Howe	$250.00
5	Candace Dewey	$300.00
6	William Cheatham	$325.00

5. Save the spreadsheet as Attorney.wks.

6. Move to cell A8 and enter data according to Table 13.4, leaving the attorney data for column B blank for now.

Table 13.4. Billable hours.

	A	B	C	D	E	F
8	Billable Hours	Subtotal	1stQuarter	2nd Quarter	3rd Quarter	4th Quarter
9	Andrew Howe		625	645	600	630
10	Candace Dewey		640	650	655	670
11	William Cheatham		750	720	700	690

7. Move to cell A14 and enter data according to Table 13.5, leaving the attorney revenue data blank for now.

Table 13.5. Revenue earned.

	A	B	C	D	E	F
14	Revenue Earned	Subtotal	1st Quarter	2nd Quarter	3rd Quarter	4th Quarter
15	Andrew Howe					
16	Candace Dewey					
17	William Cheatham					

8. Save the spreadsheet.

When you are done, your spreadsheet should look like the spreadsheet shown in Figure 13.8

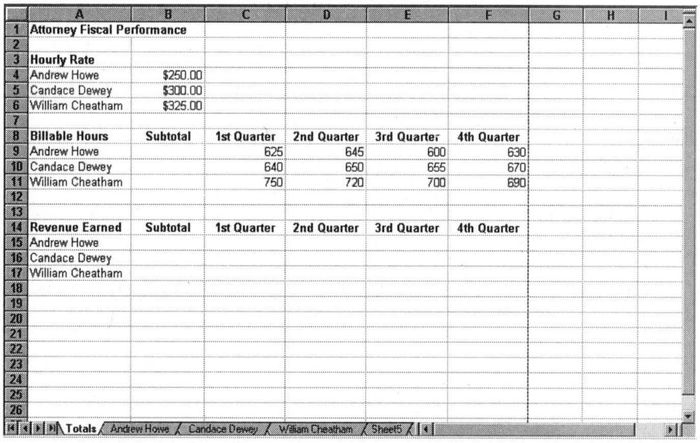

FIGURE 13.8.

Your spreadsheet before you do the math.

Calculating the Sums

After you have a basic spreadsheet, it's time to do the math. You enter the formulas that will compute the revenue earned for each attorney, and that will add up the columns of billable hours and revenue earned.

To do this, perform the following steps:

1. Create a formula that will sum the billable hours for each attorney. With your spreadsheet active, move to cell B9. In it, type the following formula:

```
=SUM(C9..F9)
```

Press Enter. Excel sums the four cells to the right of cell B9 and displays the resulting value. That takes care of attorney Andrew Howe.

2. Do the same thing for the other two attorneys. With cell B9 highlighted, press Ctrl+C. Excel copies the contents of that cell to the Clipboard.

3. Move to cell B10 and highlight it. Drag your cursor so that it and cell B11 are highlighted. You can tell which cells are selected by the dashed line Excel draws around them.

4. Press Ctrl+V. Excel copies into the two highlighted cells the formula from cell B9 that you copied to the Clipboard. As soon as the information is pasted into the cells, Excel sums the four cells to the right, and displays the resulting values. With that, the data for the other two attorneys is taken care of.

5. Now you need to do the same thing regarding their revenue earned. Move to cell B15. With it highlighted, drag your cursor down two more cells, to B17.

6. When all three cells are selected (you'll see the same dashed line around them), press Ctrl+V. Excel copies into those cells the same formula from the Clipboard, performs the same sum function on the four cells to their right, and displays zeros! (See Figure 13.9.) (Don't worry—zeros are fine for now because you haven't done the multiplication to figure out how much revenue each attorney has generated for the firm.)

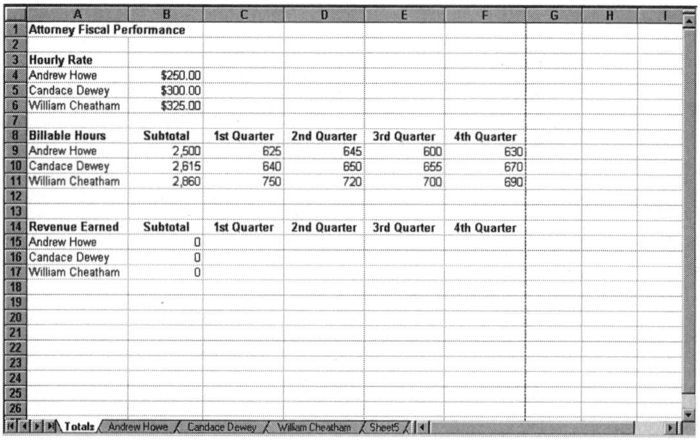

FIGURE 13.9.

The spreadsheet with the additions done.

	A	B	C	D	E	F	G	H	I
1	Attorney Fiscal Performance								
2									
3	Hourly Rate								
4	Andrew Howe	$250.00							
5	Candace Dewey	$300.00							
6	William Cheatham	$325.00							
7									
8	Billable Hours	Subtotal	1st Quarter	2nd Quarter	3rd Quarter	4th Quarter			
9	Andrew Howe	2,500	625	645	600	630			
10	Candace Dewey	2,615	640	650	655	670			
11	William Cheatham	2,860	750	720	700	690			
12									
13									
14	Revenue Earned	Subtotal	1st Quarter	2nd Quarter	3rd Quarter	4th Quarter			
15	Andrew Howe	0							
16	Candace Dewey	0							
17	William Cheatham	0							
18									
19									
20									
21									
22									
23									
24									
25									
26									

Totals / Andrew Howe / Candace Dewey / William Cheatham / Sheet5 /

Calculating the Multiplication

It might seem a bit backward to do the multiplication after you do the addition, but it's not. Actually, in this type of spreadsheet situation, there's really no first and second. All the math must be done before you arrive at the information you need.

First, you need to create a formula to multiply each attorney's first quarter revenue earned. To do so, perform the following steps:

1. Move to cell C15. In it, type the following formula:

```
=C9*$B$4
```

Excel multiplies the contents of cell C9 with the contents of cell B4 and displays the result in the highlighted cell C15.

> **NOTE**
>
> You may be wondering about the dollar signs ($) used in the multiplication formula. Excel, in its internal figuring, "thinks" in relative terms. For example, the relationship between cell C15 (where you want to see the result) and the cell containing Andrew Howe's hourly rate is to Excel "one cell over, and five cells up from the one that's highlighted now."
>
> This relative thinking works fine for arriving at the figure for his first quarter revenue earned. It breaks down, however, when you try to figure the second and subsequent quarter figures. For that reason, dollar signs are used to tell Excel to use the contents of cell B4 absolutely—in other words, to use exactly that cell's contents in the multiplication.

2. Move to cell C16 and type the following formula:

   `=C10*$B$5`

   Excel multiplies the contents of cell C10 with the contents of cell B5 and displays the result in the highlighted cell C16.

3. Move to cell C17 and type the following formula:

   `=C11*$B$6`

   Excel multiplies the contents of cell C11 with the contents of cell B6 and displays the result in the highlighted cell C17.

Next, you need to copy these formulas to arrive at the figures for each of the other three quarters. To do so, perform the following steps:

1. Move up to cell C15. With it highlighted, drag down two cells to cell C17 so that all three cells are selected.

2. Press Ctrl+C. Excel places the contents of the selected cells onto the Clipboard.

3. Move to cell D15. Drag and select all the cells from it to cell F17, and then press Ctrl+V. Excel copies the formulas from the Clipboard, performs the multiplication, and displays the resulting values. (See Figure 13.10.)

Next, you'll run two quick totals just to satisfy your curiosity. One is for the total hours worked by the attorneys, and another is for the total revenue generated.

1. Move to cell A12 and type `Total`.

2. With the cell still highlighted, press Ctrl+B to make bold the cell's text font.

3. Click the Align Right button on the Formatting toolbar to realign the cell's text font.

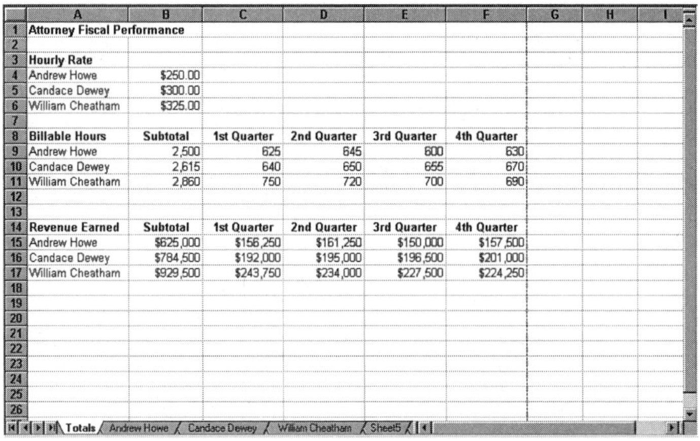

	A	B	C	D	E	F	G	H	I
1	Attorney Fiscal Performance								
2									
3	Hourly Rate								
4	Andrew Howe	$250.00							
5	Candace Dewey	$300.00							
6	William Cheatham	$325.00							
7									
8	Billable Hours	Subtotal	1st Quarter	2nd Quarter	3rd Quarter	4th Quarter			
9	Andrew Howe	2,500	625	645	600	630			
10	Candace Dewey	2,615	640	650	655	670			
11	William Cheatham	2,860	750	720	700	690			
12									
13									
14	Revenue Earned	Subtotal	1st Quarter	2nd Quarter	3rd Quarter	4th Quarter			
15	Andrew Howe	$625,000	$156,250	$161,250	$150,000	$157,500			
16	Candace Dewey	$784,500	$192,000	$195,000	$196,500	$201,000			
17	William Cheatham	$929,500	$243,750	$234,000	$227,500	$224,250			
18									
19									
20									
21									
22									
23									
24									
25									
26									

Totals / Andrew Howe / Candace Dewey / William Cheatham / Sheet5

FIGURE 13.10.
Your spreadsheet with the multiplication completed.

4. Move to cell B12. Click the Autosum button on the formula toolbar. Excel assumes that you want to sum the three cells above B12, so you can simply press Enter to accept that. Excel does the addition and displays the result in cell B12.
4. Select both cells A12 and B12, and press Ctrl+C. Excel copies to the Clipboard the formulas from both cells.
5. Move to cell A18 and press Ctrl+V. Excel copies the formulas from the Clipboard, performs the addition, and displays the result in cell B18. (See Figure 13.11.)

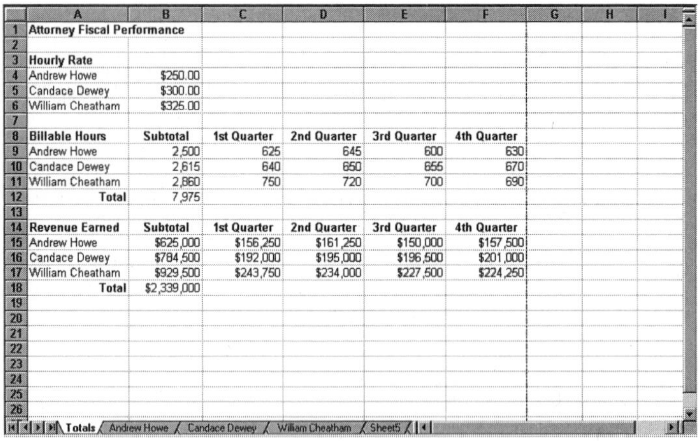

	A	B	C	D	E	F	G	H	I
1	Attorney Fiscal Performance								
2									
3	Hourly Rate								
4	Andrew Howe	$250.00							
5	Candace Dewey	$300.00							
6	William Cheatham	$325.00							
7									
8	Billable Hours	Subtotal	1st Quarter	2nd Quarter	3rd Quarter	4th Quarter			
9	Andrew Howe	2,500	625	645	600	630			
10	Candace Dewey	2,615	640	650	655	670			
11	William Cheatham	2,860	750	720	700	690			
12	Total	7,975							
13									
14	Revenue Earned	Subtotal	1st Quarter	2nd Quarter	3rd Quarter	4th Quarter			
15	Andrew Howe	$625,000	$156,250	$161,250	$150,000	$157,500			
16	Candace Dewey	$784,500	$192,000	$195,000	$196,500	$201,000			
17	William Cheatham	$929,500	$243,750	$234,000	$227,500	$224,250			
18	Total	$2,339,000							
19									
20									
21									
22									
23									
24									
25									
26									

Totals / Andrew Howe / Candace Dewey / William Cheatham / Sheet5

FIGURE 13.11.
The finished spreadsheet.

With that, you are finished with the spreadsheet part of this example. Next, you move on to the report.

Creating a Report

Now that your background data is ready, it's time to create a report that you can use to explain it (and in a chapter about Word, I think it's about time!).

Start with one of Word's built-in report templates. To begin creating a report, perform the following steps:

1. From Word's File menu, select New. The New dialog box appears.

2. Dewey, Cheatham, and Howe is a contemporary legal firm, so double-click Contemporary Report.dot to select it. (See Figure 13.12.) Word displays the report template, ready for you to modify. (See Figure 13.13.)

3. Just to be safe, save the file as Fiscal Report.doc.

FIGURE 13.12.

Click a report template to get started.

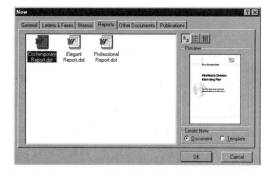

FIGURE 13.13.

The contemporary report document template before modification.

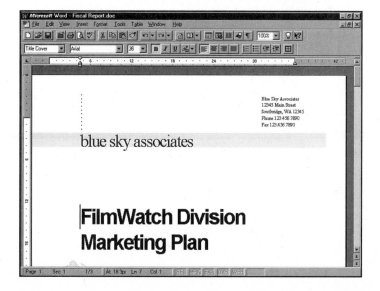

Modifying the Report

The template Word calls up is a good start. Now you need to modify the report so that it reflects the name and address of the sample legal firm. To do so, perform the following steps:

> **NOTE**
>
> This document template can be found on the CD that accompanies this book. If you use the CD, you can skip this part of the chapter. This methods used in this example also will work with any open Word document.

1. Move to the name and address frame at the top right of the form, and change it to the following:

   ```
   Dewey, Cheatham, and Howe
   1234 Main St.
   Suite 4401
   Downtown, MB 99499
   ```

2. Move to the blue sky associates logo and change it to Dewey, Cheatham, and Howe.

3. Move to the FilmWatch Division report title and change it to Firm Fiscal Report. (See Figure 13.14.)

4. Delete all the remaining text found on succeeding pages in the document.

FIGURE 13.14.

The contemporary report document template after you make modifications.

Writing the Report

With the front page finished, it's time to actually write the report. My philosophy is that reports are tools to convey specific information—not tomes to be digested. In other words, with business reports, "less is more." This example follows that philosophy.

> **NOTE**
>
> In this example, you don't actually write text for the report. You probably already know how to type, so there's no point to entering the text, especially when the task at hand is to embed an Excel spreadsheet. You can, however, work along with this example, using the document template you've just modified.

Assume that—without you actually having to do so—you are writing a report forecasting the firm's fiscal performance. You continue to write until you get to the point in the report where you want to insert the spreadsheet that you created. To insert the spreadsheet, perform the following steps:

1. From the Insert menu, select Object. Word displays its Object dialog box.

2. Click the Create from File tab. In it, down at the lower right, enable the Link to File check box. This creates an OLE link between the spreadsheet and your Word document.

3. In the File Name text box, type `Attorney.xls`. (See Figure 13.15.) If necessary, you can use the Browse dialog box to find the spreadsheet file on your hard disk.

4. Click OK, and the magic begins.

FIGURE 13.15.

The Object dialog box, ready to call up your spreadsheet.

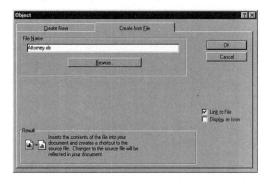

An Automagical Occurrence

When creating an OLE link, what happens in the background is—to me, at least—fascinating. The following is a simplified version of how it goes:

1. Word starts Excel, passing to it the name of the Attorney.xls spreadsheet file.

2. Excel looks for and finds the Attorney.xls spreadsheet file, loads it into memory, and then exposes it (makes it available as an object) to Word.

3. Word takes over the spreadsheet object, figures out how much room on your document it will take, creates a frame of that size, inserts the spreadsheet into that frame, and displays it for you. (See Figure 13.16.) *Voilà!*

FIGURE 13.16.

Your spreadsheet inserted into a Word document.

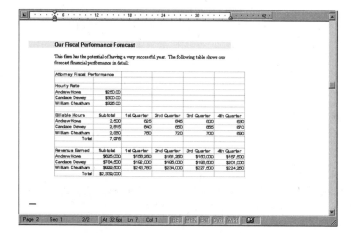

Editing a Spreadsheet from Within Word

You know, it never fails: You—under time pressure, of course—create the report just short of the deadline, and someone comes to you with a last-minute change. This must happen frequently at Microsoft because they've included in the Word and OLE business a quick and easy way to deal with the situation—you can edit the spreadsheet right while it's in your Word document.

Suppose you need to make a change to the spreadsheet. The firm has discovered that it can get another $10 per hour out of Candace Dewey's clients. Also, ol' Willy Cheatham has been losing too many cases lately. His hourly rate has got to come down $20. To make these changes, perform the following steps:

1. Move to the spreadsheet in your document and double-click it. Word unhides Excel (which has actually been running, hidden, all along) and displays in it your spreadsheet.

2. Move to cell B5, and increase Dewey's rate by $10 so that it is now $310. Excel recalculates all the numbers, based on the value in cell B5.

3. Move to cell B11, and decrease Howe's rate by $20 so that it now is $305. Excel recalculates all the numbers, based on the value in cell B11.

4. Save the spreadsheet.

After you make your changes, press Alt+Tab until Word is in the foreground of your desktop. Notice that because the spreadsheet and Word document are linked, OLE has already made the changes in your report for you. (See Figure 13.17.) "*Vachement bien,*" as the Parisians say.

FIGURE 13.17.

Your spreadsheet, with its numbers reflecting the latest information.

Our Fiscal Performance Forecast

This firm has the potential of having a very successful year. The following table shows our forecast financial performance in detail:

Attorney Fiscal Performance					
Hourly Rate					
Andrew Howe	$260.00				
Candace Dewey	$310.00				
William Cheatham	$305.00				
Billable Hours	Subtotal	1st Quarter	2nd Quarter	3rd Quarter	4th Quarter
Andrew Howe	2,500	625	645	600	630
Candace Dewey	2,615	640	660	655	670
William Cheatham	2,860	750	720	700	690
Total	7,975				
Revenue Earned	Subtotal	1st Quarter	2nd Quarter	3rd Quarter	4th Quarter
Andrew Howe	$625,000	$158,250	$161,250	$150,000	$157,500
Candace Dewey	$810,650	$198,400	$201,500	$203,050	$207,700
William Cheatham	$872,300	$228,750	$219,800	$213,500	$210,450
Total	$2,307,950				

Page 2 Sec 1 2/2 At 3.5pi Ln 7 Col 1

Looking over the spreadsheet object in your report, there's one other thing that would really improve its appearance. I refer, of course, to those rather obtrusive gridlines Excel inserts by default.

Modifying the Format of an Object

Taking out the spreadsheet gridlines in your Word document is as easy as if you were doing it in Excel. The reason is—of course—that because it's a linked OLE document, you're actually *doing it* in Excel. To modify the format, perform the following steps:

1. Double-click on the spreadsheet object in your report. Word calls up Excel and displays the linked spreadsheet.

2. From the Tools menu, select Options. Excel displays its Options dialog box. (See Figure 13.18.)

FIGURE 13.18.

Excel's Options dialog box.

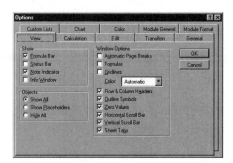

3. In the Options dialog box, select the View tab to make it active. Deselect (uncheck) the Gridlines check box under the Window Options frame. Excel removes the gridlines from your spreadsheet—both in Excel *and* in your report. (See Figure 13.19.)

FIGURE 13.19.

Your cleanly formatted report.

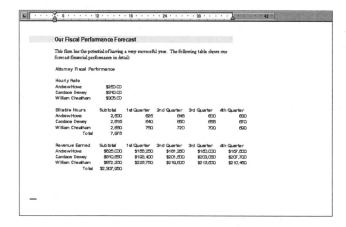

4. Save the spreadsheet in Excel.

Adding a Chart to the Report

When you get right down to it, the purpose of a report is to quickly and efficiently transmit information to your reader. As for being quick and efficient in transferring numerical concepts, words simply don't cut it as well as do pictures. For that reason, take an extra moment to embellish your report with a chart created from the Excel spreadsheet. To do this, perform the following steps:

1. Call up the spreadsheet in Excel. (Remember that you can do this by double-clicking the spreadsheet object in Word, or directly from within Excel.)

2. Use the Excel Chart Wizard to create a pie chart from the subtotaled billable hours for the three attorneys: cells A9 through B11.

3. After you create the chart, select it and press Ctrl+C to copy it to the Clipboard.

4. Open your report in Word, and move to where you want your report to appear. When there, press Ctrl+V. Word copies the pie chart into your spreadsheet. (See Figure 13.20.)

5. Save the report.

FIGURE 13.20.

Your report now contains a chart.

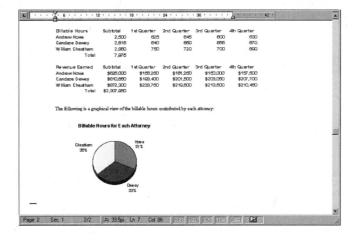

Summary

Using Word with other applications in Microsoft Office is about as seamless as it can be. The hardest part isn't even in making the connections between the software components; it's in using perhaps different applications when creating the parts of a document, and then putting them all together!

Word as a Publisher

14

*by Sue
Charlesworth*

In this chapter you look at Word as a publisher, examining its capability to produce documents that are outside the scope of those you create with a typewriter.

Publishing used to mean creating documents that went beyond the capabilities of the type-written page, using mock-ups and paste-ups, specifying typefaces, submitting the pasted-together document to a printer, reviewing proofs, and hoping that the finished article became what you had intended. With the advent of powerful word processing packages, such as Word, that run on PCs, the nature of publishing has changed.

With Word, you have at your fingertips document formatting capabilities that used to be reserved only for print shops using typesetters and other sophisticated equipment. While there still are some functions best—or only—done by the printer, you now can perform many publishing functions on your own computer, using Word. Some of the capabilities available to you through Word include the following:

- Character formatting
- Different fonts and typefaces
- Borders
- Dingbats
- Frames and objects
- Text flow
- Section and column breaks and formatting

All in all, this is a far cry from the typewriter, where your only character "formatting" was all-caps or underlining, and you had one typeface, period.

Now that you have publishing functions at your fingertips—literally—what types of documents or publications can you create with them? Let's explore.

Business Publications

Businesses need many types of documents, starting with those that establish business identity, such as letterhead and business cards, invoices, statements, estimates, and so on. Businesses need promotional materials, such as brochures, fliers, coupons, and advertisements; they need internal and external materials, such as reports to owners, catalogs, order forms, press releases, memos, newsletters, and fax sheets, not to mention letters, reports, and product documentation.

These publications influence how outsiders—and insiders—perceive the business: badly done, business communications can lose customers; well done, business communications can make the sale. Look at two quick examples. Figure 14.1 shows part of a sample flier for a freelance business writer. The writing is fair and it contains no typos, but does it inspire you to hire the writer? Compare the flier to Figure 14.2; same writer, same message, but which one would you be more likely to respond to?

Chapter 14

FIGURE 14.1.

A bland flier.

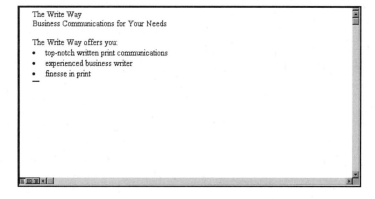

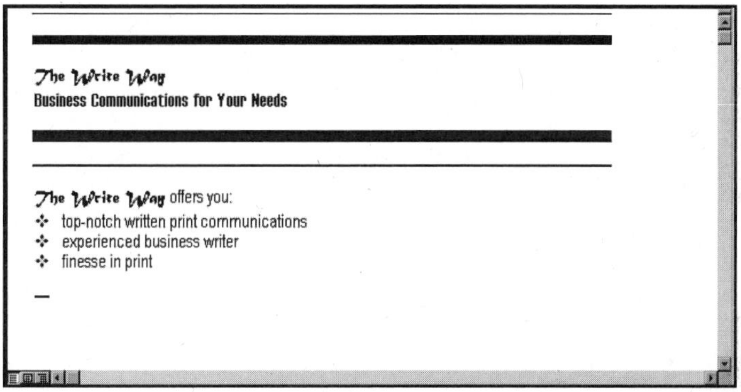

FIGURE 14.2.

A flier with pizzazz.

Suppose that you've written a report for your boss: It's an important report that highlights critical gaps in the company's customer service efforts. Your report is one of five your boss will receive this week just before her quarterly meeting with the board. She'll choose one of the reports to present to the board. Given a choice between the report in Figure 14.3 and the one in Figure 14.4, which one do you think will catch her eye?

With all the possibilities Word offers for desktop publishing, where do you start when producing your own documents? Look no further than Word's wizards and templates. When you create a new Word document, you can choose from the following wizards:

- Fax
- Letter
- Memo
- Newsletter
- Agenda
- Award
- Calendar

- Pleading
- Table

Need more? Word also provides the following templates:

- Invoice
- Purchase order
- Weekly time sheet
- Brochure
- Directory
- Press release
- Manual
- Report

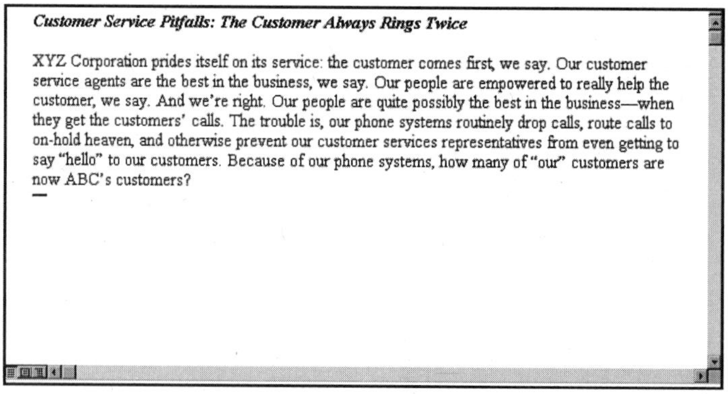

FIGURE 14.3.

A bland report.

> *Customer Service Pitfalls: The Customer Always Rings Twice*
>
> XYZ Corporation prides itself on its service: the customer comes first, we say. Our customer service agents are the best in the business, we say. Our people are empowered to really help the customer, we say. And we're right. Our people are quite possibly the best in the business—when they get the customers' calls. The trouble is, our phone systems routinely drop calls, route calls to on-hold heaven, and otherwise prevent our customer services representatives from even getting to say "hello" to our customers. Because of our phone systems, how many of "our" customers are now ABC's customers?

FIGURE 14.4.

An attention-grabbing report.

Customer Service Pitfalls

The Customer Always Rings Twice

Personal Publications

What works for improving business's images applies to your personal image, too. Publications you put out can be every bit as important to you as the year-end summary is to the corporation across town. Are you a student, or do you know one? How many essays, papers, or themes does a student generate? This former graduate student produced major papers, minor papers, analyses, take-home essay exams, and management models. Cover sheets, charts, graphics, and, of course, a lot of text, all figured into the required output. After facing stacks of papers, which paper do you think a professor would see more positively, Student A's in Figure 14.5, or Student B's in Figure 14.6?

FIGURE 14.5.

A bland cover sheet.

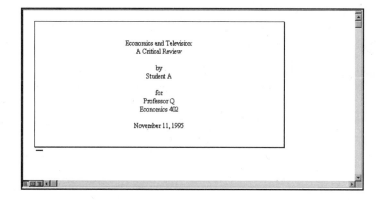

FIGURE 14.6.

An interesting cover sheet.

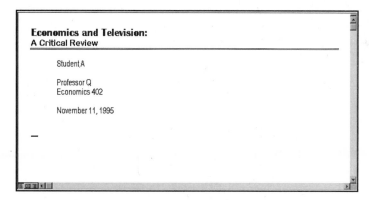

Consider another personal publication—one critical in these days of downsizing, layoffs, and buyouts—the résumé. Some sources say you have 30 seconds to make a good impression with your résumé. Which résumé would you rather have make an impression about you? The one in Figure 14.7 or the one in Figure 14.8?

FIGURE 14.7.

A bland résumé.

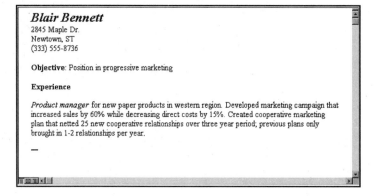

FIGURE 14.8.

A bold résumé.

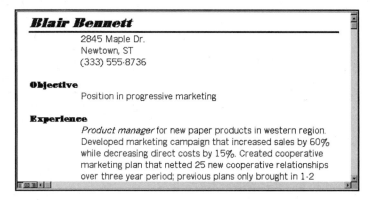

Layout

Knowing what types of documents you can publish is just the first step. As the examples in this chapter demonstrated, how you lay out and format a document plays a critical role in its success.

When laying out a publication, keep in mind the following key points:

- White space—White space, the blank areas of a document, including side, top, and bottom margins, and the spaces between lines and sections, is more than good; it's critical to a publication's success. Cramming as much text as possible on a page doesn't result in more information available to your reader; it results in a non-reader.

- Consistency—Structure your document so that your reader can identify that structure. When you use consistent formatting for major points, secondary points, sidebar material, introductions, and so on, your reader will know how to key in on those points and more easily find and read the material.

- Contrast—No, this doesn't contradict the previous point. Both consistency and contrast contribute to a publication's success. Contrast provides interest and helps clarify your publication's structure. While your document might be consistent in its structure, if all the elements look the same, your reader won't be able to determine the structure. Compare Figure 14.9 and Figure 14.10. Which figure enables you to identify structure at a glance? Make sure your contrast does contrast, however; small differences between document elements don't provide enough contrast to guide your reader. Figure 14.11 demonstrates ineffective contrast. The publication doesn't provide adequate contrast between elements. Compare it to Figure 14.12, where, once again, you can readily identify document elements.

FIGURE 14.9.

A poorly identified structure.

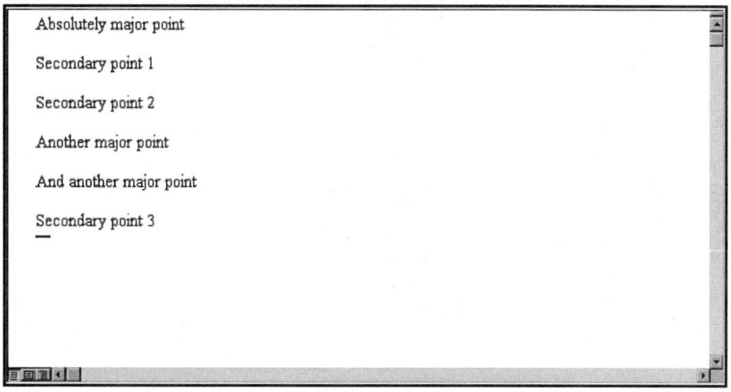

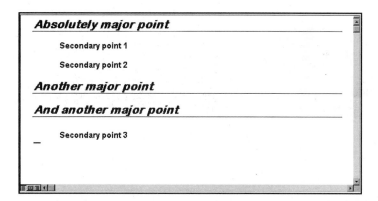

FIGURE 14.10.

A well-defined structure.

The following list discusses a few things to avoid:

- All caps—Capital letters may have been the only form of contrast and emphasis available on the typewriter, but you have other forms of emphasis now. When we read, we depend on word shape—the pattern of ups and downs created by the ascenders and descenders of letters—to help us distinguish words. Words in all caps have the same shape; thus, we have to work harder to understand what's written.

- Centered text—Our eyes and brain are more comfortable when each line begins at the same place, which makes left-justified text easy reading. Each line of centered text begins at a different place, making us work harder to read the text.

■ Underlined text—Underlining interferes with letters' descenders, confusing word shapes and making it more difficult to distinguish between letters and words. Underlining dates back to typewriters and their limited repertoire of emphasis; find a different way to highlight words or phrases.

■ Blocks of script—Long sections of script or italic type do not for easy reading make.

Now that you've been introduced to some page layout and design guidelines, you can explore how to use Word for good page design.

FIGURE 14.11.

Low contrast.

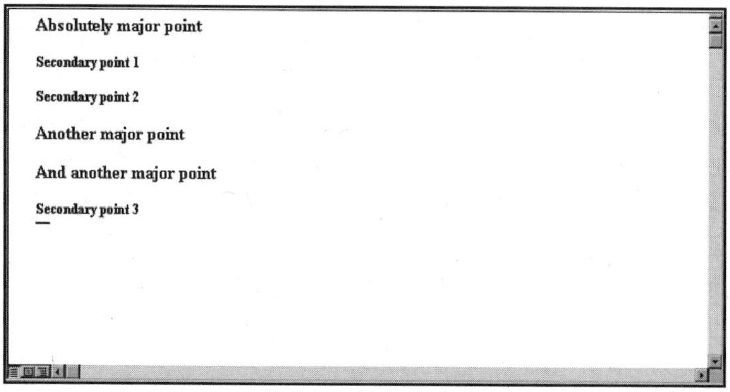

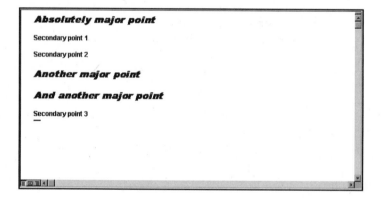

FIGURE 14.12.

High contrast.

White Space

Set generous margins to ensure adequate white space in your documents. Consider using an extra-wide left margin as a design element, as shown in Figure 14.13. This sample has the left margin set at 3 inches, with the major headings set with an indentation of –2.0 inches. Margins such as these can be especially useful for manuals and other types of teaching documents, leaving the reader plenty of room to make notes.

You also can introduce white space when setting the space before and space after attributes of paragraphs. Extra space between headings and the text they accompany helps set the headings apart. Be careful to keep the headings "attached" to their text, however, and not to the text above. In Figure 14.14, does the heading "belong" to the paragraph above it or below it? The example in Figure 14.15 makes the relationship clear.

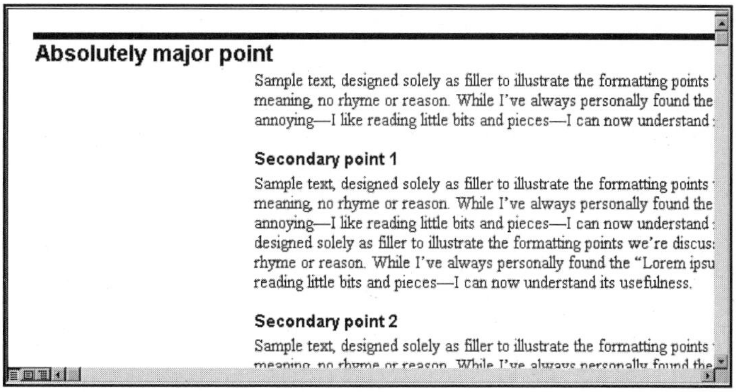

FIGURE 14.13.

Margins as white space.

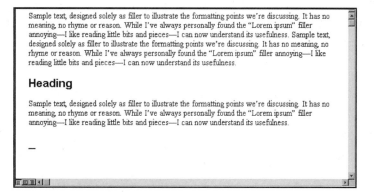

FIGURE 14.14.

An unclear heading relationship.

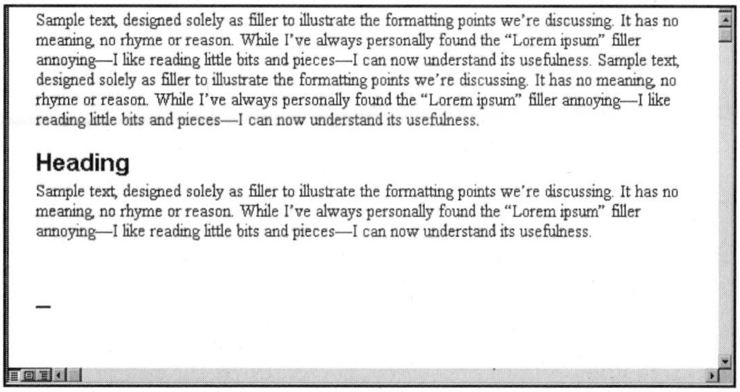

FIGURE 14.15.

A clear heading relationship.

A raging debate among desktop publishers occurs even as you read this text: Should you justify your right margins, or should you leave your right margins unjustified, with a ragged edge?

The "answer" to that question is it depends. Many people perceive a justified right margin as formal and, therefore, more desirable for more formal documents. Others insist that the drawbacks to right justification outweigh the perhaps more casual approach of a ragged-right margin. White space comes into play here, both as a positive and a negative.

With Word, when you set text with a justified right margin, Word forces extra spaces between words to make the right margin even. These extra spaces can cause "rivers" of unwanted white space to run through your text. When you have justified right margins in columns, Word has fewer words to work with when justifying and may insert whole blocks of spaces to get the right margin justified. Readers find these blocks extremely distracting. Ragged-right margins don't force extra spaces into text and help avoid those white rivers and blank areas. The extra white space at the right margin also helps open up your text.

White space in ragged right margins has a drawback. Depending on how you set Word's hyphenation, you can end up with extremely ragged-right edges. Select Tools | Hyphenation from the menu bar to help control the ragged-right margin. (See Figure 14.16.) Click Automatically Hyphenate Document to have Word hyphenate automatically. The value in the Hyphenation Zone field determines the trade-off between raggedness and number of hyphens: A smaller hyphenation zone reduces the raggedness of the right margin by hyphenating more words while a larger hyphenation zone decreases the number of hyphenated words, but increases the right margin's raggedness.

FIGURE 14.16.

The Hyphenation dialog box.

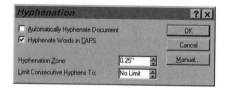

Figure 14.17 shows a paragraph set with a wide hyphenation zone; the right margin is ragged. Figure 14.18 is the same text with a narrow hyphenation zone; the right margin is much smoother.

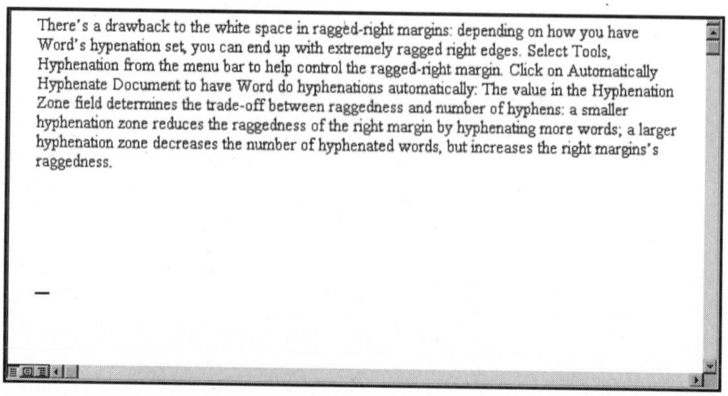

FIGURE 14.17.

A very ragged-right margin.

There's a drawback to the white space in ragged-right margins: depending on how you have Word's hyphenation set, you can end up with extremely ragged right edges. Select Tools, Hyphenation from the menu bar to help control the ragged-right margin. Click on Automatically Hyphenate Document to have Word do hyphenations automatically: The value in the Hyphenation Zone field determines the trade-off between raggedness and number of hyphens: a smaller hyphenation zone reduces the raggedness of the right margin by hyphenating more words; a larger hyphenation zone decreases the number of hyphenated words, but increases the right margins's raggedness.

FIGURE 14.18.

A smoother right margin.

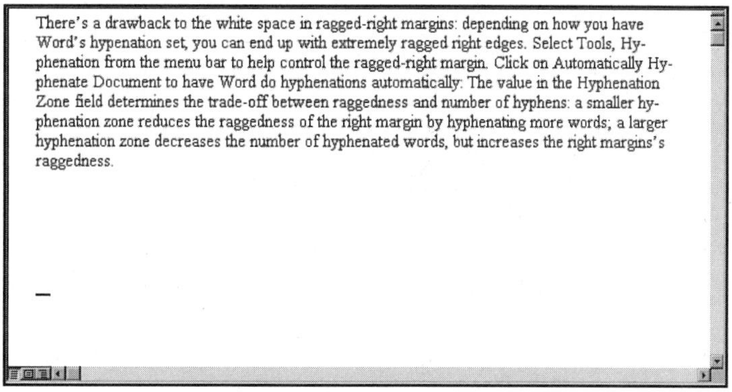

There's a drawback to the white space in ragged-right margins: depending on how you have Word's hyphenation set, you can end up with extremely ragged right edges. Select Tools, Hyphenation from the menu bar to help control the ragged-right margin. Click on Automatically Hyphenate Document to have Word do hyphenations automatically. The value in the Hyphenation Zone field determines the trade-off between raggedness and number of hyphens: a smaller hyphenation zone reduces the raggedness of the right margin by hyphenating more words; a larger hyphenation zone decreases the number of hyphenated words, but increases the right margins's raggedness.

Consistency

Word provides a powerful consistency tool for styles. Each time you begin a major topic, introduce it with the same style. Similarly, introduce different levels of topics with their own styles. Then your reader has clues and cues about your document and its content.

Text styles also can provide consistency. If you have different types of information to present in your publication, you can establish a different text style for each type of information. For example, many books that teach programming languages use a typeface to show program code that's different from the typeface used for explanatory text. As another example, you can effectively identify callouts—those little quotes from a text section that you place in margins or between paragraphs—by setting them in a different font or surrounding them with distinctive borders.

Contrast

Contrast often refers to ways to distinguish different document elements. You can establish contrast in a variety of ways. Different typefaces often distinguish between a publication's headings and its text. As stated earlier, make sure you have enough contrast in your contrast. Setting headings in a slightly larger font size doesn't make the differences jump out at your reader; using two similar serif typefaces doesn't cut it, either.

> **NOTE**
>
> Serif typefaces have little "feet" at the letter tips. Times Roman is a serif typeface. Sans serif typefaces don't have the feet. Arial is a sans serif typeface.

Create effective contrast by using a sans serif typeface for headings and a serif typeface for body text. Using the same typeface for both headings and text is effective when the headings are significantly larger. Use related type families, too. A bold, condensed version of the body font can introduce headings effectively.

Mail Merge

Remember how form letters used to look? The "form" part had obvious spaces where your name was inserted or placed your "personalized" information in standalone blocks where differences in information length weren't quite so glaring. Form letters were bad things that placed fear in the hearts of readers everywhere.

Form letters—then and now—serve exceedingly useful purposes, however. As a business owner, or a club officer, or an information gatherer, form letters enable you to produce volumes of documents tailored to specific groups of people and personalized for individuals within those groups. Using Word, you can create form letters that are highly specific, both to your reader and to you.

The Mail Merge Helper

Word avoids the use of the unsavory term "form letter" and calls its form-letter-creation process mail merge. Merging involves the following three documents:

- The data source holds the information about people you add to your mailing. A table typically forms the data source.
- The main document provides the form into which Word adds personalized information.
- The form letters are individual letters or documents that reflect the merging of the data with the form.

Word provides wizards to help with document creation and formatting. Wizards generally move you through a linear process, through which you follow steps in sequence until you complete your task. Mail merge is a little different. The process you follow to create individualized letters doesn't follow a neat linear path; you move back and forth between your main document and data source until you have both set up to your liking. To guide you through this process, Word provides the Mail Merge Helper.

To display the Mail Merge Helper dialog box, select Mail Merge from the Tools menu. (See Figure 14.19.) You'll follow the helper's steps; however, merging requires a certain amount of "bouncing" between the main document (number 1) and the data source (number 2). The text in the top box guides you through merging and supplies tips on what to do next.

You will begin with the main document. Click on Create, and then select what you want to create. Mail merge enables you to create the following:

- Form letters
- Mailing labels
- Envelopes
- Catalogs

Next, choose where Word will locate the main document. If you don't want the active document used as the main document, select New Main Document.

You now have a main document that you can edit. Unless you have a large amount of text for your form letter, however, you can do little with your main document at this point. Instead, create your data source so that you know which fields to place in your main document. Click Get Data in step 2 of the Mail Merge Helper and select Create Data Source. Word displays the Create Data Source dialog box. (See Figure 14.20.)

FIGURE 14.19.

The Mail Merge Helper dialog box.

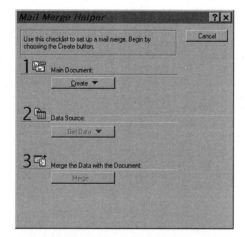

FIGURE 14.20.

The Create Data Source dialog box.

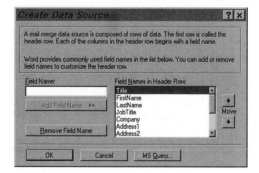

Working with the Data Source

In the Create Data Source dialog box, you specify the titles of the data fields for your mail merge. These titles form the header row of the data source table. Word provides a list of commonly used data fields to get you started. To remove fields you won't use, select the field name, and then click on Remove Field Name. Add new fields by entering their names in the Field Name text box, and then click Add Field Name. Change the order of fields by selecting a field name and then clicking the Move up or Move down arrow.

> **NOTE**
>
> As you specify the fields you want in your form letter, the order of the fields in the data source isn't critical; however, there may be a nuisance factor in having an often-used field at the bottom of the list of names.

After you specify your data fields, Word recognizes that the data source table is empty and gives you the choice of creating your data records or returning to your main document. What you do at this point is largely a matter of choice: Select Edit Main Document to place field place-holders in your main document; select Edit Data Source to add data records to your data source table. First, you'll learn about adding data records, so click on Edit Data Source.

In the Data Form dialog box that appears, you create your individual records. (See Figure 14.21.) Word presents a list of blank data fields in which you enter the value for each field. After you enter all your records, select OK. Select Add New to add the current record and leave the data form open to enter the next record. Click Delete to delete a record. To move from record to record, click the left and right arrows below the data field list. The current record number displays in the space between the arrows.

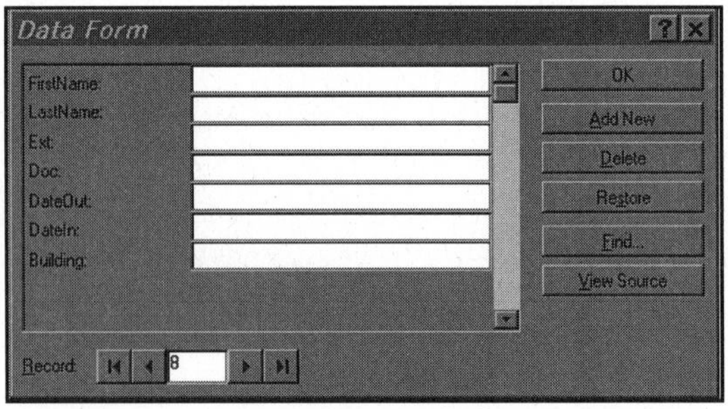

FIGURE 14.21.

The Data Form dialog box.

To find a record with a particular value, click Find, enter the value (or partial value) in the Find What box, and then specify or select the field to search in the In Field. Click Find First and Find Next to move through your records.

Working with the Main Document

After you close your data source, Word returns to your main document. Now that you have names for your data fields, you can add them to your main document.

Click the Insert Merge Field button on the mail merge main document toolbar and select the field you want from the list. Word inserts a field placeholder in your main document. Field placeholders display as the field name surrounded by chevrons: the << and >> marks. (See Figure 14.22.) When you merge your main document with your data source, Word substitutes the value in the individual fields for the field placeholders.

FIGURE 14.22.
Field placeholders.

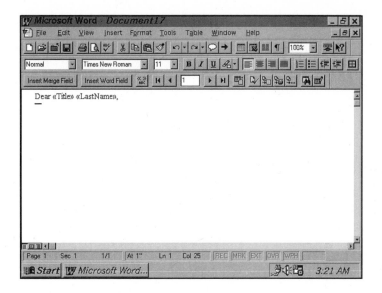

Continue to add text and field placeholders to your main document. If you want to check how a merged record will look, click on the View Merged Data button (to the right of the Insert Word Field button) on the mail merge main document toolbar. View Merged Data toggles between the main document with its placeholders and a "real" merged document.

To see how your merged documents will look and list any errors encountered during the merge, click the Check for Errors button on the mail merge main document toolbar. The Checking and Reporting Errors dialog box offers you a number of options for simulating or running a merge. (See Figure 14.23.) Once you're happy with the results, click on one of the merge buttons to run your merge.

FIGURE 14.23.
The Checking and Reporting Errors dialog box.

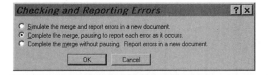

Merging the Data Source and Main Document

When you click the Merge to New Document button, Word merges the records in the data source with the main document, substituting the value of a field in the field placeholder. Word places the merge results in a single document, with each individual form letter in a separate section. You then can treat this new document as you would any other.

Clicking the Mail Merge button displays the Merge dialog box. In this dialog box, you can select a range of records to merge. Click the Query Options button to open the Query

Options dialog box. (See Figure 14.24.) The Filter Records tab enables you to select specific records to merge by using field names and comparison values. Using filters, you can pick out records in your data source that meet specific criteria. The following list provides some examples of filters:

- Specific Zip codes, to target a mailing
- Salary range, to offer special benefits packages
- Children's ages, to tailor a book purchase offer

FIGURE 14.24.

The Query Options dialog box.

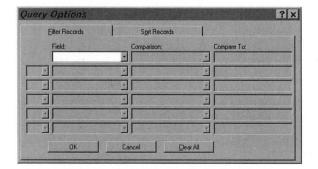

To set up your filter, select the field you want to filter by and the comparison you want to make. In Compare To, enter the value you want to filter your data field by. For the Zip code example, you'd enter ZipCode (or whatever you've called that field) in Field, then Equal to for the comparison, then a particular Zip code in the Compare To field.

In the Sort Records tab, you can specify up to three sort levels. Sorting doesn't affect which records will be used for the merge; it only arranges the newly created records in the order you specify. If you had a database composed entirely of men named John Smith, John Brown, and John Doe, you might want to sort your mail merge by last name, then by middle initial. With this sort, you'd get all your John Browns listed first; within the Brown list, the names would be arranged by middle initial. Your list would then move on to the John Does, arranged by middle initial, then finish up with the sorted John Smiths.

A Mail Merge Example

Look at a simple example of a mail merge. Your form letter will go out to individuals of a company who have checked documents out of the company library, but have not returned the documents. Figure 14.25 shows the data form for your form letter; it consists of the individual's name, company data, the name of the document, the date the document was checked out, and the date the document was checked in.

FIGURE 14.25.

The library data form.

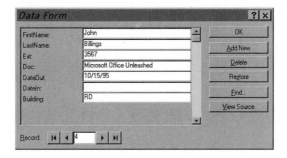

The main document, shown in Figure 14.26, is a simple reminder. You use the individual's name, document name, and check-out date, along with the person's building code, to complete the simple reminder form.

Figure 14.27 displays the merged file.

FIGURE 14.26.

The Library main document.

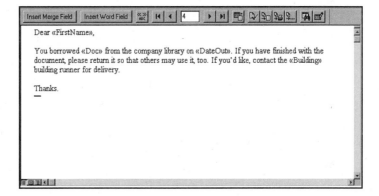

FIGURE 14.27.

The Library merged file.

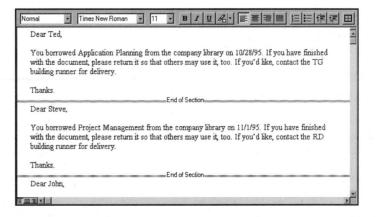

Summary

In this chapter you have explored using Word as a desktop publishing tool as well as identified some of the elements of good document design. You then read about mail merge, which enables you to create form letters by combining a main document with a data source.

Word and the
Internet Assistant

15

by Dave Speedie

Microsoft's Internet Assistant is a free add-on that allows you to create your very own Web pages for the World Wide Web. The Internet Assistant contains a Web browser that allows you to view Web pages on the Internet. The Internet Assistant also supplies you with templates and document converters that allow you to easily create an HTML document. Unlike other HTML authoring tools that have separate editing and browsing applications (which makes it difficult to create Web Pages), the Internet Assistant allows you to create professional-looking Web Pages with ease, without having to learn the complex HTML formats.

The Internet Assistant allows you to use the formatting options and toolbars to create Web pages. You are also able to use features such as AutoCorrect, Spell It and AutoFormat when creating your Web page. You can embed OLE 2.0 objects from Microsoft Excel, Microsoft Access, and Microsoft PowerPoint, for example. Also, you can create hyperlinks to other Word documents.

Using the Internet Assistant also allows you to surf the Net. On the World Wide Web you can find information on almost anything! You can view up-to-the-minute weather maps or sports scores, control a model train, locate you favorite beer home page—the list can go on and on.

Where Do I Get It?

Internet Assistant for Word for Windows 95 can be found on Microsoft's World Wide Web site. At the time this book went to press the Internet Assistant could be found at this address:

```
http://www.microsoft.com/kb/softlib/office/q_word.htm
```

Make sure that you download the 32-bit version, which is compatible with Word for Windows 95. The 16-bit version can only be used with Word for Window 6.0a and 6.0c.

How Do I Install and Set Up Internet Assistant?

To install the Internet Assistant after downloading the file, click the Start button and select Run. Next, click the Browse button and select the directory where the file is located. For Windows NT 3.51 users, in the Program Manager select File on the menu bar, and then select Run. Click the Browse button and select the directory where the file is located. At the time this book went to press the filename was WORDIA2B.EXE. Select this file and then click the OK button. Then, click the OK button in the Run dialog box.

The first prompt you receive will ask you if want to install Microsoft Word Internet Assistant. After you select Yes, you'll receive a warning screen. This warning screen states that if you accept the terms of the End User License Agreement, you should select Continue. The next screen is the licensing agreement screen. Select Accept if you agree to the terms. In the next dialog box (see Figure 15.1), click the Complete button. This starts the installation of the required files. (See Figure 15.2.)

FIGURE 15.1.

The dialog box for starting the installation.

FIGURE 15.2.

The installation screen.

When the installation of files is complete, you can click the Launch Word button to start Word for Windows 95. (See Figure 15.3.)

FIGURE 15.3.

Launching Word after installation.

What Is HTML?

HTML stands for *hypertext markup language.* HTML allows you to use several formatting qualities. You are able to use many of Word's features to design your Web page. For example, you can format text by clicking the right mouse button to bring up the shortcut menu, where you can select the Font option. You are able to create your own heading styles. You can insert a graphic, use numbered or bulleted lists, or use the horizontal rule to separate areas with a line going across your page. You are also able to create hyperlinks. This allows you to create links from your page to another location on the World Wide Web, to a bookmark, or to another HTML or Word document.

The Appearance of the Web Page

When you design your own Web page, there are several things to consider:

■ You want to ensure that the document is well formatted and well presented. You do not want to have your page cluttered with pictures and/or text. When people browse your page, they are looking for something to stand out and grab their attention. You can achieve this by having a well-formatted and well-presented page.

■ Use headers and the normal text styles where possible.

■ Use a numbered or bulleted list. They are efficient in presenting information.

■ Use horizontal rules to separate topics on your page.

Figure 15.4 shows a sample Web page.

FIGURE 15.4.

A sample Web page layout.

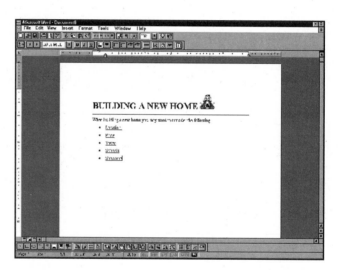

Graphics

Inserting graphics into your Web page can make it very appealing. Just remember not to use too many graphics. Here are some points to keep in mind when using graphics in your Web page:

■ If graphics are required to explain your Web page, users who only have a text-based browser will not understand your Web page.

■ If the graphic is too large to fit onscreen, users will not be able to see any text onscreen.

■ If there are a lot graphics on your page, it will take longer to download, causing users to wait a long time before they can read your page's text.

Graphics are not inserted right into your Web page like they are in a Word document. The graphics are actually linked to a file that contains the graphic. The link describes where the graphic is located. Popular browsers such as Netscape and Internet Assistant actually display the text in a Web page first; then they insert the graphic. The graphic is brought into the Web page in two or three passes. This allows the users to start reading the text before the graphic appears. The only two file formats recognized by the Internet Assistant are GIF (graphics interchange format) and JPEG (Joint Photographics Expert Group).

Here are the steps to follow in order to insert a graphic into your Web page:

1. Position the insertion point where you want the graphic to appear. Next, select Insert | Picture from the menu bar (or you can select the Picture button on the Formatting toolbar). The Insert Picture dialog box will appear. (See Figure 15.5.)

FIGURE 15.5.

The Insert Picture dialog box.

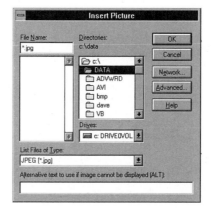

2. Notice the box labeled Alternative text to use if image cannot be displayed. Use this box to specify some text you want to display if your graphic cannot be displayed. For example, you could put `Image is currently not available` in this box.

3. If you want to have text follow the graphic, aligned on the same line as the graphic, you should select the Advanced button. (See Figure 15.6.)

FIGURE 15.6.

The Advanced Picture Option dialog box.

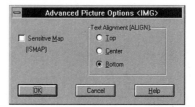

4. In the Text Alignment section, select whether you want the text that follows the graphic to be aligned with the top, center, or bottom of the graphic. Select the OK button when you are done.

5. In the List Files of Type box in the Insert Picture dialog box, select the file type of the graphic you want to bring into your Web page.

6. In the Directories box in the Insert Picture dialog box, select the directory that contains your graphic. Next, select the file from the File Name box; then select the OK button when your are done.

The graphic should now appear where you have your insertion point.

Creating an Interactive Form

Web pages can do more than present information to users—Web pages can be used to interact with the users. You can ask for the user's information when he or she comes to your Web page; you can also set up a form for a user to request more information about a product or service.

You can use text boxes, check boxes, and drop-down list boxes in your Web page. These boxes are called *form fields*. The user either types information into the form field, or selects the form field or a choice from the form field. Once the user has completed the questionnaire, he or she then selects the Submit button.

Using the Internet Assistant Forms toolbar, you can create forms on your Web page. To create a form, follow these steps:

1. Place the insertion point where you want the form field to begin.

2. Select Insert | Form Field on the menu bar. A message appears explaining to you that you are creating a form field. Select Continue.

3. Two boundaries appear on your Web page: Top of Form and Bottom of Form. You'll also notice that the Forms toolbar and the Form Field dialog box appear. Click Cancel on the Form Field dialog box.

4. Between the Top of Form and Bottom of Form boundaries, type in the text you require; then in the Forms toolbar, click the button for the type of form field you want to use on the page:

Button	Name	Description
ab|	Text Box button	Use a text box on your Web page when you want the user to enter some information.
⊠	Check Box button	Use a check box when you require the user to answer yes or no to a question.
🗔	Drop-down List Box button	Use a drop-down list box when you want the user to select an answer from a list.

You might want to customize the form fields you have inserted in your Web page. To do this, just double-click the form field you want to customize.

When you double-click a text box form field, the Text Form Field Options dialog box appears. In this box you can place text in the Default Text box. The text that appears in the text box might need to be changed occasionally. In the Text Format box you can specify formatting for your text from four options: Uppercase, Lowercase, First Capital, or Title Case. In the Type box you can select from six options: Regular Text, Number, Date, Current Date, Current Time, and Calculation. (See Figure 15.7.)

FIGURE 15.7.

The Text Form Field Options dialog box.

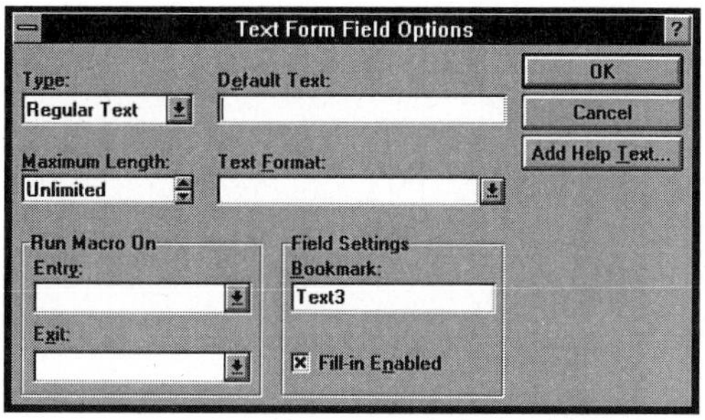

When you double-click a check box form field, the Check Box Form Field Options dialog box appears. In the Default Value section of this dialog box you can either have an × showing in the Check Box or not. If you want to have an × in the Check Box, click in the Checked button; if you do not want an × in the Check Box, click in the Not Checked button. You can also change the size of the check box in the Check Box Size section. (See Figure 15.8.)

FIGURE 15.8.

The Check Box Form Field Options dialog box.

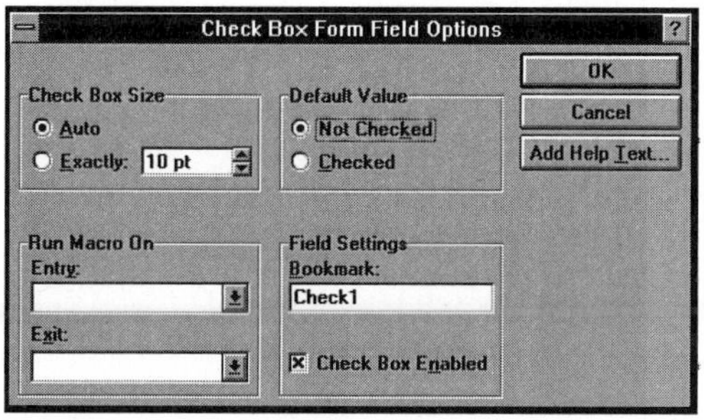

When you double-click a drop-down list box, the Drop-Down Form Field Options dialog box appears. In the Drop-Down Item box you type in the items that you want to appear in your drop-down list box; then select Add to add them to your drop-down list box. (See Figure 15.9.)

Once you have finished inserting your form fields in your Web page, you'll need to insert a Submit and a Reset Button. These buttons are found on your Forms toolbar.

FIGURE 15.9.

The Drop-Down Form Field Options dialog box.

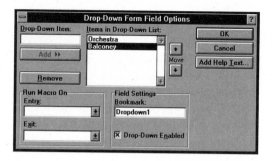

Place your insertion point where you want the Submit button to be inserted. Click the Submit button on the Forms toolbar. The Form Submit Button dialog box appears. You can change the default text that appears on the Submit button by changing the field to the right of the Text radio button. If you would like the Submit button to contain a graphic, select the Custom radio button and then select the Select Picture button. The Insert Picture dialog box appears. In the List Files of Type box select the file type of the graphic you want to bring into your Web page. In the Directories box select the directory that contains your graphic. Then, select the file from the File Name box; select the OK button when you are done.

The Submission Information section in the Form Submit Button dialog box requires you to insert information that will allow the information from your form to be received. You'll need to identify your system properly. You should contact your system administrator if you have any questions about information that should be included here.

Once a user has finished filling in the form fields and has then submitted the information, he or she will want to reset the information back to the original defaults.

Place your insertion point where you want the Reset button to be inserted. Click the Reset button on the Forms toolbar. The Reset button will appear on your Web page.

Summary

This chapter explains to you what Internet Assistant is, why you would want to use it, and where to go to download it. You have learned what file gets downloaded and how to install the application. You are now able to create professional-looking Web pages that can include hyperlinks, graphics, embedded objects, and interactive forms.

If you would like more information about Web Publishing with Microsoft Word, see *Teach Yourself Web Publishing with Microsoft Word in a Week* and *Teach Yourself Web Publishing with HTML in a Week* by Sams Publishing.

V

The Versatility of Excel

Excel Concepts

16

by
Paul McFedries
and Tom Hayes

IN THIS CHAPTER

Most worksheets are drab, lifeless conglomerations of numbers, formulas, and text. Real ho-hum stuff. If you'll be sharing your sheets with others, via e-mail, fax, floppy disk, or presentation, your numbers will have much more impact if they're nicely formatted and presented in an eye-catching layout. All the features discussed in this chapter have two things in common: They can make your day-to-day work more efficient and they can help you get more out of your Excel investment.

Formatting Numbers, Dates, and Times

One of the best ways to improve the readability of your worksheets is to display your data in a format that is logical, consistent, and straightforward. Formatting currency amounts with leading dollar signs, percentages with trailing percent signs, and large numbers with commas are a few of the ways you can improve your spreadsheet style.

This section shows you how to format numbers, dates, and times using Excel's built-in formatting options. You'll also learn how to create your own formats to gain maximum control over the appearance of your data.

Numeric Display Formats

When you enter numbers in a worksheet, Excel removes any leading or trailing zeros. For example, if you enter 0123.4500, Excel displays 123.45. The exception to this rule occurs when you enter a number that is wider than the cell. In this case, Excel tailors the number to fit in the cell either by rounding off some decimal places or by using scientific notation. A number such as 123.45678 is displayed as 123.4568, and 123456789 is displayed as 1.23+08. In both cases, the number is changed for display purposes only; Excel still retains the original number internally.

When you create a worksheet, each cell uses this format, known as the *general* number format, by default. If you want your numbers to appear differently, you can choose from among Excel's seven categories of numeric formats: Number, Currency, Accounting, Percentage, Fraction, Scientific, and Special.

- Number formats—The number formats have three components—the number of decimal places (0 to 30), whether or not the thousands separator (,) is used, and how negative numbers are displayed. For negative numbers, you can display the number with a leading minus sign, in red, surrounded by parentheses, or in red and surrounded by parentheses.

- Currency formats—The currency formats are similar to the number formats, except that the thousands separator is always used, and you have the option of displaying the numbers with a leading dollar sign ($).

- Accounting formats—With the accounting formats, you can select the number of decimal places and whether to display a leading dollar sign. If you do use a dollar sign,

Excel displays it flush-left in the cell. All negative entries are displayed surrounded by parentheses.

■ Percentage formats—The percentage formats display the number multiplied by 100 with a percent sign (%) to the right of the number. For example, .506 is displayed as 50.6%. You can display 0 to 30 decimal places.

■ Fraction formats—The fraction formats enable you to express decimal quantities as fractions. There are nine fraction formats in all, including displaying the number as halves, quarters, eighths, sixteenths, tenths, and hundredths.

■ Scientific formats—The scientific formats display the most significant number to the left of the decimal, 2 to 30 decimal places to the right of the decimal, and then the exponent. Therefore, 123000 is displayed as 1.23E+05.

■ Special formats—The special formats are a collection designed to take care of special cases. Here's a list of the special formats with some examples:

Format	Number Entered	Number Displayed
Zip code	1234	01234
Zip code + 4	123456789	12345-6789
Phone number	1234567890	(123) 456-7890
Social Security number	123456789	123-45-6789

Changing Numeric Formats

The quickest way to format numbers is to specify the format as you enter your data. For example, if you begin a dollar amount with a dollar sign ($), Excel automatically formats the number as currency. Similarly, if you type a percent sign (%) after a number, Excel automatically formats the number as a percentage. Here are a few more examples of this technique. Note that you can enter a negative value using either the negative sign (–) or parentheses.

Number Entered	Number Displayed	Format Used
$1234.567	$1,234.57	Currency
($1234.5)	($1,234.50)	Currency
10%	10%	Percentage
123E+02	1.23E+04	Scientific
5 3/4	5 3/4	Fraction
0 3/4	3/4	Fraction
3/4	4-Mar	Date

Excel interprets a simple fraction such as 3/4 as a date (March 4, in this case). Always include a leading zero, followed by a space, if you want to enter a simple fraction from the formula bar.

Specifying the numeric format as you enter a number is fast and efficient because Excel guesses the format you want to use. Unfortunately, Excel sometimes guesses wrong (for example, interpreting a simple fraction as a date). In any case, you don't have access to all the available formats (for example, displaying negative dollar amounts in red). To overcome these limitations, you can select your numeric formats from the Number tab in the Format Cells dialog box, as shown in the following steps.

To open the Format Cells dialog box and select a format, follow the steps in the following procedure:

1. Select the cell or range of cells you want the new format to apply to.

2. Select Format | Cells. The Format Cells dialog box appears.

To open the Format Cells dialog box quickly, either right-click the cell or range and then select the Format Cells command from the shortcut menu or press Ctrl+1.

3. If necessary, select the Number tab, shown in Figure 16.1.

FIGURE 16.1.

Use the Number tab in the Format Cells dialog box to select a numeric format.

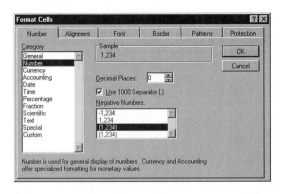

4. Select a format category from the Category list box. Excel displays the various options available for the category you choose.

5. Select the formatting options you want to use. The Sample information box shows a sample of the format applied to the current cell's contents.

6. Select OK. Excel returns you to the worksheet with the new formatting applied.

As an alternative to the Format Cells dialog box, Excel offers several keyboard shortcuts for setting the numeric format. Select the cell or range you want to format, and use one of the key combinations listed in Table 16.1.

Table 16.1. Shortcut keys for selecting numeric formats.

Shortcut Key	Format
Ctrl+~	General
Ctrl+!	Number (two decimal places; using thousands separator)
Ctrl+$	Currency (two decimal places; using dollar sign; negative numbers surrounded by parentheses)
Ctrl+%	Percentage (no decimal places)
Ctrl+^	Scientific (two decimal places)

If your mouse is nearby, you can use the tools in the formatting toolbar as another method of selecting numeric formats. Here are the four available tools:

Button	Name	Format
$	Currency Style	Accounting (two decimal places; using dollar sign)
%	Percent Style	Percentage (no decimal places)
,	Comma Style	Number (two decimal places; using thousands separator)
+.0 .00	Increase Decimal	Increases the number of decimal places in the current format
.00 +.0	Decrease Decimal	Decreases the number of decimal places in the current format

Date and Time Display Formats

If you include dates or times in your worksheets, you need to make sure that they're presented in a readable, unambiguous format. For example, most people would interpret the date 8/5/94 as August 5, 1994. However, in some countries this date would mean May 8, 1994. Similarly, if you use the time 2:45, do you mean AM or PM? To avoid these kinds of problems, you can use Excel's built-in date and time formats, which are listed in Table 16.2.

Table 16.2. Excel's date and time formats.

Format	Display
m/d	8/3
m/d/yy	8/3/95
mm/dd/yy	08/03/95
d-mmm	3-Aug
d-mmm-yy	3-Aug-95
dd-mmm-yy	03-Aug-95
mmm-yy	Aug-95
mmmm-yy	August-95
mmmm d, yyyy	August 3, 1995
h:mm AM/PM	3:10 PM
h:mm:ss AM/PM	3:10:45 PM
h:mm	15:10
h:mm:ss	15:10:45
mm:ss.0	10:45.7
[h]:[mm]:[ss]	25:61:61
m/d/yy h:mm AM/PM	8/23/94 3:10 PM
m/d/yy h:mm	8/23/94 15:10

The [h]:[mm]:[ss] format might require a bit more explanation. You use this format when you want to display hours greater than 24 or minutes and seconds greater than 60. For example, suppose you have an application in which you need to sum several time values (for example, the time you've spent working on a project). If you add, say, 10:00 and 15:00, Excel normally shows the total as 1:00 (since, by default, Excel restarts times at 0 when they hit 24:00). To display the result properly (that is, as 25:00), use the format [h]:00.

You use the same methods you used for numeric formats to select date and time formats. In particular, you can specify the date and time format as you input your data. For example, entering Jan-94 automatically formats the cell with the mmm-yy format. Also, you can use the following shortcut keys:

Shortcut Key	Format
Ctrl+#	d-mmm-yy
Ctrl+@	h:mm AM/PM
Ctrl+;	Current date (m/d/yy)
Ctrl+:	Current time (h:mm AM/PM)

TIP

Excel for the Macintosh uses a different date system than Excel for Windows uses. If you share files between these environments, you need to use Macintosh dates in your Excel for Windows worksheets in order to maintain the correct dates when you move from one system to another. Select Tools | Options, click the Calculation tab, and check the 1904 Date System check box.

Aligning Cell Contents

When you place data in an unformatted cell, Excel aligns text entries with the left edge of the cell, numbers and dates with the right edge of the cell, and error and logical values in the center of the cell. This is the default General alignment scheme. Although this format is useful for distinguishing text entries from numerical ones, it tends to make a worksheet look messy and poorly organized. To remedy this problem, Excel gives you various alignment options.

You set alignment attributes by selecting the Format | Cells command. Then choose the Alignment tab in the Format Cells dialog box, shown in Figure 16.2.

FIGURE 16.2.

Use the Alignment tab to align the contents of your cells.

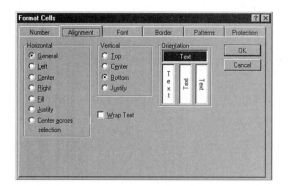

This tab is divided into four areas: Horizontal, Vertical, Orientation, and Wrap Text. The Horizontal section contains the following options (see Figure 16.3 for an example of each option):

- General—Uses the default alignment settings.
- Left—Left aligns the cell contents.
- Center—Centers the cell contents.
- Right—Right aligns the cell contents.
- Fill—Repeats the contents of the cell until the cell is filled.

■ Justify—Aligns the cell contents with the left and right edges of the cell. For text entries longer than the cell width, the cell height is increased to accommodate the text.

■ Center across selection—Centers the cell contents across the selected range.

FIGURE 16.3.

The horizontal alignment options.

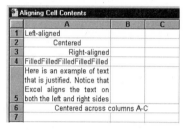

Excel's formatting toolbar also boasts several buttons that can make your alignment chores a bit easier:

Button	Name	Function
	Align Left	Left-aligns cell contents.
	Center	Centers cell contents.
	Align Right	Right-aligns cell contents.
	Center Across Columns	Centers a cell across the selection.

If you increase the height of a row (as explained in the section "Working with Columns and Rows"), the Vertical section of the Alignment tab enables you to position cell entries vertically using the following options (see Figure 16.4 for an example of each option):

■ Top—Aligns the cell contents with the top of the cell.

■ Center—Aligns the cell contents with the center of the cell.

■ Bottom—Aligns the cell contents with the bottom of the cell.

■ Justify—Justifies the cell contents vertically.

The Orientation section of the Alignment tab enables you to orient your cell entries in four ways: left to right (normal), vertically, sideways with characters running from bottom to top, and sideways with characters running from top to bottom (although this doesn't necessarily mean the top and bottom of the cell boundaries). Figure 16.5 shows an example of each option.

FIGURE 16.4.

The vertical alignment options.

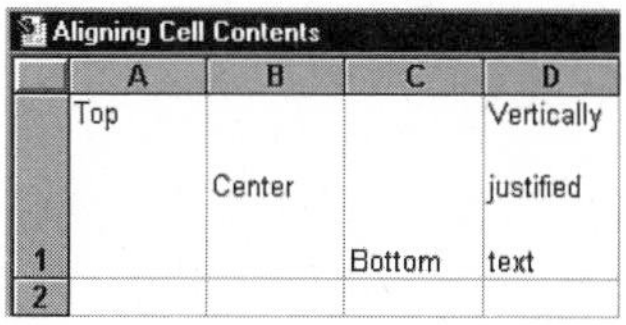

FIGURE 16.5.

The orientation alignment options.

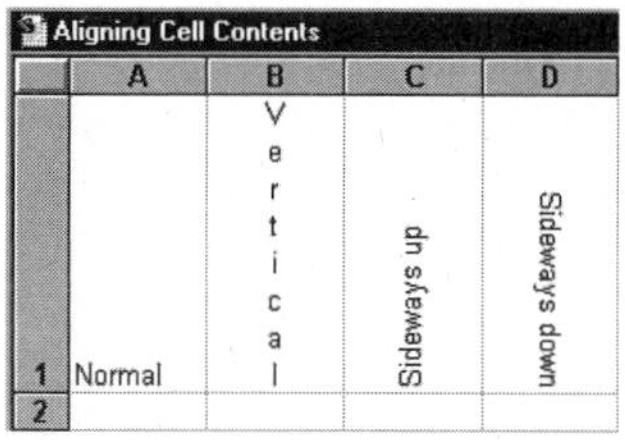

NOTE

If you choose either the vertical or the sideways orientation with a long text entry, you have to adjust the height of the cell to see all the text. See "Working with Columns and Rows," later in this chapter, for instructions on adjusting row height.

The final option in the Alignment tab is the Wrap Text check box, which enables you to wrap long cell entries so that they're displayed on multiple lines in a single cell. (See Figure 16.6.) You can left align, center, right align, or justify wrapped entries.

FIGURE 16.6.

The Word Wrap alignment option.

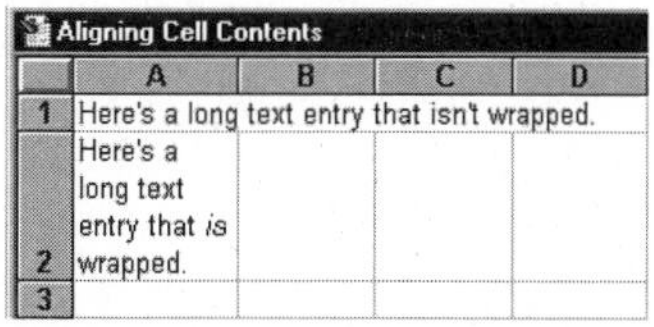

TIP

You can enter carriage returns and tabs in your wrapped cells. To enter a carriage return, position the cursor in the cell and press Alt+Enter. To enter a tab, press Ctrl+Alt+Tab.

Working with Cell Borders

Excel enables you to place borders of various weights and patterns around your worksheet cells. This is useful for enclosing different parts of the worksheet, defining data entry areas, and marking totals.

You apply cell borders by selecting Format | Cells and then choosing the Border tab in the Format Cells dialog box, shown in Figure 16.7. This tab is divided into three sections: Border, Style, and Color.

FIGURE 16.7.

The Border tab in the Format Cells dialog box.

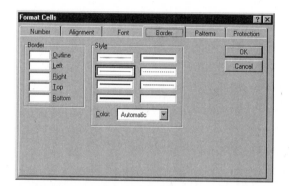

TIP

To see your borders better, turn off the worksheet gridlines. Choose Tools | Options, select the View tab, and deactivate the Gridlines check box.

The Style section contains the eight border styles you can use. The Border section applies the chosen style using the following five options:

- Outline—Applies the currently selected border style to the outer edges of the selected range.

- Left—Applies the currently selected border style to the left edge of each cell in the selected range.

- Right—Applies the currently selected border style to the right edge of each cell in the selected range.

- Top—Applies the currently selected border style to the top edge of each cell in the selected range.

- Bottom—Applies the currently selected border style to the bottom edge of each cell in the selected range.

TIP

Press Ctrl+& (ampersand) to put an outline border around the selected cells. Press Ctrl+_ (underscore) to remove all borders from the selected cells.

Follow these steps to apply a border to a cell or range:

1. Select the cell or range to be bordered.
2. Select Format│Cells, and then select the Border tab in the Format Cells dialog box.
3. Select the border location from the Border section of the dialog box. Excel displays a sample of the currently selected border style beside the Border option.
4. Select a different border style if necessary. When you select a style, a sample appears in the box to the left of the selected Border option.
5. Select OK. Excel returns you to the worksheet with the borders applied.

Figure 16.8 shows how you can use cell borders to create an invoice form. In a business document such as this, your borders should be strictly functional. You should avoid the merely decorative, and, as in Figure 16.8, you should make your borders serve a purpose, whether it's marking a data area or separating parts of the form.

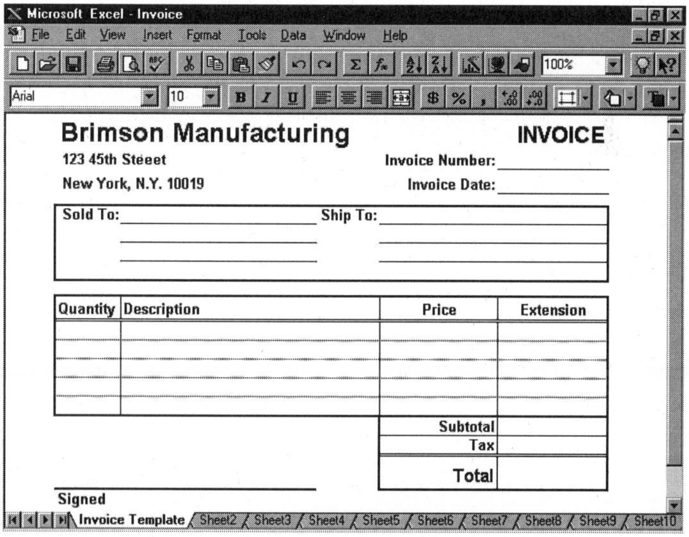

FIGURE 16.8.

Using cell borders to create an invoice form.

Working with Columns and Rows

An easy way to improve the appearance of your worksheet is to manipulate its rows and columns. This section teaches you how to adjust column widths and row heights. It also explains how to hide and unhide entire rows and columns, gridlines, and headings.

Adjusting Column Widths

You can use column width adjustments to improve the appearance of your worksheet in various ways:

■ When you're faced with a truncated text entry or a number that Excel shows as ######, you can enlarge the column so that the entry will be displayed in full.

■ If your worksheet contains many numbers, you can widen the columns to spread out the numbers and make the worksheet less cluttered.

■ You can make your columns smaller so that the entire worksheet fits onscreen or on a single printed page.

■ You can adjust the column width so that the entire worksheet creates a grid for a timeline chart.

Excel measures column width in characters. When you create a new worksheet, each column uses a standard width of 8.43 characters. The actual column width you see onscreen depends on the width of the default font. For example, the standard column width with 10-point Arial (7 pixels per character unit) is only half the size of the standard width with 20-point Arial (14 pixels per character unit). You can use any of the following four methods to adjust your column widths:

■ Enter a specific column width.

■ Use the mouse to set the column width.

■ Set the standard width for all columns.

■ Have Excel set the width automatically with the AutoFit feature.

Method One: Entering a Specific Column Width

Excel enables you to set column widths as short as 0 characters or as long as 255 characters. To enter a column width, follow these steps:

1. Select at least one cell in each column that you want to adjust.

2. Select Format | Column | Width. Excel displays the Column Width dialog box, shown in Figure 16.9. The Column Width edit box shows the width of the selected columns. (This box is blank if you've chosen columns with varying widths.)

> **TIP**
>
> To quickly open the Column Width dialog box, right-click the column header and then choose Column Width from the shortcut menu.

3. Enter the desired width in the Column Width edit box.

4. Select OK. Excel sets the column width and returns you to the worksheet.

FIGURE 16.9.

Use the Column Width dialog box to set the width for the selected columns.

When entering column widths, you can use an integer or a decimal number. If, however, you enter a width such as 10.1 and call up the Column Width dialog box for the same column, you'll notice that the Column Width edit box actually says 10.14. What happened is that Excel adjusted the column width to the nearest pixel. For 10-point Arial (Excel's default font), a character unit has 7 pixels, or roughly 0.143 characters per pixel. This means that Excel will round a column width of 10.1 to 10.14. Similarly, a width of 9.35 is rounded down to 9.29.

Method Two: Using the Mouse to Set the Column Width

You can bypass the Column Width dialog box by using the mouse to drag a column to the width you want. The following procedure lists the steps that are involved:

1. Move the mouse pointer to the column header area, and position the pointer at the right edge of the column you want to adjust. The mouse pointer changes to the shape shown in Figure 16.10.

FIGURE 16.10.

You can use the mouse to adjust the column width.

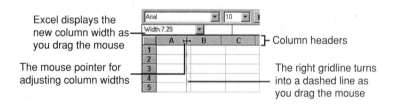

2. Press and hold down the left mouse button. The formula bar's Name box displays the current column width, and the column's right gridline turns into a dashed line, as shown in Figure 16.10.

3. Drag the pointer left or right to the desired width. As you move the pointer, the formula bar displays the new width.

4. Release the mouse button. Excel adjusts the column width accordingly.

You can use this technique to set the width of several columns at once. For every column you want to adjust, select the entire column and then perform the preceding steps on any one column. Excel applies the new width to each selected column.

Method Three: Setting the Standard Width for All the Columns

Using Excel's standard font, the standard column width is 8.43. You can change this width by following these steps:

1. Select the Format | Column | Standard Width command. Excel displays the Standard Width dialog box, shown in Figure 16.11.

FIGURE 16.11.

Use the Standard Width dialog box to set the width for all the worksheet's columns.

2. Enter the desired width in the Standard Column Width edit box.

3. Select OK. Excel applies the new column width to all the columns in the worksheet (except those not using the standard width).

Method Four: Using Excel's AutoFit Feature

If you have a long column of entries of varying widths, it might take you a few tries to get the optimum column width. To avoid guesswork, you can have Excel set the width automatically using the AutoFit feature. When you use this feature, Excel examines the column's contents and sets the width slightly larger than the longest entry.

To use AutoFit, select each column you want to adjust, and then select Format | Column | AutoFit Selection. Excel adjusts the columns to their optimal width and returns you to the worksheet.

> **TIP**
>
> To quickly set the AutoFit width, position the mouse pointer at the right edge of the column header and double-click.

Adjusting Row Height

You can set the height of your worksheet rows by using techniques similar to those used for adjusting column widths. Excel normally adjusts row heights automatically to accommodate the tallest font in a row. However, you can make your own height adjustments to give your worksheet more breathing room or to reduce the amount of space taken up by unused rows.

> **CAUTION**
>
> When reducing a row height, always keep the height larger than the tallest font to avoid cutting off the tops of any characters.

Excel measures row height in points—the same units used for type size. When you create a new worksheet, Excel assigns a standard row height of 12.75 points, which is high enough to accommodate the default 10-point Arial font. If you were to change the default font to 20-point Arial, each row height would increase accordingly.

You can use any of these three methods to adjust row heights:

- Enter a specific row height.
- Use the mouse to set the row height.
- Have Excel set the height automatically using the AutoFit feature.

Method One: Entering a Specific Row Height

Excel enables you to set row heights as small as 0 points or as large as 409 points. To enter a row height, follow these steps:

1. Select at least one cell in each row you want to adjust.
2. Select the Format|Row|Height command. Excel displays the Row Height dialog box, shown in Figure 16.12. The Row Height edit box shows the height of the selected rows. (This box is blank if you've chosen rows with varying heights.)

FIGURE 16.12.

Use the Row Height dialog box to set the height for the selected rows.

> **TIP**
>
> To quickly open the Row Height dialog box, right-click the row header, and then choose Row Height from the shortcut menu.

3. Enter the height you want in the Row Height edit box.
4. Select OK. Excel sets the row height and returns you to the worksheet.

Method Two: Using the Mouse to Set the Row Height

You can avoid the Row Height dialog box by using the mouse to drag a row to the height you want. Here's how it's done:

1. Move the mouse pointer to the row header area and position the pointer at the bottom edge of the row you want to adjust. The mouse pointer changes to the shape shown in Figure 16.13.

FIGURE 16.13.

You can use the mouse to adjust the row height.

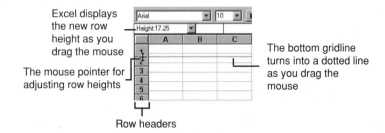

Excel displays the new row height as you drag the mouse

The mouse pointer for adjusting row heights

The bottom gridline turns into a dotted line as you drag the mouse

Row headers

2. Press and hold down the left mouse button. The formula bar displays the current row height, and the row's bottom gridline turns into a dashed line, as shown in Figure 16.13.

3. Drag the pointer up or down to reach the desired height. As you move the pointer, the formula bar displays the new height.

4. Release the mouse button. Excel adjusts the row height accordingly.

You can use this technique to set the height of several rows at once. For every row you want to adjust, select the entire row and then perform the preceding steps. Excel applies the new height to each row.

Method Three: Using Excel's AutoFit Feature

If you've made several font changes and height adjustments to a long row of entries, you might need to try several times to set an optimum row height. To save time, you can use Excel's AutoFit feature to set the height automatically to the best fit.

To try it out, select each row you want to adjust, and then select Format | Row | AutoFit. Excel adjusts the rows to their optimal height and returns you to the worksheet.

> **TIP**
>
> To quickly set the AutoFit height, position the mouse pointer at the bottom edge of the row header and double-click.

Hiding Columns and Rows

Your worksheets might contain confidential information (such as payroll figures) or unimportant information (such as the period numbers used when calculating interest payments). In either case, you can hide the appropriate columns or rows when showing your worksheet to others. The data remains intact but isn't displayed onscreen. The next two sections show you how to hide and unhide columns and rows.

Hiding Columns

Hiding a column is equivalent to setting the column width to 0. Instead of adjusting the column width directly, however, you can hide the current column (or multiple columns, if you first select a cell in each column) by using any of the following techniques:

- Select Format | Column | Hide.
- Press Ctrl+0.
- Right-click the column header and then choose Hide from the shortcut menu.
- Position the mouse pointer on the right edge of the column header; then drag the pointer to the left, past the left edge of the column header.

When you hide a column, the column letter no longer appears in the headers. For example, Figure 16.14 shows a worksheet with confidential payroll information in columns C, D, and E. Figure 16.15 shows the same worksheet with these columns hidden and their letters missing from the column headers. You still can, however, refer to cells in the hidden columns in formulas and searches.

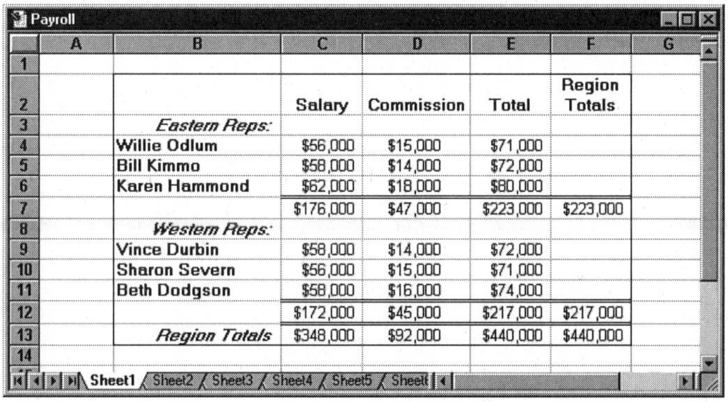

FIGURE 16.14.

Columns C, D, and E contain confidential information.

	A	B	C	D	E	F	G
1							
2			Salary	Commission	Total	Region Totals	
3		*Eastern Reps:*					
4		Willie Odlum	$56,000	$15,000	$71,000		
5		Bill Kimmo	$58,000	$14,000	$72,000		
6		Karen Hammond	$62,000	$18,000	$80,000		
7			$176,000	$47,000	$223,000	$223,000	
8		*Western Reps:*					
9		Vince Durbin	$58,000	$14,000	$72,000		
10		Sharon Severn	$56,000	$15,000	$71,000		
11		Beth Dodgson	$58,000	$16,000	$74,000		
12			$172,000	$45,000	$217,000	$217,000	
13		*Region Totals*	$348,000	$92,000	$440,000	$440,000	
14							

FIGURE 16.15.

The same worksheet with columns C, D, and E hidden.

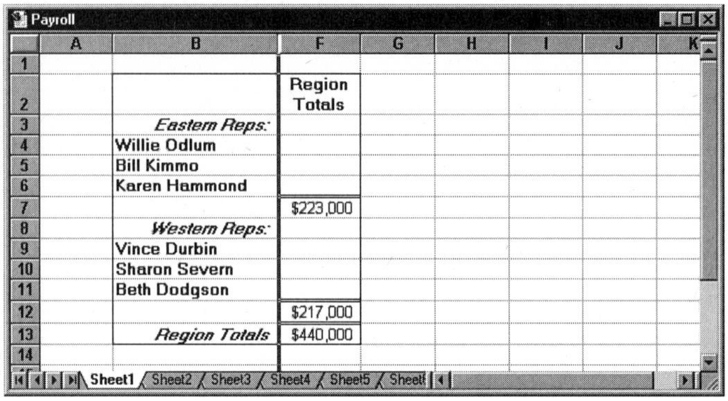

	A	B	F	G	H	I	J	K
1								
2			Region Totals					
3		*Eastern Reps:*						
4		Willie Odlum						
5		Bill Kimmo						
6		Karen Hammond						
7			$223,000					
8		*Western Reps:*						
9		Vince Durbin						
10		Sharon Severn						
11		Beth Dodgson						
12			$217,000					
13		*Region Totals*	$440,000					
14								

Payroll — Sheet1 / Sheet2 / Sheet3 / Sheet4 / Sheet5 / Sheet6

Unhiding Columns

To unhide a range of columns, first select at least one cell from each column on either side of the hidden columns. For example, to unhide columns C, D, and E, select a cell in columns B and F. Then use any of the following techniques:

■ Choose Format | Column | Unhide.

■ Press Ctrl+).

■ Right-click the selection and then choose Unhide from the shortcut menu.

What do you do, though, if you want to unhide just a single column out of a group of hidden columns (for example, column C out of columns C, D, and E)? Here are the steps to follow:

1. Choose Edit | Go To, or press F5. Excel displays the Go To dialog box.

2. Enter a cell address in the column you want to unhide. For example, to unhide column C, enter c1.

3. Select OK. Excel moves to the cell address.

4. Choose Format | Column | Unhide or Ctrl+). Excel unhides the column and returns you to the worksheet.

Hiding Rows

Hiding rows is similar to hiding columns. First, select at least one cell in every row you want to hide. Then try one of the following methods:

■ Choose Format | Row | Hide.

■ Press Ctrl+9.

■ Right-click the row header and then choose Hide from the shortcut menu.

■ Position the mouse pointer on the bottom edge of the row header; then drag the pointer up past the top edge of the row header.

As with columns, when you hide a row, the row number no longer appears in the headers. You still can, however, refer to cells in the hidden rows in formulas and searches.

Unhiding Rows

To unhide a range of rows, begin by selecting at least one cell from each row on either side of the hidden rows. For example, to unhide rows 3, 4, and 5, select a cell in rows 2 and 6. Then use one of the following techniques:

- Choose Format | Row | Unhide.
- Press Ctrl+(.
- Right-click the selected rows and then choose Unhide from the shortcut menu.

If you want to unhide a single row out of a group of hidden rows (for example, row 3 out of rows 3, 4, and 5), use the following procedure:

1. Choose the Edit | Go To command, or press F5 to display the Go To dialog box.
2. Enter a cell address in the row you want to unhide. For example, to unhide row 3, enter A3.
3. Select OK. Excel moves to the cell address.
4. Choose Format | Row | Unhide, or press Ctrl+(. Excel unhides the rows and returns you to the worksheet.

Working with Styles

Depending on the options you choose, formatting a single cell or range can take dozens of mouse clicks or keystrokes. If you plan to use a specific formatting combination repeatedly, don't re-invent the wheel each time. Using Excel's Style feature, you can summarize any combination of formatting options under a single style name and then apply the whole combination in a single operation.

Styles also save time if you need to reformat your document. Normally, you would have to select every cell containing the format you want to change (including blank cells) and then make the adjustments. With styles, you just redefine the style, and Excel updates all the associated cells automatically.

A style can contain most of the formatting features you've learned about in this chapter, including fonts, alignment, borders, and patterns, as well as number, date, and time formats. Excel also comes with several built-in styles: Comma, Comma [0], Currency, Currency [0], Percent, and Normal. Normal is the default style for the entire workbook.

Applying a Style

Here are the steps to follow to apply a style:

1. Select the cell or range you want to format.

2. Select the Format | Style command. Excel displays the Style dialog box, shown in Figure 16.16.

FIGURE 16.16.

Use the Style dialog box to apply a style.

3. Select the style you want from the Style Name drop-down list. A description of the formatting options included in the selected style appears in the Style Includes group.

4. If you don't want to use some part of the style, deactivate the appropriate check box in the Style Includes group.

5. Select OK. Excel applies the style to the selected cells.

When you apply a style to a cell, Excel overwrites the cell's existing format. Similarly, if you apply a style first and then format the cell, the new formatting overwrites the style. In both cases, however, only defined attributes change. For example, if you apply the Percent style to a cell already formatted as left aligned, the alignment doesn't change.

Creating a Style

Besides using the built-in styles supplied by Excel, you can define your own styles to suit your needs. Any style you create appears in the Style Name list for that workbook. Excel provides three ways to define styles:

- By example
- By definition
- By merging styles from another document

NOTE

It's a good idea to create a style for frequently used sections of your worksheet. For example, a Heading style would contain attributes of your worksheet headings, and a Title style would contain your worksheet title format.

Creating a Style by Example

If you have a cell that contains a format combination you want to use as a style, you can tell Excel to define a new style based on the cell format. This is called the *style by example* method, and you follow these steps to use it:

1. Select the cell that contains the format combination you want to turn into a style.
2. Select the Format | Style command to display the Style dialog box.
3. Type the new style name in the Style Name edit box.
4. Select OK. Excel creates the new style.

You can select multiple cells to use as an example. In this case, Excel assigns only formats that the cells have in common. For example, suppose that you have one cell that's left aligned with a border and another that's left aligned without a border. If you select both cells to use as your example, Excel defines the new style as left aligned only.

Using the AutoFormat Feature

Excel offers a feature that enables you to format any worksheet range easily. This feature, called *AutoFormat*, can automatically apply certain predefined format combinations to create attractive, professional-quality tables and lists.

There are 16 predefined AutoFormat combinations. Each combination uses selected format options to display numbers, fonts, borders, and patterns and to set cell alignment, column width, and row height. AutoFormat doesn't just apply a single format combination to each cell. Instead, it applies separate formatting for row and column headings, data, and summary lines (for example, subtotals and totals). If you have formatting that you want left intact, you can tell Excel to leave out the appropriate format options from the automatic format. For example, if you've already set up your font options, you can exclude the font formats from the AutoFormat table.

> **CAUTION**
>
> You can't apply AutoFormat to a single cell or to a noncontiguous range. If you try, Excel displays an error message. You can, however, select a single cell if it's within a table. Excel detects the surrounding table automatically.

Here are the basic steps to follow to use the AutoFormat feature:

1. Select the range you want to format.
2. Select the Format | AutoFormat command. Excel displays the AutoFormat dialog box, shown in Figure 16.17.

FIGURE 16.17.

The AutoFormat dialog box.

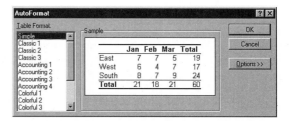

3. Select a format combination from the Table Format list box. An example of each format appears in the Sample box.
4. To exclude formatting, click the Options button, and in the Formats to Apply section that appears, uncheck the format types you want to exclude. The displayed example adjusts accordingly.
5. Select OK. Excel applies the formatting to the range you selected.

When using the AutoFormat feature, keep the following points in mind:

■ AutoFormat usually assumes that the top row and the left column in your range contain the range headings. To avoid improper formatting, be sure to include your headings when you select the range.

■ Each table format uses the typeface defined in the Normal font. To use a different typeface in all your AutoFormat tables, change the Normal font to the typeface you want.

■ The Classic table formats are designed to be used in any worksheet to make your data more readable. Headings and totals are set off with borders or shading.

■ The Financial table formats can be used in any worksheet that contains currency values. Initial data values and totals are formatted as currency.

■ The Colorful table formats are suitable for onscreen or slide presentations or for reports produced on a color printer.

- The List table formats can be used with lists and databases. Shading and borders are used to make the data more readable.

- The 3-D Effects table formats give your worksheets a professional-quality appearance suitable for any presentation.

Displaying Multiple Workbook Windows

As a user of the Windows environment, you know what an advantage it is to have multiple applications running in their own windows. Most Windows applications take this concept a step further by enabling you to open multiple documents in their own windows. However, Excel goes one better by enabling you to open multiple windows for the *same* document.

When you open a second window on a workbook, you're not opening a new file; you're viewing the same file twice. You can navigate independently in each window, so you can display different parts of a workbook at the same time. Excel even enables you to change the workbook display for every window.

Opening a New Workbook Window

To open another window for the current workbook, select the Window|New Window command. When Excel opens a new window, it changes the names appearing in the workbook title bar. Excel appends :1 to the title of the original window, and it appends :2 to the title of the second window. Figure 16.18 shows an example using the 1994 Sales workbook. Notice that the original window now has the title 1994 Sales:1, and the new window has the title 1994 Sales:2.

FIGURE 16.18.

Two windows containing the same workbook.

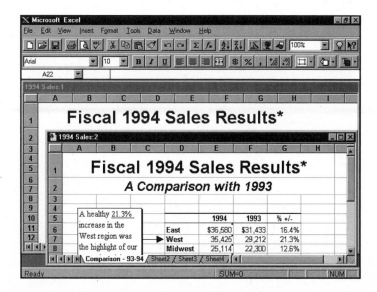

The number of windows you can open for a workbook is limited by your computer's memory. (With Windows 95's improved memory handling, however, you shouldn't have any trouble opening as many windows as you need.) Any window you open can be moved and sized to suit your taste. Because each window is a view of the same workbook, any editing or formatting changes you make in one window are automatically reflected in all the other windows.

> **NOTE**
>
> You can use multiple windows to make data entry easier. Open one window for the data-entry area, and then use other windows to display, say, a list of data codes (for example, parts numbers or general ledger accounts).

Navigating Workbook Windows

After you've opened two or more windows, you'll need to switch between them. Use any of the following techniques to navigate among workbook windows:

■ Click any visible part of a window to activate it.

■ Pull down the Window menu and select one of the windows listed at the bottom of the menu. Excel displays a check mark beside the currently active window.

■ Press Ctrl+Tab to move to the next window. Press Ctrl+Shift+Tab to move to the preceding window.

Arranging Workbook Windows

One of the problems with having several windows open at once is that they tend to get in each other's way. In most cases, it's preferable to give each window its own portion of the work area. Even though you can move and size windows yourself, you might prefer to have Excel handle this task for you. You can do this by selecting the Window|Arrange command to display the Arrange Windows dialog box, shown in Figure 16.19. The Arrange section contains the following options:

■ Tiled—Divides the work area into rectangles of approximately equal size (called tiles) and assigns each open window to a tile.

■ Horizontal—Divides the work area into horizontal strips of equal size and assigns each open window to a strip.

■ Vertical—Divides the work area into vertical strips of equal size and assigns each open window to a strip.

■ Cascade—Arranges the windows so that they overlap each other and so that you can see each window's title bar.

FIGURE 16.19.

*Use the Arrange Windows
dialog box to arrange your
open windows.*

If you have other workbooks open at the same time and you want to arrange only the current
workbook windows, activate the Windows of Active Workbook check box in the Arrange Windows dialog box. This tells Excel to apply the selected Arrange option to the current workbook
windows only. When you're done, select OK to arrange the windows.

If you don't want to include a window in an arrangement, activate the window and select the
Window | Hide command. Excel removes the window from the screen, but the window remains open in memory. To view the window again, select Window | Unhide and select the
window from the Unhide dialog box that appears.

Displaying Multiple Worksheet Panes

Another way to simultaneously view different parts of a large worksheet is to use Excel's Split
feature. You can use Split to divide a worksheet into two or four *panes* in which each pane
displays a different area of the sheet. The panes scroll simultaneously horizontally and vertically. You also can freeze the panes to keep a worksheet area in view at all times.

Splitting a Worksheet into Panes

Depending on the type of split you want, you can use one of the following two methods to
split your worksheets:

- Use the Window | Split command to split the worksheet into four panes at the selected
  cell. (Later, you can adjust the split to two panes if you like.)
- Use the horizontal or vertical split boxes to split the worksheet into two panes at a
  position you specify (horizontally or vertically).

Using the Split Command

When you use the Split command, Excel splits the worksheet into four panes at the currently
selected cell. How do you know which cell to select? Look at Figure 16.20, which shows the
Amortization worksheet with cell C6 selected.

The results of splitting the worksheet by selecting the Window | Split command are shown in
Figure 16.21. Notice that Excel places the *horizontal split bar* on the top edge of the selected
cell's row and the *vertical split bar* on the left edge of the selected cell's column. This feature is

convenient because now the loan variables are in the upper-left pane, the periods and months are in the lower-left pane, the title and column headings are in the upper-right pane, and the loan data is in the lower-right pane. The panes are synchronized so that as you move down through the loan data, the period and month values also move down.

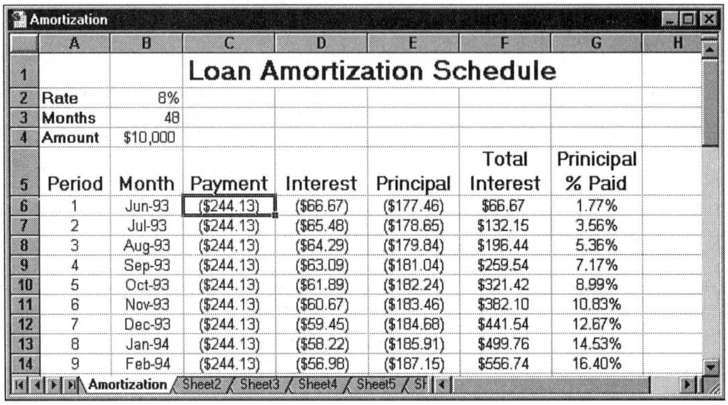

FIGURE 16.20.

The Amortization worksheet before splitting.

If the split isn't where you want it, you can always use your mouse to drag the vertical or horizontal split bar. To move both bars at the same time, drag the intersection point.

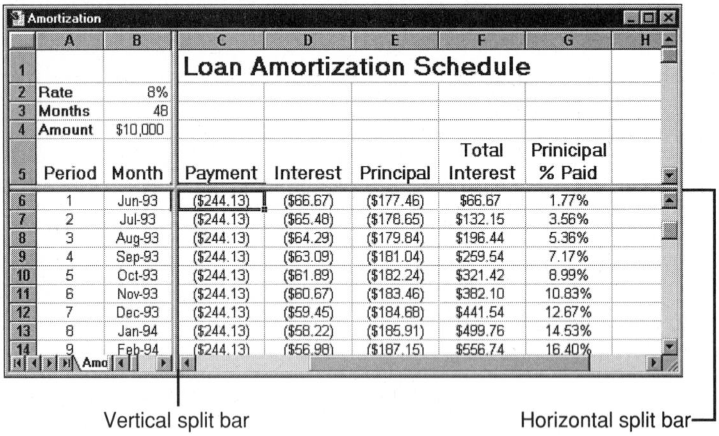

FIGURE 16.21.

The Amortization worksheet after it is split.

Vertical split bar   Horizontal split bar

Using the Window Split Boxes

Using the mouse, you can use the horizontal and vertical split boxes to create a two-pane split. The horizontal split box is the small button located between the vertical scrollbar's up arrow and the window's Close button. (See Figure 16.22.) The vertical split box is the small button to the right of the horizontal scrollbar's right arrow. (See Figure 16.22.)

FIGURE 16.22.

You can use the split boxes to split a worksheet.

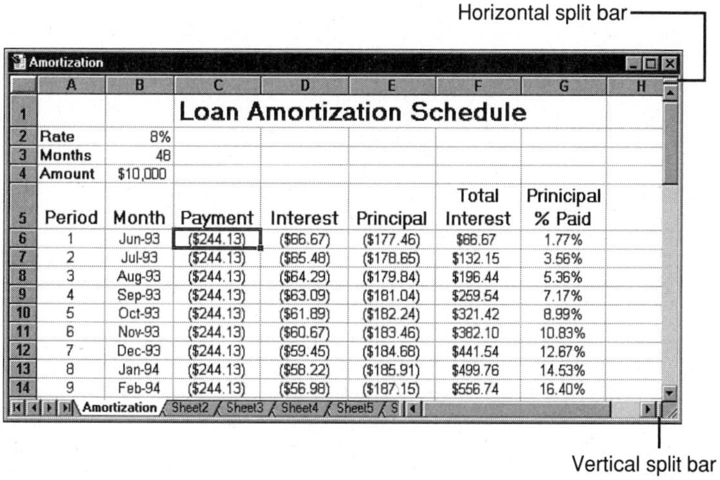

Horizontal split bar —

Vertical split bar

Follow these steps to split a worksheet using the split boxes:

1. Position the mouse pointer on the split box you want. The pointer changes to a two-sided arrow.

2. Press and hold the left mouse button. Excel displays a light gray bar to indicate the current split position.

3. Drag the pointer to the desired split location.

4. Release the mouse button. Excel splits the worksheet at the selected location. The split box moves to the split location.

TIP

To remove the split, drag the split box back to its original location, or select the Window | Remove Split command.

Freezing Worksheet Titles

One of the problems with viewing multiple panes is that the work area can get confusing when some of the panes contain the same cells. For example, Figure 16.23 shows the Amortization worksheet split into four panes, each of which contains cell C8 in its upper-left corner. Clearly, such a display is meaningless. To prevent this situation from happening, you can *freeze* your panes so that areas displaying worksheet titles or column headings remain in place.

To try it out, first split the worksheet and then arrange each pane so that it shows the desired information (title, heading, and so on). Now select the Window | Freeze Panes command. Excel replaces the thick gray split bars with thin black freeze bars.

FIGURE 16.23.

Split worksheets often can become confusing.

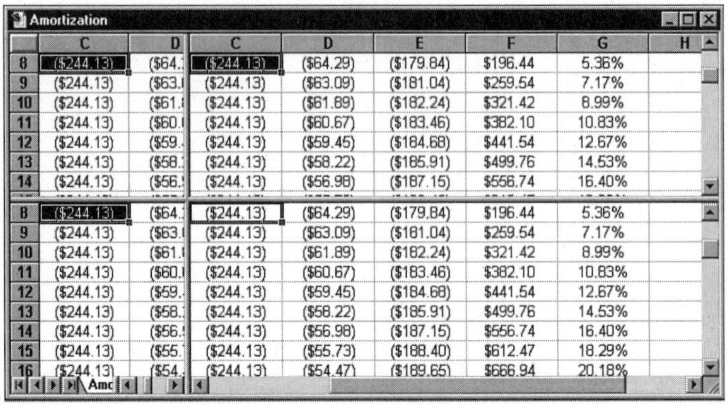

Amortization

	C	D	C	D	E	F	G	H
8	($244.13)	($64.	($244.13)	($64.29)	($179.84)	$196.44	5.36%	
9	($244.13)	($63.(	($244.13)	($63.09)	($181.04)	$259.54	7.17%	
10	($244.13)	($61.:	($244.13)	($61.89)	($182.24)	$321.42	8.99%	
11	($244.13)	($60.(	($244.13)	($60.67)	($183.46)	$382.10	10.83%	
12	($244.13)	($59..	($244.13)	($59.45)	($184.68)	$441.54	12.67%	
13	($244.13)	($58.	($244.13)	($58.22)	($185.91)	$499.76	14.53%	
14	($244.13)	($56.!	($244.13)	($56.98)	($187.15)	$556.74	16.40%	

	C	D	C	D	E	F	G	H
8	($244.13)	($64.	($244.13)	($64.29)	($179.84)	$196.44	5.36%	
9	($244.13)	($63.(	($244.13)	($63.09)	($181.04)	$259.54	7.17%	
10	($244.13)	($61.:	($244.13)	($61.89)	($182.24)	$321.42	8.99%	
11	($244.13)	($60.(	($244.13)	($60.67)	($183.46)	$382.10	10.83%	
12	($244.13)	($59..	($244.13)	($59.45)	($184.68)	$441.54	12.67%	
13	($244.13)	($58.	($244.13)	($58.22)	($185.91)	$499.76	14.53%	
14	($244.13)	($56.!	($244.13)	($56.98)	($187.15)	$556.74	16.40%	
15	($244.13)	($55.	($244.13)	($55.73)	($188.40)	$612.47	18.29%	
16	($244.13)	($54.	($244.13)	($54.47)	($189.65)	$666.94	20.18%	

Amc

Figure 16.24 shows the Amortization worksheet with frozen panes. In this case, the panes were frozen from the split position shown in Figure 16.21. For this example, the frozen panes provide the following advantages:

- No matter where you move up or down in the worksheet, the column headings and loan variables remain visible.
- As you move up or down in the worksheet, the values in the bottom panes remain synchronized.
- No matter where you move left or right in the worksheet, the period and month values remain visible.
- As you move left or right in the worksheet, the values in the two right panes remain synchronized.

FIGURE 16.24.

The Amortization worksheet with frozen panes.

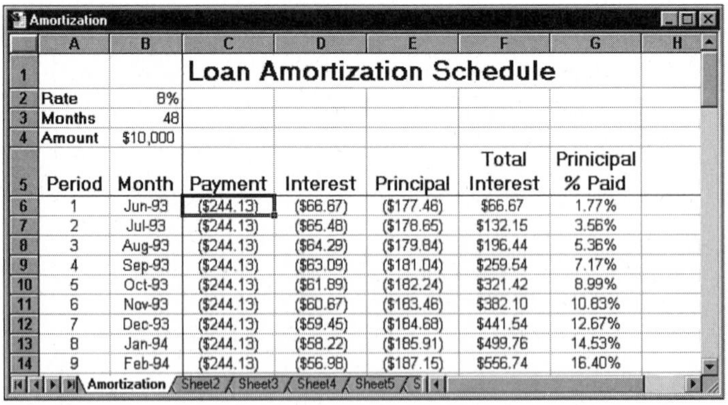

Amortization

	A	B	C	D	E	F	G	H
1			Loan Amortization Schedule					
2	Rate	8%						
3	Months	48						
4	Amount	$10,000						
5	Period	Month	Payment	Interest	Principal	Total Interest	Prinicipal % Paid	
6	1	Jun-93	($244.13)	($66.67)	($177.46)	$66.67	1.77%	
7	2	Jul-93	($244.13)	($65.48)	($178.65)	$132.15	3.56%	
8	3	Aug-93	($244.13)	($64.29)	($179.84)	$196.44	5.36%	
9	4	Sep-93	($244.13)	($63.09)	($181.04)	$259.54	7.17%	
10	5	Oct-93	($244.13)	($61.89)	($182.24)	$321.42	8.99%	
11	6	Nov-93	($244.13)	($60.67)	($183.46)	$382.10	10.83%	
12	7	Dec-93	($244.13)	($59.45)	($184.68)	$441.54	12.67%	
13	8	Jan-94	($244.13)	($58.22)	($185.91)	$499.76	14.53%	
14	9	Feb-94	($244.13)	($56.98)	($187.15)	$556.74	16.40%	

Amortization / Sheet2 / Sheet3 / Sheet4 / Sheet5 / S

TIP

To unfreeze panes without removing the splits, select the Window | Unfreeze Panes command. To unfreeze panes *and* remove the splits, select the Window | Remove Split command.

Using Outlines

Outlines? In a spreadsheet? Yes, those same creatures that caused you so much grief in high school English class also are available in Excel. In a worksheet outline, though, you can *collapse* sections of the sheet to display only summary cells (such as quarterly or regional totals, for example), or you can *expand* hidden sections to show the underlying detail.

The worksheet in Figure 16.25 displays monthly budget figures for various sales and expense items. The columns include quarterly subtotals and, although you can't see it in Figure 16.25, a grand total. The rows include subtotals for sales, expenses, and gross profit.

Suppose that you don't want to see so much detail. For example, you might need to see only the quarterly totals for each row, or you might want to hide the salary figures for a presentation you're making. An outline is the easiest way to do this. Figure 16.26 shows the same worksheet with an outline added (I'll explain shortly what the various symbols mean). Using this outline, you can hide whatever details you don't need to see. Figure 16.27 shows the worksheet with data hidden for the individual months and salaries. You can go even further. The view in Figure 16.28 shows only the sales and expenses totals and the grand totals.

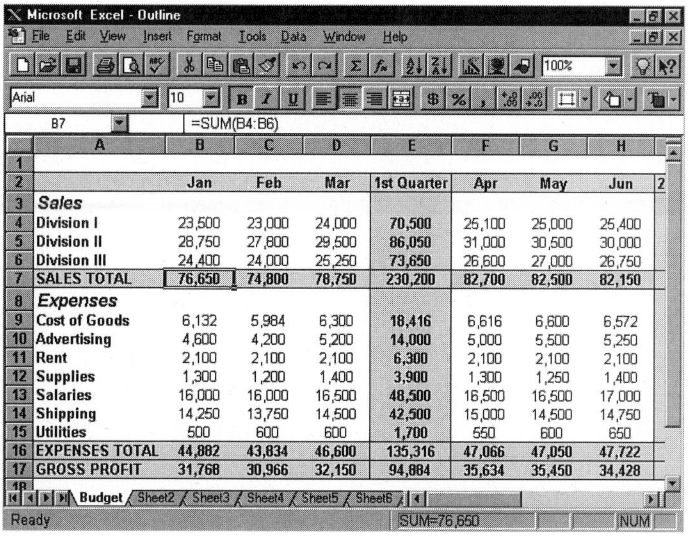

	A	B	C	D	E	F	G	H
1								
2		Jan	Feb	Mar	1st Quarter	Apr	May	Jun
3	*Sales*							
4	Division I	23,500	23,000	24,000	70,500	25,100	25,000	25,400
5	Division II	28,750	27,800	29,500	86,050	31,000	30,500	30,000
6	Division III	24,400	24,000	25,250	73,650	26,600	27,000	26,750
7	SALES TOTAL	76,650	74,800	78,750	230,200	82,700	82,500	82,150
8	*Expenses*							
9	Cost of Goods	6,132	5,984	6,300	18,416	6,616	6,600	6,572
10	Advertising	4,600	4,200	5,200	14,000	5,000	5,500	5,250
11	Rent	2,100	2,100	2,100	6,300	2,100	2,100	2,100
12	Supplies	1,300	1,200	1,400	3,900	1,300	1,250	1,400
13	Salaries	16,000	16,000	16,500	48,500	16,500	16,500	17,000
14	Shipping	14,250	13,750	14,500	42,500	15,000	14,500	14,750
15	Utilities	500	600	600	1,700	550	600	650
16	EXPENSES TOTAL	44,882	43,834	46,600	135,316	47,066	47,050	47,722
17	GROSS PROFIT	31,768	30,966	32,150	94,884	35,634	35,450	34,428

FIGURE 16.25.
A budget worksheet showing detail and summary data.

FIGURE 16.26.

The budget worksheet with outlining added.

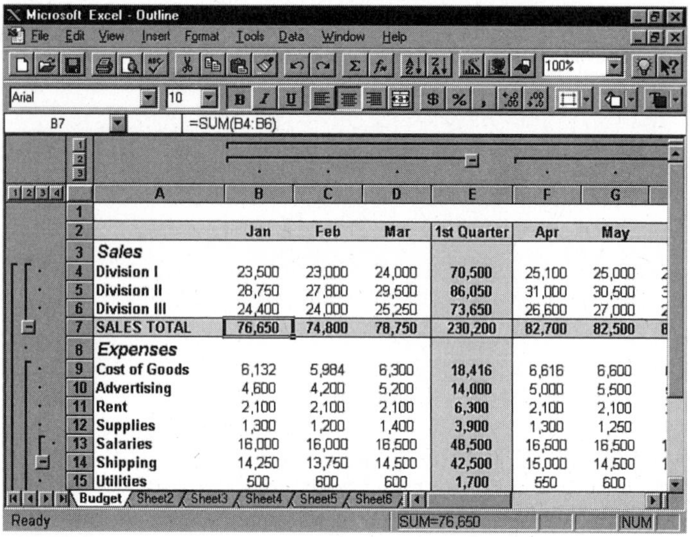

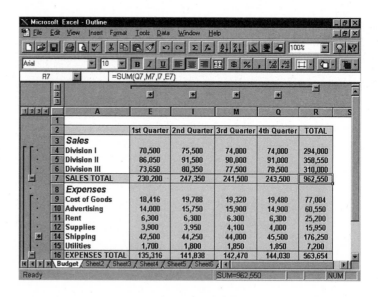

One of the big advantages of outlines is that as soon as you've hidden some data, you can work with the visible cells as though they were a single range. This means that you can format those cells quickly, print them, create charts, and so on.

FIGURE 16.27.

Outlining enables you to hide detail data you don't need to see.

FIGURE 16.28.

Outlines usually have several levels that enable you to hide even subtotals.

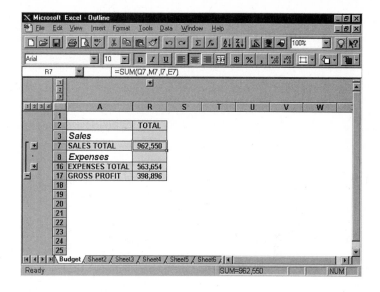

Creating an Outline Automatically

The easiest way to create an outline is to have Excel do it for you. (You can create an outline manually, too, as you'll see later.) Before you create an outline, you need to make sure that your worksheet is a candidate for outlining. There are two main criteria:

- The worksheet must contain formulas that reference cells or ranges directly adjacent to the formula cell. Worksheets with SUM() functions that subtotal cells above or to the left (such as the budget worksheet presented earlier) are particularly good candidates for outlining.

- There must be a consistent pattern to the direction of the formula references. For example, you can outline a worksheet containing formulas that always reference cells above or to the left. However, you can't outline a worksheet with, for example, SUM() functions that reference ranges above *and* below a formula cell.

After you determine that your worksheet is outline material, select the range of cells you want to outline. If you want to outline the entire worksheet, select only a single cell. Then choose the Data | Group and Outline | Auto Outline command. Excel creates the outline and displays the outline tools. (See Figure 16.29.)

FIGURE 16.29.

When you create an outline, Excel adds outline tools to the worksheet.

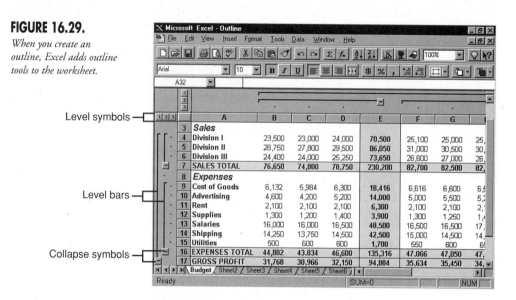

Level symbols

Level bars

Collapse symbols

Understanding the Outline Tools

When Excel creates an outline, it divides your worksheet into a hierarchy of *levels*. These levels range from the worksheet detail (the lowest level) to the grand totals (the highest level). Excel outlines can handle up to eight levels of data.

In the Budget worksheet, for example, Excel created three levels for both the column and the row data:

- In the columns, the monthly figures are the details, so they're the lowest level (level 3). The quarterly totals are the first summary data, so they're the next level (level 2). Finally, the grand totals are the highest level (level 1).

- In the rows, the individual sales and expense items are the details (level 3). The sales and expenses subtotals are the next level (level 2). The Gross Profit row is the highest level (level 1).

NOTE

Somewhat confusingly, Excel has set things up so that lower outline levels have higher level numbers. The way I remember it is that the higher the number, the more detail the level contains.

To help you work with your outlines, Excel adds the following tools to your worksheet:

- Level bars—These bars indicate the data included in the current level. Click a bar to hide the rows or columns marked by a bar.

- Collapse symbols—Click these symbols to hide (or *collapse*) the rows or columns marked by the attached level bar.
- Expand symbols—When you collapse a level, the collapse symbol changes to an expand symbol (+). Click this symbol to display (or *expand*) the hidden rows or columns.
- Level symbols—These symbols tell you which level each level bar is on. Click a level symbol to display all the detail data for that level.

TIP

To toggle the outline symbols on and off, press Ctrl+8.

Creating an Outline Manually

If you examine Figure 16.26 closely, you'll see that the Budget worksheet's rows have *four* outline levels, whereas the rows in Figure 16.29 have only three. Where did the extra level come from? I added it manually because I needed some way of collapsing the Salaries row. Because this row isn't a subtotal or some other formula, Excel ignores it (rightfully so) when creating an automatic outline.

If you would like more control over the outlining process, you can easily do it yourself. The idea is that you selectively *group* or *ungroup* rows or columns. When you group a range, you assign it to a lower outline level (that is, you give it a higher level number). When you ungroup a range, you assign it to a higher outline level.

Grouping Rows and Columns

The following procedure shows you how to group rows and columns:

1. If your detail data is in rows, select the rows you want to group. You can select at least one cell in each row, or you can select entire rows, thus saving a step later. (See Figure 16.30.) If your detail data is in columns, select the columns you want to group.

TIP

To select an entire row, click the row heading or press Shift+Spacebar. To select an entire column, click the column heading or press Ctrl+Spacebar.

FIGURE 16.30.

The Sales detail rows selected for grouping.

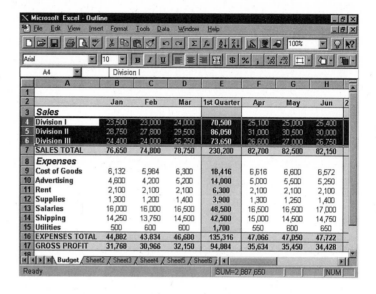

2. To group the selection, use any of the following techniques:

   Select the Data | Group and Outline | Group command.

   Press Alt+Shift+→.

    Click the Group button in the Query and Pivot toolbar.

   If you selected something other than entire rows or columns, Excel displays the Group dialog box, shown in Figure 16.31. Proceed to Step 3 to deal with this dialog box.

FIGURE 16.31.

If you didn't select entire rows or columns Excel displays the Group dialog box.

If you selected entire rows or columns, Excel groups the selection and adds the outline symbols to the sheet, as shown in Figure 16.32. In this case, you can skip to Step 4.

3. In the Group dialog box, select either Rows or Columns, and then select OK to create the group.

4. Repeat Steps 1 through 3 either to group other rows or columns or to move existing groups to a lower outline level.

FIGURE 16.32.

When you group a selection, Excel adds the appropriate outline symbols to the worksheet.

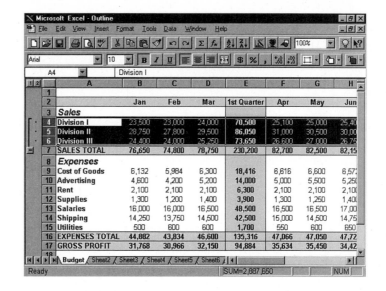

Ungrouping Rows and Columns

If you make a mistake when grouping a selection or you need to make adjustments to your outline levels, here's how to ungroup rows and columns:

1. If you're working with rows, select the rows you want to ungroup. Again, you can save a step if you select the entire row. If you're working with columns, select the columns you want to ungroup.

2. To ungroup the selection, use any one of the following techniques:

   Select the Data | Group and Outline | Ungroup command.

   Press Alt+Shift+←.

   Click the Ungroup button in the Query and Pivot toolbar.

   If you selected entire rows or columns, Excel ungroups the selection and removes the outline symbols. In this case, you can skip to Step 4.

   If you selected something other than entire rows or columns, Excel displays the Ungroup dialog box. Proceed to Step 3 to deal with this dialog box.

3. In the Ungroup dialog box, select either Rows or Columns, and then select OK to ungroup the selection.

4. Repeat Steps 1 through 3 either to ungroup other rows or columns or to move existing groups to a higher outline level.

Hiding and Showing Detail Data

The whole purpose of an outline is to enable you to move easily between views of greater or lesser detail. The next two sections tell you how to hide and show detail data in an outline.

Hiding Detail Data

To hide details in an outline, you have three methods from which to choose:

- Click the collapse symbol at the bottom (for rows) or right (for columns) of the level bar that encompasses the detail data.

- Select a cell in a row or column marked with a collapse symbol, and then select the Data | Group and Outline | Hide Detail command.

 - Select a cell in a row or column marked with a collapse symbol and then click the Hide Detail tool in the Query and Pivot toolbar.

Showing Detail Data

To show collapsed detail, you have no fewer than four methods from which to choose:

- Click the appropriate expand symbol.

- To see the detail for an entire level, click the level marker.

- Select a cell in a row or column marked with an expand symbol, and then select the Data | Group and Outline | Show Detail command.

 - Select a cell in a row or column marked with an expand symbol, and then click the Show Detail tool in the Query and Pivot toolbar.

Selecting Outline Data

When you collapse an outline level, the data is only temporarily hidden from view. If you select the outline, your selection includes the collapsed cells. If you want to copy, print, or chart only the visible cells, you need to follow these steps:

1. Hide the outline data you don't need.

2. Select the outline cells you want to work with.

3. Select the Edit | Go To command to display the Go To dialog box.

4. Select the Special button. Excel displays the Go To Special dialog box.

5. Activate the Visible Cells Only option button.

6. Select OK. Excel modifies your selection to include only those cells in the selection that are part of the expanded outline.

TIP

You also can select visible cells by pressing Alt+; (semicolon).

Removing an Outline

You can remove selected rows or columns from an outline, or you can remove the entire outline. Follow these steps:

1. If you want to remove only part of an outline, select the appropriate rows or columns. If you want to remove the entire outline, select a single cell.

2. Select the Data | Group and Outline | Clear Outline command. Excel adjusts or removes the outline.

Working with Templates

A *template* is a document that contains a basic layout (sheets, labels, formulas, formatting, styles, names, and so on) that you can use as a skeleton for similar documents. A template ensures that the worksheets, charts, or macro sheets you use frequently all have a consistent look and feel. For example, if you need to consolidate budget numbers from various departments, your task will be much easier if all the worksheets have the same layout. To that end, you can issue each department a budget template containing the worksheet layout you want everyone to use.

Creating a Template

Creating a template is similar to creating any other workbook. The following procedure outlines the required steps:

1. Set up the workbook with the settings you want to preserve in the template. You can either use an existing document or create a new one from scratch.

2. Select the File | Save As command to display the Save As dialog box.

3. Enter a name for the template in the File Name text box (you don't need to add an extension—see Step 5).

4. In the Save File as Type drop-down list, select the Template option. Excel displays the Templates folder.

5. Use the Save In list to select the folder for the template. The templates that ship with Excel are stored in the Spreadsheet Solutions folder.

6. Select Save.

Creating a New Document Based on a Template

After you've created a template, you can use either of the following methods to create a new document based on the template:

■ If you saved the template in your Excel startup directory, select the File | New command to display the New dialog box, shown in Figure 16.33. In the General tab, highlight the template and select OK. (The Workbook template, by the way, creates a default Excel workbook.)

FIGURE 16.33.

When you save a template in the startup directory, its name appears in the New dialog box.

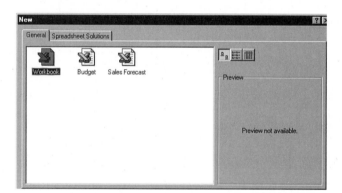

■ To use one of Excel's built-in templates, select File | New, select the Spreadsheet Solutions tab in the New dialog box, highlight the template, and then select OK.

In both cases, Excel opens a copy of the file, gives the window the same name as the template, and adds a number. The number indicates how many times you've used this template to create a new document in the current Excel session. For example, if the template is called Budget, the first new document you create is called Budget1, the second is Budget2, and so on.

Making Changes to a Template

When you want to make changes to a template, use the File | Open command, highlight the template, and select Open. After the template is open, you can make changes as you would to any other workbook. When you finish, save the file. (You don't need to specify the template type this time because Excel automatically saves the file as a template.)

Summary

This chapter shows you how to make your worksheets look their best by taking advantage of Excel's impressive array of formatting options. It also talks about changing the worksheet view, using outlines, and working with templates. If you're still hungry for more information, here are a few other places to check:

- Sometimes the best way to convey your worksheet data is through a chart. Chapter 19, "Charts and Graphics," tells you all you need to know.

- Multiple worksheet views are handy for simple what-if analyses. See Chapter 21, "Data-Analysis Tools and Techniques," for more information on what-if analysis.

- Pivot tables are often better for consolidating data by category. See Chapter 23, "Creating and Customizing Pivot Tables," to find out how they work.

Working with Ranges

IN THIS CHAPTER

Ranges are powerful tools that can unlock the hidden power of Excel. So the more you know about ranges, the more you'll get out of your Excel investment. This chapter reviews some range basics and then takes you beyond the range routine and shows you some techniques for taking full advantage of Excel's range capabilities.

A Review of Excel's Range Selection Techniques

As you work with Excel, you'll come across three situations in which you'll select a cell range:

- When a dialog box field requires a range input
- While entering a function argument
- Before selecting a command that uses a range input

In a dialog box field or function argument, the most straightforward way to select a range is to enter the range coordinates by hand. Just type the address of the upper-left cell (called the *anchor cell*), followed by a colon and then the address of the lower-right cell. To use this method, you either must be able to see the range you want to select or you must know in advance the range coordinates you want. Because often this is not the case, most people don't type the range coordinates directly; instead, they select ranges using either the mouse or the keyboard.

Selecting a Range with the Mouse

Although you can use either the mouse or the keyboard to select a range, you'll find that the mouse makes the job much easier. The following sections take you through several methods you can use to select a range with the mouse.

Selecting a Contiguous Range with the Mouse

A rectangular, contiguous grouping of cells is the most common type of range. To use the mouse to select such a range, follow these steps:

1. Point the mouse at the upper-left cell of the range (this cell is called the *anchor*); then press and hold down the left mouse button.
2. With the left mouse button still pressed, drag the mouse pointer to the lower-right cell of the range. The cell selector remains around the anchor cell, and Excel highlights the other cells in the range in reverse video. The formula bar's Name box shows the number of rows and columns you've selected.
3. Release the mouse button. The cells remain selected to show the range you've defined, and the Name box shows the address of the anchor cell.

> **TIP**
>
> Do you have to start over if you select the wrong lower-right corner and your range ends up either too big or too small? Not at all. Just hold down the Shift key and click the correct lower-right cell. The range adjusts automatically.

Selecting a Row or Column with the Mouse

Using the worksheet row and column headings, you can quickly select a range that consists of an entire row or column. For a row, click the row's heading; for a column, click the column's heading. If you need to select adjacent rows or columns, just drag the mouse pointer across the appropriate headings.

What if you want to select every row and every column (or, in other words, the entire worksheet)? That's easy: Just click the Select All button near the upper-left corner of the sheet.

Selecting a Range in Extend Mode with the Mouse

An alternative method uses the mouse with the F8 key to select a rectangular, contiguous range. You can do this by following these steps:

1. Click the upper-left cell of the range.
2. Press F8. Excel enters extend mode (you'll see EXT in the status bar).
3. Click the lower-right cell of the range. Excel selects the entire range.
4. Press F8 again to turn off extend mode.

> **TIP**
>
> After selecting a large range, you'll often no longer see the active cell because you've scrolled it off the screen. If you need to see the active cell before continuing, you can either use the scroll bars to bring it into view or press Ctrl+Backspace.

Working with 3-D Ranges

A *3-D range* is a range selected on multiple sheets. This is a powerful concept because it means that you can select a range on two or more sheets and then enter data, apply formatting, or give a command, and the operation will affect all the ranges at once.

To create a 3-D range, you first need to group the worksheets you want to work with. To select multiple sheets, you can use any of the following techniques:

- To select adjacent sheets, click the tab of the first sheet, hold down the Shift key, and click the tab of the last sheet.

- To select noncontiguous sheets, hold down the Ctrl key and click the tab of each sheet you want to include in the group.

- To select all the sheets in a workbook, right-click any sheet tab and click the Select All Sheets command.

When you've selected your sheets, each tab is highlighted and [Group] appears in the workbook title bar. To ungroup the sheets, click a tab that isn't in the group. Alternatively, you can right-click one of the group's tabs and select the Ungroup Sheets command from the shortcut menu.

With the sheets now grouped, you create your 3-D range simply by activating any of the grouped sheets and then selecting a range using any of the techniques we just ran through. Excel selects the same cells in all the other sheets in the group. (If you're from Missouri, the "Show Me" state, you can prove it for yourself by activating the other sheets in the group.)

You can also type in a 3-D range by hand when, say, entering a formula. Here's the general format for a 3-D reference:

```
FirstSheet:LastSheet!ULCorner:LRCorner
```

Here, `FirstSheet` is the name of the first sheet in the 3-D range, `LastSheet` is the name of the last sheet, and `ULCorner` and `LRCorner` define the cell range you want to work with on each sheet. For example, to specify the range A1:E10 on worksheets Sheet1, Sheet2, and Sheet3, use the following reference:

```
Sheet1:Sheet3!A1:E10
```

You'll normally use 3-D references in worksheet functions that accept them. These functions include AVERAGE(), COUNT(), COUNTA(), MAX(), MIN(), PRODUCT(), STDEV(), STDEVP(), SUM(), VAR(), and VARP().

Using Range Names

Although ranges enable you to work efficiently with large groups of cells, there are some disadvantages to using ranges:

- You can't work with more than one range at a time. Each time you want to use a range, you have to redefine its coordinates.

- Range notation is not intuitive. To know what a formula such as =SUM(E6:E10) is adding, you have to look at the range itself.

- A slight mistake in defining a range can lead to disastrous results, especially when you're erasing a range.

You can overcome these problems by using range names. You can assign names of up to 255 characters to any single cell or range on your spreadsheet. To include the range in a formula or range command, you use the name instead of selecting the range or typing in its coordinates. You can create as many range names as you like, and you can even assign multiple names to the same range.

Range names also make your formulas intuitive and easy to read. For example, by assigning the name AugustSales to a range such as E6:E10, the purpose of a formula such as =SUM(AugustSales) becomes immediately clear. Range names also increase the accuracy of your range operations because you don't have to specify range coordinates.

Besides overcoming the problems mentioned earlier, range names also bring several advantages to the table:

- Names are easier to remember than range coordinates.
- Names don't change when you move a range to another part of the worksheet.
- Named ranges adjust automatically whenever you insert or delete rows or columns within the range.
- Names make it easier to navigate a worksheet. You can use the Go To command to jump to a named range quickly.
- You can use worksheet labels to create range names quickly.

Defining a Range Name

Besides having a maximum length of 255 characters, range names must also follow these guidelines:

- The name must begin with either a letter or the underscore character (_). For the rest of the name, you can use any combination of characters, numbers, or symbols (except spaces). For multiple-word names, separate the words by using the underscore character or by mixing case (for example, CostOfGoods). Excel doesn't distinguish between uppercase and lowercase letters in range names.
- Don't use cell addresses or any of the operator symbols (such as +, -, *, /, <, >, and &), because these could cause confusion if you use the name in a formula.
- To make typing easier, try to keep your names as short as possible while still retaining their meaning. TotalProfit95 is faster to type than Total_Profit_For_Fiscal_Year_95, and it's certainly clearer than the more cryptic TotPft95.

With these guidelines in mind, follow these steps to define a range name:

1. Select the range you want to name.
2. Select the Insert|Name|Define command. The Define Name dialog box appears, as shown in Figure 17.1.

FIGURE 17.1.

Use the Define Name dialog box to define a name for the selected range.

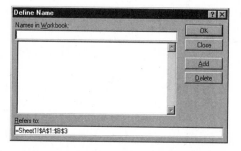

You can press Ctrl+F3 to open the Define Name dialog box quickly.

3. Enter the range name in the Names in Workbook text box.
4. If, for some reason, the range displayed in the Refers to box is incorrect, you can use one of two methods to change it:
   - Type the correct range address (be sure to begin the address with an equal sign).
   - Move the cursor into the Refers to box, delete the existing address, and then use the mouse or keyboard to select a new range on the worksheet.

If you need to move around inside the Refers to box with the arrow keys (say, to edit the existing range address), first press F2 to put Excel into edit mode. If you don't, Excel remains in point mode, and the program assumes that you're trying to select a cell on the worksheet.

5. Click the Add button. Excel adds the name to the Names in Workbook list.
6. Repeat steps 3 through 5 for any other ranges you want to name.
7. When you're done, click the Close button to return to the worksheet.

Range names are available to all the sheets in a workbook. This means, for example, that a formula in Sheet1 can refer to a named range in Sheet16 simply by using the name directly. If you need to use the same name in different sheets, you can create *sheet-level* names. These kinds of names are preceded by the name of the worksheet and an exclamation point. For example, Sheet1!Sales refers to a range named Sales in Sheet1, and Sheet2!Sales refers to a range named Sales in Sheet2.

If the named range exists in a different workbook, you must precede the name with the name of the file in single quotation marks. For example, if the Mortgage Amortization workbook contains a range named Rate, you use the following entry to refer to this range in a different workbook:

```
'Mortgage Amortization'!Rate
```

Working with the Name Box

The Name box in Excel's formula bar gives you some extra features that help make it easier to work with range names:

- After you've defined a name, it appears in the Name box whenever you select the range.
- The Name box doubles as a drop-down list. To select a named range quickly, drop the list down and select the name you want. Excel moves to the range and selects the cells.
- You also can use the Name box as an easy way to define a range name. Just select the range and click inside the Name box to display the insertion point. Enter the name you want to use and then press Enter. Excel defines the new name automatically.

Changing a Range Name

If you need to change the name of one or more ranges, you can use one of two methods:

- If you've changed some row or column labels, just redefine the range names based on the new text, and delete the old names (as described in the next section).
- Select the Insert | Name | Define command. Highlight the name you want to change in the Names in Workbook list, make your changes in the text box, and click the Add button.

CAUTION

Note that these methods don't actually change the name of the range. Instead, they just define a new name for the range while leaving the old name intact. This also means that any formulas that refer to the original range name won't get changed.

Deleting a Range Name

If you no longer need a range name, you should delete the name from the worksheet to avoid cluttering the name list. The following procedure outlines the necessary steps:

1. Select the Insert | Name | Define command to display the Define Name dialog box.
2. In the Names in Workbook list, select the name you want to delete.
3. Select Delete. Excel deletes the name from the list.
4. Repeat steps 2 and 3 for any other names you want to delete.
5. When you're done, select OK.

Filling a Range

If you need to fill a range with a particular value or formula, Excel gives you two methods:

- Select the range you want to fill, type the value or formula, and press Ctrl+Enter. Excel fills the entire range with whatever you entered in the formula bar.

- Enter the initial value or formula, select the range you want to fill (including the initial cell), and select the Edit | Fill command. Then select the appropriate command from the cascade that appears. For example, if you're filling a range down from the initial cell, select the Down command. If multiple sheets are selected, use the Edit | Fill | Across Worksheets command to fill the range in each worksheet.

> **TIP**
>
> Press Ctrl+R to select the Edit | Fill | Right command and Ctrl+D to select the Edit | Fill | Down command.

Using the Fill Handle

The *fill handle* is the small black square in the bottom-right corner of the active cell or range. You can use the fill handle to fill a range with a value or formula. Just enter your initial values or formulas, select them, and then drag the fill handle over the destination range. (I'm assuming here that the data you're copying won't create a series.) When you release the mouse button, Excel fills the range.

Note that if the initial cell contains a formula with relative references, Excel adjusts the references accordingly. For example, suppose that the initial cell contains the formula =A1. If you fill down, the next cell will contain the formula =A2, the next will contain =A3, and so on.

Creating a Series

Although you can use the fill handle to create a series, you can use Excel's Series command to gain a little more control over the whole process. Follow these steps:

1. Select the first cell you want to use for the series and enter the starting value. If you want to create a series out of a particular pattern (such as 2, 4, 6,...), fill in enough cells to define the pattern.

2. Select the entire range you want to fill.

3. Select the Edit | Fill | Series command. Excel displays the Series dialog box, as shown in Figure 17.2.

FIGURE 17.2.

Use the Series dialog box to define the series you want to create.

4. In the Series In group, select Rows to create the series in rows starting from the active cell or Columns to create the series in columns.

5. Use the Type group to enter the type of series you want. You have the following options:

   Linear—This option finds the next series value by adding the step value (see step 7) to the preceding value in the series.

   Growth—This option finds the next series value by multiplying the preceding value by the step value.

   Date—This option creates a series of dates based on the option you select in the Date Unit group (Day, Weekday, Month, or Year).

   AutoFill—This option works much like the fill handle does. You can use it to extend a numeric pattern or a text series (for example, Qtr1, Qtr2, Qtr3).

6. If you want to extend a series trend, activate the Trend check box. This option is available only if you have selected a Linear or Growth series type.

7. If you have selected a Linear, Growth, or Date series type, enter a number in the Step Value box. This number is what Excel uses to increment each value in the series.

8. To place a limit on the series, enter the appropriate number in the Stop Value box.

9. Select OK. Excel fills in the series and returns you to the worksheet.

Copying a Range

The quickest way to become productive with Excel is to avoid reinventing your worksheet wheels. If you have a formula that works, or a piece of formatting that you've put a lot of effort into, don't start from scratch to create something similar. Instead, make a copy and then adjust the copy as necessary.

Copying a Range with the Copy Command

If you prefer the pull-down menu approach, you can copy a range using the Copy command.

> **CAUTION**
>
> Before copying a range, look at the destination area and make sure that you won't be overwriting any nonblank cells. Remember that you can use the Undo command if you accidentally destroy some data. If you want to insert the range among some existing cells, see the section later in this chapter titled "Inserting a Copy of a Range."

Follow these steps to copy a range using the Copy command:

1. Select the range you want to copy.
2. Select the Edit | Copy command. Excel copies the contents of the range to the Clipboard and displays a moving border around the range.
3. Select the upper-left cell of the destination range.
4. Select the Edit | Paste command. Excel pastes the range from the Clipboard to your destination.

Inserting a Copy of a Range

If you don't want a pasted range to overwrite existing cells, you can tell Excel to *insert* the range. In this case, Excel moves the existing cells out of harm's way before pasting the range from the Clipboard. (As you'll see, you have control over where Excel moves the existing cells.) Follow these steps to insert a copy of a range:

1. Select the range you want to copy.
2. Use any of the methods described earlier in this chapter to copy the range to the Clipboard.
3. Select the upper-left cell of the destination range.
4. Select the Insert | Copied Cells command. Excel displays the Insert Paste dialog box to enable you to choose where to move the existing cells that would otherwise be overwritten. (See Figure 17.3.)

FIGURE 17.3.

Use the Insert Paste dialog box to tell Excel in which direction to move the existing cells.

> **TIP**
>
> You also can insert a copied range by right-clicking the destination cell and selecting the Insert Copied Cells command from the shortcut menu.

5. Select Shift Cells Right to move the cells to the right or Shift Cells Down to move them down.

6. Select OK. Excel shifts the existing cells and then pastes the range from the Clipboard.

Moving a Range

Moving a range is very similar to copying a range, except that the source range gets deleted when all is said and done.

Using the Menu Commands to Move a Range

To move a range with the menu commands, you need to cut the range to the Clipboard and then paste it. The following procedure details the steps involved:

1. Select the range you want to move.

2. Select the Edit | Cut command. Excel cuts the contents of the range to the Clipboard and displays a moving border around the range.

3. Select the upper-left cell of the destination range.

4. Select the Edit | Paste command. Excel pastes the range from the Clipboard to your destination.

> **TIP**
>
> For faster range moving, press Ctrl+X instead of selecting the Edit | Cut command, or right-click the source range and select the Cut command from the Range shortcut menu. You can also click the Cut button in the standard toolbar.

Inserting and Deleting a Range

When you begin a worksheet, you generally use rows and columns sequentially as you add data, labels, and formulas. More often than not, however, you'll need to go back and add some values or text that you forgot or that you need for another part of the worksheet. When this happens, you need to insert ranges into your spreadsheet to make room for your new information. Conversely, you often have to remove old or unnecessary data from a spreadsheet, which requires you to delete ranges. The next few sections describe various and sundry methods for inserting and deleting ranges in Excel.

Inserting an Entire Row or Column

The easiest way to insert a range into a worksheet is to insert an entire row or column. The following steps show you how it's done:

1. Select the row or column before which you want to insert the new row or column. If you want to insert multiple rows or columns, select the appropriate number of rows or columns, as shown in Figure 17.4.

FIGURE 17.4.

Two rows have been selected at the point where two new rows are to be inserted.

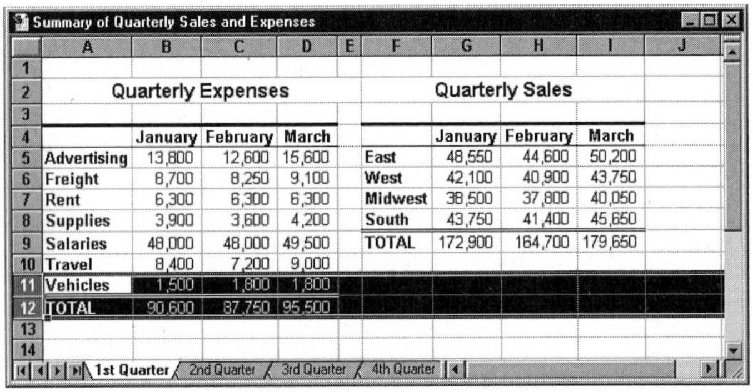

	A	B	C	D	E	F	G	H	I	J
1										
2	Quarterly Expenses						Quarterly Sales			
3										
4		January	February	March				January	February	March
5	Advertising	13,800	12,600	15,600		East	48,550	44,600	50,200	
6	Freight	8,700	8,250	9,100		West	42,100	40,900	43,750	
7	Rent	6,300	6,300	6,300		Midwest	38,500	37,800	40,050	
8	Supplies	3,900	3,600	4,200		South	43,750	41,400	45,650	
9	Salaries	48,000	48,000	49,500		TOTAL	172,900	164,700	179,650	
10	Travel	8,400	7,200	9,000						
11	Vehicles	1,500	1,800	1,800						
12	TOTAL	90,600	87,750	95,500						
13										
14										

Summary of Quarterly Sales and Expenses — 1st Quarter / 2nd Quarter / 3rd Quarter / 4th Quarter

TIP

Press Ctrl+Spacebar to select an entire column or Shift+Spacebar to select an entire row.

2. If you're inserting rows, select the Insert | Rows command. Excel shifts the selected rows down, as shown in Figure 17.5. If you're inserting columns, select the Insert | Columns command instead. In this case, Excel shifts the selected columns to the right.

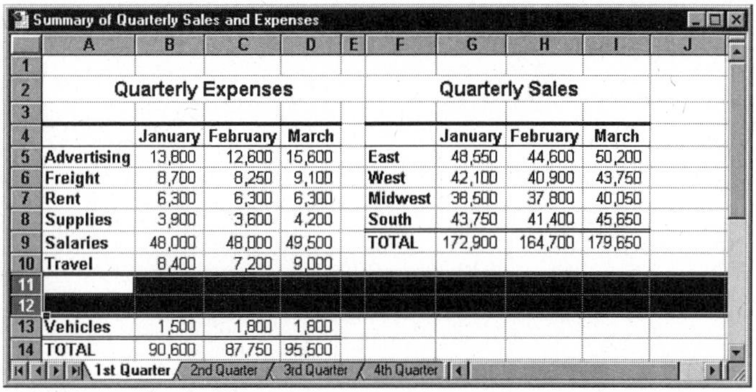

FIGURE 17.5.

When you insert rows, Excel shifts the existing cells down.

TIP

As soon as you've selected a row or column, press and hold down the Ctrl key and then press the + key to insert a row or column quickly. You also can right-click the range and then select Insert from the shortcut menu.

Inserting a Cell or Range

In some worksheets you might need to insert only a single cell or a range of cells so as not to disturb the arrangement of surrounding data. For example, suppose that you want to add a Repair line between Rent and Supplies in the Quarterly Expenses table in Figure 17.6. You don't want to add an entire row because it would create a gap in the Quarterly Sales table. Instead, you can insert a range that covers just the area you need. Follow these steps to see how this works:

1. Select the range where you want the new range to appear. In the Quarterly Expenses example, you would select the range A8:D8. (See Figure 17.6.)

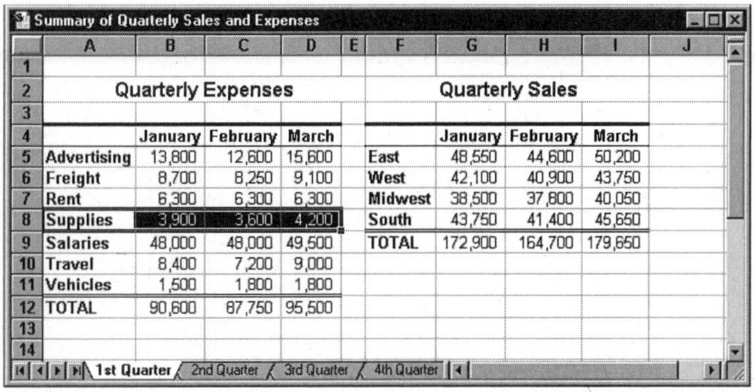

FIGURE 17.6.

When you insert cells in the Quarterly Expenses table, you don't want to disturb the Quarterly Sales table.

2. Select the Insert | Cells command. Excel displays the Insert dialog box, as shown in Figure 17.7.

FIGURE 17.7.

Use the Insert dialog box to tell Excel which way to shift the existing cells.

3. Select either Shift Cells Right or Shift Cells Down, as appropriate.

4. Select OK. Excel inserts the range.

Deleting an Entire Row or Column

Deleting a row or column is similar to inserting. In this case, however, you need to exercise a little more caution because a hasty deletion can have disastrous effects on your worksheet. (However, keep in mind that you can always select the Edit | Undo command if you make any mistakes.)

The following procedure shows how to delete a row or column:

1. Select the row or column you want to delete.

2. Select the Edit | Delete command. Excel deletes the row or column and shifts the remaining data appropriately.

Deleting a Cell or Range

If you need to delete only one cell or a range to avoid trashing any surrounding data, follow these steps:

1. Select the cell or range you want to delete.

2. Select the Edit | Delete command. Excel displays the Delete dialog box.

3. Select either Shift Cells Left or Shift Cells Up, as appropriate.

4. Select OK. Excel deletes the range.

Clearing a Range

As you've seen, deleting a range actually removes the cells from the worksheet. What if you want the cells to remain, but you want their contents or formats cleared? For that, you can use Excel's Clear command, as described in the following steps:

1. Select the range you want to clear.

2. Select the Edit|Clear command. Excel displays a submenu of Clear commands.

3. Select either All, Formats, Contents, or Notes, as appropriate.

> **TIP**
>
> To delete the contents of the selected range quickly, press Delete. You also can right-click the range and select Clear Contents from the Range shortcut menu.

Using Excel's Reference Operators

As you probably know, Excel has various operators (+, *, and &, for example) that you use for building formulas. I'd like to close our look at ranges by talking about some of Excel's *reference operators.* You use these operators when working with cell references, as discussed in the next three sections.

Using the Range Operator

The *range* operator is just the familiar colon (:), which you've been using all along. All you do is insert a colon between two references, and Excel creates a range (for example, A1:C5). There's nothing too surprising here.

Until now, though, you've probably been creating your ranges by using the reference on the left side of the colon to define the upper-left corner of the range and the reference on the right side of the colon to define the lower-right corner. There are other ways to create ranges with the range operator, however. Table 17.1 points out a few of them.

Table 17.1. Sample ranges created with the range operator.

Range	What It Refers To
A:A	Column A (that is, the entire column)
A:C	Columns A through C
1:1	Row 1
1:5	Rows 1 through 5

You also can use a range name on either side of the colon. In this case, the named range becomes a *corner* for the larger range. For example, Figure 17.8 shows a worksheet with the named range Rent that refers to B7:D7. Table 17.2 shows some sample ranges you can create with Rent as one corner.

FIGURE 17.8.

The named range Rent used in Table 17.2.

	A	B	C	D	E	F	G	H	I	J
1										
2	Quarterly Expenses						Quarterly Sales			
3										
4		January	February	March				January	February	March
5	Advertising	13,800	12,600	15,600		East	48,550	44,600	50,200	
6	Freight	8,700	8,250	9,100		West	42,100	40,900	43,750	
7	Rent	6,300	6,300	6,300		Midwest	38,500	37,800	40,050	
8	Supplies	3,900	3,600	4,200		South	43,750	41,400	45,650	
9	Salaries	48,000	48,000	49,500		TOTAL	172,900	164,700	179,650	
10	Travel	8,400	7,200	9,000						
11	Vehicles	1,500	1,800	1,800						
12	TOTAL	90,600	87,750	95,500						
13										
14										

Title bar: Summary of Quarterly Sales and Expenses
Tabs: 1st Quarter / 2nd Quarter / 3rd Quarter / 4th Quarter

Table 17.2. Sample ranges created with a range name.

Range	What It Refers To
Rent:A1	A1:D7
Rent:G2	B2:G7
Rent:E10	B7:E10
Rent:A13	A7:D13

Using the Intersection Operator

If you have ranges that overlap, you can use the *intersection* operator (a space) to refer to the overlapping cells. For example, Figure 17.9 shows two ranges: C4:E9 and D8:G11. To refer to the overlapping cells (D8:E9), you would use the following notation: C4:E9 D8:G11.

FIGURE 17.9.

The intersection operator returns the intersecting cells of two ranges.

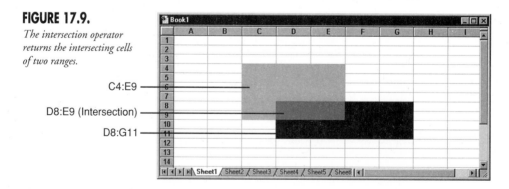

C4:E9

D8:E9 (Intersection)

D8:G11

If you've named the ranges on your worksheet, the intersection operator can make things much easier to read because you can refer to individual cells by using the names of the cell's row and column. For example, in Figure 17.10 the range B5:B12 is named January and the range B7:D7 is named Rent. This means that you can refer to cell B7 as January Rent (see cell H11).

FIGURE 17.10.

After you name ranges, you can combine row and column headings to create intersecting names for individual cells.

	A	B	C	D	E	F	G	H	I	J
1										
2		Quarterly Expenses					Quarterly Sales			
3										
4		January	February	March			January	February	March	
5	Advertising	13,800	12,600	15,600		East	48,550	44,600	50,200	
6	Freight	8,700	8,250	9,100		West	42,100	40,900	43,750	
7	Rent	6,300	6,300	6,300		Midwest	38,500	37,800	40,050	
8	Supplies	3,900	3,600	4,200		South	43,750	41,400	45,650	
9	Salaries	48,000	48,000	49,500		TOTAL	172,900	164,700	179,650	
10	Travel	8,400	7,200	9,000						
11	Vehicles	1,500	1,800	1,800		Rent for January:		6,300		
12	TOTAL	90,600	87,750	95,500						
13										
14										

Summary of Quarterly Sales and Expenses

1st Quarter / 2nd Quarter / 3rd Quarter / 4th Quarter

CAUTION

If you try to define an intersection name and Excel displays #NULL! in the cell, it means the two ranges don't have any overlapping cells.

Summary

This chapter shows you how to get the most out of your worksheet ranges. It shows you a number of ways to select a range. It also tells you about range names, the fill handle, creating a series, copying and moving a range, and how to use Excel's reference operators. For related range information, see the following chapters:

- Functions often use range arguments, and you'll be learning about functions in Chapter 18, "Manipulating the Information."

- To make your ranges look their best, you need to know how to format them. You'll find all kinds of formatting techniques in Chapter 16, "Excel Concepts."

Manipulating the Information

18

by
Paul McFedries
and Tom Hayes

IN THIS CHAPTER

A worksheet is merely a lifeless collection of numbers and text until you define some kind of relationship among the various entries. You do this by creating *formulas* that perform calculations and produce results. This chapter takes you through some formula basics, shows you a number of techniques for building powerful formulas, and talks about troubleshooting and auditing formulas.

This chapter also introduces you to Excel's built-in worksheet functions. You'll learn what the functions are, what they can do, and how to use them.

Understanding Formula Basics

Most worksheets are created to provide answers to specific questions: What is the company's profit? Are expenses over or under budget, and by how much? What is the future value of an investment? How big will my bonus be this year? You can answer these questions, and an infinite variety of others, by using Excel formulas.

All Excel formulas have the same general structure: an equal sign (=) followed by one or more *operands*—which can be a value, a cell reference, a range, a range name, or a function name—separated by one or more *operators*—the symbols that combine the operands, such as the plus sign (+) and the greater-than sign (>).

Excel divides formulas into four groups: arithmetic, comparison, text, and reference. Each group has its own set of operators, and you use each group in different ways. In the next few sections I'll show you how to use each type of formula.

Using Arithmetic Formulas

Arithmetic formulas are by far the most common type of formula. They combine numbers, cell addresses, and function results with mathematic operators to perform calculations. I've summarized the mathematic operators used in arithmetic formulas in Table 18.1.

Table 18.1. The arithmetic operators.

Operator	Name	Example	Result
+	Addition	=10+5	15
-	Subtraction	=10-5	5
-	Negation	=-10	-10
*	Multiplication	=10*5	50
/	Division	=10/5	2
%	Percentage	=10%	0.1
^	Exponentiation	=10^5	100000

Most of these operators are straightforward, but the exponentiation operator might require further explanation. The formula =x^y means that the value *x* is raised to the power *y*. For example, the formula =3^2 produces the result 9 (that is, 3*3=9). Similarly, the formula =2^4 produces 16 (that is, 2*2*2*2=16).

Using Comparison Formulas

A *comparison formula* is a statement that compares two or more numbers, text strings, cell contents, or function results. If the statement is true, the result of the formula is given the logical value TRUE (which is equivalent to any nonzero value). If the statement is false, the formula returns the logical value FALSE (which is equivalent to 0). Table 18.2 summarizes the operators you can use in logical formulas.

Table 18.2. Comparison formula operators.

Operator	Name	Example	Result
=	Equal to	=10=5	FALSE
>	Greater than	=10>5	TRUE
<	Less than	=10<5	FALSE
>=	Greater than or equal to	="a">="b"	FALSE
<=	Less than or equal to	="a"<="b"	TRUE
<>	Not equal to	="a"<>"b"	TRUE

There are many uses for comparison formulas. For example, you can determine whether to pay a salesperson a bonus by using a comparison formula to compare his actual sales with a predetermined quota. If the sales are greater than the quota, the salesperson is awarded the bonus. You also can monitor credit collection. For example, if the amount a customer owes is more than 150 days past due, you might send the invoice to a collection agency.

Using Text Formulas

So far, I've discussed formulas that calculate or make comparisons and return values. A *text formula* is a formula that returns text. Text formulas use the ampersand (&) operator to work with text cells, text strings enclosed in quotation marks, and text function results.

One way to use text formulas is to concatenate text strings. For example, if you enter the formula ="soft"&"ware" into a cell, Excel displays software. Note that the quotation marks and ampersand are not shown in the result. You also can use & to combine cells that contain text. For example, if A1 contains the text Ben and A2 contains Jerry, then entering the formula =A1&" and "&A2 returns Ben and Jerry.

Using Reference Formulas

The reference operators combine two cell references or ranges to create a single joint reference. Reference formulas are covered in Chapter 17, "Working with Ranges," but Table 18.3 gives you a quick summary.

Table 18.3. Reference formula operators.

Operator	Name	Description
: (colon)	Range	Produces a range from two cell references (for example, A1:C5)
(space)	Intersection	Produces a range that is the intersection of two ranges (for example, A1:C5 B2:E8)
, (comma)	Union	Produces a range that is the union of two ranges (for example, A1:C5,B2:E8)

Understanding Operator Precedence

You'll often use simple formulas that contain just two values and a single operator. In practice, however, most formulas you use will have a number of values and operators. In these more complex expressions, the order in which the calculations are performed becomes crucial. For example, consider the formula =3+5^2. If you calculate from left to right, the answer you get is 64 (3+5 equals 8 and 8^2 equals 64). However, if you perform the exponentiation first and then the addition, the result is 28 (5^2 equals 25 and 3+25 equals 28). As this example shows, a single formula can produce multiple answers depending on the order in which you perform the calculations.

To control this problem, Excel evaluates a formula according to a predefined *order of precedence*. This order of precedence enables Excel to calculate a formula unambiguously by determining which part of the formula it calculates first, which part second, and so on.

The Order of Precedence

Excel's order of precedence is determined by the various formula operators outlined earlier. Table 18.4 summarizes the complete order of precedence used by Excel.

Table 18.4. Excel's order of precedence.

Operator	Operation	Order of Precedence
:	Range	First
(space)	Intersection	Second
,	Union	Third
-	Negation	Fourth
%	Percentage	Fifth
^	Exponentiation	Sixth
* and /	Multiplication and division	Seventh
+ and -	Addition and subtraction	Eighth
&	Concatenation	Ninth
= < > <= >= <>	Comparison	Tenth

From this table, you can see that Excel performs exponentiation before addition. Therefore, the correct answer for the formula =3+5^2, given earlier, is 28. Notice, as well, that some operators in Table 18.4 have the same order of precedence (for example, multiplication and division). This means that it doesn't matter in which order these operators are evaluated. For example, consider the formula =5*10/2. If you perform the multiplication first, the answer you get is 25 (5*10 equals 50, and 50/2 equals 25). If you perform the division first, you also get an answer of 25 (10/2 equals 5, and 5*5 equals 25). By convention, Excel evaluates operators with the same order of precedence from left to right.

Controlling the Order of Precedence

There are times when you want to override the order of precedence. For example, suppose that you want to create a formula that calculates the pre-tax cost of an item. If you bought something for $10.65, including 7 percent sales tax, and you want to find the cost of the item less the tax, you use the formula =10.65/1.07, which gives you the correct answer of $9.95. In general, this is the formula:

$$\text{Pre-tax cost} = \frac{\text{Total Cost}}{1 + \text{Tax Rate}}$$

Figure 18.1 shows how you might implement such a formula. Cell B5 displays the Total Cost variable, and cell B6 displays the Tax Rate variable. Given these parameters, your first instinct might be to use the formula =B5/1+B6 to calculate the original cost. This formula is shown in cell E9, and the result is given in cell D9. As you can see, this answer is incorrect. What happened? Well, according to the rules of precedence, Excel performs division before addition, so the value in B5 is first divided by 1 and then is added to the value in B6. To get the correct answer, you must override the order of precedence so that the addition 1+B6 is performed first. You do this by surrounding that part of the formula with parentheses, as shown in cell E10. When this is done, you get the correct answer (see cell D10).

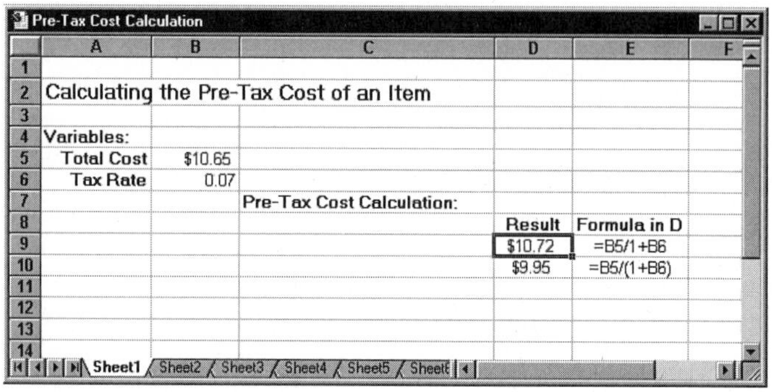

FIGURE 18.1.

Use parentheses to control the order of precedence in your formulas.

In general, you can use parentheses to control the order that Excel uses to calculate formulas. Terms inside parentheses are always calculated first; terms outside parentheses are calculated sequentially (according to the order of precedence). To gain even more control over your formulas, you can place parentheses inside one another—this is called *nesting* parentheses. Excel always evaluates the innermost set of parentheses first. Here are a few sample formulas:

Formula	First Step	Second Step	Third Step	Result
3^(15/5)*2-5	3^3*2-5	27*2-5	54-5	49
3^((15/5)*2-5)	3^(3*2-5)	3^(6-5)	3^1	3
3^(15/(5*2-5))	3^(15/(10-5))	3^(15/5)	3^3	27

Notice that the order of precedence rules also hold within parentheses. For example, in the expression (5*2-5), the term 5*2 is calculated before 5 is subtracted.

Using parentheses to determine the order of calculations enables you to gain full control over Excel formulas. This way, you can make sure that the answer given by a formula is the one you want.

CAUTION

One of the most common mistakes when using parentheses in formulas is to forget to close a parenthetic term with a right parenthesis. If you do this, Excel generates a `Parentheses do not match` message. To make sure that you've closed each parenthetic term, count all the left and right parentheses. If these totals don't match, you know you've left out a parenthesis.

Copying and Moving Formulas

I've shown you various techniques for copying and moving ranges. The procedures for copying and moving ranges that contain formulas are identical, but the results are not always straightforward. For an example, check out Figure 18.2, which shows a list of expense data for a company. The formula in cell C11 totals the January expenses. The idea behind this worksheet is to calculate a new expense budget number for 1995 as a percentage increase of the actual 1994 total. Cell C3 displays the INCREASE variable (in this case, the increase being used is 9 percent). The formula that calculates the 1995 BUDGET number (cell C13 for the month of January) multiplies the 1994 TOTAL by the INCREASE (that is, =C11*C3).

FIGURE 18.2.

A budget expenses worksheet.

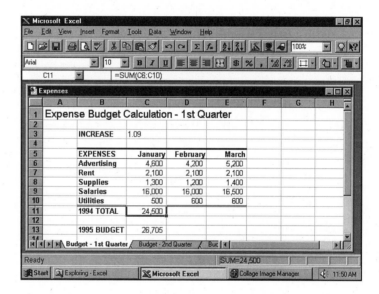

The next step is to calculate the 1994 TOTAL expenses and the 1995 BUDGET figure for February. You could just type each new formula, but you learned in Chapter 17 that you can copy a cell much more quickly. Figure 18.3 shows the results when you copy the contents of cell C11 into cell D11. As you can see, Excel adjusts the range in the formula's SUM( ) function so that only the February expenses are totaled. How did Excel know to do this? To answer this question, you need to know about Excel's relative reference format.

FIGURE 18.3.

When you copy the January 1994 TOTAL formula to February, Excel automatically adjusts the range reference.

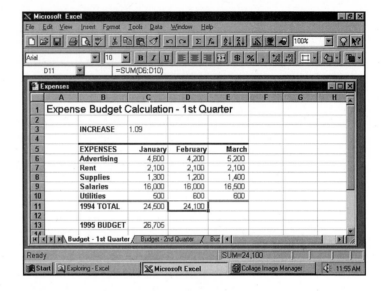

Understanding Relative Reference Format

When you use a cell reference in a formula, Excel looks at the cell address relative to the location of the formula. For example, suppose that you have the formula =A1*2 in cell A2. To Excel this formula says, "Multiply the contents of the cell one row above this one by 2." This is called the *relative reference format*, and it's the default format for Excel. This means that if you copy this formula to cell A5, the relative reference is still "Multiply the contents of the cell one row above this one by 2," but the formula changes to =A4*2, because A4 is one row above A5.

Figure 18.3 shows why this format is useful. You had to copy only the formula in cell C11 to cell D11 and, thanks to relative referencing, everything comes out perfectly. To get the expense total for March, you would just have to paste the same formula into cell E11. You'll find that this way of handling copy operations will save you incredible amounts of time when you're building your worksheet models.

However, you need to exercise some care when copying or moving formulas. Let's see what happens if we return to the budget expense worksheet and try copying the 1995 BUDGET formula in cell C13 to cell D13. Figure 18.4 shows that the result is 0! What happened? The formula bar shows the problem: The new formula is =D11*D3. Cell D11 is the February 1994 TOTAL, and that's fine, but instead of the INCREASE cell (C3), the formula refers to a blank cell (D3). Excel treats blank cells as 0, so the answer is 0. The problem is the relative reference format. When the formula was copied, Excel assumed that the new formula should refer to cell D3. To see how you can correct this problem, you need to learn about another format: the *absolute reference format*.

FIGURE 18.4.

Copying the January 1994 BUDGET formula to February creates a problem.

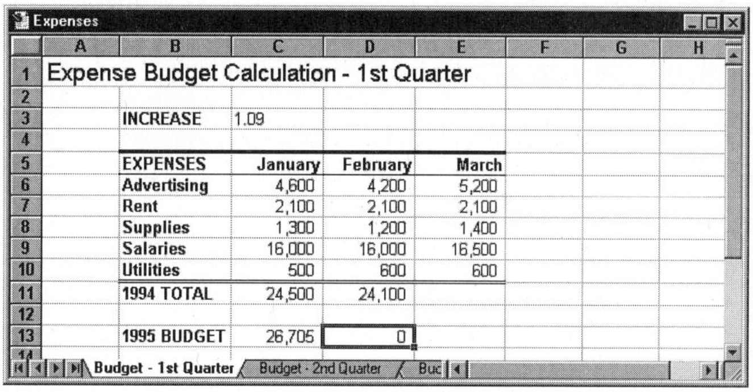

	A	B	C	D	E	F	G	H
1		Expense Budget Calculation - 1st Quarter						
2								
3		INCREASE	1.09					
4								
5		EXPENSES	January	February	March			
6		Advertising	4,600	4,200	5,200			
7		Rent	2,100	2,100	2,100			
8		Supplies	1,300	1,200	1,400			
9		Salaries	16,000	16,000	16,500			
10		Utilities	500	600	600			
11		1994 TOTAL	24,500	24,100				
12								
13		1995 BUDGET	26,705	0				

Budget - 1st Quarter / Budget - 2nd Quarter / Buc

> **NOTE**
>
> The relative reference format problem doesn't occur when you move a formula. When you move a formula, Excel assumes that you want to keep the same cell references.

Understanding Absolute Reference Format

When you refer to a cell in a formula using the absolute reference format, Excel uses the physical address of the cell. You tell the program that you want to use an absolute reference by placing dollar signs ($) before the row and column of the cell address. To return to the example in the preceding section, Excel interprets the formula =A1*2 as "Multiply the contents of cell A1 by 2." No matter where you copy or move this formula, the cell reference doesn't change. The cell address is said to be *anchored.*

To fix the budget expense worksheet, you need to anchor the INCREASE variable. To do this, change the January 1995 BUDGET formula in cell C13 to read =C11*C3. After you've made this change, try copying the formula again to the February 1995 BUDGET column. You should get the proper value this time.

> **CAUTION**
>
> Most range names refer to absolute cell references. This means that when you copy a formula that uses a range name, the copied formula will use the same range name as the original, which might produce errors in your worksheet.

You should also know that you can enter a cell reference using a mixed reference format. In this format, you anchor either the cell's row (by placing the dollar sign in front of the row address only—for example, B$6) or its column (by placing the dollar sign in front of the column address only—for example, $B6).

> **TIP**
>
> You can quickly change the reference format of a cell address by using the F4 key. When editing a formula, place the cursor to the left of the cell address and keep pressing F4. Excel cycles through the various formats.

Copying a Formula Without Adjusting Relative References

If you need to copy a formula but don't want the formula's relative references to change, you can use three methods:

- If you want to copy a formula from the cell above, select the lower cell and press Ctrl+' (apostrophe).

- Activate the formula bar and use the mouse or keyboard to highlight the entire formula. Next, copy the formula to the Clipboard (by selecting Edit | Copy or by pressing Ctrl+C); then press the Esc key to deactivate the formula bar. Finally, select the cell in which you want the copy to appear and paste the formula there.

- Activate the formula bar and type an apostrophe (') at the beginning of the formula (to the left of the equal sign) to convert it to text. Press Enter to confirm the edit, copy the cell, and then paste it in the desired location. Now, delete the apostrophe from both the source and the destination cells to convert the text back to a formula.

Working with Arrays

An *array* is a group of cells or values that Excel treats as a unit. You create arrays either by using a function that returns an array result (such as DOCUMENTS()—see the section in this chapter titled "Functions That Use or Return Arrays") or by entering an *array formula,* which is a single formula that either uses an array as an argument or enters its results in multiple cells.

Using Array Formulas

Here's a simple example that illustrates how array formulas work. In the Expenses workbook shown in Figure 18.5, the 1995 BUDGET totals are calculated using a separate formula for each month, as shown here:

January 1995 BUDGET	=C11*C3
February 1995 BUDGET	=D11*C3
March 1995 BUDGET	=E11*C3

FIGURE 18.5.

This worksheet uses three separate formulas to calculate the 1995 BUDGET figures.

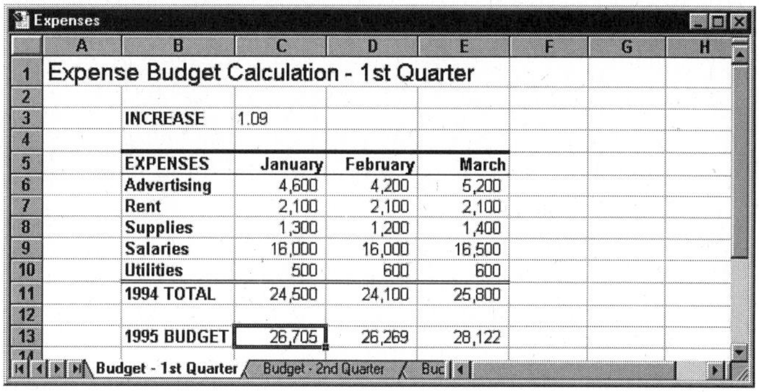

You can replace all three formulas with a single array formula by following these steps:

1. Select the range that you want to use for the array formula. In the 1995 BUDGET example, you select C13:E13.

2. Type the formula, and then in the places where you would normally enter a cell reference, type a range reference that includes the cells you want to use. *Don't*, I repeat, *don't* press Enter when you're done. In the example, you enter =C11:E11*C3.

3. To enter the formula as an array, press Ctrl+Shift+Enter.

The 1995 BUDGET cells (C13, D13, and E13) now all contain the same formula: {=C11:E11*C3}.

Notice that the formula is surrounded by braces ({ }). This identifies the formula as an array formula. (When you enter array formulas, you never need to enter these braces yourself—Excel adds them automatically.)

NOTE

Because Excel treats an array as a unit, you can't move or delete part of an array. If you need to work with an array, you must select the whole thing. If you want to reduce the size of an array, select it, activate the formula bar, and then press Ctrl+Enter to change the entry to a normal formula. You can then select the smaller range and re-enter the array formula.

TIP

To select an array quickly, activate one of its cells and press Ctrl+/.

Understanding Array Formulas

To understand how Excel processes an array, you need to keep in mind that Excel always sets up a correspondence between the array cells and the cells of whatever range you entered into the array formula. In the 1994 BUDGET example, the array consists of cells C13, D13, and E13, and the range used in the formula consists of cells C11, D11, and E11. Excel sets up a correspondence between array cell C13 and input cell C11, D13 and D11, and E13 and E11. To calculate the value of cell C13 (the January 1994 BUDGET), for example, Excel just grabs the input value from cell C11 and substitutes that in the formula. Figure 18.6 shows a diagram of this process.

FIGURE 18.6.

When processing an array formula, Excel sets up a correspondence between the array cells and the range used in the formula.

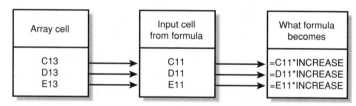

Array formula: ={C11:E11*INCREASE}

Array cell	Input cell from formula	What formula becomes
C13	C11	=C11*INCREASE
D13	D11	=D11*INCREASE
E13	E11	=E11*INCREASE

Array formulas can be confusing, but if you keep these correspondences in mind, you should have no trouble figuring out what's going on.

Array Formulas That Operate on Multiple Ranges

In the preceding example, the array formula operated on a single range, but array formulas also can operate on multiple ranges. For example, consider the Invoice Template worksheet shown in Figure 18.7. The totals in the Extension column (cells F12 through F16) are generated by a series of formulas that multiply the item's price by the quantity ordered. For example, the formula in cell F12 is this: =B12*E12.

You can replace all these formulas by making the following entry as an array formula into the range F12:F16: =B12:B16*E12:E16.

Again, you've created the array formula by replacing each cell reference with the corresponding ranges (and by pressing Ctrl+Shift+Enter).

FIGURE 18.7.

This worksheet uses several formulas to calculate the extended totals for each line.

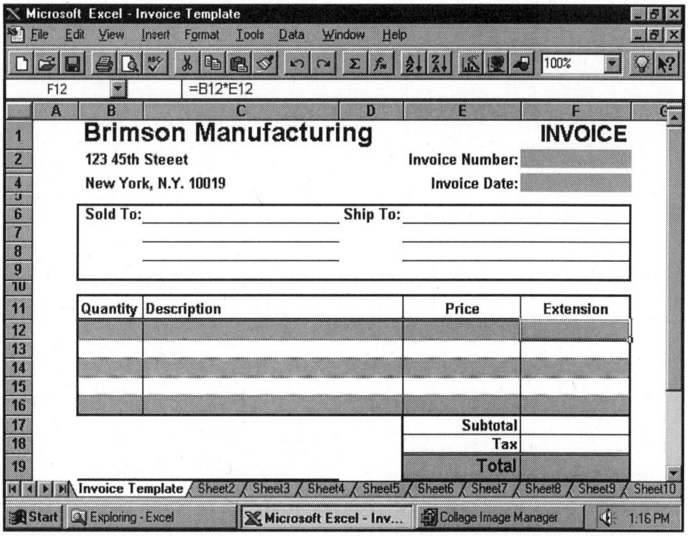

> **NOTE**
>
> You don't have to enter array formulas in multiple cells. For example, if you don't need the Extended totals in the Invoice Template worksheet, you can still calculate the subtotal by making the following entry as an array formula in cell F17: =SUM(B12:B16*E12:E16).

Using Array Constants

In the array formulas you've seen so far, the array arguments have been cell ranges. You also can use constant values as array arguments. This procedure enables you to input values into a formula without having them clutter your worksheet.

To enter an array constant in a formula, enter the values right in the formula and observe the following guidelines:

- Enclose the values in braces ({}).
- If you want Excel to treat the values as a row, separate each value with a semicolon.
- If you want Excel to treat the values as a column, separate each value with a comma.

For example, the following array constant is the equivalent of entering the individual values in a column on your worksheet: {1;2;3;4}.

Similarly, the following array constant is equivalent to entering the values in a worksheet range of three columns and two rows: {1,2,3;4,5,6}.

As a practical example, Figure 18.8 shows two different array formulas. The one on the left (used in the range E4:E7) calculates various loan payments given the different interest rates in the range C5:C8. The array formula on the right (used in the range F4:F7) does the same thing, but the interest rate values are entered as an array constant directly in the formula.

FIGURE 18.8.

Using array constants in your array formulas means you don't have to clutter your worksheet with the input values.

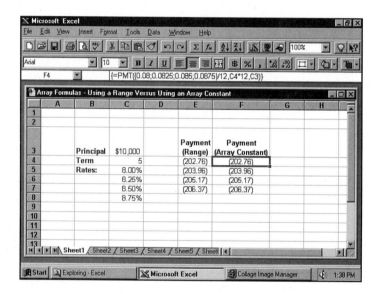

Functions That Use or Return Arrays

Many of Excel's worksheet functions either require an array argument or return an array result (or both). Table 18.5 lists several of these functions and explains how each one uses arrays.

Table 18.5. Some Excel functions that use arrays.

What the Function Uses	Array Argument?	Returns Array Result?
COLUMN()	No	Yes, if the argument is a range
COLUMNS()	Yes	No
CONSOLIDATE()	Yes	No
DOCUMENTS()	No	Yes, if multiple documents are open
FILES()	No	Yes
GROWTH()	Yes	Yes

What the Function Uses	Array Argument?	Returns Array Result?
HLOOKUP()	Yes	No
INDEX()	Yes	Yes
LINEST()	No	Yes
LOGEST()	No	Yes
LOOKUP()	Yes	No
MATCH()	Yes	No
MDETERM()	Yes	No
MINVERSE()	No	Yes
MMULT()	No	Yes
NAMES()	No	Yes
ROW()	No	Yes, if the argument is a range
ROWS()	Yes	No
SUMPRODUCT()	Yes	No
TRANSPOSE()	Yes	Yes
TREND()	Yes	Yes
VLOOKUP()	Yes	No
WINDOWS()	No	Yes
WORKGROUP()	Yes	No

When you use functions that return arrays, be sure to select a range large enough to hold the resultant array, and then enter the function as an array formula.

Working with Range Names in Formulas

You probably use range names often in your formulas. After all, a cell that contains the formula =Sales-Expenses is much more comprehensible than one that contains the more cryptic formula =F12-F2. The next few sections show you a few techniques that will make it easier for you to use range names in formulas.

Pasting a Name into a Formula

One way to enter a range name in a formula is to type the name in the formula bar. But what if you can't remember the name? Or what if the name is long and you've got a deadline looming? For these kinds of situations, Excel has a feature that enables you to select the name you want from a list and paste it right into the formula. The following procedure gives you the details:

1. In the formula bar, place the insertion point where you want the name to appear.
2. Select the Insert | Name | Paste command. Excel displays the Paste Name dialog box, as shown in Figure 18.9.

FIGURE 18.9.

Use the Paste Name dialog box to paste a range name into a formula.

TIP

A quick way to display the Paste Name dialog box is to press F3.

---

3. Use the Paste Name list to highlight the range name you want to use.
4. Select OK. Excel pastes the name in the formula bar.

TIP

You can bypass the Paste Name dialog box by using the Name box in the formula bar. When you're ready to paste a name, drop down the Name list and select the name you want.

Applying Names to Formulas

If you've been using ranges in your formulas and you name those ranges later, Excel doesn't automatically apply the new names to the formulas. Instead of substituting the appropriate names by hand, you can get Excel to do the dirty work for you. Follow these steps to apply the new range names to your existing formulas:

1. Select the range in which you want to apply the names or select a single cell if you want to apply the names to the entire worksheet.
2. Select the Insert | Name | Apply command. Excel displays the Apply Names dialog box, as shown in Figure 18.10.
3. Select the names you want applied from the Apply Names list.
4. Activate the Ignore Relative/Absolute checkbox to ignore relative and absolute references when applying names.

FIGURE 18.10.

Use the Apply Names dialog box to select the names you want to apply to your formula ranges.

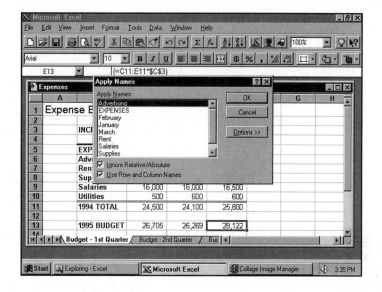

5. The Use Row and Column Names check box tells Excel whether to use the worksheet's row and column names when applying names. If you activate this check box, you also can click the Options button to see more choices.

6. Select OK to apply the names.

Naming Formulas

You can apply a naming concept for frequently used formulas and the formula doesn't physically have to appear in a cell. This not only saves memory, but it often makes your worksheets easier to read, as well. Follow these steps to name a formula:

1. Select the Insert | Name | Define command. Excel displays the Define Name dialog box.

2. Enter the name you want to use for the formula in the Names in Workbook edit box.

3. In the Refers To box, enter the formula exactly as you would in the formula bar.

TIP

Press F2 to put Excel into edit mode before you move around inside the Refers To box with the arrow keys. If you don't press F2 first, Excel assumes that you're trying to select a cell on the worksheet.

---

4. Select OK.

Now you can enter the formula name (rather than the formula itself) in your worksheet cells. For example, following is the formula for the volume of a sphere (r is the radius of the sphere): $4\pi r^3/3$.

Assuming that you have a cell named Radius somewhere in the workbook, you could create a formula named, say, SphereVolume and make the following entry in the Refers To box of the Define Name dialog box: =(4*PI()*Radius^3)/3.

About Excel's Functions

Functions are formulas that have been predefined by Excel. They're designed to take you beyond the basic arithmetic and text formulas you've seen so far. They do this in three ways:

- Functions make simple but cumbersome formulas easier to use. For example, suppose that you want to add a list of 100 numbers in a column starting at cell A1 and finishing at cell A100. Even if you wanted to, you wouldn't be able to enter 100 separate additions in a cell because you would run out of room (recall that cells are limited to 255 characters). Luckily, there's an alternative: the SUM() function. With this function, you would simply enter =SUM(A1:A100).

- Functions enable you to include complex mathematic expressions in your worksheets that otherwise would be impossible to construct using simple arithmetic operators. For example, determining a mortgage payment given the principal, interest, and term is a complicated matter at best, but Excel's PMT() function does it without breaking a sweat.

- Functions enable you to include data in your applications that you couldn't access otherwise. For example, the INFO() function can tell you how much memory is available on your system, what operating system you're using, what version number it is, and more.

As you can see, functions are a powerful addition to your worksheet-building arsenal. With the proper use of these tools, there is no practical limit to the kinds of models you can create.

The Structure of a Function

Every function has the same basic form:

```
FUNCTION(argument1, argument2, ...)
```

The function begins with the function name (SUM or PMT, for example), which is followed by a list of arguments separated by commas and enclosed in parentheses. The *arguments* are the function's inputs—the data it uses to perform its calculations.

For example, the FV() function determines the future value of a regular investment based on three required arguments and two optional ones:

FV(***rate,nper,pmt,*** *pv, type*)

rate is the fixed rate of interest over the term of the investment.

nper is the number of deposits over the term of the investment.

pmt is the amount you'll deposit each time.

pv is the present value of the investment.

type shows when the deposits are due (0 for the beginning of the period; 1 for the end of the period).

NOTE

Throughout this part of the book, when I introduce a new function, I show the argument syntax and then describe each argument (as I just did with the FV() function). In the syntax line, I show the function's required arguments in ***bold italic monospace*** type and the optional arguments in *regular italic monospace* type.

After processing these inputs, FV() returns the total value of the investment at the end of the term. Figure 18.11 shows a simple future-value calculator that uses this function. (In case you're wondering, I entered the payment value in cell B4 as negative because Excel always treats any money you have to pay as a negative number.)

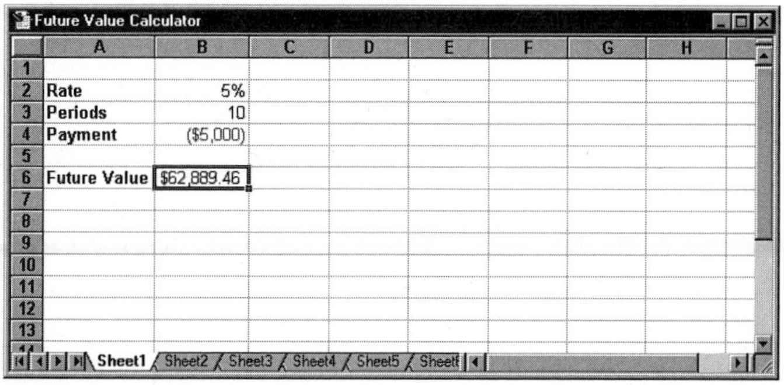

FIGURE 18.11.

The FV() function in action.

Entering Functions

You enter functions as you do any other data, but you must follow these rules:

- You can enter the function name in either uppercase or lowercase letters. Excel always converts function names to uppercase.

- Always enclose function arguments in parentheses.

- Always separate multiple arguments with commas. (You might want to add a space after each comma to make the functions more readable.)

- You can use a function as an argument for another function. This is called *nesting* functions. For example, the function AVERAGE(SUM(A1:A10), SUM(B1:B15)) sums two columns of numbers and returns the average of the two sums.

Using the Function Wizard

Although normally you'll type your functions by hand, there might be times when you can't remember the spelling of a function or the arguments it takes. To help out, Excel provides a tool called the Function Wizard. It enables you to select the function you want from a list and prompts you to enter the appropriate arguments. The following procedure shows you how the Function Wizard works:

1. To start a formula with a function, select the Function Wizard tool in the standard toolbar. Excel activates the formula bar, enters an equals sign and the most recently used function in the cell, and then displays the Function Wizard - Step 1 of 2 dialog box, as shown in Figure 18.12.

FIGURE 18.12.

Use the first Function Wizard dialog box to select a function.

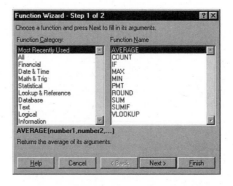

 If the standard toolbar isn't displayed, you can activate the Function Wizard by clicking the Function Wizard button in the formula bar.

> **TIP**
>
> To skip Step 1 of the Function Wizard, enter the name of the function in the cell and then either select the Function Wizard button or press Ctrl+A.

2. In the Function Category list, select the type of function you need. If you're not sure, select All.

3. Select the function you want to use from the Function Name list.

4. If you don't want to paste the function's arguments, select the Finish button to return to the worksheet. Otherwise, select the Next > button. Excel displays the Function Wizard - Step 2 of 2 dialog box.

5. For each required argument and each optional argument you want to use, enter a value or cell reference in the appropriate text box. Excel shows the current argument values and the current function value. (See Figure 18.13.)

FIGURE 18.13.

Use the second Function Wizard dialog box to enter values for the function's arguments.

Current function value

Description of current argument

Function arguments

Current argument values

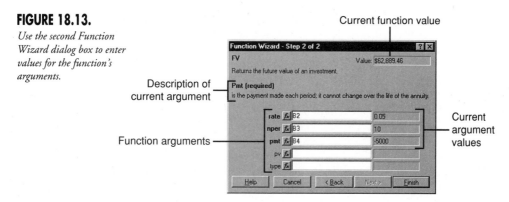

6. When you're done, select Finish. Excel pastes the function and its arguments into the cell.

Summary

This chapter shows you how to build better formulas in Excel. For related information on formulas, see the following chapters:

■ You'll find that you use ranges extensively in your formulas. To make sure your range skills are at their peak, see Chapter 17.

■ To make your formula results look their best, you need to know how to format your worksheets. You'll find all kinds of formatting techniques in Chapter 16, "Excel Concepts."

■ For more about Excel's database functions, see Chapter 22, "Working with Lists and Databases."

Charts and Graphics

19

by
*Paul McFedries
and Tom Hayes*

IN THIS CHAPTER

One of the best ways to analyze your worksheet data—or get your point across to other people—is to display your data visually in a chart. Excel gives you tremendous flexibility when you're creating charts; it enables you to place charts in separate documents or directly on the worksheet itself. Not only that, but you have dozens of different chart formats to choose from, and if none of Excel's built-in formats is just right, you can further customize these charts to suit your needs.

After you've created a chart and selected the appropriate chart type, you can enhance the chart's appearance by formatting any of the various chart elements. This chapter shows you how to format chart axes, data markers, and gridlines.

A Review of Chart Basics

Before getting down to the nitty-gritty of creating and working with charts, we'll take a look at some chart terminology that you need to become familiar with. Figure 19.1 points out the various parts of a typical chart. Each part is explained in Table 19.1.

FIGURE 19.1.

The elements of an Excel chart.

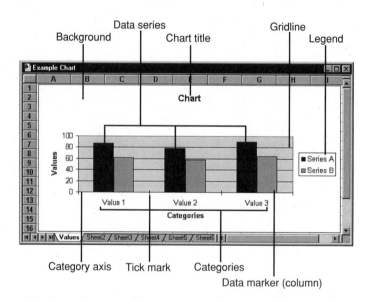

Table 19.1. The elements of an Excel chart.

Element	Description
Background	The area on which the chart is drawn. You can change the color and border of this area.
Category	A grouping of data values on the category axis. Figure 19.1 has three categories: Value 1, Value 2, and Value 3.

Element	Description
Category axis	The axis (usually the X-axis) that contains the category groupings.
Data marker	A symbol that represents a specific data value. The symbol used depends on the chart type. In a column chart, such as the one shown in Figure 19.1, each column is a marker.
Data series	A collection of related data values. Normally, the marker for each value in a series has the same pattern. Figure 19.1 has two series: Series A and Series B. These are identified in the legend.
Data value	A single piece of data. Also called a *data point*.
Gridlines	Optional horizontal and vertical extensions of the axis tick marks. These make data values easier to read.
Legend	A guide that shows the colors, patterns, and symbols used by the markers for each data series.
Plot area	The area bound by the category and value axes. It contains the data points and gridlines.
Tick mark	A small line that intersects the category axis or the value axis. It marks divisions in the chart's categories or scales.
Title	The title of the chart.
Value axis	The axis (usually the Y-axis) that contains the data values.

How Excel Converts Worksheet Data into a Chart

Creating an Excel chart is usually straightforward and often can be done in only a few keystrokes or mouse clicks. However, a bit of background on how Excel converts your worksheet data into a chart will help you avoid some charting pitfalls.

When Excel creates a chart, it examines both the shape and the contents of the range you've selected. From this data, the program makes various assumptions to determine what should be on the category axis, what should be on the value axis, how to label the categories, and which labels should show in the legend.

The first assumption Excel makes is that *there are more categories than data series*. This makes sense, because most graphs plot a small number of series over many different intervals. For example, a chart showing monthly sales and profit over a year has two data series (the sales and profit numbers) but 12 categories (the monthly intervals). Consequently, Excel assumes that the category axis (the X-axis) of your chart runs along the longest side of the selected worksheet range.

The chart shown in Figure 19.2 is a plot of the range A1:D3 in the Column Categories worksheet. Because, in this case, the range has more columns than rows, Excel uses each column as a category. Conversely, Figure 19.3 shows the plot of the range A1:C4, which has more rows than columns. In this case, Excel uses each row as a category.

FIGURE 19.2.

A chart created from a range with more columns than rows.

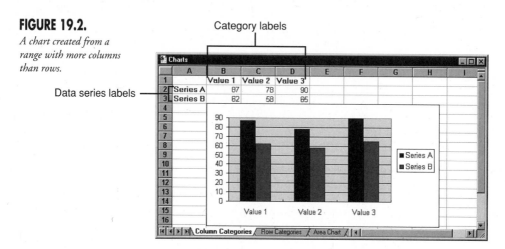

FIGURE 19.3.

A chart created from a range with more rows than columns.

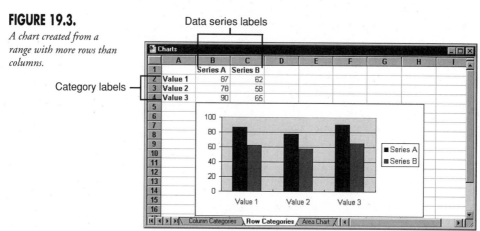

NOTE

If a range has the same number of rows and columns, Excel uses the columns as categories.

The second assumption Excel makes involves the location of labels for categories and data series:

- For a range with more columns than rows (such as in Figure 19.2), Excel uses the contents of the top row (row 1 in Figure 19.2) as the category labels, and the far-left column (column A in Figure 19.2) as the data series labels.
- For a range with more rows than columns (such as in Figure 19.3), Excel uses the contents of the far-left column (column A in Figure 19.3) as the category labels, and the top row (row 1 in Figure 19.3) as the data series labels.

NOTE

If a range has the same number of rows and columns, Excel uses the top row for the category labels and the far-left column for the data series labels.

Creating a Chart

When plotting your worksheet data, you have two basic options: you can create an *embedded chart*, which sits on top of your worksheet and can be moved, sized, and formatted, or you can create a separate *chart sheet* by using the automatic or cut-and-paste methods. Whether you choose to embed your charts or store them in separate sheets, the charts are linked with the worksheet data. Any changes you make to the data are automatically updated in the chart. The next few sections discuss each of these techniques.

Creating an Embedded Chart

When creating an embedded chart, you can use any of the following methods:

- Use the Default Chart tool to create a default chart.
- Use the ChartWizard to set chart options such as the chart type and axis titles.
- Copy a chart from a separate chart sheet.

NOTE

Because you can print embedded charts along with your worksheet data, embedded charts are useful in presentations in which you need to show plotted data and worksheet information simultaneously.

Creating a Default Embedded Chart

Excel's default chart is a basic column chart. Follow these steps to create an embedded chart using the default format:

1. Select the range you want to plot, including the row and column labels if there are any. Make sure that there are no blank rows between the column labels and the data.

2. Click the Default Chart tool on the Chart toolbar. The mouse pointer changes to a crosshair with a chart icon.

3. Position the mouse pointer at the top-left corner of the area where you want to put the chart.

4. Drag the mouse pointer to the bottom-right corner of that area. Excel displays a box as you drag. When you release the mouse button, Excel draws the chart.

> **TIP**
>
> To create a square chart area, hold down the Shift key while dragging the mouse pointer. To align the chart with the worksheet gridlines, hold down the Alt key while dragging.

> **NOTE**
>
> If, when you release the mouse button, you see a ChartWizard dialog box, Excel doesn't have enough information to create the chart automatically. Follow the steps in the next section to create the chart.

Creating an Embedded Chart with the ChartWizard

If the default chart isn't what you want, Excel's ChartWizard tool takes you through the steps necessary for setting up an embedded chart and setting various customization options. The following steps show you how the ChartWizard works:

1. Select the cell range you want to plot. (This step is optional because you get a chance to select a range later in the process.)

2. Either click the ChartWizard tool in the standard toolbar (or the Chart toolbar) or select the Insert | Chart | On This Sheet command. The mouse pointer changes to a crosshair with a chart icon.

3. Position the mouse pointer at the top-left corner of the area where you want to put the chart, and then drag the pointer to the bottom-right corner of the area. Excel displays a box as you drag. When you release the mouse button, Excel displays the ChartWizard - Step 1 of 5 dialog box, as shown in Figure 19.4.

FIGURE 19.4.

Use the ChartWizard - Step 1 of 5 dialog box to select (or adjust) the range you want to plot.

4. If you didn't do so earlier, select the cell range you want to chart, and then click the Next > button. The ChartWizard - Step 2 of 5 dialog box appears, as shown in Figure 19.5.

FIGURE 19.5.

Use the ChartWizard - Step 2 of 5 dialog box to select a chart type.

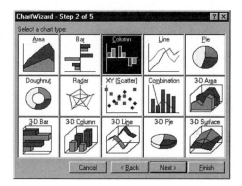

5. Select a chart type and then click the Next > button. Excel displays the ChartWizard - Step 3 of 5 dialog box, as shown in Figure 19.6.

FIGURE 19.6.

Use the ChartWizard - Step 3 of 5 dialog box to pick out a format for the chart type you selected.

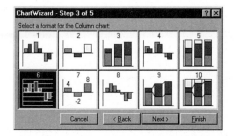

6. Select a chart format for the chart type you selected and then click the Next > button. The ChartWizard - Step 4 of 5 dialog box appears, as shown in Figure 19.7.

FIGURE 19.7.

Use the ChartWizard - Step 4 of 5 dialog box to define the layout of the chart.

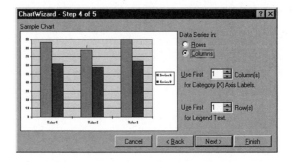

7. Select the options that define the layout of the data series and categories in your selected range. When you're done, click the Next > button. Excel displays the ChartWizard - Step 5 of 5 dialog box, as shown in Figure 19.8.

FIGURE 19.8.

Use the ChartWizard - Step 5 of 5 dialog box to add explanatory text to your chart.

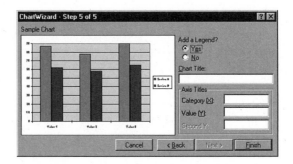

8. Select a legend option and add any titles you need. When you're done, select Finish. Excel draws the chart on the worksheet.

Activating a Chart

Before you can work with chart types, you need to activate a chart. How you do this depends on the kind of chart you're dealing with:

- For an embedded chart, double-click inside the chart box. The box border changes to a thicker, broken line.
- For a chart sheet, select the Sheet tab.

Selecting a Chart Type

After you've created a chart, you might decide that the existing chart type doesn't display your data the way you want. Or you might want to experiment with different chart types to find the one that best suits your data. Fortunately, the chart type isn't set in stone and can be changed at any time. Depending on the chart, you can use one of three methods to select a different chart type:

- Use the Chart Type dialog box.
- Use the Chart Type tool's palette of types.
- Use the chart AutoFormat feature.

Selecting a Chart Type from the Chart Type Dialog Box

Follow these steps to use the Chart Type dialog box to select a chart type:

1. Activate the chart you want to change.
2. Select the Format | Chart Type command. Excel displays the Chart Type dialog box, shown in Figure 19.9.

FIGURE 19.9.

The Chart Type dialog box.

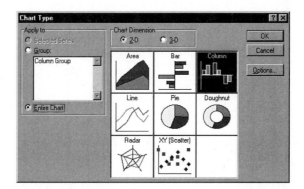

TIP

You can also display the Chart Type dialog box by right-clicking the chart background and selecting the Chart Type command from the shortcut menu.

---

3. In the Apply To group, select Entire Chart.
4. In the Chart Dimension group, select either 2-D or 3-D.
5. Select a chart type.
6. Chart subtypes are variations of the main chart type that display your data in slightly different ways. To select a chart subtype, select the Options button, activate the Subtype tab from the dialog box that appears, and choose one of the Subtype boxes.
7. Select OK.

Using the Chart Type Tool to Select a Chart Type

The following procedure shows you how to select a chart type using the Chart Type tool:

1. Activate the chart you want to change.

2. Display the Chart toolbar.

3. Drop down the Chart Type tool and select one of the chart types from the palette that appears. Using the selected chart type, Excel redraws the chart.

> **TIP**
>
> If you want to experiment with various chart types, you can "tear off" the Chart Type tool's palette. Drop the palette down, place the mouse pointer inside the palette, and drag the mouse until the palette separates. When you release the button, the Chart toolbar appears.

Selecting an AutoFormat Chart Type

To make your chart formatting chores easier, Excel comes with some built-in *AutoFormats*—predefined chart formats that you can apply easily. The following steps show you how to use the chart AutoFormat feature:

1. Activate the chart you want to change.

2. Select the Format|AutoFormat command. Excel displays the AutoFormat dialog box, as shown in Figure 19.10.

FIGURE 19.10.

The chart AutoFormat dialog box.

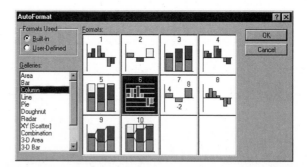

> **TIP**
>
> You also can display the AutoFormat dialog box by right-clicking the chart background and selecting the shortcut menu's AutoFormat command.

3. Highlight a chart type from the Galleries list.

4. Pick out a chart format from the Formats boxes.

5. Select OK.

Converting a Series to a Different Chart Type

If you want to create a combination chart not found among Excel's AutoFormat types or if you have chart formatting you want to preserve, you can easily apply an overlay effect to an existing chart.

For example, Figure 19.11 shows a chart with three series: sales figures for 1993, sales figures for 1994, and a series that plots the growth from 1993 to 1994. The chart clearly shows that the Growth series would make more sense as a line chart. Excel enables you to convert individual data series into chart types. To do so, follow these steps:

1. Activate the chart you want to work with.

2. Click the series you want to convert.

3. Select the Format | Chart Type command (or right-click the series and select Chart Type from the shortcut menu) to display the Chart Type dialog box.

4. In the Apply To group, activate the Selected Series option. (This option should already be selected.)

5. Select the chart type you want to use for the series.

6. Select OK. Excel converts the series to the chart type you selected. Figure 19.12 shows the preceding chart with the Growth series converted to a line chart.

FIGURE 19.11.

The Growth series would be better as a line chart.

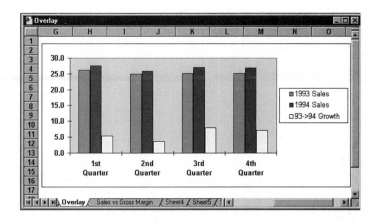

FIGURE 19.12.

The revised chart with the Growth series converted to a line chart.

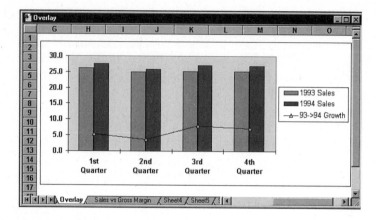

Selecting Chart Elements

An Excel chart is composed of elements such as axes, data markers, gridlines, and text, each with its own formatting options. Before you can format an element, however, you need to select it. Table 19.2 lists the mouse techniques for selecting various chart items.

Table 19.2. Mouse techniques for selecting chart elements.

Action	*Result*
Click the chart background.	The entire chart is selected.
Click an empty part of the plot area.	The plot area is selected.
Click an axis or an axis label.	The axis is selected.
Click a gridline.	The gridline is selected.
Click any marker in the series.	The data series is selected.
Click a data marker once and then click it a second time.	The data marker is selected.
Click an object.	The chart object is selected.

Formatting Chart Axes

Excel provides various options for controlling the appearance of your chart axes. You can hide axes; set the typeface, size, and style of axis labels; format the axis lines and tick marks; and adjust the axis scale. You can find most of the axis formatting options in the Format Axis dialog box, as shown in Figure 19.13. To display this dialog box, select the axis you want to format and then select the Format | Selected Axis command.

FIGURE 19.13.

Use the Format Axis dialog box to enhance the look of your chart axes.

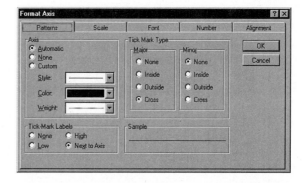

TIP

To access the Format Axis dialog box quickly, you have three options: You can double-click an axis, select the axis and press Ctrl+1, or right-click an axis and select Format Axis from the shortcut menu.

Formatting Axis Patterns

The Patterns tab in the Format Axis dialog box enables you to set various options for the axis line and tick marks. Here's a summary of the control groups in the Patterns tab:

- Axis—These options format the axis line. Select None to remove the line, or select Custom to adjust the Style, Color, and Weight. The Sample box shows you how the line will look.
- Tick Mark Type—These options control the position of the Major and Minor tick marks.
- Tick Mark Labels—These options control the position of the tick mark labels.

NOTE

The major tick marks are the tick marks that carry the axis labels. The minor tick marks are the tick marks that appear between the labels. See the next section to learn how to control the units of both the major and the minor tick marks.

Formatting an Axis Scale

You can format the scale of your chart axes to set things such as the range of numbers on an axis and where the category and value axes intersect.

To format the scale, select the Scale tab in the Format Axis dialog box. If you're formatting the value (Y) axis, you see the layout shown in Figure 19.14. These options format several scale characteristics, such as the range of values (Minimum and Maximum), the tick mark units (Major Unit and Minor Unit), and where the category (X) axis crosses the value axis. For the last of these characteristics, you have three choices:

- Activate the check box labeled Category (X) Axis Crosses At. This places the X-axis at the bottom of the chart (that is, at the minimum value on the Y-axis).

- Enter a value in the text box labeled Category (X) Axis Crosses At.

- Activate the check box labeled Category (X) Axis Crosses at Maximum Value (this places the X-axis at the top of the chart).

FIGURE 19.14.

The Scale tab for the value (Y) axis.

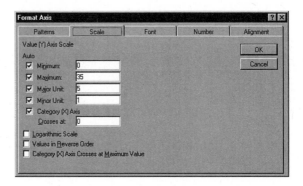

Formatting the value axis scale properly can make a big difference in the impact of your charts. For example, Figure 19.15 shows a chart with a value axis scale ranging from 0 to 50. Figure 19.16 shows the same chart with the value axis scale between 18 and 23. As you can see, the trend of the data is much clearer and more dramatic in Figure 19.16.

FIGURE 19.15.

A stock chart showing an apparently flat trend.

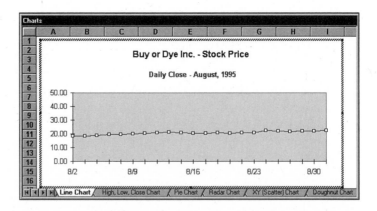

FIGURE 19.16.

The same stock chart with an adjusted scale shows an obvious up trend.

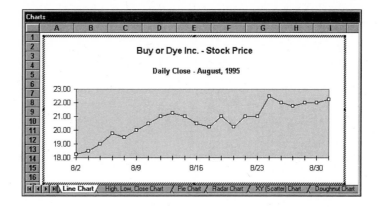

For the category (X) axis, the Scale tab appears as shown in Figure 19.17. These options mostly control where the value (Y) axis crosses the category (X) axis and the frequency of categories:

- Use the text box labeled Value (Y) Axis Crosses at Category Number to control where the Y-axis crosses the X-axis. For example, an entry of 1 (the default) places the Y-axis on the left side of the chart. If you prefer to see the Y-axis on the right side of the chart, activate the check box labeled Value (Y) Axis Crosses at Maximum Category.

- The major tick mark unit is controlled by the text box labeled Number of Categories between Tick Mark Labels. For example, an entry of 5 puts a tick mark label every five categories.

- The total number of tick marks is controlled by the text box labeled Number of Categories between Tick Marks. For example, an entry of 1 provides a tick mark for each category.

- When the check box labeled Value (Y) Axis Crosses between Categories is deactivated (the default), Excel plots the values on the tick marks. If you activate this check box, Excel plots the values between the tick marks.

- Activating the check box labeled Categories in Reverse Order displays the categories along the X-axis in reverse order.

FIGURE 19.17.

The Scale tab for the category (X) axis.

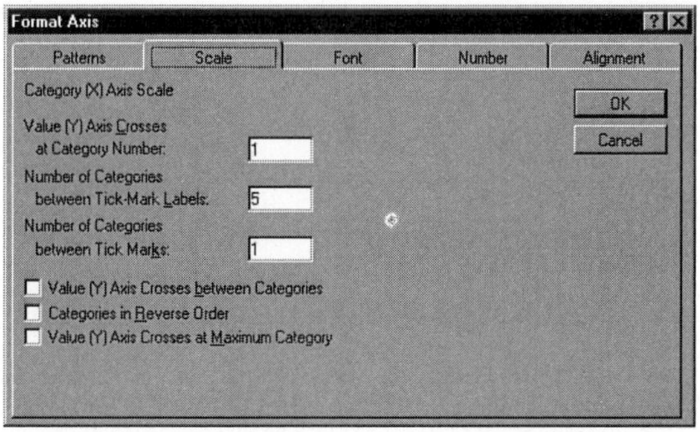

Formatting Axis Labels

You can change the font, numeric format, and alignment of the labels that appear along the axis. To change the label font, select the Font tab in the Format Axis dialog box, and then select the font options you want.

To change the numeric format of axis labels (assuming, of course, that the labels are numbers, dates, or times), you have two choices:

- Format the worksheet data series that generated the labels. Excel uses this formatting automatically when it sets up the axis labels.

- Select the Number tab in the Format Axis dialog box, and then select a numeric format from the options provided.

To format the alignment of the axis labels, select the Alignment tab in the Format Axis dialog box, and then select the option you want from the Orientation group.

TIP

You also can use the tools on the Formatting toolbar (such as Bold and Currency Style) to format the labels of a selected axis.

Formatting Chart Data Markers

A *data marker* is a symbol Excel uses to plot each value (data point). Examples of data markers are small circles or squares for line charts, rectangles for column and bar charts, and pie slices for pie charts. Depending on the type of marker you're dealing with, you can format the marker's color, pattern, style, or border.

To begin, select the data marker or markers you want to work with:

- If you want to format the entire series, click any data marker in the series, and then select the Format | Selected Series command. Excel displays the Format Data Series dialog box.

- If you want to format a single data marker, click the marker once to select the entire series, and then click the marker a second time. (Note, however, that you don't double-click the marker. If you do, you just get the Format Data Series dialog box. Click the marker once, wait a couple beats, and then click it again.) Then choose the Format | Selected Data Point command to display the Format Data Point dialog box.

TIP

You can also display the Format Data Series dialog box either by double-clicking an axis or by selecting the axis and pressing Ctrl+1. Displaying the Format Data Point dialog box is similar: Select the data point and then either double-click it or press Ctrl+1.

Whichever method you choose, select the Patterns tab to display the formatting options for the series markers. Figure 19.18 shows the Patterns tab for an area, bar, column, pie, or dough-nut chart marker. (The corresponding Format Data Point dialog box has only the Patterns and Data Labels tabs.)

FIGURE 19.18.

The Patterns tab for area, bar, column, pie, and doughnut chart data series.

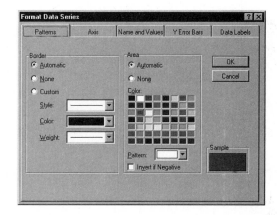

Use the Border group to either turn off the border or define the style, color, and weight of the marker border. Use the Area section to assign marker colors and patterns.

You get a different set of options when you format line, XY, or radar chart markers, as shown in Figure 19.19. Use the Line section to format the style, color, and weight of the data series line. The Smoothed Line option (available only for line and XY charts) smoothes out some of a line's rough edges. Use the Marker section to format the marker style as well as the foreground and background colors.

FIGURE 19.19.

The Patterns tab for line, XY, and radar charts.

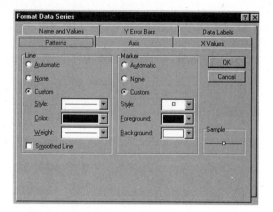

Displaying and Formatting Chart Gridlines

Adding horizontal or vertical gridlines can make your charts easier to read. For each axis, you can display a major gridline, a minor gridline, or both. The positioning of these gridlines is determined by the numbers you enter for the axis scales. For a value axis, major gridlines are governed by the Major Unit option, and minor gridlines are governed by the Minor Unit option. (The Major and Minor Unit options are properties of the value axis scale. To learn how to adjust these values, see the section earlier in this chapter titled "Formatting an Axis Scale.") For a category axis, major gridlines are governed by the number of categories between tick labels, and minor gridlines are governed by the number of categories between tick marks.

Displaying Gridlines

The following procedure shows you how to display gridlines:

1. Select the Insert | Gridlines command. Excel displays the Gridlines dialog box, as shown in Figure 19.20.

FIGURE 19.20.

The Gridlines dialog box.

TIP

To access the Gridlines dialog box quickly, right-click the plot area and select Insert Gridlines from the shortcut menu.

2. Activate the check boxes for the gridlines you want to display.

3. Select OK.

Click this tool in the Chart toolbar to display major value axis gridlines on your chart.

Formatting Gridlines

You can format the style, color, and weight of your gridlines by following these steps:

1. Select a gridline.

2. Select the Format | Selected Gridlines command to display the Format Gridlines dialog box.

> **TIP**
>
> You can also display the Format Gridlines dialog box by double-clicking a gridline, by selecting a gridline and pressing Ctrl+1, or by right-clicking a gridline and choosing Format Gridlines from the shortcut menu.

3. Use the Patterns tab to select the gridline options you want (Style, Color, and Weight).

4. Select OK.

Formatting the Plot Area and Background

You can format borders, patterns, and colors for both the chart plot area and the background. To format either of these areas, follow this procedure:

1. Select the plot area or chart background.

2. Select either the Format | Selected Plot Area command or the Format | Selected Chart Area command to display the appropriate format dialog box.

> **TIP**
>
> To quickly display the appropriate format dialog box, you can also double-click the plot area or background, you can select either one and press Ctrl+1, or you can right-click either one and select either Format Plot Area or Format Chart Area from the shortcut menu.

3. In the Patterns tab, select the options you want in the Border and Area groups.

4. If you're in the Format Chart Area dialog box, you also can select the Font tab to format the chart font.

5. Select OK.

Summary

This chapter gets you up to speed with Excel's charting capabilities. After some brief charting theory, the chapter looks at all kinds of formatting options for each of the chart elements. Here are a few other chapters to read for related information:

■ You can use charts for simple what-if data analysis. Chapter 21, "Data-Analysis Tools and Techniques," tells you how.

■ Many of the formatting options discussed for the chart elements—such as numeric formats, fonts, and alignment—are also discussed in Chapter 16, "Excel Concepts."

Exchanging Data with Other Applications

20

by
Paul McFedries
and Tom Hayes

IN THIS CHAPTER

Excel doesn't exist in a vacuum. You often have to import data to Excel from other applications (such as a database file or a text file from a mainframe). And just as often you have to export Excel data to other programs (such as a word processor or a presentation graphics package). Although these tasks are usually straightforward, you still can run into some problems. Excel therefore provides some features that can help you avoid these problems. This chapter looks at the various ways you can exchange data between Excel and other applications.

Exchanging Data with Windows Applications

To use text and graphics from another Windows application in Excel (or to use Excel data in another Windows application), you can use any of the following methods:

- Cut and paste using the Clipboard—With this method, you cut or copy data from one Windows application and paste it into another.

- Linking—With this method, you use a special paste command that sets up a link between the original data and the new copy. When you change the original data, the linked copy is updated automatically.

- Embedding—With this method, you create a copy of a file or an object from another application and paste the copy into Excel as an embedded object. This embedded copy contains not only the data but also all the underlying information associated with the originating application (file structure, formatting codes, and so on).

These methods are described in the next three sections.

> **NOTE**
>
> Linking and embedding are possible only with applications that support the object linking and embedding (OLE) standard.

Using the Clipboard

The *Clipboard* is a temporary storage location in memory for cut or copied data. It can store text, numbers, graphics, or anything you can cut or copy in a Windows application. You can then switch to a different program and paste the Clipboard data. If you don't want to embed or link the data, follow these steps to exchange data using the Clipboard:

1. Activate the application containing the original data.

2. Select the data, and then select either the Edit | Cut or the Edit | Copy command. The data is transferred to the Clipboard. Figure 20.1 shows a table in Word for Windows that has been selected and copied.

FIGURE 20.1.

A Word for Windows table that has been selected and copied to the Clipboard.

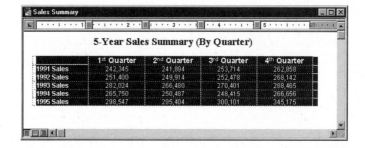

TIP

If you want to copy an Excel range to another application as a picture, select the range, hold down the Shift key, and select the Edit | Copy Picture command.

---

3. Switch to the application that you want to receive the data.

4. Move to where you want the data to appear and select the Edit | Paste command. The data is pasted from the Clipboard. Figure 20.2 shows the Word for Windows table pasted into an Excel worksheet.

FIGURE 20.2.

The Word for Windows table pasted into an Excel worksheet.

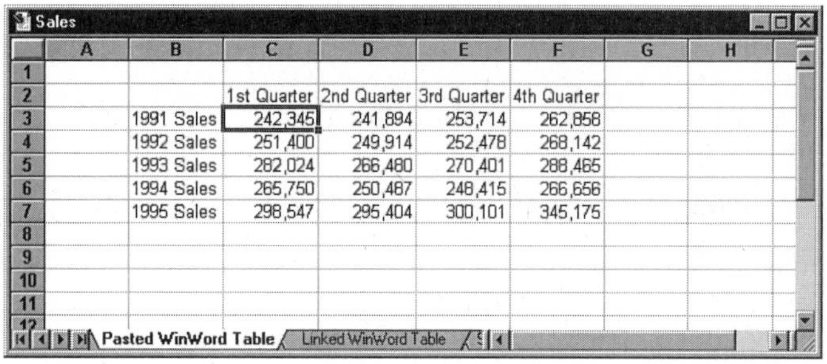

If you're pasting text into Excel, follow these guidelines when you select a location for the text:

- ■ If you want to place the text in a text box, double-click the text box to get the insertion point, and then position the insertion point where you want the text to appear.

- ■ If you want to position the text within a single cell (provided that there are fewer than 255 characters in the selection), activate either in-cell editing or the formula bar, and then position the insertion point.

- ■ If you've selected any object before pasting (such as a graphic image or text box), Excel embeds the text as a Picture object. (See the section in this chapter titled "Embedding Objects in a Worksheet.")

Linking Data

As you saw in the preceding section, when you share data via the Clipboard method, Windows sends only raw data to the client application. In other words, if you use the normal Paste command to paste data from a server file into a client application, you must manually change the copied data in the client file whenever the data in the server file is changed.

> **NOTE**
>
> Let's take a second to make sure that you're comfortable with the terminology used with object linking and embedding.
>
> For starters, an *object* is anything you can cut or copy in an application. It can be a section of text, a worksheet range, a bitmap, a sound file, or just about any data you create in an application.
>
> The program you use to create the object is called the *server application* (or sometimes the *source application* or the *object application*).
>
> The program that receives the linked or embedded object is called the *client application* (or sometimes the *destination application* or the *container application*).
>
> A document that contains objects from different applications is called a *compound document.*

By including a special *link* reference when you perform the paste, however, you can eliminate this extra work because the link updates the copied data automatically. This link tells the client application where the document came from so that the link can check the server file for changes. If the server file has been altered, the link automatically updates the client application's copy. The following procedure shows you how to copy and link data in Excel:

1. Activate the application containing the original data (the *server*).
2. Select the data, and then select Edit | Copy to copy the data to the Clipboard.
3. Switch to Excel (the *client*) and activate the cell or object that you want to receive the data.
4. Select the Edit | Paste Special command. Excel displays the Paste Special dialog box, shown in Figure 20.3.
5. In the As list, select the format you want to use for the copied data. The options you see depend on the type of data. If you're pasting text, be sure to select Text.
6. Activate the Paste Link option.
7. Select OK. Excel pastes the data and sets up the link.

FIGURE 20.3.

Use the Paste Special dialog box to select the type of object to paste and to set up the link.

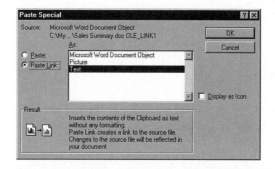

CAUTION

If Excel displays the #REF! error when you link the server data, automatic updating of remote references probably has been turned off. To turn it on, select the Tools | Options command, select the Calculation tab in the Options dialog box, and then activate the Update Remote References check box.

Figure 20.4 shows the same Word for Windows table, but this time it was pasted with a link. The array formula displayed in the formula bar is called a *remote reference formula*. It tells Excel where the server document is located so that it can update the link when necessary.

FIGURE 20.4.

The Word for Windows table pasted with a link.

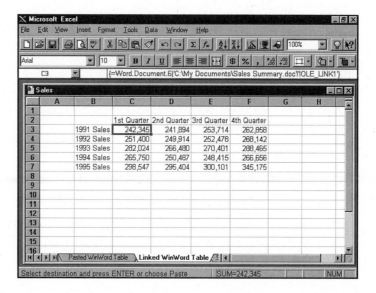

Embedding Objects in a Worksheet

When you paste a linked object in a worksheet, Excel doesn't paste the data. Instead, it sets up a remote reference formula that *points to* the data. If Excel can't find the server file—for example, if the file has been moved, renamed, or deleted—the link breaks and Excel displays a #NAME? error in any cell that used the remote reference.

Embedding differs from linking in that embedded data becomes part of the worksheet. There is no link to the original server document, so it doesn't matter what happens to the original document. In fact, there is no need for a server file at all because the embedded object maintains its native format. Also, you can easily start the server application by double-clicking one of its objects in the client worksheet. The downside to this convenience is that storing all the information about an embedded object increases the size of the workbook accordingly.

> **NOTE**
>
> In applications that support the OLE standard, an *object* is, in simplest terms, any data you can place on the Clipboard. It could be a section of text, a graphics image, a chart, or anything else you can select and copy.

There are two ways to embed an object in a worksheet:

- Copy the object from the server application and paste it in the worksheet as an embedded object.
- Insert a new embedded object from within Excel.

Embedding an Object by Pasting

If the object you want to embed already exists, you can place it on the Clipboard and then embed it in the worksheet using the Paste Special command. The following procedure shows you the steps to work through:

1. Activate the server application, and open or create the document that contains the object.
2. Select the object you want to embed.
3. Select the Edit | Copy command to place the data on the Clipboard.
4. Activate Excel and open or create the worksheet that you want to receive the data.
5. Select the cell where you want to paste the data.
6. Select the Edit | Paste Special command to display the Paste Special dialog box.
7. In the As list, select the option that pastes the data as an embedded object. You generally look for one of two clues, depending on the server application:

   The data type contains the word *Object*.

The data type contains the name of the server application.

8. If you want to see the data in the worksheet, skip to Step 10. Otherwise, you can display the object as an icon by activating the Display as Icon check box. The default icon and the Change Icon button appear. (See Figure 20.5.)

FIGURE 20.5.

You can display an embedded object as an icon.

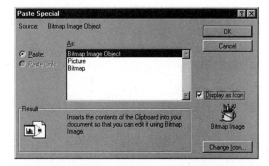

> **NOTE**
>
> Why would you want to display the object as an icon? The most common reason is that you don't need to see the data all the time. For example, the object might contain explanatory text for a worksheet model. If users of the model need to read the text, they can double-click the icon.

9. To choose a different icon, select Change Icon and then select the image from the Change Icon dialog box. To use a different icon file, select the Browse button and then select the file from the Browse dialog box. Select OK until you return to the Paste Special dialog box.

10. Select OK. Excel embeds the object in the worksheet.

Figure 20.6 shows a worksheet with a Paint object embedded normally and as an icon.

FIGURE 20.6.

A Paintbrush object embedded normally and as an icon.

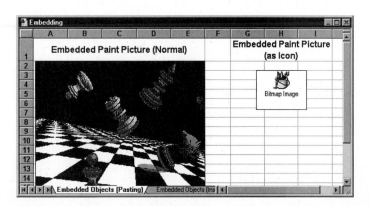

Embedding a New Object by Inserting

If the object you want to embed doesn't exist, you can use Excel to create a new object in the server application and embed it without creating a separate server document. This is, in fact, the only way to embed an object from one of the mini-applications that ship with Excel and other products. Programs such as Microsoft WordArt are not standalone applications, so you can't create separate files. You can use these programs' objects only by inserting them in the client application. Follow these steps to insert a new server object in an Excel worksheet:

1. Select the cell where you want the object embedded. (This cell represents the upper-left corner of the object.)
2. Select the Insert | Object command, and in the Object dialog box that appears, select the Create New tab, shown in Figure 20.7.

FIGURE 20.7.

Use the Create New tab to create a new object for embedding.

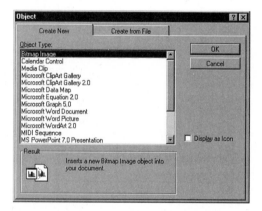

3. In the Object Type list, select the type of object you want to create.

NOTE

You can display the new object as an icon by activating the check box labeled Display as Icon.

4. Select OK. Excel starts the server application.
5. Create the object you want to embed.
6. Exit the server application. Depending on the program you're using, you usually can exit by using one of the following techniques:

    Click outside the object's frame.

    Select the File | Exit & Return to *Worksheet* command, in which *Worksheet* is the name of the active Excel worksheet. In this case, the server application asks whether you want to update the embedded object. Select Yes.

> **TIP**
>
> In some server applications, you can embed the object without leaving the application by selecting the File | Update command.

Should You Link or Embed?

Perhaps the most confusing aspect of OLE is determining under what circumstances you should link your objects or embed them. The answer lies in how OLE treats the source data. As I mentioned earlier, when you link an object, OLE doesn't bother sending the data to the client program. Instead, it only sends a reference that tells the client application which file contains the source data. This is enough to maintain the link between the two applications. When you embed an object, however, Windows crams the actual data (and a few other goodies) into the client document.

Therefore, you should *link* your objects under any of the following conditions:

- You want to keep your client documents small. The client gets just the link information and not the data itself, so there's much less overhead associated with linking.

- The object still needs some work. If you haven't yet completed the object, you should link it so that any further modifications are updated in the client document.

- You're sure the server file won't be moved or deleted. To maintain the link, OLE requires that the server document remain in the same place. If it gets moved or deleted, the link is broken.

- You need to keep the server file as a separate document in case you want to make changes to it later, or in case you need it for more OLE operations. You're free to link an object to as many client files as you like. If you think you'll be using the server data in different places, you should link it to maintain a separate file.

- You won't be sending the client file via e-mail or floppy disk. Again, OLE expects the linked server data to appear in a specific place. If you send the client document to someone else, that person might not have the proper server file to maintain the link.

Similarly, you should *embed* your objects under any of the following conditions:

- You don't care how big your client files get. Embedding works best in situations in which you have lots of hard disk space and lots of memory.

- You don't need to keep the server file as a separate document. If you need to use the server data only once, embedding it means you can get rid of the server file and reduce the clutter on your hard disk.

- You'll be sending the client document and you want to ensure that the object arrives intact. If you send a file containing an embedded object, the other person will see the data complete and unaltered.

Working with OLE 2 Applications

The latest version of object linking and embedding—version 2—includes many new features that make embedded objects even easier to create and maintain. Here's a summary of just a few of these features:

- Drag and drop objects between applications—You can move information between two open OLE 2 applications simply by dragging selected data from one application and dropping it in the other. If you want to copy the data, you need to hold down the Ctrl key while dragging.

- In-place inserting—If you select an OLE 2 object from the Create New tab in the Object dialog box, Excel activates *in-place* inserting. This means that instead of displaying the server application in a separate window, certain features of the Excel window are temporarily hidden so that the server's features can be displayed:

Excel's title bar changes to the name of the server application.

The Excel menu bar (with the exception of the File and Window menus) is replaced by the server's menu bar.

The Excel toolbars are replaced by the server's toolbars.

Any other features you need for creating the server object (such as the ruler in Word for Windows) also are added to the window.

To exit in-place editing and embed the object, click outside the object frame. Figure 20.8 shows what happens to the Excel window when you insert a Word for Windows (version 6 or later) document object.

FIGURE 20.8.

The Excel window displays many features of the Word for Windows window when you insert a Word document object.

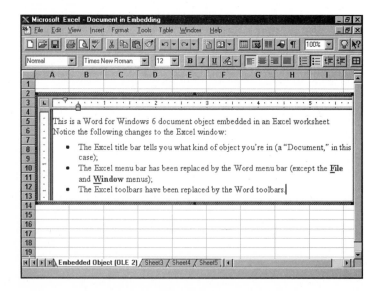

■ In-place editing—When you edit an OLE 2 object, the object remains where it is, and the Excel window changes as it does with in-place inserting. Make your changes and then click outside the object to complete the edit.

Exchanging Data with the Other Microsoft Office Programs

As you might expect, Excel data sharing works best with the other programs that come with the Microsoft Office suite: Word, PowerPoint, and Access. In the Office 95 package, the links between these programs are even tighter and more integrated than before. Microsoft's goal with this new Office suite (and, indeed, with all of Windows 95) is to turn the user's attention away from working with applications and more toward working with documents. This is a laudable goal, because for too long now, we users have been shaping our documents to fit the application we were using, rather than the other way around. We need to start thinking of applications as mere tools that help us achieve a particular result.

To that end, the Office applications boast three features that can help focus on documents:

■ The applications themselves share a common user interface. For example, the menu structures and toolbar buttons in all the Office programs are nearly identical. Also, many of the Office programs share common modules, such as the spell checker.

■ Support for OLE 2 in all the Office applications makes it easier to create and maintain compound documents.

■ The addition of the Binder application makes it easy to combine related documents from multiple applications into a single file for distribution.

Although most of your Office data sharing will follow the basic OLE steps we looked at in the preceding few sections, a few shortcuts and techniques are specific to the Office applications. The next few sections fill you in on the details.

Working with Word

As the word processor in the Office group, Microsoft Word is a popular choice as a client application because worksheets, ranges, and charts are often used to back up statements in a proposal or memo. However, exchanging data between Word and Excel isn't always straightforward because, depending on how you paste the information, it's often hard to predict the result. To help out, the next couple sections tell you exactly what to expect when sharing data between Word and Excel.

Exporting an Excel Range to Word

When you copy a range in Excel and then select Word's Edit | Paste Special command, the Paste Special dialog box gives you five data types to use for the paste. To help you decide which option is best for you, Table 20.1 summarizes each data type.

Table 20.1. Data types available for pasting an Excel range.

Data Type	Description
Microsoft Excel Worksheet Object	Embeds the range as a Worksheet object.
Formatted Text (RTF)	Pastes the range as a Word table and preserves existing formatting.
Unformatted Text	Pastes the range as plain text with tabs separating each column and linefeeds separating each row.
Picture	Inserts the range as a picture. Use this data type rather than Bitmap to preserve memory and keep screen redraws fast.
Bitmap	Inserts the range as a bitmap image. The only advantage over the Picture data type is that the bitmap image shows you exactly what the Excel range looks like.

If you copy an Excel chart to the Clipboard, Word's Paste Special dialog box offers you three data types: Microsoft Excel Chart Object, Picture, and Bitmap.

Importing Text from Word

Copying Word text to the Clipboard and then pasting it into Excel is straightforward. The Paste Special dialog box gives you a choice of three data types, as described in Table 20.2.

Table 20.2. Data types available for pasting Word text.

Data Type	Description
Microsoft Word Document Object	Embeds the text as a document object.
Picture	Inserts the text as a picture.

Data Type	Description
Text	Pastes the text as unformatted text. Places text separated by tabs into separate columns; places paragraphs into separate rows.

TIP

When Word text is on the Clipboard, selecting Excel's Edit | Paste command is the same as selecting Edit | Paste Special and choosing the Text data type.

NOTE

If you copy a Word table to the Clipboard and you would prefer to insert the content of each table cell into its own worksheet cell, use the Text data type when pasting.

Working with PowerPoint

Exchanging data between Excel and PowerPoint uses methods similar to those for Word. Here are a few things to bear in mind:

- When you're pasting a range, PowerPoint's Paste Special dialog box gives you the same data type choices as does Word.
- PowerPoint tends to insert worksheets and charts as rather small objects. To see the range properly, you need to increase the size of the object.
- If you want to insert a new worksheet object into a slide, you can use PowerPoint's Insert Microsoft Excel Worksheet button on its standard toolbar. This button works just like the one on Word's standard toolbar.

Working with Access

If your database needs to extend only to simple, flat-file tables, Excel's built-in database capabilities probably will do the job for you. For larger table and relational features, however, you'll want to use a more sophisticated application such as Access. The next couple sections show you how to share data between Excel and Access.

Exporting Excel Data to Access

To get Excel data into Access, you can use either the Clipboard or the Import Spreadsheet Wizard feature in Access.

To use the Clipboard method, you need to set up an Access table with the same number of fields as there are columns in the range you want to copy. When that's done, follow these steps to paste the data into the table:

1. In Excel, copy the data to the Clipboard.
2. In Access, open the table (datasheet view), move to the new record at the bottom of the table, and select the first field.
3. Select the Edit | Paste Append command. Access pastes the data into the table and displays a dialog box that lets you know how many records are about to be added.
4. Select Yes to return to the table.

> **CAUTION**
>
> If the Excel range you're copying has more columns than there are fields in the Access table, Access ignores the extra columns.

Importing Data from Access

Getting table records from Access to Excel can also be done in one of two ways: with the Clipboard or with the Analyze It With MS Excel feature. Here's a rundown of the Clipboard method:

1. In Access, open the table (datasheet view), and select the records you want to import.
2. Select Edit | Copy to place the records on the Clipboard.
3. In Excel, select the destination for the records.
4. Select Edit | Paste. Excel pastes the field names in the current row and the records in separate rows below.

The Analyze It With MS Excel feature can convert an Access database object into an Excel worksheet and open the new sheet in Excel all in one step. To try it out, open the datasheet, form, or report that you want to convert, and then do one of the following:

- Select the Tools | OfficeLinks | Analyze It With MS Excel command.
- Click the OfficeLinks button in the toolbar and then select Analyze It With MS Excel.

Access converts the table into an Excel worksheet, activates Excel, and then loads the new worksheet.

Importing Text Files

When you import text data, Excel usually breaks up the file according to the position of the carriage-return and line-feed characters. This means that each line in the text file gets inserted into a cell. In most cases, this is not the behavior you want. For example, if you've downloaded some stock data, you need the date, volume, and pricing values in separate columns.

Instead of making you divide each line by hand, Excel includes a TextWizard tool that can parse text files in the usual step-by-step fashion of the wizards. How you use the TextWizard depends on the format of the text. There are two possibilities:

■ Delimited text—Each field is separated by characters such as commas, spaces, or tabs.

■ Fixed width text—The fields are aligned in columns.

If you're not sure which type of file you're dealing with, just start the TextWizard as described in either of the following two procedures. In most cases, the TextWizard can determine the data type for you.

To import a text file (or to convert worksheet text into columns), follow these steps:

1. To open the text file, select the File | Open command, and then select the file from the Open dialog box. (To help out, select the Text Files option from the list labeled List Files of Type.) Excel displays the Text Import Wizard - Step 1 of 3 dialog box, shown in Figure 20.9.

FIGURE 20.9.

Use the Text Import Wizard - Step 1 of 3 dialog box to select the type of text file you're importing.

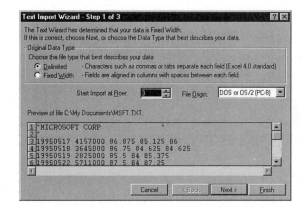

Or, if you want to convert worksheet text, select the text and select the Data | Text to Columns command. Excel displays the Convert Text to Columns Wizard - Step 1 of 3 dialog box.

2. In the Original Data Type group, activate either Delimited or Fixed Width.

3. If you're importing a text file, enter a number in the spinner labeled Start Import at Row, and then select the file's native environment from the File Origin drop-down list.

4. Select the Next > button to move to the wizard's Step 2 dialog box, shown in Figure 20.10.

FIGURE 20.10.

The Text Import Wizard - Step 2 of 3 dialog box for delimited data.

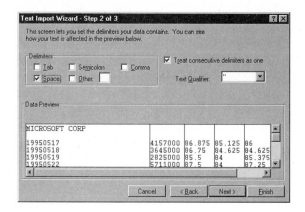

5. If you're using a delimited file, select the appropriate delimiting character from the Delimiters checkboxes. If the data includes text in quotation marks, select the appropriate quotation mark character from the Text Qualifier list.

   If you're using a fixed-width file, you can set up the column breaks by using the following techniques:

   To create a column break, click inside the Data Preview area at the spot where you want the break to occur.

   To move a column break, drag it to the new location.

   To delete a column break, double-click it.

6. Select the Next > button to move to the wizard's Step 3 dialog box, shown in Figure 20.11.

FIGURE 20.11.

Use the Step 3 of 3 dialog box to select and format the columns.

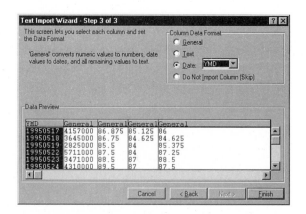

7. Select each column and then choose one of the options from the Column Data Format group. (You select a column by clicking the column header.) If you don't want a column imported, activate the Do Not Import Column (Skip) option.

8. Select Finish. Excel imports the text file, as shown in Figure 20.12.

FIGURE 20.12.

The text file imported into Excel.

	A	B	C	D	E	F	G	H	I
1	5/17/95	4157000	86.875	85.125	86				
2	5/18/95	3645000	86.75	84.625	84.625				
3	5/19/95	2825000	85.5	84	85.375				
4	5/22/95	5711000	87.5	84	87.25				
5	5/23/95	3471000	88.5	87	88.5				
6	5/24/95	4310000	89.5	87	87.5				
7	5/25/95	2715000	89.375	87	89.25				
8	5/26/95	3308000	89.25	87	87.5				
9	5/29/95	0	0	0	0				
10	5/30/95	6226000	88.375	82.625	83				
11	5/31/95	7485000	84.75	81	84.687				
12	6/1/95	3822000	85.625	83.875	84.125				
13	6/2/95	3472000	84.125	82.625	83.125				
14	6/5/95	3491000	85.375	81.75	84.75				
15	6/6/95	3065000	86.016	83.125	83.125				
16	6/7/95	4037000	84.75	82.125	84				

Summary

This chapter shows you various methods for sharing data between Excel and your other applications. It shows you the basic cut-and-paste Clipboard technique, various object linking and embedding methods, and a few techniques for exchanging data with DOS applications. It also looks at the importation of text files.

Here are some other chapters to check out for related information:

■ If the data you want exists in an external database file, you'll need to learn the querying techniques found in Chapter 24, "Using Microsoft Query."

■ If you would like to try your hand at controlling data sharing via VBA (including OLE automation), Chapter 26, "Working with Other Applications," is the place to look.

Data-Analysis Tools
and Techniques

21

by
Paul McFedries
and Tom Hayes

IN THIS CHAPTER

At times it's not enough to simply enter data in a worksheet, build a few formulas, and add a little formatting to make things presentable. We're often called on to divine some inner meaning from the jumble of numbers and formula results that litter our workbooks. In other words, we need to *analyze* our data to see what nuggets of understanding we can unearth.

This chapter looks at a few simple analytic techniques that have a many uses. You'll learn how to use Excel's numerous methods for what-if analysis and how to wield Excel's useful Goal Seek tool. This chapter also introduces you to Solver. Solver is a sophisticated optimization program that enables you to find the solutions to complex problems that would otherwise require high-level mathematical analysis.

What-if analysis, however, is not an exact science. All what-if models make guesses and assumptions based on history, expected events, or whatever voodoo comes to mind. A particular set of guesses and assumptions that you plug into a model is called a *scenario*. Because most what-if worksheets can take a wide range of input values, you usually end up with a large number of scenarios to examine. Instead of going through the tedious chore of inserting all these values into the appropriate cells, Excel has a Scenario Manager feature that can handle the process for you. This chapter completes our look at Excel's data-analysis features by examining this useful tool.

Using What-If Analysis

What-if analysis is perhaps the most basic method for interrogating your worksheet data. In fact, it's probably safe to say that most spreadsheet work involves what-if analysis of one form or another.

With what-if analysis, you first calculate a formula D, based on the input from variables A, B, and C. You then say, "What if I change variable A? Or B or C? What happens to the result?"

For example, Figure 21.1 shows a worksheet that calculates the future value of an investment based on five variables: the interest rate, period, annual deposit, initial deposit, and deposit type. Cell C9 shows the result of the FV() function. Now the questions begin. What if the interest rate were 7 percent? What if you deposited $8000 per year? Or $12,000? What if you reduced the initial deposit? Answering these questions is a simple matter of changing the appropriate variables and watching the effect on the result.

FIGURE 21.1.

The simplest what-if analysis involves changing worksheet variables and watching the result.

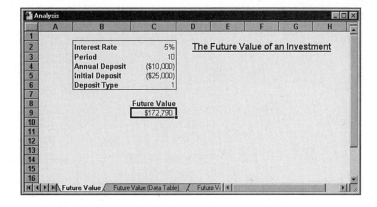

Setting Up a One-Input Data Table

The problem with modifying formula variables is that you see only a single result at one time. If you're interested in studying the effect a range of values has on the formula, you need to set up a *data table*. In the investment analysis worksheet, for example, suppose that you want to see the future value of the investment with the annual deposit varying between $7000 and $13,000. You could just enter these values in a row or column and then create the appropriate formulas. Setting up a data table, however, is much easier, as the following procedure shows:

1. Add to the worksheet the values you want to input into the formula. You have two choices for the placement of these values:

    If you want to enter the values in a row, start the row one cell up and one cell to the right of the formula.

    If you want to enter the values in a column, start the column one cell down and one cell to the left of the cell containing the formula. (See Figure 21.2.)

FIGURE 21.2.

Enter the values you want to input into the formula.

Input cell

Input values

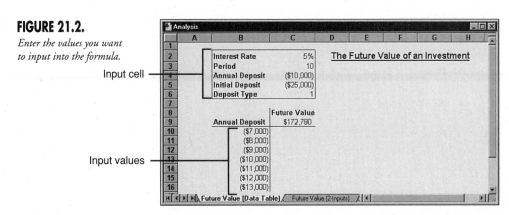

2. Select the range that includes the input values and the formula. (In Figure 21.2, this would be B9:C16.)

3. Select the Data | Table command. Excel displays the Table dialog box.

4. If you entered the input values in a row, select the Row Input Cell text box and then enter the cell address of the input cell. If the input values are in a column, enter the input cell's address in the Column Input Cell text box instead. In the investment analysis example, you enter C4 in the Column Input Cell, as shown in Figure 21.3.

FIGURE 21.3.

In the Table dialog box, enter the input cell where you want Excel to substitute the input values.

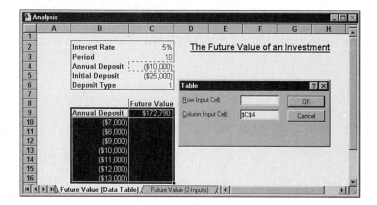

5. Select OK. Excel takes each of the input values and places them in the input cell; Excel then displays the results in the data table, as shown in Figure 21.4.

FIGURE 21.4.

Excel substitutes each input value into the input cell and displays the results in the data table.

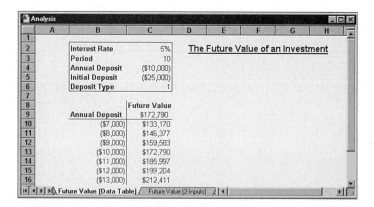

Adding More Formulas to the Input Table

You're not restricted to just a single formula in your data tables. If you want to see the effect of the various input values on different formulas, you can easily add them to the data table. For example, in our future value worksheet, it would be interesting to factor inflation into the calculations so that the user could see how the investment appears in today's dollars. Figure 21.5 shows the revised worksheet with a new Inflation variable (cell C7) and a formula that converts the calculated future value into today's dollars (cell D9).

FIGURE 21.5.

To add a formula to a data table, enter the new formula next to the existing one.

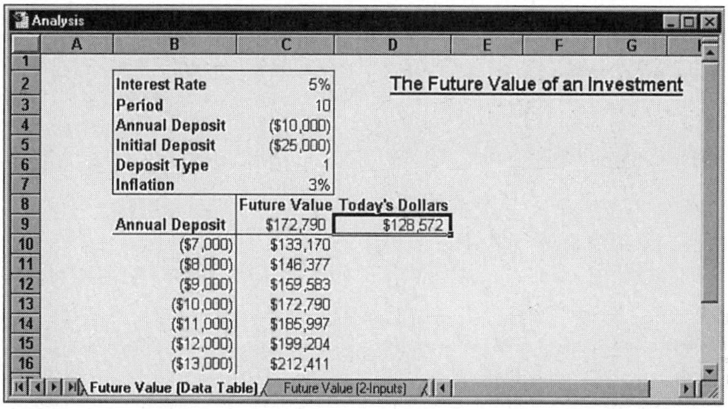

	B	C	D
2	Interest Rate	5%	The Future Value of an Investment
3	Period	10	
4	Annual Deposit	($10,000)	
5	Initial Deposit	($25,000)	
6	Deposit Type	1	
7	Inflation	3%	
8		Future Value	Today's Dollars
9	Annual Deposit	$172,790	$128,572
10	($7,000)	$133,170	
11	($8,000)	$146,377	
12	($9,000)	$159,583	
13	($10,000)	$172,790	
14	($11,000)	$185,997	
15	($12,000)	$199,204	
16	($13,000)	$212,411	

NOTE

This is the formula for converting a future value into today's dollars:

```
Future Value / (1 + Inflation Rate) ^ Period
```

Here `Period` is the number of years from now that the future value exists.

To create the new data table, follow the steps outlined earlier. However, make sure that the range you select in Step 2 includes the input values and *both* formulas (that is, the range B9:D16 in Figure 21.5). Figure 21.6 shows the results.

FIGURE 21.6.

The results of the data table with multiple formulas.

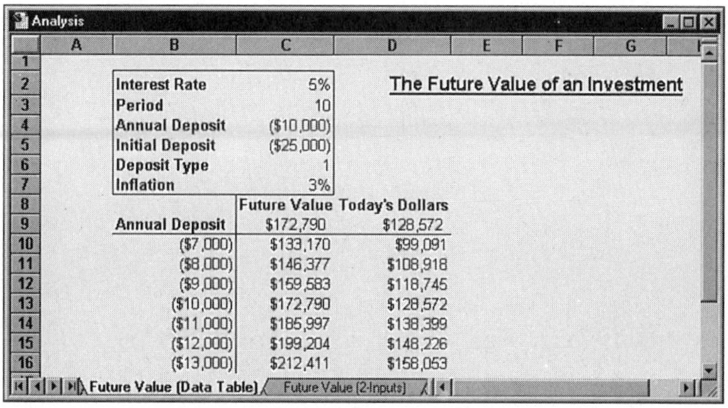

	B	C	D
2	Interest Rate	5%	The Future Value of an Investment
3	Period	10	
4	Annual Deposit	($10,000)	
5	Initial Deposit	($25,000)	
6	Deposit Type	1	
7	Inflation	3%	
8		Future Value	Today's Dollars
9	Annual Deposit	$172,790	$128,572
10	($7,000)	$133,170	$99,091
11	($8,000)	$146,377	$108,918
12	($9,000)	$159,583	$118,745
13	($10,000)	$172,790	$128,572
14	($11,000)	$185,997	$138,399
15	($12,000)	$199,204	$148,226
16	($13,000)	$212,411	$158,053

> **NOTE**
>
> After you have a data table set up, you can do regular what-if analysis by adjusting the other worksheet variables. Each time you make a change, Excel recalculates every formula in the table.

Setting Up a Two-Input Table

You also can set up data tables that take two input variables. This option enables you to see the effect on an investment's future value when you enter different values for, say, the annual deposit and the interest rate. This procedure shows how to set up a two-input data table:

1. Enter one set of values in a column below the formula and the second set of values in the row beside the formula, as shown in Figure 21.7.

FIGURE 21.7.

Enter the two sets of values you want to input into the formula.

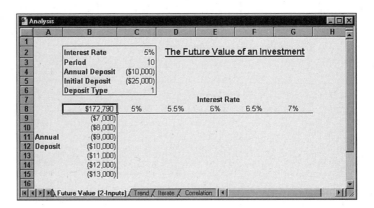

2. Select the range that includes the input values and the formula (B8:G15 in Figure 21.7).
3. Select the Data I Table command to display the Table dialog box.
4. In the Row Input Cell text box, enter the cell address of the input cell that corresponds to the row values you entered (C2 in Figure 21.7—the Interest Rate variable). In the Column Input Cell text box, enter the cell address of the input cell you want to use for the column values (C4 in Figure 21.7—the Annual Deposit variable).
5. Select OK. Excel runs through the various input combinations and then displays the results in the data table, as shown in Figure 21.8.

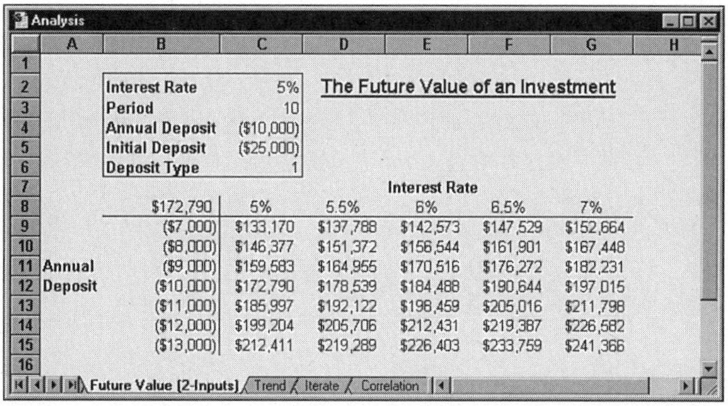

FIGURE 21.8.

Excel substitutes each input value into the input cell and displays the results in the data table.

		Interest Rate	5%	The Future Value of an Investment			
		Period	10				
		Annual Deposit	($10,000)				
		Initial Deposit	($25,000)				
		Deposit Type	1				
					Interest Rate		
		$172,790	5%	5.5%	6%	6.5%	7%
		($7,000)	$133,170	$137,788	$142,573	$147,529	$152,664
		($8,000)	$146,377	$151,372	$156,544	$161,901	$167,448
Annual		($9,000)	$159,583	$164,955	$170,516	$176,272	$182,231
Deposit		($10,000)	$172,790	$178,539	$184,488	$190,644	$197,015
		($11,000)	$185,997	$192,122	$198,459	$205,016	$211,798
		($12,000)	$199,204	$205,706	$212,431	$219,387	$226,582
		($13,000)	$212,411	$219,289	$226,403	$233,759	$241,366

TIP

As mentioned earlier, if you make changes to any of the variables in a table formula, Excel recalculates the entire table. This isn't a problem in small tables, but large ones can take a very long time to calculate. If you prefer to control the table recalculation, choose the Tools | Options command, select the Calculation tab, and then activate the Automatic Except Tables check box. To recalculate a table, press F9 (or Shift+F9 to recalculate the current worksheet only).

Editing a Data Table

When you select the Data | Table command, Excel enters an *array formula* in the interior of the data table. This formula is a TABLE() function with the following syntax:

```
{=TABLE(row_input_ref, column_input_ref)}
```

Here, `row_input_ref` and `column_input_ref` are the cell references you entered in the Table dialog box. The braces ({ }) indicate that this is an array, which means you can't change or delete individual elements of the table. (To learn more about arrays, see Chapter 18, "Manipulating the Information.") If you want to delete or move the data table, you first must select the entire table.

Working with Goal Seek

Here's a what-if question for you: what if you already know the result you want? For example, you might know that you want to have $50,000 in a college fund 18 years from now, or that you have to achieve a 30 percent gross margin in your next budget. If you need to manipulate only a single variable to achieve these results, you can use Excel's Goal Seek feature. You tell Goal Seek the final value you need and which variable to change, and it finds a solution for you (if one exists).

How Does Goal Seek Work?

When you set up a worksheet to use Goal Seek, you usually have a formula in one cell and the formula's variable—with an initial value—in another. (Your formula can have multiple variables, but Goal Seek allows you to manipulate only one variable at a time.) Goal Seek operates by using an *iterative method* to find a solution. That is, Goal Seek first tries the variable's initial value to see whether that produces the result you want. If it doesn't, Goal Seek tries different values until it converges on a solution. (To learn more about iterative methods, see "Using Iteration," later in this chapter.)

Running Goal Seek

Suppose that you want to set up a college fund for your newborn child. Your goal is to have $50,000 in the fund 18 years from now. Assuming 5 percent interest, how much will you need to deposit into the fund every year? The following procedure shows how to use Goal Seek to calculate the answer:

1. Set up your worksheet to use Goal Seek. Figure 21.9 shows the College worksheet, which I've set up the following way:

    Cell C8 contains the FV() function that calculates the future value of the college fund. When we're done, this cell's value should be $50,000.

    Cell C6 contains the annual deposit into the fund (with an initial value of $0). This is the value Goal Seek adjusts to find a solution.

    The other cells (C4 and C5) are used in the FV() function; however, for this exercise we'll assume that they're constants.

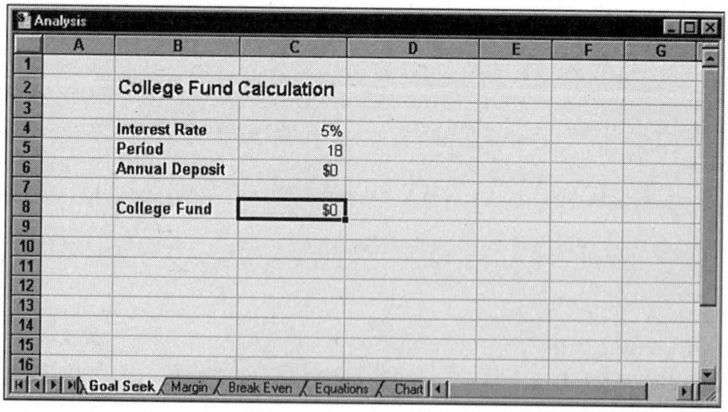

FIGURE 21.9.

A worksheet set up to use Goal Seek.

2. Select the Tools | Goal Seek command. Excel displays the Goal Seek dialog box.
3. In the Set Cell text box, enter a reference to the cell that contains your goal. For this example, enter C8.

4. In the To Value text box, enter the final value you want for the goal cell. The example's value is 50000.

5. Use the By Changing Cell text box to enter a reference to the variable cell. In the example, enter C6. Figure 21.10 shows the completed dialog box.

FIGURE 21.10.

The completed Goal Seek dialog box.

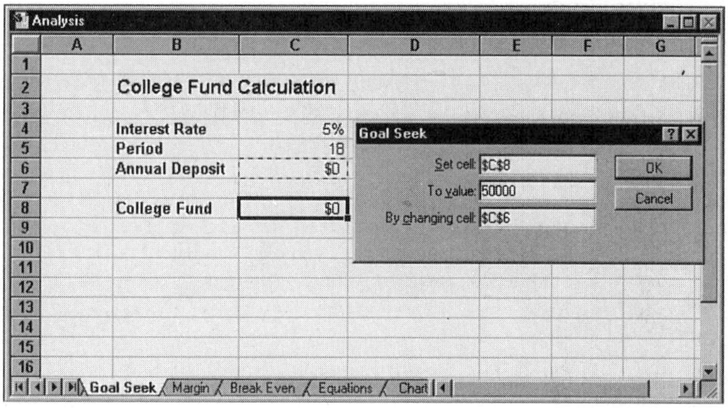

6. Select OK. Excel begins the iteration and displays the Goal Seek Status dialog box. When finished, the dialog box tells you whether Goal Seek found a solution, as shown in Figure 21.11.

FIGURE 21.11.

The Goal Seek Status dialog box shows you the solution (if one was found).

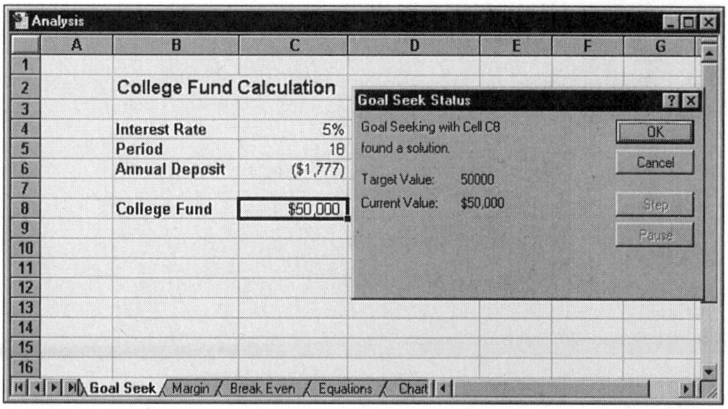

NOTE

Most of the time, Goal Seek finds a solution relatively quickly. For longer operations, you can select the Pause button in the Goal Seek Status dialog box to stop Goal Seek. To walk through the process one iteration at a time, select the Step button. To resume Goal Seek, select Continue.

7. If Goal Seek found a solution, you can accept the solution by selecting OK. To ignore the solution, select Cancel.

Goal Seek Examples

Goal Seek is a simple tool, but it can handle many types of problems. This section looks at a few more examples of Goal Seek.

Optimizing Product Margin

Many businesses use product margin as a measure of fiscal health. A strong margin usually means that expenses are under control and that the market is satisfied with your price points. Product margin depends on many factors, of course, but you can use Goal Seek to find the optimum margin based on a single variable.

For example, suppose that you want to introduce a new product line, and you want the product to return a margin of 30 percent during the first year. You're making the following assumptions:

■ The sales during the year will be 100,000 units.

■ The average discount to your customers will be 40 percent.

■ The total fixed costs will be $750,000.

■ The cost per unit will be $12.63.

Given all this information, you want to know what price point will produce the 30 percent margin.

Figure 21.12 shows a worksheet set up to handle this situation. An initial value of $1.00 is entered into the Price cell, and Goal Seek is set up in the following way:

■ The Set cell reference is C14, the Margin calculation.

■ A value of .3 (the Margin goal) is entered in the To Value text box.

■ A reference to the Price cell (C4) is entered into the By Changing Cell text box.

When you run Goal Seek, it produces a solution of $47.87 for the price, as shown in Figure 21.13. This solution can be rounded up to $47.95.

A Note About Goal Seek's Approximations

Notice that the solution in Figure 21.13 is an approximate figure. That is, the margin value is 29.92%, not the 30% we were looking for. That's pretty close (it's off by only 0.0008), but it's not exact. Why didn't Goal Seek find the exact solution?

FIGURE 21.12.

A worksheet set up to calculate a price point that will optimize gross margin.

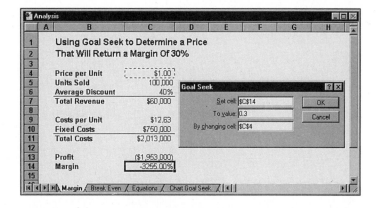

FIGURE 21.13.

The result of Goal Seek's labors.

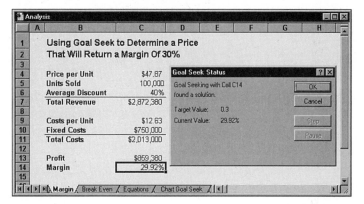

The answer lies in one of the options Excel uses to control iterative calculations. Some iterations can take an extremely long time to find an exact solution, so Excel compromises by setting certain limits on iterative processes. To see these limits, select the Tools | Options command and then select the Calculation tab in the Options dialog box that appears. (See Figure 21.14.) These two options control iterative processes:

- Maximum Iterations—The value in this text box controls the maximum number of iterations. In Goal Seek, this value represents the maximum number of values that Excel plugs into the variable cell.

- Maximum Change—The value in this text box is the threshold Excel uses to determine whether it has converged on a solution. If the difference between the current solution and the desired goal is within this value, Excel stops iterating.

It was the Maximum Change value that prevented us from getting an exact solution for the profit margin calculation. On a particular iteration, Goal Seek hit the solution .2992, which put us within 0.0008 of our goal of 0.3. Because 0.0008 is less than the default value of 0.001 in the Maximum Change text box, Excel called a halt to the procedure.

To get an exact solution, you must adjust the Maximum Change value to 0.0001.

FIGURE 21.14.

The text boxes in the Iteration group place limits on iterative calculations.

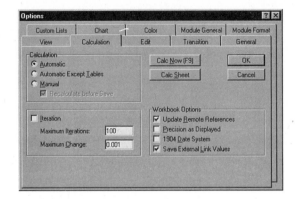

Performing a Break-Even Analysis

In a *break-even analysis*, you determine the number of units you have to sell of a product so that your total profits are 0 (that is, the product revenue equals the product costs). Setting up a profit equation with a goal of 0 and varying the units sold is perfect for Goal Seek.

To try this, we'll extend the example used in the "Optimizing Product Margin" section. In this case, assume a unit price of $47.95 (the solution found to optimize product margin, rounded up to the nearest 95 cents). Figure 21.15 shows the Goal Seek dialog box filled out as detailed here:

■ The Set Cell reference is set to C13, the Profit calculation.

■ A value of 0 (the Profit goal) is entered in the To Value text box.

■ A reference to the Units Sold cell (C5) is entered into the By Changing Cell text box.

FIGURE 21.15.

A worksheet set up to calculate a price point that optimizes gross margin.

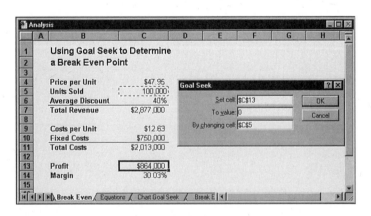

Figure 21.16 shows the solution: 46,468 units must be sold to break even.

FIGURE 21.16.

The break-even solution.

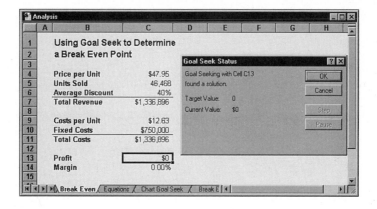

Solving Algebraic Equations

Goal Seek is also useful for solving complex algebraic equations of one variable. For example, suppose that you need to find the value of *x* to solve the following rather nasty equation:

$$\frac{(3x - 8)^2 (x - 1)}{4x^2 - 5} = 1$$

This equation, although too complex for the quadratic formula, can be easily rendered in Excel. The left side of the equation can be represented with the following formula:

```
=(((3*A2 - 8)^2)*(A2-1))/(4*A2^2-5)
```

Cell A2 represents the variable *x*. You can solve this equation in Goal Seek by setting the goal for this equation to 1 (the right side of the equation) and by varying cell A2. Figure 21.17 shows a worksheet and the completed Goal Seek dialog box.

FIGURE 21.17.

Solving an algebraic equation with Goal Seek.

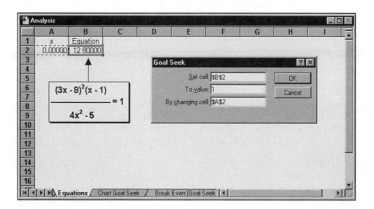

Figure 21.18 shows the result. The value in cell A2 is the solution *x* that satisfies the equation. Notice that the equation result (cell B2) is not quite 1. As mentioned earlier in this chapter, if you need higher accuracy, you must change Excel's convergence threshold. In this example, select the Tools|Options command, and in the Calculation tab type 0.000001 in the Maximum Change text box.

FIGURE 21.18.

Cell A2 holds the solution for the equation in cell A1.

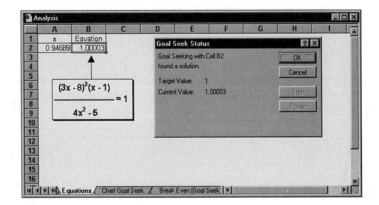

Using Iteration

A common business problem involves calculating a profit-sharing plan contribution as a percentage of a company's net profits. This isn't a simple multiplication problem, because the net profit is determined, in part, by the profit-sharing figure. For example, suppose that a company has a gross margin of $1,000,000 and expenses of $900,000, which leaves a gross profit of $100,000. The company also sets aside 10 percent of net profits for profit sharing. The net profit is calculated with the following formula:

```
Net Profit = Gross Profit - Profit Sharing Contribution
```

This is called a *circular reference formula* because there are terms on the left and right side of the equals sign that depend on each other. Specifically, Profit Sharing Contribution is derived with the following formula:

```
Profit Sharing Contribution = (Net Profit)*0.1
```

One way to solve such a formula is to guess at an answer and see how close you come. For example, because profit sharing should be 10 percent of net profits, a good first guess might be 10 percent of *gross* profits, or $10,000. If you plug this number into the formula, you end up with a net profit of $90,000. This isn't right, however, because 10 percent of $90,000 is $9000. Therefore, the profit-sharing guess is off by $1000.

So you can try again. This time, use $9000 as the profit-sharing number. Plugging this new value into the formula gives a net profit of $91,000. This number translates into a profit-sharing contribution of $9,100—which is off by only $100.

If you continue this process, your profit-sharing guesses will get closer to the calculated value (this process is called *convergence*). When the guesses are close enough (for example, within a dollar), you can stop and pat yourself on the back for finding the solution. This process is called *iteration*.

Of course, you didn't spend your (or your company's) hard-earned money on a computer so that you could do this sort of thing by hand. Excel makes iterative calculations a breeze, as you'll see in the following procedure:

1. Set up your worksheet and enter your circular reference formula. Figure 21.19 shows a worksheet for the example used earlier. If Excel displays a dialog box telling you it can't resolve circular references, select OK.

FIGURE 21.19.

A worksheet with a circular reference formula.

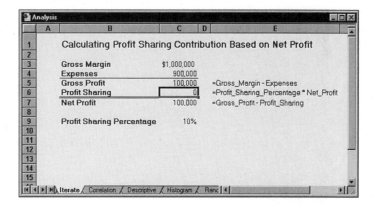

2. Select the Tools | Options command, and then select the Calculation tab in the Options dialog box.

3. Activate the Iteration check box.

4. Use the Maximum Iterations text box to specify the number of iterations you need. In most cases, the default figure of 100 is more than enough.

5. Use the Maximum Change text box to tell Excel how accurate you want your results to be. The smaller the number, the longer the iteration takes and the more accurate the calculation will be. Again, the default value is probably a reasonable compromise.

6. Select OK. Excel begins the iteration and stops when it has found a solution, as shown in Figure 21.20.

TIP

If you want to watch the progress of the iteration, turn on the Manual check box in the Calculation tab and enter 1 in the Maximum Iterations text box. When you return to your worksheet, each time you press F9, Excel performs a single pass of the iteration.

FIGURE 21.20.

The solution to the iterative profit-sharing problem.

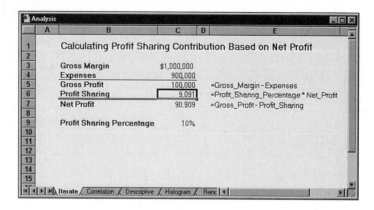

Loading the Analysis Toolpak

Excel's Analysis Toolpak is a large collection of powerful statistical functions and commands that add over 90 new functions to Excel's already impressive function list. Most of these tools use advanced statistical techniques and were designed with only a limited number of technical users in mind.

To use the tools and functions in the Analysis Toolpak, you need to load the add-in macro that makes them available to Excel. The following procedure takes you through the steps:

1. Select the Tools | Add-Ins command. Excel displays the Add-Ins dialog box.
2. Activate the Analysis Toolpak check box in the Add-Ins Available list.
3. Select OK.

NOTE

If you don't see an Analysis Toolpak check box in the Add-Ins Available list, you didn't install the Analysis Toolpak when you installed Excel. You need to run the Excel setup program and use it to install the Analysis Toolpak.

Solving Complex Problems with Solver

Earlier in this chapter you learned how to use Goal Seek to find solutions to formulas by changing a single variable. Unfortunately, most problems in business and science aren't so easy. You'll usually face formulas with at least two and sometimes even dozens of variables. Often a problem will have more than one solution, and your challenge will be to find the *optimal* solution (that is, the one that maximizes profit, minimizes costs, or whatever). For these bigger challenges, you need a more muscular tool. Excel has just the answer: Solver. Solver is a sophisticated optimization program that enables you to find the solutions to complex problems that would otherwise require high-level mathematical analysis. This section introduces you to Solver (a complete discussion would require a book in itself) and takes you through a few examples.

Some Background on Solver

Solver is a powerful tool that isn't needed by most Excel users. It would be overkill, for example, to use Solver to compute net profit given fixed revenue and cost figures. Many problems, however, require nothing less than the Solver approach. These problems cover many different fields and situations, but they all have the following characteristics in common:

■ They have a single *target cell* that contains a formula you want to maximize, minimize, or set to a specific value. This formula could be a calculation, such as total transportation expenses or net profit.

■ The target cell formula contains references to one or more *changing cells* (also called *unknowns* or *decision variables*). Solver adjusts these cells to find the optimal solution for the target cell formula. These changing cells might include items such as units sold, shipping costs, or advertising expenses.

■ Optionally, there are one or more *constraint cells* that must satisfy certain criteria. For example, you might require that advertising be less than 10 percent of total expenses, or that the discount to customers be a number between 40 percent and 60 percent.

What types of problems exhibit these kinds of characteristics? A surprisingly broad range, as the following list shows:

■ The transportation problem—This problem involves minimizing shipping costs from multiple manufacturing plants to multiple warehouses while meeting demand.

■ The allocation problem—This problem requires minimizing employee costs while maintaining appropriate staffing requirements.

■ The product mix problem—This problem requires generating the maximum profit with a mix of products, while still meeting customer requirements. You solve this problem when you sell multiple products with different cost structures, profit margins, and demand curves.

■ The blending problem—This problem involves manipulating the materials used for one or more products to minimize production costs, meet consumer demand, and maintain a minimum level of quality.

■ Linear algebra—This problem involves solving sets of linear equations.

Loading Solver

Solver is an add-in to Microsoft Excel, so you'll need to load Solver before you can use it. The following procedure takes you through the steps necessary to load Solver:

1. Select the Tools | Add-Ins command. Excel displays the Add-Ins dialog box.

2. Activate the Solver Add-In check box in the Add-Ins Available list.

3. Select OK. Excel adds a Solver command to the Tools menu.

Using Solver

So that you can see how Solver works, I'll show you an example. Earlier, you used Goal Seek to compute the break-even point for a new product. (Recall that the break-even point is the number of units that need to be sold to produce a profit of 0.) I'll extend this analysis by computing the break-even for two products: a Finley sprocket and a Langstrom wrench. The goal is to compute the number of units to sell for both products so that the total profit is 0.

The most obvious way to proceed is to use Goal Seek to determine the break-even points for each product separately. Figure 21.21 shows the results.

FIGURE 21.21.

The break-even points for two products (using separate Goal Seek calculations on the Product Profit cells).

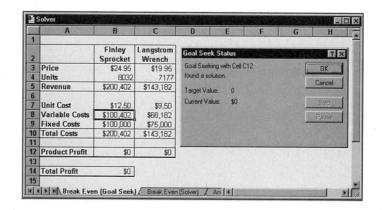

This method works, but the problem is that the two products don't exist in a vacuum. For example, there will be cost savings associated with each product because of joint advertising campaigns, combined shipments to customers (larger shipments usually mean better freight rates), and so on. To allow for this, you need to reduce the cost for each product by a factor related to the number of units sold by the other product. In practice, this would be difficult to estimate, but to keep things simple, I'll use the following assumption: The costs for each product are reduced by one dollar for every unit sold of the other product. For instance, if the Langstrom wrench sells 10,000 units, the costs for the Finley sprocket are reduced by $10,000. I'll make this adjustment in the Variable Costs formula. For example, the formula that calculates Variable Costs for the Finley sprocket (cell B8) becomes the following:

```
=B4*B7 - C4
```

Similarly, the formula that calculates Variable Costs for the Langstrom wrench (cell C8) becomes the following:

```
=C4*C7 - B4
```

By making this change, you move out of Goal Seek's territory. The Variable Costs formulas now have two variables: the units sold for the Finley sprocket and the units sold for the Langstrom wrench. I've changed the problem from one of two single-variable formulas, which are easily handled (individually) by Goal Seek, to a single formula with two variables—which is the terrain of Solver.

To see how Solver handles such a problem, follow the steps outlined in the following procedure:

1. Select the Tools | Solver command. Excel displays the Solver Parameters dialog box.

2. In the Set Target Cell text box, enter a reference to the target cell—that is, the cell with the formula you want to optimize. In the example, you would enter B14.

3. In the Equal To section, activate the appropriate option button. Select Max to maximize the target cell, Min to minimize it, or Value Of to solve for a particular value (in which case you also need to enter the value in the text box provided). In the example, you would activate Value Of and enter 0 in the text box.

4. Use the By Changing Cells box to enter the cells you want Solver to change while it looks for a solution. In the example, you would enter B4,C4. See Figure 21.22.

FIGURE 21.22.

Use the Solver parameters dialog box to set up the problem for Solver.

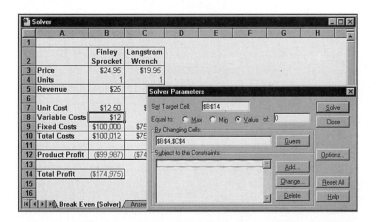

TIP

The Guess button enters into the By Changing Cells text box all the nonformula cells referenced by the target cell's formula.

NOTE

You can enter a maximum of 200 changing cells.

5. Select Solve. (I discuss constraints in the next section.) Solver works on the problem and then displays the Solver Results dialog box, which tells you whether or not it found a solution.

6. If Solver found a solution that you want to use, activate the Keep Solver Solution option and then select OK. If you don't want to accept the new numbers, select Restore Original Values and select OK or just click Cancel.

Figure 21.23 shows the results for the example. As you can see, Solver has produced a Total Profit of 0 by running one product (the Langstrom wrench) at a slight loss and the other at a slight profit. While this is certainly a solution, it's not really the one you want. Ideally, for a true break-even analysis, both products should end up with a Product Profit of 0. The problem is that we didn't tell Solver to solve the problem this way. In other words, we didn't set up any *constraints*.

FIGURE 21.23.

When Solver finishes its calculations, it displays a completion message and enters the solution (if it found one) into the worksheet cells.

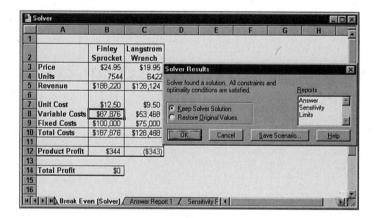

Adding Constraints

The real world puts restrictions and conditions on formulas. A factory might have a maximum capacity of 10,000 units a day; the number of employees in a company might have to be a number greater than or equal to zero (negative employees would really reduce staff costs, but nobody has been able to figure out how to do it yet); your advertising costs might be restricted to 10 percent of total expenses. All these are examples of what Solver calls *constraints*. Adding constraints tells Solver to find a solution so that these conditions are not violated.

To find the best solution for the break-even analysis, you need to tell Solver to optimize both Product Profit formulas to 0. The following steps show you how to do this:

NOTE

If Solver's completion message is still onscreen from the last section, select Cancel to return to the worksheet without saving the solution.

1. Select the Tools | Solver command to display the Solver Parameters dialog box. Solver reinstates the options you entered the last time you used Solver.

2. To add a constraint, select the Add button. Excel displays the Add Constraint dialog box.

3. In the Cell Reference box, enter the cell you want to constrain. For the example, you would enter cell B12 (the Product Profit formula for the Finley sprocket).

4. The drop-down list in the middle of the dialog box contains several comparison operators for the constraint. The available operators are less than or equal to (<=), equal to (=), greater than or equal to (>=), and integer (int). (Use the integer operator when you need a constraint, such as total employees, to be an integer value instead of a real number.) Select the appropriate operator for your constraint. For the example, select the equal to operator (=).

5. In the Constraint box, enter the value by which you want to restrict the cell. For the example, enter 0. See Figure 21.24.

FIGURE 21.24.

Use the Add Constraint dialog box to specify the constraints you want to place on the solution.

6. If you want to enter more constraints, select the Add button and repeat Steps 3 through 5. For the example, you also need to constrain cell C12 (the Product Profit formula for the Langstrom wrench) so that it, too, equals 0. When you're done, select OK to return to the Solver Parameters dialog box. Excel displays your constraints in the Subject to the Constraints list box.

NOTE

You can add a maximum of 100 constraints.

7. Select Solve. Solver again tries to find a solution, but this time it uses your constraints as guidelines.

> **TIP**
>
> If you need to make a change to a constraint before you begin solving, highlight the constraint in the Subject to the Constraints list box, select the Change button, and then make your adjustments in the Change Constraint dialog box that appears. If you want to delete a constraint you no longer need, highlight it and select the Delete button.

Figure 21.25 shows the results of the break-even analysis after adding the constraints. As you can see, Solver was able to find a solution in which both Product Margins are 0.

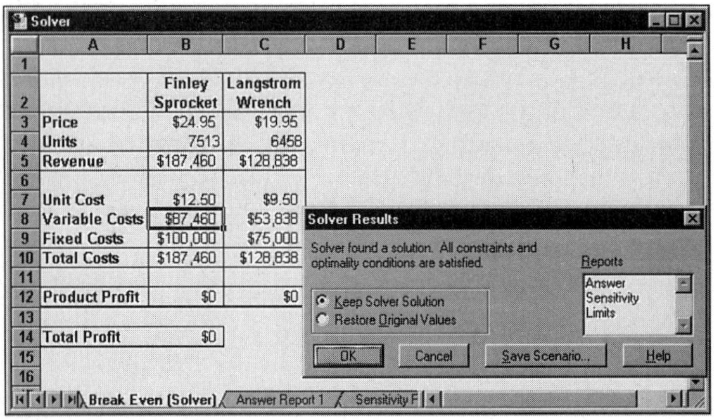

FIGURE 21.25.

The solution to the break-even analysis after adding the constraints.

How Scenarios Work

Excel has powerful features that enable you to build sophisticated models that can answer complex questions. The problem, though, isn't in *answering* questions but in *asking* them. For example, Figure 21.26 shows a worksheet model that analyzes a mortgage. You use this model to decide how much of a down payment to make, how long the term should be, and whether to include an extra principal paydown every month. The Results section compares the monthly payment and total paid for the regular mortgage and for the mortgage with a paydown. It also shows the savings and reduced term that result from the paydown.

Here are some possible questions to ask this model:

- How much will I save over the term of the mortgage if I use a shorter term and a larger down payment and include a monthly paydown?
- How much more will I end up paying if I extend the term, reduce the down payment, and forgo the paydown?

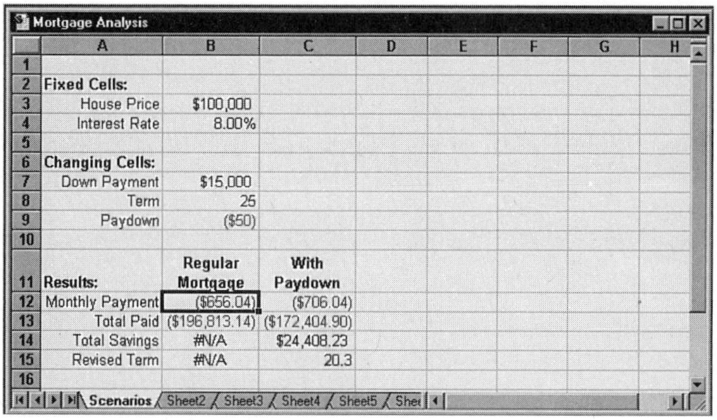

FIGURE 21.26.

A mortgage-analysis worksheet.

These are examples of *scenarios* that you would plug into the appropriate cells in the model. Excel's Scenario Manager helps by letting you define a scenario separately from the worksheet. You can save specific values for any or all of the model's input cells, give the scenario a name, and then recall the name (and all the input values it contains) from a list.

Setting Up Your Worksheet for Scenarios

Before creating a scenario, you need to decide which cells in your model will be the input cells. These will be the worksheet variables—the cells that, when you change them, change the results of the model. (Not surprisingly, Excel calls these the *changing cells.*) You can have as many as 32 changing cells in a scenario. For best results, follow these guidelines when setting up your worksheet for scenarios:

- The changing cells should be constants. Formulas can be affected by other cells, and that can throw off the entire scenario.

- To make it easier to set up each scenario and to make your worksheet easier to understand, group the changing cells and label them. (Refer to Figure 21.26.)

- For even greater clarity, assign a range name to each changing cell.

Adding a Scenario

To work with scenarios, you use Excel's Scenario Manager tool. This feature enables you to add, edit, display, and delete scenarios as well as create summary scenario reports.

Once your worksheet is set up the way you want, you can add a scenario to the sheet by following these steps:

1. Select the Tools | Scenarios command. Excel displays the Scenario Manager dialog box, shown in Figure 21.27.

2. Select the Add button. The Add Scenario dialog box, shown in Figure 21.28, appears.

FIGURE 21.27.

Excel's Scenario Manager.

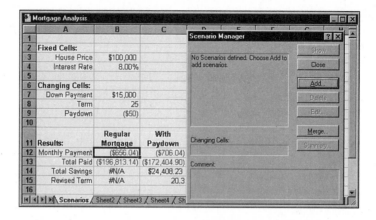

FIGURE 21.28.

Use the Add Scenario dialog box to add scenarios to a workbook.

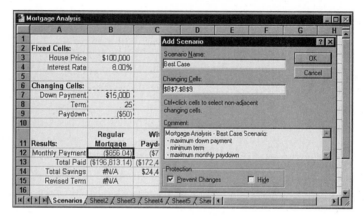

3. In the Scenario Name text box, enter a name for the scenario.

4. In the Changing Cells box, enter references to your worksheet's changing cells. You can type in the references (be sure to separate noncontiguous cells with commas) or select the cells directly on the worksheet.

5. In the Comment box, enter a description for the scenario. This will appear in the Comment section of the Scenario Manager dialog box.

6. Select OK. Excel displays the Scenario Values dialog box, shown in Figure 21.29.

7. Use the text boxes to enter values for the changing cells.

NOTE

You'll notice in Figure 21.29 that Excel displays the range name for each changing cell, which makes it easier to enter your numbers correctly. If your changing cells aren't named, Excel just displays the cell addresses instead.

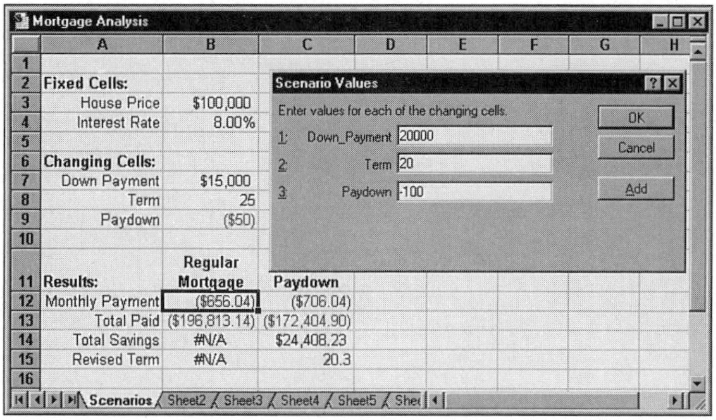

FIGURE 21.29.

Use the Scenario Values dialog box to enter the values you want to use for the scenario's changing cells.

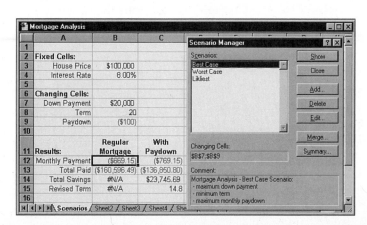

8. To add more scenarios, select the Add button to return to the Add Scenario dialog box and repeat Steps 3 through 7. Otherwise, select OK to return to the Scenario Manager dialog box.

9. Select the Close button to return to the worksheet.

Displaying a Scenario

After you define a scenario, you can enter its values into the changing cells simply by selecting the scenario from the Scenario Manager dialog box. The following steps give you the details:

1. Select the Tools | Scenarios command to display the Scenario Manager.

2. In the Scenarios list, highlight the scenario you want to display.

3. Select the Show button. Excel enters the scenario values into the changing cells, as shown in Figure 21.30.

4. Repeat Steps 2 and 3 to display other scenarios.

5. Select the Close button to return to the worksheet.

FIGURE 21.30.

When you select Show, Excel enters the values for the highlighted scenario into the changing cells.

Editing a Scenario

If you need to make changes to a scenario—whether changing the scenario's name, selecting different changing cells, or entering new values—follow these steps:

1. Select the Tools | Scenarios command to display the Scenario Manager.
2. In the Scenarios list, highlight the scenario you want to edit.
3. Select the Edit button. Excel displays the Edit Scenario dialog box (which is identical to the Add Scenario dialog box, shown in Figure 21.28).
4. Make your changes, if necessary, and select OK. The Scenario Values dialog box appears. (Refer to Figure 21.29.)
5. Enter the new values if necessary and then select OK to return to the Scenario Manager dialog box.
6. Repeat Steps 2 through 5 to edit other scenarios.
7. Select the Close button to return to the worksheet.

Summary

This chapter shows various Excel techniques for performing data analysis. You have learned how to use data tables for what-if analysis and how to use Goal Seek and iteration. This chapter also shows you how to solve complex problems by using Excel's powerful Solver tool. Finally, the chapter gives you some background on how scenarios work and how to add, display, and edit scenarios. Here are some related chapters to investigate:

■ To learn more about entering and working with arrays and array formulas, read Chapter 18.

■ For more information on Excel's charting capabilities, check out Chapter 19, "Charts and Graphics."

■ The Scenario Summary feature can create a pivot table. If you need a refresher course in pivot tables, see Chapter 23, "Creating and Customizing Pivot Tables."

Working with Lists and Databases

IN THIS CHAPTER

These days there's no shortage of dedicated database programs for the Windows market. There's the Access package that comes with Microsoft Office, of course, and there are also Windows versions of FoxPro, Paradox, and dBASE, to name a few. These high-end programs are full relational database management systems designed to handle complex, interrelated tables, queries, and reports.

Fortunately, when it comes to simple tables of data, you don't have to bother with all the bells and whistles of the big-time database systems. Excel is more than capable of handling flat-file databases (or *lists,* as they're called in Excel) right in a worksheet. You can create simple data-entry forms with a few mouse clicks, and you can sort the data, summarize it, extract records based on criteria, and lots more. This chapter introduces you to Excel lists. You'll learn what lists are, how you can use them, how to create them in your Excel worksheets, and how to work with them.

What Is a List?

A *list* is a collection of related information with an organizational structure that makes it easy to find or extract data from its contents. Examples of lists are a phone book organized by name and a library card catalog organized by book title.

In Excel the term *list* refers to a worksheet range that has the following properties:

- Field—A single type of information, such as a name, an address, or a phone number. In Excel lists, each column is a field.
- Field value—A single item in a field. In an Excel list, the field values are the individual cells.
- Field name—A unique name you assign to every list field (worksheet column). These names are always found in the first row of the list.
- Record—A collection of associated field values. In Excel lists, each row is a record.
- List range—The worksheet range that includes all the records, fields, and field names of a list.

For example, suppose that you want to set up an accounts receivable list. A simple system would include information such as the account name, account number, invoice number, invoice amount, due date, date paid, and calculation of the number of days overdue. Figure 22.1 shows how this system would be implemented as an Excel list.

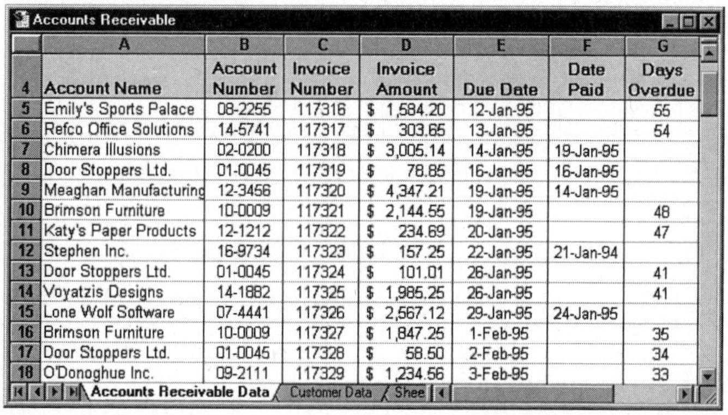

FIGURE 22.1.

An accounts receivable list.

	A	B	C	D	E	F	G
4	Account Name	Account Number	Invoice Number	Invoice Amount	Due Date	Date Paid	Days Overdue
5	Emily's Sports Palace	08-2255	117316	$ 1,584.20	12-Jan-95		55
6	Refco Office Solutions	14-5741	117317	$ 303.65	13-Jan-95		54
7	Chimera Illusions	02-0200	117318	$ 3,005.14	14-Jan-95	19-Jan-95	
8	Door Stoppers Ltd.	01-0045	117319	$ 78.85	16-Jan-95	16-Jan-95	
9	Meaghan Manufacturing	12-3456	117320	$ 4,347.21	19-Jan-95	14-Jan-95	
10	Brimson Furniture	10-0009	117321	$ 2,144.55	19-Jan-95		48
11	Katy's Paper Products	12-1212	117322	$ 234.69	20-Jan-95		47
12	Stephen Inc.	16-9734	117323	$ 157.25	22-Jan-95	21-Jan-94	
13	Door Stoppers Ltd.	01-0045	117324	$ 101.01	26-Jan-95		41
14	Voyatzis Designs	14-1882	117325	$ 1,985.25	26-Jan-95		41
15	Lone Wolf Software	07-4441	117326	$ 2,567.12	29-Jan-95	24-Jan-95	
16	Brimson Furniture	10-0009	117327	$ 1,847.25	1-Feb-95		35
17	Door Stoppers Ltd.	01-0045	117328	$ 58.50	2-Feb-95		34
18	O'Donoghue Inc.	09-2111	117329	$ 1,234.56	3-Feb-95		33

NOTE

You can use lists for just about anything you need to keep track of: inventory, accounts payable, books, CDs, and even household possessions.

Planning a List

The most important step in creating a list is determining what information you want it to contain. Although a list can be as large as the entire worksheet, in practice you should minimize the size of the range. This technique saves memory and makes managing the data easier. Therefore, you should strive to set up all your lists with only essential information.

For example, if you're building an accounts receivable list, you should include only data that relates to the receivables. In such a list, you need two kinds of information: invoice data and customer data. The invoice data includes the invoice number, the amount, the due date, and the date paid. You also include a calculated field that determines the number of days the account is overdue. For the customer, you need at least a name and an account number. You don't need to include an address or a phone number, because this information isn't essential to the receivables data.

This last point brings up the idea of *data redundancy*. In many cases, you'll be setting up a list as part of a larger application. For example, you might have lists not only for accounts receivable, but also for accounts payable, customer information, part numbers, and so on. You don't need to include information such as addresses and phone numbers in the receivables list because you should have that data in a more general customer information list. To include this data in both places is redundant.

> **TIP**
>
> Different but related lists need to have a *key field* that is common to each. For example, the accounts receivable and customer information lists could both contain an account number field. This enables you to cross-reference entries in both lists.

After you decide what kind of information to include in your list, you need to determine the level of detail for each field. For example, if you're including address information, do you want separate fields for the street address, city, state, and Zip code? For a phone number, do you need a separate field for the area code? In most cases, the best approach is to split the data into the smallest elements that make sense. This method gives you maximum flexibility when you sort and extract information.

The next stage in planning your list is to assign names to each field. Here are some guidelines to follow:

- Always use the top row of the list for the column labels.
- Although you can assign names as long as 255 characters, you should try to use short names to prevent your fields from becoming too wide.

> **TIP**
>
> If you need to use a long field name, turn on the Word Wrap alignment option to keep the field width small. Select the cell, select the Format | Cells command, choose the Alignment tab in the Format Cells dialog box, activate the Wrap Text check box, and then select OK.

- Field names must be unique, and they must be text or text formulas. If you need to use numbers, format them as text.
- You should format the column labels to help differentiate them from the list data. You can use bold text, a different font color, a background color, and a border along the bottom of each cell.

The final step in setting up your list is to plan its position in the worksheet. Here are some points to keep in mind:

- Some Excel commands can automatically identify the size and shape of a list. To avoid confusing such commands, try to use only one list per worksheet. If you have multiple related lists, include them in other tabs in the same workbook.

■ If you have any other nonlist data in a worksheet, leave at least one blank row or column between the data and the list. This technique helps Excel identify the list automatically.

■ Excel has a command that enables you to filter your list data to show only records that match certain criteria. (See "Filtering List Data" later in this chapter for details.) This command works by hiding rows of data. Therefore, if you have nonlist data you need to access, it's important not to place it to the left or right of a list.

Entering List Data

After you've set up your field names, you can start entering your list records. The following sections show you how to enter data directly on the worksheet or by using a data form.

Entering Data Directly on a Worksheet

The most straightforward way to enter information into a list is to directly type data in the worksheet cells. If you've formatted any of the fields (numeric formats, alignment, and so on), be sure to copy the formats to the new records.

Entering and deleting records and fields within a list is analogous to inserting and deleting rows and columns in a regular worksheet model. Table 22.1 summarizes these list commands.

Table 22.1. Some basic list commands.

List Action	Excel Procedure
Add a record	Select a row, and then select Insert | Rows.
Add a field	Select a column, and then select Insert | Columns.
Delete a record	Select the entire row, and then select Edit | Delete.
Delete a field	Select the entire column, and then select Edit | Delete.

If you don't want to add or delete an entire row or column (for example, if other worksheet data is in the way), you can insert or delete data within the list range. If you're inserting or deleting a row, select a list record (be sure to include each field in the record). If you're inserting or deleting a column, select a list field (be sure to include each record as well as the field name in the field).

Entering list information can be tedious. Excel offers several shortcut keys to speed up the process, as summarized in Table 22.2.

Table 22.2. Excel data-entry shortcut keys.

Key	Action
Tab	Confirms the entry and moves to the field on the right.
Shift+Tab	Confirms the entry and moves to the field on the left.
Enter	Confirms the entry and moves to the next record.
Shift+Enter	Confirms the entry and moves to the preceding record.
Ctrl+"	Copies the number from the same field in the preceding record.
Ctrl+'	Copies the formula from the same field in the preceding record.
Ctrl+;	Enters the current date.
Ctrl+:	Enters the current time.

TIP

If pressing Enter or Shift+Enter doesn't move you to another record, select the Tools | Options command. Then select the Edit tab in the Options dialog box and activate the check box labeled Move Selection after Enter.

Entering Data Using a Data Form

Excel lists are powerful information-management tools, but creating and maintaining them can be tedious and time-consuming. To make data entry easier and more efficient, Excel offers the data form dialog box. You can use this form to add, edit, delete, and find list records quickly.

What Is a Data Form?

A *data form* is a dialog box that simplifies list management in the following ways:

- The dialog box shows only one record at a time, which makes data entry and editing easier.
- You can view many more fields in a form than you can see onscreen. In fact, depending on the size of your screen, you can view as many as 18 fields in a single form.
- When you add or delete records using the data form, Excel automatically adjusts the list range.
- You get an extra level of safety when you add or delete records. Excel prevents you from overwriting existing worksheet data when you add records, and it seeks confirmation for record deletions.

■ Novice users or data-entry clerks are insulated from the normal list commands. Simple command buttons enable users to add, delete, and find data.

The good news about data forms is that Excel creates the form automatically based on the layout of your list. To view the form, you select any cell from within the list and then select the Data | Form command. (You also can select one of the field name cells or a cell in a row or column immediately adjacent to the list.)

Figure 22.2 shows the data form for the accounts receivable list. When constructing the data form, Excel begins with the field names and adds a text box for each editable field. Excel includes fields that are the result of a formula or function (for example, the Days Overdue field in Figure 22.2) for display purposes only; you can't edit these fields. The scrollbar enables you to move quickly through the list. The record number indicator in the top-right corner of the dialog box keeps track of both the current list row and the total number of records in the list. The dialog box also includes several command buttons for adding, deleting, and finding records.

FIGURE 22.2.

An Excel data form.

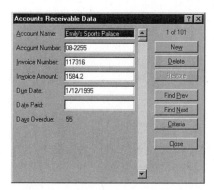

NOTE

The record number indicator is unaffected by the list sort order. The first record below the field names is always record 1.

Editing Records

You can use the data form to edit any fields in your list records, with the exception of computed or protected fields. This procedure lists the steps to follow:

1. Display the data form.
2. Select the record you want to edit.
3. Edit the fields you want to change.

4. Repeat Steps 2 and 3 for other records you want to edit.

5. Select Close to finish editing the list.

CAUTION

When you make changes to a record, Excel saves the changes permanently when you scroll to another record. Therefore, before leaving a record, check each field to ensure that it contains the data you want. To restore a record to its original data, select the data form's Restore button before you move to another record.

Adding Records

Adding records with the data form is fast and easy. Here are the steps to follow:

1. Display the data form.

2. Select the New button or press Ctrl+Page Down. Excel creates a blank record and displays New Record as the record number indicator.

3. Fill in the fields for the new record.

4. Repeat Steps 2 and 3 for other records you want to add.

5. Select Close to finish adding new records.

When you add records with the data form, Excel adds them to the bottom of the list without inserting a new row. If there is no room to extend the list range, Excel displays a warning message. To add new records, you must either move or delete the other data.

Deleting Records

Follow these steps to delete records using the data form:

1. Display the data form.

2. Select the record you want to delete.

3. Select the Delete button. Excel warns you that the record will be deleted permanently.

4. Select OK to confirm the deletion. Excel returns you to the data form.

5. Repeat Steps 2 through 4 to delete other records.

6. Select Close to return to the worksheet.

NOTE

When you delete a record from the data form, Excel clears the data and shifts the records up to fill in the gap.

Finding Records

Although the data form enables you to scroll through a list, you might find that for larger lists you need to use the form's search capabilities to quickly locate what you want. You can find specific records in the list by first specifying the *criteria* that the search must match. Excel then compares each record with the criteria and displays the first record that matches. For example, you might want to find all invoices that are over $1000 or those that are at least one day past due.

> **NOTE**
>
> You can perform only simple searches with the data form. For more complex search criteria, see "Filtering List Data" later in this chapter.

You construct the search criteria using text, numbers, and comparison operators such as equal to (=) and greater than (>). For example, to find all the invoices that are over $1000, you type >1000 in the Invoice Amount field. To find an account named Read Inc., you type read inc. in the Account Name field. The following steps take you through the procedure:

1. Display the data form.
2. Select the Criteria button. Excel displays a blank record and replaces the record number indicator with Criteria.
3. Select the field you want to use for the search.
4. Enter the criterion. Figure 22.3 shows the data form with a criterion entered for finding invoices on which the Invoice Amount is greater than 1000.

FIGURE 22.3.

The Criteria data form with a sample criterion.

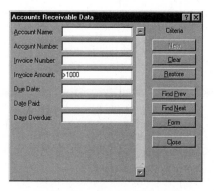

5. Repeat Steps 3 and 4 if you want to use multiple criteria (see the following discussion).
6. Use the Find Next and Find Prev buttons to move up or down to the next record that matches the criteria.

Sorting a List

One of the advantages of a list is that you can rearrange the records so that they're sorted alphabetically or numerically. This feature enables you to view the data in order by customer name, account number, part number, or any other field. You can even sort on multiple fields, which would enable you, for example, to sort a client list by state and then by name within each state.

The sorting procedure is determined by the options in the Sort dialog box, shown in Figure 22.4, which gives you the following choices:

■ Sort By—This drop-down list box contains the list field names. Select a field from this list to determine the overall order for the sort. In Figure 22.4, the Due Date field is selected; therefore, the entire database will be sorted by due date.

FIGURE 22.4.

Use the Sort dialog box to change the sort order of your lists.

■ Then By—This drop-down list also contains the list field names. Select a field from this list to sort records that have the same data in the field specified in Sort By. In Figure 22.4, for example, all the records that have the same due date will be sorted by account name.

■ Then By—Select a field name from this list to sort the records that have the same data in the fields specified by both Sort By and Then By. Figure 22.4 shows that records that have the same due date and the same account name are sorted by the Invoice Amount field.

NOTE

Although Excel enables you to sort on as many as three fields, it isn't necessary to enter a field in each of the three lists. For most sorts, you'll need to choose a field in only the Sort By list.

■ My List Has—Excel usually can differentiate between field names (the header row) and data. If Excel finds what it thinks is a header row, it doesn't include it in the sort (and it activates the Header Row option). If your list doesn't have a header row (or if you want the top row included in the sort), select the No Header Row option.

NOTE

Excel identifies the header row of a list by looking for differences in data type (most field names are text entries), capitalization, and formatting. If your list doesn't have a header row, you still can sort by using column headings (Column A, Column B, and so on).

CAUTION

Be careful when you sort list records that contain formulas. If the formulas use relative addresses that refer to cells outside their own records, the new sort order might change the references and produce erroneous results. If your list formulas must refer to cells outside the list, be sure to use absolute addresses.

For each sort field, you can specify whether the field is sorted in ascending or descending order. Table 22.3 summarizes Excel's ascending sort priorities.

Table 22.3. Excel's ascending sort order.

Type (in Order of Priority)	Order
Numbers	Largest negative to largest positive
Text	Space ! " # $ % & ' ( ) * + , - . / 0 through 9 (when formatted as text) : ; < = > ? @ A through Z (Excel ignores case) [\ ] ^ _ ' { ¦ } ~
Logical	FALSE before TRUE
Error	All error values are equal
Blank	Always sorted last (ascending or descending)

The following procedure shows you how to sort a list:

1. Select a cell inside the list.
2. Select the Data | Sort command. Excel displays the Sort dialog box.
3. Enter the sort options you want.
4. Select OK. Excel sorts the range.

Filtering List Data

One of the biggest problems with large lists is that it's often hard to find and extract the data you need. Sorting can help, but in the end you're still working with the entire list. What you need is a way to define the data you want to work with and then have Excel display only those records onscreen. This action is called *filtering* your data. Fortunately, Excel offers several techniques that get the job done.

Using AutoFilter to Filter a List

Excel's AutoFilter feature makes filtering out subsets of your data as easy as selecting an option from a drop-down list. In fact, that's literally what happens. If you select the Data | Filter | AutoFilter command, Excel adds drop-down arrows to the cells containing the list's column labels. Clicking one of these arrows displays a list of all the unique entries in the column. Figure 22.5 shows the drop-down list for the Account Name field in an Accounts Receivable database.

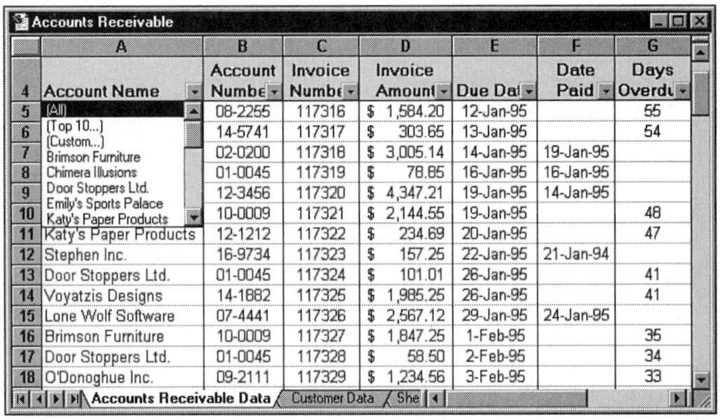

	A	B	C	D	E	F	G
4	Account Name	Account Numbe	Invoice Numbe	Invoice Amount	Due Dat	Date Paid	Days Overdu
5	(All)	08-2255	117316	$ 1,584.20	12-Jan-95		55
6	(Top 10...) (Custom...)	14-5741	117317	$ 303.65	13-Jan-95		54
7	Brimson Furniture	02-0200	117318	$ 3,005.14	14-Jan-95	19-Jan-95	
8	Chimera Illusions	01-0045	117319	$ 78.85	16-Jan-95	16-Jan-95	
9	Door Stoppers Ltd. Emily's Sports Palace	12-3456	117320	$ 4,347.21	19-Jan-95	14-Jan-95	
10	Katy's Paper Products	10-0009	117321	$ 2,144.55	19-Jan-95		48
11	Katy's Paper Products	12-1212	117322	$ 234.69	20-Jan-95		47
12	Stephen Inc.	16-9734	117323	$ 157.25	22-Jan-95	21-Jan-94	
13	Door Stoppers Ltd.	01-0045	117324	$ 101.01	26-Jan-95		41
14	Voyatzis Designs	14-1882	117325	$ 1,985.25	26-Jan-95		41
15	Lone Wolf Software	07-4441	117326	$ 2,567.12	29-Jan-95	24-Jan-95	
16	Brimson Furniture	10-0009	117327	$ 1,847.25	1-Feb-95		35
17	Door Stoppers Ltd.	01-0045	117328	$ 58.50	2-Feb-95		34
18	O'Donoghue Inc.	09-2111	117329	$ 1,234.56	3-Feb-95		33

FIGURE 22.5.
For each list field, AutoFilter adds drop-down lists that contain only the unique entries in the column.

TIP

If you want to use AutoFilter with only a single field, select that field's entire column before choosing the Data | Filter | AutoFilter command.

If you select an item from one of these lists, Excel takes the following actions:

- It displays only those records that include the item in that field. For example, Figure 22.6 shows the resultant records when the item Refco Office Solutions is selected from the list attached to the Account Name column. The other records are hidden and can be retrieved whenever you need them.

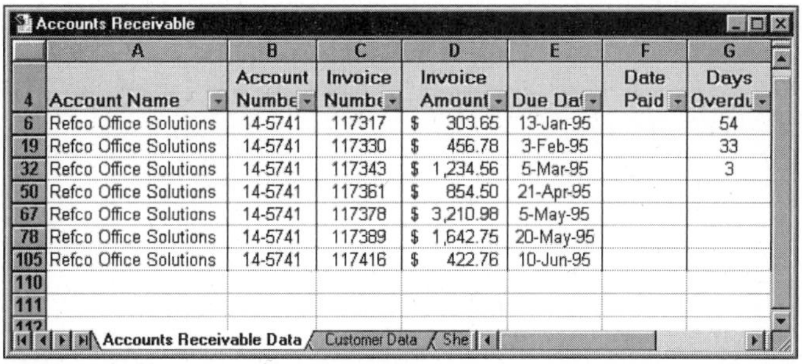

Accounts Receivable

	A	B	C	D	E	F	G
4	Account Name	Account Numbe	Invoice Numbe	Invoice Amount	Due Dat	Date Paid	Days Overdu
6	Refco Office Solutions	14-5741	117317	$ 303.65	13-Jan-95		54
19	Refco Office Solutions	14-5741	117330	$ 456.78	3-Feb-95		33
32	Refco Office Solutions	14-5741	117343	$ 1,234.56	5-Mar-95		3
50	Refco Office Solutions	14-5741	117361	$ 854.50	21-Apr-95		
67	Refco Office Solutions	14-5741	117378	$ 3,210.98	5-May-95		
78	Refco Office Solutions	14-5741	117389	$ 1,642.75	20-May-95		
105	Refco Office Solutions	14-5741	117416	$ 422.76	10-Jun-95		
110							
111							

FIGURE 22.6.
Selecting an item from a drop-down list displays only records that include the item in the field.

CAUTION

Because Excel hides the rows that don't meet the criteria, you shouldn't place any important data either to the left or to the right of the list.

- It changes the color of the column's drop-down arrow. This indicates which column you used to filter the list.
- It displays the row headings of the filtered records in a different color.
- It displays a message in the status bar telling you how many records it found that match the selected item.

To continue filtering the data, you can select an item from one of the other lists. For example, you can select the nonblank cells in the Days Overdue column to see only those Refco Office Solutions invoices that are overdue. (To learn how to select nonblank fields, see the next section.)

AutoFilter Criteria Options

The items you see in each drop-down list are called the *filter criteria.* Besides selecting specific criteria (such as an account name), you also have the following choices in each drop-down list:

- All—Removes the filter criterion for the column. If you've selected multiple criteria, you can remove all the filter criteria and display the entire list by selecting the Data | Filter | Show All command.
- Top 10—Displays the Top 10 AutoFilter dialog box (new in Excel 7), shown in Figure 22.7. The left drop-down list has two choices (Top or Bottom); the center spinner enables you to choose a number; and the right drop-down list has two choices (Items and Percent). For example, if you choose the default choices (Top, 10, and Items), AutoFilter displays the records that have the 10 highest values in the current field.

FIGURE 22.7.

Use the Top 10 AutoFilter dialog box to filter your records based on values in the current field.

- Custom—Enables you to enter more sophisticated criteria. For details, see the next section.

- Blanks—Displays records that have no data in the field. In the Accounts Receivable list, for example, you could use this criterion to find all the unpaid invoices (that is, those with a blank Date Paid field).

- NonBlanks—Displays records that have data in the field. Selecting this criterion in the Days Overdue field of the Accounts Receivable list, for example, finds invoices that are overdue.

Showing Filtered Records

When you need to redisplay records that have been filtered via AutoFilter, use any of the following techniques:

- To display the entire list and remove AutoFilter's drop-down arrows, select the Data | Filter | AutoFilter command again.

- To display the entire list without removing the AutoFilter drop-down arrows, select the Data | Filter | Show All command.

- To remove the filter on a single field, display that field's AutoFilter drop-down list, and select the All option.

Summary

This chapter shows you how to work with lists (or databases, as they used to be called) in Excel. It shows you how to set up a list, how to use forms for data entry, and how to sort and filter a list. For some list-related material, try on these chapters for size:

- If you need to fill in a list field with a series, the Fill handle or the Edit | Fill | Series command makes it easy. See Chapter 17, "Working with Ranges," for more information.

- Excel uses formatting to differentiate list data from list headers. See Chapter 16, "Excel Concepts," for details.

- Filtering and list functions are powerful tools for analyzing list data. But for large lists, they might not be enough to help you extract all the information you need. Pivot tables might be the answer, however. They're covered in depth in Chapter 23, "Creating and Customizing Pivot Tables."

Creating and Customizing Pivot Tables

23

*by
Paul McFedries
and Tom Hayes*

IN THIS CHAPTER

Lists and external databases can contain hundreds or even thousands of records. Analyzing that much data can be a nightmare without the right kinds of tools. To help you, Excel offers a powerful data-analysis tool called a *pivot table.* This tool enables you to summarize hundreds of records in a concise tabular format and then to manipulate the table's layout to see different views of your data. This chapter introduces you to pivot tables and shows you various ways you can use them with your own data.

How Pivot Tables Work

In the simplest case, pivot tables work by summarizing the data in one field (called a *data field*) and breaking it down according to the data in another field. The unique values in the second field (called the *row field*) become the row headings. For example, Figure 23.1 shows a database of sales by sales representatives. With a pivot table, you can summarize the numbers in the Sales field (the data field) and break them down by Region (the row field). Figure 23.2 shows the resulting pivot table. Notice how Excel uses the four unique items in the Region field (East, West, Midwest, and South) as row headings.

Region	Quarter	Sales Rep	Sales
East	1st	A	192,345
West	1st	B	210,880
East	1st	C	185,223
South	1st	D	165,778
Midwest	1st	E	155,557
South	1st	F	180,567
West	1st	G	200,767
Midwest	1st	H	165,663
East	2nd	A	173,493
West	2nd	B	200,203
East	2nd	C	170,213
South	2nd	D	155,339
Midwest	2nd	E	148,990
South	2nd	F	175,660
West	2nd	G	190,290

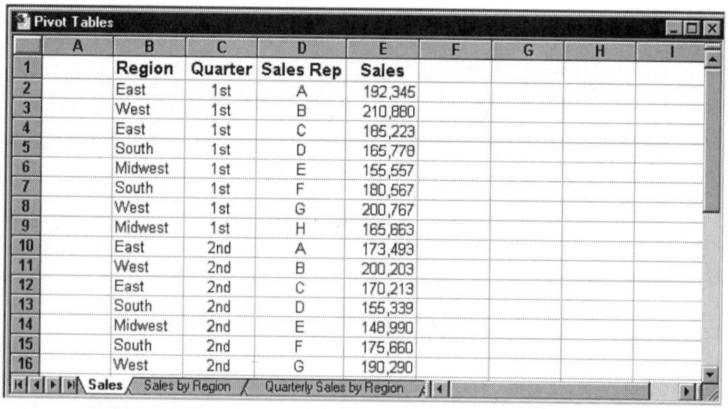

FIGURE 23.1.
A database of sales by sales representatives.

Sum of Sales	
Region	Total
East	1,463,655
Midwest	1,340,875
South	1,409,544
West	1,477,884
Grand Total	5,691,958

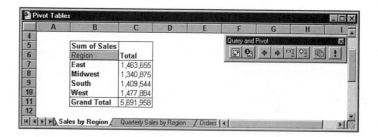

FIGURE 23.2.
A pivot table showing total sales by region.

You can further break down your data by specifying a third field (called the *column field*) to use for column headings. Figure 23.3 shows the resulting pivot table with the four unique items in the Quarter field (1st, 2nd, 3rd, and 4th) used to create the columns.

FIGURE 23.3.

A pivot table showing sales by region for each quarter.

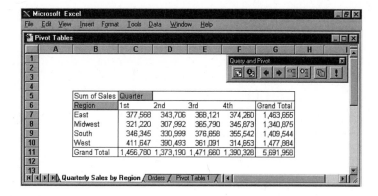

The big news with pivot tables is the *pivoting* feature. If you want to see different views of your data, you can, for example, drag the column field over to the row field area, as shown in Figure 23.4. The result, as you can see, is that the table shows each region as the main row category, with the quarters as regional subcategories.

FIGURE 23.4.

You can drag row or column fields to "pivot" the data and get a different view.

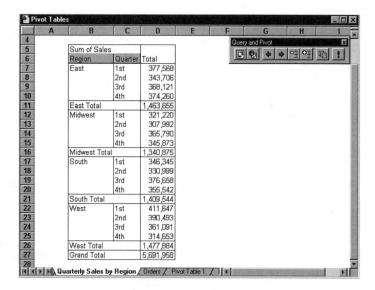

Some Pivot Table Terms

Pivot tables have their own terminology, so here's a quick glossary of some terms with which you need to become familiar:

- Source list—The original data. You can use one or more Excel lists, an external database, an existing pivot table, or a crosstab table from Excel 4.0.

- Field—A category of data, such as Region, Quarter, or Sales. Because most pivot tables are derived from lists or databases, a pivot-table field is directly analogous to a list or database field.

- Item—An element in a field.

- Row field—A field with a limited set of distinct text, numeric, or date values to use as row headings in the pivot table. In the example you just studied, Region is the row field.

- Column field—A field with a limited set of distinct text, numeric, or date values to use as column headings for the pivot table. In the second pivot table, shown in Figure 23.3, the Quarter field is the column field.

- Page field—A field with a limited set of distinct text, numeric, or date values that you use to filter the pivot-table view. For example, you could use the Sales Rep field to create separate pages for each rep. Selecting a different sales rep filters the table to show data for only that person.

- Pivot-table items—The items from the source list used as row, column, and page labels.

- Data field—A field that contains the data you want to summarize in the table.

- Data area—The interior section of the table in which the data summaries appear.

- Layout—The overall arrangement of fields and items in the pivot table.

Building Pivot Tables

Excel provides the PivotTable Wizard to make creating and modifying your pivot tables easy. The PivotTable Wizard uses a four-step approach that enables you to build a pivot table from scratch:

1. Specify the type of source list to use for the pivot table.

2. Identify the location of the data.

3. Define the row, column, page, and data fields for the table.

4. Select a location, name, and other options for the table; then create the table.

Throughout the rest of this chapter, the list shown in Figure 23.5 is used as an example. This is a list of orders placed in response to a three-month marketing campaign. Each record shows the date of the order, the product ordered (there are four types: Printer stand, Glare filter, Mouse pad, and Copy holder), the quantity and net dollars ordered, the promotional offer selected by the customer (1 Free with 10 or Extra Discount), and the advertisement to which the customer is responding (Direct mail, Magazine, or Newspaper).

Figure 23.6 shows a simple pivot table for the Orders database. In this example, the quantity shipped is summarized by product and advertisement. The row headings are taken from the Product field, and the column headings are taken from the Advertisement field. The Promotion field is used as the page field to filter the data.

FIGURE 23.5.

The Orders list that is used as an example throughout this chapter.

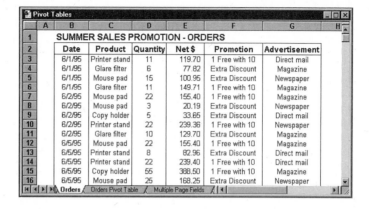

FIGURE 23.6.

A simple pivot table created from the Orders database.

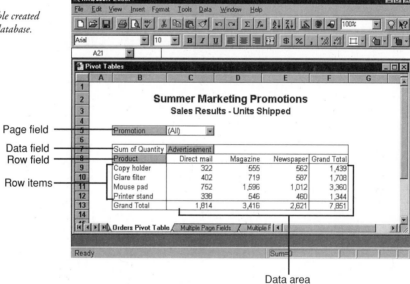

Navigating the PivotTable Wizard

The PivotTable Wizard dialog boxes, like those for other Excel wizard tools, contain several buttons that enable you to navigate the PivotTable Wizard quickly. (See Table 23.1.)

Table 23.1. PivotTable Wizard navigation buttons.

Button	Description
Help	Displays a Help window for the current step
Cancel	Closes the PivotTable Wizard without creating the table

continues

Table 23.1. continued

Button	Description
<Back	Goes back to the preceding step
Next>	Goes to the next step
Finish	Creates the pivot table

Creating a Pivot Table

The steps you use to create a pivot table vary depending on the source data you're using. You can use four types of data:

- Microsoft Excel List or Database—A multicolumn list on a worksheet. The list must have labeled columns.

- External Data Source—A separate database file in Access, dBASE, FoxPro, SQL Server, or some other format. You retrieve the data from Microsoft Query (as explained in Chapter 24, "Using Microsoft Query").

- Multiple Consolidation Ranges—A collection of lists with row and column labels in one or more worksheets. Each range must have a similar layout and identical row and column labels.

- Another Pivot Table—Another pivot table in the same workbook.

Creating a Pivot Table from an Excel List

The most common source for pivot tables is an Excel list. You can use just about any list to create a pivot table (even, as you'll see, a list in an unopened workbook), but the best candidates for pivot tables exhibit two main characteristics:

- At least one of the fields contains *groupable* data; that is, the field contains data with a limited number of distinct text, numeric, or date values. In the Sales worksheet shown in Figure 23.1, the Region field is perfect for a pivot table because, despite having dozens of items, it has only four distinct values: East, West, Midwest, and South.

- Each field in the list must have a heading.

So, given a list that fits these criteria, follow these steps to create a pivot table:

1. Select a cell inside the list you want to use. (This isn't strictly necessary, but doing so saves you a step later.)

2. Select the Data|PivotTable command. Excel displays the PivotTable Wizard - Step 1 of 4 dialog box, shown in Figure 23.7.

You also can start the PivotTable Wizard by clicking the PivotTable Wizard button in the Query and Pivot toolbar.

FIGURE 23.7.

The PivotTable Wizard - Step 1 of 4 dialog box, which appears when you start the PivotTable Wizard.

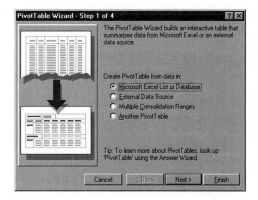

3. Make sure the Microsoft Excel List or Database option is activated, and then select Next>. You then see the PivotTable Wizard - Step 2 of 4 dialog box, shown in Figure 23.8.

FIGURE 23.8.

The PivotTable Wizard - Step 2 of 4 dialog box for an Excel list.

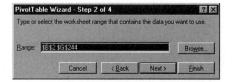

4. If you selected a cell in the list, the correct range coordinates should already be displayed in the Range text box. If not, enter the range either by typing the address or by selecting the range directly on the worksheet. Select Next> to display the PivotTable Wizard - Step 3 of 4 dialog box, shown in Figure 23.9.

FIGURE 23.9.

The layout used to create the pivot table shown in Figure 23.6.

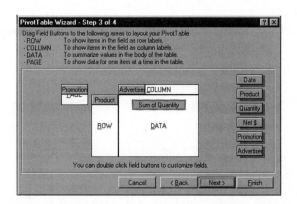

5. Specify the layout of the pivot table by dragging the field labels on the right to the appropriate areas. For example, to add a row field, drag a label and drop it anywhere inside the ROW box. Figure 23.9 shows the layout used to create the pivot table you saw in Figure 23.6. When you're finished, select Next> to display the PivotTable Wizard - Step 4 of 4 dialog box, shown in Figure 23.10.

FIGURE 23.10.

Use the PivotTable Wizard - Step 4 of 4 dialog box to specify the table location and display options.

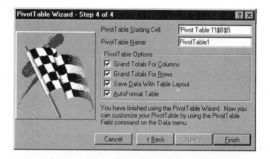

TIP

You can customize each field by double-clicking on the label. (You also can customize the fields after you've created the pivot table.)

---

6. Use the PivotTable Starting Cell text box to select the upper-left corner of the range you want to use for the table. You can type a reference or select it directly on the worksheet (or even on another sheet).

7. Enter a name for the table in the PivotTable Name box.

8. Use the check boxes in the PivotTable Options group to refine the table's display:

Grand Totals For Columns—Activate this check box to add an extra row at the bottom of the pivot table to show grand totals for each column.

Grand Totals For Rows—Activate this check box to add an extra column on the right of the pivot table to show grand totals for each row.

Save Data With Table Layout—To make pivot-table updating faster, Excel stores a hidden copy of the source data in a memory cache along with the table layout. If the source list contains a large amount of data, you might not want Excel to store a copy. In this case, deactivate the Save Data With Table Layout check box. When you make changes to the pivot-table layout, Excel uses the source data directly to update the table.

AutoFormat Table—Activate this check box to format the pivot table using Excel's default AutoFormat.

NOTE

It's a good idea to let Excel AutoFormat the pivot table. This way, when you pivot the data, the formatting pivots as well. (If you don't use AutoFormat, you must reformat the pivot table every time you pivot the data.)

9. Select the Finish button. Excel creates the pivot table in the location you specified and displays the Query and Pivot toolbar.

Formatting a Pivot Table

For your final pivot-table chore, you need to look at the various ways you can format the table to make it look its best for reports or presentations. The next three sections cover AutoFormatting the table, changing the name of a field, and changing the numeric format for the data field.

Using AutoFormat to Format a Pivot Table

As you might have found out the hard way, if you apply your own formatting to a table, Excel discards the formatting when you re-create or reorganize the table. To avoid having to reformat the table with each change, use the AutoFormat feature to format your pivot tables. Excel maintains the AutoFormat no matter how you alter the table.

To try this out, select a cell in the table, choose Format AutoFormat from the menu and then select a format from the Table Format list in the AutoFormat dialog box. Figure 23.11 shows the Orders pivot table formatted with the Colorful 2 AutoFormat.

FIGURE 23.11.

The Orders pivot table formatted with the Colorful 2 AutoFormat.

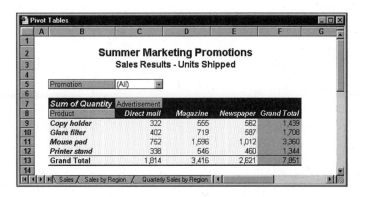

Changing the Data Field's Numeric Format

Numeric formatting applied to the data field with the Format | Cells menu choice is also lost each time you reorganize your pivot tables. To maintain a permanent numeric format in the data field (or to change the existing numeric format), follow these steps:

1. Display the PivotTable Field dialog box for the data field.
2. Select the Number button. Excel displays the Format Cells dialog box, shown in Figure 23.12.

FIGURE 23.12.

Use this version of the Format Cells dialog box to select a numeric format for your data field.

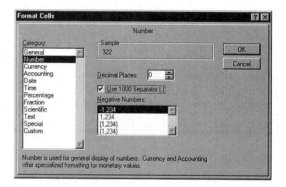

3. Select the numeric format you want to use. (See Chapter 16, "Excel Concepts," for details.)
4. Select OK to return to the PivotTable Field dialog box.
5. Select OK to return to the worksheet.

Changing the Name of a Pivot Table Field

Excel sometimes creates generic names for your pivot table fields. For example, if your pivot table consolidates data from multiple ranges, Excel uses names such as Row, Column, and Page1 for the table fields. Similarly, if you group items based on their labels, Excel creates new fields with names like Product2 and Promotion3.

To change these generic names, or any row, column, or page field names, you can use either of the following techniques:

■ Select the cell containing the field label and use the formula bar to edit the field name.

■ Display the PivotTable Field dialog box for the field, edit the field name that appears in the Name text box, and then select OK.

Deleting Fields from a Pivot Table

If you'd like to simplify the pivot table, you can knock things down a dimension by removing a row, column, or page field. (You can also remove a data field if your pivot table has multiple data fields.) Excel gives you three methods for removing a field:

- Drag the field off the pivot table.
- Use the PivotTable Wizard.
- Delete the field from the PivotTable Field dialog box.

Deleting a Field By Dragging

To remove a row, column, or page field from the pivot table, you can use your mouse to drag the field out of the pivot area. (You can't use this method to delete a data field.) The *pivot area* is defined by two ranges:

- The rectangular range that holds the row fields, the column fields, and the data fields
- The two rows of cells directly above the row fields (that is, the area where the page field normally appears)

When you drag a row, column, or page field out of this area, the mouse pointer changes to a field icon with an X through it. When you release the mouse button, Excel deletes the field from the table.

Deleting a Field Using the PivotTable Wizard

You can also use the PivotTable Wizard to remove a row, column, data, or page field from the pivot table. Follow these steps:

1. Select a cell inside the pivot table you want to work with.
2. Select the Data | PivotTable command (or click on the PivotTable Wizard button in the Query and Pivot toolbar) to display the PivotTable Wizard - Step 3 of 4 dialog box.

> **TIP**
>
> You also can display the PivotTable Wizard - Step 3 of 4 dialog box by right-clicking on a pivot table cell and selecting PivotTable from the shortcut menu.

3. Use your mouse to drag the field label you want to remove and drop it off the table area.
4. Select the Finish button. Excel removes the new field and redisplays the pivot table.

Deleting a Field Using the PivotTable Field Dialog Box

The third and final method uses the PivotTable Field dialog box to delete a row, column, page, or data field. The following procedure takes you through the necessary steps:

1. Select a cell in the pivot table field you want to delete.

2. Display the PivotTable Field dialog box (as described at the beginning of this chapter).

3. Select the Delete button. Excel deletes the field and returns you to the worksheet.

Summary

This chapter introduces you to pivot tables and shows you how to create them from Excel lists. You have learned various techniques for customizing your pivot tables. Here are some chapters that contain related information:

■ For coverage of creating and working with charts, check out Chapter 19, "Charts and Graphics."

■ To get an explanation of querying external data sources, see Chapter 24.

■ Pivot tables are just one of Excel's many data-analysis features. To learn more about analysis with Excel, see Chapter 21, "Data-Analysis Tools and Techniques."

Using Microsoft Query

For the most part, the biggest problem with Excel lists is getting the data onto the worksheet in the first place. If the data doesn't exist in any other form, you have no choice but to enter it yourself. In many cases, however, the data you need already exists in a separate file elsewhere on your computer, or perhaps on a network server.

Excel provides several tools for accessing data files in non-Excel formats. Excel's File | Open command can handle files in xBASE and Lotus 1-2-3 formats, and the TextImport Wizard can convert delimited or fixed-width text files into Excel. These methods, however, often fall short for three reasons:

- If you need only a small piece of a huge file, it's wasteful to import the entire file into Excel. Besides, databases with tens of thousands of records aren't all that uncommon, so a file import might choke on Excel's 16,384-row limit.

- Many databases contain related tables. For example, a database might include a table of customer data and a table of order data related by a common Customer ID field. If you need data from both tables, you're out of luck because there's no way for Excel to honor the relationships between the two tables.

- The data you need might be in a file format not supported directly by Excel, such as SQL Server or Paradox.

To solve all these problems, Excel comes with a separate program called Microsoft Query that you can use to access external database files from programs such as dBASE, Access, FoxPro, and SQL Server. This chapter shows you the basics of Microsoft Query and explains how to open external databases, extract the information you need, and return that information to Excel.

About Microsoft Query

Microsoft Query is a small but powerful database application designed to provide you with easy access to various database formats. You can use Microsoft Query as a standalone program or via an Excel add-in.

A *query* is a request to a database for specific information. It combines criteria conditions with functions to retrieve the data with which you want to work. Microsoft Query enables you to construct queries easily by using pull-down menu commands and drag-and-drop techniques. Query takes these actions and constructs *SQL* (Structured Query Language) statements that do the dirty work of retrieving and filtering the data.

You also can use Microsoft Query to edit and maintain your database files. You can add and delete records, modify field contents, sort records, join databases, and even create new database files. The beauty of Microsoft Query is that you can do all this with many different database formats and maintain a consistent interface.

Understanding ODBC

The data you can work with in Microsoft Query depends on the *open database connectivity (ODBC) drivers* you installed with Excel. These drivers serve as intermediaries between Query and the external database. They take care of the messy problems of dealing with different database file structures and communicating between incompatible systems.

Each ODBC driver is a *DLL* (dynamic link library; a set of subroutines) that tells an ODBC-enabled application (such as Microsoft Query) how to interact (via SQL) with a specific data source. The go-between for the application and the driver is the ODBC Driver Manager, which keeps track of the location of the database, the database filename, and a few other options.

Figure 24.1 shows how Excel, Microsoft Query, the ODBC Driver Manager, the ODBC device driver, and the database fit together.

FIGURE 24.1.

The relationship between Excel, Query, the ODBC components, and the database.

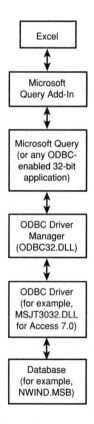

Here are the basic steps you'll follow each time you need to access an external database:

1. Use the Microsoft Query add-in to start Query from Excel.
2. Use the ODBC Driver Manager to specify the database to use.

3. Use Microsoft Query to load tables, filter the data, and format the layout of the data (which is all done via the appropriate ODBC driver).

4. Return the query results to Excel.

Excel provides ODBC drivers for the sources listed in Table 24.1.

Table 24.1. Excel's ODBC device drivers.

Database	Versions	Driver DLL
Access	1.0, 1.5, 2.0	MSRD2X32.DLL
Access	7.0	MSJT3032.DLL
dBASE	III, IV, 5.0	MSXB3032.DLL
Excel (XLS files)	3.0, 4.0, 5.0, 7.0	MSXL3032.DLL
FoxPro	2.0, 2.5, 2.6	MSXB3032.DLL
Paradox	3.x, 4.x, 5.x	MSPX3032.DLL
SQL Server	1.1, 4.2, NT, Sybase 4.2	SQLSRV32.DLL
Text		MSTX3032.DLL

Extra drivers for Btrieve (version 5.1), ODBC ODS Gateway, and other databases are available from Microsoft or from third-party vendors.

Some Notes About Databases and Tables

Although the terms *database* and *table* are often used interchangeably, they have distinct meanings in Microsoft Query (and, indeed, in relational-database theory as a whole). To wit, a *table* is a collection of data organized into records and fields. It's directly analogous to an Excel *list*, in which a row is the equivalent of a record and a column is the equivalent of a field. A *database* is a collection of tables (and, like Access databases, can include other objects as well, such as forms and reports).

You'll often find that two or more of a database's tables are "joined" by a *relational key* field. For example, suppose you have a table that contains data for your customers. This data includes the customer ID, the customer name, the customer address, and more. The same database might also have a table of orders placed by these customers. This table probably includes fields for the amount ordered and the date the order was placed, but it also needs to record which customer placed the order. You could enter the customer's name, address, phone number, and so on, but that would be wasteful because all that data already resides in the Customers table. A better approach is to include the CustomerID field and then relate the two tables using that field. For example, if an order is placed by a customer with ID 12-3456, you can find out, say, that customer's address simply by looking up 12-3456 in the Customers table.

Figure 24.2 shows a graphical representation of this relationship (this figure was taken from a Microsoft Query screen).

FIGURE 24.2.

Two tables related via a common CustomerID field.

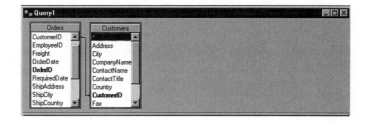

The last thing you need to know before beginning is that many tables include a field that contains only unique values. This so-called *primary-key* field ensures that no two table records are alike and that there is an unambiguous way to reference each record in the table. For the Customers table, as long as you assign a unique ID number to each customer, you can use the CustomerID field as the primary key. Similarly, you can create an OrderID field in the Orders table, assign unique numbers to the field (such as invoice numbers), and use that as the primary key. As you'll see, Query displays primary-key fields in bold. (See Figure 24.2.)

Loading the Microsoft Query Add-In

As mentioned earlier, you can run Query either as a standalone program or via Excel's MS Query add-in. Your concern in this chapter is using Query as an adjunct to Excel, so it concentrates solely on working with Query via the MS Query add-in program. Assuming that Query is installed on your system, the following steps outline the procedure for loading the MS Query add-in:

> **NOTE**
>
> If you didn't install Query when you set up Excel, you can load it onto your system by running the Excel (or Microsoft Office) setup program and selecting the Add/Remove button. You need to add Microsoft Query, Excel's MS Query add-in, and the necessary ODBC drivers for the data with which you are going to work.

1. Select the Tools | Add-Ins command. Excel displays the Add-Ins dialog box, shown in Figure 24.3.
2. In the Add-Ins Available list, activate the check box beside the MS Query Add-In item.
3. Select OK to return to the worksheet.

FIGURE 24.3.

*Use the Add-Ins dialog box
to select the add-ins you
want to load.*

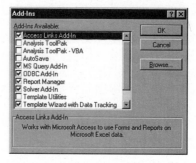

When you load the MS Query add-in, Excel modifies the Data menu by adding the Get External Data command. As you'll see in the next section, this command starts Microsoft Query so that you can work with an external database.

Starting Microsoft Query

To retrieve data from an external database file, you switch to Microsoft Query and specify the information you need. To display the Microsoft Query window, follow the steps given next.

> **NOTE**
>
> To run Microsoft Query as a standalone program, use Explorer or My Computer to display the \Program Files\Common Files\MSQuery folder, and double-click on the Msqry32 file.

1. Select the Data | Get External Data command, or click the Get External Data button in the Query and Pivot toolbar. Query loads and then displays the Select Data Source dialog box, shown in Figure 24.4. If you're starting Query for the first time, this dialog box is blank. Skip to the next section for instructions.

FIGURE 24.4.

*Use the Select Data Source
dialog box to choose the
data source with which you
want to work.*

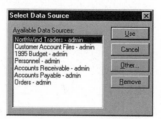

2. Highlight a data source in the Available Data Sources list.
3. Select Use to open the source. Query displays the Add Tables dialog box, shown in Figure 24.5.

FIGURE 24.5.

Use the Add Tables dialog box to select the tables you want to include in your query.

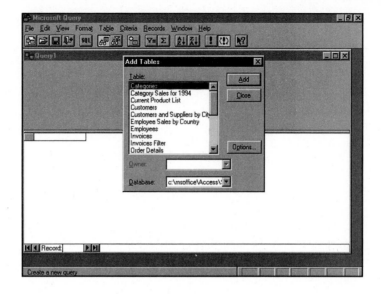

4. For each database file you want to work with, highlight it in the Table list, and select the Add button.

5. When you've finished adding tables, select Close.

CAUTION

After you start Microsoft Query, Excel goes into a state of "suspended animation." This means you won't be able to work with Excel until you exit Query. If for some reason you lose your link with Query (Excel uses a DDE link to communicate with Query, and DDE is notoriously flaky), you might end up with both programs locked up. If this happens, try pressing Esc or Ctrl+Break to interrupt the macro that Excel uses to communicate with Query.

Working with Data Sources

A *data source* is a pointer that defines the data with which you want to work. This includes the ODBC driver and the location of the file (or files). Data-source locations generally fall into two categories:

- A single database file that includes multiple tables. For example, an Access database file would be a data source.

- A directory (or folder) of database files, each of which contains only a single table. For example, a directory of FoxPro or dBASE (versions III and IV) files would be a data source.

Defining a Data Source

Before you can work with Microsoft Query, you need to define at least one data source. As you saw in step 4 in the preceding section, you then use this data source to select which tables to include in the query. You'll usually define your data sources from within Query, but you also can use the Control Panel's 32-bit ODBC utility. The next two sections explain both methods.

Defining a Data Source Using Query

This procedure outlines the steps you need to follow to define a data source:

1. If you're in the Select Data Source dialog box, select the Other button. If you're in the Microsoft Query window, select the File | New Query command (or click the New Query button in the toolbar), and then select Other. Query displays the ODBC Data Sources dialog box.

2. Select New. Query displays the Add Data Source dialog box, shown in Figure 24.6.

FIGURE 24.6.

Use the Add Data Source dialog box to select a driver for the database with which you want to work.

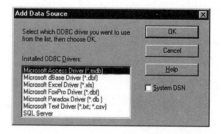

3. In the Installed ODBC Drivers list, highlight the driver for the database you want to work with and then select OK. Query displays a Setup dialog box for the driver. The layout of the dialog box varies from driver to driver. Figure 24.7 shows the Setup dialog box for an Access source.

FIGURE 24.7.

The Setup dialog box for an ODBC Access data source.

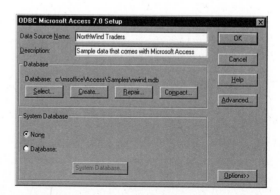

4. In the Data Source Name text box, enter an identifier for the source. This is the name that will appear in the Select Data Source dialog box when you start Query.

5. Use the Description text box to enter a description for the source.

6. Select the data source using the appropriate method:

   ■ If you're defining an Access data source, choose the Select button, highlight the database name in the Select Database dialog box that appears, and then select OK.

   ■ If you're defining a dBASE, FoxPro, or Paradox data source, use the Version drop-down list to select the version number of the program that created the files; then choose Select Directory to specify the directory (folder) where the files reside.

   ■ If you're defining an Excel data source, use the Version drop-down list to select the version number of Excel that created the files, and then choose Select Workbook to specify the workbook file that contains the list or lists.

   ■ If you're defining a text data source, choose Select Directory to specify the directory (folder) where the files can be found.

   ■ If you're defining a SQL Server data source, use the Server combo box to enter the name of a SQL Server on your network.

7. Fill in the other dialog box options, as necessary.

8. Select OK to return to the ODBC Data Sources dialog box.

9. Select OK to return to the Select Data Source dialog box.

10. Highlight the source you want to work with, and then select Use. The Add Tables dialog box appears.

11. For each database file you want to work with, highlight it in the Table list and select the Add button. When you're done, select Close. Query displays a new query file.

Deleting a Data Source

There are many reasons why you might no longer need a particular data source:

■ The database file or directory that a data source points to might get removed from the system or network.

■ You've defined a new data source that uses a different ODBC driver.

■ You have no further use for the data referenced by the data source.

Whatever the reason, you should delete unneeded data sources to keep the Available Data Sources list uncluttered and to prevent errors (for example, by trying to access a database that no longer exists). Deleting a data source requires two separate procedures: you first remove the data source from Query and then delete the data source in the 32-bit ODBC utility. Here are the complete steps:

1. In Query, select the File|Table Definition command to display the Select Data Sources dialog box.

2. In the Available Data Sources list, highlight the data source you want to remove.

3. Select the Remove button.

4. Select Cancel to return to Query.

5. Open the Control Panel window, and select the 32-bit ODBC icon.

6. In the User Data Sources (Driver) list, highlight the data source you want to delete.

7. Select the Delete button. A dialog box appears asking if you're sure you want to delete the data source.

8. Select Yes.

9. Select Close to return to the Control Panel.

A Tour of the Microsoft Query Window

After you've added one or more tables, Microsoft Query creates a new query file and displays it in a window, as shown in Figure 24.8. To get you comfortable with the layout of this window, here's a rundown of the various features (not all of which might be currently visible on your screen):

- Table pane—The query file's window is divided into three panes. The top pane is the *table pane*. It displays one or more boxes that represent the tables you added to the query from the Add Tables dialog box. Each box displays the name of the table at the top, followed by a list of the database field names. You can toggle the table pane on and off by selecting the View|Tables command, or by clicking the Show/Hide Tables toolbar button.

- Criteria pane—This is the middle pane, and it's where you define the criteria for your query. Note that the criteria pane isn't displayed when you begin a new query. To toggle the criteria pane on and off, select the View|Criteria command, or click the Show/Hide Criteria button in the toolbar.

- Data pane—The bottom pane displays the results of the query (called, appropriately enough, the *result set*). This area is empty initially, so you have to add fields from the databases included in the query.

- Navigation buttons—You use these buttons to move from record to record in the result set.

To move from pane to pane, either use your mouse to click the pane you want to work with or press F6 to cycle through the panes. (You can also press Shift+F6 to cycle backward through the panes.) To change the size of a pane, use your mouse to drag the bar that separates each pane from its neighbor.

FIGURE 24.8.

The Microsoft Query window.

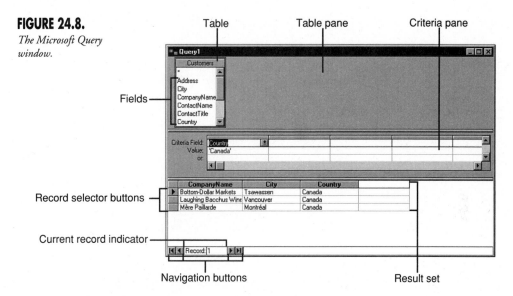

Adding Fields to the Data Pane

To get the information you want from an external database, you need to add one or more table fields to the query window's data pane. After you've added fields, you can move them around, edit them, change their headings, and more. This section shows you various methods for adding fields to the data pane. The next section takes you through the basics of working with table fields.

Adding a Field with the Mouse

You might find that your mouse provides the most convenient method for adding fields to the data pane. You can try two basic techniques:

- Double-click on a field name. Query adds the fields to the next available column in the data pane.
- Drag the field from the field list and drop it inside the data pane. Drop the name on an existing field to position the new field to the left of the existing field.

If you want to add multiple fields at once, hold down Ctrl and click on each field. (If the fields are contiguous, you can select them by clicking on the first field, holding down Shift, and then clicking on the last field.) Then drag the selection into the data pane.

If you want to place all the fields inside the data pane, you have two ways to proceed. If you want the fields to appear in the order in which they appear in the table, either double-click on the asterisk (*) field or drag the asterisk field and drop it inside the data pane. If you want the fields to appear in alphabetical order, double-click on the table name and then drag any of the fields into the data pane.

Filtering Records with Criteria

You also can filter the records in an external database; the process is similar to the one you learned for lists. This section leads you through the basics of filtering records with criteria.

Creating Simple Criteria

Excel's AutoFilter enables you to set up simple criteria such as showing only records in which the State field is CA or in which the Account Number field is 12-3456. Query enables you to create similar filters, and the process is almost as easy, as you'll see in these steps:

1. Move to the column that contains the field you want to use to filter the records.

2. Select the value in the field you want to use as a criterion.

 3. Click the Criteria Equals button in the Query toolbar. Query filters the data based on the selected field value.

4. Repeat steps 1 through 3 to filter the records even further.

Entering Simple Criteria in the Criteria Pane

As you learned in Chapter 22, "Working with Lists and Databases," you can set up a criteria range in a worksheet to use when filtering your records. The equivalent in Microsoft Query is the *criteria pane*. You can add field names to this pane and then set up criteria that range from simple field values to complex expressions for compound and computed criteria.

If you use the technique described in the preceding section for entering simple criteria, you'll see that Query displays the criteria pane automatically and adds the field names and values to the criteria pane.

You also can enter simple criteria directly in the criteria pane (this is handy, for instance, if you don't have a mouse and can't use the Criteria Equals tool). The following procedure shows you the necessary steps:

1. Display the criteria pane, if necessary, and move the cursor into the first header of the Criteria Field row.

2. Use the drop-down list to select a field to use for the criterion. (Alternatively, you can drag a field from the table pane and drop it on the criteria pane.)

3. Select the cell below the field name (that is, on the Value row) and enter the field value you want to use for the criterion. Enclose text in single quotation marks (for example, `'CA'`) and dates in number signs (for example, `#1995-01-15#`). For more information see the section "Entering Criteria Expressions in Microsoft Query."

4. To run the query, move the cursor to a different cell, select a different pane, or press Enter. (This is assuming, of course, that the Automatic Query feature is activated. If it's not, you need to run the query by hand.)

Figure 24.9 shows a sample query that filters the Customers table to show only those records in which Canada appears in the Country field.

FIGURE 24.9.

A query that uses a criterion to filter data from the Customers table.

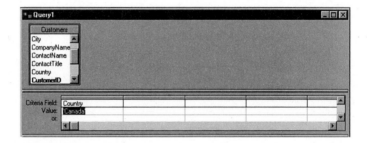

Entering Criteria Expressions in Microsoft Query

Entering criteria expressions in Microsoft Query is similar to entering them in Excel. You should, however, be aware of the following differences:

- Enclose text in single quotation marks (for example, `'CA'`) rather than double quotation marks. In most cases, Query adds the single quotation marks for you.

- Enclose dates in pound signs (for example, `#1994-01-15#`). Again, Query usually recognizes a date and adds the pound signs for you.

- If you're working with numbers, you can use the normal comparison operators such as equal to (=), not equal to (<>), greater than (>), and less than (<). For example, suppose you have an Invoices table with an Amount field. To filter the table to show only those invoices on which the amount is greater than or equal to $1000, you add the Amount field to the criteria pane and enter the following criterion: `>=1000`.

- To use wildcard characters, you must include the keyword `Like` and then use an underscore to substitute for a single character, or a percent sign to substitute for a group of characters. For example, to find all records in which the NAME field includes the word Office, you type `Like '%Office%'` in the criteria pane's NAME field.

Returning the Query Results to Excel

When you have the result set you want, you can import the data into Excel by following this procedure:

1. Select the File | Return Data to Microsoft Excel command. Query switches to Excel and displays the Get External Data dialog box, shown in Figure 24.10. You also can click the Return Data to Excel button to return the query results.

FIGURE 24.10.

Use the Get External Data dialog box to set a few options for the external data you're returning.

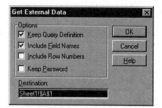

2. Select the options you want to use for the returned data:
   - Keep Query Definition—Activate this check box to keep a copy of the query definition in the worksheet. This way, you can refresh the data at any time.
   - Include Field Names—Activate this check box to add the result set's field names as column headers in the returned data.
   - Include Row Numbers—Activate this check box to include the result set's record numbers as the first column in the returned data.
   - Keep Password—If the data source requires a password, activate this check box to save the password with the data. This way, you can access the same data source (say, to refresh the data) without having to reenter the password.

3. Use the Destination box to select the top-left corner of the range you want to use for the data.

4. Select OK. Excel pastes the result set into the worksheet.

Summary

This chapter introduces you to Microsoft Query, the tool that enables Excel users to access external data. It provides an overview of Query and the ODBC drivers that are the nuts and bolts of the whole process. You learn how to start Query, set up a data source, add tables, create a result set using fields and criteria, and then return the results to Excel.

Understanding Objects

25

by
Paul McFedries
and Tom Hayes

IN THIS CHAPTER

Many of your VBA procedures perform calculations using simple combinations of numbers, operators, and Excel's built-in functions. You have probably found, however, that most of your code manipulates the Excel environment in some way, whether it's entering data in a range, formatting a chart, or setting Excel workspace options. Each of these items—the range, the chart, and the Excel workspace—is called an *object* in VBA. Objects are perhaps the most crucial concept in VBA programming; they are explained in detail in this chapter.

What Is an Object?

The dictionary definition of an object is "anything perceptible by one or more of the senses, especially something that can be seen and felt." Of course, you can't *feel* anything in Excel, but you can *see* all kinds of things. To VBA, an object is anything in Excel that you can see *and* manipulate in some way. For example, a range is something you can see, and you can manipulate it by entering data, changing colors, setting fonts, and so on. A range, therefore, is an object.

What isn't an object? Excel for Windows 95 is so customizable that most things you can see qualify as objects, but not everything does. For example, the Maximize and Minimize buttons in workbook windows are not objects. Yes, you can operate them, but you can't change them. Instead, the window itself is the object, and you manipulate it so that it is maximized or minimized.

You can manipulate objects in VBA in one of two ways:

- You can make changes to the object's *properties*.
- You can make the object perform a task by activating a *method* associated with the object.

To help you understand properties, methods, and objects, let's put things in real-world terms. Specifically, let's look at your computer as though it were an Excel object. For starters, you can think of your computer in one of two ways: as a single object and as a *collection* of objects (such as the monitor, the keyboard, the system unit, and so on).

If you describe your computer as a whole, you mention things like the name of the manufacturer, the price, the color, and so on. Each of these items is a *property* of the computer. You also can use your computer to perform tasks, such as writing letters, crunching numbers, and playing games. These are the *methods* associated with your computer. The sum total of all these properties and methods gives you an overall description of your computer.

But your computer is also a collection of objects, each with its own properties and methods. The system unit, for example, has all kinds of properties: the height, width, and weight, the type of processor, the size of the hard disk, and so on. Its methods would be things such as turning the computer on and off and inserting and removing disks.

If you like, you can extend this analysis to lower levels. For example, the system unit is also a collection of objects (the hard disk, the motherboard, and the power supply).

In the end, you have a complete description of the computer, both in terms of what it looks like (its properties) and in terms of how it behaves (its methods).

The Object Hierarchy

As you've seen, your computer's objects are arranged in a hierarchy with the most general object (the computer as a whole) at the top. Lower levels progress through more specific objects (such as the system unit, the motherboard, and the processor).

Excel's objects are arranged in a hierarchy as well. The most general object—the `Application` object—refers to Excel itself. Beneath the `Application` object, Excel has nine other objects, as outlined in Table 25.1. Notice that, in most cases, each object is part of a *collection* of similar objects.

Table 25.1. Excel objects beneath the `Application` object.

Object	Collection	Description
AddIn	AddIns	An Excel add-in file. The `AddIns` collection refers to all the add-ins available to Excel (that is, all the add-ins that are listed in the Add-Ins dialog box).
AutoCorrect	None	Contains the settings for the AutoCorrect feature.
Debug	None	The VBA Debug window.
Dialog	Dialogs	A built-in Excel dialog box. The `Dialogs` collection contains all the Excel built-in dialog boxes.
Name	Names	A defined name. The `Names` collection is a list of all the defined names available to Excel, including built-in names such as `Database` and `Print_Area`.
MenuBar	MenuBars	A menu bar. The `MenuBars` collection contains the Excel menu bars, both built-in and custom.
Toolbar	Toolbars	A toolbar. The `Toolbars` collection is a list of all the built-in and custom toolbars that are available.
Window	Windows	An open window. The `Windows` collection contains all the open windows.
Workbook	Workbooks	An open workbook. The `Workbooks` collection is all the open workbooks.

Most of the objects in Table 25.1 have objects beneath them in the hierarchy. A `Workbook` object, for example, contains `Worksheet` objects and possibly `Chart` objects and `Module` objects. Similarly, a `Worksheet` object contains many objects of its own, such as `Range` objects and an `Outline` object.

To specify an object in the hierarchy, you usually start with the uppermost object and add the lower objects, separated by periods. For example, here's one way you could specify the range B2:B5 on the worksheet named Sheet1 in the workbook named Book1:

```
Application.Workbooks("Book1").Worksheets("Sheet1").Range("B2:B5")
```

As you'll see, there are ways to shorten such long-winded hierarchic paths.

Working with Object Properties

Every Excel object has a defining set of characteristics. These characteristics are called the object's *properties*, and they control the appearance and position of the object. For example, each `Window` object has a `WindowState` property you can use to display a window as maximized, minimized, or normal. Similarly, a `Range` object has a `Font` property that defines the range font, a `Formula` property for the range formula, a `Name` property to hold the range name, and many more.

When you refer to a property, you use the following syntax:

```
Object.Property
```

For example, the following expression refers to the `ActiveWindow` property of the `Application` object:

```
Application.ActiveWindow
```

One of the most confusing aspects of objects and properties is that some properties do double duty as objects. (See Figure 25.1.) The `Application` object has an `ActiveWindow` property that tells you the name of the active window. However, `ActiveWindow` is also a `Window` object. Similarly, the `Window` object has an `ActiveCell` property, but `ActiveCell` is also a `Range` object. Finally, a `Range` object has a `Font` property, but a font is also an object with its own properties (`Italic`, `Name`, `Size`, and so on).

FIGURE 25.1.

Some Excel properties can also be objects.

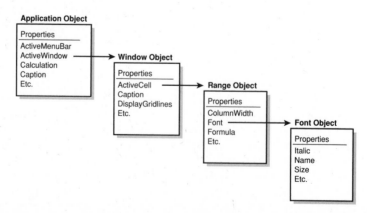

In other words, lower-level objects in the object hierarchy are really just properties of their parent objects. This idea can often help you reduce the length of a hierarchical path (and thus save wear and tear on your typing fingers). For example, consider the following object path:

```
Application.ActiveWindow.ActiveCell.Font.Italic
```

Here, an object such as `ActiveCell` implicitly refers to the `ActiveWindow` and `Application` objects, so you can knock the path down to size, as follows:

```
ActiveCell.Font.Italic
```

Common Object Properties

Each Excel object has a number of properties. Table 25.2 is a list of frequently used properties associated with the some of the common objects mentioned previously.

Table 25.2. Frequently used properties of some common Excel objects.

Property	Description
	Application
ActiveWindow	The active window
ActiveWorkbook	The active workbook
Calculation	The calculation mode
Caption	The name that appears in the title bar of the main Excel window
ScreenUpdating	Turns screen updating on or off
StandardFont	The standard font name for new worksheets
	Workbook
ActiveSheet	The active sheet
FullName	The full name of the workbook, including the path
Name	The name of the workbook
Path	The full path of the workbook, excluding the name of the workbook
Saved	Returns `False` if changes have been made to the workbook
	Worksheet
Name	The name of the worksheet
ProtectContents	Protects the worksheet cell's contents
Visible	Hides or unhides the worksheet

continues

Table 25.2. continued

Property	Description
	Window
ActiveCell	The active cell
Caption	The name that appears in the window's title bar
DisplayGridlines	Turns the grid lines on or off
DisplayHeadings	Turns the row and column headings on or off
Visible	Hides or unhides the window
WindowState	Sets the window view to maximized, minimized, or normal
	Range
Column	The first column of the range
Font	The font of the range
Formula	The range formula
Name	The range name
Row	The first row of the range
Style	The range style
Value	The value of a cell
Worksheet	The worksheet that contains the range

> **NOTE**
>
> To learn how to refer to individual workbooks, worksheets, and windows, see the section in this chapter titled "Working with Object Collections."

Setting the Value of a Property

To set a property to a certain value, you use the following syntax:

Object.Property=value

Here, *value* is the value you want to use. *value* can be either a constant or a formula that returns a constant, and it can be any one of the following types:

- A numeric value. For example, the following statement sets the size of the font in the active cell to 14:

```
ActiveCell.Font.Size = 14
```

■ A string value. You denote a string by surrounding it with double quotation marks. The following example sets the font name in the active cell to Times New Roman:

```
ActiveCell.Font.Name = "Times New Roman"
```

■ A logical value (that is, `True` or `False`). The following statement turns on the `Italic` property in the active cell:

```
ActiveCell.Font.Italic = True
```

Returning the Value of a Property

Sometimes you need to know the current setting of a property before changing the property or performing some other action. You can find out the current value of a property by using the following syntax:

```
variable=Object.Property
```

Here, *variable* is a variable or another property. For example, the following statement stores the contents of the active cell in a variable named `cellContents`:

```
cellContents = ActiveCell.Value
```

Working with Object Methods

An object's properties describe what the object *is*, whereas its *methods* describe what the object *does*. For example, a `Worksheet` object can recalculate its formulas using the `Calculate` method. Similarly, a `Range` object can sort its cells by using the `Sort` method.

How you refer to a method depends on whether it uses any arguments. If it doesn't, the syntax is similar to that of properties:

```
Object.Method
```

For example, the following statement saves the active workbook:

```
ActiveWorkbook.Save
```

If the method requires arguments, you use the following syntax:

```
Object.Method (argument1, argument2, ...)
```

NOTE

Technically, the parentheses around the argument list are necessary only if you'll be storing the result of the method in a variable or in an object property.

For example, the `Range` object has an `Offset` method that returns a range offset from the specified range. Here's the syntax:

```
Object.Offset(rowOffset, columnOffset)
```

Object is the `Range` object.

rowOffset is the number of rows to offset.

columnOffset is the number of columns to offset.

For example, the following expression returns a cell offset five rows and three columns from the active cell:

```
ActiveCell.Offset(5, 3)
```

To make your methods clearer to read, you can use VBA's predefined *named arguments*. For example, the syntax of the `Offset` method has two named arguments: *rowOffset* and *columnOffset*. Here's how you would use them in the previous example:

```
ActiveCell.Offset(rowOffset:=5, columnOffset:=3)
```

Notice how the named arguments are assigned values by using the `:=` operator.

> **TIP**
>
> Another advantage to using named arguments is that you can enter the arguments in any order you like, and you can ignore any arguments you don't need (except necessary arguments, of course).

> **NOTE**
>
> In this example, the `Offset` method returns a `Range` object. It is quite common for methods to return objects, and it's perfectly acceptable to change the properties or use a method of the returned object.

Common Object Methods

Each Excel object has several methods you can use. Table 25.3 summarizes a few of the most frequently used methods associated with the common objects discussed earlier.

Table 25.3. Frequently used methods for common Excel objects.

Method	Description
	Application
FindFile	Displays the Find File dialog box
Quit	Exits Excel
Undo	Cancels the last action
	Workbook
Activate	Activates a workbook
Close	Closes a workbook
Protect	Protects a workbook
Save	Saves a workbook
Save As	Saves a workbook under a different name
Unprotect	Unprotects a workbook
	Worksheet
Activate	Activates a worksheet
Calculate	Recalculates a worksheet
Copy	Copies a worksheet
Delete	Deletes a worksheet
Move	Moves a worksheet
Protect	Protects a worksheet
Unprotect	Unprotects a worksheet
	Window
Activate	Activates a window
Close	Closes a window
	Range
Clear	Clears everything from the range
ClearContents	Clears the contents of each cell in the range
ClearFormats	Clears the formatting of every cell in the range
Copy	Copies the range
Cut	Cuts the range
Offset	Returns a range that is offset from the specified range
Paste	Pastes the Clipboard contents into the range
Select	Selects a range
Sort	Sorts the range

Working with Object Collections

A *collection* is a set of similar objects. For example, the Workbooks collection is the set of all the open Workbook objects. Similarly, the Worksheets collection is the set of all Worksheet objects in a workbook. Collections are objects, so they have their own properties and methods, and you can use the properties and methods to manipulate one or more objects in the collection.

The members of a collection are called the *elements* of the collection. You can refer to individual elements using either the object's name or by using an *index* (that is, the order in which the object appears in the collection). For example, the following statement closes a workbook named Budget.xls:

```
Workbooks("Budget.xls").Close
```

On the other hand, the following statement uses an index to make a copy of the first Picture object in the active worksheet:

```
ActiveSheet.Pictures(1).Copy
```

If you don't specify an element, VBA assumes you want to work with the entire collection.

> **NOTE**
>
> It's important here to reiterate that you can't refer to many Excel objects by themselves. Instead, you must refer to the object as an element in a collection. For example, when referring to the Budget.xls workbook, you can't just use Budget.xls. You have to use Workbooks("Budget.xls") so that VBA knows you're talking about a currently open workbook.

Common Object Collections

Here's a list of collections you are likely to use most frequently:

- Sheets—Contains all the sheets in a workbook. This includes not only worksheets, but also modules, charts, and dialog sheets. The available methods include Add (to create a new sheet), Copy, Delete, Move, and Select.

- Workbooks—Contains all the open workbooks. Use this collection's Open method to open a workbook. The Add method creates a new workbook.

- Worksheets—Contains all the worksheets in a workbook. The Visible property enables you to hide or unhide the collection. The methods are the same as for Sheets.

- Windows—Contains all the open windows. The Arrange method enables you to arrange the collection onscreen (for example, tile or cascade).

Using the Object Browser

The *Object Browser* is a handy tool that shows you the objects available for your procedures as well as the properties and methods of each object. You also can use it to move quickly between procedures and to paste code templates into a module. To display the Object Browser, activate a module and then either select the View | Object Browser command or click on the Object Browser button in the Visual Basic toolbar. You'll see the Object Browser dialog box, shown in Figure 25.2.

FIGURE 25.2.

VBA's Object Browser.

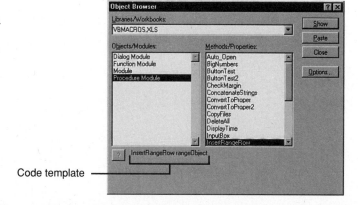

Code template

TIP

You also can press F2 to display the Object Browser.

Here's a rundown of the Object Browser's features:

■ Libraries/Workbooks—This drop-down list contains all the libraries and workbooks referenced by any module in the current workbook. (A *library* is a file that contains information about the objects in an application.) You'll always see at least two libraries in this list: The Excel library lists the Excel objects you can use in your code, and the VBA (Visual Basic for Applications) library lists the functions and language constructs specific to VBA.

■ Objects/Modules—When you highlight a library in Libraries/Workbooks, the Objects/Modules list shows the available objects in the library. When you highlight a workbook, Objects/Modules shows the modules in the workbook.

■ Methods/Properties—When you highlight an object in the Objects/Modules list, Methods/Properties shows the methods and properties available for that object. When you highlight a module, Methods/Properties shows the procedures contained in the module. To move to one of these procedures, highlight it and then click on the Show button.

■ Code template—This section displays code templates you can paste into your modules. These templates list the method, property, or function name followed by the appropriately named arguments, if there are any. (See Figure 25.3.) You can paste this template into a procedure and then edit the template.

FIGURE 25.3.

The Object Browser displays code templates that you can paste into your procedures.

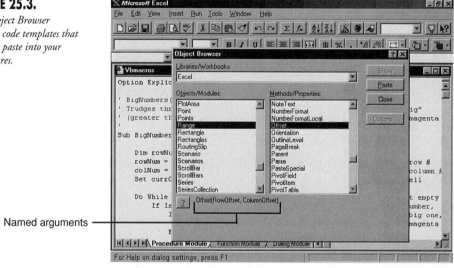

Named arguments

Follow these steps to paste code templates:

1. In a VBA module, place the insertion point where you want the code template to appear.

2. Display the Object Browser, as described previously.

3. Select a library from the Libraries/Workbooks list and then select an object from the Objects/Modules list.

4. Use the Methods/Properties list to highlight the method or property you want to use.

5. If you would like to display a Help screen for the selected method or property, click the ? button, read the Help screen that appears, and then return to the Object Browser.

6. Click the Paste button. VBA returns you to the module and pastes the code template into the procedure.

Assigning an Object to a Variable

As you learned in Chapter 24, "Using Microsoft Query," you can declare a variable as an Object data type by using the following form of the Dim statement:

```
Dim variableName As Object
```

After you've set up your object variable, you can assign an object to it by using the Set statement. Set has the following syntax:

```
Set variableName = ObjectName
```

variableName is the name of the variable.

ObjectName is the object you want to assign to the variable.

For example, the following statements declare a variable named budgetSheet to be an object and then assign it to the 1995 Budget worksheet in the Budget.xls workbook:

```
Dim budgetSheet As Object
Set budgetSheet = Workbooks("Budget.xls").Worksheets("1995 Budget")
```

Working with Multiple Properties or Methods

Because most Excel objects have many different properties and methods, you'll often need to perform multiple actions on a single object. This is accomplished easily with multiple statements that set the appropriate properties or run the necessary methods. However, this can be a pain if you have a long object name.

For example, take a look at the FormatRange procedure shown in Listing 25.1. This procedure formats a range in the Sales worksheet with six statements. The Range object name—Worksheets("Sales").Range("B2:B5")—is quite long and is repeated in all six statements.

Listing 25.1. A procedure that formats a range.

```
Sub FormatRange()

    Worksheets("Sales").Range("B2:B5").Style = "Currency"
    Worksheets("Sales").Range("B2:B5").WrapText = True
    Worksheets("Sales").Range("B2:B5").Font.Size = 16
    Worksheets("Sales").Range("B2:B5").Font.Bold = True
    Worksheets("Sales").Range("B2:B5").Font.Color = RGB(255, 0, 0) ' Red
    Worksheets("Sales").Range("B2:B5").Font.Name = "Times New Roman"

End Sub
```

To shorten this procedure, VBA provides the With statement. Here's the syntax:

```
With object
    [statements]
End With
```

object is the name of the object.

statements is the statements you want to execute on *object*.

The idea is that you strip out the common object and place it on the With line. Then all the statements between With and End With need only reference a specific method or property of that object. In the FormatRange procedure, the common object in all six statements is Worksheets("Sales").Range("B2:B5"). Listing 25.2 shows the FormatRange2 procedure that uses the With statement to strip out this common object and make the previous macro more efficient.

Listing 25.2. A more efficient version of FormatRange().

```
Sub FormatRange2()

    With Worksheets("Sales").Range("B2:B5")
        .Style = "Currency"
        .WrapText = True
        .Font.Size = 16
        .Font.Bold = True
        .Font.Color = RGB(255, 0, 0) 'Red
        .Font.Name = "Times New Roman"
    End With

End Sub
```

NOTE

You can make the FormatRange2 procedure even more efficient when you eliminate the repetition of the Font object. In this case, you can *nest* another With statement inside the original one. The new With statement would look like this:

```
With .Font
    .Size = 16
    .Bold = True
    .Color = RGB(255, 0, 0)
    .Name = "Times New Roman"
End With
```

Summary

This chapter introduces you to the all-important subject of objects. You have learned what an object is and how Excel's objects are arranged in a hierarchy, with the Application object at the top. You have examined object properties, methods, collections, and variables, and you have learned how to use the Object Browser.

Working with Other Applications

26

by
Paul McFedries
and Tom Hayes

IN THIS CHAPTER

Your VBA code will likely spend most of its time working with Excel objects and their associated properties and methods. However, there will be times when you need your code to interact with other applications. Happily, VBA offers a number of functions and methods for working with other applications inside your procedures. This chapter shows you how to start other programs; how to send them keystrokes; how to work with DDE; and how to use DLLs in your procedures.

Starting Another Application

I suppose that the most obvious way to work with another application is simply to start it up and work with it directly. As is usually the case with computer tasks, there is a hard way and there is an easy way to do this. The hard way in this case is to open the Start menu and then either wade through all those submenus to launch the program from its icon or select the Run command and enter the program's executable filename in the Run dialog box.

The easy way, especially if you use the other application frequently while working in Excel, is to use the Shell function to start the program from a VBA procedure:

```
Shell(pathname,windowStyle)
```

pathname is the name of the file that starts the application (or the name of a data file associated with the executable file). Unless the file is in the Windows folder, you should include the drive and folder to make sure that VBA can find the file.

> **NOTE**
>
> The parts of code that appear in a boldfaced, italicized, monospaced font (for example, *font*) are mandatory parameters.

windowStyle is a number that specifies how the application window will appear:

windowStyle	Window Appearance
1, 5, 9	Normal size with focus
2 (or omitted)	Minimized with focus
3	Maximized with focus
4, 8	Normal without focus
6, 7	Minimized without focus

If successful, Shell returns a number (called the *task ID number*). If unsuccessful, Shell generates an error.

Listing 26.1 shows an example of the Shell function.

Listing 26.1. Using the `Shell` function to start an application.

```
Sub StartControlPanelIcon(cplFile As String)

    On Error GoTo BadStart

    Shell "CONTROL.EXE " & cplFile, 1
    Exit Sub

BadStart:
    MsgBox "Could not start Control Panel!", _
        vbOKOnly + vbExclamation
End Sub

' This procedure calls StartControlPanelIcon with
' "ODBCCP32.CPL" to open the Data Sources dialog box
'
Sub ChangeDataSource()
    StartControlPanel ("ODBCCP32.CPL")
End Sub
```

The Windows Control Panel is a frequently used accessory that lets you control many aspects of the Windows environment, including printer settings, fonts, and colors. The `StartControlPanelIcon` procedure takes advantage of the fact that you can start any Control Panel icon directly by using the following command-line syntax:

`CONTROL.EXE cplFile`

Here, `cplFile` is a CPL (Control Panel Library) file that corresponds to the Control Panel icon you want to start. Table 26.1 lists some of the Control Panel icons and their corresponding CPL files.

Table 26.1. Control Panel icons and their CPL files.

Icon	CPL File
32bit ODBC	ODBCCP32.CPL
Accessibility Options	ACCESS.CPL
Add/Remove Programs	APPWIZ.CPL
Date/Time	TIMEDATE.CPL
Display	DESK.CPL
Find Fast	FINDFAST.CPL
Fonts	MAIN.CPL Fonts
Keyboard	MAIN.CPL Keyboard
Mail and Fax	MLCFG32.CPL
Microsoft Mail Post Office	WGPOCPL.CPL

continues

Table 26.1. continued

Icon	CPL File
Modems	MODEM.CPL
Mouse	MAIN.CPL Mouse
Multimedia	MMSYS.CPL
Network	NETCPL.CPL
Passwords	PASSWORD.CPL
Printers	MAIN.CPL Printers
Regional Settings	INTL.CPL
System	SYSDM.CPL

The StartControlPanelIcon procedure takes a cplFile argument that specifies the Control Panel icon with which you want to work. The procedure sets up an On Error handler just in case Control Panel doesn't start properly. Then it runs the Shell function to load Control Panel and run the module specified by cplFile.

The ChangeDataSource procedure shows an example of how you call StartControlPanelIcon. In this case, the Data Sources dialog box appears so you can set up or modify an ODBC data source.

NOTE

Use the ChDir statement if you need to change to an application's directory before starting the program:

ChDir *Path*

The *Path* argument is a string that specifies the directory to change to.

CAUTION

Don't enter statements after a Shell function if you want the statements to execute only when you've finished with the other application. The Shell statement runs an application *asynchronously,* which means that VBA starts the program and then immediately resumes executing the rest of the procedure.

Activating a Running Application

Once you have some other programs up and running, your VBA application may need to switch between them. For example, you might want the user to switch between Excel and the Control Panel to change various settings. To switch to any running application, use the `AppActivate` statement:

```
AppActivate(title,wait)
```

title is the name of the application as it appears in the title bar, or its `task ID` number (as returned by the `Shell` function).

wait is a logical value that determines when Excel switches to the application. If *wait* is `True`, `AppActivate` waits until you activate Excel before switching. If *wait* is `False` or omitted, `AppActivate` immediately switches to the application.

Note that for some applications the title bar may include both the name of the application and the name of the active document. If *title* doesn't match any application's title bar exactly, VBA tries to find a title bar that *begins with title*.

> **NOTE**
>
> If the application you want to activate is a Microsoft application, you can use the `Application` object's `ActivateMicrosoftApp(index)` method. Here, *index* is a constant that represents the Microsoft application you want to activate: `xlMicrosoftAccess`, `xlMicrosoftFoxPro`, `xlMicrosoftMail`, `xlMicrosoftPowerPoint`, `xlMicrosoftProject`, `xlMicrosoftSchedulePlus`, or `xlMicrosoftWord`.
>
> If the application isn't running, `ActivateMicrosoftApp` starts it. For example, the following statement activates Microsoft Word:
>
> ```
> Application.ActivateMicrosoftApp xlMicrosoftWord
> ```

Sending Keystrokes to an Application

As you'll see later in this chapter, you can use DDE to run a server application's macro commands. But the majority of Windows applications don't have a macro language. What's to be done with these less-sophisticated programs?

Well, one solution is to simply load the application using the `Shell` function and let the user work with the program directly. This is fine if the user is familiar with the application, but your real goal here is to control programs from within a VBA procedure. The solution is to use the `SendKeys` statement to send keystrokes to the application. You can send any key or key combination (including those that use the Alt, Ctrl, and Shift keys), and the result is exactly the same as if you typed it yourself. Here is the syntax of the `SendKeys` statement:

SendKeys *string*,*wait*

string is the key or key combination you want to send to the active application. For letters, numbers, or punctuation marks, enclose the character in quotes (for example, "a"). For other keys, use the strings outlined in Table 26.2.

wait is a logical value that determines whether VBA waits for the keys to be processed before continuing the procedure. If *wait* is True, VBA waits for the application to finish processing the keys before moving on to the next statement in the procedure. It doesn't wait if the *wait* argument is False or omitted.

Table 26.2. Strings to use for the SendKeys method's *string* argument.

For...	Use...
Backspace	"{BACKSPACE}" or "{BS}"
Break	"{BREAK}"
Caps Lock	"{CAPSLOCK}"
Delete	"{DELETE}" or "{DEL}"
Down arrow	"{DOWN}"
End	"{END}"
Enter (keypad)	"{ENTER}"
Enter	"~" (tilde)
Esc	"{ESCAPE}" or "{ESC}"
Home	"{HOME}"
Insert	"{INSERT}"
Left arrow	"{LEFT}"
Num Lock	"{NUMLOCK}"
Page Down	"{PGDN}"
Page Up	"{PGUP}"
Right arrow	"{RIGHT}"
Scroll Lock	"{SCROLLLOCK}"
Tab	"{TAB}"
Up arrow	"{UP}"
F1 through F12	"{F1}" through "{F12}"

> **NOTE**
>
> For most of the keys listed in Table 26.2, you can send the key multiple times by enclosing a number within the braces. For example, to send the up-arrow key three times, use {UP 3}.

By combining these keys with the Alt, Ctrl, and Shift keys, you can create any key combination. Just precede a string from Table 26.2 with one or more of the codes listed in Table 26.3.

Table 26.3. Codes for the Alt, Ctrl, and Shift keys.

For...	*Use...*
Alt	% (percent)
Ctrl	^ (caret)
Shift	+ (plus)

All you have to do is start a program with Shell, and then you can send whatever keystrokes you need. (You can sometimes get away with activating a running application with AppActivate and then sending the keys, but I've found this doesn't work consistently. You'll need to experiment with the applications you want to use.) For example, you can close any active Windows application by sending the Alt+F4 key combination, as follows:

```
SendKeys "%{F4}"
```

Listing 26.2 shows a more complex example that dials a phone number using the Phone Dialer accessory.

Listing 26.2. Controlling an application using the SendKeys statement.

```
Sub LoadAndDialPhoneDialer()

    Dim msg As String, buttons As Integer, response As Integer
    On Error GoTo BadStart

    msg = "About to dial the following number:" & _
        Chr(13) & Chr(13) & _
        "    " & ActiveCell & _
        Chr(13) & Chr(13) & _
        "Please make sure your modem is turned on."
    buttons = vbOKCancel + vbExclamation
    response = MsgBox(msg, buttons)

    If response = vbCancel Then Exit Sub
```

continues

Listing 26.2. continued

```
    ' Copy the contents (a phone number?) of the current cell
    ActiveCell.Copy

    ' Start Phone Dialer without the focus
    Shell "DIALER.EXE", 1

    ' Paste the copied phone number with Ctrl+V and
    ' then press Enter to select the Dial button
    SendKeys "^v~", True

    ' Wait five seconds to give the modem time to dial
    Application.Wait Now + TimeValue("00:00:05")

    ' Close the dialog boxes and exit Phone Dialer
    SendKeys "~{ESC}%{F4}"

    Application.CutCopyMode = False

    Exit Sub

BadStart:
    MsgBox "Could not start Phone Dialer!", _
        vbOKOnly + vbExclamation
End Sub
```

This procedure uses a modem and the Phone Dialer accessory to dial the phone number contained in the active cell. After displaying a message box that tells the user the number that will be dialed and to make sure his or her modem is on, the procedure copies the active cell and starts Phone Dialer.

A SendKeys statement sends Ctrl+V and then Enter to paste the phone number and select the Dial button. After a few seconds, Phone Dialer displays the Call Status dialog box. Go ahead and pick up the receiver, but don't press Enter to clear the dialog box. The procedure waits 5 seconds to give your phone time to dial, and then another SendKeys statement sends the following keys: Enter (to remove the dialog box), Esc (to cancel the Dialing dialog box), and Alt+F4 (to exit Phone Dialer). Finally, the CutCopyMode property is set to False to take Excel out of copy mode.

NOTE

Keep in mind that the SendKeys statement is case sensitive. For example, the strings "^P" and "^+p" both send the key combination Ctrl+Shift+P. If you just want to send Ctrl+P, "^p" is the string to use.

TIP

Include the following characters in braces ({}) to send them in a `SendKeys` string: `~ % ^ ( ) + { } [ ]`. For example, you send a percent sign as follows:

```
SendKeys "{%}"
```

Using Dynamic Data Exchange

DDE is an internal communications protocol that enables some Windows applications to exchange data and even execute each other's commands. Because it's implemented unevenly in different applications, DDE is nowhere near as clean (or as straightforward) as OLE, but it's often the only choice we have. The good news is that VBA provides plenty of tools to control the DDE protocol at the procedure level. The next few sections examine each of those tools.

DDE: The Basics

Human conversations can take two forms: static and dynamic. A static conversation—such as the exchange of letters or e-mail—is one where information is passed back and forth intermittently. A dynamic conversation, on the other hand, is one where information is exchanged continuously. Face-to-face meetings and telephone calls are examples of dynamic conversations.

So a *dynamic* data exchange, then, is one in which two applications continuously send data and commands to each other. As in OLE, the two applications involved in this process are called client and server. The *client* is the application that initializes the conversation and sends requests for data (the client is also sometimes called the *destination*). The *server* is the application that responds to the client's requests by executing its own commands and sending its data (the server is also called the *source*).

DDE conversations unfold in three stages:

1. Initiate a link between the client and the server. This link—it's called a *channel*—is the path along which the two applications will communicate. In our case, VBA will be initiating the conversation, so it will be the client.

2. Work with the server. Once the link is established, the client can exchange data with the server and can control the server by invoking its internal macro commands or by sending keystrokes.

3. Terminate the link. When the client is finished working with the server, your procedure needs to close the channel.

Initiating a Link Between VBA and a Server Application

Just as you need to call someone before you can have a phone conversation with them, so too must your procedure "call" a server application to initiate a DDE conversation. To establish a channel between VBA and another DDE application, use the DDEInitiate method:

```
object.DDEInitiate(app,topic)
```

object is the application object.

app is the DDE name of the server application with which you want to open a link.

topic is the "topic of conversation" that the two applications will be using. For most applications, you use either System (the application as a whole) or the name of a document in the application (that is, the name as it appears in the title bar).

The DDE name used in the *app* argument depends on the application—it's almost always the name of the executable file that starts the application (without the extension). For example, the DDE name for Excel is Excel, for Word for Windows it's Winword, and for Access it's MSAccess. For other applications, check your documentation or contact the application's technical support department.

Make sure you include the full pathname of a document in the DDEInitiate method's *topic* argument if you're trying to access a document that isn't already open. Here's an example:

```
DDEInitiate("Winword", "C:\WINWORD\MEMO.DOC")
```

If DDEInitiate is successful, it returns an integer identifying the channel. You'll need to refer to this number in all subsequent DDE exchanges between the client and server.

The server application needs to be open before you can initiate a DDE session. So one decision you need to make before running the DDEInitiate method is whether you want to open the server beforehand with the Shell function or whether you want DDEInitiate to handle it for you. In most cases, a Shell function is the way to go because the DDEInitiate startup method has two annoying quirks:

▪ Excel displays a dialog box similar to the one shown in Figure 26.1. You need to select Yes to start the application. If you like, you can prevent this message from appearing by setting the Application.DisplayAlerts property to False.

FIGURE 26.1.

The dialog box Excel displays if you let DDEInitiate start a server application that isn't already running.

- If the application isn't in the current directory or the DOS search path, DDEInitiate won't be able to find it. You can solve this problem by first using the ChDir statement to change to the application's directory:

```
ChDir "C:\WINWORD"
```

Listing 26.3 shows a sample Function procedure that uses the DDEInitiate method.

Listing 26.3. Using the DDEInitiate method to open a DDE channel.

```
Function OpenHailingFrequencies() As Integer
    Dim channel As Integer

    On Error GoTo BadConnection

    ' Start WinWord and establish the DDE connection
    Shell "C:\MSOffice\Winword\Winword.exe", 6
    channel = DDEInitiate("Winword", "System")

    MsgBox "A channel to Word is now open.", vbInformation
    ' Return the channel number
    OpenHailingFrequencies = channel
    Exit Function

BadConnection: _
    MsgBox "Could not open a channel to Word!", vbExclamation
    ' Return 0
    OpenHailingFrequencies = 0

End Function
```

The OpenHailingFrequencies procedure is designed to open a DDE channel between Excel and Word for Windows. A variable named channel is declared to store the channel number returned by the DDEInitiate method. An On Error GoTo handler is established just in case something goes wrong. (This is always a good idea, because DDE connections are notoriously flaky.)

Next, a Shell function starts Word for Windows without focus and then the DDEInitiate method is run. If all goes well, the channel number is stored in the channel variable, a MsgBox function tells the user the connection has been established, and then the channel number is returned. If an error occurs, the code jumps to the BadConnection label, displays an error message, and returns 0.

When your procedure is finished with its DDE conversation, you need to terminate the link between the client and server. You do this by running the DDETerminate method:

```
DDETerminate channel
```

Here, *channel* is the channel number returned by the DDEInitiate method.

Controlling the Server Application

Once you have an open channel, you can use the DDEExecute method to control the other application. You can either send commands the server application understands (such as commands from its macro language, if it has one) or you can send keystrokes. DDEExecute has the following syntax:

DDEExecute(***channel, string***)

channel is the channel returned by the DDEInitiate method.

string is a text string representing the commands to run in the application.

The tricky part of the DDEExecute method is the ***string*** argument; its form depends entirely on the application. Excel and Word for Windows enable you to use their macro commands, provided that you enclose the commands in square brackets ([ ]). Other applications also enable you to use their macro commands, but they don't support the square-brackets standard. Other programs have no macro language, but they do have special DDE commands. Finally, there are applications without special commands to use, but they enable you to control the application by sending keystroke sequences with the DDEExecute method.

> **NOTE**
>
> To send keystrokes with DDEExecute, use the same key formats I showed you earlier for the SendKeys statement. For example, the DDEExecute(Channel,"^v") statement sends the key combination Ctrl+V to the application linked to VBA by Channel. Note, however, that you can't use DDEExecute to send keys to a dialog box. For that you need to use the SendKeys method.

Listing 26.4 uses several examples of the DDEExecute method.

Listing 26.4. Using DDEExecute to control a server application.

```
Sub CreateWordLink()

    Dim channel As Integer
    On Error GoTo BailOut

    ' Start Word
    Application.StatusBar = "Starting Word..."
    Shell "C:\MSoffice\Winword\Winword.exe", 6

    ' Initiate channel with System topic
    Application.StatusBar = "Initiating DDE conversation..."
    channel = DDEInitiate("Winword", "System")

    ' Open the document we want to work with
    Application.StatusBar = "Opening Word document..."
```

```
    DDEExecute channel, "[FileOpen ""C:\My Documents\DDE_Test.doc""]"
    DDETerminate channel

    ' Initiate new channel with document
    Application.StatusBar = "Initiating DDE conversation with document..."
    channel = DDEInitiate("Winword", "C:\My Documents\DDE_Test.doc")

    ' Get the text from the first line of the document
    Application.StatusBar = "Getting text..."
    DDEExecute channel, "[StartOfDocument]"
    DDEExecute channel, "[EndOfLine 1]"
    DDEExecute channel, "[EditCopy]"

    ' Paste and link the copied text
    Application.StatusBar = "Pasting and linking text..."
    Worksheets("Sheet1").Activate
    Range("A1").Select
    ActiveSheet.Paste link:=True

    ' Quit Word and terminate channel
    Application.StatusBar = "Quitting Word..."
    DDEExecute channel, "[FileExit 2]"
    DDETerminate channel

    Application.StatusBar = False
    Exit Sub

BailOut:
    DDETerminate channel
    MsgBox "DDE operation failed!", vbExclamation
    Application.StatusBar = False

End Sub
```

The CreateWordLink procedure loads Word for Windows, executes several Word commands—including copying some text—and then pastes the copied text into Excel with a DDE link.

The procedure begins by setting up an error handler and starting Word. (The Application object's StatusBar property is used throughout the procedure to keep the user abreast of what's happening.) A channel is opened to Word's System topic and the return value is stored in the channel variable. The first DDEExecute method runs WordBasic's FileOpen command to open a file named DDE_Test.doc. You've now finished your conversation with the System topic, so DDETerminate closes the channel.

You can now start up a new conversation, but this time with the DDE_Test.doc file as the topic. The procedure executes three WordBasic commands; these commands move to the start of the document (StartOfDocument), select the entire first line (EndOfLine 1), and copy the selection to the Clipboard (EditCopy).

The next few lines paste and link the copied data. First, the cell where the data will be pasted is selected (this is mandatory when pasting linked data) and then the Paste method uses its link argument to paste the text with a DDE link to Word.

Finally, one last DDEExecute method sends the WordBasic command for quitting Word: FileExit 2. (Note that the 2 means that Word doesn't save any documents.) Then, another DDETerminate closes the second channel.

Exchanging Data with the Server Application

As you've seen, each DDE conversation between the client and server is established on a specified topic. Everything else the two applications "discuss" in the current DDE session is limited to subjects related to the topic. For example, in the preceding section you saw how the server's commands are a fit subject to include in the conversation.

We'll now turn to another subject you can use in your DDE dialogs: data items. Each server application that supports DDE defines one or more items that can be shared with the client. For example, a typical spreadsheet item is a cell, and a typical word processor item is a bookmark (that is, a named chunk of text). These items are always composed of simple text and numbers; graphics and other high-level objects can't be transferred in a DDE conversation.

The next two sections show you how to use the DDERequest and DDEPoke methods to exchange data items between the client and server.

Receiving Data from the Server

If the server has data you would like to transfer to a worksheet cell, you can establish a DDE link between the two applications and then use the DDERequest method to retrieve the data:

DDERequest(*channel, item*)

channel is the channel returned by the DDEInitiate method.

item is a string that specifies the data item you want to retrieve from the server.

Listing 26.5 runs through an example.

Listing 26.5. Using DDERequest to retrieve data from an application.

```
Sub RequestWordData()

    Dim channel As Integer, wordData As Variant
    On Error GoTo BailOut

    ' Start Word
    Application.StatusBar = "Starting Word..."
    Shell "C:\MSOffice\Winword\Winword.exe", 6

    ' Initiate channel with System topic
    channel = DDEInitiate("Winword", "System")

    ' Open the document we want to work with
    Application.StatusBar = "Opening Word document..."
```

```
    DDEExecute channel, "[FileOpen ""C:\My Documents\Memo.doc""]"
    DDETerminate channel

    ' Initiate new channel with document
    channel = DDEInitiate("Winword", "C:\My Documents\Memo.doc")

    ' Find keyword and add a bookmark
    DDEExecute channel, "[StartOfDocument]"
    DDEExecute channel, "[EditFind .Find = ""ACME""]"
    DDEExecute channel, "[SelectCurSentence]"
    DDEExecute channel, "[EditBookmark .Name = ""Gotcha""]"

    ' Retrieve the bookmark
    wordData = DDERequest(channel, "Gotcha")
    Worksheets("Sheet1").[A1].Value = wordData

    ' Quit Word and terminate channel
    DDEExecute channel, "[FileExit 1]"
    DDETerminate channel

    Exit Sub

BailOut:
    DDETerminate channel
    MsgBox "DDE operation failed!", vbExclamation

End Sub
```

The idea behind the RequestWordData procedure is to find a particular section of text in a word document and then read it into Excel. The procedure begins, as before, by setting up an error handler, starting Word, establishing the channel, and then opening the document.

The first DDEExecute method moves to the start of the document; the second DDEExecute looks for the text string "ACME" in the document; then the entire sentence containing "ACME" is selected, and a final DDEExecute creates a bookmark named "Gotcha" for the selected sentence.

To retrieve the text, the DDERequest method asks Word for the "Gotcha" item and stores it in the wordData variable. (Note that the wordData variable is declared as a variant. This is required because the DDERequest method always returns an array.) The retrieved data is stored in cell A1 of Sheet1, and then Word is closed (note that FileExit 1 saves changes) and the channel is terminated.

> **NOTE**
>
> You can use DDERequest to get a list of all the server's open documents. Just initiate a DDE channel on the System topic and then use DDERequest to return the Topics item. Here is an example:
>
> ```
> openFiles = DDERequest(channel, "Topics")
> ```
>
> Here, openFiles is a variant variable. The server will return the list of open files as an array.

Sending Data to the Server

Like all good conversations, the exchange between the client and server is a two-way street. Therefore, just as your procedures can request data from the server, so too can the client send data to the server. This is handled by the DDEPoke method:

DDEPoke(*channel*,*item*,*data*)

channel is the channel returned by the DDEInitiate method.

item is a string that specifies the data item to which the data will be sent.

data is the data you want to send to the server application (it must be plain text or numbers).

Listing 26.6 shows you an example.

Listing 26.6. Using DDEPoke to send data to an application.

```
Sub SendDataToWord()

    Dim channel As Integer, pokeData As Variant
    On Error GoTo BailOut

    ' Start Word
    Application.StatusBar = "Starting Word..."
    Shell "C:\MSOffice\Winword\Winword.exe", 6

    ' Initiate channel with System topic
    channel = DDEInitiate("Winword", "System")

    ' Open the document we want to work with
    Application.StatusBar = "Opening Word document..."
    DDEExecute channel, "[FileOpen ""C:\My Documents\Memo.doc""]"
    DDETerminate channel

    ' Initiate new channel with document
    channel = DDEInitiate("Winword", "C:\My Documents\Memo.doc")

    'Get the data to be sent
    PokeData = Worksheets("Sheet1").[A1].Value

    'Send it to the "Gotcha" bookmark
    DDEPoke Channel, "Gotcha", PokeData

    ' Quit Word and terminate channel
    DDEExecute channel, "[FileExit 1]"
    DDETerminate channel

    Exit Sub

BailOut:
    DDETerminate channel
    MsgBox "DDE operation failed!", vbExclamation

End Sub
```

This procedure performs the opposite function of the procedure in Listing 26.5. Here, VBA takes text from a cell and sends it to a bookmark in Word. The procedure begins by setting up the error handler, starting Word, and then establishing the link. The cell data to send is stored in the pokeData variable, and then the DDEPoke method sends it to the "Gotcha" bookmark in the Word document. The link is then terminated and the procedure exits.

Summary

This chapter walks you through a number of techniques for working with other applications. The most straightforward of these techniques is the simple Shell function, which starts another application. You can activate any running application by using the AppActivate statement, and you can send keystrokes to a running application by using the SendKeys method.

You have also learned about dynamic data exchange. This protocol lets DDE-enabled applications "talk" to each other and exchange data items. VBA has several DDE functions that let you initialize a DDE channel, execute the server application's commands, send data back and forth, and terminate the link.

Here's a list of related chapters:

- Chapter 20, "Exchanging Data with Other Applications," shows you how to use DDE and OLE to work with other applications directly.
- To access external databases, you can use Microsoft Query. See Chapter 24, "Using Microsoft Query," for details.

IN THIS PART

The Organizaton of Access

Access Concepts

27

*by Matt Kinney,
Craig Eddy, and
Dwayne Gifford*

This chapter introduces you to Microsoft Access for Windows 95, the data-organizing component of the Microsoft Office 95 suite. Designed to help you create personal and departmental databases, this version of Access builds on the previous releases of Access to provide an easier system to program and use.

Getting Started

A *database* is an integrated repository of data that is usually shared among users. Databases serve two primary purposes: They provide information to users and they capture data about entities and relationships. Every database has software called the *database management system* (DBMS) that controls the storage and retrieval of the data contained in the database. Microsoft Access uses the relational model for its database management system. The relational model views all data as groups of tables or relations that consist of a fixed number of columns and rows. Relational database management systems (RDBMSs) are one of the largest segments of the database market—they comprise everything from client/server systems to desktop RDBMS databases.

Access for Windows 95 adds several major enhancements and features that are directed at end users and developers alike. The first noticeable new feature is the new Windows 95–compliant interface. The features of the interface that encompass the Windows 95 look and feel are not covered here, except where they introduce a new feature due to the Windows 95 functionality.

32-Bit Implementation

One of the features that may not be immediately apparent to users is the fact that Access for Windows 95 is 32 bit (at least it might not be apparent to users until they experience the speed that 32-bit Access provides). Also included is a 32-bit open database connectivity (ODBC) driver that allows developers to use the Access engine via ODBC. An especially useful aspect of this implementation is that future versions of Visual Basic will be able to use the 32-bit Access engine, thus giving developers a noticeable speed improvement over the 16-bit version of the application.

Database Window

The familiar database window, which is what many users first work with in Access, has been greatly enhanced to provide more flexibility and functionality. You can now hide objects you don't want others to see, automatically create a shortcut to a database object, and drag and drop data to Microsoft Excel or Microsoft Word. You can also display icons for the database objects in four different views—list, details, and large or small icons—to see more information about an object, such as its creation date or a description. Figure 27.1 shows the database window in details view.

FIGURE 27.1.

The maximized database window in details view.

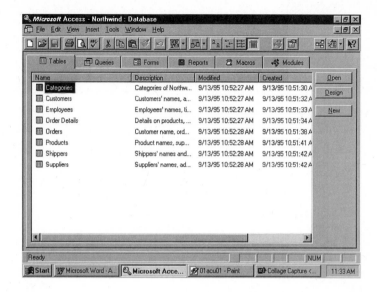

Briefcase Replication

One of the most significant new features in Access is the briefcase replication functionality. *Briefcase replication* allows you to create replicas, or "special copies" of a database, to distribute to users in different locations so that each can work on his or her copy of the database independently of other users. Replicas allow for data synchronization so that all the replicas can be put together into a single entity, incorporating all the changes that have been introduced in the individual users' copies.

Briefcase replication requires that Briefcase be installed on your computer. Briefcase is installed as part of the Typical setup option in Windows. Synchronization with another replica is as simple as selecting the database file in Briefcase and selecting Update Selection in the Briefcase menu. Note, however, that once you convert a nonreplicable database (a database for which a replica has not been created) into a replicable database (a database for which a replica has been created), there is no going back—you cannot convert it back to a nonreplicable database.

Performance Analyzer

The Performance Analyzer is a feature that assists not only the developer, but the end user as well. Performance Analyzer optimizes any or all of the objects in a database. When the analyzer is complete, three kinds of performance suggestions are displayed: Recommendation, Suggestion, and Idea. When you click an item in the list, information about the optimization is presented below the list. Access can perform Recommendation and Suggestion optimizations for you; however, Idea optimizations must be performed manually. Idea optimizations present a list of instructions to follow in the Suggestion Notes section (kind of like a cue card). (See Figure 27.2.) Performance Analyzer does not provide suggestions for how to improve the system you are running Access on or how to improve Access performance itself.

FIGURE 27.2.

*The Performance Analyzer
results window.*

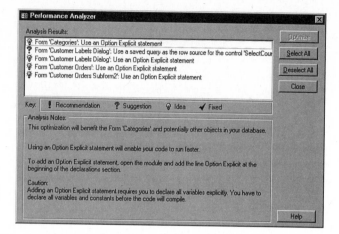

Database Splitter

The Database Splitter wizard splits a database into two files: one that contains the tables (or the back-end components) and one that contains the queries, reports, forms, and other Access objects (or the front-end components). This allows an administrator to distribute the front-end files to users while keeping a single source of data on the network. This results in less overhead and traffic on the network, because the only time the network is used is to retrieve or modify data, not every time a user wants to go to another form or report. This results in a significant performance improvement in a multiuser environment.

Table Analyzer

The Table Analyzer, shown in Figure 27.3, is used to analyze the table objects in the database and to normalize the data. *Normalization* is the process of taking duplicate information in one or more fields and splitting the information into related tables to store the data more efficiently. Normalization is defined by a set of five rules, the first three of which were defined by Dr. E.F. Codd and are used to design relational databases. Access can either normalize the tables you specify or normalize all tables automatically. The Table Analyzer is especially useful if you are importing a large flat-file database into Access, because normalizing the database enables you to take advantage of relational database features. Also included in the Table Analyzer is the ability to create a query in order to view information from the split tables in a single datasheet. This saves the user or developer from having to create this query after normalization; this should make it easier to convert any reports or forms to use the new normalized table(s).

Chapter 27

FIGURE 27.3.

The Table Analyzer Wizard.

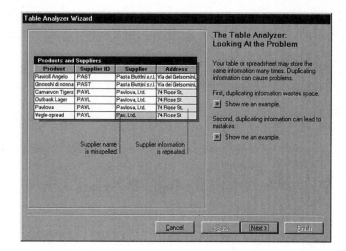

Table Design

Table design is greatly enhanced in Access for Windows 95, with new features that make designing tables easier and make the tables much more powerful. A table can now be created by entering data in a blank datasheet. When the datasheet is saved, Access evaluates the data entered and creates the field types and formats as well as deletes any unused columns. You can also rename the fields (columns) you'll be using by double-clicking the column and then typing in a name for it. Note that all column names must follow Access object-naming rules. The data entered should be of a consistent format to enable Access to create an appropriate data type and display format. You can then go to the design view to customize the table definition further as well as define validation rules.

Another significant enhancement to table design is the Lookup Wizard, shown in Figure 27.4. The Lookup Wizard creates a field that displays a list of values that are retrieved or "looked up" from another table. The Lookup Wizard can also be used to create a list of user-defined values. A major benefit of this approach is that the field created by the Lookup Wizard is automatically added to any query that includes the field. In other words, a field created with the Lookup Wizard needs to be created only once, whereas other combo box or list box fields must be created every time.

FIGURE 27.4.

The Lookup Wizard.

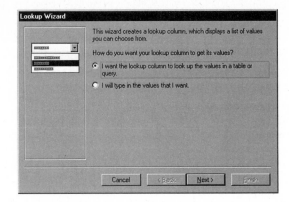

Data Manipulation

Access for Windows 95 includes new features that allow the user to get data easily from the database into other documents, to spell check and error correct, and to filter records in a new way. Because of Windows 95's drag-and-drop functionality, you can now select data from a datasheet and drag it into an Excel or a Word document, or you can save it as a rich text format document, which can be opened by most word processors and used to create a Windows help file. This allows for easier presentation and analysis of data by the end user. Access now has the functionality to automatically spell check text and memo fields, similar to the AutoCorrect function, as it now shares the spell checking engine in Office 95. Therefore, any changes or words added to the spell check dictionary in Access 95 will also show up in all Microsoft Office 95 applications. It also capitalizes different words, such as the days of the week, automatically. Although this feature results in extra overhead, it's well worth it to have your data be free of typographic errors.

Two new record-filtering techniques have also been introduced in Access. *Filtering* is the process of specifying parameters so that only a subset of the entire recordset is displayed. You can now choose from the Filter By Selection and Filter By Form options. Once a filter is created using these methods, you can elect to save the filter as a query, thus bypassing the query design grid altogether. Access also allows you to do new things with filters such as base a new form or report on filtered data, save a filter with a report, form, or table, save a filter sort order, apply filters automatically, and apply a filter to a subform.

> **NOTE**
>
> A saved filter does not appear as a separate object in the database window unless it is saved as a query.

In Filter By Selection, you specify which records you want to work with by highlighting or selecting them directly on the form or datasheet. Once a subset is selected, you can then create another subset of the subset in order to narrow even further the scope of the records. This is by far the easiest way for an end user to create a filter with the least amount of effort and hassle.

Filter By Form allows you to enter the values for the records for which you are searching. A value can either be typed in or picked from a list in the fields. This method is similar to the one used in the query design grid and is probably more familiar to experienced Access users.

Query Features

Access includes several new features that make querying easier and more efficient. The new Simple Query Wizard allows you to create a select query, a query that returns data based on specified parameters for one or more tables. It also allows for the creation of calculations such as sums, counts, totals, and averages on a table or tables. The filter characteristics discussed previously can now equally apply to a query's datasheet view to narrow the scope of focus even further in the query's results. Also, you can now sort a query's records on demand from the datasheet in ascending or descending order. In previous versions of Access you could only specify a sort order in the query design window.

In Access 2, Microsoft introduced the feature of enforcing referential and domain integrity at the table level. This meant that the developer no longer had to write code to enforce these rules for every update done to the data. Access automatically created joins or relationships between fields in different tables or queries in query design view if the fields had the same name and data type and no relationship was already defined between the fields. (A join tells Access how the data is related.) In Access for Windows 95 this feature can be turned off so that automatic joining does not occur. However, you can still create joins yourself. Figure 27.5 shows the Table/Queries Options screen with Enable AutoJoin turned on.

FIGURE 27.5.

The Tables/Queries tab of the Options dialog box with the Enable AutoJoin option turned on.

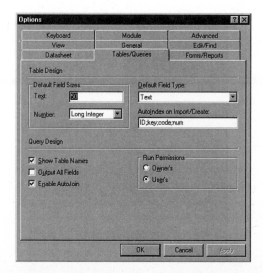

Form and Report Design

It is now easier than ever to create great-looking forms and reports in Access. The new Form and Report Wizards are greatly enhanced, and there is a new wizard called the Subform/Subreport Wizard. You can also create a report or form based on a query you have already filtered, and the new form or report inherits the filter from the query. The appearance of a form or report can be greatly enhanced with the new autoformatting capability, the addition of background pictures, as well as the new formatting toolbar. The creation and formatting of controls, special effects, and screen tips make designing top-quality forms a breeze. New drag-and-drop object support as well as support for the new OCX custom controls are also added.

The new Form and Report Wizards allow you to create a multiple table form or report without first having to create a query. The Form Wizard, shown in Figure 27.6, allows you to effortlessly create a form linked to another form, a form with a subform, or a form with two subforms. Access presents a list of options based on the data you specify for the form. The Report Wizard, shown in Figure 27.7, can just as easily create reports that summarize, group, or total data. If you have difficulty linking a subform to its main form or a subreport to its main report, simply use the Subform/Subreport Field Linker function in the new Subform/Subreport Wizard. As with all Access wizards, tell it what you want to do, and the wizard will "magically" do your bidding.

FIGURE 27.6.

Field selection using the Form Wizard.

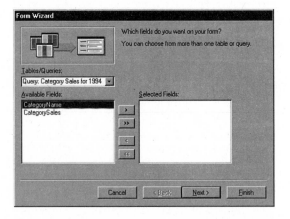

Form and report appearance has been enhanced as well. If you don't like the way your report or form looks, simply use the AutoFormat function to change the look of your entire report or only selected aspects of it. Access also provides a selection of predefined form and report formats and templates that you can use and customize. You can also create your own predefined formats for future use or distribution. You can now have a background picture or logo on your form or report by simply entering the picture's filename as the Picture property of the form or report. To add special effects or color, you can use the new formatting toolbar, which makes many formatting tasks available at your fingertips.

FIGURE 27.7.

Making grouping selections using the Report Wizard.

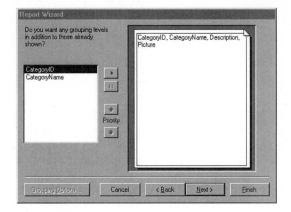

Control creation and appearance can also enhance the look and feel of your forms and reports. Access can now create a default control for the field you drag from the field list. If you use a wizard, Access automatically creates the correct control for you on the form or report. You can now copy a format from one control to another using the Format Painter. Many new special effects have been added. They include etched, shadowed, and chiseled as well as flat, raised, and sunken. Your Access forms and reports can now have the screen tips functionality, as well. Simply enter the message you want to display in the ControlTip property, and when the user moves the mouse over the control and is there for a moment, your tip will appear!

The Access Interface

The Microsoft Access for Windows 95 interface includes several features that make it easy to accomplish tasks in Access quickly. Because Access is Windows 95 compliant, it offers all the benefits and advances provided by the Windows 95 operating system. You are now able to customize just about any feature you can think of to make your Access life easier. This includes the interface, the Access Start Up window, always keeping objects hidden that you specify to be hidden, colors, and other effects you use routinely.

The Windows 95–compliant interface of Microsoft Access offers many advantages and has a new visual appeal. Also, the integrated help system and the right-click floating menus are very valuable. You can automatically have your forms and reports designed with the 3-D effects that are standard in Windows 95 as well as use the large and small icon views in the database window. (See Figure 27.8.) The ability to define custom characteristics for your databases and search on those characteristics is a distinct advantage if you work on many different databases at one time.

FIGURE 27.8.

Access in large icon view.

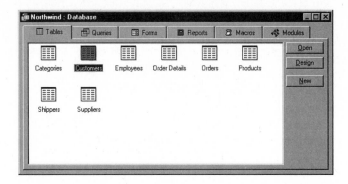

One of the most handy features in Access is the customizable toolbars and custom menus, which allow you to build your own menus to replace Access 95's default menus. You can now customize the Access environment to your liking or to the type of development you are currently doing. The new Button Editor, shown in Figure 27.9, allows you to edit an existing button image or design a new one from scratch. The new formatting toolbar in the form and report design view allows you to customize the appearance of your forms and reports. The formatting choices previously available through the palette are available on this toolbar. You can also have buttons that include drop-down lists and portable palettes. Your custom toolbars can either be for the entire Access application or just for individual databases.

FIGURE 27.9.

The Button Editor.

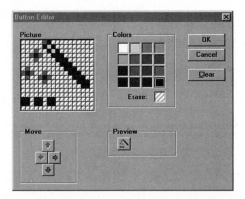

NOTE

To prevent others from customizing your toolbars, you can disable the shortcut menu on the toolbar.

The ability to add a custom menu bar complete with your custom commands is a very helpful feature of Access. Custom menu bars are created using the Menu Builder, or you can create one by using macros. However, the Menu Builder is by far the easiest way to create custom menus. The creation of custom commands is somewhat more involved—you must edit the macros that the Menu Builder creates or else create your own macros from scratch. Your menu bars can either be specific to a particular view (that is, design view) or be global, which allows you to control the tasks that others perform in your database or application.

If you often choose the same set of tasks repeatedly, you can customize the Access environment to those settings so that they are used by default. From the Tools menu, select Options. You'll see the Options dialog box, shown in Figure 27.10, which has several tabs in it. Select the tab for the options you want to set; then select the options you want to use. You can click Apply if you want to see the settings immediately without closing the window; otherwise, click OK to apply the settings and close the window.

FIGURE 27.10.

The Options dialog box.

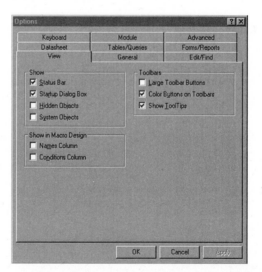

If you change the environment settings in Access, Access will save the option settings in your workgroup information file, not in your user database. Because these changes are global, they apply to any database and anyone in your group who uses the same workgroup information file.

The Database Container

The database container is just what it sounds like, a container for database objects. A *database* is simply a collection of the objects defined in the following list:

- Table—Tables are the fundamental structure of the database. Tables store data as records (rows) and fields (columns).

- Query—Queries are used to change, view, and analyze data. The form and report objects often use a query object as their record source.

- Report—Reports are a way to present your data in printed form in the manner you specify. Reports are fully customizable. However, you can use the predefined report objects that come with Access.

- Form—Forms are used for several purposes and do not necessarily have to present data from a table or query object. You can use a form to present data, as a data entry vehicle, or as a dialog box to get user input.

- Macro—Macros are used to automate common tasks. They often contain a series of statements to accomplish a task, such as showing a form or report.

- Module—A module is a collection of Visual Basic for Applications procedures, functions, declarations, and constants that are used to control an Access database. They can often be used to provide greater control and functionality over a macro object.

Within each of these objects there may be collections of other objects (for example, in the table object there is a Fields collection). A full discussion of the database container and the data access object is covered later in this book. However, the basics outlined in this list should provide you with a good "jumping off" point. The data access object (DAO), which includes the database container, is a fundamental component of Access and should be fully understood before moving further into Access and Visual Basic development.

Creating a Database

Access has two convenient methods for creating databases. The more user-friendly approach is to use the Database Wizard, which creates all the tables, forms, and reports for the database type you choose. The other, more work-intensive method, is to create a blank database and add the tables, forms, and reports separately. This method leads to more flexibility for the developer; however, it means that each element must be defined separately. At any rate, you can extend and modify your database definition any time after it has been created.

Creating a Database Using the Database Wizard

The simplest method of creating a database is by using the Database Wizard. When Access first starts, a window is displayed that allows you to open an existing database or create a new one. (See Figure 27.11.) From this window, select Database Wizard and then click OK. If you have already been working in Access, you can click the New Database icon in the main toolbar (that is, if you haven't customized it).

FIGURE 27.11.

The opening selection screen.

In the list, double-click the type of database you want to create. If the exact type you want is not in the list, either create a blank database or select the type that is the closest match to the type you want (you can modify it later).

At this point you'll be led through several screens that allow you to further define your database, finishing up with an application that includes forms, reports, and a database waiting for your data.

Creating a Database Without Using the Database Wizard

If you are just starting Access, you'll be presented with options to create a new database or open an existing one. If this box is displayed, click Blank Database and select OK. (Refer to Figure 27.11 for an example of this screen.)

If you have been working in Access and want to create a new database, select the New Database icon from the main toolbar and then select the Blank Database icon in the Database Wizard. (See Figure 27.12.)

FIGURE 27.12.

The Database Wizard with Blank Database selected.

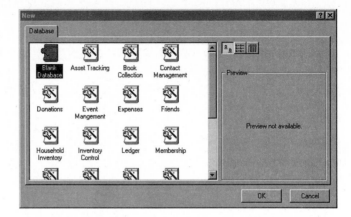

You'll then see then database window with your blank database in it. A blank database is like an empty container waiting for you to put something in it. Next you'll need to add objects, such as tables, forms, and reports, to the database.

Summary

In this chapter you've learned about the new features of Access for Windows 95 as well as some of the basic concepts behind Access databases. With this overview, you can begin to consider your options for designing and creating your own Access databases.

In Chapter 28, "Effective Database Design," you'll see some examples of database designs, and we'll discuss their effect on creating your own databases.

Effective Database Design

28

by Craig Eddy

Millions of databases have been designed and published, especially in the decade and a half since the introduction of the personal computer. Thanks to all this experience, database models have evolved from stacks of punched cards all the way to object-oriented relational databases. This chapter discusses the design of an effective relational database. Here are some key points that define an effective relational database:

- It is easily adapted to meet future changes in application needs.
- Its table layout and relationships are easily understood.
- It provides acceptable performance and disk space utilization.
- Additional data tables can be integrated into the database with ease.

The importance of database design cannot be overlooked without serious consequences to both performance and maintainability. In fact, good database design is the single most important factor in creating an effective database. The design must be flexible, logical, and methodical. By the time you finish this chapter, you'll have learned how to design such a database.

Relational Databases

There is no single strict definition of a relational database. It can best be described as a set of data tables, each modeling a single entity and having certain "key" fields in common with other tables. These key fields establish the relational links between the data tables. The relational database model excels in providing the ability to collect, organize, and report on data that may be of a different nature but is in some way related. This section discusses relational databases in-depth and provides definitions for a few database terms used in this chapter.

The Microsoft Access database used as the chapter's example is a personal information manager (PIM). It's shown in Figure 28.1.

Definitions of Relational Database Terms

Most objects used in a relational database closely parallel objects used in spreadsheet applications and flat-file databases; therefore, the terms are not difficult to visualize or understand. While this section will not serve as a complete dictionary of relational database terms, it will go a long way toward helping you create effective relational databases.

Field

The term *field* refers to the basic building block of any database, relational or not. A field is the database's way of representing a single piece of information or an attribute of an object. Fields should always be atomic, meaning that they cannot be broken into multiple pieces of information. Fields are given a data type that defines the kind of data stored in the field.

FIGURE 28.1.

The relationship diagram for a Microsoft Access personal information manager.

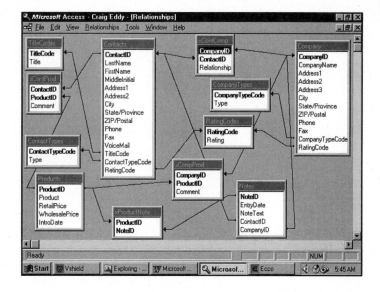

Record

A *record* is a collection of data for a specific object or table. In the sample PIM database, a contact record is the row of data stored for each contact. Each record in the database should contain a unique piece of information—in the PIM database, each record should represent a different person.

Because a relational database does not store or retrieve records in any set way, there is no physical order to the records. In other words, there is no concept of a record number as there is in many other database systems.

Table

A *table* is a collection of fields. The data contained in a table is stored as a record. Each table in a database should represent a different entity. For example, the PIM database contains separate tables for contacts, companies, notes, and products. Although these are all related in some way, they are completely different objects. The fact that a table can only represent a single entity should not be overlooked—it is one of the keys to creating an effective relational database. Figure 28.2 shows the contact and company tables in datasheet view.

Key Field

A field is said to be a "key" when it is used to relate two or more tables to each other. Keys are fields that these related tables have in common. The values stored in key fields are duplicated among the related tables. For example, in the Notes table of the sample PIM, CompanyID and ContactID are key fields that relate a note to either a contact, a company, or both. Therefore, if a note is created that relates to Federated Oil, the note's CompanyID field will contain the value 2—Federated Oil's company ID. (See Figure 28.2.) Keys are classified as either primary, foreign, or composite, depending on their use and the fields that comprise them. These keys are discussed in the section "The Three Types of Keys."

FIGURE 28.2.

The Contacts and Company tables shown in datasheet view.

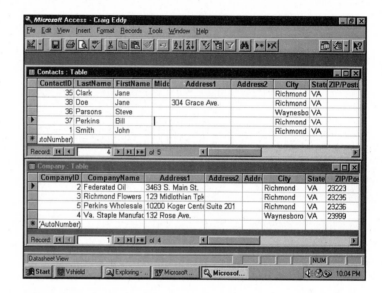

Relationships and Joins

A *relationship* is what a key establishes between two or more tables. The note used in the previous example is related to a company. The fact that the note has a value in its CompanyID field establishes a relationship between this particular note and Federated Oil. A *join* is a sort of virtual table created when the user requests information from different tables that participate in a relationship. The key fields are used to find matching records in the different tables participating in the join. Figure 28.3 illustrates a join created to return the company name and phone number along with the details of the note used in the previous example.

A little explanation might be helpful here. The top datasheet window shows the Company table. Federated Oil's CompanyID is 2. There is only one note in the database. It is shown in the middle datasheet window. The CompanyID for the note record is 2. The join query whose results are displayed in the bottom datasheet window takes all the records in the Notes table, matches their CompanyID values with the Company table, and combines fields from both tables to produce the bottom datasheet window. As you can see, the CompanyName and Phone columns of the bottom datasheet window match the information stored in the Company table for the record whose CompanyID is 2 (Federated Oil).

FIGURE 28.3.

An example of a join that combines the Company and Notes tables.

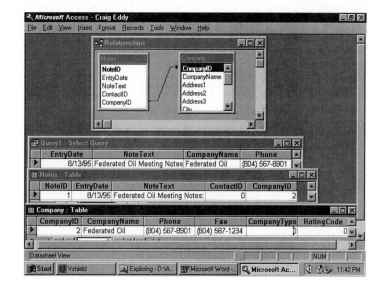

Self-Joins

A more advanced form of join is called the *self-join*. This is a join in which a table is joined to itself based on a field or combination of fields that have duplicate data in different records.

The Three Types of Keys

As mentioned previously, there are three different types of keys. A database's keys really do unlock the relationships contained within the database, but only if they're correctly implemented. Each table in a relational database must have a unique identifier that consists of one or more fields. Without it, there is no way to retrieve a unique record from the related tables to create the joined table.

> **TIP**
>
> Give each key field the same field name throughout the database. This makes creating joins between the tables easier. It also aids in understanding the database design since the company identifier is called CompanyID in all tables in which it appears.

Primary Keys

A field that is the unique identifier for a table is called that table's *primary key*. The selection of which field to use as the primary key for a table is one of the most important decisions made when designing a database. The primary key *must* uniquely identify each record in the table and must never have duplicated values. For this reason, I recommend that the AutoNumber data type be used to create a new field in a table. The AutoNumber field guarantees that a duplicated value is never inserted in the primary key field. Access automatically inserts a unique value in this field when a record is inserted in the database and never lets that value be modified or deleted once it is inserted.

The primary keys of the PIM database are shown in boldface type in the relationship diagram. (Refer to Figure 28.1.)

Composite Keys

There are often cases in which a record cannot be uniquely identified by a single field. In these cases, a composite key is used to identify unique records. A *composite key* is the group of fields that uniquely identify a record. A composite key is also the primary key for that table. While duplicate values are allowed within any of the fields of a composite key, there cannot be duplicate values across all the fields that make up the composite key.

An example explains this concept in a clearer way. The xContComp table is used to relate contacts and companies. It has a composite key made up of its ContactID and CompanyID fields. A contact can be related to many different companies by inserting a record for each contact/company combination. Likewise, a company can have many related contacts in the same way. However, the same contact/company combination cannot be repeated in the table. Figure 28.4 shows the xContComp, the Contacts, and the Company tables. From this example, you can see that Bill Perkins (ContactID = 37) is related to both Perkins Wholesale (CompanyID = 5) and Va. Staple Manufacturers (CompanyID = 4). You cannot insert another record into xContComp that has a CompanyID value of 4 and a ContactID value of 37 because doing so would violate the uniqueness of the composite key.

Foreign Keys

If you understand the concepts of primary and composite keys, then you will easily grasp the concept of foreign keys. Essentially, a *foreign key* is a field (or group of fields) in one table that has duplicate values in the primary (or composite) key of a related table. For example, the Notes table has ContactID and CompanyID fields. These are foreign keys in the Notes table but are the primary keys of the Contacts and Company tables. The Relationships window shown in Figure 28.3 graphically displays the relationship between foreign and primary keys. It is this relationship that actually allows Access to join data between tables.

Referential Integrity

The term *referential integrity* refers to the ability to maintain links among tables. Basically, maintaining referential integrity means that every foreign key field value in a table must map to a corresponding record in the table that has this field as its primary key. For instance, if a note were created with a value of 99 for its CompanyID field (given the existing data shown in Figure 28.4), there would be no corresponding record in the Company table. This note record would be termed an "orphan" record because it has no "parent" record in the Company table (this requirement of having parent records is analogous to the network database model discussed in the opening section of this chapter).

FIGURE 28.4.

An example of the use of composite keys.

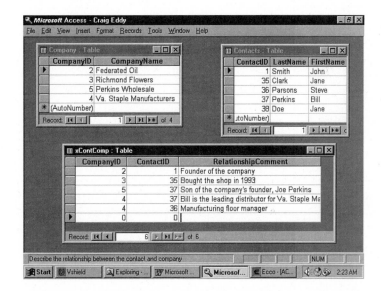

NOTE

Access can be made to enforce referential integrity and thus prevent the creation of orphan records. This mechanism is part of the Relationships window (select Relationships from the Tools menu). To change the referential integrity settings, select a relationship (by clicking the line joining two tables) and then select the menu item Edit | Relationship.

The Three Different Types of Relationships

The real power of a relational database is the ability to combine primary and foreign keys to establish relationships between data tables. There are three different types of relationships that can be created using the relational data model. These relationships and examples of each are discussed in this section. Essentially, the type of relationship created between tables determines the format of the data retrieved when the tables are joined.

One-to-One

The simplest (and least used) type of relationship is the *one-to-one* relationship. This means that for every record in one of the tables in the relationship there is a single corresponding record in all the other tables that take part in the relationship. Because these tables could easily be combined into a single table (thus avoiding having to join the tables), this type of relationship is used only in special circumstances.

One-to-Many

A *one-to-many* relationship is a relationship in which a record in one table has one or more related records in another table. The one-to-many relationship is by far the most common relationship in a relational database. Strictly speaking, the PIM database contains nothing but one-to-many relationships.

In the PIM database, there is a one-to-many relationship between the Contacts table and the Notes table. Each contact can have many notes referencing it. The key field ContactID is used to join the tables in the relationship.

Many-to-Many

A *many-to-many* relationship is a relationship in which many records in one table may have many records in another table. Strictly speaking, many-to-many relationships are not allowed in a relational database. Instead, an intermediate table is created that holds the primary keys from the two original tables as foreign keys. The xContComp table is an example of such an intermediate table. It allows a contact to be related to many companies and vice versa. (Refer to Figure 28.4.) The many-to-many relationship between the Contacts and Company tables is broken into two one-to-many relationships with the xContComp table.

Although there is a third field in the xContComp table that allows for a description of the particular relationship, this is not necessary. The table can consist merely of the two foreign key fields.

Steps to Creating a Relational Database

This section describes the methods used in creating a database "from scratch." The process of creating a database structure is known as *data modeling*. The term *modeling* is used because a database is used to model a real-world system or collection. This section presents a methodical means of modeling data and creating an effective database.

Identifying Required Data

The first step in creating a database is to determine what information needs to be tracked and the overall objective of tracking this information.

The questions to answer in this stage should deal with how the data will be used. It is important to answer as fully as possible these high-level questions up front because the answers will determine how best to structure the data within the database. By studying current forms and reports, you can get a good feel for the amount and types of data to be tracked. You'll also need to analyze the business process to gain some insight into how the data is collected. This insight will help you in organizing the data into logical tables.

Collecting the Identified Fields into Tables

The next step of the process is to arrange the fields you identified in the previous step into logical tables. One of the requirements of a table is that it model one and only one entity. This means that fields containing contact information should be stored in a separate table from fields containing company information. Also, the collection of fields used should describe the entity in question as fully as possible.

Along the way, watch for fields that are candidates for lookup tables. A *lookup table* is a table that holds a list of possible values for a field in the main table. If the data being modeled has a field that consistently has repeated values, this field is a good candidate for a lookup table. The lookup table will most likely consist of two fields: a primary key field (the AutoNumber data type is recommended) and a description field that contains the values being repeated. The main table's field would then be replaced with a foreign key field that matches the primary key of the lookup table. In the sample PIM the CompanyTypes, ContactTypes, TitleCodes, and RatingCodes tables are lookup tables.

The use of lookup tables prevents data inconsistencies that can occur when free-form text is entered into fields. However, lookup tables may not always be warranted. The drawback to using lookup tables is that a join must be created between the base table and the lookup table in order to retrieve a meaningful description of the data stored in the lookup table. This can often degrade performance. A balance must be struck between the desire for consistent data and performance.

Identifying Primary Key Fields

Every table must have a unique identifier for each record. This can be one field or a set of fields. Attempt to identify candidates for the primary key at this stage. I recommend that if the table in question is not an intermediate table for a many-to-many relationship, an AutoNumber field be added to the table to serve as the primary key.

Drawing a Simple Data Diagram

Now comes the task of creating a diagram (similar to the one shown in Figure 28.1) for the new database. Draw each entity in its own box and be sure to include the primary key fields. After each entity (table) is drawn, draw the links between the tables by connecting primary (and composite) keys to foreign keys.

While these links are being drawn, check for links that would benefit from intermediate tables. These links are usually present when there are links in different directions between two tables. For example, if the Contacts table were thought of first, it would be natural to have a CompanyID field present to associate the contact with the employer. However, if the Company table were designed first, you might think to add a ContactID field to designate a contact at that company. This raises two questions, however:

- What if the contact were a consultant who had associations with several companies. Should you add a limited number of extra CompanyID fields to the Contacts table?

- More than likely there will be more than one contact at any given company that you'd like to track in the database. Should you add additional ContactID fields to the Company table?

The answer to both of these questions is no. Instead of adding a limited number of fields to either table, you should add an intermediate table (the XContComp table in the sample PIM) to hold the links between contacts and companies. This way, a contact can be associated with any number of companies and vice versa.

Normalizing the Data

The process of modifying a database's structure so that it conforms to the relational model is known as *normalization*. The basic goal of normalization is to remove redundant data from the database. In the process, the final database is made more flexible and better able to absorb the inevitable changes to its structure. Now is the best time to make sure the new tables follow these recommendations!

Normalization involves the following processes:

- Ensure that each table's fields are uniquely identified by the table's primary key.
- Ensure that each field of the database represents a single piece of information. Do not store city and state names in the same field, for instance.
- Remove redundant data from tables. Each record of the database should contain unique data. Each unique piece of information should only be stored in one place (except for key fields, which have duplicated values throughout the database).
- Remove repeating groups if there is a possibility that more fields will be added to the group. For instance, if a table stores EntryDate, ReviewDate, and DueDate fields and there is a chance that more date fields will be added to the table later, a date lookup table should be added. This table would have at least three fields: the primary key field from the original table, a field that would store a value representing which of the three (at present) different types of dates (entry date, review date, and due date) a given record represented, and a date/time field to store the actual date value.

Identifying Field-Specific Information

Once the complete structure has been created, it is time to start defining the physical layout of the tables. Here's the recommended process:

1. Create sensible field and table names. These should describe the data but not be excessively long.
2. Identify the data type for the field: text, numeric, currency, yes/no, and so on. For text fields, determine the maximum length that will be allowed. For numeric fields, determine the range of numbers that will be stored.
3. Determine if there are any validation rules, defaults (a value that will be inserted automatically when a new record is added), or input formatting that should be applied to the field.

Creating the Physical Tables

The last step of the design process is to use Access to create the physical database tables. Access has several wizards that greatly aid in the creation of new or linked tables. I recommend that you create some tables using the wizards and then experiment in the design view for the tables.

Summary

This chapter shows you how to design effective databases. However, all the reading in the world is no substitute for on-the-job training. The best way to learn the ins and outs of database design is to design a lot of different databases. Fortunately, Microsoft Access makes database design and construction (nearly) painless and very time efficient.

Always remember these two key points:

- An effective database design is flexible, logical, and methodical by nature.
- The power of relational databases lies in the relationships that can be created between diverse tables.

Querying Data: The QBE Grid and Select Queries

Queries enable you to extract specific information from a database. That information could be from one table or from multiple tables. There are two ways to query data in Access. The first is through the Query module of the Access database container, and the second is as an SQL statement for the record source of a form or a report. The ability to query information is considered the brain of a relational database system. You could enter information all day long, but if that information couldn't be queried, it might as well be kept in a flat file.

New Query Features

The Query module of Access for Windows 95 has several new features. These new features make it easier to manage, locate, and share information. This enables people who extract data from Access 95 databases to make more informed decisions quickly. Here are a few of the major features:

- Filter by form/datasheet—This enables the end user to type information needed to formulate a query, and Access builds the underlying query. The data is then placed in form view for the end user.

- QuickSort queries—The Ascending and Descending Sort buttons have appeared in the toolbar in previous versions. In Access for Windows 95, the Sort Ascending and Sort Descending buttons appear on queries when they're viewed in datasheet view. In previous versions, this feature was available only for tables.

- The Simple Query Wizard—This new feature enables the user to select information from different tables. The Simple Query Wizard handles the inclusion of the related tables and establishes relations between the necessary tables with intelligent joining technology. The end result is the information that the user picked.

- The Pivot Table Wizard—This wizard enables the user to create a Microsoft Excel pivot table based on an Access table or query. The advantage is that the Excel pivot table can give users the ability to change the criteria of a pivot table on-the-fly.

- Improved relationships dialog—In previous versions of Access, if you had two tables and dragged one field from the table on the left to the table on the right, your join would be different than if you dragged one field from the table on the right to the table on the left. Now, you can drag a field from either side of a one-to-many relationship, and Access executes the join intelligently.

- Background joins between wizards—Intelligent joining technology is an option that can be turned on or off (the default is On). It automatically figures out the joins between tables in a query, based on field names and field types.

- Top values—This enables the user to select the top numbers or percentages for a given field in the query.

- Enhanced properties—Properties for queries in the past were limited. With Access for Windows 95, the user has enhanced properties not only on the query itself but on each individual field in the grid.

■ New objects—Eight objects are available: Auto Form, Auto Report, New Table, New Query, New Form, New Report, New Macro, and New Module. All can be summoned from a Query window.

Using the QBE Grid

In Access, data is stored in tables. Simple queries involve sorting all the records in one table by one field. More complex queries sort all the records in one table by two or more fields. Relational databases enable the user to sort records in two or more tables by two or more fields. Queries are used to view, change, and analyze data in different ways. Query data can also be used as the source for forms and reports.

Access makes the querying process simple by placing all the tables with the necessary information in a query and drawing lines to show the relationships between the tables. Whether a query is accessed from the Query module of the database container or through the Query Builder on the record source of a form or a report, the QBE grid looks and functions the same way. The Access QBE grid is shown in Figure 29.1.

FIGURE 29.1.

The Access Query window is divided into two sections: the table pane and the query grid.

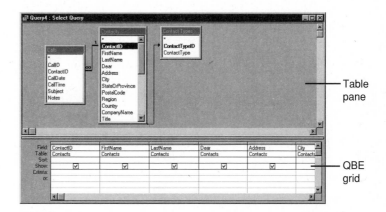

The upper half of the Query window shows the relationship between the tables being queried. This is called the table pane. The lower half of the window shows the fields from the tables and the criteria by which the data is to be queried. This is called the query grid or the QBE grid. The Access method of QBE (query by example) is arguably the best and easiest method of querying data available. However, it does have limitations. The following list shows some of the limits for Access queries:

■ The maximum number of tables in one query is 32.

■ The maximum number of fields in a recordset is 255.

■ The maximum size of a recordset is 1GB.

■ The maximum number of sorted fields in a query is 10.

- The maximum number of nested queries is 50.
- The maximum number of characters in a cell in the QBE grid is 1024.
- The maximum number of ANDs in a WHERE or HAVING clause is 40.
- The maximum number of characters in an SQL statement is approximately 64,000.
- The maximum number of characters for a parameter in a parameter query is 255.

A query can be viewed in its design view, datasheet view, or SQL view. The query's design view is just a means for the user to come up with the criteria needed for a particular form or report. Access takes the query generated by the user and builds a SQL statement. This SQL statement performs the work of the query.

Adding to the Query Window

Adding to the Query window can be divided into two segments: adding tables or other queries during the creation of the query itself and adding tables or other queries to an existing query.

During the creation of a blank query, all the tables and queries are listed in a Show Table window. By highlighting the desired tables or queries and clicking the Add button, those items are placed in the table pane of the Query window. You can perform the same function by double-clicking each item in the Show Table window.

Another way to add tables or queries to an existing query is from the menu. Select Query | Show Table to add a new table or query to the query. Microsoft has provided a Show Table button that serves as a shortcut to adding tables to an existing query.

To add to the Query window, click the Add Table button. It pulls up a Show Table window. This window gives the user the option of viewing just the tables for that database, just the queries, or both.

Follow these steps for yet another way to add tables or queries to a query:

1. Position the current query so that it takes up half your screen.
2. Press the F11 key to bring up the database container.
3. Position the database container so that it takes up the other half of your screen.
4. Click the Table or Queries module that contains the items to be placed in the query.
5. Click the desired table or query to highlight it and, while holding down the mouse button, drag the item into the table pane of the Query window.
6. When the mouse pointer is over the table pane of the Query window, you see a small, white box with a plus sign attached to the pointer. Release the mouse button to drop the desired table or query onto the table pane.

Just adding tables or queries to the query is only the first step in producing a query. To produce a query, you must have at least one table or query and one field in the query grid. A query is a compilation of data. This data can be subject to different criteria. The output of a query is the data it produces. A query can't run unless it has at least one output field. Output fields are obtained by placing fields from the objects in the table pane of the query into the query grid. To make an output field, click a desired field needed for the query output and drag it to the query grid.

If you want all the fields in a table or query to be dragged to the query grid, double-click the title bar that appears at the top of every table and query. This highlights all the fields for the table. Click and hold any of the highlighted fields and drag them to the query grid. When the mouse button is released, all the fields appear in the query grid.

Another method of bringing all the fields in a table or query to the query grid is to click the asterisk that appears at the top of the table or query. This asterisk brings all the fields to the query grid. This asterisk acts like the asterisk wildcard that you use when you're trying to find a file using the Explorer. For example, to find all the files that start with ACC, you would enter ACC* in the Named line of the Find All Files dialog box.

When you drag just the asterisk to the query grid, even though all the fields are present in the Datasheet view, only the asterisk appears in the query grid. If you need to set criteria for a particular field, that field needs to be visible, so it must be dragged to the query grid individually.

The click-and-drag method of moving fields from the table pane to the query grid can be expedited by double-clicking each desired field. If you need all the fields from a table to be moved to the grid, double-clicking the asterisk can achieve that result.

> **TIP**
>
> Multiple fields can be added to the query grid at one time. If the fields are consecutive, you can highlight the first field, hold down the Shift key, and click the last field. All the fields in between are highlighted. If the fields are scattered throughout the table, hold down the Ctrl key while clicking the desired fields.

Setting Query Properties

Every object has properties. That also goes for objects in the database container. Setting query properties can be done to the query object as a whole, or on the individual objects within the query. This section covers setting properties to the query object as a whole, followed by information on setting properties to the individual tables and fields within a query.

When the Queries tab of the Database window is active, a list of all the queries is visible. In Access for Windows 95, every individual query object can have properties assigned to it. Highlight a query and click the Properties button on the toolbar to see its properties.

For every object, the user can assign a description. Each description can be 255 characters long. The Properties dialog box shows when the object was created, when it was modified, and who owns it. At the bottom of the dialog box are two check boxes that pertain to the attributes of the object. When the Hidden check box is checked and applied, the object is no longer visible in the database container window. This enables you to set security on an object-by-object basis in the database. The second check box deals with the ability to make this individual object replicable.

> **NOTE**
>
> If you put the letters USYS in front of an object name, that object doesn't appear in the database container window. USYS means user system objects. The object can be unhidden by viewing the system objects.

To view objects that are hidden, select Tools | Options. Click the View tab and check Hidden Objects. This unhides all the objects that were hidden in the properties sheet. Notice that there is also a check box for system objects. This unhides any objects with a prefix of USYS or MSYS.

> **CAUTION**
>
> USYS objects are objects created by the developer and hidden from the end user by the prefix USYS. MSYS objects are objects created by Microsoft and hidden from the developer with the prefix of MSYS. Giving users access to any system objects isn't recommended. They could inadvertently corrupt the database.

Everything discussed about setting properties so far has dealt with the whole query as an object. Within each query, there are also objects. Every object, including tables, fields, and joins, has properties. To access the properties for an object, highlight the object and select View | Properties. You can also highlight the object and click the Properties button on the toolbar. Another way to get to the properties for an object is to highlight the object and click the right mouse button. A different way to get to the properties of some of the objects is to double-click the joins or the table pane itself in the Query window and get to that object's properties. If you double-click the table, all the fields in that table are highlighted. If you double-click a field in a table, that field is automatically placed in the query grid.

Bring up the table pane's property sheet by double-clicking the table pane or right-clicking the table pane and choosing Properties from the shortcut menu. This is a detailed property sheet for the query. The Description line has the same information as the Description line from the Properties dialog box accessed from the database container.

So far, properties concerning the query as a whole object have been covered. Each query object contains several objects. Those objects are tables, other queries, and fields. You can observe the properties for each object by clicking the desired object and selecting View | Properties in design view.

The two properties for tables are Alias and Source.

Alias enables the user to give a name to a table. Normally, this isn't important, but there are situations in which this might be helpful. If there are two copies of the same table in one query, this feature is helpful. For example, a user needs a query on employees and supervisors. The Employee table contains a list of all the employees and their supervisors. Supervisors are also employees, so the user needs two copies of the Employees table. As the tables are added, the first table is called Employee. The second table is called Employee_1. The user has the option of using the Alias feature to rename the second table to Supervisors. It's easier to make a distinction between two tables with different names than two tables with similar names.

The other property for the tables in a query is called Source. This line shows where the table is coming from. If the table is coming from the current database, this line is blank. If the table is coming from another Access database or another back-end database such as Oracle, the property reflects the source of the table.

The purpose of queries is to extract data and make it available to the user. Data is made available by running queries. Queries can't run unless there is at least one field in the QBE grid. Each individual field in the QBE grid has properties.

The Properties dialog box for a field has two tabs. The first tab is the General tab, which has four attributes. The Lookup tab has one attribute. The following are the five attributes for field properties:

- Description—This feature functions exactly like the Description feature found in the design view of a table. It enables the user to enter up to 255 characters for a description, which appears in the status bar when a form is created. If the field isn't from a table in the current database, the description is automatically filled in by Access with the connection information used for the field.

- Format—Format enables the user to customize the way datatypes are displayed and printed. Usually, either the Format or Input Mask of a field is filled out when the user wants to control the display of a field. If both are filled out at the same time for the same field, the Format line takes precedence.

- Input Mask—Input Mask is similar to Format in that it controls the way you want to display data. In fact, a wizard is available that builds the code in correct syntax based on the type of output you selected. The Input Mask Wizard itself is shown in Figure 29.2.

FIGURE 29.2.

The Input Mask gives the developer several commonly used input masks to choose from.

NOTE

The difference between Format and Input Mask is that the Input Mask can control how the data is entered. You can use certain symbols in a mask that make the field a mandatory field. If a form is created based on a query that has a mandatory field, the user must enter information that conforms to the input mask. For example, you could set the Input Mask of the Postal Code field to 00000. When a form is built based on this query, the user can't enter only three digits in the Postal Code field. The user must enter a five-digit postal code.

- Caption—Caption functions the same way as it does in the design view of a table. The caption is the text that appears in the label of a field. Even though a caption can be 2,048 characters long, if there isn't enough room for the caption to appear, it is truncated.

- Display Control—Display Control is found on the lookup tab of the properties for a field in the QBE grid. Three types of controls are available—a text box, a list box, and a combo box. Each control has its own attributes, which become visible when the control is selected. When a form is based on a query where a lookup control has been set, all the configurations for that control stay with the field. When that field is pulled from the field list onto a form, the lookup control with all the appropriate properties remains with the field. For example, the customer type field is set to combo box. When a form is based on this query, as you pull the customer type field onto the form, it appears as a combo box with all the properties already set.

> **NOTE**
>
> All the field properties found in a query can be found in a table. If you set a single field's properties to perform an action in the table and have a query based on that table, the properties for that single field don't follow through to the query. You can have different properties for the same field in several different queries. The attributes for a field in a form are based on the record source of the form. If the form is based on a table, the attributes for the field are the same as they are in the table. If the form is based on a query, the attributes for the field are the same as they are in the query.

Different Types of Query Joins

Query joins are the lines that are visible between two or more tables. They relate the tables and queries in the table pane of the grid to each other. These lines can be created manually or automatically. To create a join line, simply click one field in one table and drag it to a field in another table. Actually, there is more to a query than dragging any field to another field, but the join line itself is produced by dragging a field from one table to another table.

Microsoft Access can automatically create join lines between tables if the AutoJoin option is turned on. Access uses one of two sources of information that you might have already provided. The first way Access can automatically create a join line is based on a relationship that already exists. If you've already created a relationship, Access uses the relationship schema when automatically creating a join between two or more tables or queries. The other way that Access automatically creates joins is based on the naming conventions used to create the fields in a table. If two tables have exactly the same name and comparable datatypes, Access automatically joins the two tables by the fields that have the same name.

> **NOTE**
>
> Whether the join line is automatically drawn when two or more tables or queries are placed in the table pane of the query or you draw the line by dragging one field in one table to the matching field in the other table, the line can have symbols attached to it. Only two types of symbols can exist—either a 1 or an infinity symbol ( ). There are only three relationship types: one-to-one, one-to-many (signified by the infinity symbol), and many-to-one.

You can access the Join Options dialog box in several ways. You can double-click an existing join line. You can highlight an existing join line and right-click to show the Join Properties line item. You can highlight an existing join line and select View | Join Properties. Finally, if no join line is available, you can create one by dragging a field from one table to the field of another table. With the line created, you can perform one of the previously mentioned methods for accessing the Join Options dialog box. This is the same way joins are created and classified in the Relationships window, which is available by bringing up the database container and selecting Tools | Relationships.

There are only three types of joins in an Access query:

- Inner join is the first option. This is usually the default join. This join selects records from the two tables where the values of the joined field are equal in both tables. The join doesn't have an arrow on either end of the line.

- Left join is the second option. A left join is also commonly known as a left outer join, which is a reserved word in Microsoft Access. left outer joins include all the records from the table on the left side of the join even if there are no matching record values in the table on the right side of the join. Records from the right table are combined with records from the left table only when they match.

- Right join is the third option. A right join is also commonly known as a right outer join, which is a reserved Microsoft Access word. This join includes all the records from the table on the right and all the records that have a matching value from the table on the left. Records from the left table are combined with the records from the right table only when they match.

As stated earlier, when two or more tables are added to a query, joins are automatically drawn based on a relationship that already exists, or on fields with the same name if the AutoJoin feature is turned on. If lines aren't automatically drawn, you or the user can draw them by clicking one field in a table and dragging it to another field in another table. Properties for the join are set when you click the join line and bring up the join's properties. If you select option #1, the join becomes an inner join and includes only the records from both tables where the fields by which they are joined have the same value. If you select option #2, the join becomes a left outer join; if you select option #3, the join becomes a right outer join. In Figure 29.3, it appears as if both queries are left outer join queries, but they are not. Only the one on the left is a left outer join query.

So far, the discussion has been of the three different types of joins. Knowing the different types of joins is only half the battle. Knowing when to use each join is the other half. Figure 29.4 shows the three types of joins—left outer join, inner join, and right outer join. Each query contains the same two tables: Contacts and Contact Types. Each query is joined by the same field: Contact Type ID. Each query has only one output field: Last Name.

FIGURE 29.3.

Both queries only appear to be left outer join queries.

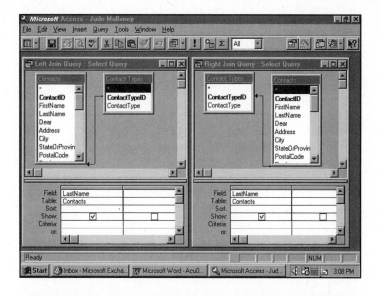

FIGURE 29.4.

Left outer join, right inner join, and right outer join queries in Design view.

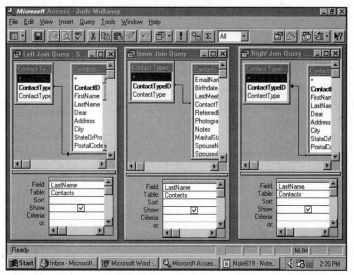

Each query is using the same data tables joined by the same fields, yet they are joined differently. The SQL view of each query is shown in Figure 29.5. The type of join is defined by the words left, inner, and right.

FIGURE 29.5.

It's easy to determine whether the query contains a left outer join, inner join, or right outer join in SQL view.

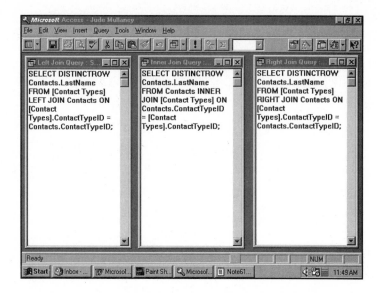

Even though all three queries have the same tables, joined by the same fields, and have the same field in the QBE grid, the output is different. Figure 29.6 shows the data output for each query.

FIGURE 29.6.

The queries might look the same, but the joins result in different outcomes.

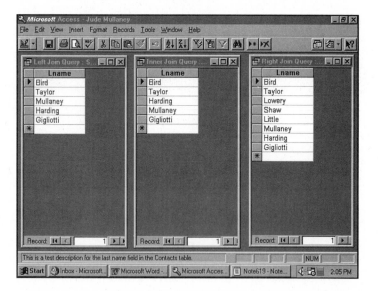

Relationships and Referential Integrity

When establishing relationships between tables, it's important to understand that they aren't created in the Query module of the database container. The relationship isn't a query even though it looks similar to a query. It is actually created from the database container and affects the database as a whole.

It's possible to create relationships based on queries, but referential integrity isn't enforced. Referential integrity ensures that relationships between records in related tables are valid. This prevents the user from accidentally deleting or changing related data.

Changing the AutoJoin Option

Relationships are logical joins, or lines drawn between tables for the database as a whole. Joins in a query are the lines drawn between tables and pertain only to the query itself. Once the query is closed, the joins are no longer relevant.

An option called AutoJoin is available to the developer. You can access AutoJoin by selecting Tools | Options. When the option is enabled, Access automatically creates an inner join between two tables on two conditions. The first condition is that the fields have the same name. The second condition is that one of the fields must be a primary key.

It's also possible to create a join between two tables if the AutoJoin feature isn't activated, but you must create the join manually by clicking one field in the first table and dragging it to another field in the second table. If the AutoJoin feature is turned on, more than one join can be created between the same two tables. If the join created by the AutoJoin isn't desired for the current query, you must delete it by highlighting the join line and pressing the Delete key. If the join that is created by the AutoJoin is desired and a second join is required, you just need to create the second join by dragging one field from the first table to another field in the second table.

Because the join created by the AutoJoin option is an inner join, you can change the join at any time. Highlight the join line and click the right mouse button to bring up the Join Properties dialog box. Select the desired join, either #2, left outer join, or #3, right outer join, and click OK to save.

Analyzing Query Performance with Analyzer

Often you develop a query but aren't satisfied with it. The query might be sluggish or not performing to your satisfaction. What is a developer to do? Access for Windows 95 has come up with a way to analyze the query and all the objects within that database to give suggestions to the developer. It's called the Analyzer.

You can access the Analyzer by selecting Tools | Analyze from the database container and clicking Performance. Once the Performance Analyzer has been launched, a dialog box like the one in Figure 29.7 appears. You then have the ability to choose one object in the database or all the objects in the database.

FIGURE 29.7.

The Performance Analyzer enables the developer to choose objects in the database.

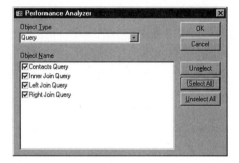

You can select an individual object type from the drop-down list or select all objects from the drop-down list. By selecting All, you can see every object that was created for this database. All the objects appear in the Object Name list. You can pick and choose the individual objects to be analyzed by checking the box associated with the object. If you want the entire database analyzed, you can click Select All, and the whole database can be analyzed.

Depending on the size of the database and the complexity of its objects, the analyze process can take several minutes. Once the process has finished, Access displays a dialog box like the one in Figure 29.8.

FIGURE 29.8.

The Analyzer offers advice on how to increase the speed of an object within a database or the entire database itself.

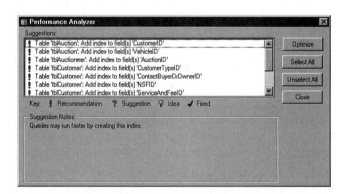

When the Performance Analyzer is finished grinding away, it returns advice to you. This advice is broken down into three categories: Recommendations, Suggestions, and Ideas. Recommendations have a red exclamation point for an icon. Suggestions have a green question mark, and Ideas have a yellow light bulb. The suggestion list shows the icon, the object module, the name of the object in question, and a brief suggestion of how to improve it.

If you click Recommendation or Suggestion, Access gives a proposal on how to increase its performance. When the item is highlighted, the Optimize button is enabled. Access can make the changes to the database automatically. All the hints with a light bulb icon are Ideas, and Access can't optimize the object if the advice is only an idea. Developers must perform the idea optimizations themselves.

> **CAUTION**
>
> The Performance Analyzer can make some changes automatically, but be careful. Some recommendations and suggestions might not be what you intend for the database.

Optimizing Queries

A developer can take several actions on his own to increase the speed of his queries, including the following:

- Index the join fields in both tables. This includes tables joined from different sources. If there are multiple index fields to be queried by, the query's speed increases if you use the indexed fields in the order they appear in the table's index window. If fields are not or cannot be indexed, use sorts on those fields only when absolutely necessary.

- Choose the appropriate datatype size for each field, especially the join fields. If you always choose a Long Integer as a datatype, you might not be utilizing the database to its best ability.

- In the QBE grid, choose only those fields that need to be shown. Showing all the fields slows down the display of the datasheet. Depending on the size or complexity of the query, this slowdown could be a few minutes.

- Nested queries shouldn't have calculated fields. If it's necessary to have calculated fields in nested queries, try to have the calculation performed in the top level of the query or have a control on the form that performs the calculation.

- Group Bys also slow down queries, so try to keep them to a minimum. If they are needed, the placement of Group Bys is important. Calculate aggregates on the same table as the field that is to be totaled. If the number of Group Bys is reduced, the speed is increased. At times Group Bys are necessary for extracting data from the database in the format needed. First and Last Functions might be more appropriate than Group Bys.

- Total queries that have joins might be faster if the single query is made into two queries. The first query performs the join and then adds that query to a new query to calculate the totals.

■ Restrictive query criteria might perform faster depending on which side of the join the criteria is placed on. Criteria on one field might perform differently if the criteria is set on the one side rather than the many side.

■ Make Table queries can be used to create tables if the data being used doesn't change often. Any form or report runs faster when it's based on a table as opposed to a query.

■ Crosstab queries utilizing fixed column headings run faster than nonfixed column headings.

Using Each of the Standard Query Types

A finite number of queries are available. Queries are like colors. Even though several thousand different colors are available, each color is derived from the three primary colors—red, blue, and yellow. Although there may be several different variations of queries, there are only two types of queries—queries that are acted on and queries that are viewed. These are called Action queries and Select queries. The following sections describe the different types of Action and Select queries and when to use them.

Action Queries

Action queries are queries where the data resulting from the query is acted upon. Changes are made to the records in one operation. There are four types of Action queries: Make Table, Delete, Append, and Update.

> **TIP**
>
> Access can't perform an AutoForm or AutoReport operation on any of the Action queries. They aren't considered valid queries for the basis of an AutoForm or AutoReport.

Make Table Queries

Make Table queries do exactly what the name implies. They make tables based on one or more other tables that utilize part or all the data from each table. What is the purpose of making a new table when the old ones work just fine? Developers use Make Table queries for several reasons. One reason is that you need to send information from the Employee table to another database, and the Employee table contains sensitive information. You would make a table with just the name and address and be able to export that make table to another database.

Developers use the Make Table query to create a query of history information. The make table retains all the information on a table or group of tables up to a specific date. The make table retains the information and could be considered a backup table. Make tables created for the purpose of holding history information have a two-pronged benefit. First, they enable you to retain all the information in smaller groups—say yearly. Any information needed can be quickly generated based on a yearly make table. Second, with a make table containing the history information of years gone by, those records could actually be deleted from the real tables, thus increasing the speed of any forms or reports based on those tables. You don't move old records as you think of a move with the Explorer. You simply copy the older records to another table and delete the older records from the main table.

If you had several forms or reports based on the same two or more tables, you could increase the speed of the forms and reports by creating a make table. The key phrase in the previous statement is "several forms or reports." If only one table or report was based on a multitable query, it wouldn't be any faster because the query still has to run. If the form or report is used only periodically, a query running to generate a dynaset or a query running to generate a make table takes the same amount of time. However, if there were several different forms or reports, it would make sense to have a Make Table query. The first time the query is run, speed doesn't increase, but each time a form or report is run after the query has generated the make table, the speed does increase. The speed increases because forms and reports run faster when based on tables than when based on queries.

To create a Make Table query, create a new, blank query with the desired tables. Pull the fields into the QBE grid and set the criteria, if any. Select Query | Make Table or click the Query Type button on the query's design toolbar and select Make Table. A Make Table dialog box appears. Type the name of the new table you're creating, as shown in Figure 29.9.

FIGURE 29.9.

When creating a Make Table query, type the name of the new table here.

A different database can be accessed from here. Before the Make Table query is created, click the datasheet view of the query to make sure the results of this query are the ones needed. The make table is created when the query is actually run. After the query is run, check the Table module of the database container. The new table should be there. Open the new table to see the records. As new records are added to the original table, they don't appear in the make table unless the Make Table query is run again. If the Make Table query is run again, new records that match the criteria set by the query are added to the new table.

Append Queries

The Append query does exactly what it says it does—it adds. Suppose you need to combine the Contact table with a Customers table. The two tables are similar in fields except the Contact table has more fields than the Customer table. The Append query takes the records from one table and matches the fields in the other table. All records are appended to the table, and those fields that don't match are ignored.

To create an Append query, create a new, blank query with the table whose records will be appended to another table. In design view, select Query | Append or click the Query Type button on the toolbar. The Append dialog box appears. Type the table name that these records are to be appended to. A different database can even be accessed from here. Drag the fields from the table into the QBE grid. Specifications can be set in the QBE grid. Notice in Figure 29.10 that there is an extra line in the QBE grid of an Append query. It is the Append To line. Here is where the matching field name in the other table is entered.

FIGURE 29.10.

An Append query has an extra line in the QBE grid where the matching field name is entered.

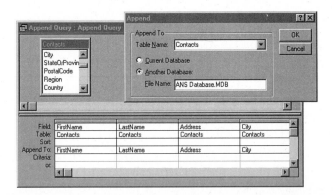

Once the Append query is run, the records are added to the other table. If seven records match the criteria, seven new records appear in the other table. In this case, the seven records were added to another database. If new records are added to the table in the current database, the changes aren't reflected in the other database until the Append query is run again. Then the new records are added to the other database.

> **WARNING**
>
> Access automatically renumbers any record that is appended if the AutoNumber field isn't placed on the QBE grid. If the original AutoNumber field is needed to remain with the record, place the AutoNumber field on the QBE grid. Any duplicate AutoNumber values aren't appended.

Update Queries

Update queries give you the ability to change data on a global scale. For example, if all the employees get an annual raise of 5 percent, their salaries are increased by 5 percent through an Update query. If all the customers' area codes in the Charlotte area changed to 701, the change could be made through an Update query.

To create an Update query, open a new, blank query and add the tables needed to make the change. In design view, select all the criteria that are needed for the update. If all the contacts that were categorized as Buyers became Sellers, the field that needs to be changed is ContactTypeID. First, set the criteria to read only those records where the ContactTypeID is 1 (in the ContactType table, Buyer = 1). Look at the query in datasheet view to make sure the right records are being changed.

Next, select Query | Update or click the Query Type button on the toolbar. Only when the query is run does the update take place. If the view is changed to Datasheet, the same information appears as before the query was changed to Update. Notice in Figure 29.11 that an Update To line is added to the QBE grid. To change all the Buyers to Sellers, the ContactTypeID number for Sellers (2) must be added to the grid. If the words Buyer and Seller are used instead of 1 and 2, an error occurs. This error occurs because the field pulled down is the ContactTypeID, not ContactType. Access is looking for a number, not a string.

The changes are made to the data only when the query is run. In Figure 29.11, three records are changed from Buyer to Seller. New records can be added to the table, and their ContactTypeID can reflect that the contact is either a Buyer or a Seller. Only when the Update query is run again do all the Buyers become Sellers.

FIGURE 29.11.

When the Update query is selected, an Update To line is added to the QBE grid.

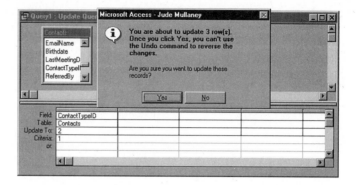

Delete Queries

The Delete query gives you the ability to delete records from one or more tables in a single action. As helpful as this can be, it can also be very dangerous. If the Delete query is based on one table, when the query is run, the records that match the criteria are deleted. If the Delete query is based on more than one table, two Delete queries must be run. A Delete query can delete records from only one table at a time. For example, if all the contacts in North Carolina need to be deleted, two Delete queries need to be run—one on the calls associated with the North Carolina contacts and one on the North Carolina contacts themselves.

To create a single-table Delete query, open a new, blank query with the table containing the records to be deleted. Pull down the asterisk field that represents all the fields in the table and place it in the first column of the QBE grid. In the other columns, pull down additional fields to set the criteria. Set the criteria for the query to reflect the records that need to be deleted. View the query in datasheet view before running the Delete query. If the datasheet view doesn't reflect the records that need to be deleted, return to design view and check the criteria until the results of the datasheet equal the records that need to be deleted.

Select Query | Delete Query or click the Query Type button on the toolbar and select Delete. Click the Run icon (the exclamation point) to activate the delete. Access tells you how many records are affected by the Delete query and gives you the option of canceling the delete. Remember, once the delete has taken place, nothing can undo the delete. The only way to retrieve the records that are deleted from a Delete query would be to restore them from a backup of the database.

Select Queries

The first type of queries discussed was Action queries; the second type of query is Select queries. Select queries are queries where the data resulting from the query is viewed. There are two types of Select queries: Simple Select queries and Crosstab queries.

Simple Select Queries

Simple Select queries are the most common of all the queries. They enable you to extract data from different tables and view it. Limited manipulations can be made with Select queries. Select queries are so common that a Select Query Wizard is available. The Wizard lists all the existing tables and queries and asks for the fields that should appear in the query. From that information, the Wizard creates the Select query.

> **TIP**
>
> For the Query Wizard to work flawlessly, the relationships for all the tables might need to already be established. If no relationship exists between the tables needed in the Wizard, the query can still be created if a standard naming convention was used when the table fields were created.

To create a Simple Select query without the Wizard, open a new, blank query and add the tables desired for the query. A relationship must exist between two or more tables in a query. If a relationship isn't automatically established when the tables are entered into the table pane of the query, it is because either the table fields don't adhere to a standard naming convention or no relationship was established in the relationship window of the database. You can establish a relationship for this query by dragging a field from one table to a related field in the other table. This kind of relationship appears only in this query.

By dragging fields from the tables to the QBE grid, a Simple Select query is built, as shown in Figure 29.12. Criteria can be set on Select queries. Select queries can calculate sums, averages, counts, and other types of totals on one or more tables.

FIGURE 29.12.

A Simple Select query.

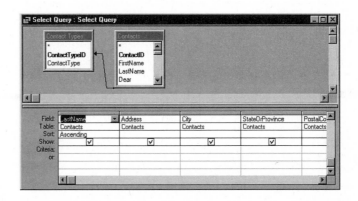

Crosstab Queries

The second type of Select query is Crosstab queries. They're somewhat like Simple Select queries in that they can calculate sums, averages, counts, and other types of totals on one or more tables. They differ from Simple Select queries in that Crosstab queries display information not only down the left column of the datasheet (like a Simple Select query), but also across the top. Crosstab queries are similar in appearance to pivot tables. Crosstab queries have row headings as well as column headings. Simple Select queries can produce the same information as Crosstab queries, but the Crosstab queries give a more concise datasheet.

To create a Crosstab query without the help of a wizard, open a new, blank query and add the tables needed for the desired result. Add the fields from the tables into the QBE grid. Select Query | Crosstab or click the Query Type button on the design toolbar, as shown in Figure 29.13.

FIGURE 29.13.

You can create a Crosstab query by selecting Crosstab from the Query Type button.

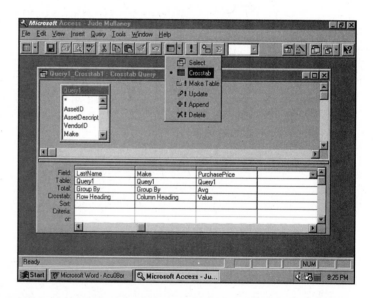

> **TIP**
>
> When you're creating a Crosstab query, there must be at least three output fields. One field must be a row heading, one field must be a column heading, and one field must be a value.

When the Crosstab query is selected, Access automatically adds a Total row and a Crosstab row to the QBE grid. There must be at least three output fields in a Crosstab query—one for the column heading, one for the row heading, and one for a value, as shown in Figure 29.13.

There might be occasions where data is missing or data that has been appended to the table or query in the Crosstab and fields might be missing. This missing data might be data in the row or column headings of your Crosstab query. When data for headings is missing, Access returns a < > sign, which means that this field is null. You can prevent a null sign from appearing in a heading by typing Is Not Null in the Criteria cell in the design grid for that field. This means that any time a heading comes across a null field, that record isn't considered for the Crosstab query. However, if you need to know that there are records that should be visible in the query even if there is a null heading field, you can use the Nz function. This function is an expression that is placed in the Criteria cell of the heading field and returns a string Unknown instead of a null.

NOTE

Data in Crosstab queries can't be edited.

You can't create an AutoForm or AutoReport based on an Action query or a Crosstab query. However, you can display Crosstab data on a form or report without creating a separate query in the database. This is achieved by adding a PivotTable control on the form or report. With the Excel Pivot Table, row and column headings can be changed on-the-fly, enabling users to analyze the data in different ways.

Summary

Access for Winodws 95 includes several new features that make querying more efficient. This chapter covers the new query features available, such as the Filter by Form button. It also covers the design and new properties of a basic query. The differences between relationships and joins are discussed, as well as the different types of joins. The AutoJoin option is described, and the six standard query types are covered—Make Table, Append, Update, Delete, Simple Select, and Crosstab. The Performance Analyzer is examined and illustrated.

Creating and Using Simple Forms

Jud
Cra
Ted

IN THIS CHAPTER

This chapter gives a basic overview of forms and shows why forms are used and how to use them. It includes a section that details the design and customization of forms, which explains even more about the capabilities of forms. These capabilities are not utilized in the AutoForm or other Form Wizards.

An Introduction to Forms

Access forms can give databases a professional image in a relatively short time. Splash screens and main menus are just a few examples of items that appear in mass-distributed, professional software products. Forms give flexibility to databases by being either very simple or very complex.

Creating Simple Forms with AutoForm

The AutoForm feature in Access enables you to create quick and dirty data entry forms in the blink of an eye (depending on the speed of the computer). AutoForms are fast and ask no questions. They are only performed on existing tables or queries, and there are several places where the AutoForm Wizard can be accessed. You can access the AutoForm Wizard from either the Tables module or the Query module at the database container. You can also access it from the Forms module, but only when a new form is created. When you access the AutoForm Wizard from either the Tables or the Query module, record source for the new form is the object that was highlighted when the AutoForm button was pressed. However, you can also invoke it from the Forms module by creating a new form and selecting the table or query that the form is to be based on and click on the AutoForm Wizard option. For this example, the AutoForm Wizard is being invoked on the Vendor Invoice query.

To understand how the AutoForm places its fields, it is necessary to look at the query (or table, as the case may be) that the AutoForm is being based on. Figure 30.1 shows the Vendor Invoice query in design view.

FIGURE 30.1.

The query that the AutoForm wizard is being based on.

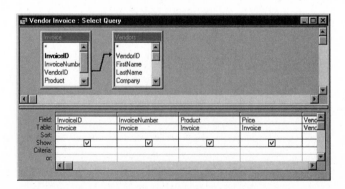

The forms produced by the AutoForm Wizard are not much to look at. They have background pictures assigned to them and usually appear in a single-column format, unless there are many fields in the base table or query. Each field has a label, which in most cases appears to the left of the field, as shown in Figure 30.2. All the fields that are on the form are present in the query. Their order of appearance on the form also follows the order of appearance on the query. The same goes for a table-based AutoForm. The fields appear on the form in the same order as in the query.

In this case, the query on which the AutoForm is based contains a table that has a field where the DefaultControl property is changed from Text Box to Combo Box. This feature is inherited by the AutoForm, and the field is placed on the form as a combo box.

FIGURE 30.2.

The AutoForm Wizard produces quick forms using all the fields in the table or query on which the AutoForm is based.

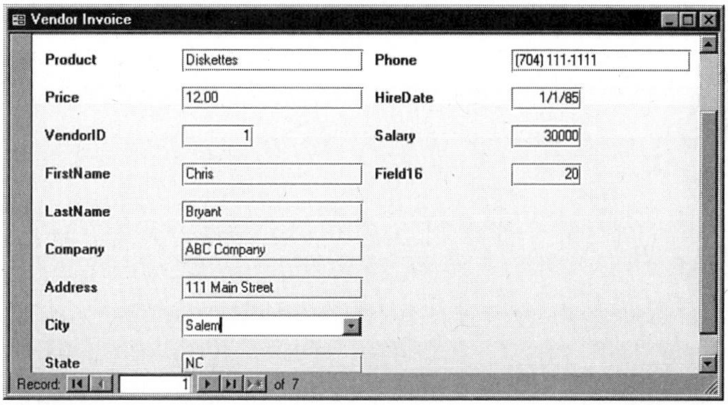

TIP

If fields in a table have their Default Control property changed, the AutoForm Wizard will use the Default Control property when creating the form. In addition, any of the caption properties found in the table will also appear in the form created by AutoForm.

Notice that the form generated by the AutoForm already has a background and font specifications to the labels and colors assigned to them. You can change all these items so that every time the AutoForm wizard is used, a specific background is used and certain colors, fonts, and pitches are used. You can achieve this by opening the form in design view. Make the desired changes to the labels and fields. The form now becomes the template for the changes to the AutoFormat wizard. From the Format pull-down menu, choose AutoFormat.

Press the Customize button in the lower-right corner of the dialog box. The Customize button allows you to perform one of three actions:

■ Create a new AutoFormat template based on the current form and background selected

- Change the current AutoFormat template based on the current form and background
- Delete the current AutoFormat template

Once the background and font, style, and color changes have been selected, click OK. The AutoFormat will now create all new forms using the new template. You can change this option as many times as desired. Each time it is changed, new forms will use the new template. Any old forms will not automatically be updated. They will retain their existing backgrounds and colors.

> **NOTE**
>
> When basing an AutoForm on a query, the query must be a Select Query, not an Action Query. There are only two queries that fall into the Select Query category: the Select query and the Crosstab query. The AutoForm wizard will not work on an Action Query.

Creating Simple Forms with the Form Wizard

Form Wizards, such as the Form Wizard, the Chart Wizard, and the Pivot Table Wizard, are different from the AutoForm Wizards, such as the AutoForm Columnar, AutoForm Tabular, and AutoForm Datasheet Wizards. The AutoForm Wizards do not allow for any developer interaction during the creation of the form—only after the form has been created. Form Wizards differ by asking you questions about the tables and queries to be used for the form, which fields from each can be used, sort orders, backgrounds, and the like. In Access 2.0, when a Form Wizard is used, you can choose only one table or query. In Access for Windows 95, this has been changed. You can now choose certain fields from different tables and queries.

> **NOTE**
>
> When using multiple tables and queries, it is necessary to have the relationships between those tables and queries established. When the relationships are established, the joins (inner, outer left, or outer right) will be used in the creation of the SQL statement needed for the Record Source property of the form.

The only way to access the Form wizards is by clicking the New button in the Forms module of the database container. The first dialog box is a modal form, which means that the developer must click the OK button or the Cancel button to proceed in Access.

NOTE

When a modal form is on the screen, you must answer the question being posed by the modal form before you can proceed in that piece of software. All hotkeys, such as Esc and F11, are turned off.

TIP

If the wizard being used is not an AutoForm-type wizard, there is no need to select a table or query to base the form on here.

After you have selected an option—in this case the Form Wizard Option—you press the OK button to proceed. The next screen allows you to choose the fields that are to appear on the new form. Access for Windows 95 gives you the ability to choose multiple fields from multiple tables and/or queries. This is a major enhancement from the 2.0 version. This part of the wizard determines the SQL statement that will appear on the Record Source property of the new form. In Access 2.0, you could only choose one table or query.

In Figure 30.3, tables and queries are selected from the drop-down box that appears in the upper section of the box. The fields associated with the highlighted table or query are displayed below, in the box on the left. Any field that appears in the box on the right are considered selected fields and will appear on the new form. To move fields from the left box to the right box, click the greater-than keys between the two boxes.

FIGURE 30.3.

The Form Wizard allows the developer to choose fields from more than one table or query.

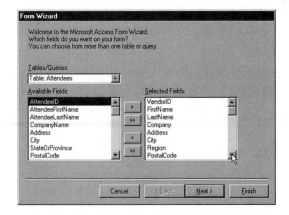

NOTE

All the tables are available and only the Select-type queries will appear in the drop-down list. Remember, Action-type queries cannot have forms or reports based on them.

What happens if there are two or more objects from which fields are selected? Those objects must have an existing relationship before the wizard will continue. Access displays a message box stating that one or more objects are not connected. The developer then has the choice to go into the relationships window of the database and rectify the situation or to return to the wizard and allow the developer to remove the fields that are causing this error to occur.

NOTE

If you choose to modify the relationships of the database, the wizard will be canceled.

The next step in the Form Wizard process concerns the layout of the fields. The developer has three choices: Columnar, Tabular, and Datasheet.

Once the layout has been determined, the background style is next. Eight different formats ship with Access for Windows 95. If the developer has modified any of the formats or added and deleted different formats, those changes will be reflected here.

The fourth and last step in the wizard allows the developer to modify the name of the form. A suggestion is already in place, and it is based on the name of the table or query that the form is being based on. The screen gives the developer a choice to go directly into the form and begin entering data or go directly into the design view of the form to make modifications. The Access help files can also be displayed.

This is the end of the Form Wizard. The developer can create a sophisticated and professional data entry form in a fraction of the time that it would take to create it from scratch. It is not as fast as an AutoForm wizard, but it does allow more flexibility in the customization.

Opening and Using a Form

Forms can be opened a number of ways. The most common is through the database container window in the Forms module. However, end users may get confused with the database container window. To shield this from the end user, developers can launch forms from buttons on other forms, from a macro, or from Visual Basic for Applications (VBA). You can even open forms from the database container without hitting the Open button. Drag the desired form from the database container to the application background. Access automatically opens the form. The pointer changes to reflect the fact that an object is being dragged.

Forms should always be used instead of tables or query datasheets. With forms, you can control what the user enters, how it is entered, and what is required before you can move to the next record. Direct access to tables or query datasheets gives you the ability to modify and delete existing data as well as adding data. This could be hazardous if the user is a novice to Access or Windows.

When forms are opened from other forms, a button usually launches them. A common example of one form being used to launch other forms is a main menu. Main menus may have several different buttons that launch several different forms. In the toolbox there is a button called the command button (shown in the margin). This tool, when coupled with the wizard, helps developers through the process that is needed to have a button launch another form.

> **TIP**
>
> The wizard button that appears in the upper-right corner of the toolbox must be activated in order for the Command Button Wizard to run. Click the Wizard button first, then create the command button.

On the form, click and drag a small square about the size of the desired button. As soon as the box is drawn, the wizard is launched. There are several different actions that a button on a form can perform. Those actions are listed in the wizard dialog box. Since this example deals with opening a form, the operation to be performed is a forms operation and the action is the Open Form action.

The next screen in the wizard asks for the name of the form that is to be opened when the button is pushed. In this case, the Vendors form will be opened.

The following screen deals with how the form being launched is to be opened. It can display specific data that can be linked to the form the button is sitting on. It can also just open and display all the records in the form.

There are only two more screens left in the Command Button Wizard. After choosing how the form should open, you must choose how the button appears. The button can either display a line of text or a picture. You can use one of the more than 220 button pictures that ship with Access, or you can choose a custom picture through the Browse button.

The final screen in the Command Button Wizard is where you give the button a name. The suggestion from Access is usually pretty generic, like Command2. It is wise to rename the button to something that reflects what the button does when pushed (for example, Vendors for the button that opens the Vendors form).

Forms do not have to be opened from a button. They can be opened through a macro. Macros function like small bits of VBA code. Look at the macro in Figure 30.4. The action being performed is the OpenForm action.

FIGURE 30.4.

The Vendors form will be opened by this macro action.

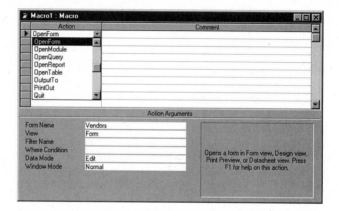

The lower half of the macro contains the action arguments information. These boxes must be filled out before the macro will work correctly. In Figure 30.4, the arguments are filled out as follows:

- The Form argument determines the form to be opened, which comes from the drop-down list. In this case it is the Vendors form.

- The View argument determines how the form is opened. It can be Form, Design, Print Preview, or Datasheet View.

- The Filter Name argument is either a query or a sort order for the records. This is not a required field.

- Where Condition refers to the Where clause in a SQL statement. A builder button can help developers build the Where condition.

- The Data Mode argument is how the form will be opened for the user. It determines whether users will be allowed add, edit, or read-only access to the records in the form.

- Window Mode refers to the size of the window that the form will be displayed in when it is opened. It can be Normal, Hidden, Icon, or Dialog.

Now that all the argument information has been filled out, close and save the macro. Once the macro has been created, it can be called from a form. Open any form in design view. Pull up the toolbox and turn off the wizard button. Click on the Command Button tool and draw a small box on the form. A blank button will appear on the form. Pull up the properties box for that command button, which is shown in Figure 30.5. This is where the macro code will be attached to the command button without the help of the wizard.

You should ask yourself what action the end user will want to do to bring up the form. The action that you decide on is called an *event*. On the command button's property sheet, click on the Event tab to display all the events that pertain to the button. There are 12 actions or events that the end user could do to the command button. Usually, users will click or enter on the button. This is the action that the macro will be attached to. From the On Enter property, click the drop-down list to display all the macros available. Select the desired macro, and the code behind the button is finished. The only thing left to do is change the caption that appears on the button to reflect what it does. The end user does not know that Command3 means "open the Vendors form." The caption for the button can be found under the Format tab of the button's property sheet.

FIGURE 30.5.

Macro code is attached to an event on a command button that appears on a form.

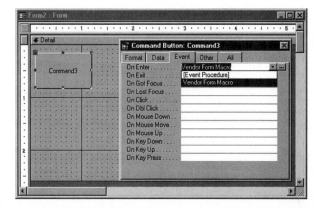

TIP

You can override the DefaultView and the ViewsAllowed properties of a form with the `View` argument of the macro.

There is one other way a form can be opened: through VBA code called the `OpenForm` method. This differs from the `OpenForm` action that appears in a macro. In fact, the correct syntax of the `OpenForm` method is almost exactly like the action arguments in the macro, and its correct syntax is shown here:

```
DoCmd OpenForm formname ,[view] [,filtername] [,wherecondition]_ [,datamode]_
    [,windowmode] [,openargs]
```

The syntax can actually be reduced to the following:

```
DoCmd OpenForm formname
```

When the syntax is reduced, Access accepts the defaults for each of the arguments that are preceded by commas. The `View` argument is defaulted to `Normal`. `FilterName` is left blank. `WhereCondition` is also left blank. `DataMode` is defaulted to `Edit`, and `WindowMode` is defaulted to `Normal`. The difference between the `OpenForm` action that appears in macros and the `OpenForm` method that is available in code is the `OpenArgs` argument. This argument allows for Visual Basic arguments and expressions to be entered.

> **TIP**
>
> The `WhereCondition` argument in the macro's `OpenForm` action allows up to 256 characters. The `OpenForm` method's `WhereCondition` argument increases the number of characters to 32,768.

No matter how forms are opened—from the database container, through buttons on other forms, from a macro or through code—the forms can switch among the three views—Form view, Design view, and Datasheet view—and the views can be accessed from the View pulldown menu or through the View button on the upper-left corner of the form.

Subforms

A subform is a form that is displayed on another form. A form/subform combination can be thought of as a main/detail form or a parent/child form. An example of a form/subform is shown in Figure 30.6. Note that subforms are often viewed in datasheet mode but that's not a requirement. However, the main form cannot be viewed in datasheet mode when a subform is present.

FIGURE 30.6.

A form/subform example.

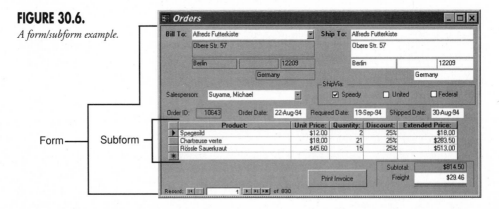

A subform is a completely separate form that is embedded in another form. You add a subform to a form using the Subform/Subreport control. You can also create the subform by dragging the name of the subform from the Forms tab of the database window onto the main form. The two forms are "linked" using the LinkChildFields and LinkMasterFields properties. The field names that are used to relate these two forms are placed in these properties.

Subforms are especially effective at showing data from tables or queries participating in one-to-many relationships. For example, you could create a form with a subform to show data from an orders table and a line items table. The main form would contain order detail information such as customer name and address, ship-to address, and shipping method. The subform would contain the items arranged in a particular order. It would contain fields such as stock number, item description, item cost, and quantity.

Adding Subforms

Subforms are most often used to display dependent records in a one-to-many relationship. The Quarterly Orders in the Northwind database, shown in Figure 30.7, is an example of this type of form.

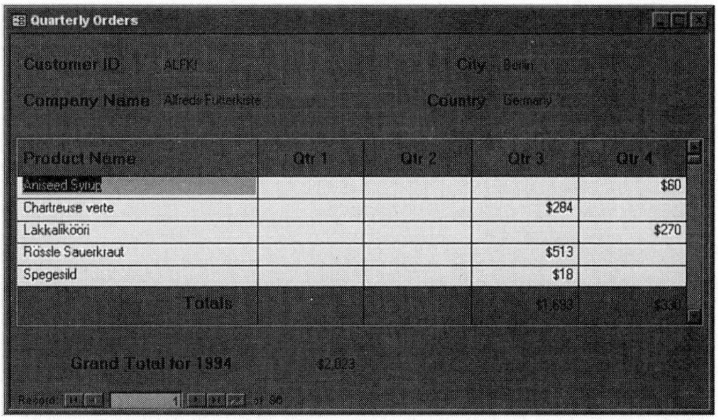

FIGURE 30.7.

The Quarterly Orders form in form view.

> **NOTE**
>
> This chapter concentrates on those things that make the main form and subform actually work together.

Let's look at how the main form was made. We'll start with the basic header design already complete. The header section of the form contains information about the *one* side in the one-to-many relationship, as shown in Figure 30.8.

Before adding the subform, let's look at how the subform was made. Notice that in Figure 30.9 this form has a header and footer that have the column names and column sums. This form uses a query as the data source. The subform contains information about the *many* side in the one-to-many relationship.

FIGURE 30.8.

The Quarterly Orders form in design view and without the subform.

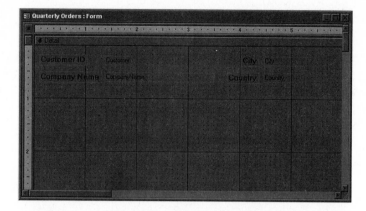

FIGURE 30.9.

The Quarterly Orders subform in design view.

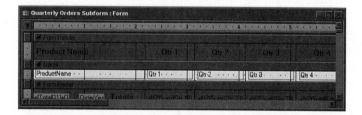

FIGURE 30.10.

The Quarterly Orders form with a subform in design view.

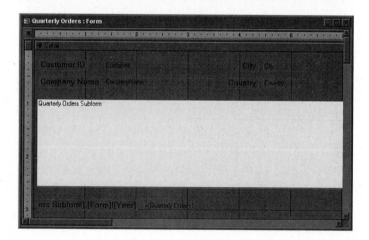

Now we will add the subform to the main form. There are two methods for adding a subform to a main form. The first uses the Subform Wizard to add the subform to the main form. Simply click the Subform/Subreport button on the toolbar and follow the instructions to pick and bind the form together.

The second and more direct method is to simply drag and drop the subform from the database window onto the main form. Place and size the form as needed and then establish a connection between the main form and subform by setting the LinkChildFields and LinkMasterFields properties of the subform. Now the subform's data will change in sync with the main form's header as the database is navigated.

While this is one of the most common uses for subforms, this is still a simple application. One of the more advanced uses of subforms involves the use of VBA code to change the subform while the application is running.

Adding Controls to a Form

To add a control to a form, click the toolbox button for the desired control. The button will change to its pressed state. Move the mouse onto the form, press the left mouse button where you want the control located, and then drag the mouse to size the control. You can also simply click on the form, and the control will be added using a default size.

If you want to add several controls of the same type to a form, you can "lock down" the toolbox button by double-clicking on it. This allows you to add several labels to the form without having to reselect the label tool each time. To release the lock, either click the button again or press the Esc key.

If the Control Wizard is active, adding a control with an associated Control Wizard will cause that wizard to be activated.

To make a copy of a selected control (or group of selected controls), use the Duplicate item on the Edit menu. Access will create a duplicate of the selected control(s) directly below the selected control(s).

> **WARNING**
>
> The Control Wizard will not be activated when you're creating a duplicate. Also, any code associated with a control will not be copied to the new control.

Types of Controls

An Access form can contain one of three types of controls: bound, unbound, and calculated. The differences between these types are discussed in this section.

Unbound Controls

An unbound control is used to convey information to the user or to receive from the user input that will not be stored in the database. Here are some examples of using unbound controls:

- A label for a text box is used to describe what the text box represents.
- Text boxes or drop-down list boxes can be used to select different scenarios on a what-if form.

■ A line can be placed on a form to separate different sections of the form.

■ A company logo can be placed on the form to add graphical effects.

When a control is added using the toolbox and no Control Wizard is activated, the control will automatically be unbound.

Bound Controls

Bound controls are used to display and edit data from the database. The term "bound" refers to the fact that the control is tied to a field of a table, query, or SQL SELECT statement. The most common type of bound control is the text box, but nearly any control can be a bound control (with the exception of lines, rectangles, page breaks, command buttons, image frames, and labels).

When a bound control is added to a form, it will default to the control specified in the DisplayControl property for the field to which it is bound.

A bound control will inherit many of the formatting and text properties defined for the field to which it is bound (Caption, Description, Input Mask). These properties can be changed on the form using the control's property sheet.

To add a bound control to the form, the field list must be visible. You can turn the field list on and off using the Field List item of the View menu. These are the steps:

1. Select a single field, a group of fields (by holding the Ctrl key to select sequential fields or holding down the Shift key to select multiple fields that are not sequential), or all fields (by double-clicking the title bar of the Field List window).

2. Drag the mouse from the field list to the form. The cursor will change to a small box (or group of boxes, if more than one field is selected). Place the upper-left corner of the box where the upper-left corner of the first bound control should be placed.

3. The control(s) will be placed on the form and a label will be placed to the left of each control. The text of the label will be the Caption property for the field to which the control is bound.

You can also change an unbound control to a bound control using the control's Control Source property. Doing so, however, will not cause the control to inherit many of the field's properties (except for ValidationRule, ValidationText, and DefaultValue, which are always enforced for the field).

Calculated Controls

Calculated controls use expressions to derive their data. Expressions are combinations of operators, fields, control names, functions, and constants. Although text boxes are the most common form of calculated controls, any control having the Control Source property can be a calculated control. For example, a calculated control can be used to compute sales tax on an order entry form.

All expressions must begin with an equal sign. For example, this is an expression: `=[States]![SalesTaxRate]*[OrderForm]![OrderTotal]`. The `[States]![SalesTaxRate]` part refers to a table of states where one of the fields is SalesTaxRate. The `[OrderForm]![OrderTotal]` part refers to the control named OrderTotal on the form named OrderForm (probably the current form).

To create a calculated control while in design view, follow these steps:

1. Select the type of control to be used from the toolbox and position the control on the form (see the section "Adding Controls to a Form").

2. Enter the expression using one of the following methods:

   ■ If the control is a text box, the expression can be entered directly into the control. Click inside the text box portion until the blinking edit cursor is visible. Type the expression into the edit box.

   ■ If the control is not a text box or if you don't want to enter the expression directly, double-click the control to open its property sheet. Move to the Control Source property. Here you can enter the expression as text or use the Expression Builder (click the Build button to the right of the ControlSource text box). The Expression Builder shown in Figure 30.11 is an extremely useful tool for creating expressions because it allows you to browse all the objects in the database, including controls from other forms, fields from queries, and built-in functions.

FIGURE 30.11.

The Expression Builder in action.

Of Combo Boxes, List Boxes, and Option Groups

Combo boxes, list boxes, and option groups are a group of controls that make the Control Wizard extremely helpful. If the Control Wizard feature is enabled (the Control Wizard button of the toolbox is pressed), adding one of these controls to a form will cause the Control Wizard to activate. The wizards for the combo box and list box are very similar and are dealt with together later.

In the following examples, you'll create a new form by selecting Design View and the Orders table in the New Form dialog box.

The Combo Box and List Box Wizards

These wizards allow you to easily bind a combo box or list box to another table or query in the database. The steps followed in the wizard are similar to the steps you follow when using the Lookup Wizard for a table field. In this example you'll create a new customer name field on a form based on the Orders table of the Northwind database.

Make sure that the toolbox is visible and that the Control Wizard feature is enabled. Click the Combo Box button on the toolbox and place a combo box on a blank form. The Combo Box Wizard activates.

The three options will determine how the combo box relates to the Orders table. Since you're adding a combo box that will allow the user to select a customer name, you'll choose the first option (I want the combo box to look up the values in a table or query). If you were adding a control to allow the user to select an order from all orders in the database, you'd choose the third option. If you wanted to have a predefined set of values from which to pick, you'd choose the second option. Press the Next button.

This dialog box of the wizard is where you'll choose the data source. The data source will be the table or query that provides the list of data to be displayed in the combo box. Choose Customers and click Next.

The next dialog box is where you'll choose which fields should be included in the combo box. Since you'll be using the combo box to pick a CustomerID for an Orders record, you need to choose not only the CompanyName field but also the CustomerID field. Select the fields shown and click Next.

The next dialog box allows you to define how the columns will look in the combo box. Note also the AutoLookup check box. Because you chose the Customers table and the CustomerID field and because the Orders and Customers tables are related via this field, the wizard is smart enough to assume that you want to use this field as the key field for the combo box. Unchecking the AutoLookup combo box will cause the CustomerID column to be displayed as well. Leave AutoLookup enabled. Also leave the column width as is and click Next.

The final dialog box allows you to specify the label text for the label to be placed next to the new combo box. A default is chosen based on the columns chosen. Click Finish to close the wizard and create the control. After you've returned to design view, it is necessary to set the Control Source property of the new combo box to the CustomerID field of the Orders table. Open the property sheet for the new combo box by double-clicking the control. On the Control Source property use the drop-down box to specify the CustomerID field.

Finally, switch to form view and cycle through the records using the record selector at the bottom of the form. The text in the combo box will change. You can change the customer associated with an order by using the drop-down portion of the new combo box and selecting a new customer. Because of the way this control was created, if you enter into the edit box text that isn't a valid CompanyName, you'll get a validation message stating that you must choose an item that is in the list. This way a customer must appear in the Customers table before it can have an Orders record.

Navigation in a Form

Navigation in a form refers not just to the fields that appear on the form but to the records within the form. When you are working on a form, you can navigate around the form by several different methods. The first is to use the Enter key. The Enter key accepts the data that the user entered into the field and moves the focus to the next field. The Tab key performs the same action; however, the user does not need to enter in any data. If there are hotkeys associated with buttons on the form, the user can hold down the Ctrl key and press the corresponding underlined letter.

NOTE

The tab order of the form can affect the way the Tab key and the Enter key move the user around the form. To change the tab order, select Tab Order from the View pull-down menu when the form is in design view.

You can move from record to record by moving to the last field on the current form and pressing Enter. This action will bring you to the first field on the next record. The same does not go for the Tab key. If you are on the last field on the form and press the Tab key, the focus is moved back to the first field on the same record. It loops you around all the fields on the same record. You can also use the Page Up and Page Down keys to move to the next sequential record. If you hold down the Ctrl key and press Home or End, you will move to the first and last record in the dataset, respectively.

> **TIP**
>
> You can move to the first record in the form by holding down the Ctrl key and pressing the Home key. You can move to the last record in the set by holding down the Ctrl key and pressing the End key.

The developer can choose to turn on the navigation buttons on a form. Navigation Buttons is a property that appears on the form's property sheet, which is shown in Figure 30.12.

FIGURE 30.12.

Navigation Buttons is a property of the form.

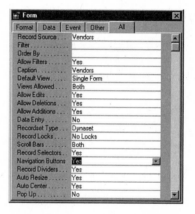

These buttons give you a graphical way of moving around the records. When this feature is turned on, the navigation buttons appear on the bottom-left corner of the form. The buttons are visible in Figure 30.13. The buttons show which record is currently on the screen. The triangle pointing to the left allows the user to move back one record. The triangle pointing to the right allows the user to move forward one record. The other two triangles that are pointing (left and right) to vertical lines allow the user to move to the very first record or to the very last record respectively. There is one other button in the navigation button area: the triangle pointing to an asterisk. When this button is pushed, you are moved to the next blank record and are ready for data entry.

You can use either the keyboard or the mouse to navigate through a form. This can be done through mouse clicks on the navigation buttons or by pressing the Page Up and Page Down keys on the keyboard.

FIGURE 30.13.

When the navigation buttons are turned on, they appear on the bottom-left corner of the form.

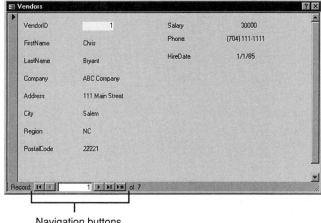

Navigation buttons

Editing Data on a Form

Editing data on a form actually means that you can add, edit, or delete information in individual fields or information on entire records. You can control what the user can do when a form is opened. In Figure 30.14, there are several new properties that give the developer more flexibility when it comes to allowing users to edit data.

FIGURE 30.14.

A few new properties give the developer more control of editing data.

Six properties pertain to the editing of data. They are Allow Edits, Allow Deletions, Allow Additions, Data Entry, Recordset Type, and Record Locks:

- Allow Edits is either on or off. This allows the user to save records when using the form. When turned off (No) it prevents the changing of any of the data displayed by the form.

- Allow Deletions is either on or off. When this property is set to No, the user can view and edit existing data; however, they cannot delete any records. When it is set to Yes, the user can delete records provided the referential integrity rules are not broken.

■ Allow Additions is either yes or no. When this is turned on (Yes), the user can add a record to the form. When it is set to No, the user cannot add records. The Add Record button on the Navigation Button group is not activated.

■ Data Entry is either set to Yes or No. This is different from Allow Additions in that when this feature is turned on, the form automatically opens to a new, blank record. The user does not have the capability to view existing records. Errors will occur if Allow Additions is set to No and Data Entry is set to Yes. When this feature is set to Yes, the form must have a record source.

■ Recordset Type can only be set to Dynaset, Dynaset (Inconsistent Updates), or Snapshot. It deals with the multiple tables and their fields being bound to controls on the form. The bound controls can be edited if Recordset Type is set to Dynaset. Snapshot removes the ability of the user to edit the bound controls. This is similar to the AllowUpdating property in Access 2.0.

■ Record Locks deals with the multiuser application environment. It can only be set to No Locks, All Records, or Edited Record. No Locks means that two or more people can edit the same record. He who saves first wins. All others will get a message stating that the record has been changed. The only option from there is to either dump the changes, overwrite the changes of the person who saved it first, or copy a version of the changes to the Clipboard and view the saved changes. The Edited Records option allows the user to edit a record while locking out the other users. Depending on the size of the record, Access may also lock down other records stored around the edited record. This prevents other users from editing records that are not being used by any other user. The All Records option locks all the records in the form and their underlying tables. Only one person at a time is allowed to edit any records on the form.

Saving the Form

There are several ways to save a form's data. Selecting Save from the File pull-down menu is one way. Another way is to close the form. Any changes made to the design of the form will send up a flag in Access and display a message box stating that changes have been made since the last save of the form. You are then allowed to save the new changes over the old form, dump the new changes, or cancel the close process and return to the form.

Figure 30.15 shows the Vendors form. The record that is visible has been changed. Developers and users can tell that the record has been changed by looking at the record selector that appears to the left of the record. Notice the little pencil that is right above the mouse pointer. This is an indication that lets the user as well as the developer know that the current record is in the process of being modified. The user can press the Tab key as well as the Enter key, and the record will still show the little pencil. Only when the focus is moved to the next record or the form is closed will the changes be written.

FIGURE 30.15.

The record has been changed since its last save.

This indicates to user that the current record is being modified

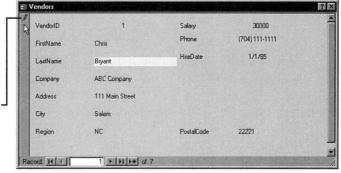

The record can be saved by doing one of the following:

- Using the navigation buttons at the bottom of the form
- Pressing the Enter key until the focus is moved to the next record
- Pressing the Page Down key (or Page Up if the record is the last in its set)
- Holding down the Ctrl key and pressing the End key (or the Home key)
- Holding down the Shift key and pressing the Enter key
- Closing the form
- Pressing the record selector button

These are ways the user can save the record. The developer may or may not provide a Save button on the form. If the Save button exists, pressing it will also save the form.

Creating a Sample Form

This section covers two simple sample forms. These forms will give any application a sophisticated look. The first form is a Splash form. This form appears when the application is first executed.

Create a new, blank form. On that form place an image and a label stating the name of the application. Figure 30.16 shows a splash screen. The logo was placed on the form using the Image button in the toolbox. The title Vendor Software is a label. The font and pitch have been changed. The Fore color is black, but the back color as well as the line color have been turned transparent so there are no lines on the splash screen. The properties for the form show that there is not a record source. Turn off RecordSelectors and Navigation Buttons. Make sure the AutoResize and AutoCenter properties are set to Yes.

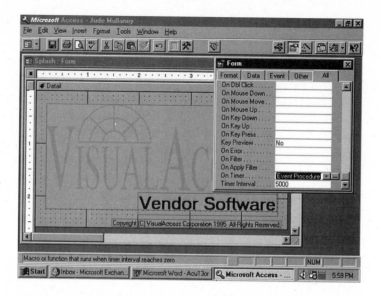

FIGURE 30.16.

The splash screen in its design view.

To make this perform like a real splash screen, the Timer property should be set to 5000 cycles (1 second = 1000 cycles). After the 5 seconds have passed, the On Timer event will be fired. Now comes the VBA code that was discussed earlier. On the On Timer event, press the ellipsis (...) button to activate the Code Builder. The object of the splash is to bring up the form for a few seconds and then make it go away. Enter the following code into the code section. The first line of code is closing the splash screen and the second line of code is opening the MainMenu form, which has yet to be created:

```
Private Sub Form-Timer ()

    DoCmd.Close
    DoCmd.OpenForm "MainMenu"

End Sub
```

Close the form and save it as Splash.

Now create the MainMenu form. Create another new, blank form. On that form, use the Label tool to create the name of the software and the MainMenu label. Use the Command Button tool to create a button that launches the Vendors form. It should look like the form in Figure 30.17.

Notice that there is no record source. The RecordSelectors and Navigation buttons have also been turned off. Make sure that the AutoResize and AutoCenter properties are set to Yes. An Exit button added takes the user out of the software entirely. When the Vendors button is pushed, the Vendors form will launch. Close the form and save it as MainMenu. Make sure that if you used a space between the two words in the code above, you stay consistent.

Now you need to tie it all together. From the database container, open a new, blank macro. The only action to be performed in this macro is the OpenForm action. In the Action

Arguments section of the OpenForm action, choose Splash from the drop-down list on the Form Name argument, as shown in Figure 30.18.

FIGURE 30.17.

The Main Menu form in its design state.

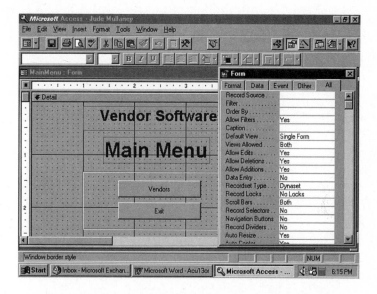

FIGURE 30.18.

The macro ties it all together.

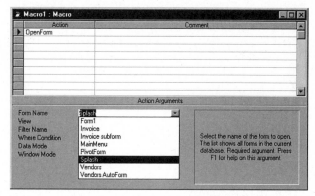

Close the macro and save it as AutoExec. AutoExec is a special, reserved word in Access and it is the very first macro that is launched when the software is first opened. Anything in the AutoExec macro will run without the end user having to do anything until the MainMenu form appears on the screen.

Test the database by closing and reopening it. It should open the splash screen first, then go to the MainMenu screen second. Try it.

Summary

This chapter covers the more than 25 new features of the Access for Windows 95 Forms module. It also reviews the basics concerning forms. It covers the different types of record sources that forms could be based on and also discusses the option of not using any record source for forms. The chapter also covers the new features of the Auto Wizard and Form Wizard. This chapter also covers adding controls and subforms to a form. Opening, navigation, editing, and saving forms are also discussed. Finally, it is all pulled together in the section on sample forms, which opens a splash form and closes it and then opens the MainMenu form. From there, an end user can immediately open the Vendors form for data entry.

Designing and Customizing Reports

by

IN THIS CHAPTER

Printing a report from Access is often the final result of the database effort. No matter how great the user interface, printed output is more easily understood by most people. Even though reports can be rows and columns of courier text, people have high expectations for the look of the report. In the days of DOS, people did not seem to question a report that rivaled the look of a teletype printout, but now a report has to be functionally correct as well as cleverly formatted. This chapter focuses on creating the back-end data structures that make up a good report, along with the powerful formatting tools that are included in Microsoft Access for Windows 95.

Microsoft Access is an excellent tool for data publishing. *Data publishing* is the database equivalent of desktop publishing. Many people use Microsoft Access just as a publishing tool, publishing data that has been attached to their company mainframe or an existing database. Reports in Access are now created much like laying out newsletters in PageMaker or Quark. Access tools, known as *controls*, are used to create lines, words, and pictures. Knowledge gained from creating the company newsletter can now be used in making the company reports. Microsoft has included functional similarities between desktop publishing applications and Access. For instance, holding down the Shift key while drawing with the Line tool produces a straight line.

What's New in Access for Windows 95

Microsoft Access for Windows 95 has gained revolutionary new functionality over the previous version. In the reporting area, although no revolutionary changes have been made in this release, some bells and whistles have been added to make your work easier. For example, the new print preview in Access mimics the print preview of Microsoft Word, and you now have the ability to attach a report to an e-mail. Word users will feel right at home with Access because of the similarities between generating an Access report and formatting a Word document. The advances made with reporting in Access follow a general trend with all the new Windows 95 products—tighter integration and standardization within the Microsoft Office applications. Access now looks and feels even more like Word and Excel, sometimes to the point that it is easy to forget which program is being used. Here's a list of the new features of Access:

■ More intuitive Report Wizards—There's no need to second guess what groups and totals reports are—a sample is created in the wizard window. The wizard can be instructed to pull fields from multiple tables, and Access generates the query. Access does not require a query first for multitable reports. (See Figure 31.1.)

■ An improved print preview—Users can now preview many pages at once as well as pick the desired Zoom level, just like in Microsoft Word.

■ An improved formatting toolbar—Formatting tools from Word and Excel now appear on the Access toolbar. Useful tools such as the Format Painter make the task of reformatting a control simple.

■ A new formatting feature called Control Morphing—Remember the drudgery of having to delete a text box control and then recreate it as a label? Now there is Control

Morphing. From the Format menu just select the Change To option, which can convert a text box into a label.

FIGURE 31.1.

The new and improved Report Wizards give sample previews.

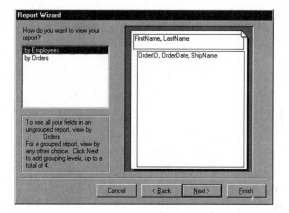

- Improved help—In accordance with the Windows 95 help engine, Microsoft Access now has more ways to get your questions answered.
- Tabbed dialog boxes—The Property Sheet and Print Setup now have tabs that are consistent with Windows 95.
- A new menu called Insert—Access now has an Insert menu for easy insertion of pictures, objects, and the report expressions of Date/Time or Page Numbering.
- Sending a report through e-mail—The sought-after feature of including a report in an e-mail message is now available.
- Background pictures—One of the new report properties, the Picture property, allows a report to have a background image or a *watermark*.

Creating a Report Instantly Using the AutoReport Tool

Microsoft Access has the tools and flexibility that enable beginners to quickly see results and advanced developers to generate complex documents. Microsoft's answer for the I-want-it-now managers is a feature called the AutoReport, which is identical to the AutoForm feature for form creation. AutoReport takes a chosen table or query and generates a report with the click of the mouse. This is an excellent way to get a jump start on report creation.

Here are the steps for creating an instant report using AutoReport:

1. Open the sample database \\access\samples\nwind.mdb (also referred to simply as Northwind). In the database window, click the Table tab to show the predefined tables that are in Northwind. Click on a table to select it for the upcoming report.

By selecting a table, you are setting the source of records for the report.

2. Click the drop-down box for the New Object tool, located on the far-right side of the database toolbar.

3. Choose AutoReport.

FIGURE 31.2.

The print preview of a report using the AutoReport feature.

Report Header

Detail Section

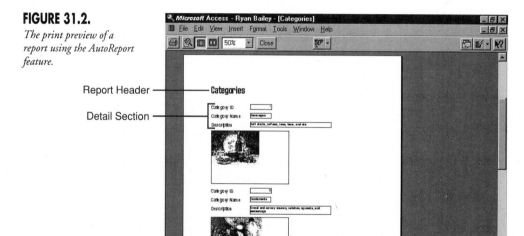

AutoReport displays the completed work in print preview. Exploring print preview will reveal how to display the report in different ways and how to change the printing properties. To make report modifications, choose the Close button to enter the design view.

The Architecture of Access Reports

The serious developer will need to know the wheres and whys of reporting to do complex publishing. As demonstrated previously, the AutoReport feature brings report publishing to beginning users. For elaborate reporting the developer needs to focus on where the data is coming from for the report and how the objects and sections of the report are meshing with each other. This section gives some insight into approaching reports from a molecular level.

How Reports Are Structured

When Access is instructed to run a report, it works with the controls that either the developer or the wizard has inserted into its sections in order to format a page of information. Notice the report sections that the wizard has generated in Figure 31.3.

FIGURE 31.3.

Design view of a columnar Access report.

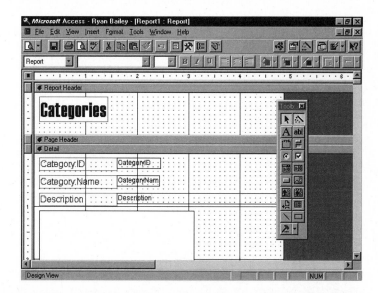

Notice that the sections begin with the Report Header and end with the Report Footer and that they then work their way inward. The following diagram represents this sectional construction:

Report Header

      Page Header

            Detail Section

      Page Footer

Report Footer

Compare the report in design view (refer to Figure 31.3) to print preview (refer to Figure 31.2); notice that the controls are printed in their corresponding sections:

- The label called Categories is in the Report Header; it appears only at the top of the first page of the report.

■ Notice that the Page Header is zero height, which means no header will appear on page two.

■ The Detail section is where the individual records get printed. The Detail section can also be thought of as where the records get "cycled."

■ Notice that there are two controls that have the word *Title* in them. One is a descriptive label and the other is a bound control that displays data from the underlying table.

■ The following section is the Page Footer; notice the text box expressions `=Now()` and `="Page " & Page & " Of " & Pages`. These expressions display the date/time and page numbering, respectively. The final section of all reports is the Report Footer.

■ The Report Footer is zero height, which means it will not display anything.

NOTE

A *control* is an element placed on forms and reports. Examples include labels, text boxes, OLE picture controls, lines, and rectangles. All controls have properties that can be set in the property sheets.

Types of Reports

Actually there is only one type of report—the type with sections that contain controls that are displayed onscreen, and ultimately on paper. However, by manipulating a report's section height and width, along with section properties and page setup, you can display a report in many creative ways. After learning the fundamentals of reporting, you will have more control with reporting. Until then, you can use the wizards Microsoft has created, which break the report creation process into five major report categories:

■ Columnar report—A report where one record on each page is displayed vertically.

■ Tabular report—A report where rows of records going across like a spreadsheet are displayed horizontally. Multicolumn reports that snake the text flow in columns is a type of tabular report.

■ Grouping report—A report where data is grouped with totals.

■ Label report—A report where columns of data are spaced out in groups (for example, mailing labels).

■ Chart report—A report that has a graph only.

NOTE

An excellent way to learn about reporting is to examine the work of others. The sample database Northwind contains sample reports that are worthy of investigation.

Establishing the Data Source for a Report

An Access report needs a recordset as its underlying source. This recordset can either be a table or a query. If report information comes from more than one table, a query will have to be built first (or the Report Wizard will have to be used). Forms and reports are identical in how they are tied to tables and queries.

TIP

The Report Wizard in this release of Access will create a query if the fields are chosen from two different tables. However, if the report is extremely complex and pulls records from multiple tables, then you should create and save a query first.

NOTE

In Access, a table and query are functionally the same: They are rows and columns of data. A report does not care if its record source is of either type—it treats them the same.

NOTE

Treat forms and reports as identical twins when working with them. All the knowledge gained from building forms can be used in building reports. There is substantial similarity in the controls and properties of both. Think of a form as the part of Access that a user views on the monitor, and a report as the part that come out of the printer.

Report Creation from the Bottom Up

This new movement to "wizardize" routine tasks in the Microsoft Office has to be put in perspective. The Report Wizards are an excellent vehicle for end users to quickly publish data and for developers to learn. Accomplished Access developers use the wizards' power when they feel it's appropriate. Most real-life reports have to follow existing models, so a wizard will not work in this situation. Use the wizards in the beginning, but try to stop using them as a crutch as soon as possible. This will force you to learn fundamental reporting skills. Creating a report from the bottom up is an excellent first step.

Preliminary Foundations

The first step is to question what fields are involved in the report. Do all the fields for the report reside in a single table, or will a query need to be created to bring these fields into one recordset? If the fields come from more than one table, can the Report Wizard handle the task, or is this situation so complex that it requires query creation? Will this report need subreports?

The second step in the creation of any report is to think toward the finished product. In other words, what will the report look like when it is finished? Taking a few minutes to sketch it on paper provides a blueprint from which to work and saves a considerable amount of time in the long run.

> **NOTE**
>
> If the report is so complex that it is based on two or more unrelated queries, a subreport might be required.

The next step is to create and test the query that underlies the upcoming report. Most reports are based on queries.

Initiating the Report Generation Process

Here are the steps for generating reports:

1. Click the Report tab of the database window.
2. Click on the New button, located on the right side of the database window.
3. In the New Report dialog box, choose a table or query on which to base the report.

There are now several choices:

- Design View—Use this option to start from scratch with a blank report.

- Report Wizard—Use this option to create a report by answering a series of questions.
- AutoReport—Use this option to create an instant columnar or tabular report.
- Chart Wizard—Use this option to construct a chart using Microsoft Graph.
- Label Wizard—Use this option to build mailing labels.

> **NOTE**
>
> It is recommended that you use one of the Report Wizards to begin a report. The wizard saves you time by doing most of the formatting and page setup. Afterwards, go into design view and customize the report.

Building a Single Table Report Using the Report Wizard

The only way to really learn reporting is to do it. The following is a step-by-step creation of a popular report style—the Grouping report. This report answers the request, "Show me all the employees of Northwind Traders grouped by title; display the employee's name, city, and phone number, sorted by last name, then first name."

> **NOTE**
>
> Realize that wizards do not have to be used to create reports. Their only purpose is to save developers time in the report creation process. Wizards can only be used with a new report; they cannot be invoked again for the same report after the report is finished.

Hands On: Using the Report Wizard

The following sections show you step by step how to use the Report Wizard.

Step 1: Select the Record Source

Click the New button while in the Report tab of the database window. Single-click the Report Wizard and choose the Employees table, which will be the underlying source of data for this report. Choose OK.

Step 2: Select the Fields

From the Employees table, which fields need to be displayed? To select fields to be on the report, use the > button to move them from the Available Fields box to the Selected Fields box. For this report select Title, FirstName, LastName, City, and HomePhone. After you complete each step, choose the Next button.

Step 3: Which Fields Will Be the Grouping Fields?

This step is the trickiest. Determine what field is repeated in the record source by which you are grouping. In this example there are many people with the title Sales Representative; therefore, double-click the field Title to declare it as the grouping field. By moving the field Title into the grouping box, this tells Access to group all the people in Sales, for example.

Step 4: Which Fields Will Sort the Data?

By default, the grouping field (Title, in this case) is sorted alphabetically. This step asks you which field or fields determine the sort order within the grouping. The grouping on Title was established in the previous step. The example we are using will sort by the last name and then the first name. To do this, first double-click on LastName, and then FirstName.

Step 5: What Look Will the Report Have?

This step of the wizard is very powerful. Access has many onscreen options for the block layout of the report. Depending on the choice, a preview of the layout is shown. In the background Access is setting numerous report options.

Step 6: What Is the Style of the Report?

In this step you pick an appropriate style. As each of the choices is clicked on, Access displays an example of the final results of the formatting. Choose the format that most closely resembles the need. Afterward, in the report design, individual settings can be changed.

> **NOTE**
>
> Remember that *all* the settings the wizard generates can be modified after the report is finished.

The Final Step

Type in an appropriate title for this report, choose whether you want to see the report in design or preview, and then choose the Finish button.

> **NOTE**
>
> Despite the time the wizard takes to compose a report, it is well worth the time to use the wizard. Manually creating the same report would take much longer.

Print Preview Unleashed!

The print preview has been completely rebuilt for Access for Windows 95. This new utility is almost indistinguishable in look and features from the print preview in Microsoft Word.

The Many Ways to View a Report

Here's a list of the various ways you can view your reports:

- Use the mouse as a magnifying glass to zoom in on and out off the report by clicking it.
- Use the toolbar's One Page and Two Page tools.
- Use the toolbar's Zoom Control drop-down box. (Unfortunately, zoom levels are not customizable—you can't specify 66%, for example.)
- Use the View menu's Zoom and Pages options.
- Right-click to bring up the shortcut menu, which contains the Zoom and Pages options, as well.

How Grouping Works in Reporting

Display the Sorting and Grouping dialog box (shown in Figure 31.4) by choosing it from the View menu. By examining the previously created Employees by Title report, you can get some clues as to what the wizard did. Notice that Title is the first entry in the box, and its property Group Header is set to Yes. This is all that is needed to initiate grouping; it establishes another section in the report. If the LastName field's property Group Header is set to Yes, then another section appears. From a sorting aspect, LastName and FirstName have been chosen, and the sort order is ascending (A–Z).

FIGURE 31.4.

The Sorting and Grouping dialog box defines the report's structure.

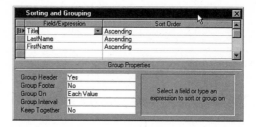

Building a Multitable Report Using the Report Wizard

This new feature of Access is one of the most exciting in this upgrade. It really shows the latitude of Access: It is a tool that is useful for everyone from complete beginners to serious developers. In previous versions of Microsoft Access, if the report was based on more than one table, a query had to be created. In this version, multitable reports can be built using the Report Wizard. Access generates a SQL statement as fields are selected from different tables. The wizard then displays previews of the various "models" of chosen data. This wizard is identical to the one in previous versions except for one difference: If a table or query is not chosen in Step 1, then an added feature is brought up that gives you the capability to pick fields from multiple tables:

1. Selecting fields from more than one table. In the Report tab of the database window, choose New. Select the choice Report Wizard and click OK. *Do not* choose a table or query as the record source. If you leave the field blank, Access invokes another step in the wizard. This hidden step allows the selection of different fields from different tables. First choose a table, and then choose the fields from the table needed. Second, choose a related table and the fields accordingly. Repeat as necessary. The tables chosen do not have to have direct relationships or relationships at all.

2. Choose the view. Access interpolates the fields and tables and provides different ways to display the information.

3. Choose the grouping. Access intelligently groups the data as it is picked from the Field list. The Priority buttons allow fields to be moved higher or lower in the grouping chain.

4. Answer the formatting and layout questions until the report is completed. By making onscreen selections, a sample preview is displayed onscreen. After a few experiments, you'll understand these layout decisions.

When the process is complete, investigate the Record Source property for this report. You will find that a SQL statement has been generated that pulls from the requested tables. By choosing the Recordsource Builder button, you will see that the query is laid out in the QBE. This

Report Wizard finds all the linking tables necessary and includes them in the query. For this step to be successful, the tables must be related.

CAUTION

If Access finds that the tables chosen in the wizard do not have a relationship, then it asks you to establish them or to choose other fields.

Multitable Reports and Relational Databases

Creating simple reports takes a knowledge of manipulating controls. Creating complex multitable reports can require a tight knowledge of the relational model of databases and the actual data in the database. The previous method is excellent for insight into the background needed for complex reports. However, complex reporting is not possible unless proper relational rules have been followed and relationships thought out. Consider the following points before you begin the report definition process:

- Are the tables normalized for minimal redundancy? Normalization in the database world means that information is not repeated in the database unless a business rule dictates differently. Assume that John Smith is a single person who has one address. This address should only occur once in the database. This address should be in the database in the Contact table one time, not multiple times in every order that John Smith makes.

- Are relationships established? This goes way back to the roots of good database design. To check the relationships, press F11 to display the database window or choose Edit | Relationships. Relating tables is not mandatory for proper report design. However, having relationships between tables is an essential part of a bulletproof application.

- Is there a need to base this query on another query? A query to Access is a recordset as a table is a recordset. You can base a query on other queries (that is, recordsets). This technique is useful when you have a series of calculations in a report or when you are trying to speed up reports that pull from multiple tables.

- Will a subreport be necessary? A subreport is literally a report within a report. Subreports can show parent/child relationships like a main form/sub form, or they simply show unrelated data from an unrelated table. Subreports are discussed later in this chapter.

- Should special functions be written to execute in the query? Many reporting problems such as complex If...Then expressions will require the writing of code (VBA). A good place to start is to look in the Access Help file for the keyword Select Case.

Customizing Reports

Forms and reports are very similar in how they manipulate controls, sections, and properties. An entire book could be written on the tricks and techniques used in form and report design. This section covers the foundations of customization, which should serve as a basis from which you can use your own creativity.

Many developers rush into report creation and assume that the customizing process will be just as intuitive as using the wizards. Unfortunately, they are often frustrated: They are tricked because 90 percent of the report is built in a few minutes, but the last 10 percent can take several hours. By studying the techniques covered in the following sections, you can drastically cut the time it takes to complete that last 10 percent. For example, you can use the power trick of automatically sizing a text box control by double-clicking one of its selection handlebars. The techniques discussed in these sections are best learned through hands-on experimentation.

Toggling Between Design View and Print Preview

Reports only have two views: design view and print preview. Previewing is split up into the actual print preview or the layout preview, a formatted sample of records. The View menu shows all views; it appears in both print preview and design view.

The shortcut for toggling between the views is to choose the Close Button in print preview to enter the design view. In design view the toolbar choices are Layout Preview and Print Preview:

■ Layout preview—This view provides a quick, formatted sample of records and gives an instant example of the formatting.

■ Print Preview—This view provides the actual formatting of *all* the records.

NOTE

From the database window, hold down the Ctrl key and double-click a report to enter design view.

Manipulating Controls

Selecting, moving, and sizing controls in order to get the desired layout can be a very tedious process. Some power features to accelerate the design process are presented in the following sections.

> **NOTE**
>
> Controls are any of the elements placed on forms or reports. Examples are text boxes, lines, and pictures.

Moving and Sizing Controls

You can move a control and its label together by placing the cursor on the border of a selected control and then dragging. (The key combinations of Ctrl+arrow keys can also be used to move the control.) You can move a control independently of its label by placing the cursor on the large black square in the left corner of the selected control and then dragging.

> **NOTE**
>
> Hold down the Ctrl key while moving a control to unenable Snap to Grid.

You can size a control by placing the cursor on one of its sizing handles and then dragging. (The key combinations of Shift+arrow keys can also be used to size the control.)

> **NOTE**
>
> To size a control automatically, double-click one of its sizing handles.

The Four Methods for Selecting Controls

When more than one control is selected, they can be manipulated, moved, sized, or deleted as a group. Here are the methods for selecting multiple controls:

- Hold down the Shift key while clicking the separate controls.
- Choose Select All from the View menu.
- Click the Reports background and drag a square around the controls to capture them as a group.
- Click either of the rulers that line the upper- or left-hand edge of the report to "shoot" and select.

FIGURE 31.5.

Dragging a square around a group of controls will select them.

Drag the pointer in the background

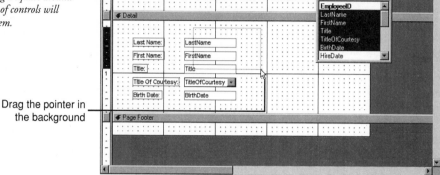

FIGURE 31.6.

Shooting the controls by clicking the ruler will select many controls at once.

Click in the ruler to select horizontally

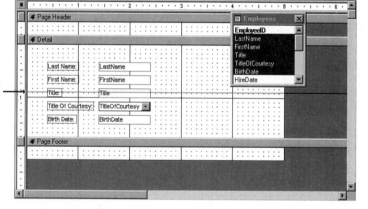

Deleting and Re-establishing Controls

To delete a control, simply select it and press the Delete key.

To re-establish a control, follow these steps:

1. Display the report's field list by choosing View | Field List.

2. Drag the field(s) off the list and onto the report. (Hold down the Ctrl key to select more than one field.)

> **NOTE**
>
> The field list displays the fields in the underlying table or query. If a field is not on the field list, it can't be shown on the report.

Creating Controls with the Toolbox

You can display the toolbox by choosing View | Toolbox or the wrench and hammer icon on the toolbar. The toolbox is a construction kit for controls. Reports generally only have label controls, text box controls, and lines for separating the two.

Follow these steps to create any type of control:

1. Display the toolbox by choosing View | Toolbox.
2. Click a tool (the Line tool, for example).
3. Drag and draw a line. (Hold down the Shift key to draw a straight line.)

Changing Control Properties

Changing control properties is the final step in manipulating a report. Everything in Access has properties. The report has properties; each control has properties; and each report section has properties. By changing a property to Yes or No, you can make changes to the entire structure of the report.

Here are four methods for displaying the Property sheet:

■ Choose the View menu; then select Properties.

■ Click the Properties tool on the toolbar.

■ Right-click a control; then choose Properties.

■ Double-click any control or section.

The most crucial report property is the Record Source property. (See Figure 31.7.) If the developer deletes the contents of this property, the report no longer has data to display. By choosing the drop-down list box of the Record Source property, the data source can be redirected to another table or query.

FIGURE 31.7.

The Record Source property defines the report's underlying recordset.

> **NOTE**
>
> To see the Help screen for any property, press F1 while the cursor is inside a property.

> **TIP**
>
> When the property sheet is open, click any element of the report to show its properties. To see the overall report properties, click the square located in the upper-left corner of the report window (where the two rulers meet).

Modifying a Report to Display One Grouping per Page

Often a page break is needed in an Access report. You can create one by setting the section property called Force New Page. Here are the steps:

1. Open the Northwind sample database.
2. Double-click the report called Summary of Sales by Year. Notice that each year gets repeated one after the other. The task is to put each year on a separate page.
3. From the View menu choose Report Design.
4. Once in the design view, click the View menu again and display the properties.
5. Click the background area of the ShippedDate Footer to display its properties.
6. Choose the All tab in the property box.
7. Change the second property down, Force New Page, to After Section. This forces a page break after this section is formatted on the report.
8. Print preview the report to see that each group (that is, each year) is on a separate page.

Making Massive Changes Using the Format Menu

The new features in the Format menu for this version include AutoFormat, Control Morphing, and some new sizing tools.

Formatting with AutoFormat

Identical in functionality to the AutoFormat feature in Word and Excel, the AutoFormat feature in Access can be very useful. If a report has been built from scratch or modified and needs a new look, then AutoFormat reformats every control.

FIGURE 31.8.
*AutoFormatting a report
can make many changes at
once and give a consistent
look.*

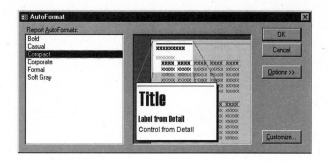

Aligning and Sizing Multiple Controls

The Format menu changes depending on the report element chosen. If several controls are selected, then the Format menu contains the option to align or size them.

TIP

Right-clicking a selected control brings up the Align option.

NOTE

Here's an aligning secret. Because labels and controls are linked to each other, aligning columns can become very frustrating. Try selecting only the labels, aligning them in the opposite direction, moving one label where the group should align, and then realigning the labels to the desired position.

Redefining the Defaults for Controls

When controls are created from the tools in the toolbox or dragged off the field list, they assume the default Size and Font properties. As a developer, you have the ability to change these defaults. With the following technique, report-developing time can be radically decreased. Here's how to redefine a text box control's default properties:

1. Set the Size, Font, and other properties as needed.
2. From the Format menu, choose Change Default.

All new text boxes for this report will now assume the new default setting.

Building a Report from Scratch and Modifying Its Controls

Creating a report from scratch is an excellent way to learn what the Report Wizards do and how to harness their power. For the casual user the following example will be helpful in the occasional report modification; for a developer it will provide insight into reporting fundamentals. An example of when you would have to rely on building from scratch is when the report needed has to resemble an existing report:

1. Initialize a blank report. In the database window select the Report tab, the New button, and then OK. A blank report based on no recordset is generated.

> **TIP**
>
> To change the Normal template for blank reports, choose Tools | Options | Forms/Reports. In the Report Template box, type in the name of a report in the database.

2. Set the record source. From the report design window select View | Properties or double-click the square box to the left of the horizontal ruler to display the report properties. Set the record Source property to the Table Categories.

3. Place the fields. Choose View | Field List to display the field list. Drag each field needed on the form into the Detail section. To drag more than one field at a time, hold down the Ctrl key and click the needed fields.

4. Arrange the fields. Using the customizing techniques discussed earlier in this chapter, move, size and change the fields inside the Detail section. Don't forget that by selecting individual controls, you can change the Font, Border, Alignment, and Size properties.

> **TIP**
>
> Using the key combination Ctrl+arrow keys moves controls in fine increments; Shift+arrow keys sizes the controls. Also, the Format menu contains useful design tools.

5. Display one record per page. Double-click the background of the Details section to show its properties. Set the Force New Page property to After Section.

6. Preview the report and fine tune. Click the Print Preview tool to see how the report will print.

Working with Subreports

A subreport is one report inserted into another, where the two underlying data sources have a relationship. A subreport is very useful in showing information from two or more tables. The premise for a main report/subreport is the same for a main form/subform. In the database there are two tables with a one-to-many relationship (also known as a *parent–child relationship*). A subreport displays the children of the parent report. Although this can be accomplished with a Grouping report, often times the situation requires the use of a subreport. Subreports are particularly useful when the parent record and multiple child records from unrelated tables need to be shown.

Creating Subreports

Subreporting can be accomplished through the Subreport Wizard or by manual construction. Use of the wizard is recommended for beginners because the concept of subreports is often confusing. To invoke the Subreport Wizard, turn on the Wizard tool in the toolbox; then click the Subreport tool and draw a box on the report. At this point, the Subreport Wizard will initiate.

> **TIP**
>
> The topic of subreports can be a complex one—online help is an excellent resource for this feature.

FIGURE 31.9.

Main reports/subreports are based on one-to-many relationships. One category can have many products.

A relationship

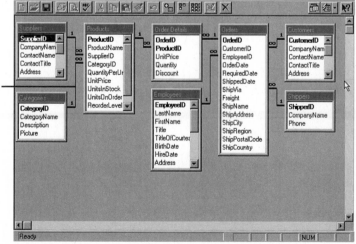

FIGURE 31.10.

A subreport showing the children of the main report.

Parent records

Child records

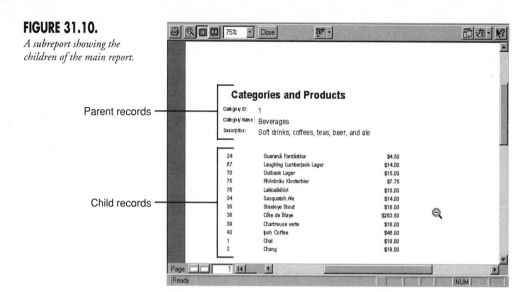

Creating a Subreport Without the Wizard

You can embed subreports in reports to display information from various tables, whether they are related or not. Although it can be confusing to beginning and advanced Office users, it can be a powerful feature.

The process of building a main report/subreport contains multiple steps:

1. Ensure that the two tables have a one-to-many relationship. In the database window, choose Edit|Relationship to investigate how the tables relate to each other. Take note of the field that links the two tables. An established relationship is not necessary for subreporting, but it's a good idea that should not be overlooked.

2. Compose and save a report based on the parent table.

3. Create and save a report based on the child table. Be sure to include the linking field in the soon-to-be subreport.

4. Open the main report in design view. Using the Subreport tool with the Wizard tool turned off, draw a rectangle where the subreport will go.

5. Display the subreport's properties; set the Source Object property to the name of the saved subreport.

6. Examine the subreport properties Link Child Fields and Link Master Field. If Access did not automatically fill in these properties, you need to set them manually.

> **CAUTION**
>
> The architecture of subreports hinges on the Link Child Fields and Link Master Fields properties. If these properties are left blank, the subreport will not work. Fortunately, Access automatically sets these properties for you if the related fields have the same name.

Building a Subreport with the Subreport Wizard

Microsoft recognized that subreports were a major headache to many users. The Access development team responded with a Subreport Wizard. The Subreport Wizard can be invoked after the main report has been created. Here's how to bring up the Subreport Wizard:

1. Click the Wizard tool on the report toolbox.
2. Click the Subreport tool.
3. Draw a rectangle on the report.
4. Answer the wizard's questions.

> **NOTE**
>
> The main report does not have to be based on records. For example, the parent record could come from a reference to a form, a global variable, a parameter query, or a field in another section of the report. Creative use of subreports can greatly extend reporting in Access.

The Many Ways to Publish a Report

With the ever-increasing need to distribute information across the Internet and across platforms, Microsoft has given us new ways to take reports out of our computers and share them with others. Publishing a report can occur in many ways. Printing on paper, which is the classic end result of a report, is now not the only choice.

Publishing on Paper

While printing the report on paper is an obvious choice, it is not the only one. By choosing File | Page Setup, the printing parameters can be changed for the printed page. Inside the Print Setup box, you will find many consistencies within the Microsoft Office, such as margin settings, printer setup, and paper orientation.

Publishing to E-mail

Reports can now be embedded into a MAPI-compliant mail package such as Microsoft Exchange. While viewing the report in print preview, click the File menu and choose Send. Three choices for formatting come up: Formatted Text (RTF), Spreadsheet (XLS), or Text Only (TXT). The next box is the Microsoft Exchange E-mail dialog box, complete with the report displayed as a ready-to-ship embedded icon.

Exporting in Another Format

If the report needs to be viewed by someone who does not have Access but has a word processor, spreadsheet, or desktop publisher, then export it in a common file format. To do this, choose File | Save As/Export. In the Save As dialog box, select To an External File; then choose OK. In the bottom of the box you can choose the format to export.

Publishing to Word or Excel Through Office Links

Using the Office Links tool, located in the middle of the toolbar, a report can be published to Word or Excel. Access opens the chosen program and transports the data to that program.

The Office Links feature of Access can start with a report in print preview and turn it into a Microsoft Word document or a Microsoft Excel spreadsheet. If you click the Office Links drop-down box and then choose Publish It with MS Word, Access opens Word and transfers the formatted text. The process is the same with Microsoft Excel.

> **NOTE**
>
> This export feature can be performed programmatically through the macro action OutputTo.

> **NOTE**
>
> Subreports are now transferred to Microsoft Word when you use the Office Links feature. This was a major limitation of the previous version. However, the transfer of some report elements, such as rectangles and lines, occasionally does not make the voyage from Access to Word.

TIP

To stretch your concept of what a report is capable of, investigate the catalog report in Northwind.

Summary

If you study the techniques and examples in this chapter, your report creation time will be greatly decreased. The tools available in Access 95 give an incredible amount of creativity in data publishing. With the new freedom in report building there will also be new frustrations. Because Access can do so much, it can become confusing. Complex reporting will be easy after you study the literature, read the help screens, investigate examples, and get lots of practical experience. As with other elements of Microsoft Office, nothing is more beneficial than hands-on experience.

Creating Access Macros

32

by Ewan Grantham

In Access you can use macros to automate tasks by building lists of actions that occur in response to events, such as a command button being clicked. You build the list in the order in which you want these actions to occur. The list can cover all the features available through the menus, as well as some that aren't. By using macros, you can automate the process of importing and exporting data, create buttons that perform complex queries, and perform other useful functions.

In Access 95 three new macro actions have been added that enhance your ability to manipulate objects as well as the appearance of applications. These new actions are shown in Table 32.1.

Table 32.1. New Access 95 macro actions.

Action	Description
Save	Saves the specified database object or the active object if a specific object is not named.
SetMenuItem	Sets the state of menu items on custom menus (including shortcut and global menus) for the active window. Items can be enabled/disabled and checked/unchecked.
ShowToolbar	Displays or hides a built-in toolbar or a custom toolbar. You can display a built-in toolbar in all Microsoft Access windows or just the view in which the toolbar is normally displayed.

In the rest of this chapter you'll learn about creating simple and complex macros, working with existing macros, associating macros with various events, and troubleshooting your macros.

Writing Access Macros

Unlike writing a VBA program, where you can be as structured or unstructured as you want, writing a macro tends to be a very regimented process. For example, look at Figure 32.1, which shows the initial screen for creating a new macro. You'll notice that each line has an Action and a Comment column. The actions from which you can select are shown in the drop-down list.

Once you choose a possible action, the arguments for that action appear in the bottom panel, as shown in Figure 32.2. Notice that the default arguments for a TransferDatabase action (import/export data to a supported database) are already filled in.

Just as there was a list of supported actions for the macro, many of the arguments for an action also have drop-down lists. Figure 32.3 shows that there are quite a few choices for a target database.

Not all the arguments contain drop-down lists, however, so you still have to be somewhat aware of what you are trying to do. But with all these lists, you can see how easy it is to build sophisticated macros quickly without being too technical.

FIGURE 32.1.

The opening screen for a new macro.

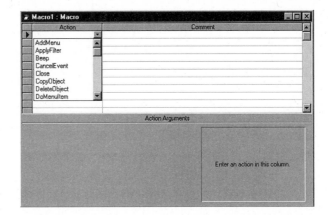

FIGURE 32.2.

Macro arguments for `TransferDatabase`.

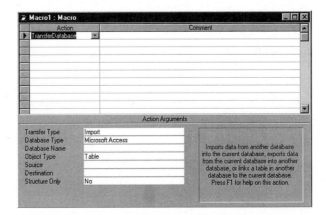

FIGURE 32.3.

The argument drop-down list.

The argument drop-down list

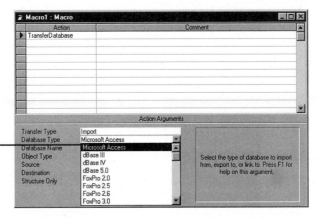

Creating a Simple Macro

To illustrate this a little more clearly, I'll show you how to create a simple macro for importing a text file. This is one way to bring in data from a larger system. To do this, you need to select the Macro tab from the database window and then select the New button. At this point your screen should show empty Action and Comment columns. (Refer to Figure 32.1.) Now go into the first Action field and click the button on the right side of the field in order to access the drop-down list. For this macro, scroll down to the TransferText option and select it. Your screen should now look like the one shown in Figure 32.4, which shows the `TransferText` action and the default arguments.

FIGURE 32.4.

The start of a macro using `TransferText`.

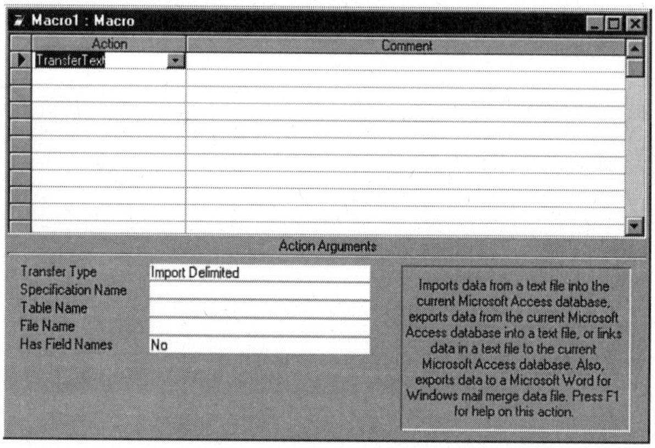

Now click the first argument (`Transfer Type`). This brings up a button you can click for a drop-down list of the different possible values for the argument. The `Specification Name` and `Has Field Names` arguments also have drop-down lists. The other two arguments (`Table Name` and `File Name`) have to be typed in. The final version of this macro might look like the example shown in Figure 32.5.

FIGURE 32.5.

The final version of the sample macro.

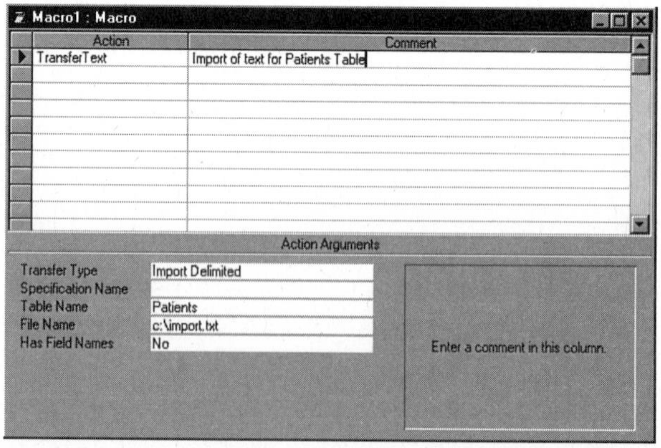

Notice that the comment has also been filled in. This is especially important in longer macros where you may have several of the same actions for different tables or forms.

Now you can exit the macro. You'll be prompted to save your changes and to name the macro. Because you can use up to 255 characters (including spaces), you should try to use a meaningful name, such as Import for Patients Table.

Part of the trick to writing macros is knowing what actions are available to you. To learn about the actions you can use, check out the online help for Access under the macros topic, or look at your Access user manual. Another way to find out more about the macro actions is to scroll through the drop-down list, select actions that look interesting, and then press the F1 key to bring up more information about that action.

Using the *SendKeys* Action

One of the more complex actions is the SendKeys action. By using SendKeys, you can enter information into an open Access dialog box or another active Windows application. An example where this action might be helpful is the import used in the sample macro. Suppose you are bringing down large amounts of data—you probably don't want to store the data uncompressed because of all the disk space it takes up. Therefore, you would want to keep the data in a zip file and then use a Windows-based Unzip program and the SendKeys action to unpack the import file when you need to use it again.

If you are sending literal text data (such as a name), it needs to be in quotation marks for most arguments (although there are exceptions). To send keystrokes that are used for commands or movements, use the special key arguments listed in Table 32.2.

Table 32.2. Special key arguments.

To Get This Key	Use This Keystroke Argument
Keyboard Characters	
Alt	%
Backspace	{BACKSPACE} or {BS} or {BKSP}
Break	{BREAK}
Caps Lock	{CAPSLOOK}
Clear	{CLEAR}
Ctrl	^
Delete	{DELETE} or {DEL}
Down arrow	{DOWN}
End	{END}

continues

Table 32.2. continued

To Get This Key	Use This Keystroke Argument
Keyboard Characters	
Enter	{ENTER} or ~
Esc	{ESCAPE} or {ESC}
Function key	{Fx} (where x is a number from 1–16)
Help	{HELP}
Home	{HOME}
Insert	{INSERT}
Left arrow	{LEFT}
Num Lock	{NUMLOCK}
Page Down	{PGDN}
Page Up	{PGUP}
Print Screen	{PRTSC}
Right arrow	{RIGHT}
Shift	+
Scroll Lock	{SCROLLLOCK}
Tab	{TAB}
Up arrow	{UP}
Reserved Characters	
Braces { or }	{{} or {}}
Brackets [or]	{[} or {]}
Caret ^	{^}
Percent %	{%}
Plus +	{+}
Tilde ~	{~}

When you press two keys in combination, such as Alt+F, specify this action as

%F

To press Alt+F, followed by P (without the Alt), use

%FP

If a key is held down while two or more keys are pressed, enclose the group of following keys in parentheses. The following example is the equivalent of Alt+D+V:

%(DV)

When you want to send the same keystroke many times, add a number specifying how many times to repeat. To move up three times, for example, use the following:

```
{UP 3}
```

Running Your Macro

There are several ways to run a macro once it's written. The first way is to select the Run button that appears when your macro is open for editing. You can also go to the menu in this case and select the Run option. You'll notice that you have the choice of Start or Single Step. You'll generally want to use Start, except when you are troubleshooting a macro.

Similarly, you can run a macro by clicking the Macro tab on the database window and then double-clicking its icon. If your macro depends on having a particular form already open, you need to open the appropriate form and then select Tools | Macro from the menu. You will then get the Run Macro dialog box shown in Figure 32.6, where you can type in or select the macro to run.

FIGURE 32.6.

The Run Macro dialog box.

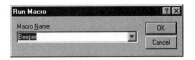

You can also have one macro run another macro by using the RunMacro action. In general, though, you'll usually run a macro as a result of a specific event occurring. Here is a list of events that will kick off a macro:

- Clicking a button
- Moving between fields
- Making changes in a record
- Opening or closing tables and forms
- Pressing a shortcut key
- Selecting a custom command from a custom menu

Most macros can be run by any of these methods; however, a particular form or record might need to be active in order for a macro to complete successfully.

Modifying Existing Macros

Once you have a macro, you might decide to make changes to it. Or you might need to modify someone else's macro to do a specific task for you. For these tasks Access provides some of the reusability of an object-oriented development environment.

Now bring up the Import for Patients Table macro you created earlier. You'll see a screen that lists all the macros available for the database. (See Figure 32.7.)

FIGURE 32.7.

A listing of macros.

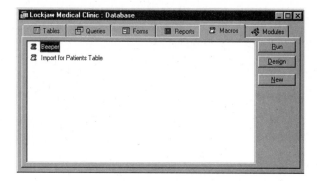

Click the icon for the macro and then click the Design button. This brings the macrosheet back up. To modify this macro, you're going to add a few steps to make the import process a little more robust. Since you are going to be doing these types of imports regularly, you'll want to first import the data into a temporary table. That way any major problems occur there, rather than possibly affecting the data in the table that the application uses. Doing it this way also allows for more flexibility in merging the data into the application table.

To make this modification, begin by clicking in the action that is already shown. Now go to the Insert menu and select Row (which should be the only available option). You should now have an empty row above the TransferText row. Click the button on the right side of the field to access the drop-down list and then select OpenQuery. Your screen should now look like the one shown in Figure 32.8.

FIGURE 32.8.

The current version of the Import for Patients Table macro.

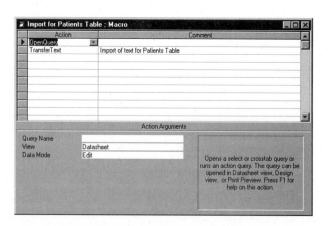

Even though you probably don't have a query by this name, type in `Empty Temp Patients` as the query name and then enter an appropriate comment. You can do this to add a number of rows at the top (or between other rows in longer macros). Next, click the `TransferText` action to bring up its argument table again. Change the table name from Patients to Temp Patients. Change the comment to reflect the change in tables as well. Again, this is something that can be done to as many lines as needed.

Finally, click the action below the TransferText row. At this point new steps can continue to be added as needed. For the purpose of this example, one more action is needed: another `OpenQuery` action, used to copy the records from the temp table to the application table. Name it Move Records from Temp Patients and add a comment. The end result is now ready to be saved. (See Figure 32.9.)

FIGURE 32.9.

The final version of the sample macro.

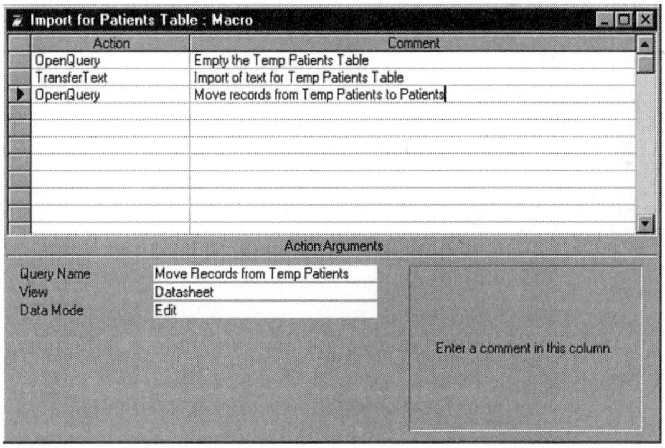

So you can modify a macro by inserting new rows, changing the arguments for current rows, and adding additional rows. With these tools you can change the actions of an existing macro, alter one macro to accomplish a similar process, or correct an error in a macro.

Adding Macros to Events

As mentioned earlier in this chapter, you'll usually associate a macro with an event. These events can occur throughout the use of an Access database. Depending on what you are trying to do, you may want a macro in a form, in a section of a form, in a report, or in a section of a report. All these options are covered in this section.

Adding Macros to Forms

To add a macro to a form, you can either create a control that you associate the macro with or edit the event properties of the form or field to call the macro. In either case, the form must be opened in design view to allow changes to be made. At the form level you edit the event properties by first clicking somewhere in the form design window (but not on the form itself). Then a right mouse click will bring up a floating menu, with one of its options being Properties.

Selecting Properties gives you a tabbed properties form like the one shown in Figure 32.10. It has all the events that are associated with the overall form.

FIGURE 32.10.

Event properties for forms.

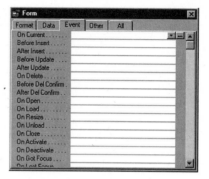

To associate your macro with one of these events, simply click the button for the drop-down list, which will show the macros that are currently available. (See Figure 32.11.) As an alternative, you can click the button with the three periods and then choose the Macro Builder option to begin building your macro directly. At the form level you can also click the Other tab and then associate a macro with the Menu Bar option.

FIGURE 32.11.

Choosing the macro for the event.

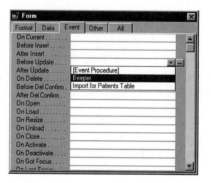

To determine which event to use, think about when you want your actions to occur and then match the macro accordingly. If you are unsure how a specific event works, click in the field for the event and then press F1 to bring up the online help for the event.

Each section of the form (Header, Detail, and Footer) has its own events. To work with these events, click in the section you want to work with and then click with the right button to bring up the floating menu. Select Properties and then click the Event tab. You'll see a group of choices like the ones shown in Figure 32.12. Notice that there are fewer options available at this level.

Finally, you can use this process to work with events at the field level. For this, click the field you want to work with and then click with the right mouse button to bring up the floating menu. Again, select Properties. The options are shown in Figure 32.13. It is important to remember that these macros are associated only at the level at which you defined them. In other words, an After Update defined at the field level will not be activated if you update a different field. So if your macro can be used by more than one field, you will want it associated with either a section or a form-level event.

FIGURE 32.12.

Events for a section of the form.

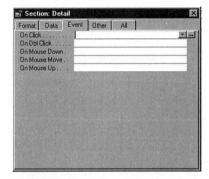

FIGURE 32.13.

Events for fields on the form.

Macros can also be associated with controls on the form. The events will vary somewhat depending on the type of control being worked with. As an example, in Figure 32.14 a command button has been defined, and a macro has been associated with one of its events. You can also associate a macro with a command button when the button is created by specifying it as a Run Macro button in the Command Button Wizard.

Like forms, controls have certain events you tend to use fairly often. You can learn more about these events by pressing the F1 key to access the online help.

Adding Macros to Reports

Reports are another area where macros can be very useful. Just like forms, reports have two levels of events. Access 95 adds some additional events to reports—my favorite is the OnNoData event, which allows you to handle empty tables more gracefully.

FIGURE 32.14.

Events for a command button on the form.

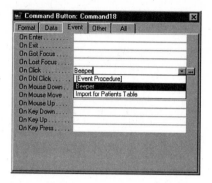

Figure 32.15 shows the events associated with the report object. Again, this is brought up by clicking in an area of the report design window that is not part of one of the report sections, right-clicking to pull up the floating menu, and then selecting the Properties option.

FIGURE 32.15.

Events for a report.

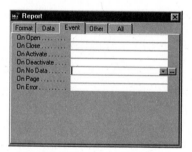

For more details on these events you can again rely on Access 95's online help to assist you in choosing the proper event for your macro.

Within a report there are also sections, and each section can have the events associated with it set up with a corresponding macro. These events are listed in Table 32.3.

Table 32.3. Report section events.

Event	Description
OnFormat	Runs a macro after Access has accumulated or calculated the data for the section but before printing the section.
OnPrint	Runs a macro after the data in a section is laid out but before printing.
OnRetreat	Runs a macro when Access returns to a previous report section during report formatting.

Troubleshooting Macros

While it is nice to think that all macros you write will run correctly the first time you code them, the reality is that sometimes they won't. Usually you'll build a simple macro, test it, get it working, and then add some more complex statements, and so on, until you get the final version of your macro. One way that you'll know that your macro isn't working is when you see the Action Failed dialog box. (See Figure 32.16.) This dialog box shows you which macro has failed, what step it was on when it failed, and the arguments that were being used for that step.

FIGURE 32.16.

The Action Failed dialog box.

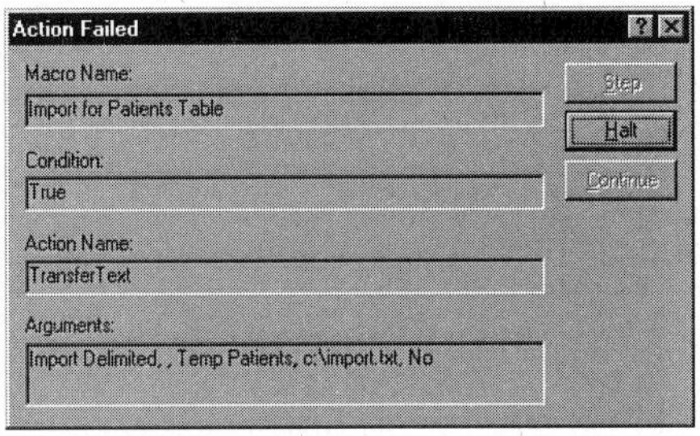

If you get the Action Failed dialog box, you'll want to jot down the macro name and the step as well as any open forms, reports, or queries. Then, select the Halt button to close the dialog box. If you don't already have the macrosheet open for the offending macro, you need to open it and see if you can figure out why that step caused the particular failure. You should examine whether what you thought should happen matched what appeared to be happening (particularly a problem with reports), whether the logic in the conditions matches what you thought you coded, and whether there was a condition in the data being analyzed that you didn't expect.

After you've looked at these items, if there is still no apparent problem, it's time to try stepping through the macro by using the Macro Single Step button. To do this, begin by opening the macro and any forms or reports that would normally be open when it runs. Then, click the Single Step button, which is to the right of the Run (!) button, to start the Single Step process. Then run the macro. As the macro goes through each step, you get a dialog box (similar to the one shown in Figure 32.17) that shows the step being executed. The information about that step is displayed in the dialog box.

You have three choices at each step: You can click Step (which is the default) to take you to the next action, click Halt to stop execution of the macro, or click Continue to run the macro from that point on without stopping until the end of the macro or an error is encountered.

Something else you can do to help in troubleshooting is to use the MsgBox action to display a message at a particular step in the macro. For example, your message can let you know if you've executed an action that you didn't think you would (in which case you should check your Condition statement) or can give you the value of a variable with which you are working.

FIGURE 32.17.

The Single Step dialog box.

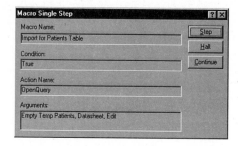

In longer macros where you might have several similar actions, you probably won't want to single-step through the macro. In this case, you'll want to use the StopMacro action to stop the macro after the point where you think the error is occurring. Then, by moving this action back and forth, you can make sure you are working on the correct action.

Once the macro has been debugged, you'll probably want to finish your macro by adding a SetWarnings action to the beginning of it with the argument Off. That way, system messages (particularly confirmations for queries) will not appear to the end user. Along the same line, you may want to add an Echo action to turn off screen updates while your macro is running. This is a good idea because, if you are switching between several forms or reports, the macro will run much faster.

Summary

In this chapter you've learned about macros—not only what they are, but also the basics of coding, modifying, and troubleshooting them. You should now be more comfortable with deciding when to use them as well as how to make sure they run when you want them to.

Using OLE and OLE Automation

33

by Ricardo Birmele

IN THIS CHAPTER

In earlier chapters you learned about OLE in general. You now know that it's a technology that enables you to make various Office applications "talk" with each other, using each other's exposed objects.

In this chapter you're going to put some of that knowledge to work. You're going to create an Access database that stores OLE objects. Then you'll incorporate OLE automation to make it easier for you to manipulate those stored OLE objects.

The Project: Clever Ideas and a Way to Remember Them

Did you ever get a really, really *good* idea. One that you just couldn't wait to tell someone about?

There are two problems with really good ideas. First, it is often hard to describe the idea to yourself well enough so that you can remember it later. Second, it is often hard to describe the idea to others well enough so that they can understand it.

The project in this chapter is a database application that enables you to easily remember and describe your clever ideas. It stores a picture and a description of an idea in an Access database. It uses OLE and OLE automation to augment Access's limited picture drawing and description writing capabilities. When you're done, you'll have an application you can build on to create even more sophisticated solutions.

You'll start with a simple table to store the data. You'll add to that a form to make your data entry easier. On that form you'll place controls that will automate your use of OLE.

Creating the Database

To create a database, follow these steps:

1. If it's not already running, start Access and open a blank database. Name it Clever Ideas. (See Figure 33.1.)
2. With the Tables tab selected, click New in the database container to create a new table. Access displays its Table Design dialog box.
3. Create a table that contains the following four fields:

Field Name	Datatype	Description
Idea Name	Text	A name for my idea
Idea Category	Text	A category for my idea
Picture	OLE object	A place to sketch my idea
Comments	OLE object	A place to describe my idea

FIGURE 33.1.

Opening a blank database.

4. Save your table, giving it the name Clever Ideas. (See Figure 33.2.)

FIGURE 33.2.

The Clever Ideas table design.

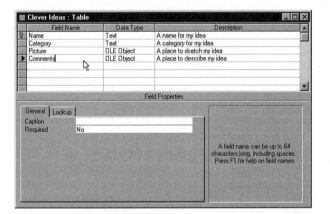

Getting to OLE Quickly

After you create this table with its OLE object fields, you can use them right away. To do so, perform the following steps:

1. Click the Table View button at the extreme left end of your table design toolbar. Access displays your table in datasheet view. (See Figure 33.3.)

FIGURE 33.3.

You can enter object data using OLE and the datasheet view.

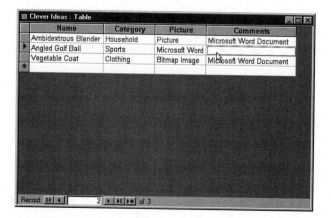

2. Because the Name field is a key field in your sample table, you'll always need to enter data into the Name field. Also, because the Name field is a text field, just move to the field and start typing the name for your idea. Enter a name there now.

3. Move your mouse cursor to the picture column and right-click on it. From the pop-up menu that appears, select Insert Object. (See Figure 33.4.) The Insert Object dialog box appears. (See Figure 33.5.)

FIGURE 33.4.

Choose Insert Object from the pop-up menu.

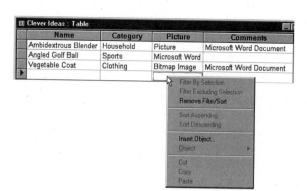

FIUGRE 33.5.

The Insert Object dialog box.

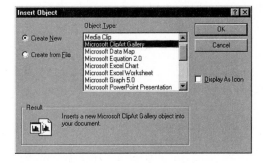

4. Choose a graphical object to insert into your picture field by moving down the Object Type list box. If you want to use clip art, Microsoft includes a ClipArt Gallery with Word for Windows. If you would rather draw something yourself, choose Paintbrush Picture or Microsoft Draw. After you make your choice, click OK.

NOTE

Microsoft WordArt is a name that can fool you. It's not a drawing program in the sense that you use lines and circles to create pictures. Instead, it's an application that enables you to manipulate text objects. For example, you can use it to easily create a fancy word logo.

I chose to use PaintBrush to sketch an idea for a combination Tesla coil and fog generator. (See Figure 33.6.) After you finish with the sketch, click on the File menu. Its Exit option will say something similar to `Exit & Return to Clever Ideas: table`. This message tells you that while you are using another application, its product will become part of your database's table. (See Figure 33.7.)

FIGURE 33.6.

A sketch in the making.

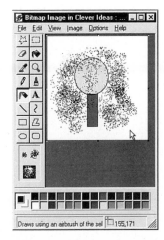

FIGURE 33.7.

Exiting this application places its output into your table.

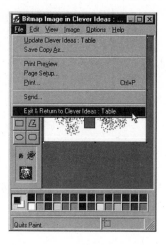

That's all there is to creating an OLE object and inserting it into your table. As you can see from Figure 33.8, Access notes the existence of the object within your file with the words Bitmap Image.

FIGURE 33.8.

OLE objects become part of your table.

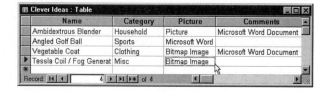

Activating Your Object In-Place

One of the more useful capabilities of OLE objects enables you to activate and edit the objects in-place. While you can't see the objects themselves in your table, you can see the type of objects they are. After the objects are in your table, you can treat them just as you would any other type of data. In other words, you can delete an OLE object, copy it, move it, or edit it.

That's where *in-place activation* (also known as *visual editing*) comes into play. To edit an OLE object that already exists in your table, perform the following steps:

1. Display your database table in datasheet form.

2. Right-click an OLE object field that contains an OLE object and choose Bitmap Image Option from the pop-up menu. (See Figure 33.9.)

3. Access displays a secondary pop-up menu that gives you the option of opening, editing, or converting the object. Click the Edit option on the secondary pop-up menu. Access calls up its server application, loads the object into that server application, and then Windows displays it for you to edit.

FIGURE 33.9.

Access "knows" the type of object pointed to by the OLE object field. It also knows what type of manipulations you can perform on it.

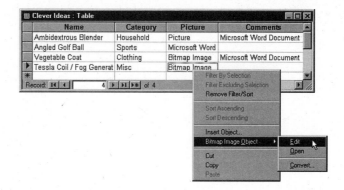

After you are done with your edits, save the newly edited object back to your database by selecting the appropriate Exit option from the object's File menu.

Creating a Form for Your Project

No Access database would be complete without a form to use for entering and viewing data. Because your database is simple—comprised of a single table—your form can be simple, too. To create a form, perform the following steps:

1. Run Access and call up the Clever Ideas database.

2. In Access's database container, click the Forms tab to make it active.

3. Click the New button to display the New Form dialog box.

4. In the New Form dialog box, make sure that the name of the Clever Ideas table appears in the drop-down list box in the lower-right corner of the dialog box. Access knows that Clever Ideas is the table from which the form object's data is supposed to come. Also make sure that Design View is selected in the large list box at the right of the dialog box. (See Figure 33.10.)

FIGURE 33.10.

New forms begin with the New Form dialog box.

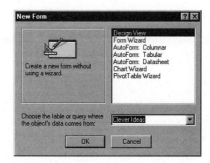

5. Click OK and Access creates a blank form. You can place in it the fields from the Clever Ideas table.

Placing Fields on the Form

With the form open in design view, you are ready to place in it fields from the Clever Ideas table. To do so, perform the following steps:

1. Referring to Figure 33.11, click the Field List button in the form design toolbar, and drag down field names from the field name box onto the form itself.

FIGURE 33.11.

A suggested form field layout.

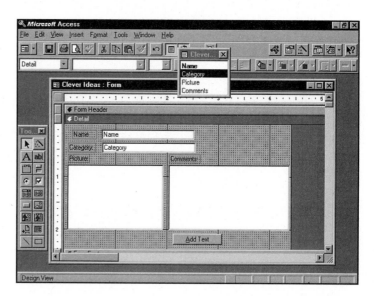

2. Add a command button just below the comments field. Later, you'll attach code to it that will enable you to use OLE automation. For now, in the Format tab in the Properties dialog box, assign the button the &Add Text caption property. In the Other tab, give the button the cmdAddText name property.

> **NOTE**
>
> When you use an ampersand (&) in a caption, Access underlines the next letter following it. Access also creates an internal link between that letter and an internal command invoked by the user pressing that letter and the Alt key. That command automatically runs the code associated with the key's Click event. This means that the user can press Alt+A or click the command button to cause it to invoke its task.

3. If the Properties dialog box isn't active, click the Properties button on the toolbar. When the form appears, select the Picture OLE object field.

4. Return your attention to the Properties dialog box and select the Format tab. In the Size Mode property at the top of the list, choose ZOOM from the drop-down list. Doing this ensures that you will see the entire picture object, regardless of its size when it is manipulated in its server application. (See Figures 33.12 and 33.13.)

FIGURE 33.12.

A clipped image may give too close a look at the object.

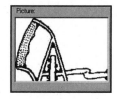

FIGURE 33.13.

Zooming provides a better view.

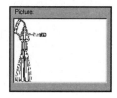

Bound and Unbound Fields

Fields on an Access form can be bound or unbound. *Bound* fields are *connected* to a field in the underlying table. They automatically display the contents of the underlying field. *Unbound fields*, on the other hand, do not display the contents of the underlying field; they display whatever you programmatically "tell" them to, such as the results of a calculation.

Because you dragged the field names to the form, they are automatically bound fields. They will display the text or OLE object contained in the corresponding field in the Clever Ideas table.

Displaying OLE Images

You now have a form. To insert an object into the Picture or Comments fields, follow these steps:

1. Select the Picture or Comments field.

2. Select Object from the Insert menu. Access displays the Insert Object dialog box you saw back in Figure 33.5.

3. Choose an object type from the list in the dialog box and click OK. Access calls up its server application, activates it, and then stores the data in the appropriate OLE object field in your Clever Ideas table.

Inserting an OLE Object Automatically

You might remember from earlier in this chapter that you can double-click an OLE object field with the table in datasheet view to display the Access Insert Object dialog box. Unfortunately, that's not true with OLE object forms. As a matter of fact, if you were to do so, you would see Access display an error dialog box similar to the one shown in Figure 33.14.

FIGURE 33.14.

Access tells you that you first have to link or embed an object before you can edit it.

One solution is to create an Access macro that is evoked whenever you double-click an empty OLE Object field. To do that for the Picture field in your Clever Ideas database, perform the following steps:

1. With the database container window active, click on its Macros tab.

2. Click the New button. Access displays a blank macro sheet.

3. Type `AutoInsertObject` in the Macro Name field. This will become the name for this macro.

4. In the Action field, select `DoMenuItem`. Access places it in the Action field.

5. Give `DoMenuItem` the following arguments:

Argument Name	Argument Parameter
Menu Bar	Form
Menu Name	Insert
Command	Object

6. Save the macro sheet as MyMacros. (See Figure 33.15.)

FIGURE 33.15.

A macro can consist of a single line.

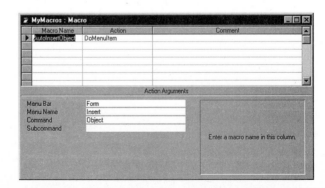

Adding the Macro to an Event

With the macro created, all you need to do is to add its name to the On Double Click event in the Clever Ideas form property sheet. To do so, perform the following steps:

1. Call up the Clever Ideas form in design view.

2. Select the picture OLE object frame. Access indicates that it is active by displaying a border and sizing handles around it.

3. With the Properties dialog box active, click on the Event tab. Access displays the contents of the Event tab.

4. Sliding your mouse cursor down to the On Dbl Click event, select MyMacros.AutoInsertObject from the drop-down list box. (See Figure 33.16.)

5. Save the form.

FIGURE 33.16.

The OnDbl Click *event is called when a user double-clicks on a control.*

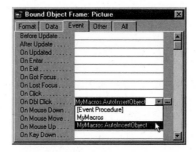

Now when you double-click the picture OLE object field, Access will automatically display its Insert Object dialog box. As you can see with the table in datasheet view, you can select an object type to insert into your field. If there's an object already in the field, Access will call up the object's server application so you can edit the object.

OLE Automation

Sometimes it's easier for your user to click a button and be presented with an specific object type. Access makes this easy with OLE automation. In your Clever Ideas form, you'll add code to the Add Text button. To do so, perform the following steps:

1. With the form in design view, select the Add Text command button.

2. In the Properties dialog box, select the On Click event on the Event tab.

3. Click the Builder button to the right of the blank field. (It's the one with an ellipsis on it.) Access displays its Choose Builder dialog box.

4. Choose the Code Builder option. Access displays its code builder form, into which you should type the following code:

```
Private Sub cmdAddText_Click()
On Error GoTo AddTextErr
Comments.Class = "Word.Document"
Comments.OLETypeAllowed = acOLEEmbedded
Comments.Action = acOLECreateEmbed
Comments.Action = acOLEActivate
AddTextErr:
    MsgBox Error$ & Chr$(13) & "Unable to embed word document"
    Resume AddText

AddText:

End Sub
```

5. Select Compile all Modules from the Run menu. Access compiles all the code modules in your application, apprising you of any errors.

6. Click the Save button on the toolbar.

Examining the Code

Take a closer look at each line of code to see what it does.

This is the necessary first line for the code subroutine:

```
Private Sub cmdAddText_Click()
```

It lets you know that this code is associated with the cmdAddText command button and is invoked by that control's Click event.

Here you provide an out in case the code runs into an error during its execution. The statement points to an embedded routine:

```
On Error GoTo AddTextErr
```

This statement sets the property that determines the type of object to be embedded into the Comments field:

```
Comments.Class = "Word.Document"
```

The words to the left of the assignment operator comprise the object's fully qualified class name. Its syntax comprises the object's server application name, a period, and the type of object that server is providing.

If you want to, you also could add another period and a version number. In this case, the result could be "Word.Document.6." If you do add another period and version number, however, that version of the server application would have to be loaded on the machine running your Access database application. In this case, this syntax avoids the version number and yields a more general usage. In other words, this way the routine simply looks for Microsoft Word for Windows, regardless of the version installed on your computer.

This indicates whether you want the object to be linked or embedded into the comments OLE object field:

```
Comments.OLETypeAllowed = acOLEEmbedded
```

If you want it to be linked, you could use the constant `acOLELinked` in place of `acOLEEmbedded`.

This statement creates a placeholder in memory for the object to be embedded:

```
Comments.Action = acOLECreateEmbed
```

This is the last step necessary to prepare for the OLE operation.

Finally you come to the statement that actually calls up the OLE server application:

```
Comments.Action = acOLEActivate
```

These three lines provide an error handling routine for this procedure:

```
AddTextErr:
    MsgBox Error$ & Chr$(13) & "Unable to embed word document"
    Resume AddText
```

All it does is advise you of the error's occurrence through a message box, and then allows the procedure to continue without "bombing out."

This line is nothing more than a way of saying "keep on going" to the computer as it works its way through this procedure:

```
AddText:
```

Every Access BASIC subroutine must end with this statement:

```
End Sub
```

Access OLE, Constantly

Access includes a number of intrinsic constants. Many of these constants are to be used specifically for OLE operations. They behave like any other programming constants you might be familiar with.

OLE Action Constants

When an OLE object "does something," it performs an action. You indicate what action it is to perform by using this syntax:

```
OLE_Object.Action = foo
```

where `foo` is one of the constants in Table 33.1.

Table 33.1. Action constants.

Constant	Action
acOLEActivate	Activates a server application
acOLEClose	Closes an OLE object
acOLECopy	Copies an OLE object to the Windows Clipboard
acOLECreateEmbed	Creates a placeholder for an embedded OLE object
acOLECreateLink	Creates a placeholder for a linked OLE object
acOLEDelete	Deletes an OLE object
acOLEFetchVerbs	Obtains the verbs available for an OLE object
acOLEInsertObjDlg	Calls up the Insert OLE Object dialog box
acOLEPaste	Pastes an OLE object from the Windows Clipboard
acOLEPasteSpecialDlg	Calls up the Paste Special dialog box
acOLEUpdate	Updates the contents of an OLE object field

OLE Application Constants

There are a number of constants you can use when manipulating OLE objects. These include the ones in Table 33.2.

Table 33.2. Application constants.

Constant	Action
acOLEActivateDoubleClick	Activates a server application when the field is double-clicked
acOLEActivateGetFocus	Activates a server application when the field gets the focus
acOLEActivateManual	Activates a server application only with direct user intervention
acOLEChanged	Determines whether an OLE object has been changed
acOLEClosed	Determines whether an OLE object has been closed
acOLECreateFromFile	Creates an OLE object from a server application file
acOLECreateNew	Programmatically creates a new OLE object
acOLEDisplayContent	Shows the contents of an OLE object
acOLEDisplayIcon	Displays an icon to represent an OLE object

Constant	Action
acOLEEither	Allows the insertion of either a linked or an embedded OLE object
acOLEEmbedded	Allows the insertion of only an embedded OLE object
acOLELinked	Allows the insertion of only a linked OLE object
acOLENone	Determines whether there is no OLE object
acOLERenamed	Determines whether an OLE object has been renamed
acOLESaved	Determines whether an OLE object has been saved since it was last modified
acOLESizeAutoSize	Automatically sets up the size of a field that is to hold an OLE object
acOLESizeClip	Formats an OLE field so that it clips the display of its OLE object
acOLESizeStretch	Formats an OLE field so that it stretches the display of its OLE object to fit the field
acOLESizeZoom	Formats an OLE field so that it zooms the size of the OLE object to fit the field
acOLEUpdateAutomatic	Automatically updates the contents of an OLE object field
acOLEUpdateFrozen	Updates an OLE object without changes
acOLEUpdateManual	Manually updates an OLE object

OLE Verb Constants

Verbs are similar to actions in that when you call them, they cause something specific to happen to an OLE object. The difference between them is that actions are more general calls, and verbs are calls that can be used only with OLE objects. (See Table 33.3.)

Table 33.3. OLE verb constants.

Constant	Action
acOLEVerbHide	Hides the server application for an embedded OLE object
acOLEVerbInPlaceActivate	Activates an embedded OLE object within the OLE object field on your form, without server application menus being available

continues

Table 33.3. continued

Constant	Action
acOLEVerbInPlaceUIActivate	Activates an embedded OLE object within the OLE object field on your form, with server application menus being available
acOLEVerbOpen	Opens a server application window and edits an OLE object
acOLEVerbPrimary	Obtains the default verb for an OLE object
acOLEVerbShow	Edits an OLE object

Summary

Now you know how to use OLE in Access. It's a fascinating and emerging technology. My best advice is to experiment, experiment, experiment. If nothing else, that process may give you new, clever ideas to store in your Clever Ideas database.

Interacting with Other Microsoft Office Products

34

by Ewan Grantham

Microsoft had a number of design goals for Access for Windows 95. One of the major goals was to make sharing data between Access and the other Office applications easier. This has been done, in part, by adding a number of functions to the OFFICE.DLL, which has common code used by all Office 95 applications for items such as the File Open dialog box, the Spell Check Wizard, and Auto Correct. Access has also been made more consistent with the other Office 95 applications with the addition of the Format Painter and the AutoFormat tools.

Changes have been made to the Office suite itself, particularly with the addition of the Office Binder, which also improves the transfer of data to and from Access, as well as builds compound documents. As part of this change, the easiest way to move data now is to select the region of data, copy or cut it, and then paste it into the target application. With Excel, Word, and Access, this data will come across properly formatted without further intervention.

One question that always comes up when looking at integrating data and/or applications is which way the integration should go. In other words, should you bring Excel data into Access, or bring the Access data into Excel. With Office 95, there is little difficulty in working with the data either way. However, you can usually figure out the best way to go by thinking about how you (or the person you're designing this for) work. If you normally do a lot of data entry or sophisticated queries, you probably want to remain in Access. If you mainly crunch numbers or do analysis of trends, then you want to stay in Excel. The application you are most comfortable working with should be your interface.

Another consideration is whether you want to actually move the data or just create a link to it. In general, if the data is to be updated often in both applications, you'll want to create a link. That way, you avoid doing a lot of imports, exports, and reconciliations. On the other hand, if you are just trying to put out some information for a report or are moving the data to a particular platform from which it will be worked on in the future, then moving the data through some form of export and import is probably your best option.

In this chapter you'll learn how to move data between Access 7 and the other Office 95 applications using somewhat more powerful methods than cut and paste. After you learn these methods, you'll know how to integrate the Office 95 tools more tightly in order to build custom solutions to your problems.

Working with Word

Access and Word tend to be used together in a business setting because of the need for tracking things such as mailing addresses (which Word doesn't do well) and creating memos and reports (which Word does do well). Because of this, there are several different methods available for sharing data between the two applications.

Using the Mail Merge Wizard

The first way to share data between the two applications is to use the Microsoft Word Mail Merge Wizard (if you are using Microsoft Word version 6.0 or later) to create a mail merge document. Once this link has been established, you can open your document in Microsoft Word at any time to print a new batch of form letters or labels using the current data in Microsoft Access. In order to set this up, you need to open the Database window and click the name of the table or query you want to export. Then, in the Tools menu, select OfficeLinks | Merge It. (See Figure 34.1.)

FIGURE 34.1.

Setting up a Merge It link from Access.

Once you've done this, the Mail Merge Wizard is automatically loaded. This wizard allows you to use an existing document or to create a new one. Figure 34.2 shows the Mail Merge Wizard.

FIGURE 34.2.

Running the Mail Merge Wizard in Access.

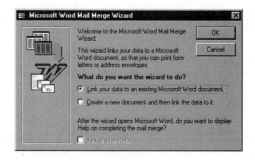

Creating a Mail Merge Data Source File

Another method of exporting Microsoft Access data, which can be used by any version of Microsoft Word, is to create a mail merge data source file. This can then be used with the mail merge feature of Word. While this method is a little more complex, it provides more flexibility because the resultant file can be sent to remote or networked users. It also allows you to archive information on who was sent what, if that is an essential part of your business.

To export to a Microsoft Word mail merge data source file from Access 7, you need to do the following:

1. Open the Database window in Access for the database with which you want to work.

2. Next, click the name of the table or query you want to export. Then in the File menu, click Save As | Export.

3. In the Save As dialog box (see Figure 34.3), click the option To an external File or Database; then click OK.

FIGURE 34.3.

The Save As/Export dialog box for a table.

4. In the Save As Type box, click Word for Windows Merge.

5. Click the arrow to the right of the Save In box and then select the drive or folder to export to.

6. In the File Name box, enter the filename or accept the default. At this point, your screen should look like the one shown in Figure 34.4.

FIGURE 34.4.

Ready to export the table to be used by MS Word.

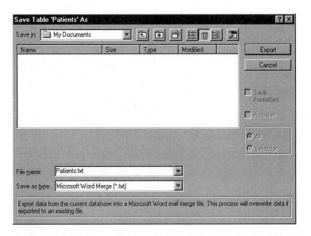

When you click the Export button, Microsoft Access creates the data source containing the field names and all the data from your table.

When you create a Word Mail Merge file, Microsoft Access uses the field names from the table or query. Because Word for Windows has different formatting rules than Access, field names longer than 20 characters are truncated, and characters other than letters, numbers, and underscores are converted to underscores.

In a Word mail merge file, the first record in the file contains the field names and is called the header row. All the other records are data rows. The field names in the header record must match the field names in the main document. If they don't match, edit the field names either in the export file (you can open this in Word for Windows) or in the main document so that they do match.

Creating a Rich Text Format File

Using a rich text format file to share data between Access and Word is very similar to the method described in the previous section, but is designed to handle the output of a datasheet, form, or report in which you want to carry the data as well as the formatting. A rich text format (RTF) file preserves formatting such as fonts, colors, and styles. RTF files can be opened with Microsoft Word (6 and 7) as well as other Windows word processing and desktop publishing programs.

To create an RTF file from Access 7, do the following:

1. In the Database window, click the name of the object you want to save. To save a selection of a datasheet, open the datasheet and select that portion of the datasheet before continuing. In Figure 34.5 a section of the NorthWind database's Customer table has been selected.

FIGURE 34.5.

A selection of customer records from the NorthWind database.

2. From the File menu, click Save As | Export.
3. In the Save As dialog box, click the option To an external File or Database; then click OK.

4. In the Save As Type box, click Rich Text Format.

5. Click the arrow to the right of the Save In box and then select the drive or folder to save to.

6. In the File Name box, enter a name for the file (or use the suggested name) and then click Export.

Figure 34.6 shows the RTF file loaded into Word 6. Notice that the filename has automatically been converted to an eight-character name for compatibility with Windows 3.*x* word processors.

FIGURE 34.6.

How Word 6 displays the Access 7 RTF file.

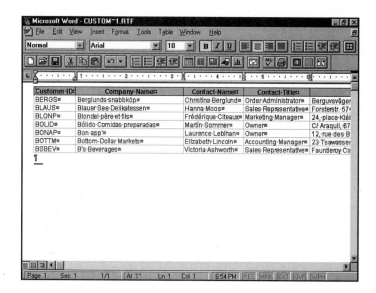

You can also use the OutputTo action in a macro to save an object in another application's file format (such as RTF). When you use this action, you specify the database object you want to output; the object doesn't have to be open or selected in the Database window. To learn more about using macros in Access, read Chapter 21, "Data-Analysis Tools and Techniques."

Creating an RTF File and Autoloading Word

By going through the process somewhat differently, you can create an RTF file as well as load Word automatically in order to start working on the file. This is particularly useful if you are building an application in which you want to use Word's text-editing capabilities without having user intervention.

Here's the process:

1. In the Database window, click the name of the table, query, form, or report you want to save and load into Microsoft Word. To save a selection of a datasheet, open the datasheet and select that portion of the datasheet before continuing.

2. From the Tools menu, select OfficeLinks | Publish It With MS Word. The output is saved as an RTF file in the folder where Access for Windows 95 is installed. Word automatically starts and opens it.

The resultant file looks exactly the same as an RTF file.

Working with Excel

The following sections explain how you can work with Excel XLS files.

Creating an Excel Spreadsheet Format (XLS) File

Creating an XLS file is similar to the technique used for saving Access data from forms, reports, and datasheets to RTF. Saving output to Microsoft Excel version 5.0 or 7.0 preserves most formatting (fonts and colors, for example) from the original Access form or report. When saving to Microsoft Excel, report group levels are saved as Microsoft Excel outline levels, while a form is saved as a table of data.

Here's the process:

1. In the Database window, click the name of the object you want to save. To save a selection of a datasheet, open the datasheet and select the portion of the datasheet that you want to export.

2. From the File menu, select Save As/Export.

3. In the Save As dialog box, click the option To an External File or Database; then click OK.

4. In the Save As Type box, click Microsoft Excel.

5. Click the arrow to the right of the Save In box and then select the drive or folder to save to.

6. In the File Name box, enter a name for the file (or use the suggested name), select the Save Formatted check box, and then click Export.

Figure 34.7 shows what the NorthWind data looks like when its loaded in Excel. Compare this to what the data looked like originally and how MS Word displayed the RTF version of the same data.

FIGURE 34.7.

How Excel displays an XLS file created in Access.

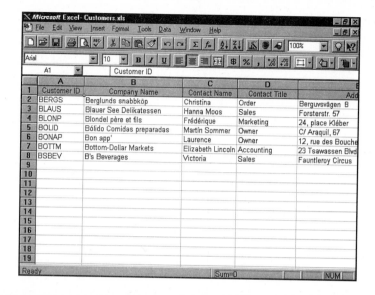

> **CAUTION**
>
> With one exception, if you export to an existing spreadsheet file, Access deletes and replaces the data in that spreadsheet. The exception occurs when you export to an Excel workbook, in which case the data is copied to the next available worksheet.

Creating an XLS File and Autoloading Excel

Just like Word, Excel can be automatically loaded with the information exported to it. Here's the process:

1. In the Database window, click the name of the table, query, form, or report you want to save and load into Microsoft Excel. To save a section of a datasheet, open the datasheet and then select that portion of the datasheet before continuing.

2. From the Tools menu, select OfficeLinks | Analyze It With MS Excel. The output is saved as a Microsoft Excel (XLS) file in the folder where Microsoft Access is installed. Microsoft Excel automatically starts and opens it.

The end result looks the same as if the file had been exported and then loaded. This method saves a couple steps and also makes it easier to integrate Excel into an overall solution.

Excel, Access, and OLE

As part of the overall philosophy of more tightly integrating the various Office 95 elements, a package called AccessLinks comes with Excel as an add-in (to Excel) in order to make working directly with Access forms and reports easier. To use the AccessLinks add-in program, you must have both Access and Excel installed. If the Access Form, Access Report, and Convert To Access commands do not appear in Excel's Data menu, you need to install the AccessLinks add-in program. Here's how to do it:

1. From the Tools menu (in Excel), click Add-ins.
2. In the Add-ins Available box, select the check box next to the add-in you want to load.

If the add-in you want to load does not appear, click Browse and then locate the add-in. If the add-in is not installed on your computer, then you should check the Excel User Manual for instructions on how to load the add-in from your original disks or CD-ROM.

In addition to looking at AccessLinks, we'll also look at other ways to link information between Excel and Access.

These solutions rely on the underlying OLE 2 technology that is part of the Office 95 (and Windows 95) architecture. OLE (which stands for *object linking* and *embedding*) has been around for a while. In the previous version of OLE (2.*x*), Access was able to work with other OLE applications, but now the latest version allows Access to be an OLE server. What this means in real terms is that Access for Windows 95 has the ability to more closely control what happens with data coming in and going out.

Using Access Forms in Excel

The first step is to create a new Access form from Excel that is built around the linkage of the spreadsheet. To do this, follow these steps:

1. From the Data menu in Excel, click Access Forms.
2. A dialog box will be loaded, as shown in Figure 34.8, for specifying information about the worksheet and on linking it to Access.

FIGURE 34.8.

The dialog box for specifying in which database to put the link and form.

3. Select either the New Database or Exiting Database option; then click OK.

4. In either case, Access is loaded with a defined link to the spreadsheet.

5. The Access Form Wizard is then loaded using the linked table with data from the spreadsheet. The wizard then guides you through building a data entry form for the Excel list. You can enter additional data into the list by clicking the Forms button, which is placed on the worksheet by the Access Form Wizard.

Be aware that there is a significant amount of time that can pass between Steps 3 and 4, and again between Steps 4 and 5. So, if it seems that nothing is going on, wait a couple minutes and see what happens before killing the process.

Once you have a form created, you may want to use the existing form again. To do so, simply click one of the cells and then click the Forms button on your worksheet. If Excel cannot find the form, the Locate Microsoft Access Form dialog box allows you to browse your folders for the MDB file that is linked with your worksheet.

Using Access Reports in Excel

Using Access reports is very similar to using the Access forms. Here's the procedure:

1. From the Data menu, click Access Reports.

2. A dialog box, like the one shown in Figure 34.8, will prompt you for the database in which to put the link and report.

3. Select either the New Database or Existing Database option; then click OK.

4. In either case, Access is loaded with a defined link to the spreadsheet.

5. The Access Report Wizard is then loaded using the linked table with data from the worksheet. It then guides you through building a report for the Excel data.

Again, be aware that there is a significant amount of time that can pass between Steps 3 and 4 and between Steps 4 and 5. So if it seems that nothing is going on, wait a couple minutes and see what happens before killing the process.

Once you have a report created, you may want to use this report again. To do so, simply click one of the cells and then click the Report button that was placed on your worksheet. If Excel cannot find the report, the Locate Microsoft Access Report dialog box allows you to browse your folders for the MDB file that is linked with your worksheet.

Linking Access Tables to Excel Data

You may have already worked with linking tables between different Access databases or between an Access database and an external database such as DB2, Oracle, or Paradox. You can also use this same process to link your table to an Excel worksheet.

To do this, begin by opening the database in which you want to create the link. Then, go to the File Menu, select Get External Data, and then select Link Tables. (See Figure 34.9.)

FIGURE 34.9.

Selecting the menu options to create a linked table.

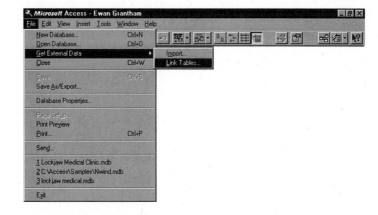

You'll then get the Link dialog box, which gives you the default option of linking to another Access database. Instead, use the drop-down list to select Microsoft Excel as the file type; then navigate through the folders to find the Excel worksheet you want. See Figure 34.10 for an example of what you will see on your screen.

FIGURE 34.10.

Specifying the worksheet to link to.

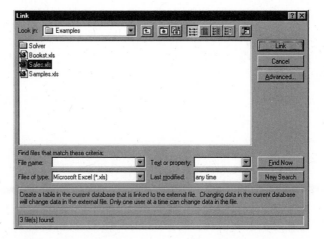

Once you click Link, the Link Spreadsheet Wizard is loaded. This wizard shows you how it interprets what it sees on your worksheet. In the example shown in Figure 34.11, some rows were added to make the worksheet more attractive (the link starts at Row 4 instead of the default Row 1). Also, because the headers are not in the top row, that option remains unselected.

FIGURE 34.11.

Working with the Link Spreadsheet Wizard.

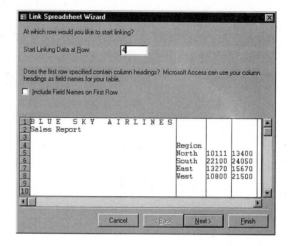

When you click the Next button, one more screen will come up. You use this screen to give your linked table a name. Either use the default name or type in a different name; then press the Finish button. If you look at a list of the tables in your database, you'll now see that one of them has a small Excel icon next to it. This indicates that it's a linked table (that is, it's linked to an Excel spreadsheet).

To remove the link, simply delete the linked table from your database. Although the link is deleted, the original worksheet remains intact.

Creating an Access Table from Excel Data

If you'll be working primarily with a set of data from Access in the future, your best option is to create an Access table from your Excel worksheet. Here's the procedure for doing this:

1. Select a cell in your worksheet list.
2. From the Data menu, click Convert To Access.
3. You now get a dialog box in which you can specify the database you want to put the new table in, or you can create a new database that will contain this table. (See Figure 34.12.)

FIGURE 34.12.

Specifying where the new table should go.

4. The Access Table Analyzer Wizard is then loaded (along with Access). This wizard guides you through the steps for permanently converting your Excel data to an Access table in a database.

Working with Pivot Table Dynamic Views

There are times when using the cross-tabulation features of a pivot table on a form would be nice (for instance, when analyzing sales patterns). With Access for Windows 95, you can now create a form that has a pivot table embedded in it, but uses the data from your Access table or query.

The process is run through the PivotTable Wizard. To get to this, you first open the database that has the table or query from which your data comes. Then, go to the Forms tab and click the New button. You'll see a number of choices in a list on the right side, but the one you want for this process is the PivotTable Wizard. Click OK and you'll see a screen like the one shown in Figure 34.13, which is the first window of the PivotTable Wizard.

FIGURE 34.13.

The opening window of the PivotTable Wizard in Access for Windows 95.

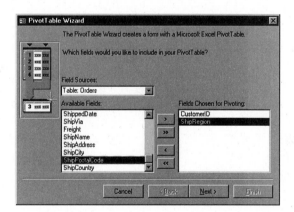

You'll notice that the table Orders is being used, and that two fields from that table have been selected. Any query or table in Access can supply one or more fields to this form. Clicking Next brings up the layout screen, which is shown in Figure 34.14, and contains a diagram of the pivot table along with the fields that can be used to build it.

The next step is to drag the fields into the right places in order to provide the answers needed. In this case, a comparison of Customers to Regions is being created; therefore, the fields are arranged so that Customer ID has been defined as the row, ShipRegion as the column, and Count of Customer ID as the result. (See Figure 34.15.)

Selecting Next brings up the final window in the PivotTable Wizard where you can make some final changes to your form before actually creating it. The default name has been changed (as you can see in Figure 34.16) to better represent what will actually be displayed on the form.

Using *(Pivot)* to indicate that this is a pivot table form is a good way to help differentiate this form from others in the database as well as to let users know that this form might be a bit slow to load.

FIGURE 34.14.

The pivot table layout window in the PivotTable Wizard.

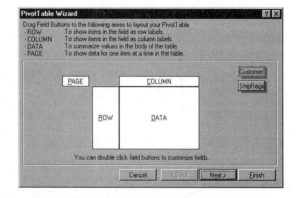

FIGURE 34.15.

The layout window with the fields arranged for the form.

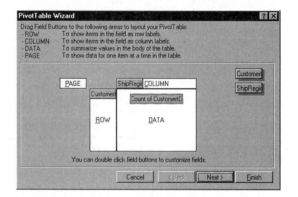

FIGURE 34.16.

The final window in the PivotTable Wizard with the recommended changes.

At this point it is a good idea to consider whether this table is really going to be a good PivotTable candidate (actually before starting would have been better, but that's not how it always works).

By using Customer ID and Region, the pivot table will have as many rows as there are customers. What you would really want to do is to summarize some of this data before comparing it (by dollar amount or by type of customer, for example). The summarization could be done in a table (if the base table is large) or through a query (for smaller tables). I bring this up because one of the problems that is often faced when using Access to get data from large corporate databases is the tendency to try to "suck an elephant through a straw."

A better pivot table example is shown in Figure 34.17, where the pivot table shows the relationship between who is doing the shipping of products in each region. Already, you can see some interesting trends, particularly for the CA region.

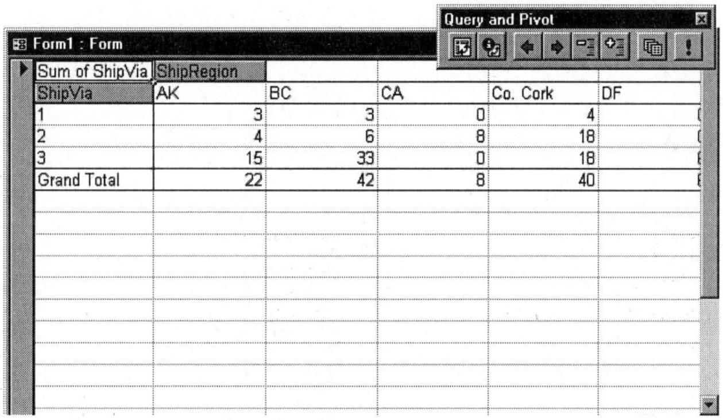

FIGURE 34.17.

The pivot table form, showing who is doing how much shipping in each region.

Having walked through this example, you should feel comfortable enough to try this feature for yourself. Think of some business questions you're interested in examining and then try using pivot table form.

Embedding and Linking Excel Worksheets in Access

The next section on Word and Access has a full walkthrough of this process, but a quick walkthrough specific to Excel is presented here. Here are the basic steps:

1. Create a field in the table that will hold your data with a type of OLE object.

2. Create a form that includes that field. If you use one of the Access Form Wizards, a bound object frame will automatically be created for you; otherwise, you'll need to do this yourself.

3. When it's time to enter data into the OLE field, use the Insert menu option and select Object.

4. Select the type of object you want (most likely Excel worksheet in this case) and the icon that represents it (if you choose to use an icon rather than always showing all the contents).

5. Either create a new worksheet or specify an old one to be embedded or linked.

6. When you are done with the Excel object, be sure to select the Close and Return To option from the File menu.

Word, Access, and OLE

When it comes to using Word and Access, the main forms of sharing data are though exports between the two products (covered earlier in the chapter) and through embedding and linking. As discussed earlier, there are times when you want to link and times when you want to embed. As a quick example of when you would want to do one or the other with Word, consider the following:

- *Link.* You have an employee table for a group of computer consultants. You want to be able to search through your database for the ones who have Access experience. Once you find them, you want to be able to print out their résumés. The résumés should be linked Word documents so that changes to the résumés will be picked up automatically.

- *Embed.* You run a publishing house and have to track chapters that are being written for books that you publish. You want to be able to call up various versions of a chapter to track changes. The chapters should be embedded so that you can lock them from further changes.

So, if you have a document that must always be available and that is fairly static, you want to embed it. If you have a document that changes often, it should probably be linked. The one thing to keep in mind if you choose to link, however, is that if the base file is moved or renamed, the link will be broken.

The first step to linking or embedding is to have a field in the table that will be storing the type of OLE object. Figure 34.18 shows a table that tracks patient visits to a medical clinic and stores the doctor's and nurse's notes for the visit.

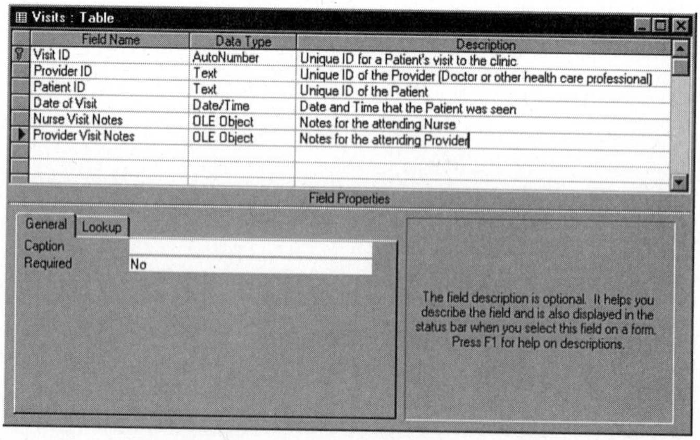

FIGURE 34.18.

An example of a table used to store some OLE data.

Now that a table has been created that can store the data, a way has to be found to get it into the table. In this case, one of the Form Wizards will be used to help you do that. Therefore, click the Forms tab in the Database window and then select New. When the next screen comes up, choose AutoForm: Columnar (remember that you could use any form type, this just happens to be my preference for this table) and then select the table (in this case, Visits). Now click OK; your screen should see look something like the one shown in Figure 34.19.

FIGURE 34.19.

The default columnar version of the form for the Visits table.

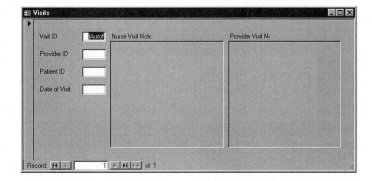

A couple problems immediately become apparent. First, the titles for the Nurse's field are cut short. More importantly, the space set aside for the linked or embedded information hardly leaves enough room to display the other fields on the table. This is because the default action is to show the contents of the OLE object fields. However, by working with the form in design mode, the Display Type property for these two fields can be changed from Content to Icon; then you can resize the fields to take up less of the screen. The drawback to this is that you have to double-click the icon to read the notes.

After cleaning up the form, it's time to run it and show how the Word document ends up as part of the record. Therefore, when you double-click the form's icon, the data for the record is typed in. Next, click inside the bound area (called a *bound object frame* in the Access documentation) and then either click again with the right mouse button or go to the Insert menu and select Object (as shown in Figure 34.20).

FIGURE 34.20.

Preparing to add Word data to the Access form.

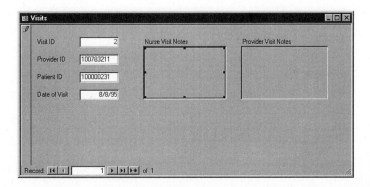

There are a number of different types of objects that could be selected, but in this case, Word document will be selected.

If the Word document is supposed to be linked, then the Create From File option must be used. To embed, the Create New option is used. If you want to embed an existing object, use Create New and then load the document into Word.

You can also change the icon that will appear for this document at this point. There is a group of icons for each of the Microsoft products. The icon choices are somewhat different for items to be linked than for embedded items.

For this example, Create New was chosen, which caused an instance of Microsoft Word to be loaded with a blank document for text entry. As much or as little can be typed in here as needed. When the text entry is finished, the Close and Return To option that will be on the Word File menu needs to be selected, as shown in Figure 34.21.

FIGURE 34.21.

Almost finished. (Note that the Close and Return To option includes the name of the form.)

Returning to the form, the Doctor's notes will be entered as a linked document, and the final version of the record will look like Figure 34.22. All that remains is to save the information and go on to the next record.

FIGURE 34.22.

A record with an embedded and a linked form.

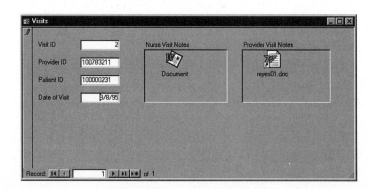

Enabling Microsoft Mail

One other way to share Access data is by sending your data through electronic mail. The information can be output as a Microsoft Excel (XLS), rich text format (RTF), or MS-DOS text (TXT) file. Here's the procedure for doing this:

1. Open the database that contains the object you want to send (if it isn't already open).
2. In the Database window, click the name of the object you want to attach. If you want to send just part of a datasheet, open the datasheet and select that portion before continuing.
3. From the File menu, select Send.
4. Click the file format you want to attach and then click OK.

Once you've clicked OK, Access opens a new mail message and attaches the output of the object in the format you've selected.

> **NOTE**
>
> If the Send command isn't available, your electronic mail program might not be installed properly. Another possibility is that it might not support messaging application programming interface (MAPI). Check your program's documentation to confirm that it supports MAPI, and if it does, try reinstalling the mail application to make the Send command available.
>
> You can use the SendObject action in a macro to attach an output file to an electronic mail message. When you use this action, you can specify the database object you want to attach, and the object doesn't have to be open or selected in the Database window.

Summary

This chapter introduces you to many of the methods available for moving data between Access and other Office 95 tools. You now have a large toolkit of solutions; you can pick the best one for your particular need the next time you have to share data with your other applications.

While drag-and-drop will work, it is not nearly as customizable as using the Mail Merge Wizard to move information into Word. And while you can do some good analysis with Excel, you can do even better analysis when you partner Excel and Access together through tools such as the PivotTable Wizard.

So when you run into a situation in which you wish your data were available in a different tool, don't just wish—exchange that data.

Putting It All Together

35

by Dwayne Gifford

One of the hardest tasks when developing an Access application is bringing it all together. You must be aware of some very important issues beforehand or they will come back to haunt you at the end of the application. Some of these issues are the actual structure of the application, making sure the data is compatible with applications that might need to use your data, and making sure you're compliant with them because you might need their data. These are only a few of the issues you will run into when you try to put the application together.

Structuring an Access Application

All applications need to be designed from somewhere. In most Access applications, they start in one of two places—either from the database up or from the interface down. The methods described in the following sections are just two of many that can be used.

Database-Up Design

When the analyst begins to work on the application, he or she works with the database architect to make sure that all database rules are followed and that the design of the application meets the application's requirements. After the design has been laid out, the database architect starts building the tables and the relationships that are required for the application. When the table layout is finished, the analyst starts building the form layouts for the client to approve. When the forms have been approved, the developers develop the forms. At this point the analyst starts the layouts for any further requirements by means of reports or other forms.

User Interface-Down Design

Starting from the interface makes it a bit more difficult to make sure the database rules and relationships are followed properly. When developing applications with Access, this is the design that is usually followed because most end users are limited in their ability to develop applications in Access. They can continue only until the form doesn't do everything they want it to do, or more users need to use it and they're running into record locks, or it's just too big for them to support. At this point the IS (information systems department) group is called in to fix the problem and add enhancements.

In almost all cases the table structure needs to be rebuilt, making sure that the database relationship is followed and making sure that all the needs of the database are met. In this type of design, the first step is to get an analyst to work with the client to get the layouts for the forms approved. After the forms have been approved, the database architect can work on rebuilding the tables for the database. The last step is for the developers to make any required changes to the forms. This design is very similar in process to the database-up design, except that in this design, there is usually already an application to work form.

Standardizing Data and Code

Very few standalone applications exist anymore, and if they're still around, some won't be for much longer. Most applications need to share data with more than one application and receive data from more than one application. When designing the application, it's important to get a database architect involved early. He can help in designing the table layouts, and he can also guide the use of other applications data. He has an understanding of where the new application might benefit from other applications' data. Also, later on, when the architect works on other applications, he can borrow data from this application. Note that it's much more productive to borrow functionality from other applications than to rebuild the functionality each time a new application is built. For example, let's say that your order entry system is outdated. A new application will take orders and will need to bill the customers. Instead of rebuilding the billing system for the new application, the new application can share its data in a format that the billing system will understand, and the billing system will bill the customers for the new application.

Creating Common Data Formats

Most companies have a set of data that is used in some way in all applications. This data, referred to as *common data*, often includes the products or goods that the company will sell or customer information. One of the biggest problems facing IS groups these days is trying to get a common format to common data. Usually after an application has been put in place, the IS group finds out that another application actually has some of the data that this application needs for the user to do his job properly. However, the format that the user sets up on the new application isn't the same as the other application, so he is required to type the data in manually. This isn't a big problem when the user is using only one application, but as time passes and cutbacks occur, he needs to use more than one application and no longer has time to update the old application. This application becomes useless in no time because it isn't up to date.

Standardizing Code for Applications

One of the biggest problems facing Access development teams is making sure they set a standard that they will follow when programming the application. This is vital because, for example, if one developer needs the ability to clear the form, he or she develops this piece of code without checking with the other developers. When a second developer needs a new form cleared, this developer programs the same code without checking with anyone. If this continues, soon each form has its own clear form function.

At the outset of the application development, it's important to assign one developer to program all common tasks. These tasks include form handling operations that aren't form specific, generic control handling, or any generic operations that aren't application specific. If another developer needs a form operation function developed, this developer needs to talk with the standard code developer. This way the code becomes portable, which means that the code is generic to any form handling or any control handling. Once it has been coded, it can be used over and over by being ported to other applications.

Naming Conventions

Another important issue about standardizing code is making sure that the developers are following the same naming conventions. This is necessary so that if a developer leaves and a new developer comes on board, this new developer can ask questions of the other developers and get good foundation questions answered. Many times I have come on board to help develop an application and no one can answer my simple questions about the other developers' code because they haven't been using the same standard. Imagine starting a new job and none of the application's developers are still around, and each form in the application uses a different naming convention. Just think how long it would take you to get an understanding of how the application works.

It's important to set the naming conventions for everything in the application. This means that you follow the same naming convention for naming the controls, forms, reports, macros, queries, and modules, as well as the variables in the VBA code. Numerous naming conventions are used in the marketplace, and technically there are no right or wrong choices, as long as the same naming convention is used throughout the application. It's important that the programmers stay consistent with this, even if it's a Friday night and they want to leave early. In this case, the naming convention is often forgotten.

Planning for Performance

One of the biggest problems an application runs into is performance. It's important to look at this early in the application's development. One way to plan for this is to make sure that the tables that will be used in queries are indexed. This helps to achieve the best available performance. Also, if at all possible avoid multiple table joins to get at required data. Both of these issues come back to proper database architecture from the start. One of the ways to improve performance is with list boxes. List boxes can be populated in three ways. The first is to use a table and reference the column or columns you wish to have shown. The second is to write the Select statement in the control source, and the third is to create a query and then reference the query from the control source. All three methods work great in their own way. Following is a list of which method to use when populating the list box, depending on how it will be used. These guidelines will help you get the ultimate performance from a form:

- If it's static data coming from one table, use the table itself and reference the columns.

- If it's static data coming from two or more tables, write a query that loads the required data.

- If it's data coming from one or more tables that need to be queried as other data changes, write the Select statement in the control source.

User Interface Guidelines

One of the biggest problems with applications that are built in Access is that they don't always follow the Windows interface guidelines. Instead of this book giving you a new guideline to follow, it's more important to emphasize the importance of following the Microsoft Windows interface guidelines. These guidelines did not change much from Windows 3.*x* to Windows NT, but with the new release of Windows 95, it's important to learn the new guidelines. The simple and sure method of following the guidelines is to make your application duplicate the look and actions of Access itself.

Running the Application

When you give the user the application, it's important to give him his own taskbar item or shortcut item to use when he wants to open the application. This is because you don't want users searching through folders on their computer trying to remember what you called the application. Also, by doing this you can add any required command-line parameters. If the program has been turned into a standalone application, it's important to remember to create a setup program for the application. The reason for this setup program is to make sure all files get placed on the user's computer in the correct folder. To turn an application into a runtime Access application, you need to use the Access ADT. The Access ADT is a package of wizards and applications that will assistant you in putting a professional look and feel into your application.

Startup Options

When a database starts up, users need to be able to get to the starting window or dialog box to work from. Access for Windows 95 has two ways to achieve this. The first method is to use the Startup dialog box, and the second is to use the AutoExec macro. Both have their own purposes, and I suggest you use both to your advantage.

The Startup Dialog Box

To open the Startup dialog box, shown in Figure 35.1, select Tools | Startup. In this dialog box are 13 items that can be set for the current database. Each item is explained in the following list:

- Application Title—This item lets you use your title instead of Microsoft Access. To add the title, click the text box and type your title for the application. This title appears as the caption for the application in the task list instead of Microsoft Access.

- Application Icon—If you know the icon filename, you can type it in or click the button to the right of the text box. This button lets you navigate your way to the icon folder. By default it shows you icon files only. To make it also show executable files, type `*.exe` in the Filename text box at the bottom and press Enter.

Whatever icon you select becomes the icon for this application, so when the application is minimized this icon appears instead of the Access icon. Also, if you tab between applications, this is the icon displayed.

FIGURE 35.1.

The Startup dialog box.

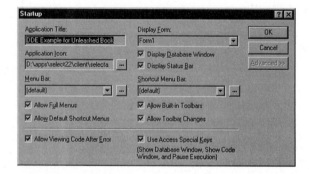

- Menu Bar—This is how you tell the database which menu bar to use as the default menu bar. If you set this, the default menus no longer run, so I suggest not setting this until you're about to release the application to the end users. If you haven't built the menu yet, click the builder button, which is located to the right of the list box. You're placed into the Menu Builder Wizard, where you can build the macro.

- Allow Full Menus—If you want to limit the menu access to the users, turn this option off.

- Allow Default Shortcut Menus—To enable the users of the database to use the default shortcut menus, select this option.

- Display Form—This is the default start form. If you want the users always to start at one form, select that form from the list box. If you have not created the startup form yet, refer to the section "Defining the Switchboard" later in this chapter. This section will help you build your startup form.

- Display Database Window—This is important because you usually don't want a user to be able to view the Database window at startup. If you turn this option off, the Database window isn't displayed at startup. If you want the Database window to be visible at startup, turn this option on.

- Display Status Bar—This option is covered in the section titled "Keeping the User Informed." I strongly suggest leaving this option on.

- Shortcut Menu Bar—To set a shortcut menu bar, select the macro from the list box that you want to run as the default shortcut menu. If you want to use a shortcut menu and haven't set it up, click the button with the three dots to the right of the list box. You're placed in the Menu Builder Wizard.

■ Allow Built-in Toolbars—If you don't want the users to be able to see the default toolbars, turn this option off.

■ Allow Toolbar Changes—If you want the user to be able to modify the toolbars, leave this option on.

The next two options are available when you click the Advanced button:

■ Allow Viewing Code After Error—By turning this option off, you can make sure that the users won't see the code if an error occurs. This option also turns the Ctrl+Break option off and on when you're running code.

■ Use Access Special Keys—Selecting this option ensures that all the shortcut keys available in Access are deactivated and no longer usable.

The AutoExec Macro

Previous versions of Access didn't have a Startup dialog box, so you needed to program a macro and name it AutoExec. The other way to run a macro at startup is to use the command-line option. To do this, you need to add /X *macro* after the database name, with *macro* being the name of the macro. To have Access run the macro when the database starts, you name the macro AutoExec. You can also perform other options with a macro that the Startup dialog box can't handle, such as finding out who the current user is.

Defining the Switchboard

One of the most important parts of developing an application is setting up the starting and ending point of an application. To help you with this, Access has a Wizard called Switchboard Manager. To open the Switchboard Manager, you need to click on Tools|Add-ins|Switchboard Manager. If the current database does not have a switchboard, the dialog box shown in Figure 35.2 is opened, which asks you whether you would like to create a switchboard.

FIGURE 35.2.

Switchboard confirmation to create the initial switchboard.

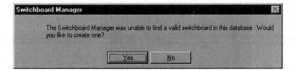

If you click No, you are returned to the database window. If you click Yes, the wizard creates a new table labeled Switchboard Items, which is made of the columns shown in Table 35.1.

Table 35.1. Columns I added to the Switchboard Items table.

Name	Description
SwitchboardID	This ID number tells the switchboard form which pane of the switchboard the current item belongs to.
ItemNumber	This is the order in which the item is to appear on the switchboard form for the current SwitchboardID.
ItemText	This is the text that will appear in the itemnumber position.
Command	This is a number between 0 and 8. For information on available commands, see Table 35.2.
Argument	This is the form name, report name, macro name, function name, or switchboard number that the command will carry out.

After the table is built, a form named SwitchBoard is created. After the form has been built, the window shown in Figure 35.3 is opened with the default switchboard of Main Switchboard already entered for you.

FIGURE 35.3.

Switchboard Manager with the default switchboard.

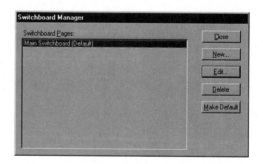

You have five options available from Figure 35.3: Close, New, Edit, Delete, and Make Default. Close ends the current Switchboard Wizard and returns you to the database window. New opens the Name the New Switchboard dialog box, which defaults to New Switchboard Page. To change the name, type in the new name of the switchboard and press Enter. If you don't want to add a new switchboard page, click the Cancel button. If you click the Delete button, you are prompted to confirm the deletion of the currently selected switchboard page. The Make Default button places the word *default* beside the currently selected switchboard page and removes the word *default* from the old default switchboard page. This tells the switchboard form which page to open first. The Edit button opens the page shown in Figure 35.4, with the switchboard defaulted to the currently selected switchboard page shown in Figure 35.3.

FIGURE 35.4.

The Edit Switchboard Page dialog box.

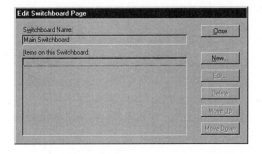

Here you are able to add, edit, and delete items for the currently selected switchboard page. As you add items, they are placed in the order in which you add them. If at any time you want to change the order, click on the item and then click either the Move down or the Move up button. These buttons move the current item one spot up or down, depending on which button you click. If this is the first time in the Edit Switchboard Page dialog box for the current page, two options are available: Close and New. The Close button returns you to the window in Figure 35.3. The New button opens the window shown in Figure 35.5.

FIGURE 35.5.

The Edit Switchboard Item dialog box.

To add a new item, follow these three steps:

1. Enter the name of the item in the Text text box.
2. Select the command from the Command list box.
3. Depending on the command you selected, you might need to select the appropriate third item. The label changes depending on the command selected. If you selected Design application or Exit application, you are not asked for the third item.

The Switchboard Manager limits you to eight command items per switchboard page and the switchboard is able to run any of the commands listed in Table 35.2.

Table 35.2. Commands available from the switchboard.

ID Number	Command Name	Command Description
1	Go to Switchboard	This command changes the current switchboard to the switchboard number that is in the argument column.

continues

Table 35.2. continued

ID Number	Command Name	Command Description
2	Open Form in Add Mode	Opens the form in the argument column in Add mode.
3	Open Form in Edit Mode	Opens the form in the argument column in Edit mode.
4	Open Report	Opens the Report that is in the Argument column.
5	Design Application	This really stands for Customize Switchboard.
6	Exit Application	Closes the current application and leaves Access still open.
7	Run Macro	Runs the macro that is in the argument column.
8	Run Code	Runs the function that is in the Argument column.

When you see a command of 0 in the table, you will also notice that it is the starting point for a new switchboard page. This tells the switchboard form what to change its caption to and where the new page starts.

NOTE

Even though the Switchboard Wizard limits you to eight command buttons, the code is already there for you to add more buttons as needed. To do this, you need to edit the switchboard form and add a new command button and label just as you did for the other eight items. Make sure that you continue the naming convention for the labels and command buttons. Then go into the Switchboard Items table and add the item manually. For an example of this, see SwitchBoard.MDB on the CD-ROM that accompanies this book. In the function FillOptions, you need to change Const conNumButtons = 8 to be Const conNumButtons = ?, depending on how many control buttons you added. After you do this, the switchboard will operate without any problems.

After you have added the items to the switchboard page, you can edit them by selecting an item from the list and clicking on the Edit button. This brings you back to the window shown in Figure 35.5, but the currently selected item information is filled in for you to edit. If you want to delete the currently selected item, click the Delete button. A delete item confirmation is displayed. Click OK to delete the item and Cancel to not delete the item and be returned to the window shown in Figure 35.4. If you want to change the name of the currently selected switchboard page, click on the Switchboard Name text box and change the name. When you close the Edit Switchboard Page dialog box and return to the Switchboard Manager, the currently selected switchboard page name is the one you typed in the Edit Switchboard Page dialog box.

> **NOTE**
>
> Remember that as you add new switchboard pages, you must add the `goto Switchboard` command to the Main page in order to get to the page, and then you must add a command item to get back to the Main page. To see an example of this, refer to the SwitchBoard.MDB sample on the CD-ROM included with this book.

When you click on a command button that performs the action `goto Switchboard`, it changes the filter on the form to use the new page instead of the old page. This, in turn, forces a reload of the form based on the new information.

The Drill-Down Concept

When you start at the top of a dataset, you see all the available records. The idea of drilling down is to get to the bottom of the dataset, where there is only one record available. There are three steps to this process. The first two steps take care of the data retrieval and requerying of the data, and the third step is to display the information retrieved:

1. Prompt the user for information that will help narrow down the number of records available.

2. If more than one record is available, repeat Step 1. Otherwise, go to Step 3.

3. When only one record is left, display this record in whatever format the user wants to see it in.

This view can be achieved in many ways, but two controls come with the ADT for Access for Windows 95 that help you achieve this type of view. They are the Data Outline control 1.1 and TreeView control.

The Way to Open a Form

There is only one way to open a form, but you can call the `openform` event two different ways: through a macro and from inside VBA code. The best of the two is from VBA code. If you add a button to a form and use the Button Wizard, you will notice that it creates the call in VBA code. As mentioned earlier, it's important to set up a standard code for all generic calls, and opening a form is a generic call. The best way to open a form is to create a standard function that opens the form. This function requires seven arguments: the form name, the type of view, the filter name, the `where` condition, the data mode, the window mode, and opening arguments. These arguments are listed in Table 35.3. The reason for these arguments is that these are the seven arguments that `Docmd.OpenForm` takes. The only mandatory parameter is the form name—the rest are optional parameters.

Table 35.3. Arguments for `Docmd.OpenForm`.

Argument	Description
FormName	A valid string of a form in the current database.
View	Any of the following constants: acNormal, acDesign, acPreview, or acFormDS. acNormal opens the form in normal mode. acDesign opens the form in design mode. acPreview opens the form in print preview. acFormDS opens the form in datasheet mode. If left blank, acNormal is assumed.
filtername	A string expression of a valid query name in the current database.
WhereCondition	A string expression made up of a valid SQL where clause without the where.
Datamode	One of the following constants: acAdd, acEdit, or acReadonly. acAdd is used to allow adding new records only. acEdit is used for editing and adding new records, and acReadonly is used to open the form in read-only mode. The default is acEdit.
WindowMode	The following constants are valid: acNormal, acHidden, acIcon, or acDialog. acNormal opens the form in normal mode; acHidden opens the form hidden; acIcon opens the form minimized; and acDialog opens the form as a dialog box.
OpenArgs	A string expression that is used to set the OpenArgs property of the form being opened.

The following example gives you an idea of what a generic open routine looks like. In the example, all parameters that the open form call can take are passed in, and all optional parameters for the open form are also optional for the subroutine:

```
Sub OpenLocalForms(stFormName, formProperty, Optional FormView As Variant,
➥Optional FormFilter As Variant, Optional FormWhere As Variant, Optional
➥formdata As Variant, Optional FormWindow As Variant, Optional formArg As
➥Variant)
    lblTypeofOpen.Caption = formProperty
DoCmd.OpenForm stFormName, FormView, FormFilter, FormWhere, formdata, FormWindow,
➥formArg
End Sub
```

In the `OpenForm` routine for the sample application, I added one extra parameter—`formProperty`. I added this parameter because the forms that I have coded have `Property Get`, `Property Let`, and `Property Set` added. This enables me to open the form with additional options. Also notice that I made all parameters except `stFormName` and `formProperty` optional parameters. The following line of code is an example of how to call the `OpenLocalForms` routine:

```
Call OpenLocalForms(stDocName, 1, , , "FilePath = 'Bob'", , 3)
```

This call opens the form that the string `stDocName` is equal to. `Property Let` is equal to 1, `FormView` is left blank, `FormFilter` is blank, `FormWhere` is set to `"FilePath = 'BOB'"`, `formdata` is left blank, and `FormWindow` is set to 3. This opens the form with only the records that met the filter you passed in. In this case, the filter is only records that have a `FilePath = Bob`. Also, the form is opened as a dialog box. By making one standard `OpenForm` routine, you can make sure that all forms are being opened the same way.

Switching Out Subforms

One of the best examples of how to switch out subforms is included in the Setup Wizard application that is shipped with Access for Windows 95 ADT. The idea of switching out the subforms is that you will have one main form that can display one subform at a time. When the user opens the main form, it displays the default subform. When the user wants to move to the next subform, you need to change the `SourceObject` property of the control for the subform. To do this you need to have some code that places the correct string value into the `SourceObject` property. The code would look something like this:

```
Me!subView.SourceObject = FormName
```

`SourceObject` is set to *FormName*. This value is the name of a form in the current database. When you're doing this, it's important to make sure that all subforms are the same size; otherwise, the main form looks different each time it changes to a new subform. The idea here is to make sure the user doesn't notice a difference as he scrolls through the subforms. Also, when you set the `SourceObject` equal to the new form, the `Load` event for this new subform is called. Before this event is completed, the `Unload` event of the old form is called if the form has an `Unload` event set up. If you want to look at the Setup Wizard, you need to open WZSTP70.MDA with the Shift key pressed. The form to start with is stp_frmSetup. When the user clicks the Next or Back button, a routine is called to switch out the subforms. Make sure you don't make any changes to this database. If you do, it isn't guaranteed to function properly and perform the setup of other programs.

Using the Tab Metaphor

In many cases, a form contains so much information that it becomes almost impossible to read, or it doesn't fit on the screen. Usually a form contains information that is important and is referred to as the main or header information. This is the information the user wants to view all the time, and the rest can be grouped together. One of the ways to group information is to use a tab metaphor. To do this, you can use the tab control that comes with the Access for Windows 95 ADT or the Sheridan Tab that comes with Visual Basic 4.0. This control gives you the ability to group information together under its own tab. When the user needs to see the information, he can click the tab. Clicking the tab brings the information into focus and causes the other data to be removed from focus. Figure 35.6 shows what a tab control looks like and how it can group the information together and still make sure the header information is always visible.

FIGURE 35.6.

A form with a tab control being used.

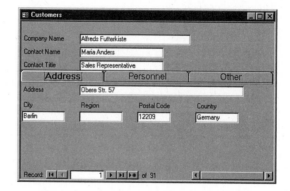

This form includes tabs for Address, Personnel, and Other. Each of these tabs contains information relating to the tab name. For example, if you want to find out personnel information on the customer, you simply click the Personnel tab.

A Generic Form for Printing Reports

One of the most common mistakes in any application is enabling the user to print from the currently active form. This is impossible to support and fix if something goes wrong. The best idea is to have one common place to do all the printing from. This enables you to keep all the code required for printing in one common location. Also, imagine if you needed to fix one of the reports that isn't printing properly. If you had the ability to print from everywhere, you would need to take out of service not only this report but also the form. This definitely isn't a good idea. Figure 35.7 shows an example of a generic form for printing.

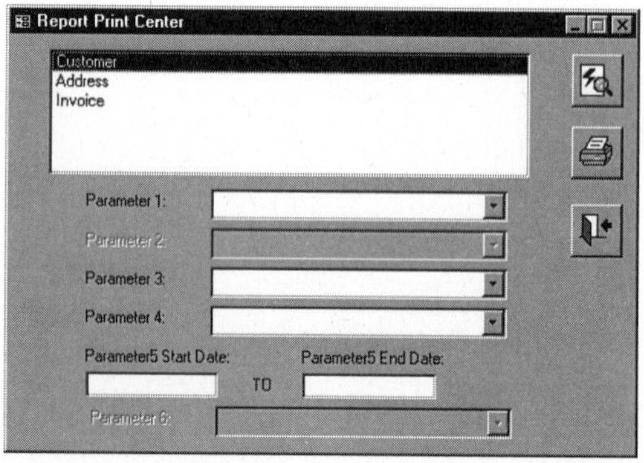

FIGURE 35.7.

A generic form for printing.

When you set up the printing form, it's important to remember to set the following options:

Option	How to Set It
Views Allowed	Set to Form
Allow Edits	Set to Yes
Allow Deletions	Set to No
Allow Additions	Set to No
Scroll Bars	Set to Neither
Record Selectors	Set to No
Navigation Buttons	Set to No
Auto Center	Set to Yes
Border style	Set to Thin. This ensures that the user can't adjust the size of the form.
Min Max Buttons	Set to Min Enabled. This ensures again that the user can't make changes to the form.

These are only suggestions, but it's important to remember that when you set up a generic form, no user should be able to make changes to the form. Another idea to use when working with generic report printing forms is to use a table that contains a list of parameters used to populate the report form. This table contains a column for report names and one for each available parameter on the report form. These parameter columns are of type Yes/No. For each control or group of controls on the form, there is a matching parameter column in the table. Thus, if you have 20 possible parameters for any given report, there should be 20 parameter columns in the table. Therefore, by having a Report Name column, you can populate the Report Option list box from this column in the report table. Table 35.4 is a sample table outline for the report table.

Table 35.4. A report table sample.

Column Name	Column Type	Default
Report	Name String, FieldSize 35, Description name of report to appear in list box	
Parameter1	Yes/No	No
Parameter2	Yes/No	No
Parameter3	Yes/No	No

continues

Table 35.4. continued

Column Name	Column Type	Default
Parameter4	Yes/No	No
Parameter5	Yes/No	No
Parameter6	Yes/No	No

As you can see in Figure 35.7, I have grouped the start date and end date to one parameter (Parameter5) so that if a start date is required an end date is also required. Remember that this is only a suggestion, but it makes support much easier. It also makes the development of reports faster because if you need a new report created you know what parameters are already available.

Referring to Controls from a Query

To have a query use a parameter that is based on a form, you need to create the query and in the Criteria section add something like the following:

```
=forms![Customers]![CompanyName]
```

The form tells the query to look at the form collection. The Customers form provides the form name, and the Company Name form tells it what control to reference. Remember to use the preceding syntax, because if you start using Screen.Activeform and not the actual form name, you could run into invalid results because the form you want lost the focus before this call. This means that you're referring to the wrong control. If the form happens to be in design mode when you make the call, Null is assumed.

Keeping the User Informed

It's very important to keep users informed about what you're doing. There are two ways to do this: through a macro or through VBA code. To do this through a macro you need to add the following line to your macro: Action set to Echo, Echo On to No. The text that you want to display is typed in Status Bar Text. In VBA code, the following line would need to be added: DoCmd.Echo False, "Text to be placed on the Status Bar." By adding either of these, you place the text of the message in the status bar at the bottom of the screen. In some cases this isn't enough information to be passed on, or it might be something where the user should be able to cancel out of the operation. To accomplish this you need to open a dialog form. This dialog form is similar to a MsgBox dialog box, but you need to pass information to it throughout the transaction. Figure 35.8 is a sample dialog box that gives the users information on the operation and gives them the option to cancel the operation by clicking the Cancel button.

FIGURE 35.8.

A generic status form.

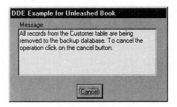

When you set up this form, it's important to remember to set a few of the form options. The following list is in addition to the list setting up the print form:

Option	How to Set It
Allow Edits	Set to No
Auto Modal	Set to Yes
Border style	Set to Dialog
Min Max Buttons	Set to None
Modal	Set to Yes
Control Box	Set to No

These extra options are set to make sure the user is unable to do other work while this critical operation is occurring and to make sure that he can't minimize or close the form while it's still working. The only ways out of this form are to cancel the operation or to let it finish, at which time the Cancel button changes to an OK button and the user knows the task has completed. Figure 35.8 includes a text box for the information you wish to display to the users and the Cancel button. You could also add a progress indicator bar to this form. However, when you do this you will find yourself programming this functionality instead of making the application function correctly.

Exiting the Application on the Close of the Main Form

It's important that when the user closes the main form, the application also closes. It's also important to remember that if the user is running Access and not a runtime version of Access, you shouldn't close Access on the close of the main form. There are two ways to accomplish this. The first is to create a macro that is called whenever a Close button is selected. The second is to create a VBA function that receives a parameter of *FormName*. Whether the form closes and activates the main form or closes the application depends on the form. Following is an example of VBA code that closes a form or the application depending on who calls the function:

```
Sub CloseForm(strName As String)
    If strName = "Main" Then
        DoCmd.SelectObject acForm, strName
        CloseCurrentDatabase
```

```
    Else
        DoCmd.SelectObject acForm, strName
        DoCmd.Close
        DoCmd.OpenForm "Main"
    End If
End Sub
```

To have the form call this subroutine, all that is required is a `Call closeform(me.name)`. It compares the name passed in to the word main. If the form that placed the call is main, the application is closed, leaving Access open. Otherwise, the calling form is closed and the main form is opened.

One Way to Program in Access

When you start programming in Access, in most cases you start looking for the fastest way to get it done. In most cases this is to use the macro language. This is okay as you learn, but it limits your application's capabilities as you start requiring more complicated applications. The next step in development is to use the basic VBA code that is available to you. For more information on VBA code, refer to Chapter 53, "Getting Started with VBA" and Chapter 54, "Advanced VBA Programming." After spending some time using VBA code, you will want to start using VBA code to its fullest. The only way to achieve this is to have a full Understanding of Jet, data access objects (DAO), and Microsoft Access objects (MAO). MAOs offer the programmer and application developer some very powerful features. If you stay with the macro environment you can still get to these commands, but you're limited. For example, `Runsql` in the macro window enables you to use only 256 characters. If you were making the same call `Docmd.RunSQL`, you could use 32,768 characters.

Summary

When you develop an Access application, you should always take your applications to the next level, making them look and feel more professional.

Using Access in the Client/Server Model

This chapter explains the client/server model for database applications and how to use Access as part of a client/server database solution. It contains hints on designing the application and optimizing its performance, as well as special considerations for working with particular database servers.

Client/Server Defined

Client/server architecture, illustrated in Figure 36.1, is a form of distributed processing in which one process (the client) initiates a transaction by sending a message to another process (the server). Client/server architecture is the basis of many modern operating systems and software applications. In operating systems such as Windows 95, Windows NT, and UNIX, separate processes are assigned to system services. When a program needs a service, such as when it's printing a document, a message is sent from one program to another. This architecture isolates services from one another and simplifies application development by sharing common services among programs. This is why you need not concern yourself with setting up Access 95 when a new printer is installed. When the printer is installed in Windows, it's automatically available to Access (and to all other Windows programs).

FIGURE 36.1.

Client/server architecture.

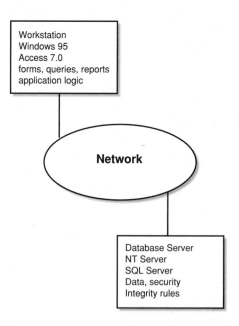

Microsoft Exchange is an example of a client/server application for electronic mail and group communications. The client portion is the exchange inbox that resides on each workstation. It enables users to read their mail, compose new messages, and move their messages among folders even if they aren't connected to other users on a network. The server portion is the exchange server or another mail server (for example, Microsoft Mail). When a workstation connects to the network (through either a local area network connection or dial-up networking), the client communicates with the server and transmits and receives new messages. Schedule+ works in a similar fashion as a client/server application.

In a client/server database, the client (also called the front end) is the program that runs on a user's workstation. The server (sometimes called the database engine or back end), which might be running on another computer on the network, stores data and processes requests for information sent by clients. For instance, Access might be used as a front end to incorporate data in a Microsoft SQL Server database running on a DEC Alpha or other computer.

Using Access as a client/server front end is different from running Access on a file server. The file server merely makes a database file available to several workstations so that they can share data. When a user needs the data, the file is read from the file server hard disk and is sent to the workstation across the network. The workstation must perform all the processing to select rows from the table or join multiple tables. The file server doesn't really help with the processing. In a client/server database, on the other hand, the workstation submits a request for information in the form of a SQL query. The database server processes the query and returns only the rows that the user requested. The database server assists with processing and greatly reduces the network traffic and the work that the workstation must do. After the data reaches the workstation, Access simply formats the data and displays it for the user.

You could even argue that Access is inherently client/server, in that front-end functions are separated from data-management functions handled by the Jet engine. The Jet engine is essentially the native database server for Access. Fortunately, Access can also connect to other database engines. For the purpose of this chapter, I will address only the use of Access as a front end to a database engine.

If this is your first client/server project, you might want additional sources for general information on client/server architecture. You will find much more information on client/server concepts in *Client/Server Computing,* Second Edition (Sams Publishing, 1994). Also, many magazines cover client/server databases, including *DBMS, Data Based Advisor, Database Programming and Design, Software Magazine,* and *Client/Server.*

When to Use a Client/Server Database

Why would you want to use Access as a front end? When would you need to go to client/server architecture for a database application? Several requirements might force you to go client/server.

The most common situation for switching from Access standalone or on a LAN to client/server is when you have large data requirements or large numbers of concurrent users. Although Access performs well with a few hundred or a few thousand records in a table, it tends to bog down with hundreds of thousands or millions of records. Imagine, if you will, a database containing the income-tax returns of all U.S. residents for the past 10 years. This database wouldn't fit well on the laptop computer I'm using to write this chapter, or even on a high-performance file server. Client/server solves this problem because I can run the database server on any computer, not just on a PC. I could have terabytes of storage and dozens of processors on a mainframe or even a supercomputer. Client/server architecture allows enterprisewide access to your database.

A related reason to switch to client/server architecture is to improve the speed of searches and other database transactions. Database server software is highly optimized and can provide much faster processing than the Jet engine, which is suitable for small and medium-sized databases.

Database engines such as Microsoft SQL Server, Sybase SQL Server, Informix, CA-Ingres, and DB/2 provide better security and reliability than Access alone can offer. Some of these products have special support for multiprocessor servers, whereas others have highly efficient optimization algorithms, and often they offer special functions Access is lacking.

Client/server architecture is useful in a heterogeneous computing environment. Imagine that your organization has 500 people with PCs, 75 with UNIX workstations, and 25 with Macintoshes. Access isn't available for UNIX or the Mac, but client/server offers you a way out of this problem. Other UNIX and Mac packages can access data on the database server. You therefore can have all the computer users in the company sharing the same corporate data, reducing redundant data entry.

A final reason to switch to client/server is to provide friendlier, more responsive tools to look at data in mainframe systems. The increased productivity of Windows applications compared to their terminal-based predecessors, combined with the prospect of cost savings, is driving the trend toward downsizing mainframe applications (legacy systems). A legacy system is a system that was built long ago, and the people who built it might not even be at your organization any longer. Still, the data in the system is valuable, and you can't give up the old system overnight. With Access, you can allow users to read and write legacy data, and potentially move the application to a larger or smaller database server as needed.

Access as a Front End

Access 95 works as a front end in a client/server database by means of linked tables. These were called "attached" tables in Access 1.0 and 2.0. Data in a linked table isn't actually stored in the Access database. Instead, the Access table contains a pointer to the location where the information is physically stored, such as a dBASE file or an Oracle database table. See Table 36.1.

Table 36.1. Layers in an Access client/server application.

Layer	Function
Access User Interface (Database windows)	Displays on user workstation; interacts with user.
Jet Engine	Fetches data requested by Access; enforces referential integrity and validation rules.

Layer	Function
ODBC Driver Manager	Links from Access to all ODBC data sources.
ODBC Driver (SQL Server, Oracle, other)	Links from ODBC Driver Manager to a particular data source; may be provided by a third party.
Network Library (NetLib, SQL*Net)	Network communications software that allows data to be exchanged between client and server.
Database Server (SQL Server, Oracle, Informix)	Software that processes requests for data and sends resulting rows or messages to client.

Built-in and ODBC Drivers

Access can link to other database formats through either built-in drivers or Open Database Connectivity (ODBC). Built-in drivers are provided for other Microsoft Access databases; FoxPro files (versions 2.0, 2.5, 2.6, and 3.0); Paradox files (3.*x*, 4.*x*, and 5.0); dBASE III, IV, and V files; Microsoft Excel files; Lotus 1-2-3 files; fixed-length text; and variable-length text. Access can also export to Word for Windows mail merge, although there is no driver for Access to read Word files directly. The built-in drivers enable you to import, export, and link to these foreign data files.

The typical Access installation doesn't include all the drivers for linking data, not even the ODBC drivers. To include the drivers, run the Setup utility and choose Add/Remove. (Or, when you first install Access, choose Custom installation and select all the drivers.) The dialog box shown in Figure 36.2 appears. Select Data Access and then click the Change Option button. The Data Access options are displayed, as shown in Figure 36.3.

FIGURE 36.2.

Selecting the Data Access option.

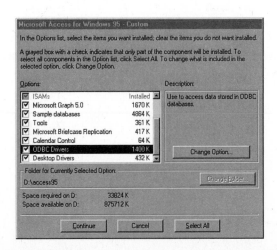

FIGURE 36.3.

The Data Access options.

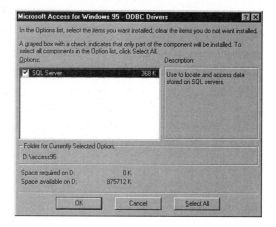

ODBC as a Translator

In addition to the built-in drivers, the standard that makes it easy to link Access to SQL and other data sources is open database connectivity (ODBC). This is the most popular standard for sharing data files in Windows. ODBC can connect an ODBC client to both relational and nonrelational data sources.

Access can act as an ODBC client or an ODBC server. The focus in this chapter is on Access as an ODBC client, but other applications (such as Excel and Crystal Reports) can serve as front ends to Access databases.

ODBC needs a driver for each data source. ODBC drivers are usually provided by the vendor of the server. The driver must be 32-bit and compliant with ODBC 1.0.

ODBC doesn't include its own networking capability, so you need a network library in addition to the ODBC driver for your server. For instance, you might use the Oracle SQL*Net, Named Pipe Net-Libraries, DECNET, or FTP 2.2 with Net-Library. If you encounter problems with your net library, you should search Microsoft TechNet for your net library. You might need patches or upgrades to the net library to work with Access 95. Microsoft TechNet is a great source of technical information on all Microsoft products, especially for advanced topics. TechNet members receive a monthly CD-ROM with the latest information and several other benefits. To enroll, call Microsoft at (800) 344-2121, extension 115.

Creating SQL Pass-Through Queries

Pass-through queries are a powerful feature introduced in Access 2.0. They enable you to send SQL statements to the server just as you enter them, without being parsed or generated by Access. With pass-through SQL, you can take advantage of server-specific features such as SQL extensions or stored procedures.

Access pass-through queries don't use the graphical design features of the Query window. This means that you receive no help from Access in formulating the query or checking its syntax. You therefore might save time and reduce errors by following these steps instead:

1. Write the query in whatever interactive query tool your server provides. The query tool will check the query syntax and perhaps assist with table and field names.

2. Fully test the query in its native environment.

3. Copy the query into an Access pass-through query or an Access module using cut and paste.

Steps for Creating a SQL Pass-Through Query

Here are the steps in Access to create a pass-through query:

1. Click the Queries tab in the Database window, and then click New.

2. Click New Query. There is no Query Wizard for SQL pass-through queries, so choose Design View.

3. Close the Show Table dialog box without choosing a table or query.

4. Choose Query | SQL Specific | Pass-Through.

5. The Query Properties sheet (see Figure 36.4) is normally displayed at this point. If you don't see the Query Properties sheet, display it by choosing View | Properties or clicking the View Properties tool on the toolbar.

6. Enter the ODBC connection string in the `ODBC Connect Str` property.

Be careful not to switch the query type of a pass-through query, because you will lose the SQL you have been typing.

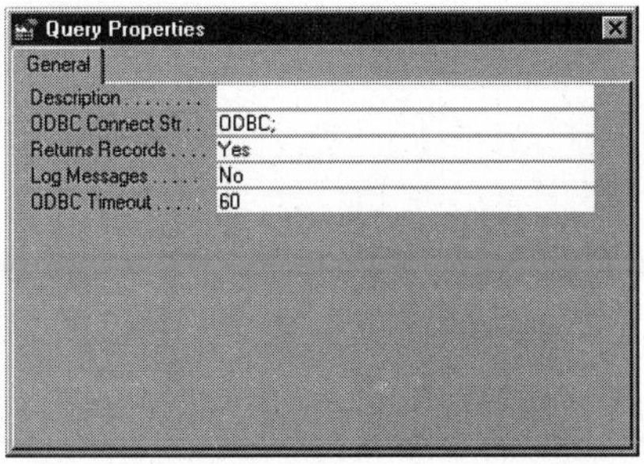

FIGURE 36.4.

The Properties window in a SQL pass-through query.

Pass-Through Query Properties

The properties of pass-through queries are different from those of Access select queries:

Property	Description
Returns Records	Set to yes if the query will return rows; set to no for other queries.
Log Messages	Set to yes to create a table to store messages returned by the server.
ODBC Timeout	Set the time in seconds before the query times out.

ODBC Connection String Builder

In SQL pass-through queries, Access provides help for constructing an ODBC connection string so that you don't have to write it from scratch.

The ODBC connection string builder is available only in pass-through queries; it's not available in the Source Connect Str property in the Query Properties window. Note that the ODBC connection string builder isn't installed as a standard option. You must run Setup, choose Add/Remove, and then check the Developer Tools option.

Click the button with the three dots next to the ODBC Connect Str property. Access then assists you with building a connection string. A dialog box appears with a list of the installed ODBC data sources, as shown in Figure 36.5. For this example, I am using the Pubs database that comes with Microsoft SQL Server.

FIGURE 36.5.

The ODBC connection string builder.

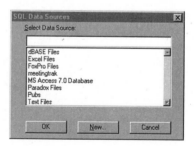

After you specify the data source, you might be prompted for a username and password. (See Figure 36.6.) If you wish, you can store the password in the connection string so that you won't be prompted for it again when you run the query. (See Figure 36.7.)

Now that you have answered all the questions posed by the ODBC connection string builder, a finished ODBC connection string is entered in the connection string property. (See Figure 36.8.)

To see whether your connection is working, write a simple query in SQL. For instance, a query of SELECT * FROM AUTHORS will yield the result shown in Figure 36.9. This proves that the ODBC connection is working and that you are retrieving rows from the server.

FIGURE 36.6.

The username and password dialog for the ODBC connection string builder.

FIGURE 36.7.

Choosing whether to store the password in the connection string.

FIGURE 36.8.

The completed ODBC connection string.

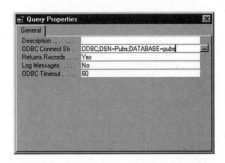

FIGURE 36.9.

*The result of SELECT * FROM AUTHORS.*

au_id	au_lname	au_fname	phone	address	
172-32-1176	White	Johnson	408 496-7223	10932 Bigge Rd	Menl
213-46-8915	Green	Marjorie	415 986-7020	309 63rd St. #4	Oakla
238-95-7766	Carson	Cheryl	415 548-7723	589 Darwin Ln.	Berke
267-41-2394	O'Leary	Michael	408 286-2428	22 Cleveland Av	San J
274-80-9391	Straight	Dean	415 834-2919	5420 College Av	Oakla
341-22-1782	Smith	Meander	913 843-0462	10 Mississippi D	Lawre
409-56-7008	Bennet	Abraham	415 658-9932	6223 Bateman S	Berke
427-17-2319	Dull	Ann	415 836-7128	3410 Blonde St.	Palo
472-27-2349	Gringlesby	Burt	707 938-6445	PO Box 792	Covel
486-29-1786	Locksley	Charlene	415 585-4620	18 Broadway Av	San F
527-72-3246	Greene	Morningstar	615 297-2723	22 Graybar Hou	Nash
648-92-1872	Blotchet-Halls	Reginald	503 745-6402	55 Hillsdale Bl.	Corva
672-71-3249	Yokomoto	Akiko	415 935-4228	3 Silver Ct.	Waln

Record: 1 of 23

If you don't enter an ODBC connection string when you write the query and you don't use the ODBC connection string builder, you will be prompted to choose a data source each time you run the query.

Saving the Results of a Pass-Through Query

You might want to store the results of a pass-through query in an Access table for later use. A simple way to accomplish this task is to create a make table query based on the pass-through query, including all the fields you want to store in the local table. Each time you run the make table query, it will create a new table that stores the results of the pass-through query. If you don't want to continue duplicating this data in new tables, you can use an update query instead or delete the table before the make table query is run.

For this example, you'll run a stored procedure called SP_HELP that is included with SQL Server. This procedure returns a list of objects that are contained in the database.

1. Start by defining a pass-through query, as described earlier. In the SQL window, type SP_HELP.

2. Run the query to see which rows are returned. The result should look something like Figure 36.10. You will be prompted to choose the data source and enter your name and password.

FIGURE 36.10.

The results of running the SP_HELP stored procedure.

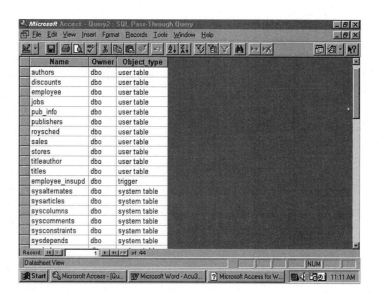

3. Close the query and save it as qrySP_HELP.

4. Create a new query and choose qrySP_HELP as the input for the query in the Show Table dialog box.

5. Change the query type to make it a make table query.

6. In the Make Table dialog box, enter tblSP_HELP as the table name and click OK.

7. Double-click the asterisk (*) in the qrySP_HELP data model to select all the fields from the query. The query will look like Figure 36.11.

8. Run the query.

FIGURE 36.11.

A make table query based on the SP_HELP stored procedure.

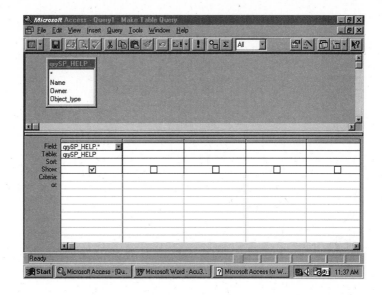

9. Go to the Database window. Access has created two new tables—`tblSP_HELP` and `tblSP_HELP1`. The first table contains the rows produced by the stored procedure, and the second contains an entry for each field definition in that table, as shown in Figure 36.12.

FIGURE 36.12.

Tables produced based on the SP_HELP stored procedure.

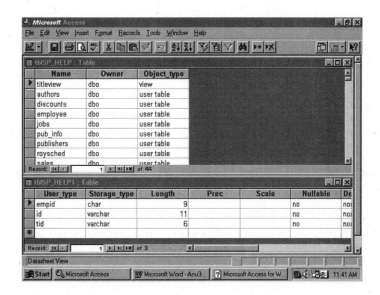

You can create a pass-through query in Access Basic as well. Follow these steps:

1. In the Database window, choose Modules and then New.

2. Create a new subprocedure by clicking the Insert Procedure button on the toolbar.

3. Make the procedure a sub rather than a function and enter `CreatePassThroughSQL` as the subprocedure name.

4. Enter the following in this procedure:

```
Public Sub CreatePassThroughSQL()
    Dim dbs As DATABASE, qdf As QueryDef, strSQL As String
    Set dbs = CurrentDb
    strSQL = "SELECT au_lname , au_fname * FROM Authors ORDER BY au_lname"
    Set qdf = dbs.CreateQueryDef("qrySelectAuthors", strSQL)
    DoCmd.OpenQuery qdf.Name

End Sub
```

Next, test the procedure by going to the Debug window. Click the Debug Window tool on the toolbar, press Ctrl+G, or select View | Debug Window.

Using the SQL *IN* Clause

Another way to retrieve data from outside the Access database is to use an `IN` clause in a SQL query. An outside table can be used as either the source or the destination for a query. The `IN` clause specifies the database where the foreign table is stored. In xBASE products, the filename and table name are identical, as in the following instance:

```
SELECT CompID FROM Companies
IN "C:\DBASE\DATA\COMP" "dBASE IV;"
WHERE City = "New York";
```

An alternative syntax is also supported. This syntax combines the database type and path in the second argument for `IN`:

```
SELECT CompID FROM Companies
IN "" "dBASE IV; [DATABASE=C:\DBASE\DATA\COMP;]
WHERE City = "New York";
```

The same syntax is used with `INSERT INTO` and `SELECT INTO` statements.

Optimizing the Performance of a Client/Server Application

It isn't enough to build your client/server application as you would build any other Access database but just attach the tables to a database server. Although this technique might work, it would be unlikely to perform well.

Client/server architecture provides you with many options for improving the performance of an application. Unfortunately, the sheer number of parameters you can tune might make client/server development confusing at first. Many optimization techniques are also trade-offs between different types of performance, or between performance and some other factor, such as the portability of the application. The following sections give you general guidelines for getting the most out of your client/server application.

Make the Server Do the Work

In general, the goal of client/server database design is to divide the work between the workstation and the server to take advantage of the strengths of each and avoid their respective weaknesses.

The workstation is best suited for these activities:

- Presenting an attractive and useful user interface
- Formulating queries based on user input and submitting them to the server
- Formatting data on the screen
- Formatting data in a report
- Performing calculations based on retrieved data

The server is best suited for these activities:

- Storing large data sets
- Retrieving, sorting, and manipulating shared data
- Optimizing queries
- Enforcing data integrity rules that apply to all applications

Therefore, it follows that the server should do as much as possible to sift through all the data and return only the rows that the user wants to view or process on the workstation.

Avoid Local Joins and Selects

When you join tables in a query, a database evaluates rows from each table to find which records in one table are related to which records in the other. In client/server architecture, this join operation can be performed on the server or on the client. If a join is performed on the server, only the selected rows (the final result of the join) are transmitted across the network to the workstation. To perform a join locally, rows from both tables to be joined must be sent to the workstation before the join can be carried out. In most cases, particularly when large numbers of records are involved, it's more efficient to perform the join on the server than on the client.

In addition to avoiding local joins, you should steer clear of functions that aren't supported by the server and therefore must be performed by the client.

Joins from Tables from Different Servers

Access enables users to join tables from different servers, even servers that are different types (such as Sybase and Oracle). Unfortunately, the join can be performed on neither of the servers because they don't have distributed join support for each other. The join will therefore be performed on the workstation.

Operations That Can't Be Processed on the Server

Like many other database products, Access adds special features that go beyond the ANSI and ISO standards. The extensions listed next force local query processing because they can't be handled by the server.

The following are the extensions to SQL that are offered by Access but aren't available in most database servers:

- Top *n* or Top *n* Percent
- TRANSFORM (crosstab)
- IN (remote database connection)
- DISTINCTROW (allow duplicates)
- WITH OWNERACCESS (allow query without table rights)

Similarly, user-defined functions can't be processed on the server, forcing the rows to be processed on the workstation. If a user-defined function is frequently used in a client/server application, it will pay to convert it into a stored procedure on the server.

You should also avoid the following items:

- Joining queries that contain aggregation or the DISTINCT SQL keyword: Joins that require calculations for each row of the sets to be joined will force your server to do a significant amount of hard work. If you frequently need to perform these types of queries, you might want to store the results of the aggregation for this purpose.

- ORDER BY expressions not supported by the server: Performance suffers if the workstation must sort a large data set. All the rows would have to be sent to the workstation for processing.

- Multiple levels of GROUP BY: Consider the impact of grouping and sorting operations. You might find that sorting beyond one or two levels has no benefit for presenting data and hurts performance. If you sort customers by last name and first name, you probably don't also need to sort them by postal code and phone number in that query.

- Crosstab queries with more than one aggregate: Most servers can't handle crosstab-style aggregation and therefore end up sending all the detail rows to the workstation.

- Operations with more than one SQL statement, such as nested SELECT: Retrieving with criteria expressed as constants is nearly always faster than using the result of a subquery.

- Access extensions to SQL: All these special Access functions force rows to be returned to the workstation rather than processed on the server:
  - Special Access operators and functions (for example, financial functions)
  - User-defined functions in Access Basic that use remote fields
  - Mixing data types without explicit type conversion
  - Heterogeneous joins between local and remote tables or multiple ODBC sources
  - Functions supported by some but not all servers
  - Outer joins
  - Numeric, string, and date functions
  - Data conversion functions

Make the Criteria Match the Server Data Structure As Much As Possible

Assume that shipping methods are stored as integers but entered by the user as a full name in the combo box of a data-entry form. The following is an example of a bad query:

```
SELECT * FROM Orders WHERE [What Shipping Method?] = IIF (Shipping Method = 1 ,
"Federal Express" , IIF (Shipping Method = 2 , "UPS" , "US Mail" ))
```

The following example selects based on the value in the field rather than evaluating the value and determining whether the immediate IF applies. This query yields better performance:

```
SELECT * FROM Orders WHERE [Shipping Method] = IIF (What Shipping Method? =
"Federal Express" , 1 , IIF ([What Shipping Method?] = "UPS" , 2 , 3 ))
```

Use Stored Procedures if They Are Supported by Your Server

Stored procedures are precompiled SQL programs that can be invoked from the workstation. They run much faster than ad hoc SQL statements that must be compiled at runtime. Many servers, such as Microsoft SQL Server, Sybase SQL Server, and Oracle, offer this feature.

Minimize Unnecessary Calls for Server Data

The less often you have to fetch data from the server, the faster your application will run. The following suggestions will reduce the frequency at which you go to the server.

Open Forms Without Retrieving Data

By default, when opening a form, Access opens the recordset underlying the form, retrieves all rows, and displays the first record from the recordset. This method would be inefficient at best in a client/server environment. For instance, if you opened a Customer form that contained millions of records, it would consume significant server and network resources to open the recordset and send a page of records to the workstation. Moreover, the likelihood that the user would even need to edit that particular record becomes increasingly small as the number of records grows larger.

Place a button on the form to allow the user to search for records based on criteria furnished by the user. In a Customer form, the user might enter a Customer ID or a last name. When the button is clicked, the workstation sends the query to the server, and a small number of rows is returned to the workstation and displayed.

Ask Only for What You Need

As your parents might have taught you, there is virtue in taking only what you can use right now. This lesson is as true in client/server database implementation as it was in kindergarten.

Only fetch rows and columns that the user needs. When you use the asterisk (*) rather than listing the fields from a table by name, the database will retrieve all the fields from the table. Don't select fields with * unless you really need all the fields.

Download Reference Tables

You can significantly improve response time by storing reference tables on the workstation rather than the server. The more frequently these tables are consulted, the more they should be located on the server. If the tables are static, they will be easy to update. Otherwise, you should consider a provision for synchronizing workstation copies with a master copy on the network.

The following code updates a local department reference table from a server-based reference table. You could allow users to run the procedure by clicking a button or include the code in an AutoExec function that runs each time the application is opened:

```
Sub UpdateDeptRecords()
    Dim dbs As DATABASE

    ' Return Database variable pointing to current database.
    Set dbs = CurrentDb
    dbs.Execute "delete * from tbldepts"
    dbs.Execute "INSERT INTO tbldepts SELECT * FROM tblRemoteDepts"

End Sub
```

Create Temporary Local Tables for Users to Manipulate Server Data

In some applications users need to retrieve data from the server and then perform analysis on this data, such as what-if calculations, statistics, or graphs. If this user performs a number of queries on the same data, it might be worthwhile to create a temporary local (or file server) table where this data can reside. This technique reduces the server workload and network traffic and provides better response time for the user. For instance, a business analyst might request sales totals by product type and location for a specified period. Without a local table, if graphs were generated showing this data broken down in several dimensions, the database would be requeried for each form or report as it was run.

Create Views on the Server and Link Them

Views are a powerful feature for controlling access to specified rows and columns and joining tables on the server. If your server supports the technique, you can link the view instead of linking the tables and creating the view in Access.

Avoid Operations That Move the Cursor Through Recordsets

Moving the cursor to the last of 100,000 records is time-consuming, because the server must handle all the records between the record 1 and record 100,000. Relational databases aren't optimized for navigational operations, and in most cases simply moving to a record based on its location in a recordset isn't necessary for a business function. Relational databases are designed to find records based on the values in their fields rather than their relative locations.

Transactions on Attached Tables

Transactions enable you to group several actions together and ensure that they aren't left partially completed. Remember that attached tables must be opened as dynasets rather than tables.

Also, create and close the dynaset on the attached SQL Server table outside the transaction itself, as shown in the following examples:

This is incorrect:

```
Dim MyDyna As Dynaset
BeginTrans
    MyDyna = CreateDynaset("Table1")
    'Inserts/Updates/Deletes here
    MyDyna.Close
    CommitTrans/Rollback
```

This is correct:

```
Dim MyDyna As Dynaset
MyDyna = CreateDynaset("Table1")
BeginTrans
    'Inserts/Updates/Deletes here
CommitTrans/Rollback
MyDyna.close
```

Use Attached Tables Whenever Possible

Although it's possible to open tables directly in code, attached tables are faster, more convenient, and more powerful. Attached tables are visible as objects in the Database window, and users can access them for queries, forms, and reports.

Use *ForwardOnly* Snapshots if You Do Not Need to Update or Scroll Backward

By default, Access lets you scroll both forward and backward in snapshot recordsets. If you don't need this capability, use the dbForwardOnly flag to specify a recordset that allows only forward scrolling. The recordset will be placed in a buffer area and would perform faster than a default snapshot.

Using Remote Data Caching

Access automatically handles caches for remote data behind datasheets and forms, but you can improve the performance of dynasets by explicitly managing the CacheStart and CacheSize properties to set the number of records that will be cached. You can force the cache to be filled with the FillCache method, as shown in Listing 36.1.

Listing 36.1. Using the FillCache method to fill a range of data.

```
Dim MyRecordset As Recordset, MyDatabase As Database
Set MyDatabase = CurrentDB.OpenDatabase("",0,0,_
"ODBC;DATABASE=MySqlDb;DSN=
 orpSQL;UID=Guest;PWD=")
' Open ODBC database.
Set MyRecordset = MyDatabase.OpenRecordset("OrderDetail",DB_OPEN_DYNASET)
    ' Open local recordset.
MyRecordset.FindFirst "CustID = 1001"
MyRecordset.CacheStart = MyRecordset.Bookmark
 ' Start caching records at Customer ID 1001.
MyRecordset.CacheSize = 12     ' Set cache size to 12 records.
MyRecordset.FillCache     ' Fill cache.
...' Display rows.
```

Do Not Use Combo Boxes Based on Large Numbers of Records

Although it might make sense to have a combo box that enables the user to choose a state when entering an address, it makes less sense to have a combo box to choose a customer in an Orders form if you have millions of customers. In a case like this, replace the combo box with a dialog box. The user would enter criteria in the top of the dialog box and click a button to see matching records. The user would then select the desired record and click a Done button to return to the main form.

Use Snapshot Recordset Objects to Populate Combo Boxes

Because the content of combo boxes is often static and the recordsets for combo boxes are often small, you can get extra speed from using snapshots rather than dynasets to populate combo boxes. On the other hand, you should use dynasets if the user will be allowed to add new values to the combo box list.

Use Background Population to Take Advantage of Idle Time

During idle time, Access retrieves rows from the server by creating a server table called MSysConf. You can change the settings for background population to reduce the network traffic by increasing the interval between each retrieval or reducing the number of rows that are retrieved at a time.

First, you must create a table called MSysConf on the server. It should have the following columns:

Column Name	Data Type	Allows Null?
Config	A data type that corresponds to a 2-byte integer	No
chValue	VARCHAR(255)	Yes
nValue	A data type that corresponds to a 4-byte integer	Yes
Comments	VARCHAR(255)	Yes

Next, add up to three records to the MSysConf table as follows:

Config	nValue	Meaning
101	0	Doesn't allow local storage of the login ID and password in attachments.
101	1	(Default) Allows local storage of the login ID and password in attachments.
102	D	D is the delay, in seconds, between each retrieval (default: 10 seconds).
103	N	N is the number of rows retrieved (default: 100 rows).

Using Access with Specific Products

To get the best results with Access as a front end, you should understand the behavior of the particular database server product you're using. You must be aware of special features the engine offers (or lacks) and of how to tune it for optimum performance. Although most of the popular database engines conform to the SQL 92 standard, they also offer their own proprietary extensions to SQL.

Field types aren't the same for all database products. You therefore must consider how your Access field types will map to the database server or vice versa. For instance, some databases don't have counter fields, OLE fields, or even time fields.

Field and table names have different formats in Access and server databases. For instance, Access allows spaces in field names, but spaces are prohibited in SQL Server. Many server products allow periods in table names, but periods aren't permitted in Access. Access automatically allows for this restriction and renames tables as it attaches them, substituting an underscore for the period. Another interesting naming convention is that Access appends the table name to the owner name of an attached table. If you attach to a table called Customers on Watcom SQL, for instance, your Access table name will be admin_Customers if you use the default user account. This means that SQL using the original table name of Customers will no longer work with the attached table. You can rename the attached table and remove the username portion to solve this problem.

Access 95 offers declarative referential integrity, a feature that isn't yet supported by all server vendors. Declarative referential integrity means that the developer need only define the relationship and specify the rules for enforcing referential integrity for them to be universally enforced. Microsoft SQL Server 6.0 offers declarative referential integrity as well. In some products, such as SQL Server 4.*x*, triggers are in place of declarative referential integrity. A trigger is a SQL procedure that is run automatically when a certain event occurs (in this case, an INSERT, UPDATE, or DELETE).

Access fields have the Required property to make a value in a field mandatory before the record can be saved. Some servers lack this feature. You can work around this difficulty by using NOT NULL as the default value for a required field.

In general, you should reoptimize your queries after they have been migrated to the server. The optimization schemes used by servers are quite different and might even differ from one server version to the next.

Security schemes on the server are likely to differ from the Access security model. You can opt to redefine all your security rules on the server or to enforce them both at the application level and on the server. Ultimately, server security is more important than application security, because it's the last line of defense for your data. If you have security at both levels, maintaining user names, passwords, and privileges will be more complicated.

Microsoft SQL Server 6.0

Of all the servers, Access is best integrated with Microsoft SQL Server. This should be no surprise because Microsoft produces both products. Their features therefore are coordinated, and special interoperability is provided.

The Upsizing Wizard has been written for Microsoft SQL Server to automate moving from Access to SQL Server.

Sybase SQL Server

Access is also compatible with Sybase, because Microsoft SQL Server is a descendant of Sybase SQL Server. Migrating from Microsoft SQL Server to Sybase SQL Server is therefore relatively painless. The field types are the same, and both products use the same SQL extensions in Transact-SQL.

In the future, there is no guarantee that this interoperability will continue as the feature sets of Microsoft SQL Server and Sybase SQL Server diverge.

Oracle 7.x

Although Oracle offers many of the same features as SQL Server, these features are implemented differently. For instance, Oracle uses a different language (PL/SQL) for stored procedures than SQL Server (Transact-SQL) uses.

Oracle enables the developer to choose whether a trigger is executed before or after the action on the table takes place. In SQL Server, the trigger always runs after the action.

Oracle field types are different from Access or SQL Server field types. For instance, Oracle uses a special field type ROWID in place of the time stamp used by SQL Server. Oracle indexes also include two options, hash and sequence indexes, not found in SQL Server.

Some extensions of SQL exist in Oracle that aren't supported in SQL Server, and vice versa. For instance, there is no SQL Server equivalent for the ON CASCADE of Oracle; a trigger must be written to provide the same functionality.

If you're migrating an Oracle application to SQL Server, you can import the tables into Access, create the relationships in Access, and then use the Upsizing Wizard to transfer the data model to the SQL Server.

Exporting Tables to a Client/Server Database

After you have chosen a server, you need to figure out how to move your data in the server but your application in Access.

It's often easier to develop the application in Access and then move the data to the server. This is because the developer can work standalone or on a file server without being concerned about server features or performance.

You can even use Access as an intermediary when transferring tables from one server to another. If you have sufficient disk space on your workstation or the file server, you can import tables from the old server into Access and then export them to the new server. You can also attach tables from both servers and use Append queries to move the data from one server to the other.

Exporting tables to a server database is nearly as easy as exporting them to another format such as dBASE or Lotus. It also uses the same menu options. Follow these steps to export a table to a client/server database:

1. Select the table to be exported in the Database window. Choose File | Save As | Export.
2. Choose To An External File Or Database in the Save As dialog box and then click OK.
3. Choose ODBC Databases for the Save As Type (it's the last item on the list) and then click Export.
4. Choose the ODBC data destination or click New to define a new data source.
5. If prompted, enter the username and password for the destination database.

You can also create tables with DLL pass-through queries. For instance, the following are examples of queries that create tables.

This query creates a new table called This Table with two text fields:

```
CREATE TABLE [This Table] ([First Name] TEXT, [Last Name] TEXT);
```

This query creates a new table called MyTable with two text fields, a date/time field, and a unique index composed of all three fields:

```
CREATE TABLE MyTable ([First Name] TEXT, [Last Name] TEXT,
[Date of Birth] DATETIME, CONSTRAINT
MyTableConstraint UNIQUE ([First Name], [Last Name], [Date of Birth]));
```

This query creates a new table with two text fields and an integer field. The SSN field is the primary key:

```
CREATE TABLE People ([First_Name] TEXT, [Last_Name] TEXT,
SSN INTEGER CONSTRAINT MyFieldConstraint
 PRIMARY KEY)
```

Creating Indexes on New Tables

After you create the table, you should define the indexes. Servers such as SQL server won't automatically create indexes on tables you export from Access. You can use the tools provided by your server vendor, or you can write a pass-through query in Access, such as the following one. This query creates an index consisting of the fields Home Phone and Extension in the Employees table:

```
CREATE INDEX NewIndex ON Employees ([Home Phone], Extension);
```

This query creates an index on the Employees table using the Social Security Number field. No two records can have the same data in the SSN field, and no null values are allowed:

```
CREATE UNIQUE INDEX MyIndex ON Employees (SSN) WITH DISALLOW NULL;
```

This query creates an index on an attached table. The table's remote database is unaware of and unaffected by the new index:

```
CREATE UNIQUE INDEX MailID ON MailList ([Client No.])
```

Summary

Access can be used to develop standalone and LAN applications, but it can also serve as a powerful and flexible front end for client/server applications. This means that you can upsize applications for dozens or hundreds of users or use Access as a data analysis tool for report writing, queries, and business graphics.

As this chapter shows, Microsoft has included many special Access features specifically for client/server operations. The most important of these is probably the pass-through query, which allows you to take advantage of stored procedures and other server features. You can expect even tighter integration of Access and database engines in the future.

In order to develop an efficient client/server application, you must master not only Access but also your database server software. You face many trade-offs in striving for the best performance from the application. There are few fixed rules here; many things can be determined only by trial and error. Still, the rewards of using Access with client/server architecture are worth the effort.

IN THIS PART

PART

The Presentation of PowerPoint

Designing an Effective Presentation

37

by Sue Charlesworth

Presentations enable you to communicate your ideas to groups of people. Using a variety of presentation formats and techniques, you can present textual material, tables, graphs, drawings, and other types of information to your audience, to inform, persuade, train, or otherwise influence their thinking. In the Office suite, PowerPoint provides the framework and engine for creating eye-catching presentations.

PowerPoint's presentational building blocks are slides, which are individual "chunks" of information in the form of text, graphics, tables, charts, media clips, and other Office objects. Slides generally convey information in telegraphic or shorthand style—short phrases or "bursts" of text, pictures, charts, or graphs. Save long sentences and flowing prose for reports—presentations use short, pithy lines to make text easy to grasp.

In this chapter, you'll explore the creation of a PowerPoint presentation with an emphasis on *design* and learn to choose the elements of an *effective* presentation. Here are some of the design topics examined:

- Organizing the presentation's contents using an outline
- Selecting the right template for a presentation
- Determining the layout for individual slides
- Adding animation effects to slides
- Choosing transitions from slide to slide

Outlines—Organizing Content

PowerPoint makes it easy to create sharp-looking presentations; well-designed templates, predefined slide layouts, and predetermined text placement all help you easily place your information on slides. All the pretty backgrounds and fancy type in the world won't help your presentation make its point if *you* haven't done your work first. In other words, if you haven't put time and thought into the design of the presentation, all the flash in the world won't make it effective. In fact, too much flash can hinder the effectiveness of what you have to say.

In PowerPoint, outlines provide a convenient means for organizing the content of your presentation. The abbreviated style of outlines is ideally suited to presentations, and the hierarchic arrangement of information readily adapts to text slides. In PowerPoint, the top level of an outline's structure becomes the title of a slide and lower levels of the outline form bulleted text hierarchies.

You can create a PowerPoint presentation without developing an outline first. For short presentations where you have a clear picture of the information you want to present and how that information fits together, it might be easier to create slides directly, without going through the outlining stage. But for longer presentations, as with any informative endeavor, an outline helps you organize your content, making it easier for you to create an effective presentation.

Let's now turn our attention to the creation of a presentation, beginning with an outline.

Creating the Outline

In PowerPoint, you can create an outline for your presentation in one of two ways:

- Clicking the Outline View icon at the bottom of the screen
- Selecting View | Outline from the menu bar

PowerPoint switches to outline view, automatically opens the outline toolbar, and positions the cursor in the slide for adding text. The first line of a slide in outline view is the title. To add lines of outline text, click the demote button to move the text down a level (for the first line of text on the slide) or press Alt+Shift+→. Press Enter to add a new line at the same level as the previous line. Click the promote button to move the text up a level, or press Alt+Shift+←. Continue to add text lines to your slide, changing levels to reflect the hierarchical relationship of your information. (See Figure 37.1.)

FIGURE 37.1.

The outline view.

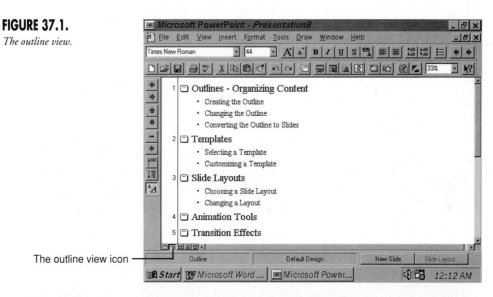

The outline view icon

TIP

If you have a text document in an outline format, select Insert | Slides From Outline from the menu bar, and then select the outline document. The outline becomes PowerPoint slides.

For easier viewing of your slide's titles (which, remember, are the top level of your outline), click the Show Titles button of the outline toolbar. PowerPoint collapses your outline to show only the titles. Click on the Show All button to expand your outline so that all levels display.

Changing the Outline

As you develop your outline, PowerPoint makes it easy for you to rearrange the order of information in a level or to shift the position of a slide or group of slides. To change the order of information within a level, move the cursor to the left of the line you want to move. When the cursor changes to a double-headed arrow, click the left mouse button to select the line, and then drag the line to its new position. To change the position of a slide and all its information, move the cursor to the left of a slide title, then click and drag the slide. To move a group of slides, select additional slides by holding down Ctrl (for slides out of sequence) or Shift (for slides in order), and then drag the group.

Converting the Outline to Slides

Here are the two ways to change from outline view to slide view (thereby "converting" your outline to slides):

- Clicking the Slide View icon
- Selecting View | Slides from the menu bar

Each major heading from the outline becomes a slide, with the top-level heading becoming the slide's title. Each outline line converts to a bulleted text line, with different levels corresponding to the outline's levels. (See Figure 37.2.)

FIGURE 37.2.

Making a slide from an outline.

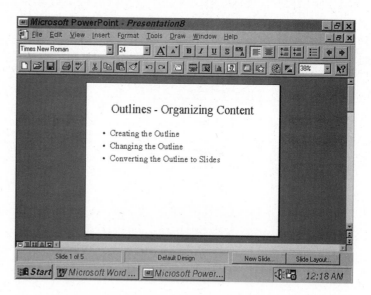

Outlining the MicroMouseMike Presentation

Throughout this chapter—and the rest of the PowerPoint section—we'll be looking at a particular presentation as an example of using PowerPoint. This sample presentation outlines the roll-out plans of a new product—the MicroMouseMike—a combination cordless computer pointing device and hand-held microphone. The presentation is aimed at the employees of Stand Up Routines, the creator of the MicroMouseMike.

Figure 37.3 shows part of the outline for the MicroMouseMike roll-out presentation. The presentation's developers have organized the content into what, when, where, who, why, and how points, followed by a brief business analysis of strengths, weaknesses, opportunities, and threats.

FIGURE 37.3.

Part of the MicroMouseMike outline.

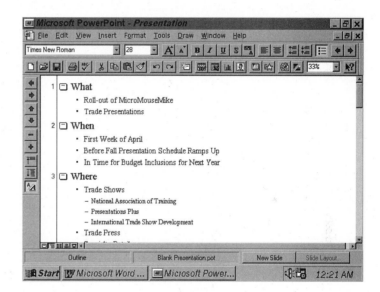

AutoContent

The outline is admittedly a good way to organize your content, but what if you're not sure what your content should be? PowerPoint provides the AutoContent Wizard to give you a starting point for presentations. Use the AutoContent Wizard to help you create the following presentations:

- Recommending a strategy
- Selling a product, service, or idea
- Training
- Reporting progress
- Communicating bad news

There are many more topics you can create with the AutoContent Wizard. To access the AutoContent Wizard, select AutoContent Wizard for Create a New Presentation Using in the PowerPoint dialog box, or you can select AutoContent Wizard from the Presentations tab in the New Presentation dialog box.

AutoContent presentations are not complete in and of themselves. They provide the template for a presentation, basic slides within the presentation topic, and suggestions for the information to put in each slide. It's up to you to flesh out the presentation.

> **TIP**
>
> Don't forget to delete the suggested text. You don't want development hints to show up as part of your presentation.

Templates

Once you have the content of your presentation laid out, it's time to turn your attention to how your presentation will look. You can, if you choose, design the look of the overall presentation from scratch, designating background colors and patterns, font type and size for each level of information on a slide, bullet shape and color for each level, placement and alignment of the title text, and so on. To be effective, your presentation design should consider the following details:

- The legibility and readability of different fonts at different sizes
- Color theory and psychology
- The presentation medium—color overheads, black-and-white overheads, onscreen slides, or 35mm slides
- Placement of headers, footers, and other recurring information

Designing an effective presentation format from scratch takes a lot of work and expertise, encompassing many factors that most of us don't want to deal with. It is for us that PowerPoint includes presentation templates.

PowerPoint's templates address the issues of presentation design and provide professional, predesigned presentation layouts. Fonts and sizes have already been plugged in, with an eye toward legibility and readability. Colors don't clash or send out hostile vibrations. Bullets fit with the feel and color scheme of the rest of the presentation. All you have to do is pick an appropriate template for your purpose, make changes to the template to suit your needs, and then add your information.

Selecting a Template

Next to the content, the overall design of your presentation is probably the most important part of an effective presentation. Starting with a professionally designed template gets you pointed in the right direction. The next issue, however, is *which* template to use.

When you create a new presentation, you select a template. When PowerPoint displays the New Presentation dialog box, you'll need to select the Presentation Designs tab. Select a template to preview it in the preview window. (See Figure 37.4.) Move through the templates to find one you want and then apply it. That template forms the base of your presentation.

FIGURE 37.4.

A preview of a template.

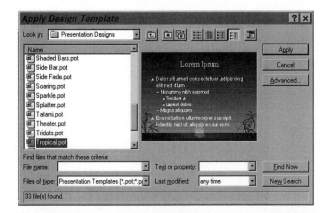

> **NOTE**
>
> Yes, you can create a "blank" presentation without a template. Actually, it's a presentation with a template called Blank Presentation.POT. Even then, the template isn't truly blank. The "blank" template provides basic font types and sizes, bullets, and text placement guidelines. Every presentation should have at least that much to its framework.

If you want to change the template of an open presentation, select Format I Apply Design Template from the menu bar or click the Apply Design Template button on the toolbar. The Apply Design Template dialog box lists the available templates and previews the template selected. As discussed previously, preview the different templates and select the one you want to apply to your presentation.

But how do you decide which template to choose? Think about the purpose of your presentation: What information do you want to convey, to whom, and in what kind of setting? What overall tone do you wish your presentation to have? A presentation about this quarter's financial results to the Board of Directors will look very different from one delivered at a sales pep rally. When choosing your presentation template, the following points might help:

- Is your presentation formal or informal?

- Is your presentation internal—for your employees or the members of your group, or external—for customers, prospects, students, the Board, or some other set of people?

- Are you presenting good news or bad?

- Are you selling something or are you summarizing progress on a project?

The Cheers (see Figure 37.5) or Tridots templates, for example, probably wouldn't be best suited for serious, formal presentations, but they might be just right for highlighting this quarter's spectacular results at an employee meeting. Tropical could be an excellent backdrop for presenting a sales competition where the prize is a trip to Hawaii or for a travel agency's pitch for obtaining vacation sales. World or International might be great for presentations on global sales trends or markets or for a business student's report on multinational organizations. What about that serious, formal presentation to the Board of Directors? Why not use Azure (see Figure 37.6), Double Lines, or White Marble?

FIGURE 37.5.

A preview of the Cheers template.

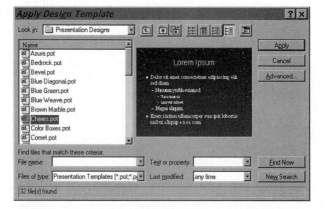

FIGURE 37.6.

A preview of the Azure template.

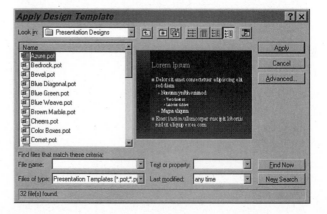

You'll have other considerations when choosing your template, of course, but the previous list and discussion offer some starting points.

Customizing a Template

One of PowerPoint's templates might be just right for your presentation. If so, great! That's one fewer thing to worry about on your way to an effective presentation. Often, however, a template is just right *except* for the background color, or the title alignment, or the font. Or perhaps you need the company's logo to appear on each slide. Using the template as a starting point, you can make changes to the overall presentation so that it is just right for your needs.

Every presentation has a Slide Master. The Slide Master is the "control center" for your presentation, setting the base fonts and bullets, including their size and color, and designating where common information appears on slides. Anything you change on the Slide Master, or anything you add, shows up on all slides in your presentation. Put your company's logo (or that of your customer or prospect) on the Slide Master to have it appear on all the slides of your presentation.

To open the Slide Master, do either of the following:

■ Select View | Master | Slide Master from the menu bar.

■ Press Shift and click the Slide View icon.

The Slide Master (see Figure 37.7) also displays *placeholders*, which are areas on a slide reserved for particular information. Placeholders on a Slide Master include the following areas:

■ Title area

■ Object area (where different kinds of Office objects can be placed)

■ Date area

■ Number area (where slide numbers that are automatically incremented display)

■ Footer area (where you can enter the information you want to appear on every slide)

You can change the size and placement of the placeholders.

> **CAUTION**
>
> When you place objects outside the Slide Master's planned areas, be sure to check all your slides to verify that slide text doesn't conflict with the other objects.

With the Slide Master open, you can also change the background, background colors, and other colors of the presentation. Select Format | Slide Color Scheme to change the colors of the Slide Master. (See Figure 37.8.) The Standard tab presents a number of different predefined color schemes. The Custom tab allows you to change the color of individual elements of your presentation. Select Format|Custom Background to change custom background colors, patterns, or textures.

FIGURE 37.7.

The Slide Master.

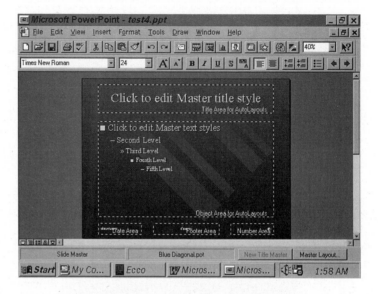

FIGURE 37.8.

The Color Scheme dialog box.

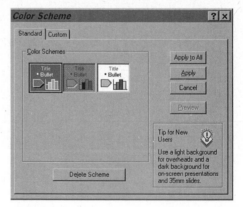

Here are a few more tips for slide design:

- Sans serif typefaces (those without the little "feet" at the letter tips) are more legible than serif typefaces (those with the little "feet"). *Legibility* refers to the ability to easily recognize letters and words. You're aiming for legibility in your slides.

- In general, type that is smaller than 18 points will be too small for your audience to read. If you have a large room or an older audience, or simply wish to ensure that everyone can read your slides, use larger type.

NOTE

PowerPoint type defaults to 32 points for first-level items, 28 points for second-level items, 24 points for third-level items, and 20 points for fourth- and fifth-level items. The type sizes of the first three levels should be adequate for most audiences. If you can spare the room, it wouldn't hurt to bump up each level by 4 points.

- Use light backgrounds with dark type for overheads, and use dark backgrounds with light type for onscreen slide shows or 35mm slides.
- Make sure you have good contrast between background and type
- Don't cram too much information on one slide. Limit yourself to main points: five per slide is close to the maximum.
- Use landscape (horizontal) slides rather than portrait (vertical) slides. Vertical slides require smaller type sizes to fit in information and lend themselves to overcrowded slides. Horizontal slides, with their longer lines, are easier to read, and force you to be more compact with your information.

TIP

The predefined slide color schemes usually include at least one scheme with a dark background and one with a light background. Use dark backgrounds for onscreen presentations and 35mm slides; use light backgrounds for overheads.

NOTE

When you make changes to the Slide Master, the changes affect that presentation only—the template itself does not change.

TIP

When trying out different templates or backgrounds, create a new, temporary presentation and copy just a few of your slides into it. Check out the proposed changes against these few slides, and you'll see the effects of your changes much faster than if you apply them to your entire presentation. Include slides that represent all your slide types (text, graphic, and chart) to make sure you like all the types with the new colors and styles. When you're happy, go back to your real presentation and make the same changes.

The MicroMouseMike Template

The sample presentation, as stated earlier, describes the product roll-out plans for the MicroMouseMike. As you'll remember, the presentation is aimed at the employees of Stand Up Routines, the creator of the MicroMouseMike. The product is ready to hit the shelves, and Stand Up Routines wants to generate enthusiasm and increase product awareness in its employees by promoting the roll-out internally. The presentation will be informative without being "teachy" or "preachy."

After examining all the templates and applying the top template candidates to the MicroMouseMike presentation, Stand Up Routines has decided to use the Wet Sand template for the presentation. Wet Sand, they feel, gives an unexpected feeling of informality and adds interest to the presentation. They have also decided to change the type face for the body and title of the slides to an interesting sans serif style (Kabel, not provided by Windows 95) in order to provide good legibility and to continue the feeling of informality and fun. Figure 37.9 shows one of the slides with the Wet Sand template.

FIGURE 37.9.

A MicroMouseMike slide with the Wet Sand template.

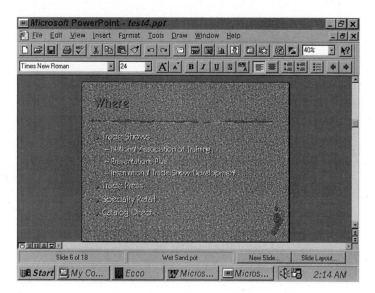

Slide Layouts

Now that the content and overall presentation have been determined, we turn our attention to the layout of the individual slides. When you first create your content outline and change from outline view to slide view, all your slides will have a simple bulleted text layout. To change the layout of any slide, select the Slide Layout button from the bottom of the screen. PowerPoint then displays thumbnails of all the available slide layouts. Select the layout most suited for the information presented in the slide.

You have slides with bulleted text that you have "created" from your outline, but you probably still have slides you want to add. You might even want to add some pictures, too. While you can have an effective presentation using text alone, graphic and different visual formats can add interest to your information. Use one of the following techniques to create new slides:

- Click the New Slide button at the bottom of the screen.
- Select Insert | New Slide from the menu bar.
- Click the Insert New Slide button on the toolbar.
- Press Ctrl+M.

PowerPoint opens the New Slide dialog box, allowing you to choose the layout of your slide. (See Figure 37.10.)

FIGURE 37.10.

New slide layouts.

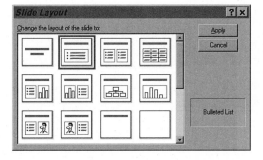

Choosing a Slide Layout

In many cases, the most appropriate layout to use is fairly obvious: Bulleted List for plain text; Table for tabular information; Graph for some form of chart. Other times, however, you'll need to make some design decisions. Do you want a slide of text followed by the chart it describes, or do you want to combine the text and graph on one slide? If so, is the slide more effective with the text on the left or on the right? Because the text area on a two-part slide is obviously going to be smaller, can you effectively make your point in a smaller area with a smaller font size? If you decide to put four objects (clip art, charts, or some other Office object) on the slide, do they complement each other without making the slide look too cluttered or busy?

After creating the layout for a graph or organization chart, double-click in the area indicated on the new slide to open the application and then create the representation of your information. Refer to Chapter 43, "Using the Graph Tools," for creating graphs and Chapter 45, "The Office Toolbox," for creating organization charts. Double-clicking in an object layout opens a list of objects you can place in your slide. In the table layout, double-clicking sets up the insertion of a Word table.

You can change the layout of a slide at any time by clicking the Slide Layout button and selecting a new layout. Common sense tells you that a bulleted list won't "translate" into an organization chart. Changing slide layouts is most effective for those layouts where you are swapping out the left and right sides or the top and bottom of a slide, or when you have just created the slide and realize that you want a different layout.

Changing the MicroMouseMike Presentation

Looking over their MicroMouseMike roll-out presentation, the folks at Stand Up Routines realize that they need to make a few changes. First of all, the text they entered in parts of the original outline is too long to fit on one slide. Also, they need some visual interest.

To take care of the too-long text, they reconsider the layout of the Who and Threats slides. The Who slide looks too cluttered when they put the To and By sections in two columns on the same slide; therefore, they decide to create a new slide by splitting Who into two slides. For the Threats slide, they change the layout to 2-Column Text and cut and paste the slide text into two columns. Even though the slide may look a little "busy," they decide that they don't want to split the Threats slide into two slides and that the two columns of text is acceptable. (See Figure 37.11.)

FIGURE 37.11.

The Threats slide with two columns of text.

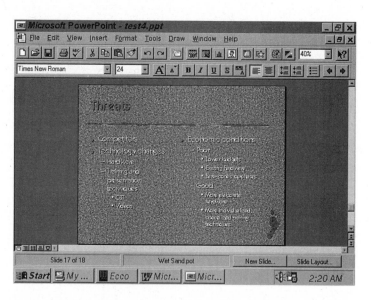

To add visual interest, Stand Up Routines adds clip art to the When and Business Analysis slides. To do this, they select the Text & Clip Art slide layout, double-click in the clip art side, and then select the graphic they want for the slide. They also create a new Where - Breakdown slide (see Figure 37.12) to add a chart showing the proportion of attention given to the different roll-out areas.

Chapter 37

FIGURE 37.12.

The Where - Breakdown slide with a graph.

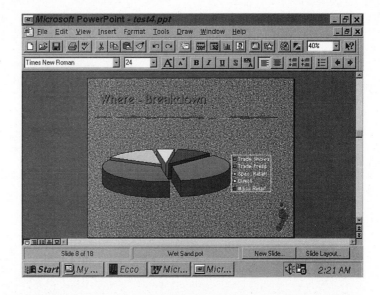

> **NOTE**
>
> This discussion does not cover the creation of the graph. See Chapter 43 for information on graphs.

Animation Tools

For onscreen presentations in PowerPoint, you can add animation or action within a slide. *Animation* specifies how text lines, clip art, or other objects appear on a slide.

Before adding animation, activate the animation effects toolbar (see Figure 37.13) by either of the following two methods:

- Clicking the Animation Effects button on the toolbar
- Selecting View | Toolbars from the menu bar and then selecting Animation Effects

> **NOTE**
>
> You won't be able to create animation without the animation effects toolbar.

To add animation for graphics, select an object and then the desired effect from the animation effects toolbar. Repeat this for as many objects on the slide as you want to animate.

FIGURE 37.13.

The animation effects toolbar.

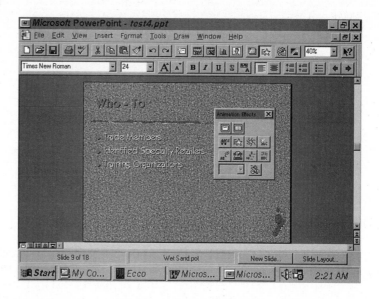

When you specify animation for graphics, the animation order increments automatically. If you want your objects to appear in a different order, select the object and then change the number of its order.

To further refine your animation (or to create animation) click the Animation Settings button on the animation effects toolbar. In the Animation Settings dialog box (see Figure 37.14), you can specify the following items:

- Whether or not to "build" (animate) an object
- The specific effect to take place
- What sound, if any, will accompany the effect
- What to do with the object when its turn is over

FIGURE 37.14.

The Animation Settings dialog box.

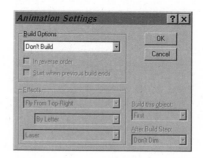

NOTE

You must specify the effect for each individual object separately. You can't select a group of objects and then apply an effect to all of them at once. Don't forget this step, or you might find yourself wondering why your sun sets but your moon doesn't rise.

To remove animation from an object, select the object, click the Animation Settings button on the animation effects toolbar, and then select the Don't Build option from the Build Options list.

To add animation for text, click in a text box and then select the animation effect. The text animation you choose affects all text in that text box; therefore, you don't have to (and can't) specify effects by line.

TIP

By default, text effects take place by first-level paragraphs. Therefore, the first-level text will appear using whatever effect you've chosen, followed by any second- or lower-level text. The animation stops before the next first-level paragraph. Use the Animation Settings dialog box to change the levels at which the animation "stops" before requiring your input to go on.

Remove text animation by clicking the Build Slide Text button on the animation effects toolbar to toggle the effects off.

CAUTION

Animation effects are lots of fun to develop, but a little goes a *long* way when you're at the receiving end. Use animation effects sparingly to be most effective.

CAUTION

Absolutely, positively preview your slide show, complete with animation, before you show it to someone else. It is too easy to pick a text effect that puts up a line of text a letter at a time, blanking out each letter before moving on to the next. This is not a particularly good way to impress your boss.

Following the same reasoning, assigning random effects to a slide might not work well for your presentation. By definition, you don't know what you'll get with a random effect—there's no way to preview it.

TIP

If you want to use flying text, use it in the slide title rather than the body of the slide. This way, you've emphasized the title, which you probably want to do anyway, and have not detracted from the information in the slide itself.

TIP

Forgotten which slides have animation effects? In the slide sorter view, slides with animation effects have a little icon below the slide. In addition, when you select a slide, its animation effect, if any, is displayed in the toolbar.

Animation and MicroMouseMike

Given that right now you are reading a book (a notoriously static medium), seeing examples of animation effects in the MicroMouseMike sample presentation is all but impossible. However, I will provide you with descriptions of the animation effects so that you can get ideas for incorporating them into your presentations.

Since the MicroMouseMike is a wireless, hand-held, combination PC mouse and microphone, you can develop a slide like Figure 37.15, which shows a PC, a mouse, and a microphone (all available from the Office Clip Art Gallery) with plus signs between them. You can animate the three objects in turn using the flying effect to have them "land" in the appropriate place on the slide.

For a How slide, or one similar, consider adding the text effect of "moving" through the bulleted points, dimming a line after it's been addressed. To do this, click in the text box, select the Build Slide Text button from the animation effects toolbar, and then click the Animation Settings button. Next, click the arrow below After Build Step and select Other Color. Use a shade of gray (or another appropriate color) that is slightly lighter than the background. In your presentation, as you move through the slide, the previous bullet points are dimmed out.

FIGURE 37.15.

The MicroMouseMike slide.

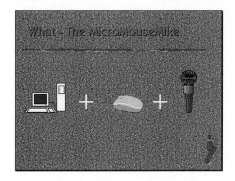

Transition Effects

The last weapon in PowerPoint's visual effects arsenal that we explore is transition effects. While animation effects take place within a slide, transition effects occur between slides. Transitions move your presentation gracefully from slide to slide, so you don't have an abrupt change from one slide to another.

To add a transition to a slide, go into slide sorter view (see Figure 37.16) and select a slide; select multiple slides to apply the transition to all of them. Click the Slide Transition button on the toolbar or select a transition from the drop-down Transition list. In the Slide Transition dialog box (see Figure 37.17), you can specify the following items:

- The effect
- The effect's speed
- How to advance the slide
- A sound

In addition, a preview window shows a demonstration of the effect.

A transition icon appears below the slide. Click the transition icon to preview the transition for that slide. You can also apply a transition while in slide view by selecting Tools | Slide Transition from the menu bar.

> **NOTE**
>
> The transition chosen for a slide takes effect when the presentation changes to that slide. If the first slide of a presentation has a transition, the effect will display as that slide opens the presentation.

FIGURE 37.16.

The slide sorter view.

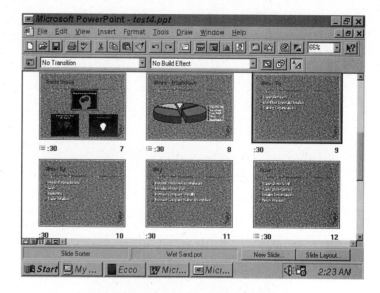

FIGURE 37.17.

The Slide Transition dialog box.

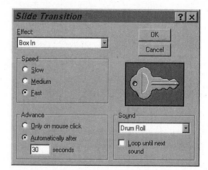

TIP

Be careful when combining a transition and an animation effect on the same slide. The transition, a pause, and then text flying onto your screen one letter at a time might be too much.

NOTE

Animation, whether text or graphic, and transitions only take effect during onscreen presentations or slide shows.

Summary

This chapter explores the design of an effective PowerPoint presentation. It starts with using an outline as a means to organize the content of a presentation. Once an outline is created, it can be "converted" to slides. Next, the chapter looks at templates as the way to add a "look" to the presentation. PowerPoint's predesigned templates save you from the burden of determining all the pieces of the presentation and their visual components. A template might not address all of your needs, but you can customize a presentation through the use of the Slide Master. The chapter then discusses the layout of individual slides and the kinds of information a slide can hold.

Exploring animation and transition effects finishes this chapter's look at presentation design. Animation and transitions add further visual interest to an onscreen presentation. Animation occurs within a slide, to either text or graphics, while transitions move the presentation smoothly from one slide to the next.

Throughout this chapter, the MicroMouseMike product roll-out presentation is used as an example to demonstrate design techniques and PowerPoint operation.

Making the
Presentation

38

*by Sue
Charlesworth*

Now that you have the content of your presentation settled, along with simple animations and transitions, you can turn your attention to the mechanics of making the presentation. This chapter also looks at the issue of notes—how you provide additional information besides what's on your slides, either for yourself or for your audience.

Creating and Using Notes

When determining the content of your presentation, you kept the actual amount of information on a slide to a minimum—just the high-level points to provide the framework for the topics you want to present. How do you, then, keep track of the details you want to cover for each slide? What if you want to provide those details to your audience, too? Simple. Use PowerPoint's notes.

Notes allow you to have paper printouts that contain both your slides and additional information you enter in notes. Consider the following ways you can use notes:

- As your presentation notes.
- As additional details for your audience.
- As a copy of your presentation with a blank area for your audience to take their own notes. Have you ever been to a conference where they distribute hard copies of the presentations with three-slides-per-page printouts with lines for notes and wanted to do the same thing? Keep reading and find out how.
- As a student guide. If you use a presentation as your primary teaching medium, you can put additional information on notes pages for your learners.
- As an instructor's guide. Again, if you teach from your presentation, you may have points you wish to make or other information associated with a particular slide. Add this information as notes, and you have your instructor's guide, perfectly in sync with the information you're giving your learners.

To create notes, select View | Notes Pages from the menu bar, or Notes Pages from the icons at the bottom of the screen. The note page displays the current slide with the notes area below. (See Figure 38.1.) Click in the notes area and type whatever text you wish for each slide.

If you're creating handouts for your audience, you might want to consider the master formatting tools on the Notes Master. Select View | Master | Notes Master from the menu bar, or press Shift while selecting the Notes Pages icon to open the Notes Master. In the Notes Master (see Figure 38.2), you can specify a header and footer and add the date and page numbers. You can also specify how the text within the note body itself will appear by changing the font. What you enter on the Notes Master then prints on every note page.

To print your notes, select File | Print from the menu bar. In the Print dialog box, move to Print what and select Notes Pages from the list. Click on Black and White to print the slide in black and white, instead of a gray version of your color slide. Notes pages print in portrait layout, with a half-sized representation of your slide on the top portion of the page and your text on the bottom portion.

Chapter 38

FIGURE 38.1.

The notes view.

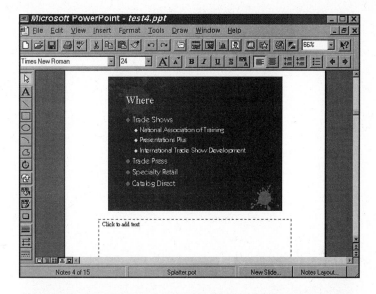

FIGURE 38.2.

The Notes Master.

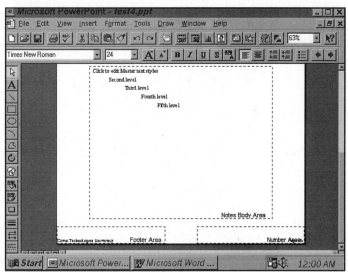

NOTE

Be sure to check Black and White for printing, even if you are already viewing your slides in black and white. If you don't, your color slide prints in black and gray and looks ugly.

To print your notes with more layout options, select Tools | Write-Up from the menu bar. Write-Up (see Figure 38.3) allows you to choose from a number of layouts and then switches to Word (starting it up, if necessary) so you can add notes to your slides in Word. Once in Word, your slides and notes are formatted either as a table (for notes or blank lines next to the slides) (see Figure 38.4) or as individual pages with a slide in the top portion of the page and notes below. You manipulate your notes using Word.

FIGURE 38.3.

The Write-Up dialog box.

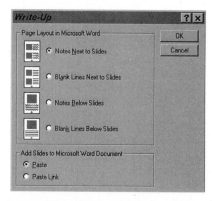

FIGURE 38.4.

PowerPoint notes in Word.

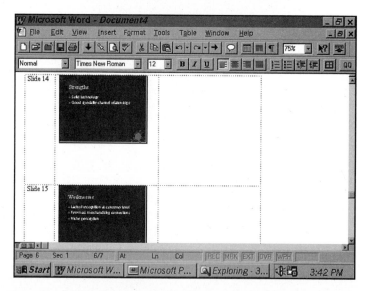

CAUTION

Change your slide view to black and white (by selecting View | Black and White from the menu bar) before using Write-Up and printing in Word. Without this step, you get ugly, potentially unreadable gray versions of your color slides.

TIP

Do you want notes for yourself, plus handouts with blank lines for your audience? Print out your notes from PowerPoint and then use Write-Up to create your handouts. The Blank Lines options in Write-Up print lines on the handouts, ignoring any note text you may have added.

Handout Material

Handouts are simply printouts of your slides; just the slides, no notes. To print handouts, select File | Print from the menu bar. In the Print dialog box, move to Print what and select Handouts (two, three, or six slides per page). Make sure to check Black and White before printing.

Handouts print in portrait format, with the arrangement of slides dependent on which number of slides per page you chose. Two slides per page print one above the other, half size. Three slides per page print three slides along the left side of the page, with the right side blank. Six slides per page print three slides each along the left and right sides of the page. The size of the slides in three-per-page and six-per-page is the same.

Because handouts are just printed slides, you can't change to a handout view. You can, however, format parts of your handout pages using the Handout Master (by selecting View | Master | Handout Master from the menu bar). On the Handout Master (see Figure 38.5), you can specify a header and footer and add the date and page numbers. What you enter on the Handout Master then prints on every handout page.

FIGURE 38.5.

The Handout Master.

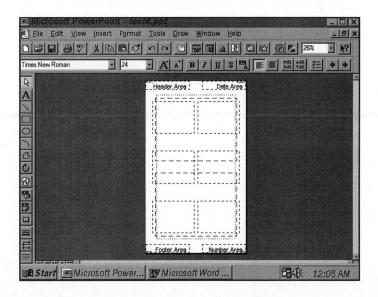

NOTE

The boxed areas on the Handout Master can't be changed; they just show the outlines of the different-sized slide areas.

Making a Presentation from a PC

And now (imagine here either a dramatic hush or a blood-stirring drum roll, depending on your mood), we talk about actually giving your presentation, showing it to someone other than yourself, your spouse, or your roommate: someone like your boss, or her boss, or the Board of Directors, or the rest of your Marketing 101 class.

A presentation from a PC (also called an onscreen slide show or an electronic presentation) shows your slides, one at a time, moving from one slide to the next automatically or on a mouse click from you. In PowerPoint, you activate your electronic marvel from the menu bar by selecting View | Slide Show, or by selecting the Slide Show icon.

TIP

Make sure you select the presentation's first slide before starting Slide Show from the icon. The slide that is active is the first slide to display.

Controlling Your Slide Show

Starting your slide show from the menu gives you a little more control of the show. When you start from the icon, as noted above, the active slide in the presentation is the first slide displayed. Using the menu, however, you first see the Slide Show dialog box. (See Figure 38.6.) In the Slide Show dialog box, you choose to show all slides or some of your slides, designating beginning and ending slide numbers. You also select how the slides will change (or advance) from one to the next and if the presentation will continuously loop through the slides.

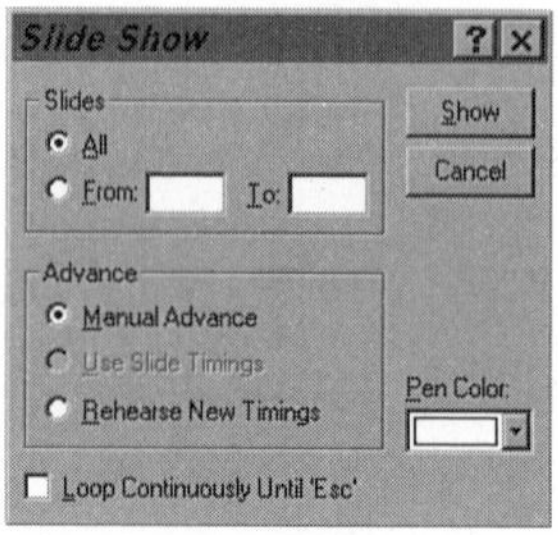

FIGURE 38.6.

The Slide Show dialog box.

If you want complete control of your presentation, select Manual Advance. With this setting, PowerPoint waits for your mouse click (or keystroke) before advancing to the next slide in your presentation. You can move through individual slides as quickly or as slowly as you wish. To move to the next slide, click on the left mouse button or press the N key on the keyboard; press the P key to move to the previous slide.

Often, you'll need to make your presentation within certain time constraints. You'll have an overall time limit and within that limit, you'll want to devote specific amounts of time to different slides and subjects. You can set your presentation to change slides according to times you determine. To set slide timings manually, select Tools | Slide Transition from the menu bar, or right-click on a slide in the Slide Sorter view and select Slide Transition.

In the Advance section of the Slide Transition dialog box (see Figure 38.7), select Automatically after and supply the number of seconds you wish to spend on this slide. Set the advance time for each slide. PowerPoint displays the number of seconds you've indicated for each slide below the slide in the Slide Sorter view.

FIGURE 38.7.

The Slide Transition dialog box.

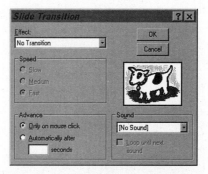

NOTE

You must enter a value in *seconds*. If you want your slide to display for 3 minutes, enter 180 seconds. The Slide Sorter view translates the seconds into minutes figures.

Rather than using this manual, brute force method of entering the timing for each slide, you can automatically set the timings as you move through the presentation. When in the Slide Show dialog box (select View | Slide Show from the menu bar, or press Shift while selecting the Slide Show icon), click on Rehearse New Timings, then the Show button. PowerPoint begins your presentation and displays the Rehearsal dialog box. (See Figure 38.8.)

In the Rehearsal dialog box, the time on the left is the cumulative time of the entire presentation so far. The time on the right is the time spent so far on the current slide. Practice what you want to say for each slide, then click on the right-arrow key to record the time and advance to the next slide. If you want to redo the timing for a slide, click on the Repeat button. The time counters (for both the cumulative time and the current slide's time) reset and you can begin your timing again. Click on the pause button (|‖|) to suspend timing until you click it again.

FIGURE 38.8.

The Rehearsal dialog box.

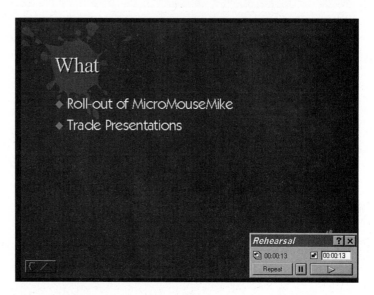

When you've worked through your presentation, PowerPoint displays a dialog box giving the total time of the presentation and asking if you want to record the slide timings for view in Slide Sorter. When you select Yes, PowerPoint saves the slide timings and displays the number of seconds for each slide below the slide in the Slide Sorter view. (See Figure 38.9.)

FIGURE 38.9.

The Slide Sorter view with slide timings.

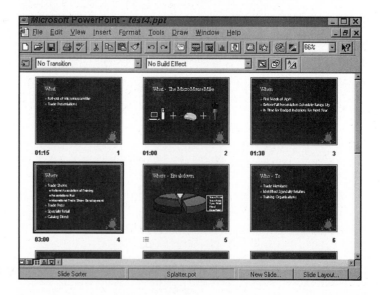

To run your presentation using your slide timings, whether entered manually or through Rehearsal, select Use Slide Timings in the Slide Show dialog box. Your presentation runs automatically, changing slides after the times you designated.

> **NOTE**
>
> If you want to know how long each slide takes to present, but don't want to lock yourself into the timings, rehearse your presentation to work out your speed. Don't save the timings and, when actually giving your presentation, use manual advance and present each slide as you rehearse.
>
> PowerPoint does have a Slide Meter feature that compares your recorded timings with your actual slide presentation speed. During your slide show, click the right mouse button and select Slide Meter. (See Figure 38.10.)

FIGURE 38.10.

The Slide Meter feature.

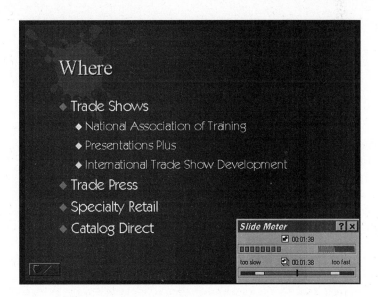

You can set up your presentation to run unattended, looping continuously through the slides. Rehearse and record timings, making sure you give enough time for someone to read and digest each slide, then run your presentation using slide timings and selecting Loop Continuously Until Esc.

TIP

Use a looping presentation at trade shows, in information booths, or anyplace you want to show your information without giving a "live" presentation. Add well-planned animations and transitions to help keep your viewers' interest.

NOTE

To stop any slide show at any time, press the Esc key.

Branching Within Your Presentation

During an interactive slide show (one where your audience is alive and well and asking questions, instead of one where you show each slide in order, no matter what), you may want to change the order in which you show your slides. Use the Slide Navigator to move quickly from slide to slide. Right-click in the current slide, select Go To, and then select Slide Navigator. The Slide Navigator (see Figure 38.11) lists your slides by number and title, allowing you to select a particular slide and go quickly to it. The Last Slide Viewed box keeps your place, noting where you were before jumping around in your presentation.

FIGURE 38.11.

The Slide Navigator.

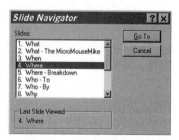

NOTE

Yes, you can use the P and N keys to move to the previous and next slides, respectively. That method, however, takes extra time and may appear unprofessional.

When you anticipate branching to a different slide, set up the "branch" in advance by following these steps:

1. Place a drawing or clip art object (see Figure 38.12) in the slide from which you'll branch.

2. Select the object, and then select Tools | Interactive Settings (see Figure 38.13) from the menu bar.

3. In the Interactive Settings dialog box, select Go To.

4. Click on the arrow to view the options available for branching.

5. Select Slide.

6. From the Go To Slide dialog box, select the slide to which you want to branch.

7. Select OK in Interactive Settings.

FIGURE 38.12.

A clip art object for branching.

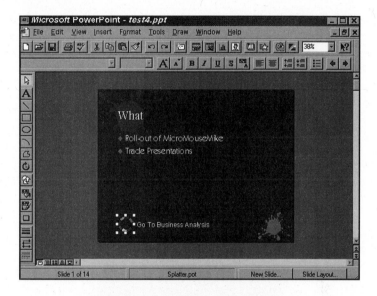

FIGURE 38.13.

The Interactive Settings dialog box.

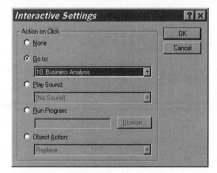

When you run your slide show, click on your branch object (the cursor changes to a pointing hand when over a branching object) to jump to the designated slide.

NOTE

You may have more than one branching object in a slide.

TIP

Use this branching feature to personalize (and keep high interest during) presentations. At a certain point in your presentation, have your audience vote on what they want to see next. Click on the appropriate object, and your audience sees its own presentation.

Branching to Another Presentation

Within this branching concept, you may find that it makes more sense to have your branches be separate presentations. Consider branching to separate presentations when

- You want different slide templates for different branches
- Several smaller files become easier to handle than one huge, slow file
- Presentations you want to show already exist
- Multiple people are creating different parts of the presentation

Setting up a branch to another presentation is similar to, but more complicated than, branching within a presentation. To branch to another presentation, follow these steps:

NOTE

These steps assume that you have already created the other presentation.

1. In the slide from which you'll branch, select Insert | Object from the menu bar, and then select Create from File.
2. Click on Browse and select the file you want to branch to.
3. If you want changes in the branch presentation to be reflected in your current presentation, click on the Link box. Otherwise, with the Link box unchecked, PowerPoint inserts the contents of the branch presentation *at that point in time* into your current presentation and changes in the branch presentation do not appear in your current presentation.
4. Click on OK to exit the Insert Object dialog box.
5. PowerPoint inserts a thumbnail of the branch presentation's first slide. Size the thumbnail as required.

6. Select the thumbnail, then Tools | Interactive Settings from the menu bar.

7. In the Interactive Settings dialog box, select Object Action, and then select Show.

When you run your slide show and click on one of the thumbnails (the cursor changes to a pointing hand when over a "hot spot"), PowerPoint branches to the new presentation. Once the embedded slide show finishes, it returns control to your original presentation. To move on the next slide, click somewhere outside the thumbnail hot spot.

NOTE

You can have more than one branching thumbnail on a slide.

TIP

Be creative with the branch presentations, so they display well as thumbnails. If you branch to more than one presentation from the same slide, give each presentation a different template. (See Figure 38.14.) Make the first slide of the branch presentations a clip art or drawing object that readily communicates the subject of the presentation. Depending on how you size your thumbnails, the title of the branch presentations may not be readable, but you'll have an "icon" to represent each branch.

FIGURE 38.14.

Branch presentation thumbnails.

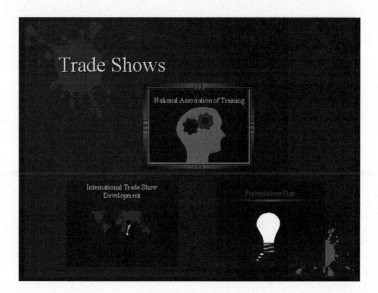

Beyond the Software: Presentation Hardware and Other Goodies

Knowing how to create your presentation using PowerPoint is well and good, but there's another big component to your presentation: the hardware you'll use to show it. At the lowest level, you can give your presentation on a desktop or laptop PC. The size of the screen or monitor and the number of people you can crowd around the display will have a considerable impact on the presentation's effectiveness. Be particularly careful with laptops with passive matrix screens; these screens can only be viewed from straight on and anyone at the edges will completely miss out on your presentation.

Another, more effective, hardware option for giving your presentation is the LCD panel. An LCD panel intercepts the video from a PC and displays the image on the panel. When you place the LCD panel on an overhead projector, the projector picks up the image and displays it on a wall screen. Using an LCD panel with an overhead projector allows you to show your presentation in any situation where an overhead projector is effective. Here are a few warnings about LCD panels:

■ You limit your presentation quality to the resolution of the panel.

■ LCD panels can project the screen image darker than it is on the PC. A higher light output from the overhead projector can help alleviate this problem.

An LCD projector intercepts the video from a PC and projects the image, greatly magnified, onto a screen. LCD projectors give you more flexibility than the LCD panel/overhead projector arrangement, as you can place the projector farther away from the screen and get a larger projected image. As with LCD panels, the resolution of the image from an LCD projector can vary. LCD projectors cost considerably more than the LCD panel/overhead projector combination.

Using a standard mouse—or worse, a laptop's pointing device—during a presentation can be frustrating. With a mouse, you're limited by the length of the mouse cord, so you may be inappropriately tethered to the PC. I, at least, find the mouse buttons to be confusing when I give a presentation—I want the right button to advance a slide and the left button to move back a slide. Of course, I could specifically switch the mouse buttons for my presentation, but I share the presentation facilities with other groups and if I forgot to change the button configuration back, I'd be lousing *them* up.

Consider, then, one of the hand-held pointing devices specifically geared to presentation giving. These devices usually have the advance button on the right and provide cursor-moving capabilities at your fingertips. You can get cordless versions of these devices, too, so you no longer have a tether.

If you're using a big screen of some sort, think about how you will point at things on your slides. If you're close enough to the screen, you can use one of the collapsible, antenna-like pointers. Keep in mind, however, that getting that close to the screen might place you in the light source: then you're half-blind and your shadow may block important parts of the slide. Also, check out conditions before giving your presentation. Will your audience be able to see your pointer?

A laser pointer provides a good alternative to the antenna pointer. You can use it from where you stand so you don't block the screen and distract your audience by moving toward the screen. Laser pointers can be trickier to use than you'd think, though. You may need practice to move the pointer slowly enough so your audience can pick out what you're highlighting. Sweeping that little red dot around in circles can distract your audience or make them dizzy. Don't shine the pointer in anyone's eyes, yours included.

Interacting with Your Presentation

In addition to making your presentation interact with your audience, you can interact with your presentation in a number of ways.

Annotations

You can annotate, or write or draw on, your slides during a presentation. To turn on the annotation "pen," right-click, and select Pen, or press Ctrl+P. The cursor changes to a pencil. Hold down the left mouse button and move the mouse to "write" on the presentation slide. Annotations appear on the screen only and do not change the content or appearance of the slides themselves.

> **TIP**
>
> To erase an annotation, press E.

Meeting Minder

PowerPoint's Meeting Minder allows you to make notes about your presentation as you go along. For example, if your presentation is the agenda for a departmental meeting and you want to make minutes of the meeting and note action items as your meeting progresses, use Meeting Minder to "automate" those tasks.

Access Meeting Minder during a presentation by right clicking, then selecting Meeting Minder. (See Figure 38.15.) Choose the tab you want to use:

- Notes Pages allows you record notes to be added to the slide's notes page.
- Meeting Minutes provides you room, by slide, to take minutes.
- Action Items, similarly, provides space to cumulatively record action items determined during the meeting.

FIGURE 38.15.

The Meeting Minder.

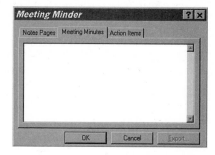

PowerPoint automatically transfers Notes Pages information to the slides' notes; Meeting Minutes and Action Items require a little work on your part for them to finish up. Before closing your presentation, right-click and select Meeting Minder. Click on the Export button (see Figure 38.16) and select the export options you'd like for Meeting Minder. Click on Export Now. A Word document headed "Meeting Minutes" opens. (See Figure 38.17.) This document contains the minutes and action items you noted in Meeting Minder.

FIGURE 38.16.

Meeting Minder export options.

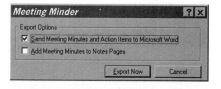

FIGURE 38.17.

Meeting Minder minutes in Word.

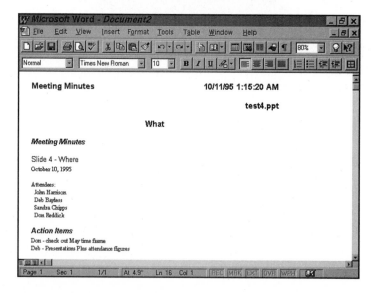

The Pack and Go Wizard

Quite often, in the world of electronic presentations, the computer you create your presentation on won't be the one you show it on. What if that other computer doesn't have PowerPoint? Must you lug around your PowerPoint disks or Office CD to install on the other computer, wasting your time and breaking licensing laws right and left? Must you hope and pray that your "target" computer already has PowerPoint loaded? No, all you "must" do is run the Pack and Go Wizard to package your presentation—and a PowerPoint viewer, if needed—on a disk to install on the target computer.

To run the Pack and Go Wizard (see Figure 38.18), select File | Pack and Go from the menu bar, and follow the instructions the wizard gives you. As with other Office wizards, this one is fairly self-explanatory. Pay attention, however, to the following selections in the wizard:

- Include linked files—If your presentation includes linked files, selecting this button ensures that the linked files get packed up, too.

- Embed True Type fonts—Selecting this button ensures that the fonts you use in your presentation are the same ones that show up in your presentation.

- Include PowerPoint Viewer—If the computer on which you'll show your presentation doesn't have PowerPoint, pack the Viewer and you'll be able to run your presentation on that computer, too.

FIGURE 38.18.

The Pack and Go Wizard opening screen.

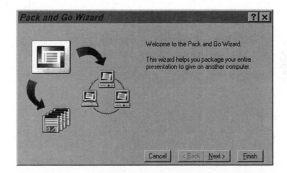

TIP

Just to be safe, it's probably a good idea to always include the viewer. You may need an extra disk to make room for it, but wouldn't you rather *know* that you'll have PowerPoint?

Once the wizard has packed everything up, it's time to move to the target computer and unpack. Put the Pack and Go disk (or the first one, if PowerPoint produced more than one) in the disk drive and run pngsetup.exe. Specify a destination folder, and let the wizard do the rest.

To show your presentation (if you didn't check out your presentation right away to see if the viewer really does work), go into the directory you specified and run pptview.exe. Select the presentation, specify if you want to loop or use automatic timings, and select Show. Your presentation runs just as if it were on the machine where you created it.

> **CAUTION**
>
> If you're viewing a presentation that branches to other presentations, don't try to view immediately after you've finished setting up the presentation on the target computer. You can't guarantee which of the presentations will run first.

> **NOTE**
>
> Keep your disk(s) handy after you've set up your Pack and Go presentation on the other machine. Despite indications to the contrary, you'll need to have the (first) disk in the disk drive when you exit the setup.

Choosing Your Output Medium

Now that you know most of the mechanics of giving your presentation, it's time to examine the output medium itself: Given the choices of electronic presentations, overhead transparencies, 35mm slides, and just plain paper, which should you use when?

Electronic—Onscreen—Presentations

One of the greatest benefits of electronic presentations is flexibility. You can easily make last-minute changes—or even changes on-the-fly during the presentation. Because the file is the presentation medium, you don't have additional output worries. You have flexibility, too, in the order of your slides. Changing to different slides is no harder than bringing up the Slide Navigator and selecting where you want to go. You no longer even have the annoying rapid-fire clicks to a slide you want to show. In addition, branching allows you to jump to other parts of your presentation, or to other presentations.

As discussed earlier, the computer on which you show an electronic presentation can be a disadvantage. If you're using a laptop to make a presentation to a group, your effectiveness is limited by the small size of the screen and the display's characteristics. A desktop computer likely has a better monitor, but you still have limitations regarding how many people can cluster around the screen.

For electronic presentations, a projection system is the way to go, if one is available. The big screen makes viewing a pleasure for all attendees, and you (the presenter) have room to move around and point things out. One drawback to the projection system output device: Generally, you'll darken the room for best viewing. Often, people know that they don't have to be as (or look as) attentive during a darkened-room presentation; while the lights are off, your audience may be gone (mentally), too.

An additional benefit of electronic presentations is the lack of further production costs. Create the slide in your computer and that's that: no printing, no reproduction, no ink or toner consumed.

Electronic presentations given on laptops or desktop PCs provide for the most informal presentations. Granted, a laptop-based presentation may be an excellent way to make a sales pitch to a limited number of people at a customer's site, but it's still not up to the level of other output media. Video project–based presentations are a step up on the formality scale, but work well only for small to mid-sized audiences.

Overhead Transparencies

Of the three output media, overhead transparencies are the second most flexible, but only in terms of changing the order of your presentation. You can swap out transparencies fairly easily, but count out last-minute changes to the transparencies themselves. You can use markers to write on the overhead, but you're stuck with what you put on the thing originally.

Do put your transparencies in some kind of sleeve or sheet protector. The sleeves provide holes for storing your overheads in binders, protect your slides from scratches, and provide extra weight to keep your slide firmly planted on the overhead projector. Make sure you use crystal-clear sleeves, though, or your slides may appear dim or discolored. Consider using the sleeves with "wings." The wings give you room to make notes about the overhead.

Many sources indicate to use a light background with dark letters for overhead transparencies. Feel free, however, to try out dark backgrounds with light text, but be certain that your overheads are readable and legible. Consider the cost of dark backgrounds, though. Colored ink or toner or film isn't cheap. Producing all those slides in color could prove to be burdensome to your budget.

Overhead transparencies still lend themselves to less-than-formal situations and smaller-sized audiences. (Would you really want to worry about putting overheads on the projector the right way out, the right way up, and completely straight, when giving an important presentation to the Board of Directors?)

35mm Slides

35mm slides probably provide the most professional presentation and are the most suitable medium for formal presentations. 35mm slides offer excellent color and image quality. You can change images more quickly using slides than overhead transparencies—and you don't have to worry about slides being crooked.

Using 35mm slides as your output medium brings up a host of issues that many of us aren't used to dealing with, however. With 35mm slides, you have to determine where and how you will get your presentation file converted into slides. You also need to decide whether you want plastic or glass mounts for your slides. Plastic mounts are cheaper than glass and are appropriate for informal presentations. Glass mounts provide sharper image focus and are less likely to pop out of focus, which can be a problem with plastic mounts. Once you have your slides, you have to arrange them and load them into cassettes, making sure you get them all in the right way. You have to worry about the possibility of all your slides falling out of their cassettes 3 minutes before you're due to begin.

> **TIP**
>
> Number the slides in your presentation. That way, if you have a 3-minutes-before-you're-due-to-begin-type disaster, at least you'll have the numbers to guide your reloading chore.

One consideration for producing the slides themselves: Send your file to Genigraphics. Genigraphics Corporation is a service bureau that has provided PowerPoint users the necessary options to have their PowerPoint slides converted to 35mm slides, digital color overheads, posters, or large display prints. Run the Genigraphics Wizard (by selecting File | Send to Genigraphics from the menu bar) and follow the instructions to get your information to Genigraphics and your output back from them.

Summary

This chapter looks at creating and using notes and handouts to accompany your presentation. Then it concentrates on the mechanics of actually giving your presentation, including hardware considerations, adding annotations, and using the Meeting Minder. The Pack and Go Wizard allows you to move your presentation from one machine to another without all the extra baggage of including PowerPoint, too. Finally, the chapter explores some of the issues involved with different presentation output media.

Multimedia Presentations

39

by Sue Charlesworth

IN THIS CHAPTER

You've seen simple animations in PowerPoint, but its multimedia capabilities go far beyond flying text, drive-in clip art, and dissolve transitions. With PowerPoint, your presentations can include sounds and video, with video clips including either movies or animations.

What Is Multimedia?

Multimedia involves effects in two or more media. In today's computing, multimedia generally means including video (or motion of some kind) and sound in a presentation, software package, or some other form of output.

Multimedia seems to have burst into the computing scene relatively suddenly. A number of improvements in technology helped bring on this explosion of sight and sound. Some of the factors contributing to multimedia's rise are

- Cheaper, more powerful processors
- Cheaper, improved CD-ROM technology
- Cheaper memory
- Improved sound cards
- Improved graphics cards

We had become used to increasingly sophisticated graphics and special effects in movies, TV, and videos; when the technology to put motion and sound in software became affordable, multimedia took off.

Why Use Multimedia Presentations?

As stated, we've come to expect sophisticated audio and visual effects in our entertainment and, increasingly, in our software, including games, informative and educational software, and business applications. Multimedia is *the* thing in user-oriented output; put somewhat baldly, without multimedia, you're at a competitive disadvantage. Other factors being equal, someone else's product, whether it's software or a business presentation, may well be deemed better than yours, if theirs is multimedia and yours is not.

Perceptions (and marketing ploys) aside, we do have high expectations of what we see. If presentations don't catch—and keep—our interest, we become easily bored and turn off. Movement and sound—the stuff of multimedia—help catch and hold our attention.

In addition, different people learn in different ways: Some people learn by seeing (which could include reading); some learn by hearing; others learn by doing. While even multimedia presentations can't do much about those who learn by doing, they can address themselves to the learn-by-seeing folks by providing video clips and pictures, in addition to text. Learn-by-hearing people can benefit from sounds and video sound tracks, in addition to the presenter's material.

The more of your information you include in your presentation, the less you have to provide. If the material you want to cover is all in the presentation, you won't have to worry about forgetting to make important points; similarly, if different people make the same presentation, you'll be assured of consistency among presenters.

The Trials and Tribulations of Multimedia

Yes, multimedia can be good when it brings heightened interest and new forms of communication to output. However, multimedia presentations can be stunningly bad (literally, sometimes). Too much motion, too much sound, too many lights, too many cameras, and too much action can produce presentations that no one wants to sit through. If they're done well, multimedia presentations can bring new interest and effectiveness to your presentations; if they're done poorly…well, you could lose your audience more easily than if they become bored. A well-done single-media PowerPoint presentation can be far more effective than a poorly done multimedia one.

In addition to the possibility of media overkill, multimedia brings with it hardware considerations simply not needed with single media. You could show a single-media presentation on many existing computer systems; for a successful multimedia presentation, you must have a powerful enough processor, sufficient memory, and adequate sound and graphics cards. Multimedia-capable systems aren't as plentiful as single media–capable systems; if your presentation is part of a traveling road show and you're dependent on computer systems at your different destinations, you may find your finely tuned multimedia presentation falling flat on its face.

Multimedia presentations take up a lot of space, too. *Your* hard disk may have enough space for your wondrous creation, but will the one at your presentation site have enough? Do you want to make and load all those backup disks? Or, if you use compression software and you don't need *quite* so many disks, will you remember to bring along a copy of the decompression software?

Multimedia PowerPoint Presentations

Now that we have the warnings and doom and gloom out of the way, let's look at creating multimedia presentations in PowerPoint. Throughout this chapter I'll assume that you've taken all the warnings to heart and that we have the appropriate multimedia muscle, for both development and deployment. Here we go.

Basic Multimedia

You get basic multimedia capabilities with PowerPoint's slide animation and transitions. Animation and transitions also add sound to your presentation. With text or object animation, the Effects box of the Animation Settings dialog box provides a drop-down list of sounds available. PowerPoint "matches" sounds to the animation effects—the "drive in" animation effect is teamed with screeching brakes, for instance—but you can change to any sound offered. (See Figure 39.1.)

FIGURE 39.1.

Screeching brakes sound.

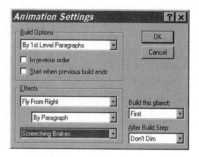

Similarly, you can add sounds to slide transitions. In the Slide Transition dialog box, select a sound from the Sound drop-down list. Checking the Loop until next sound box does just what it says—the sound repeats until some other sound replaces it.

CAUTION

Looping sounds can get *very* irritating *very* quickly. Use it with extreme care! Don't forget to turn looping sounds off. They're there until another sound turns them off. If you forget to set another sound and you have breaking glass sounding throughout the rest of your presentation, you may not have an audience when the presentation finishes. Test your presentation before giving it.

NOTE

You can add a sound to a slide transition even if you don't use a transition effect. (See Figure 39.2.)

More Advanced Multimedia

You can transform your presentation into a multimedia marvel by adding audio (sound) and video (either live or animation) clips from other sources. Because these clips are not part of the PowerPoint package, you'll need to add them as objects.

FIGURE 39.2.

Sound but no motion.

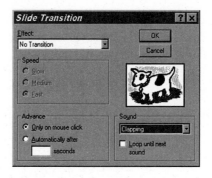

PowerPoint offers a number of ways to add video or audio clips to slides. You can select one of the following:

- Insert | Movie or Insert | Sound from the menu bar
- Insert | Object | Video Clip or Insert | Object | Wave Sound
- The Object slide layout (by double-clicking in the object area, then selecting Video Clip or Wave Sound)
- The Text & Media Clip or Media Clip & Text slide layout (by double-clicking in the media clip area, then selecting Insert Clip and the appropriate medium from the menu bar)

The last method opens the Microsoft Media Player.

Multimedia clips are available from any number of sources. For videos, look for Video for Windows clips (those with the .avi extension); for sounds, look for wave (wav) files. The Microsoft Office 95 CD-ROM offers some samples. The Valupack folder on the CD has a wealth of goodies. In the Video folder, the Fourpalm folder contains "live" video clips; the Tcvisual folder has a number of animations. In the Audio folder, check out the Network offerings. The Effects, Elements, and Music folders contain a variety of wav files just begging for use as slide transitions, background music, or special effects.

Controlling Your Clips

After you've inserted your clip in a slide, you can edit the clip so it better meets your needs. You have access to controls that can help you change both the video and sound tracks to meet your presentation's needs.

Video Clips

Right-click on the multimedia object, and then select Edit | ...Object. (What's between Edit and Object depends on the type of object you've inserted.) Media Player opens, along with your multimedia object, and you can edit your object.

Because we're dealing with different kinds of media, Media Player responds differently to each kind. If you open a sound, Media Player responds with a sound editor; if you open a video, Media Player opens its video editor. (See Figure 39.3.)

FIGURE 39.3.

Media Player for video.

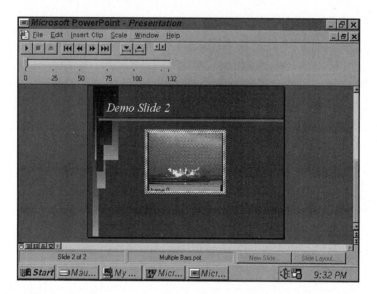

The Scale option from the Media Player menu bar (remember, we're looking at the video version) enables you to select how you want to view the clip: by time, frames, or tracks. When you change the Scale, the units marked on the slider change to reflect the new scale reference.

NOTE

The slider itself doesn't indicate which scale is active, nor do the Scale menu selections; the caption area below the clip, however, does.

TIP

Most of us are probably more concerned with how long a clip takes than how many frames it contains. The Time Scale, therefore, may be your best choice.

Edit | Options from the Media Player menu offers you a number of ways you can control or change the appearance of the video in your presentation. (See Figure 39.4.) Select Auto Repeat to have the video player loop.

FIGURE 39.4.

The Options dialog box.

If you want to control the video while it plays in your presentation, leave Control Bar On Playback checked. When the video plays in your presentation, you'll have access to simple controls—start, pause, stop, and a slider. If you choose to have the control bar, PowerPoint also displays a caption for the video. The caption defaults to the filename; change the caption if you want something a little more friendly or descriptive.

Edit | Selection allows you to select exactly which part of the video you want to play. Depending on the Scale chosen, the Set Selection dialog box (see Figure 39.5) reflects either frames or time. Click on the up and down arrows next to the From, To, and Size fields to edit the start and stop points of the video.

FIGURE 39.5.

The Set Selection dialog box.

NOTE

Editing by frames could probably come in handy here. But you still need to know what frames to use as starting and stopping points.

TIP

If the video you want is a little too long, or just right except for that bit right at the end, edit it here to fit your needs.

Use the play control buttons to see how your clip looks, so you can make sure it's just right before you add it to your presentation.

Audio Clips

To change the volume of your system as it plays your clip, select the video object, right-click, and select Open Video Clip Object. The Media Player opens, but this time it's a free-floating dialog box and has the menu option Device. (See Figure 39.6.) Select Device to open the Volume Control dialog box. (See Figure 39.7.) Adjust the sliders to control the video's volume.

FIGURE 39.6.

Media Player as a free-floating dialog box.

FIGURE 39.7.

The Volume Control dialog box.

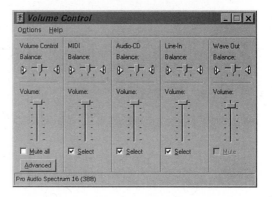

While still in the Volume Control dialog box, select Options from the menu bar, then select Advanced to put the Advanced button on the Volume Control dialog box. Clicking on the Advanced button opens the Advanced Controls for Volume Control dialog box (see Figure 39.8), where you can adjust bass and treble values.

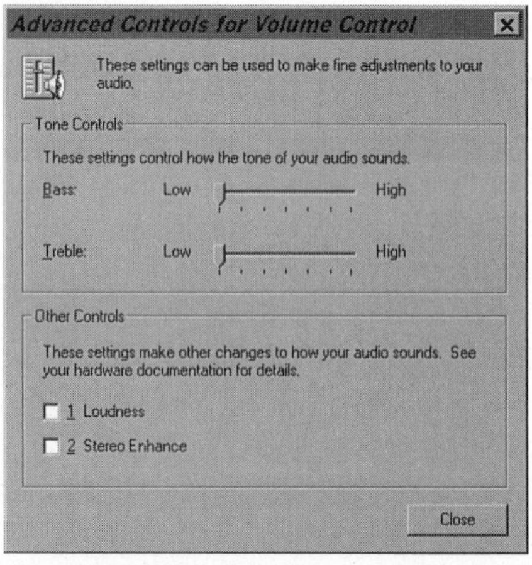

FIGURE 39.8.

Advanced controls for volume control.

Playing Your Clips

If you insert your video or audio clips as described, you'll need to click on each clip during your presentation to have them all play. Further tweaking of your clips allows you to have them play automatically during your presentation.

Select a clip and right-click. Select Animation Settings from the pop-up menu. In the Animation Settings dialog box, click on the arrow next to the Play Options field and select Play from the list. (See Figure 39.9.) At this point, you won't need to click on the specific clip to have it play during your presentation; however, you will need to click somewhere in your presentation.

FIGURE 39.9.

The Animation Settings dialog box with Play options.

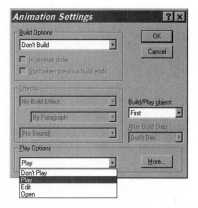

For completely automatic clip playing, after you've selected the Play option, click on the More button. In the More Play Options dialog box, in the Start group, click on the Automatically button. (See Figure 39.10.) Click on the up and down arrows if you want to specify a number of seconds to delay playing the clip.

FIGURE 39.10.

The More Play Options dialog box.

> **NOTE**
>
> As discussed in the "Speed of Presentation" section, it takes time for PowerPoint to fire up and play media clips, particularly video clips. If you're planning the time between clips, be sure to take this additional setup time.

Performance and Quality Considerations

As attention catching as multimedia is, it doesn't come without a price. Audio and video files take a lot of disk space and require a lot of processing power. Memory, particularly the lack of it, affects performance. Multimedia presentations also rely heavily on hardware capabilities for their quality. Graphics and sound cards become important.

Monitors, on the other hand, probably become less important, at least for the presentations themselves. While you may still have the presentation-on-a-laptop scenario, much of multimedia's impact could be lost on that tiny screen. For truly effective multimedia presentations, you'll probably need some kind of projection system. If, however, you design your presentation as a standalone, single-person viewing station, you will need to be concerned about monitor size and quality.

> **NOTE**
>
> Hooking up a laptop to an overhead projection unit does keep laptops in the multimedia game. You're still concerned with the quality of the laptop's screen, though, and then you've got the projection hardware to play with, too.

> **NOTE**
>
> Monitor quality does, of course, play a large role in creating the presentation. If you do a lot of multimedia presentations, a large-screen, high-quality monitor will help you keep your eyesight and your sanity. You'll be a lot less likely to use that monitor for the actual presentation, though, given the limited number of people you can fit around it.

Quality of Output

No matter what visuals you put in your multimedia presentation, they'll fall flat if they don't look good when played. The physical size of a video clip window affects the presentation's quality. Many video clips are no bigger than a few inches on each side. You could resize the window, of course, but there's a reason for the original dimensions. Increasing the size of a video window, particularly for a "live" one, produces a grainy image. Grainy images look blocky and blurry and don't lead to overall good impressions of the presentation. Animations, depending on their level of detail, don't suffer so much from graininess, but their edges can become quite "jaggy." Sharp, clear pictures, therefore, will be small in relation to the overall size of the slide and screen.

Quality of the picture aside, you need to be concerned with the smoothness of the movie or animation. If your processor, memory, and video card constrain your video clips, they'll look jerky, pause, or skip sections. The sound may not keep in sync with the picture.

> **TIP**
>
> PowerPoint helps you with the window-sizing issue. Select the video object, and then choose Draw | Scale | Best Scale For Slide Show from the menu bar. PowerPoint resizes the video window for optimum skip-free playing.

Sound reproduction can also cause problems. If you have a clip of someone giving important information verbally, you'll want your audience to hear the voice clearly. Your sound card comes into play here. Pay attention to the volume of any sound or video clips. You want your audience to hear your presentation, but not be blasted away by it. Test your presentation under the conditions under which it will be played—same equipment, same area, same background conditions, if possible. Know how to get to the volume controls. You can't change the volume of a clip during a presentation, so know how to control volume through the speakers.

Speed of Presentation

It takes time for PowerPoint to set up a video clip to run. Once the clip starts, PowerPoint takes awhile to fire up the object, during which time you and your audience watch the "working" cursor. When the clip is finished, it takes PowerPoint some time to close things down, too. Be sure to account for these waiting times when planning your presentation.

Hardware Considerations

PowerPoint's help files list these minimum recommendations for your computer to run multimedia presentations:

- 486 processor running at 66MHz (a Pentium yields better video results)
- 16MB or more of memory
- 30MB hard disk space
- "Soundblaster compatible" card
- External speakers
- VGA 256-color graphics adapter, with 16-bit or 24-bit adapters recommended for better results with video

With several of these recommendations, more is better. The faster your processor (the clock speed, measured in MHz) or the more powerful (a Pentium chip as opposed to a 486 chip), the better. The more memory you have, the better. Sound cards, speakers, and graphics adapters come in different qualities; higher-quality hardware usually results in higher-quality output. (Higher-quality hardware also results in higher prices, but such is life.)

What happens if your system doesn't meet the hardware requirements? That depends. In general, your presentation's quality degrades in the areas where your hardware lacks oomph. We've mentioned a number of the problems earlier in this chapter. You do have some options for improving performance, whether you're straining the capabilities of your top-end system or straining just to get your older setup to work. Here are some things to consider:

- Keep the size of your video window small. Besides the picture-quality issues, bigger windows use more system resources.

- Don't have competing media. While a video clip with a sound track runs as a unit, an audio loop in the background could affect performance.

- Do you need both an audio and a video track? If you create your own multimedia clips, rather than rely on what someone else provides, leaving off the audio can help keep quality up.

One more hardware issue is disk space. While disk space may not affect the running of your presentation, it certainly has a bearing on creating and storing your presentation. Multimedia isn't cheap, space-wise. For example, an "empty" (no text) 10-slide presentation with the Cheers template takes up 139KB of disk space; adding a checkerboard transition to all slides has minimal impact, increasing disk space to 140KB; with a drumroll sound transition on all the slides, disk space used jumps to 159KB. Including a 5^1/$_2$-second video clip bumps the file size to 456KB.

Putting It into Practice—A Multimedia Presentation

To look at actually putting a multimedia presentation together, we return attention to the MicroMouseMike. The roll-out plans for the MicroMouseMike included a demonstration at the Presentations Plus trade show. Now, we'll start building that presentation.

First, some background. This presentation serves a different purpose than the one for employees, so we choose a different template. This time it's Comet; Comet adds some excitement, without detracting from the video clips in the slides. A change to the Slide Master gives us an extremely legible sans serif font for all slide text. (We don't want our audience to have to work to read our slides; a trade show presents enough distraction without making it easy for our audience to tune out.) We won't worry about outlining the content; we'll assume that all that's already been done and we're putting in the multimedia parts. Figure 39.11 shows the outline for the first part of the presentation.

FIGURE 39.11.

*The MicroMouseMike
presentation outline.*

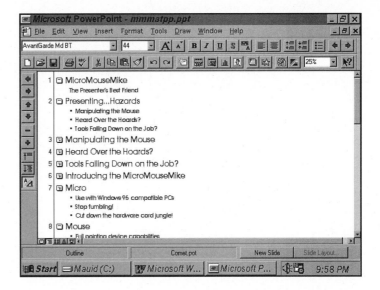

The MicroMouseMike presentation at the Presentations Plus trade show is designed as a fairly simple, informational presentation. The MicroMouseMike folks intend to use it to attract people to the booth and keep their attention long enough for them to learn something about the MicroMouseMike. A person will emcee the presentation, reading a script. By using a person tied in to a separate sound system, the verbal audio requirements won't use up PC resources. The MicroMouseMike folks have a superb presentation system, so they won't have to worry about resources otherwise. (The mighty MicroMouseMike, of course, serves as the combined mouse and microphone.)

Unless otherwise noted, audio clips referenced come from the Network folder of the Office 95 CD. All audio and video clips come from the Valupack folder of the CD.

> **NOTE**
>
> This is a book, not a multimedia presentation. You can't see or hear what the next sections discuss. Use your imagination, and by all means, try out the effects yourself.

For the first slide, the presentation's introduction, we'll add a longish piece of music for the slide transition. For this, we've chosen pentium.wav, from the Music folder. In Slide View, select the first slide, right mouse click, select Slide Transition, and go to the Sound box in the Slide Transition dialog box. Move all the way to the bottom of the list for Other Sound, then work your way through the directories to select pentium.wav. The presenter will speak over this music clip to introduce the MicroMouseMike, the Presenter's Best Friend.

The next four slides form a group and we add multimedia effects accordingly. Dealing with the hazards of presenting shows, broken glass forms the sound theme. Each line of text in the first of these slides flies in to the sound of breaking glass (one of the "standard" sounds) and the transition from this slide to each of the next three is also broken glass. (In slide view, select all four of the slides and add the same transition.) Because the last three slides of this group contain video clips, we won't "clutter" them with visual transitions, too.

The three video slides of the group contain video clips from the Fourpalm Movies folder: The first has mouse.avi; the second, kayaker.avi; and the third, sidewalk.avi. Use any method discussed in this chapter to insert the movie objects. Give each the optimum non-skipping size by selecting Draw | Scale | Best Scale For Slide Show from the menu bar. On each slide, change the caption to reflect the top, not the filename: Select the video object, right-click, select Edit Video Clip Object or Open Video Clip Object, select Edit | Options from the menu bar, and change the caption. The mouse movie runs about 12 seconds, too long for presentation, so we cut it down to around 6 seconds in length: Select the mouse video object, right-click, and select Video Clip Object Edit. Move the slider to make the clip about 6 seconds long. (See Figure 39.12.)

FIGURE 39.12.

Changing video clip time.

The next slide, Introducing the MicroMouseMike, comes right from the employee presentation. We'll have each of the three objects fly in from the upper right, accompanied by the flyby.wav sound from the Elements folder.

TIP

After you've used an "Other Sound," PowerPoint adds that file to the top of the sounds list. Scroll to the top for the flyby sound after you've put it in the first object.

On the next slide, we'll insert separate audio objects for each line of text. (See Figure 39.13.) Use Animation Settings to time the audio clips so they play after the presenter reads the line. We'll add keyboard.wav for the first line, boing1.wav for the second, and tear.wav for the third. Line up the sound icons at the right side of the slide, so they don't distract from the main message. The keyboard sound is fairly subtle; increase its volume several times by right-clicking on the sound object, selecting Edit Wave Sound Object to open Media Player for sounds (see Figure 39.14), and then selecting Effects | Increase Volume from the menu bar (see Figure 39.15). You may need to increase the volume three or four times.

FIGURE 39.13.

Audio objects for text lines.

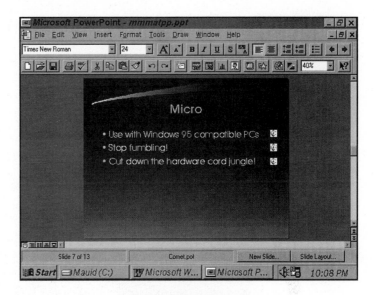

FIGURE 39.14.

Media Player for audio objects.

FIGURE 39.15.

Increasing volume.

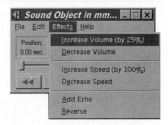

That's all we're going to cover for this presentation. As you've seen, PowerPoint offers many ways to add multimedia capabilities to presentations, and we could add much more life to our MicroMouseMike show. A few last reminders, though. Like animations and transitions, multimedia is *fun!* (Insert elflaff.wav here.) It's also hazardous (breaking glass) to the health of your presentation. Overused, or used poorly, multimedia can create loud (both visually and aurally), distracting, obnoxious, overbearing...the list could go on and on...presentations. Don't make your multimedia presentation the modern equivalent of the neighbor's vacation slides (out of focus, missing heads, boring...). Err on the side of understatement, rather than overstatement, in a multimedia presentation.

Summary

Multimedia, the ability to include sound and motion, in presentations offers a lot of punch; it also requires more hardware power than a single-media presentation. Hardware weaknesses can degrade the quality of an otherwise perfectly constructed presentation.

PowerPoint's animation and transition capabilities add basic motion to presentations; you can also add sound effects to slide animations and transitions. Beyond these basic native abilities, video and sound clips can be added to your presentations as objects. Microsoft's Media Player helps you control these clips.

Factors that influence the quality of your presentation (outside of design) include

- The type of your computer's processor
- The speed of your computer's processor
- How much memory your machine has
- The quality of your graphics and sound cards

In general, the more or the higher, the better.

Problems that can show up in your presentations because of inadequate hardware include

- Grainy, blurry, or blocky images
- Jaggy images
- Jerky movies
- Movies that skip or pause
- Sound out of sync with the picture

In the last part of this chapter, we looked at putting multimedia objects into a presentation.

Integrating OLE Objects into PowerPoint

40

by Sue Charlesworth

IN THIS CHAPTER

Through OLE (object linking and embedding) you can insert all or part of another Office application's file—an object—in a PowerPoint presentation; OLE also enables you to edit or update the information in that object. The main differences between linking and embedding involve which application stores the object's information and how information in the object gets updated.

With linking, the parent application—the one in which the object was created—stores the object's information. The host application—the one in which the object is placed—only receives a copy of the object that refers to the original. The parent application updates the data in the object; the linked copy in the host application reflects any changes made in the original application. In PowerPoint, as with other Office applications, you use the Paste Special command to link objects.

Embedding, on the other hand, stores the object and its data in the host application file itself; the object becomes part of the host file. You update information in the object by double-clicking on the object; the object's application opens so you can edit its data. When you close the object, the change is reflected in the host application. With embedding, the original file remains unaffected by changes to the object. You use the Paste command to embed objects.

Building Presentations from Word Documents

Using OLE, you can use Word documents to build PowerPoint presentations. In general, you can look at three ways to create PowerPoint presentations from Word documents: as straight text, as outlines, and as tables.

Linking and Embedding Word Text

Blocks of Word text, when placed in a PowerPoint slide, look like blocks of Word text. No fancy transformations happen when linking or embedding. Normal font sizes in documents don't make for easy reading in a presentation, nor do paragraphs provide the telegraphic, bullet-pointed style effective for presentation reading. In short, straight Word text often doesn't make sense for linking or embedding in a PowerPoint presentation. (See Figure 40.1.)

Having said that, a few instances come to mind where linking or embedding Word text in a presentation makes sense. A document with a particular format could make an effective addition to a presentation. For example, a meeting agenda produced through Word's Agenda Wizard might be reproduced in a presentation given during the meeting. Figures 40.2 and 40.3 show an example of this use. Or you might want to display printed quotes in a presentation, where the text format of the object adds impact to the presentation.

Chapter 40

FIGURE 40.1.

Embedded Word text.

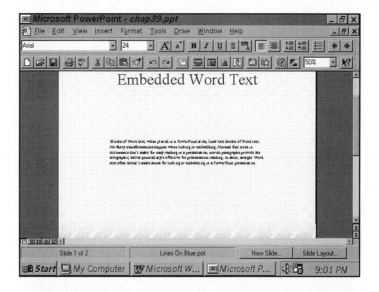

FIGURE 40.2.

A Word agenda document.

To embed Word text in a PowerPoint slide, copy the text you want to embed in the slide. In PowerPoint, paste the text in the desired slide. You can use any Office method for pasting the text: Right-click in your document and select Paste from the pop-up menu; select Edit | Paste from the menu bar; or press Ctrl+V.

FIGURE 40.3.

*Word agenda text in a
PowerPoint slide.*

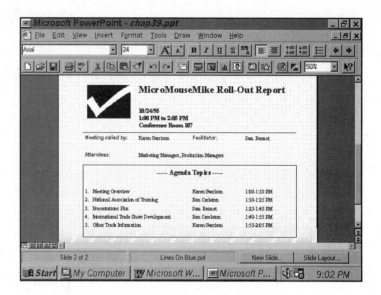

To paste the text into the slide in a different format, select Edit | Paste Special from PowerPoint's menu bar. Leave the Paste button active and select the format you'd like to use for the pasted text (see Figure 40.4):

- Picture pastes the text into the slide as a drawing-type object.

- Formatted Text preserves any formatting (bold, italic, or fonts) and pastes in the text at default presentation text size.

- Unformatted text pastes the text into the slide at default presentation text size and formatting.

FIGURE 40.4.

Paste Special formats.

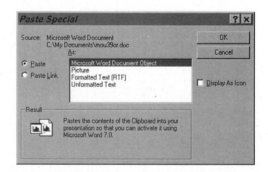

To link Word text in a PowerPoint slide, copy the text and you want to link in the slide. In PowerPoint, select Edit | Paste Special from the menu bar, and then choose Paste Link.

> **NOTE**
>
> You can link or embed entire Word files in a PowerPoint slide. To do so, select Insert | Object from the menu bar. Click on the Create from File button. Click on Browse to select the file. Click on OK to embed the file; select Link, and then click OK to link the file.

Embedding Word Outlines

Word outlines, when specially embedded in a PowerPoint presentation, become presentation outlines: Heading 1 text lines become slide titles; Heading 2 and lower lines form the bullet point lines of a slide. Office provides two ways to embed Word outlines in PowerPoint presentations: one from the Word side, the other from the PowerPoint side.

> **NOTE**
>
> This embedding uses the heading styles to create slides; you don't necessarily have to work from the Outline View in Word.

In Word, select File | Templates from the menu bar. In the Templates and Add-Ins dialog box, click on the Attach button. Move to the \Msoffice\Winword\Macros directory, select Present7.dot, and click the Open button. (See Figure 40.5.) Back in the Templates and Add-Ins dialog box, select Open. The Present7 template contains the PresentIt macro; PresentIt takes the lines with heading styles from the Word file, opens PowerPoint if necessary, creates a new PowerPoint presentation, and embeds the Word outline as a slide outline in PowerPoint.

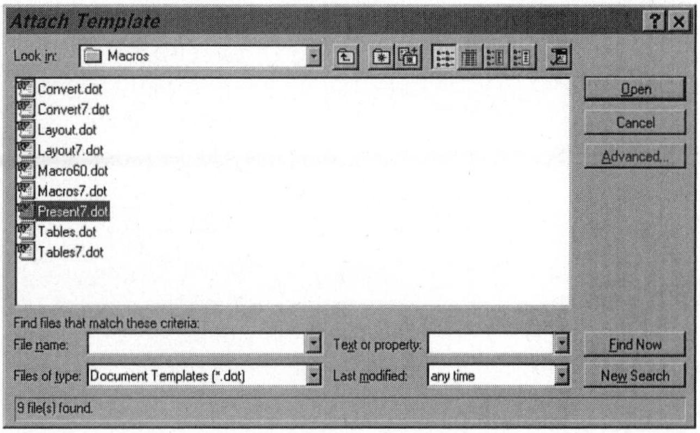

FIGURE 40.5.

Attaching the Present7 template.

Run the PresentIt macro by selecting View | Toolbars from the menu bar, then select Microsoft and click OK. From the Microsoft toolbar, click on the Present It icon on the far right. (See Figure 40.6.) Alternatively, select Tools | Macro from the menu bar, select PresentIt, and select Run. (See Figure 40.7.) When the macro finishes, you'll be in PowerPoint with a new presentation, ready to develop it further.

FIGURE 40.6.

The Microsoft toolbar with the Present It icon.

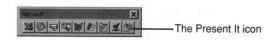

The Present It icon

FIGURE 40.7.

The PresentIt macro from the macro list.

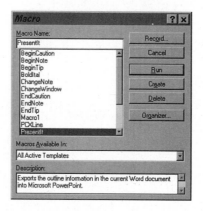

To build a presentation from a Word outline while in PowerPoint, select Insert | Slides from Outline from the menu bar. (See Figure 40.8.) Navigate through your directory structure to find your Word file, and select Insert. The Word file outline becomes slides in the active presentation.

FIGURE 40.8.

The Insert Slides from Outline menu option.

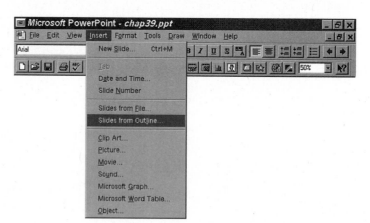

NOTE

Once you've embedded a Word outline into a PowerPoint presentation, you can't double-click the object to edit it. The outline has become multiple slides, so you have no one object to click on. Also, there is no need to be able to edit the outline through Word; PowerPoint has all the capabilities necessary for manipulating the outline.

Embedding Word Tables

You can embed Word tables from the PowerPoint side. You insert a Word table object in a PowerPoint slide by selecting a slide layout for a table (see Figure 40.9), or by selecting Insert | Microsoft Word Table from the menu bar. The Insert Word Table dialog box allows you to specify the number of columns and rows in the table. Click OK, and a Word table of the dimensions specified opens. As with other embedded objects, editing takes place within Word; the table object itself exists in the PowerPoint slide.

FIGURED 40.9.

Table slide layout.

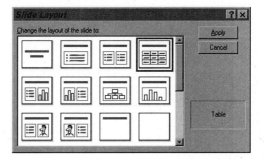

Adding Excel Charts

You can also link and embed Excel charts in PowerPoint slides. To link an Excel chart in a PowerPoint slide, open the Excel worksheet, select and copy the chart, move to the PowerPoint slide, select File | Paste Special from the menu bar, and then choose Paste Link. When you double-click the linked chart, its parent worksheet opens and you can edit the Excel file. Any changes to the Excel file that update the chart are reflected in the chart in the PowerPoint slide.

To embed an existing Excel chart in a PowerPoint slide, open the Excel worksheet, select and copy the chart, move to the PowerPoint slide, and paste the chart into the slide. Use any method to paste the chart into the slide. When you double-click on the embedded chart, Excel, the chart, and its worksheet open within the PowerPoint slide. (See Figure 40.10.) Edit the chart or worksheet to make changes to the chart in the slide. Changes to the embedded chart do not affect the original Excel file from which you copied the chart.

FIGURE 40.10.

An embedded chart.

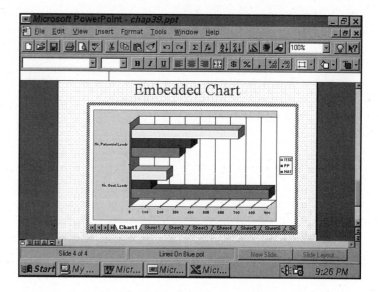

You can also embed a new Excel chart in a PowerPoint slide. Select Insert | Object from the menu bar, and then select Microsoft Excel Chart. PowerPoint embeds a new default chart into the slide. Double-click on the chart to open it and change the data to meet your needs.

> **NOTE**
>
> If you select multiple charts from a worksheet and try to link or embed them in a slide, PowerPoint gets confused and doesn't recognize the type of object you're dealing with. If you continue, PowerPoint pastes the charts in the slide as a picture. To put multiple linked or embedded charts on a single slide, link or embed them one by one.

Summary

Object linking and embedding enables you to place objects of other Office types in PowerPoint presentations. With linked objects, the object's information is stored in the parent application; editing the object changes the data in the parent file. With embedded objects, the object becomes part of the PowerPoint file; editing the object does not affect the file from which it came. The Paste Special function links objects; Paste embeds objects.

You can add Word text, outlines, and tables to PowerPoint slides. You can embed or link text, although straight text doesn't translate well to presentations. Using the Present7 template and macro, you can transform Word outlines (or, rather, the various Word headings) into slides. You embed Word tables into slides from the menu or from the Table slide layout option.

You can also use Excel charts as OLE objects in PowerPoint slides. Copy a chart, then paste it to embed it in a slide; use Paste Special to link the chart in the slide. Create a new embedded chart by selecting Microsoft Excel Chart from the list opened by from Insert | Object.

PART

Making Time with Schedule+

Schedule+ for Yourself

41

by Sue Charlesworth

Think about how you organize your work: If you are a manager, you might organize your day around projects; a salesperson, around contacts; a consultant, around appointments. No matter your line of work, your preferred or required manner of organizing your workday, or your work hours, Schedule+ has the tools to help you organize your tasks, time, and contacts.

Starting Schedule+

Here's a list of ways you can start Schedule+:

- Select Schedule+ from the Program list in the Windows 95 Start menu.
- Select Schedule+ from the appropriate directory in Windows Explorer.
- Select one of the Schedule+ icons from the Office shortcut bar.

> **NOTE**
>
> Either of the first two options opens the Schedule+ main screen. Selecting one of the Schedule+ icons from the Office shortcut bar brings up one of the Schedule+ main tasks. The icons are identical, so use ToolTips or memorization to determine which is which.

From left to right (or top to bottom, if you have moved your Office shortcut bar), here's a list of the tasks:

- Make an appointment
- Add a task
- Add a contact

The selected view overlays the main Schedule+ screen.

Enter your logon name (this is how Schedule+ will refer to you throughout) and then click OK. (See Figure 41.1.) You're now on your way to better organization!

FIGURE 41.1.

The logon screen.

The Main Schedule+ Screen

The main Schedule+ screen in Figure 41.2 consists of a menu bar and a toolbar along the top of the screen, a status bar at the bottom, and three main areas. The largest area contains a view selected from a series of tabs along the left side of the area. The active tab appears on top of the other tabs. On the right are the Date Navigator (a calendar with the current date highlighted and arrow buttons to change the month) and the To Do list. The status bar displays the current time, date, and, if a time-related slot is selected, the active time slot.

FIGURE 41.2.

The main Schedule+ screen.

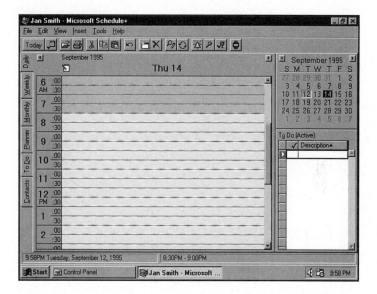

The Date Navigator

The Date Navigator, which appears in the top-right part of the main Schedule+ screen, provides an easy way to move rapidly from date to date. (See Figure 41.3.) Today's date is indented, and the currently selected date is highlighted. A boldface number indicates a date with an appointment scheduled. To move to a date in the current month, click that date. Any date-related views change to the selected day. To move from month to month, click the left arrow in the upper-left corner of the Date Navigator to move back a month and click the right arrow in the upper-right corner to move forward a month.

FIGURE 41.3.

The Date Navigator.

The To Do List

The To Do list in the main Schedule+ screen is an abbreviated version of your To Do list. (See Figure 41.4.) Double-click a task in the list to open the To Do view. Click in the ✓ column of an item to show that it is finished. To create a new To Do task, type its description in the Description column of an empty line or double-click the button at the left side of an empty line to open a new item.

FIGURE 41.4.

The To Do list.

Views

Each of the tabs in the main area provides a different view of your Schedule+ information. Here's a list of the default tabs provided:

- Daily
- Weekly
- Monthly
- Planner
- To Do
- Contacts

These views and their functions are examined in more detail in the following sections.

The Daily View

Here's where you keep track of your daily time-related activities. The Daily view shows the Appointment Book, where you can keep track of what appointments you have scheduled at specific times and how long each one lasts. (See Figure 41.5.) Icons indicate other aspects of an appointment: if it has a reminder set, is recurring, tentative, or private, or has a location noted. The Appointment Book distinguishes between work hours and nonwork hours by shading the nonwork times.

Double-click a time slot to open the Appointment dialog box. Here you can enter details about a new appointment or change existing appointment information. Typing in a time slot will also add an appointment.

Use the Date Navigator as previously described to move from date to date. When you select a new date, the Appointment Book changes to reflect the activities for that day. Click the left- or right-arrow buttons at the top of the Appointment Book area to move backward or forward a day, respectively. Clicking the Today button (at the left of the toolbar) immediately displays the Appointment Book for the current date. Click the Go To Date button to display a calendar of the current month; use the calendar like the Date Navigator to move from date to date.

FIGURE 41.5.

The Daily view.

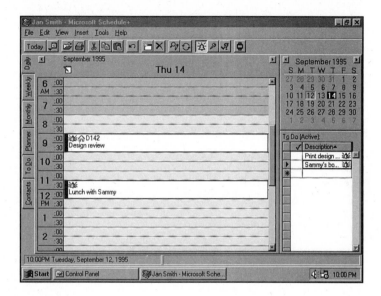

Changing Your Daily View

Select the Number Of Days option from the View menu to change the number of days (up to seven) visible in the Appointment Book.

> **NOTE**
>
> This option is different in the Weekly view. In the Weekly view, the day columns are wider and the Date Navigator and To Do list no longer show onscreen. When displaying multiple days in the Daily view, the Date Navigator and To Do list remain.

From the Tools menu, select Options and then the General tab to change the starting and ending hours of your workday.

> **TIP**
>
> Shift workers, you can use the Day Starts At and Day Ends At options to accommodate your workday.

Use the split bars at the margins of the areas to resize the areas of the main Schedule+ screen. For example, moving the divider between the Appointment Book and the other areas to the left will display another month in the Date Navigator and more columns of the To Do list. Figure 41.5 shows the Daily view with the Date Navigator and To Do list expanded.

The Weekly View

Use the Weekly view for a week-at-a-glance view of your schedule. (See Figure 41.6.) The Appointment Book displays a week of appointments. The Weekly view gives more room for each day by removing the Date Navigator and To Do list from the screen.

FIGURE 41.6.

The Weekly view.

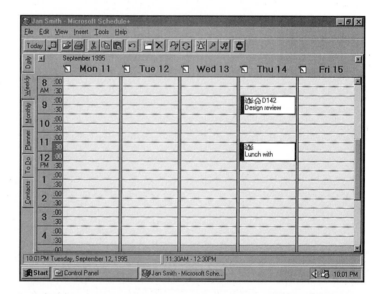

> **NOTE**
>
> The Weekly tab, with its longer appointment lines, is great if your time commitments are more important than having a calendar and a to do list displayed.

To move quickly to other days, click the left- or right-arrow buttons at the top of the Appointment Book area to move backward or forward a day, respectively. Clicking the Today button (at the left of the toolbar) immediately displays the weekly Appointment Book, including today's date. Click the Go To Date button, located at the far left of the toolbar, next to the Today button, to display a calendar of the current month; you can use the calendar like the Date Navigator to move from date to date.

Click the Daily tab for access to the Date Navigator.

The Monthly View

The Monthly view displays an entire month at a time, with today's date highlighted. (See Figure 41.7.) Days in the calendar show as many appointments, tasks, and events as possible in the available space.

FIGURE 41.7.

The Monthly view.

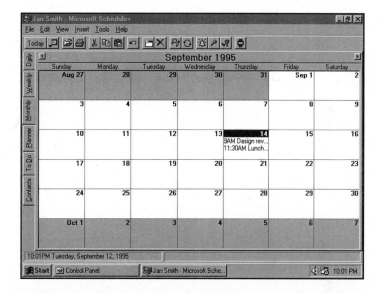

The date navigation tools operate differently in the Monthly view than in the other views. In the Monthly view, the Appointment Book is not opened; rather the selected date is merely highlighted. For easy access to appointments, click the Daily or Weekly tabs.

The Planner View

The Planner view gives you a multiple-week view of your busy time periods. (See Figure 41.8.) Nonwork hours are again shaded. The Date Navigator is present for rapid date changes, as are the left- and right-arrow buttons on the main area as well as the Today and Go To Date buttons on the toolbar.

FIGURE 41.8.

The Planner view.

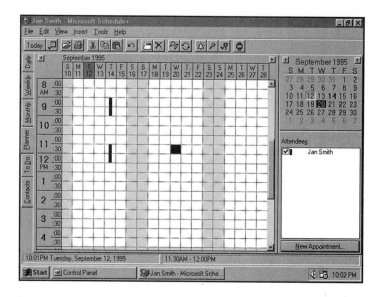

In the networked mode of Schedule+, the Planner view is a meeting planner. This view, therefore, includes a list of meeting attendees. In the standalone mode, as discussed here, the only attendee is you (whatever name you gave when opening Schedule+).

Double-click a colored time block to see the scheduled attendee (you). Click on the arrow to the right of the name to see a summary of the appointment. Click the New Appointment button (at the bottom right of the screen) to open the Appointment dialog box.

The To Do View

The To Do view shows you details about your To Do list and the tasks on it. (See Figure 41.9.) Double-click a task or the button on the left side of the view to display the Task view. Create a new task by double-clicking the button at the left side of an empty line. Click in the ✓ column of an item to show that it is finished.

> **NOTE**
>
> The To Do view is not associated with dates; therefore, you cannot access dates in this screen. For quickest date access, click the Daily tab and then use the Date Navigator or the date-changing buttons.

FIGURE 41.9.

The To Do view.

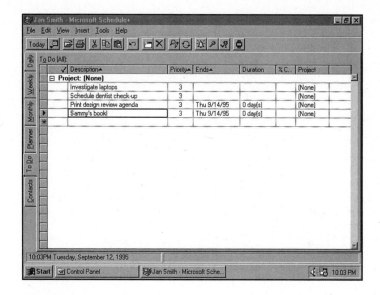

Changing Your To Do View

To change your To Do view, select Tools | Options from the menu bar. In the Defaults tab, establish the defaults for your tasks. Here's a list of the defaults you can set:

- Task reminders and their start information
- Default task priority
- Default project priority
- Default task duration
- Default estimated effort

The Contacts View

The Contacts tab allows you to see and manage your contacts list. (See Figure 41.10.) This view includes an abbreviated list of contacts and a business card–type view of each one. Double-click the button on the left side of the view to display the Contact dialog box. You can create a new contact by entering information in the fields of an empty line in the contacts list or in the "business card" section.

> **NOTE**
>
> The Contacts tab is not associated with dates; therefore, you cannot access dates in this screen. For quickest date access, click the Daily tab and then use the Date Navigator or the date-changing buttons.

FIGURE 41.10.

The Contacts view.

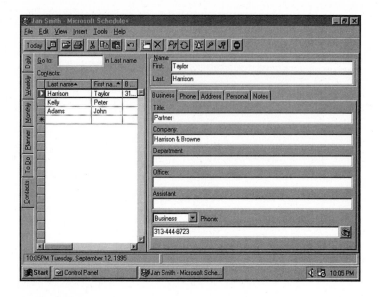

View Customization

Options from the Tools menu offer a variety of ways to change how your views look. Use the General tab (see Figure 41.11) to set the following items:

- The starting day of the week for the Weekly view
- When the workday begins and ends in the Weekly view
- The time scale displayed in the Appointment Book
- The time scale used for drag-and-drop appointment time changes

The General tab also enables reminders, the daily reminder, and audible reminder alarms.

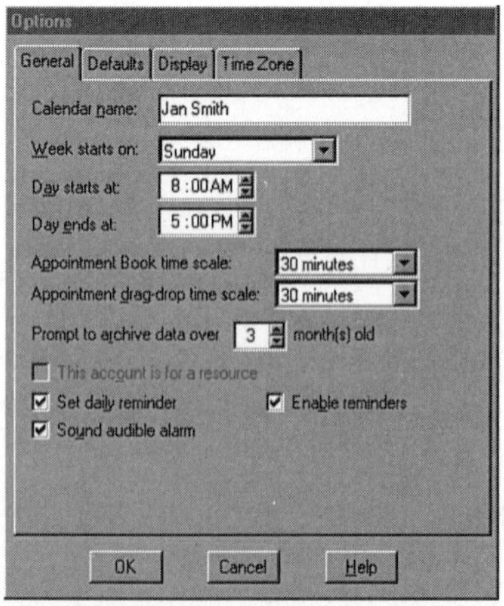

FIGURE 41.11.

The General tab in the Tools \ Options menu.

Use the Defaults tab (see Figure 41.12) to set automatic reminders for appointments as well as the amount of time before an appointment to show the reminder.

FIGURE 41.12.

The Defaults tab in the Tools | Options menu.

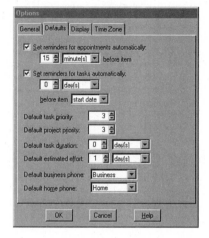

The Display tab allows you the change the appearance of your Appointment Book, Planner, grids, and pages. (See Figure 41.13.) Click the arrows for the drop-down lists of options for backgrounds and for Planner color selections.

Also, use the Display tab to show (or not show) the following items:

- ToolTips.
- Gridlines.
- Week numbers in the calendar.
- Events.
- The Time pop-up window. The Time pop-up window displays the date and time when you click a time slot in the Appointment Book.
- Location. When this box is checked, the "Where" notation of an appointment displays with the appointment in the Appointment Book.
- A list of recently used files.

You can also use the Display tab to change the font size of displays.

TIP

Leave ToolTips on at least until you become familiar with Schedule+. You can turn them off if they become annoying. ToolTips take a while to display anyway, so leaving them on won't slow down your work.

FIGURE 41.13.

*The Display tab in the
Tools | Options menu.*

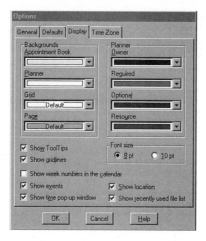

In the Time Zone tab (see Figure 41.14) you set a time zone as the primary time zone, give it a code heading, and indicate if Schedule+ should adjust for daylight savings time. You can also specify a secondary time zone with its own code heading and daylight savings time adjustment.

FIGURE 41.14.

*The Time Zone tab in the
Tools | Options menu.*

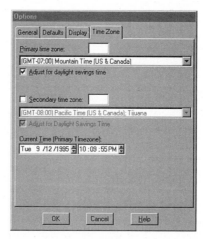

TIP

Is the company's home office in Chicago while you're in Denver? Does your sister live on the other coast? Specify another time zone as the secondary time zone so you can instantly see what time it is there in comparison to where you are.

You may also set the current time and date for the primary time zone in this tab. Click the part of the date or time (that is, the day of the week, the month, or the hour) you want to change and then click the up or down arrow to change its value.

The View menu allows other customization options. Use the Status Bar and Toolbar selections to toggle on or off the status bar at the bottom of the screen and the toolbar at the top.

The Tab Gallery

Select Tab Gallery to change the tabs your schedule uses. The Tab Gallery dialog box (see Figure 41.15) displays a list of available tabs, the tabs your schedule uses, Add and Remove buttons for adding or removing tabs from your schedule, and Move Up and Move Down buttons for changing the order of tabs in your schedule. When you select a tab from the Available Tabs list, Schedule+ displays a preview and description of the view's format in the Preview and Description windows. The Remove Tab option in the View menu deletes a tab from your views.

FIGURE 41.15.

The Tab Gallery dialog box.

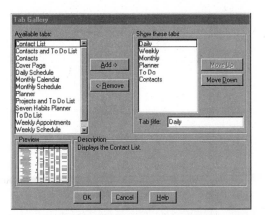

FIGURE 41.16.

The Monthly Schedule view.

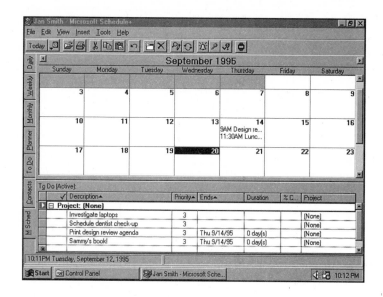

If you choose more tabs than fit onscreen, click the up or down arrows below the tabs to scroll through them.

Time Scheduling: Appointments

Create a new appointment in one of the following ways:

- Double-click in an empty time slot in the Appointment Book
- Click in an empty time slot, then right-click and select New Appointment
- Click the New Appointment button in the Planner view
- Select Insert|Appointment from the menu bar
- Click the Insert New Appointment button on the toolbar if the focus is on a time slot in the Appointment Book

The Appointment dialog box will be displayed.

The Appointment Dialog Box

Here's a list of ways to display the Appointment dialog box (see Figure 41.17):

- Double-click a time slot in the Appointment Book
- Click a day in a monthly display, then right-click and select New Appointment
- Select a time slot and then the Insert New Appointment button on the toolbar
- Select Insert|Appointment from the menu bar

FIGURE 41.17.

The Appointment dialog box.

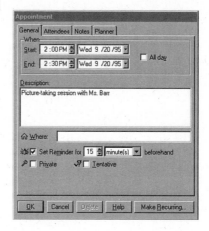

In the Appointment dialog box you enter or change the details of an appointment. In the General tab you set the appointment's start and end times. The start time defaults to the time of the slot from which you entered the Appointment view; the end time is determined by the Appointment Book time scale period set in Options. If you wish to set the appointment start and end times for a day other than the current day, click the down arrow next to either of the dates, and the Date Navigator is displayed. Select the All Day box if you want to schedule an all-day appointment; the entire day will be blocked out.

> **CAUTION**
>
> The *entire* day, all 24 hours of it, is blocked out for an all-day appointment. This could be inconvenient if you only want the workday blocked out. Set start and end times to account for your business day if you need to set appointments for outside work hours.

Use the Description box to enter a description of your appointment (this is the description used in the Appointment Book and other references). The Location box allows you to indicate where the appointment will take place. If you enter a location (and the Show location option is turned on), the Location icon displays with the appointment.

You can set a reminder (again, depending on whether reminders are turned on) and specify how long beforehand Schedule+ reminds you of the appointment. The Private box refers to networked Schedule+ and indicates if others can view this appointment. The tentative box allows you to "pencil in" appointments. Tentative appointments don't appear as busy times in the Planner and are shaded in all other appointment views.

If your appointment happens in a regular pattern, click the Make Recurring button to establish the appointment's pattern. Once you've set an appointment to recur, Schedule+ enters all specified instances of the appointment.

> **TIP**
>
> Do you have team meetings every other week? a standing tennis match on Saturday mornings? Enter your activity once and have Schedule+ fill in all its occurrences.

The Attendees tab of the Appointment dialog box refers to meetings set up in the networked mode of Schedule+. You'll not need it in standalone operation.

The Notes tab gives you ample room to record additional information about the appointment.

> **TIP**
>
> Use the Notes tab to make notes about topics you'd like to discuss in your appointment. In the networked mode, distribute your meeting agenda here.

The Planner tab displays a small version of the Planner view. The networked mode of Schedule+ uses the Auto-Pick button to determine a time suitable for all stated meeting attendees.

Appointments in the Appointment Book

Depending on the size of the appointment column in the Appointment Book, an appointment displays its description and the icons indicating options set. In addition to its icon, a tentative appointment is shaded.

If you schedule two activities to occur over the same time period, Schedule+ displays both appointments.

On the left side of an appointment is a duration bar, which indicates the scheduled length of the appointment. If the appointment doesn't begin or end exactly on one of the time scale marks, the duration bar indicates the time, even though the Description box may extend to a time scale mark.

To change the time of an appointment, move the cursor to the appointment's left border. When the cursor becomes a four-headed arrow, drag the appointment to its new time. To change the length of an appointment with the duration bar, move the cursor until it is on the appointment's bottom border. When the cursor becomes a double-headed arrow, drag the bottom of the appointment to the new end time. Select and drag the left border of an appointment to move it to a new date. Drop the appointment on the new date in the Date Navigator.

Copying and Deleting Appointments

Copy appointments by selecting the appointment and then using Copy and Paste to copy the appointment to its new time. Or you can press the Ctrl key and drag the appointment to its new time.

> **TIP**
>
> Copy appointments when you have an activity that occurs more than once, but not in a pattern or not often enough to make it a recurring appointment.

To delete an appointment, select it and then click the Delete button on the toolbar, or select Edit | Delete Item from the menu bar.

Events

What do you do with special days that don't have appointments, or with activities that happen on a certain day but don't have a specific time? Here's the Schedule+ answer: Record them as events. To create an event, select Insert | Event from the menu bar or click the notepad icon in the Appointment Book. In the Event dialog box (see Figure 41.18), select the event's starting and ending dates, add a description, and determine if the event is private.

FIGURE 41.18.

The Event dialog box.

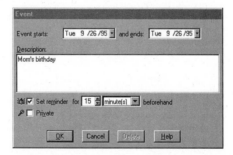

> **CAUTION**
>
> Schedule+ allows you to set a reminder for an event, but given the non-time-specific nature of events, this option makes little, if any, sense.

Once a day has an event, the Notepad icon changes to show "writing" on it. If you have elected to show events in the Options menu item, the event description will appear above the day in the Appointment Book.

Create recurring annual events by selecting Annual Event from the Insert menu or by selecting Insert Annual Event from the Notepad icon. Annual events have only the annual date of the event, rather than starting and ending dates.

Contacts

The Contacts view allows you to see and manage your contacts list. (See Figure 41.19.) This view includes an abbreviated list of contacts and a business card–type view of each contact. Double-click a contact or the button on the left side of the view to display the Contacts view. Here's a list of the ways to create a new contact:

- Enter information in the fields of an empty line in the contacts list.
- Enter information in the fields of the "business card" section.
- Double-click the button to the left of an empty contact line.
- Select Insert | Contact from the menu bar.
- Select the Insert New Contact button on the toolbar.

FIGURE 41.19.

The Contacts view.

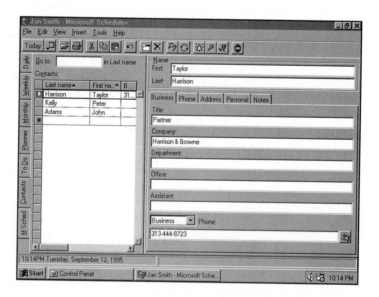

With the last three options in the previous list, Schedule+ displays the Contact dialog box. (See Figure 41.20.) In the Business tab, enter the contact's name, address, work information, and phone number. Click the Phone Number arrow to display a list of phone number types. Select different types to enter different phone numbers. To dial a selected phone number, click the Dial Phone button, located above the phone number.

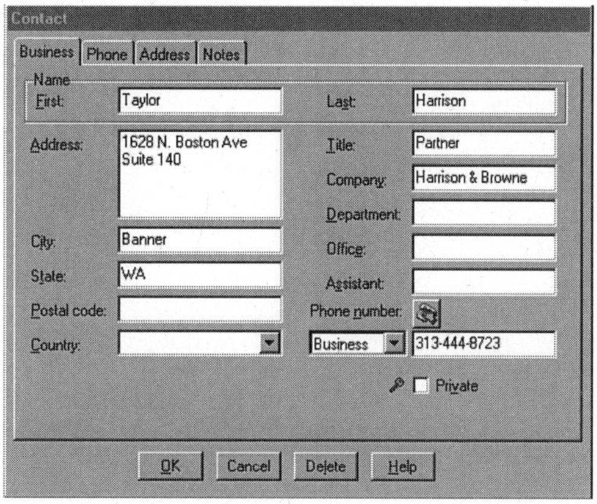

FIGURE 41.20.

The Contact dialog box.

NOTE

Contact information is the same, no matter where it is entered. A phone number entered through a column in the contact list is accessible from the business card section's phone fields, as well as from the Contact dialog box.

The contacts list can be sorted. Select View | Sort from the menu bar and then choose up to three fields on which to sort. After a field has been sorted, an up arrow after a field name indicates that the field is in ascending order; a down arrow, descending order. See Figure 41.21 for sorted contacts columns.

NOTE

Clicking the button with the column name also sorts the tasks. The first click sorts the column in ascending order. To reverse the order of the sort, hold down the Ctrl key and click. Another click resorts the contacts in ascending order.

FIGURE 41.21.

Sorted contacts columns.

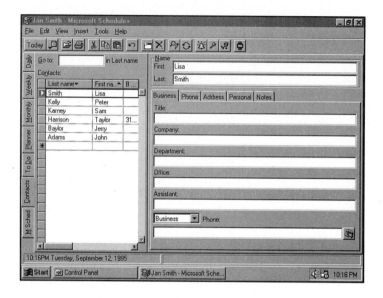

Columns in the Contacts List

The columns in the contacts list correspond to the fields in the Contact dialog box. Customize the columns displayed in the contacts list by selecting View | Columns from the menu bar. The following list shows which columns are displayed with which options:

- All—All contacts columns
- Typical—Last name, First name, Business phone, Company, Title, and Home phone
- Few—Last name, First name, and Business phone

> **TIP**
>
> Is one of the predetermined column displays almost but not quite what you need? Choose the one closest to your needs, and add or delete columns to make your contacts list just right.

You can completely customize your column display by selecting View | Columns | Custom from the menu bar. The Columns dialog box (see Figure 41.22) displays a list of available fields, a list of the fields your contacts list will show, Add and Remove buttons for adding or removing fields from your contacts list, and the Move Up and Move Down buttons for changing the order of the columns in the list. Change the width of a column by increasing or decreasing the number of its pixels.

FIGURE 41.22.

The Columns dialog box for contacts.

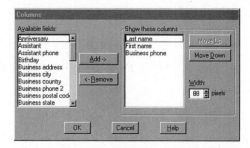

Moving a field "up" in the Columns list places it to the left in the Contacts grid; moving a field "down" places it to the right in the grid.

Contacts and Other Views

You can create appointments or tasks associated with a contact. Select a contact, and then select Insert | Related Item from the menu bar. To create an appointment, select Appt from Contact. An Appointment dialog box opens, with the contact's name in the description. Finish entering the appointment as needed. Create a task by selecting Task from Contact. The contact's name is the task's description.

The Contacts view is not associated with dates; therefore, you cannot access dates in this screen. For date access, click the Daily tab and then use the Date Navigator or the date-changing buttons.

Deleting Contacts

To delete a contact, select it and then click the Delete button on the toolbar. Or you can select Edit | Delete Item from the menu bar.

The To Do List

The To Do list consists of the tasks you have created. (See Figure 41.23.) Each task is a row in the list's grid format; the different pieces of information about a task are fields arranged in columns.

FIGURE 41.23.

The To Do list.

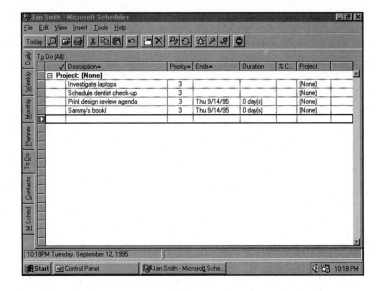

Tasks

Here is a list of the ways to create a new task:

- Double-click the button to the left of an empty task row in the To Do list
- Select Insert | Task from the menu bar
- Select the Insert New Task button from the toolbar

The Task Dialog Box

In the Task dialog box you enter or change the details of a task. (See Figure 41.24.) In the General tab, select Ends to set an end date for the task. Leave the date, if acceptable, or click the down arrow to display a calendar. Click the desired end date; then click the left- or right-arrow button to change months. If you selected Ends, you may specify a start date for the task, changing the number and measure of time as necessary.

Use the Description box to enter a description of your task (this is the description used in the To Do list). To assign the task to a project, click the down arrow to display a list of your projects. If you have no projects or you choose not to assign one, the task will belong to the (None) project. Select a priority for the task using the up and down arrows. If you have specified an end date for the task, you can set a reminder for it; you can also designate a task as private.

If your task occurs on a regular basis, click the Make Recurring button to establish the task's pattern. Once you've set a task to recur, Schedule+ enters all specified instances of the task.

FIGURE 41.24.

The Task dialog box.

Do you have status reports due the 15th and 30th of each month? annual reviews to prepare and give? a quarterly sales meeting to plan? Enter your task once and have Schedule+ fill in all its occurrences.

In the Status tab you track the progress of the task. (See Figure 41.25.) You can update the percentage complete, add the actual and estimated effort for task completion, and enter the date the task was completed. If you want to associate a contact with the task, click the arrow to display a list of your contacts or enter the contact name in the Contact box. Click the New contact button to create a contact. You can add billing information and mileage associated with the task, if desired. The Role field refers to the Seven Habits tool, which is covered in Chapter 42, "Extending Schedule+."

FIGURE 41.25.

The Status tab in the Task dialog box.

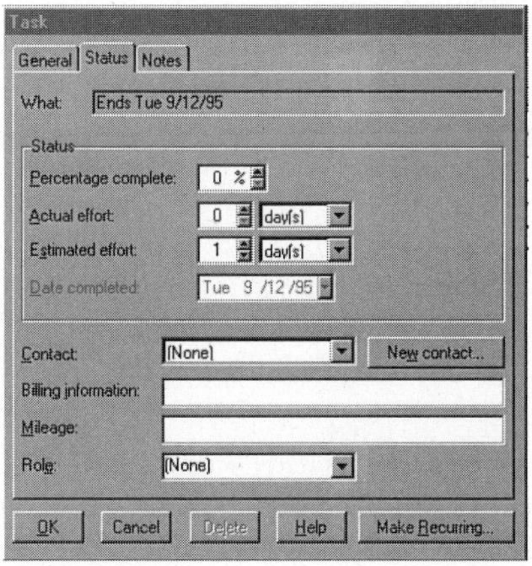

The Notes tab gives you ample room to record additional information about the task.

> **NOTE**
>
> The To Do view is not associated with dates; therefore, you cannot access dates in this screen. For quickest date access, click the Daily tab and then use the Date Navigator or the date-changing buttons.

Tasks and Appointments

You can associate a task with a time in the Appointment Book. Here's a list of ways to create this relationship:

- Click a task in the Daily view and drag it to the desired time.
- Use Copy and Paste to add the task to a time slot.
- Select the task; then select Insert | Related Item from the menu bar. When you select Appt from Task, the Appointment dialog box opens.

Columns in the To Do List

The columns in the To Do list correspond with the fields in the task. Customize the columns displayed in the To Do list by selecting View | Columns from the menu bar. The following list shows which columns are displayed with which options:

- All—All task columns
- Typical—Done (✓), Description, Priority, Ends, Duration, %Complete, Project
- Few—Done (✓), Description, Priority, Ends
- Description Only—Description

> **TIP**
>
> Is one of the predetermined column displays almost but not quite what you need? Choose the one closest to your needs, and add or delete columns to make your To Do list just right.

You can completely customize your column display by selecting View | Columns | Custom from the menu bar. The Columns dialog box (see Figure 41.26) displays a list of available fields, a list of the fields your To Do list will show, Add and Remove buttons for adding or removing fields from your To Do list, and the Move Up and Move Down buttons for changing the order of the columns in your To Do list. Change the width of a column by increasing or decreasing the number of its pixels.

FIGURE 41.26.

The Columns dialog box for tasks.

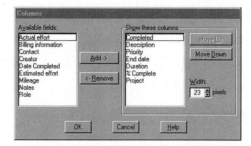

Moving a field "up" in the columns list places it to the left in the To Do grid; moving a field "down" places it to the right in the grid.

Copying and Deleting Tasks

You can copy tasks by selecting the task and then using Copy and Paste to copy the task. Or you can press the Ctrl key and drag the task to its new location.

Copy tasks when you have an activity that occurs more than once, but not in a pattern or not often enough to make it recurring.

To delete a task, select it and then click the Delete button on the toolbar. Or you can select Edit | Delete Item from the menu bar.

Task Tracking

In addition to listing your tasks, the To Do list is a powerful task tracking tool. You can group and sort tasks by up to three criteria each and filter the tasks so that all tasks, or only those with a specific status, display on the To Do list. The Group By, Sort, and Filter options are all found on the View menu.

The filter used for a To Do list is displayed in the status bar.

Projects

Organize your tasks by grouping related tasks into projects. To create a project, select Insert | Project from the menu bar. In the Project dialog box you give the project a name, assign it a priority, and determine if it is private. (See Figure 41.27.)

FIGURE 41.27.

The Project dialog box.

> **NOTE**
>
> A project's tasks can have different priorities than the priority of the project itself.

Sorting Tasks

You sort tasks using the Sort command from the View menu. Tasks can be sorted on as many as three fields. In the Sort dialog box you select the columns to be sorted and the type of sort (ascending or descending) for Schedule+ to use. (See Figure 41.28.) Once a column is sorted, the arrow after the field name indicates whether it is listed in ascending or descending order.

FIGURE 41.28.

The Sort dialog box.

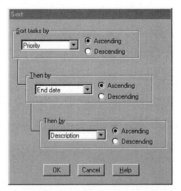

> **NOTE**
>
> Clicking the button with the column name also sorts the tasks. The first click sorts the column in ascending order. To reverse the order of the sort, hold down the Ctrl key and click. Another click resorts the tasks in ascending order.

Grouping Tasks

When you group tasks, they are arranged by categories or fields that you specify. The category occupies a new line in the To Do list; levels of categories are indented. To collapse the tasks in a group, click the icon to the left of the group line; click again to expand the group.

Select Group By from the View menu to group your To Do list. You can group by as many as three fields. (See Figure 41.29.)

FIGURE 41.29.

The Group By dialog box.

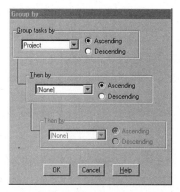

TIP

To easily track the tasks associated with a particular project, group your tasks by project.

Summary

In this chapter you've learned about Schedule+ and its tools for managing your personal information in the form of appointments, contacts, and tasks. Schedule+ presents its information in the form of views or tabs. Standard tabs provide daily, weekly, and monthly views of your appointments and other time-related activities, contact information, and a to do list with task management. Views are fully customizable to display information as you use it.

Extending Schedule+

42

by Sue Charlesworth

In this chapter you'll explore Schedule+ in more depth by watching Jan Smith, an imaginary worker, use Schedule+ to plan a project. Next, you'll examine Schedule+ with other products and then finish up with a look at the Seven Habits tool, a way to integrate the principles of Stephen Covey's *The Seven Habits of Highly Effective People* with Schedule+.

The Schedule+ Example

Jan Smith, our fictitious hero, arranges his company's annual awards week. This year, the awards week will be held in Hawaii for the company's top sales producers, the contributors of the year's top five suggestions, members of the sales and upper management teams, and their respective spouses. Jan figures he will need to have contacts within the company with the divisional sales managers as well as with various officers and staff members at corporate headquarters. In addition, he will work extensively with a travel agent and with the staff of the selected hotel in Hawaii. Jan sees his activities fall into two broad categories: getting the list of attendees and setting up all the activities and transportation for the week in Hawaii.

Jan realizes that he primarily needs to see his daily schedule, his contacts, and the two project categories: people and place. Also, he'd like ready access to a yearly calendar so he can refer to future dates. In Schedule+ Jan goes into View|Tab Gallery from the menu bar to set up his tabs. He adds the Project To Do tab so he can easily keep his projects and their tasks in view, the Yearly Calendar tab, and he arranges the Project To Do, Contacts, and Yearly tabs. (See Figure 42.1.)

FIGURE 42.1.

Jan's views.

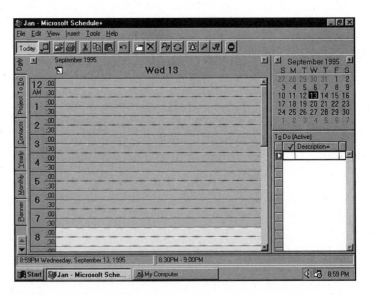

Next, Jan selects his Project To Do tab and sets up his projects—one called People and another called Place—by clicking the button to the left of an empty project line. (See Figure 42.2.) Then it's time for the tasks. This is Jan's first, rough guess at the tasks he'll need to complete, and he enters them in no particular order. Figure 42.3 shows his first list. Note that the tasks have default values only and aren't assigned to projects.

FIGURE 42.2.

Creating a project.

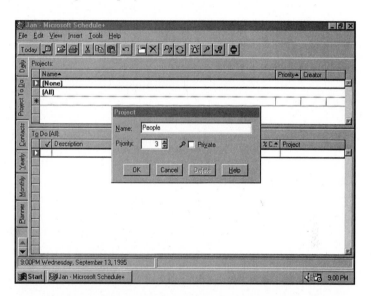

FIGURE 42.3.

The first To Do list.

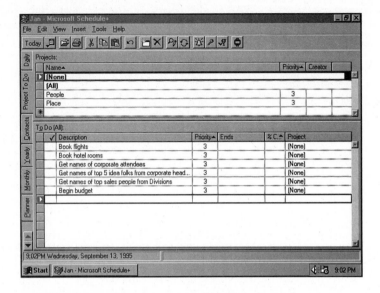

Now Jan assigns his tasks to projects. He clicks the Project field of a task and selects the appropriate project from the pull-down list. Once he has all the tasks assigned a project (see Figure 42.4), he clicks the button to the left of the project name, and the tasks for that project are displayed in the To Do portion of the projects to do view. (See Figure 42.5.)

FIGURE 42.4.

The To Do list with projects.

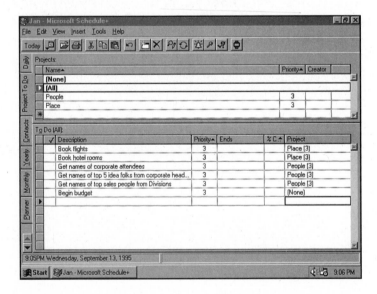

Chapter 42

FIGURE 42.5.

The list of tasks for the People project.

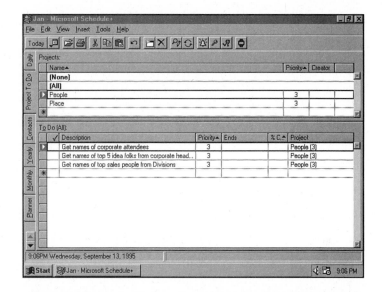

Since the default information for the tasks isn't quite right, Jan changes it to meet his needs. First, because he doesn't care how long each task takes, Jan deletes the Duration column by double-clicking the column heading and selecting Remove from the Columns dialog box. Next, Jan needs to change the priority of some tasks, so he clicks the Priority field and then clicks the up or down arrow to adjust the value. (See Figure 42.6.) For those tasks with an end or due date, he double-clicks the Ends field, selects the down arrow to display the Date Navigator calendar, and chooses the appropriate date. For those tasks that don't have end dates, he double-clicks the Ends field and then clicks the checkmark to turn off an ending date.

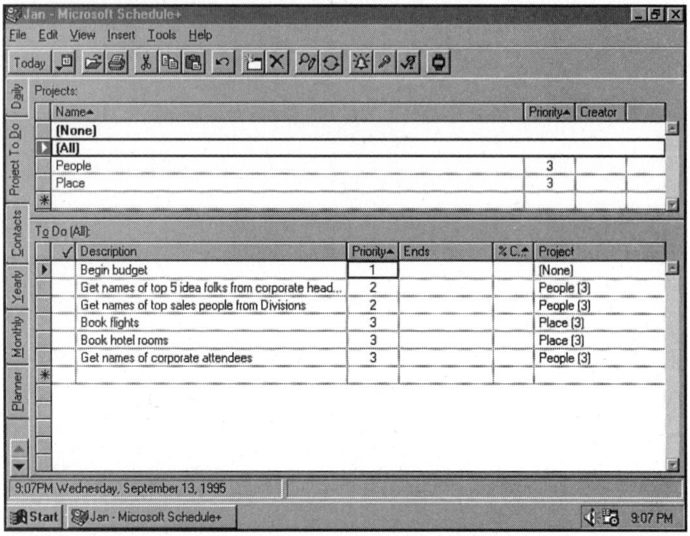

FIGURE 42.6.

*Changing the priority
of some tasks.*

TIP

You can also turn off the end date for tasks by double-clicking the button at the left of
the task and then clicking the checkmark by Ends in the General tab.

NOTE

When you enter information directly into fields in your To Do list, you don't get the
defaults that Schedule+ provides you when you enter tasks from the To Do dialog box.
If you use the To Do dialog box to enter a task, you'll get an end date; if you enter a
description directly in the To Do list, you'll have no end date.

CAUTION

Schedule+ defaults to today's date as a task's ending date. If you don't change the date,
all your tasks will be in red tomorrow, with warnings that they're overdue.

Next Jan selects the Contacts tab. For his company contacts, Jan adds the names and data for
the divisional sales managers and for his contacts at corporate headquarters. Then he adds the
travel agents' information as well as the names of the Groups and Meetings staff at the Hawaiian hotel. (See Figure 42.7.)

FIGURE 42.7.

Jan's contacts.

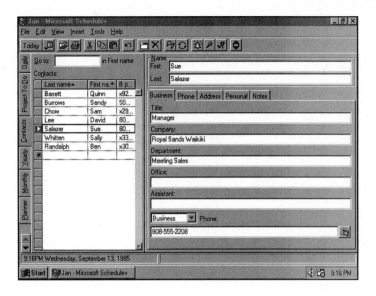

In addition to the columns Schedule+ provides in the Contacts view, Jan want to see the company name of his contacts. He double-clicks a column heading to bring up the Contacts dialog box and then adds a Company column before the Business Phone column. Jan also changes the order of the contact names so that the first name is displayed first. Jan realizes he'd like his contacts grouped by project, too. Checking out the Group By option in the View menu, Jan sees that he can't group contacts by project (Project isn't one of the fields available for contacts), so he chooses to group them by company name. Finally, Jan uses split bars to make more room to view his contacts list and to resize column widths. (See Figure 42.8.)

FIGURE 42.8.

The customized contacts view.

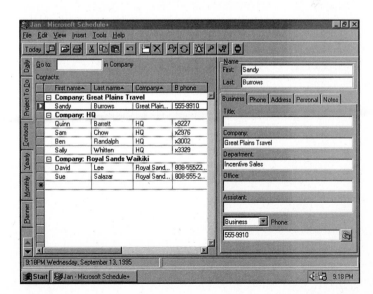

Now it's two months later and Jan wants to get a good picture of where he is. His To Do list is a hodgepodge of tasks completed, tasks partly done, and tasks barely started. (See Figure 42.9.) As he begins cleaning up his To Do list, Jan decides he doesn't need to see his completed tasks anymore, so he selects View | Filter from the menu bar and then Not Yet Completed to see only active tasks. To see how close to completion his remaining tasks are, Jan clicks the %C field of each task and then clicks the up arrow to update the status.

FIGURE 42.9.

Jan's To Do list, showing some tasks completed, some partly completed, and some barely started.

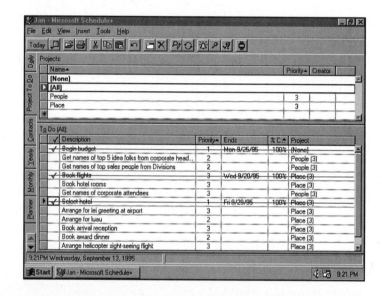

TIP

You can also update the Percentage Complete field by double-clicking the button at the left of the To Do list to display the Tasks dialog box and then switch to the Status tab and update the Percentage Complete field.

Jan wants to see his most critical tasks first, in order of percentage completed. He selects Sort from the View menu and then selects % Complete for the first sort and Priority for the second sort.

TIP

Don't forget that you can sort your tasks by clicking the column headings.

Simply sorting on his tasks doesn't make the tasks as easy to distinguish as he'd like. Instead, Jan groups his tasks (by selecting View|Group By from the menu bar) by % complete and then by priority.

This grouping still isn't what Jan wants, because he doesn't like all the lines from the "nested" grouping. (See Figure 42.10.) He settles for grouping his tasks only by priority and sorting additional columns when he needs his tasks to be arranged further. (See Figure 42.11.)

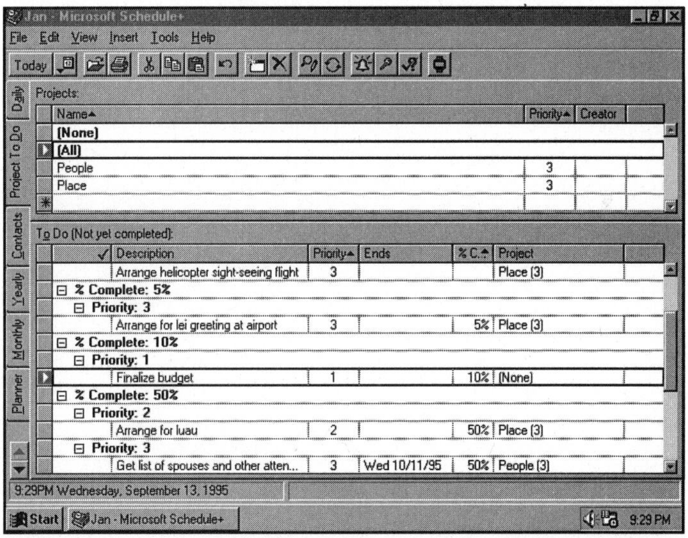

FIGURE 42.10.

Contacts with multiple groupings.

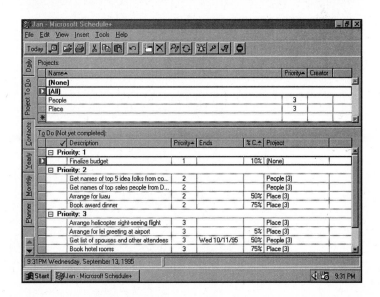

FIGURE 42.11.

Contacts grouped by priority.

TIP

To collapse tasks within a group, click the – icon to the left of the grouped by field name; expand the tasks by clicking on the + icon.

Some of Jan's tasks are directly related to a contact. For these tasks, he double-clicks the button to the left of the task and selects the Status tab in the Tasks dialog box. Clicking the arrow next to the Contact field drops down a list of his contacts. Once Jan selects a contact, that person is associated with the task. (See Figure 42.12.) Jan adds a Contact column in his To Do list by double-clicking a blank column heading, adding the Contact field, and then moving the Contact field to the appropriate location. (See Figure 42.13.)

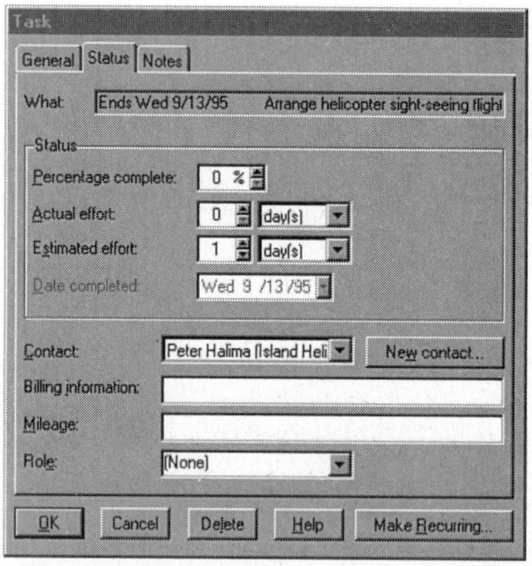

FIGURE 42.12.

Adding a contact to a task.

FIGURE 42.13.

The To Do list with the Contact column.

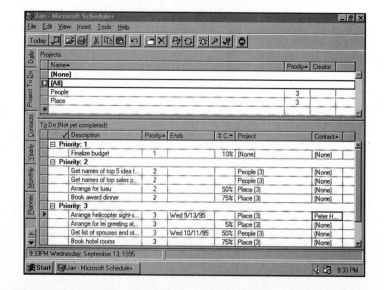

Now that his tasks are in order, Jan turns to his contacts. With the addition of more contacts, grouping by company isn't acceptable; he still wants to view his contacts by project. With no grouping for contacts by project, Jan improvises. For each contact, he adds the project name (Place or People) to the User 1 field in the Notes tab. (See Figure 42.14.) He doesn't need that field for his contacts; he'll group on it instead. Selecting View | Group By from the menu bar, Jan groups his contacts by the User 1 field. (See Figure 42.15.)

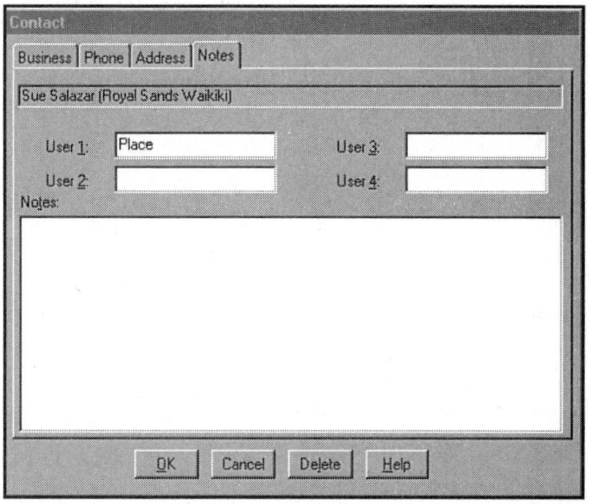

FIGURE 42.14.

The project name in the User 1 field.

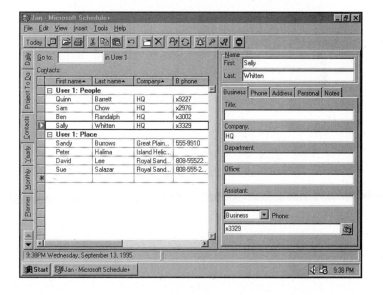

FIGURE 42.15.

The contacts grouped by project.

To help make his life (as well as his contacts' lives) a little easier, Jan adds a second time zone to his date views. The corporate headquarters is in a different time zone, and Jan is used to making the mental adjustment for time there. The time difference for Honolulu, however, is a different matter. From Tools | Options on the menu bar, Jan selects the Time Zone tab, enters DEN for his primary time zone, selects the check box labeled Secondary time zone, enters

HNL for his secondary time zone, and selects Hawaii from the pull-down list. (See Figure 42.16.) (Note that Hawaii doesn't go on daylight savings time, so that option isn't available.) Now Jan will be less likely to call his Hawaiian contacts at unsociable hours. (See Figure 42.17.)

FIGURE 42.16.

Adding a secondary time zone.

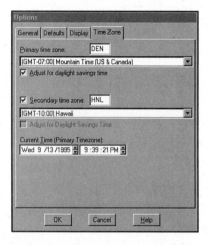

FIGURE 42.17.

The daily view with a secondary time zone.

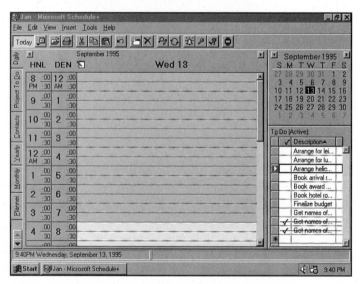

Using Schedule+ with Other Products

We're done with Jan Smith and his awards week work and are ready to move on to other aspects of Schedule+.

Chances are you have other means of tracking your time and projects, and Schedule+ won't always be the method of choice. However, you can integrate Schedule+ with other products in a number of ways.

The Timex Data Link Watch

Schedule+ provides a wizard for easy transfer of data to and from the Timex Data Link watch. To access the Timex Data Link Watch Wizard, select File | Export | Timex Data Link Watch from the menu bar, or select the Timex Watch Wizard button from the toolbar. Enter the appropriate information in the different dialog boxes of the Watch Wizard to specify which information Schedule+ sends to the Data Link watch. When your watch is ready, follow the instructions in the Export To Watch dialog box. The Microsoft/Timex Data Link Transmission screen appears. After the transmission is completed, Schedule+ asks you if the transmission was OK.

Exporting Data

In addition to exporting your Schedule+ data to the Timex Data Link Watch, you can also export your data in a format for easy transfer to another Schedule+ system, or in a variety of text formats for transfer to systems that can read specially delimited text files. One common format uses comma-separated values; the Text Export Wizard discussed in the following section gives you hints on creating comma-separated export files.

Schedule+ Interchange

The Schedule+ Interchange format makes it easy for you to copy your Schedule+ data and to transfer it to another computer. To use the Interchange command, select File | Export | Schedule+ Interchange from the menu bar and then specify a date range and the type of data you want to export. Schedule+ suggests a default filename with an .SC2 extension.

> **TIP**
>
> Use the .SC2 extension for your Interchange files. Schedule+ expects to see this extension when importing an Interchange file.

Once your file is in its new location, start Schedule+, select File | Import | Schedule+ Interchange from the menu bar, and then select the import filename. Schedule+ imports your data into the open file.

Exporting Plain Text

Choosing File | Export | Text from the menu bar allows you to export your Schedule+ data as plain text. Following the Text Export Wizard, determine what kind of data you want to export, what date range you want, how you want to delimit your data, the fields you want to export and in what order, and the file you want created.

Output for Paper Systems

You can format and print your Schedule+ information to fit in a loose-leaf planner. Select File | Print from the menu bar; then determine the information you want printed and its format. You might need to experiment to find out which paper format fits your system.

The Seven Habits Tool

The Seven Habits tool is based on Stephen R. Covey's books *The Seven Habits of Highly Effective People* and *First Things First*. Our look at the tool will be brief; refer to Covey's books to get further ideas on how the tool can benefit you.

The Seven Habits Wizard walks you through Covey's six-step organizing process which, in turn, helps you determine your mission, roles, and goals (three of the tabs in the Seven Habits tool). To start the wizard, select Tools | Seven Habits Tools from the menu bar and then click the Wizard button. Use the Next and Back buttons to move through the wizard.

Once you have completed the Seven Habits Wizard, your answers display in the appropriate tab (Mission, Roles, or Goals) of the Seven Habits tool. You can at that point edit your information and continue to develop your Seven Habits.

To complete the Seven Habits tool without the wizard (but with extra help for getting started) select Seven Habits Quick Start from the Tools menu. The Seven Habits Quick Start displays the Seven Habits tool with information about developing your own Mission, Roles, and Goals tabs. Select the tab you'd like to work with, read Quick Start's instructions, and use the Next and Back buttons to navigate through Quick Start.

In addition to the Seven Habits tool, Schedule+ provides a Seven Habits tab, which you can add to your views. This view displays your daily appointments and your To Do list, including tasks related to your Seven Habits roles. You may also select the Role field for sorting and grouping your tasks. This helps you keep the Seven Habits in mind as you carry out your activities.

Summary

In this chapter you watched Jan Smith as he used Schedule+ to organize his company's awards week in Hawaii. Jan worked primarily with projects, tasks, and contacts—customizing his views to suit his particular needs.

In addition, you learned about using Schedule+ with other products, such as the Timex Data Link Watch, and with file exports. Finally, you learned about the Seven Habits tool, which is based on the works of Stephen R. Covey. This tool presents a different way of organizing your tasks.

PART

The General Objects

Using the Graph Tools

43

by Sue Charlesworth

This chapter looks at Microsoft Graph, the first of Office's object applications. As we explore Graph, we'll use some sample data to demonstrate Graph's uses and capabilities.

Although the sample data is somewhat simplistic, it is sufficient to highlight Graph's functions. The sample information shows six months of data on product defects, breaking out the number of defective parts found at three different places: on the manufacturing line (Line), in quality assurance (QA), and at the customer site (Cust). Table 43.1 shows the data.

Table 43.1. Defects by month and where found.

Month	Line	QA	Cust
Jan	10	12	8
Feb	6	10	6
Mar	7	7	7
Apr	8	4	3
May	6	4	1
Jun	5	3	0

What Graph Is

Graph is a charting tool designed to enable you to present numeric data graphically in non-charting Office applications. Graph consists of two major parts: the datasheet, which is like a minimal spreadsheet with cells, rows, and columns of data; and the chart, which is the graphed representation of the data in the datasheet.

The Office products that use Graph are Word, PowerPoint, and Access. In this chapter, we'll look at Graph in Word and PowerPoint.

What Graph Isn't

Graph isn't a full-blown spreadsheet; it has no mathematic capabilities. If you need spreadsheet functions, use Excel. Graph also isn't a Word table; while Graph presents your data in a tabular fashion, you don't have extensive formatting functions. But then, you don't need to format the numerals themselves; it's the data that the numerals represent that's important in Graph.

The most important thing to remember is that Graph isn't a standalone program. You can't save a graph by itself; it has to be part of one of the other Office documents. You can't start Graph up by itself; you must insert a Graph object from within Word, PowerPoint, or Access. A graph, along with other Office objects, is embedded within its "parent" document.

Since You Can't Get There from Here, How Do You Get There?

To insert a graph object in Word, select Insert | Object from the menu bar, then double-click on Microsoft Graph 5.0 in the Object Type list in the Create New tab. (See Figure 43.1.) A graph object opens with a datasheet and chart, including sample data. (See Figure 43.2.)

FIGURE 43.1.

Creating a Graph object.

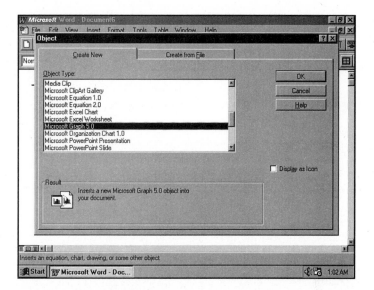

FIGURE 43.2.

A new Graph object.

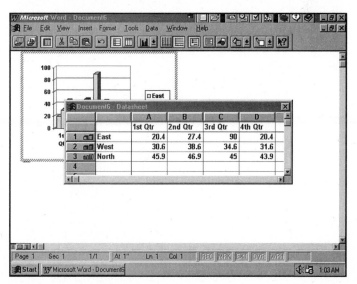

In PowerPoint, do one of the following:

- Select Insert | Object from the menu bar, and then select Microsoft Graph 5.0 Chart from the Object Type list.
- Select Insert | Microsoft Graph from the menu bar.
- Select a slide layout of a graph, and then double-click to open a Graph object.

When you're in Graph, the toolbar changes to the Graph toolbar. The menu bar remains the same, although a few selections in individual menus may be specific to Graph, unlike the normal Word or PowerPoint selections.

> **NOTE**
>
> You can't customize the Graph toolbar, and you lose any customizations you've added to the parent application's toolbar. Mostly, this isn't a problem, because Graph does different things than do Word or PowerPoint, but losing navigation buttons (next window, for example) could be annoying.

Because a graph is an object, not an Office application, you can't save a graph directly. Office saves graphs as embedded objects within the parent file. In fact, if the only thing you have in a Word document is a graph, the filename prompt when saving is EMBED MSGraph.doc. Despite the name, the file is a Word doc file, not a Graph file.

Just the Facts, Ma'am: Using the Datasheet

The datasheet in Graph looks like a simple spreadsheet: It has a series of cells formed at the intersection of a column and a row. The cursor is a fat white plus sign, as in Excel. Table 43.2 shows how to select different elements of the datasheet.

Table 43.2. Selecting datasheet elements.

To Select This	Click This
A cell	The cell
A row	The button at the left of the row
A column	The button at the top of the column
The entire datasheet	The top-left button
A block of cells	A corner cell through the desired range of cells

To deactivate a row or column, double-click its button. Graph grays out the data in that row or column, changes the button's appearance so that it looks flat, and removes that data from the chart.

Now that you know some of the basics of the datasheet, you can put data in it.

> **NOTE**
>
> If your datasheet "disappears," click on the View Datasheet icon on the Graph toolbar to bring it back.

Direct Data Entry

You can enter data directly into the Graph datasheet. To do so, simply click the desired cell and type in the information.

> **TIP**
>
> Don't forget column and row headings. Graph uses these to label the chart.

To delete information by cell, click in the cell and press the spacebar, delete key, or backspace key. To delete information by row or column, select the row or column, then

- Select Edit | Delete from the menu.
- Select Edit | Clear from the menu, and then select All or Contents.
- Right-click and select Delete or Clear.

> **NOTE**
>
> Entering headings is rather brutish compared to Excel's labor- and sanity-saving tricks. If you've got a large amount of data with headings that form some series, consider building the spreadsheet in Excel.

Indirect Data Entry

Often, you won't just have your data displayed graphically. You'll probably lay it out as a table or list in your primary document. As you'll already have entered your data in one place, simply cut and paste it into your datasheet.

You can use your data now. Assume that you've got your data in a Word document in the table shown in Figure 43.3. To transfer the information into Graph, follow these steps:

1. Select the table.
2. Select Insert|Object from the menu bar.
3. Select Microsoft Graph 5.0 Chart from the Object List.

FIGURE 43.3.

A table of data for Graph examples.

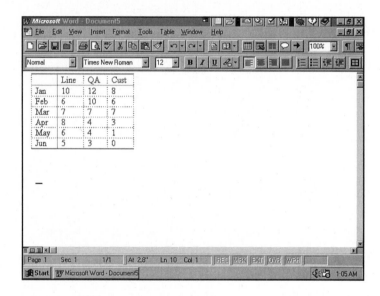

Graph opens with the ChartWizard. (See Figure 43.4.)

FIGURE 43.4.

The ChartWizard opening window.

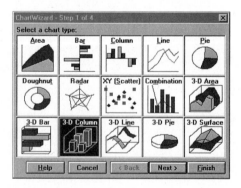

The ChartWizard walks you through the creation of your chart, using the data from your Word table in four steps:

1. Select a chart type. Graph defaults to a 3-D column chart, but select 3-D Bar.

2. Select a format for the chart type: format 4.

3. Determine data series, first row, and first column properties. Keep the defaults.

4. Add a legend and titles, if desired. Keep the legend, add the title Six Month Defect Location, and leave the axis titles blank.

See Figures 43.5 through 43.8 to see these four steps illustrated.

FIGURE 43.5.

Selecting the chart type.

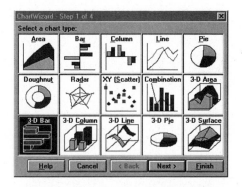

FIGURE 43.6.

Selecting the chart format.

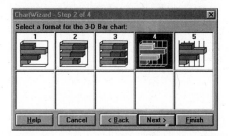

FIGURE 43.7.

Setting data series, row, and column properties.

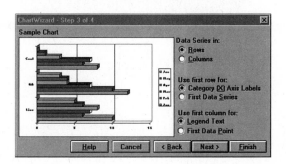

FIGURE 43.8.

Adding a legend and titles.

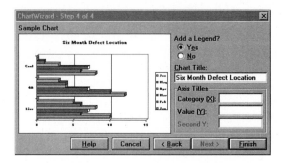

Graph now displays the datasheet with your data and the chart that you specified. (See Figure 43.9.)

FIGURE 43.9.

The datasheet and chart with defect data.

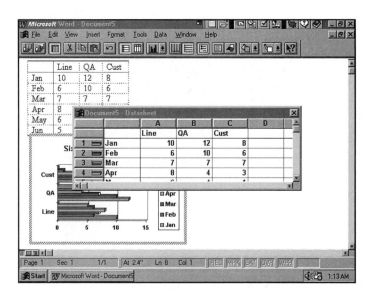

You can also import your data from an Excel spreadsheet. Once you're in Graph, click on the Import Data button on Graph's toolbar. Select your Excel filename to import its data into the Graph datasheet.

> **CAUTION**
>
> Despite the warning that says Graph will overwrite the sample datasheet information, not all of the sample data goes away. You will need to clean up the datasheet and delete the unwanted information.

Formatting Your Data

You can make any number of points with your data. In this case, you might want to emphasize the number of defects found at each location, rather than the number of defects found per month. You might want to show the number of defects found each month as a portion of the total number of defects discovered, or if there are any trends by month or by location. Graph makes it easy to represent your data in different ways.

To change the chart type, click the Chart Type button on the Graph toolbar, and then select the new chart type. To specify rows as the primary data series, click the By Row button; to specify columns as the primary data series, click the By Column button. With this data, selecting By Row plots the data by number of defects found per month, broken down by location; selecting By Column plots the data by number of defects found per location, broken down by month.

> **NOTE**
>
> You can also select Data | Series in Rows, or Data | Series in Columns from the menu to specify your data series.

> **TIP**
>
> Forget how you're looking at your data? Check the indicators on the datasheet. If you selected By Row, there will be a depiction of the chart type and colors in the row labels; if you selected By Column, the indicators will be in the column headings.

Now let's look at the major chart types and what they emphasize.

Pie Charts

A pie chart shows the proportion of parts to the whole. Pie charts depict only one set of data; Graph ignores other sets. With this data, if you select By Row, the pie chart shows what proportion of the total number of defects is found each month; with By Column, the chart shows what proportion of the total number of defects is found at each location.

Figure 43.10 shows a pie chart of the month data; Figure 43.11 shows a pie chart of the location data.

FIGURE 43.10.

A pie chart showing months.

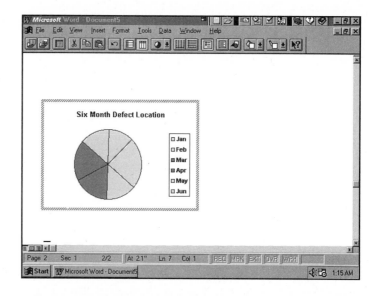

FIGURE 43.11.

A pie chart showing location.

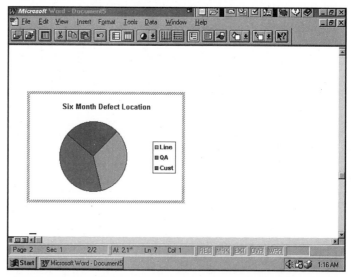

CAUTION

Unless you duplicate your data table and use two graphs, as we did here, a pie chart can't show comparisons between two sets of data.

Column Charts

A column chart displays variation over time or comparisons between items. Values display vertically. Column charts can also be 3-D.

> **CAUTION**
>
> Be careful with 3-D column charts. Displaying data categories behind one another, as shown in Figure 43.12, can make the information hard to read.

FIGURE 43.12.

A three-dimensional column chart.

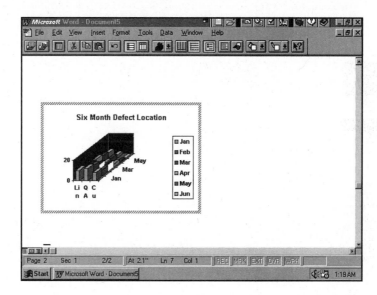

Bar Charts

Bar charts are similar to column charts and can also show variations over time and comparisons between items. Bar charts display values horizontally. You can also make 3-D bar charts.

Area Charts

Area charts emphasize the amount of change in values; they often display values cumulatively, rather than individually, and can point out trends. Area charts can be 3-D.

> **CAUTION**
>
> As with column charts, be careful with 3-D area charts. Displaying data categories behind one another can make the information hard to read.

Line Charts

A line chart emphasizes trends or changes in data over a period of time.

FIGURE 43.13.

A 3-D line chart.

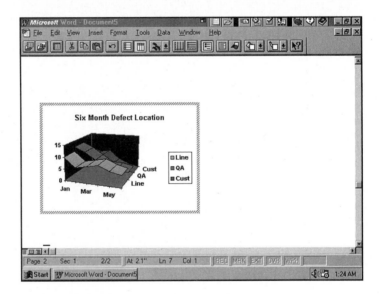

Fine-Tuning Chart Formatting

Once you have your chart type chosen, use AutoFormat (by selecting Format|AutoFormat from the menu) to select the specific way to represent your data within the chart type. Figures 43.14 and 43.15 both show area charts, but with different AutoFormatting.

For another way to choose how a chart will show your data, select Format|Chart Type from the menu, and then select the Options button to view subtypes available for the chart type.

FIGURE 43.14.

A 3-D Area Chart, with AutoFormat set to 4.

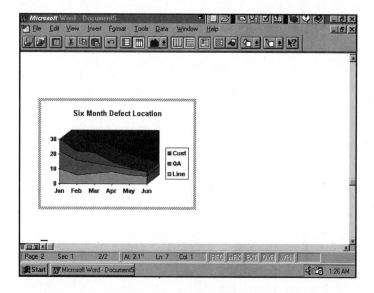

FIGURE 43.15.

A 3-D Area Chart, with AutoFormat set to 7.

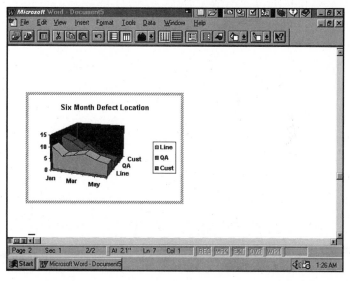

If you have a 3-D chart, you can select Format | 3-D View from the menu. This option allows you to change the elevation, rotation, and perspective of your 3-D chart. A wireframe depiction of your chart type shows the new angles of view.

Changing a Chart's Look

In addition to changing the chart type and specific presentation, you can also change specific attributes of your chart. The following list gives quick highlights of some customizations for your chart:

■ Click on the Vertical Gridlines and Horizontal Gridlines buttons to add visual references of data values.

■ Click on an individual data series, and then on the color or pattern button to change the series' color or pattern.

■ If you want only a pattern with no color, select None for color and then select your pattern.

> **CAUTION**
>
> If you have a particular series selected and then change chart type, only the selected series will change. You'll end up with two different charts, one on top of the other. Make sure you're changing the entire chart.

> **TIP**
>
> If you're going to produce your chart in black and white only (as a Word document, say, or a photocopied color presentation), test colors to make sure they show up distinctively enough in black and white, or use patterns to distinguish between data series.

To add text to your chart, click on the Text Box button and then click and drag the cross-hairs to add a text box. When you release the mouse, you have an insertion point and are ready to add your text.

Use the Drawing button to display the Drawing toolbar. The Drawing tool isn't covered here (look for it in Chapter 44, "Using Drawing Tools"), but you can use it to place additional graphics on your chart.

> **TIP**
>
> Use a combination of text boxes and lines to create callouts.

Graph and Its Parent Applications

As stated earlier, Graph cannot exist on its own, so we turn our attention to Graph's relationship with its parent applications. The following list summarizes some changes you make to your graph in its parent document:

- Change a graph's size by clicking the graph, selecting a handle, and dragging.
- Double-click the graph to open it.
- In Word, add a border to the graph.
- In Word, format the graph as a frame, which give you more flexibility in the graph's relationship with text in the document.

If you plan to use the same data in both a Word document and a PowerPoint presentation, create the graph in one application, and then add it to the other with a link to the original graph. Let's say that you've created a report about product defects and now need to build a presentation covering the same information. Select the graph in Word, copy it, and then switch to PowerPoint.

In PowerPoint, create a Graph slide, select Edit | Paste Special from the menu, and select Paste Link and Microsoft Graph 5.0 Object. (See Figures 43.16 and 43.17.) You have pasted a copy of your Word graph into PowerPoint, and this copy is linked to your Word document. When you change the graph in Word, Office reflects the same changes in PowerPoint, without you having to duplicate your editing in PowerPoint.

FIGURE 43.16.

A graph slide in PowerPoint.

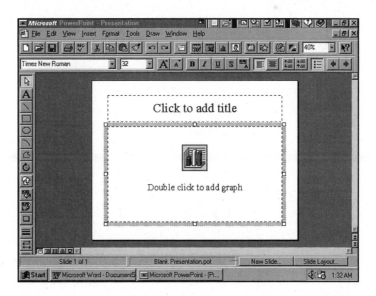

FIGURE 43.17.

*The Paste Special dialog
box for a linked graph.*

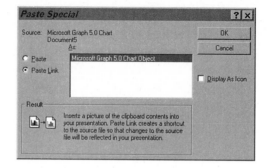

Summary

This chapter looks at Microsoft Graph 5.0, which enables you to graphically represent data in applications that are normally not set up for charting, such as Word and PowerPoint. A graph contains a datasheet, which looks like a simple spreadsheet, and the chart itself. Graphs are objects and as such cannot exist outside the parent application in which they've been created.

You can enter data directly into the graph datasheet or you can import data from another Office application such as Word or Excel. Importing data from another Office source enables you to create data in one application and use it again in another. Importing also gives you the freedom to create the data in an application where it is easier to do so.

Once you have your data, you select a chart format to represent it. In chart formats, you can show your data from different points of view by using your columns or your rows as the data series. Different forms of charts highlight different aspects of your data. Chart subtypes enable you to further refine the presentation of your data.

To use data in more than one application and synchronize changes to the data, paste the graph into the second application as a special link. Then, any changes made in the original graph are automatically reflected in the linked graph.

Using Drawing Tools

44

by Sue Charlesworth

IN THIS CHAPTER

With Office 95's drawing tool, you can make drawings right in your documents, presentations, and spreadsheets. While the tool is essentially the same in Word, PowerPoint, and Excel, each Office application has a slightly different implementation of the drawing tools. In this chapter you'll look at the basics of the drawing tools, you'll see how to create and manipulate drawings, and you'll create a sample drawing.

Office's drawing tool isn't a full-blown vector-based program where you can draw bézier curves, edit nodes, and add lenses and other special effects. You can, however, draw lines, rectangles, ellipses, arcs, and freeform shapes, and color, rotate, flip, and group your shapes. If you need a complex drawing, your best bet would be to create it in another program, then insert it into your Office document as an object or paste it into a frame. If you want simple, easy-to-do drawings—or if Office is the only tool you have available—the Office drawing tools will get you by.

Office drawings are not quite objects like other Office objects discussed in this section. You can directly access the drawing tool from within applications, so you don't need to insert an object; in fact, Office doesn't identify drawing objects to insert. While individual shapes may be called objects, this is just to identify them as items.

The Drawing Tools in Office Applications

As stated, Word, PowerPoint, and Excel each has its own implementation of the drawing tools. Despite the differences, each application does have the following drawing functions:

- Line
- Rectangle
- Ellipse
- Arc
- Freeform
- Group
- Ungroup
- Bring to front
- Send to back
- Select drawing

NOTE

The ToolTip for the button may not read exactly as in the preceding list and the buttons themselves may be somewhat different from application to application, but they do the same thing in each application.

Table 44.1 shows which specific drawing tools are available in Word, PowerPoint, and Excel.

Table 44.1. Drawing tools in Office applications.

Tool	Word	PowerPoint	Excel
Text box	✓		✓
Text tool		✓	
Callout	✓		
Format callout	✓		
Fill color	✓	✓	
Line color	✓	✓	
Line style	✓	✓	
Bring in front of text	✓		
Send behind text	✓		
Flip horizontal	✓	✓	
Flip vertical	✓	✓	
Rotate right	✓	✓	
Rotate left		✓	
Reshape	✓		
Snap to grid	✓		
Align drawing objects	✓		
Create picture	✓		
Insert frame	✓		
Arrow			✓
Freehand			✓
Filled rectangle			✓
Filled ellipse			✓
Filled arc			✓
Filled freeform			✓
Create button			✓
Drop shadow		✓	✓
Pattern			✓
Free rotate tool		✓	
AutoShapes		✓	
Arrowheads		✓	
Dashed line		✓	

Word

Word provides no menu access to drawing tools. To access these tools, click on the Drawing button on the toolbar, and the Drawing toolbar appears.

> **NOTE**
>
> Selecting Format | Drawing Object from the menu allows you to change drawing object defaults.

Excel

Excel has no menu access to drawing tools. To access these tools, click on the Drawing button on the toolbar, and the Drawing toolbar appears as a free-floating toolbar. If you want the drawing toolbar to be located with the other toolbars, click in and hold the toolbar (not one of the buttons) and drag the toolbar to the top of the screen.

Excel's unique drawing tools will create the following:

- Filled shapes (rectangles, ellipses, arcs, and freeform shapes)
- Buttons (used for Excel macros)
- Arrows (select the arrow and double-click to edit the arrow's characteristics)
- Freeform lines
- Drop shadows

In addition, Excel offers a pattern tool.

PowerPoint

Although PowerPoint has a Draw item on the menu bar, you must use toolbars to create drawing objects. From the menu bar, select View | Toolbars | Drawing and Drawing+ to display the drawing toolbars.

PowerPoint's main claim to fame in drawing tools is AutoShapes: a series of preset tools that allow you to easily create multisided shapes.

Creating Drawing Objects

Now that you've seen which application has what tools, turn your attention to actually *creating* drawing objects.

To create an object, click on the appropriate button on the toolbar. The cursor changes to cross-hairs, showing that the drawing tool is active. Move the cursor to where you want your drawing object, and then click and drag in the application. (See Figure 44.1.) To constrain your object to a symmetrical shape—a square, circle, or quarter-circle arc—hold down the Shift key while drawing. (See Figure 44.2.) Hold down the Ctrl key and drag to draw the shape around its horizontal or vertical axis. If you want to make a series of the same shape, double-click on the tools' button to keep the shape active; to deactivate the shape, select another button, click in the document without dragging, or press the Esc key.

FIGURE 44.1.

A shape.

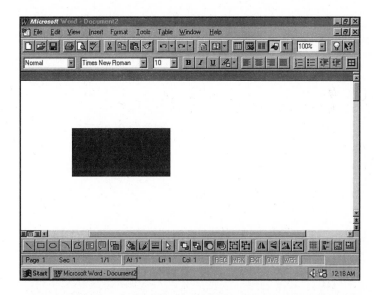

FIGURE 44.2.

A circle.

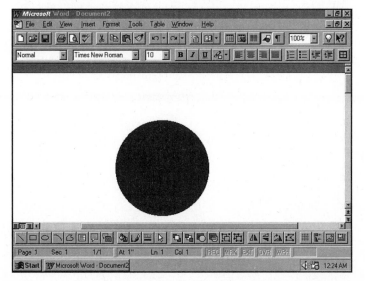

814

The freeform tool works a little differently than the other shape tools. First, the freeform tool has two modes, freeform curve (Figure 44.3) and multiple connected lines (Figure 44.4). When you hold down the left mouse button and draw, you get completely freeform curves. When you click the left mouse button and release, you draw a line from that point to where you next click, allowing you to draw multisided shapes. Second, each mode finishes shapes differently than the other tools. In the freeform curve mode, you must double-click to deactivate the tool. In the multiside mode, bringing a line close to the starting point closes the shape and deactivates the freeform tool.

FIGURE 44.3.

A freeform curve.

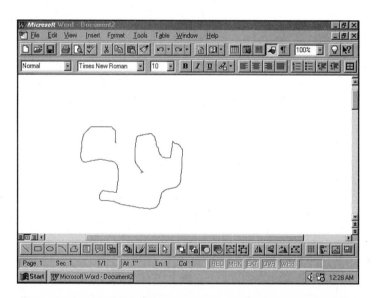

FIGURE 44.4.

Connected lines.

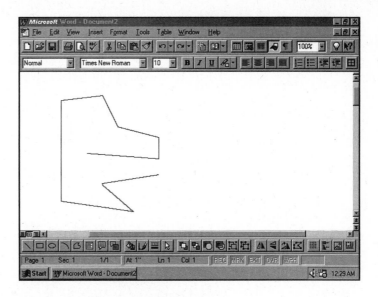

Manipulating Drawing Objects

Unless you're perfection itself, your drawing objects won't be exactly right when you first put them in your document. They won't be in the right place, or they'll be too short or too long or the wrong color. Fortunately, you can move, resize, reshape, color, and otherwise change your objects so they look the way you want.

To change drawing objects, you first have to select them. When you move the cursor over a drawing object, the cursor changes. In Word, it becomes a selection pointer with a double-headed arrow; in Excel, the cursor becomes a selection pointer. In PowerPoint, how the cursor reacts depends on what kind of slide or frame you have active. If you are in a text frame, the cursor changes from the I-bar to a selection pointer. In other frames, the cursor is and remains a selection pointer. To select an object, left-click when the cursor indicates that it's over a drawing object.

> **CAUTION**
>
> In PowerPoint, you can "layer" drawing objects and frames. If you put a drawing object in a blank slide and then change the slide layout to text or some other kind of frame, you won't be able to get to the drawing object to select it. You can, however, put a drawing object on top of a text frame and select and manipulate the object from that "top" layer. Be careful of the order in which you add drawing objects and frames.

Resizing Drawing Objects

To resize an object, select the object, move the cursor over a sizing handle, and then drag the handle. Dragging one of the corner handles resizes the object in proportion to the original shape; dragging one of the side, top, or bottom handles resizes the width or length of the object without affecting the other dimension. Drag outward to make the object larger; drag inward to make it smaller.

Filling Drawing Objects

In Word and PowerPoint, objects are created with fills. Word objects fill with white; PowerPoint objects fill with a default color. These fills are defaults; if you wish to change the fill color, or to have no fill at all, click on the fill color button to select your new choice. In Excel, you specifically designate whether you wish to create "transparent" unfilled objects or filled objects. Unfilled Excel objects cannot be filled; you must specifically create a filled object.

> **NOTE**
>
> If you've gotten just the right shape in Excel, and then decide you want it filled, you're out of luck. You'll have to create a new filled object. This shouldn't be too much of a problem, though, because Excel probably wouldn't be your first choice of application for creating drawings.

Filled objects overlay any text, cell contents, or other objects. Unfilled objects appear simply as outlines. (See Figure 44.5.) Use the bring forward and send backward buttons to change the layering of filled objects. In Word, you can also put objects in front of or behind text.

FIGURE 44.5.

Filled and unfilled ellipses.

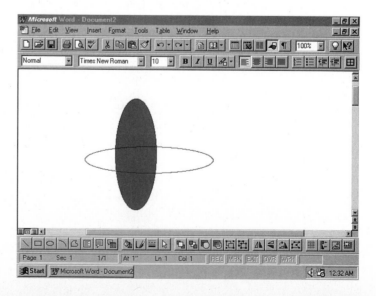

Moving Drawing Objects

To move an object, select it, then drag it to its new location. Filled objects will lie on top or in front of text or other objects.

Flipping and Rotating Objects

In Word and PowerPoint, you have additional tools for object manipulation. Flipping allows you to "rotate" an object on its horizontal or vertical axis. Rotating rotates the object 90 degrees. Figure 44.6 shows a rotated and flipped object. In PowerPoint, you also have the Free rotate button, which allows you to rotate a shape to any angle. With the object selected, click on the Free rotate button. The sizing handles change to circles and the cursor becomes a set of curved arrows. Click on one of the rotating handles and drag the object to its new angle. (See Figure 44.7.)

FIGURE 44.6.

Rotated and flipped trapezoids.

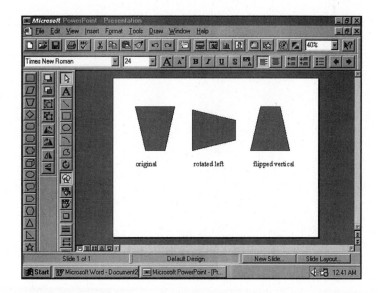

FIGURE 44.7.

A free rotated rounded rectangle.

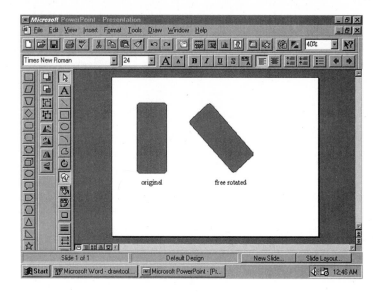

Grouping Objects

You can group objects to keep them together as a unit. Select the objects you want to group, and then click on the Group button. The sizing handles change to encompass the grouped object. Groups can be moved, resized, and colored as a unit. (See Figure 44.8.) To ungroup objects, select the group, and then click on the ungroup button. The objects return to their individual states.

> **NOTE**
>
> Click on the Select Drawing Objects button on the drawing toolbar to change the cursor from an insertion point to a selection arrow. When the selection arrow is active, you can press and hold Shift and click on multiple objects to select them, or click and hold the left mouse button, and then drag to "marquee" select a group of objects at one time. You must completely enclose an object with the dotted-line marquee for it to be selected.

> **NOTE**
>
> Any changes made to a group of objects stay with the individual objects when they're ungrouped.

FIGURE 44.8.

Ungrouped and grouped filled objects.

Text in Objects

In Word and Excel, you can add a text box to a drawing by selecting the text box tool and drawing a box. Inside the text box, you can add whatever text you'd like. In PowerPoint, you have a text tool that creates a text frame in which you can type.

AutoShapes

PowerPoint has an additional drawing tool called AutoShapes. When you click on the AutoShapes button on PowerPoint's Drawing toolbar, the AutoShapes toolbar displays. With AutoShapes, you can create drawing objects such as arrows, hexagons, octagons, and rounded rectangles. To create an AutoShape, select the shape you want, and then drag the cross-hair cursor in the slide. As with ellipses and rectangles, hold the Shift key when you drag to create a symmetrically proportioned AutoShape.

> **TIP**
>
> You may need the same drawing in different Office documents (for example, in a Word document and in a PowerPoint presentation) covering the same information. Rather than create the drawing twice, use the Office copy and paste capabilities to duplicate the drawing from one application to another.

A Drawing Example

Suppose you need to create a diagram depicting your company's latest manufacturing process. The drawing, you recognize, will be somewhat elementary, but the only tool you have is Office and you need the drawing *now*. Because you'll want the drawing for both a presentation and a report, you decide to create your diagram in PowerPoint, and then copy it into a Word document. AutoShapes will be a big help.

To begin, create a presentation and a blank slide. From the menu, select View | Toolbar | Drawing and Drawing+. Click on the AutoShapes button to activate the AutoShapes toolbar. Select the star AutoShape, move the cross-hair cursor to the upper-left corner of your slide, hold down Shift, and drag to create an even star. Make sure the star is selected, and then color it yellow by clicking on the fill button, selecting Other color, and clicking on a yellow honeycomb. (See Figure 44.9.) Next, click on the right arrow and draw an arrow to the right of the star. Color the arrow gray.

> **NOTE**
>
> The fill dialog box displays a number of colors without requiring you to go to Other colors. Depending on the default color scheme for your slide, the color you want may be one of the standard colors displayed in the fill dialog box.

FIGURE 44.9.

Selecting a color.

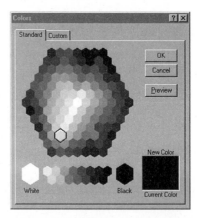

> **CAUTION**
>
> Changing the design template of your presentation may also change the color fills of your objects. After you change the design template, make sure you like the new colors.

Next, draw a cube, elongate it slightly, color it dark blue, and add another arrow. (See Figure 44.10.) For consistency, select your original arrow, copy it, and then paste a new one next to the cube. Now add a rounded rectangle. Click on the fill tool, and then on Textured. Select the Paper texture. (See Figure 44.11.) Copy and paste your arrow again, position it below the paper rectangle, and click on Rotate right to point the arrow down. Move the arrow away from the paper rectangle, if you need to.

FIGURE 44.10.

The completed cube.

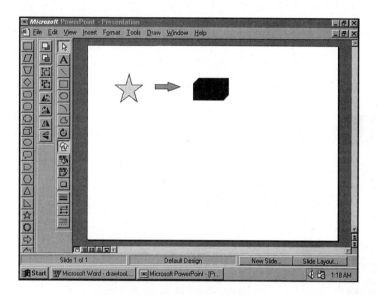

FIGURE 44.11.

The Textured Fill dialog box.

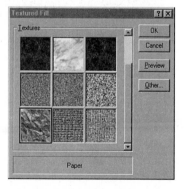

Click on the cross tool, move the cursor below your last arrow, hold the Shift key, and draw a cross. Select the free rotate tool, move the cursor over one of the rotate handles, and move the cursor until the cross has rotated to become an ✕. Select the fill tool, and then select Shaded. In the Shaded Fill dialog box, select the Preset button, click on the arrow next to Preset Colors, and choose Chrome. Then select the Shade Style From Center, click on the left variant (Figure 44.12), and click OK. Click on the drop shadow tool to add a shadow. (See Figure 44.13.) Select one of your right arrows, and copy and paste it. Move the new arrow to the left of the ×. Click on flip horizontal to change the arrow to point left.

FIGURE 44.12.

The Shaded Fill dialog box.

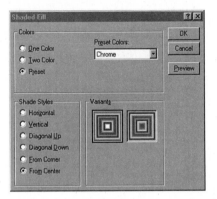

Select the seal tool and draw a somewhat flattened seal shape next to the arrow. Select the fill tool, and then select Patterned. Select the diamond checks, then choose a bright green for the foreground and a purple shade for the background. (See Figure 44.14.) Click OK. Click on the line color tool and make the seal's outline black. Select the line style tool to make the outline very heavy. (See Figure 44.15.) Add a balloon to the left of the seal (using the balloon tool, and then flip horizontal). Double-click on the balloon to activate the text tool and type We're done! Resize the balloon to accommodate the entire text. (See Figure 44.16.)

FIGURE 44.13.

The completed cross.

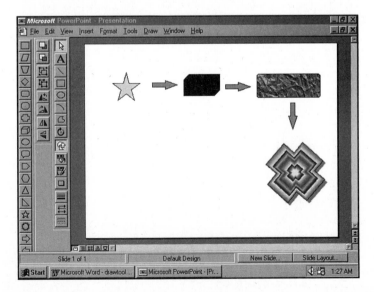

FIGURE 44.14.

The Pattern Fill dialog box.

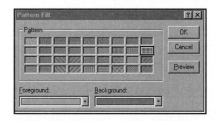

FIGURE 44.15.

The completed seal.

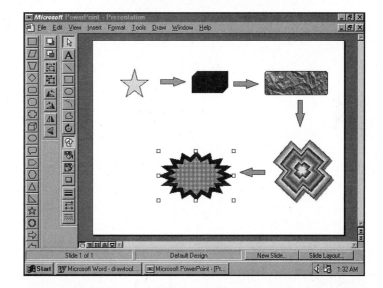

FIGURE 44.16.

We're done!

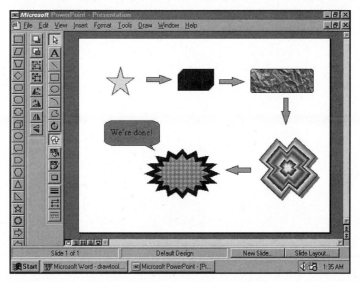

You probably wouldn't really create a diagram that looks like this one. Too many shapes, colors, styles, patterns, and textures make for an unreadable drawing. In the absence of a dedicated graphics tool, however, Office's drawing tools allow you to create diagrams, simple drawings, and other graphics to illustrate your documents.

Summary

This chapter looks at the drawing tools in Office applications. While the drawing tools in Word, PowerPoint, and Excel are quite similar, there are differences between the tools available in each Office application.

The Office drawing tools offer basic drawing capabilities with a number of tools for manipulating the created shapes. PowerPoint, with its AutoShapes and fill tools, has the most powerful drawing abilities.

The Office Toolbox

45

by Sue Charlesworth

Having explored one Office "object"—Graph—and another application—the Drawing tool—similar to an Office object, we now turn our attention to other Office objects. WordArt, Equation, and Organization Chart are true Office objects: They have no life of their own—they are unable to exist outside a Word document, PowerPoint presentation, or Excel spreadsheet; they can only be accessed from the Insert|Object menu selection; and they can't be saved as files by themselves.

Unlike the Drawing tool, WordArt, Equation Editor, and Organization Chart are created and manipulated almost identically. Only PowerPoint differs from the others, due to its inherently graphic orientation. Functionality of the object tools is otherwise identical across Office applications. Our discussion of these objects, therefore, is nonspecific; we will explore the object applications themselves without regard to their host Office application.

Starting WordArt, Equation Editor, and Organization Chart

To access WordArt, select Insert|Object|Microsoft WordArt 2.0 from the menu bar. WordArt opens a text frame in its host application, a text editing box, a toolbar, and a menu bar specific to WordArt. Double-click in an existing WordArt object to open it for editing.

CAUTION

If you had an older version of Office installed previously, you may also have WordArt 1.0 on your Object menu; make sure you select WordArt 2.0.

To open Equation Editor, select Insert|Object|Microsoft Equation 2.0 from the menu bar. Equation Editor opens a frame in the host application and displays the Equation Editor toolbar. As with other Office objects, double-click in an existing equation to open it.

NOTE

Equation Editor in PowerPoint is slightly different. No frame is opened; an editing window displays instead, with the toolbar at the top of the window.

CAUTION

If you had an older version of Office installed previously, you may also have Equation 1.0 on your Object menu; make sure you select Equation 2.0.

Organization Chart is much the same; select Insert | Object | MS Organization Chart 2.0. Office creates a frame in the host application and opens Organization Chart as a window with a menu bar, toolbar, and default organization chart. Once the frame is created, open an organization chart by double-clicking it in its parent application.

TIP

Notice that the menu selections for these Office objects aren't necessarily where you would expect them. Equation presents no problems: However, because WordArt is one word, it follows other Word objects; and Organization Chart, because it uses "MS" rather than "Microsoft," follows all the Microsoft entries.

NOTE

As mentioned earlier, PowerPoint's graphic bent treats these objects a little differently. PowerPoint doesn't need to create a frame to hold a graphic object, so WordArt, Equation Editor, and Organization Chart don't insert frames in PowerPoint. PowerPoint also has a slide type for Organization Chart, although you can still insert an organization chart from the menu.

WordArt

WordArt is a tool to manipulate text into different shapes and patterns. With WordArt, you can "pour" text into waves, triangles, arches, and other shapes, tilt your text at various angles, rotate it, and add other text effects.

When you open WordArt (by selecting Insert | Object | Microsoft WordArt), you have a menu bar, a toolbar, a text frame, and a text entry window called Enter Your Text Here. (See Figure 45.1.) You enter your text in the text window, and then click on various formatting options on the toolbar. To see the effects of your manipulations on the text itself, click on the Update Display button in the text window; the text and its effects display in the text frame.

WordArt's Special Effects

One of the main effects in WordArt is produced by the shape box (the first tool on the left on the toolbar). WordArt's basic shape defaults to Plain Text; click on the arrow to display all the shapes available for your text.

FIGURE 45.1.

The WordArt window and toolbar.

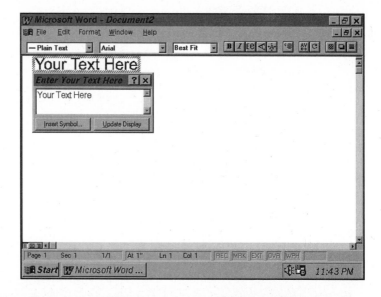

TIP

Some of the shapes are specifically geared to a certain number of lines. The circle shapes work best with two lines of text, with the first line forming the top of the circle and the second line the bottom. The two button shapes (Figure 45.2) work best with three lines of text: The first line forms the top curve; the second text line forms the middle bar; and the third text line becomes the bottom curve.

FIGURE 45.2.

A WordArt button.

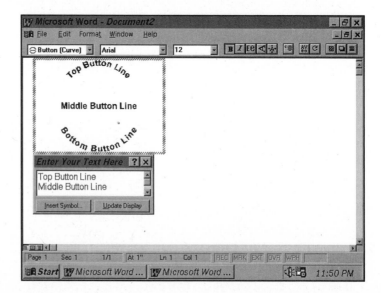

> **NOTE**
>
> You don't have to have a fancy shape to take advantage of WordArt's other features. However, the shapes are lots of fun to play with!

Next on the toolbar is the font box. Click on the arrow to show a list of all available fonts, and select the one you want.

> **NOTE**
>
> WordArt doesn't provide ToolTips, so you're on your own for determining what the buttons on the toolbar do.

The font size box allows you to change the size of your text. The font size defaults to Best Fit, where WordArt sizes the font to fit the text into the frame. However, clicking on the arrow provides you with a list of other sizes you can choose.

> **NOTE**
>
> The WordArt effects, including the font, affect the entire WordArt text. You can't apply special effects to only a word or two.

The bold and italic buttons work as you'd expect. The middle button of the group makes all text, upper- and lowercase alike, the same height. The button with the sideways A flips text on its side, and the far-right button of the group stretches text to the edges of the frame. The next button to the right is for text alignment (left, right, center). The button with the AV and double arrow allows you to change the spacing between the letters in your text, moving the letters close together or far apart. When you click on the button with the circular arrow, you can add special effects such as text rotation and change other properties of your text. The exact properties available depend on the type of shape you are using.

The last three buttons shade, shadow, and outline your text. The shading button also allows you to change the color of your text.

> **CAUTION**
>
> In shading, clear applies a transparent fill to your text. If you choose Clear, your text may seem to disappear entirely, which is an unsettling experience. Also, watch out for foreground and background colors. The normal shading color is black; if you choose white and you've made white letters, you'll also experience disappearing text.

A further "gotcha" in shading—in fact, in all of WordArt—is that you can't restore your text to a default style or undo your changes. If you've done something really bizarre and you can't remember what "normal" is, you may have to start again from scratch. If you've created a WordArt effect you'd like to keep, you might want to save your file before doing any exotic WordArt work.

WordArt Examples

You want to create stationery for your store, The Needle Nook. Open WordArt and enter The Needle Nook in the text box. Then select Arch Up (Curve) from the Shapes box (second row, far left). Leave the font Arial, and change the size to 64. Select Bold, and then click on the Special Effects button. In the Special Effects dialog box, change the arc angle to 90 degrees. For shading, select the bottom-right pattern. There! You've created a logo for your store. (See Figure 45.3.)

FIGURE 45.3.

The Needle Nook's logo.

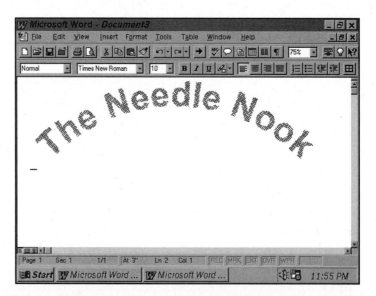

TIP

Resizing the WordArt frame within its parent application doesn't distort the WordArt. Adjust the frame edges to size and fit your WordArt as needed.

Now you want to create reasonably priced but unique name tags for your company's spring sales meeting. Open WordArt and enter three lines of text in the text box: I'm Part of the

Spring Thing for the first line, Hi! I'm for the second, and a participant's names for the third. Select Button (Pour) for the shape, select a fancy font, and select a font size of 24. (See Figure 45.4.) Unfortunately, there is no way to automate text entry in WordArt, so you'll need to create a separate name tag for each person and add each name.

FIGURE 45.4.

The Spring Thing name tag.

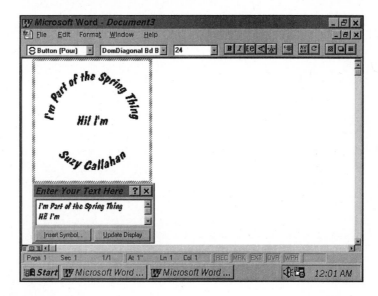

Equation Editor

Equation Editor allows you to create correctly formatted mathematic equations. Equation Editor does not do the calculations or computations; it just provides a way to create a printable equation and place it in your document, spreadsheet, or presentation.

If Equation Editor doesn't do the calculations, what is its benefit? Equation Editor offers two main advantages:

- More symbols than are available from the Symbols font
- Automatic adjustments for mathematical typesetting conventions, setting font sizes, spacing, and formats

Using Equation Editor

When you open Equation Editor, it displays a text frame, where you can see the equation you're creating, as well as the Equation toolbar. (See Figure 45.5.) The Equation toolbar is somewhat different from other Office toolbars; it has no buttons. Instead of buttons, the Equation toolbar presents two rows of boxes that represent *palettes*, or groups of related symbols or fill-in equation templates. When you click on one of the palette boxes, the palette of available options drops down, allowing you to select the one you need.

FIGURE 45.5.

The Equation Editor toolbar.

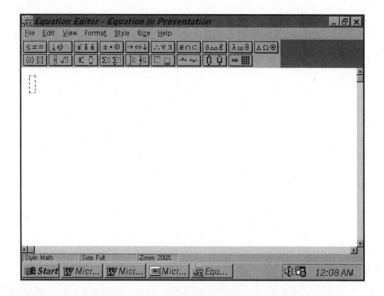

> **NOTE**
>
> This is another place where PowerPoint is a little different from Word and Excel. PowerPoint opens Equation Editor as a window, with the Equation toolbar along the top and editing space below.

> **CAUTION**
>
> If you use default equation sizing in PowerPoint, when you exit the Equation Editor, the equation placed in your presentation is tiny, if not minuscule. No one (including you) will be able to read it. You'll need to change the font size in Equation Editor or enlarge the equation in the slide.

The top row of the Equation toolbar offers a variety of symbols, including

■ Relational symbols (less than, greater than, not equal)

■ Primes, bars, and hats

■ Set symbols (union, subset)

■ Uppercase Greek alphabet

■ Lowercase Greek alphabet

The bottom row of the Equation toolbar provides templates for equation construction. Select a template, fill in your numbers or symbols, and you've created a correctly spaced and formatted equation. The templates in the Equation toolbar include

- Brackets and braces
- Subscripts and superscripts
- Integrals
- Fractions
- Summations
- Matrices

If you're not quite sure what a symbol or template is, the status line at the bottom of the screen displays the name of the palette, if a palette is selected, or the name of the individual symbol or template.

NOTE

Equation Editor doesn't provide ToolTips for the toolbar.

TIP

With a palette open, use the arrow keys to "snake" through the palette to see what all the palette's options are. Pay attention, though; the left- and right-arrow keys will move you to the next palette over, if you press them while you're at the left or right edge of the palette. The up- and down-arrow keys simply continue in the current column.

Constructing an Equation

When you click on a template in a palette, Equation Editor inserts that template into your equation. The template provides slots, indicated by boxes made of dashed lines, where you put your values or variables. You can nest templates; in any slot, you can insert another template.

To construct an equation, insert the following:

- The desired template(s)
- Symbols from the Equation toolbar
- Regular letters—uppercase or lowercase—from the keyboard
- Numerals from the keyboard in whatever order you need

TIP

Although you can enter some characters from the keyboard, such as < for less than or the left-hand side of an angle bracket pair, it's probably better to enter these from the Equation Editor to take advantage of the automatic spacing and formatting. Other characters, however, like the plus, minus, and equal signs, you must enter from the keyboard.

NOTE

You can't enter spaces into an equation with the spacebar. If you need spaces not accounted for in standard mathematical formatting, insert a space from the Spaces and ellipses palette.

CAUTION

Equation Editor has no copy and paste facilities. You can't copy numbers from elsewhere, and you can't cut something from within your equation to move it to another part of the equation. You can, however, select what you have entered, and then choose a template. Equation Editor places the text inside the template. Even with this ability to "surround" text, plan your equation carefully; you might still be surprised by the placement of symbols and have to retype information. (This is the voice of experience speaking.)

NOTE

What? No copy and paste in Equation Editor? How in the world are you going to get your formula from PowerPoint into Word without retyping the whole thing? Relax. Although you can't copy and paste *within* Equation Editor, you can copy the entire equation, as embedded in its host document, and paste it into another document.

To edit your equation, use the arrow keys to move left and right and up and down in the equation or template. With fractions, superscripts, subscripts, and all the complexities of an involved formula, you may need to concentrate to identify the part of the equation you're editing. Equation Editor's insertion point helps guide you. In addition to the standard vertical insertion point, Equation Editor also provides a horizontal bar. The vertical insertion point indicates the point in a slot where a character, a symbol, or a template will be placed next. The horizontal bar indicates the active slot.

TIP

The horizontal bar, in particular, helps you determine your location in your equation. Generally, as you move to higher-level, more-encompassing slots, the horizontal bar becomes longer.

CAUTION

Be careful where you are in your equation if you are about to insert another template, symbol, or character. If you've just entered a subscript, you'll probably want to move to the normal flow of the equation before adding something else. Watch the insertion point's horizontal bar to orient yourself in the equation. It is far too easy to enter the next part of your equation in an undesirable place.

If you enter a series of information in rows and you want to align your information in columns, select Format from the menu bar, and then select the alignment you want.

TIP

Have you ever tried to align a column of numbers in Word? Have you spaced your numbers out carefully, only to have them be misaligned when printed? Have you inserted a table so you could right-justify just that part of your text? Have you tried to figure out decimal point tab alignment? What about the times when your numbers didn't have decimal points? Use Equation Editor. Insert an equation, type in your lines of numbers, select Format|Align Right, and it's done.

Here's another neat alignment trick: If you have a series of equations with equal signs, you can align around the equal signs. For example, economics offers us this series of equations:

$$MS = (\tfrac{1}{v})\$GNP$$
$$MS = (\tfrac{1}{v})P \times Q$$
$$V \times MS = P \times Q$$
$$M \times V = P \times Q$$

They look very nice when aligned around the equal signs.

Equation Examples

Let's look now at creating some specific examples of equations. For these, we turn to statistics, economics, and other business disciplines to provide the raw materials. The first examples come from statistics.

> **NOTE**
>
> What the equation means or does is immaterial to our discussion. We only want to see how to construct the equation on paper, not to understand what all the symbols mean.

Select Insert|Object|Equation 2.0 from the menu bar. Once you're in the Equation Editor, follow these steps:

1. Type SSTO=.
2. From the Summation templates palette, select Summation with underscript limit.
3. Move the insertion point to the underscript slot and type all.
4. From the Spaces and ellipses palette, select Thick space.
5. Type i (still in the underscript).
6. Move the insertion point outside the slot next to the summation sign.
7. Repeat steps 2 through 6, using all j for the underscript.
8. From the Fence templates palette, select Parentheses.
9. Type X.
10. From the Subscript and superscript templates palette, select Subscript.
11. Move the insertion point to the subscript and type ij.
12. Move the insertion point to the right (outside the subscript but within the closing parenthesis) and type -X.
13. From the Embellishments palette, select Over-bar.
14. Repeat step 13.
15. Move the insertion point to the end of the equation.
16. From the Subscript and superscript templates palette, select Superscript.
17. Move the insertion point to the superscript and type 2.

Figure 45.6 shows the completed equation.

FIGURE 45.6.

The first equation.

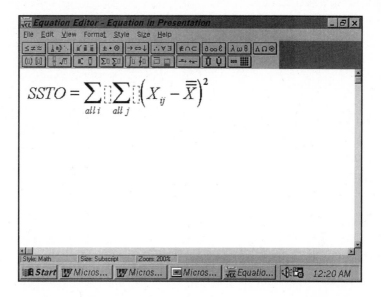

If you want to change the style of part of your equation, select Style from the menu bar, and then select the style you want to change. For example, the sample shown in Figure 45.6 uses the default style selection Math and all text is in italics. If you want regular text, select Text from the Style menu when you enter text characters.

> **CAUTION**
>
> Don't forget to change the style back to Math when you want italicized characters to represent variables.

In the next example, we won't go quite so step by step, assuming that by now you have a feel for how Equation Editor works:

1. Open Equation Editor.
2. Type z=.
3. Enter a full-size vertical fraction.
4. In the top of the fraction, enter a set of parentheses.
5. Inside the parentheses, enter a lowercase x with an over-bar and a subscript of lowercase a.
6. Move outside the subscript and enter -, then a lowercase x with an over-bar and a subscript of b.
7. Move outside the parentheses and enter -.

8. Enter a new set of parentheses.

9. Inside the parentheses, enter a lowercase Greek alphabet mu with a subscript of lowercase a, move to the right of the subscript and enter a -, and a lowercase Greek alphabet mu with a subscript of lowercase b.

10. Move to the bottom of the fraction and enter a square root sign.

11. Inside the square root sign, enter a slash fraction.

12. In the left-hand part of the slash fraction, add a lowercase Greek alphabet sigma with a subscript of a.

13. Move the insertion point to the right of the subscript and insert a superscript 2.

14. Move the insertion point to the right-hand portion of the slash fraction and type n and add a subscript a.

15. Move the insertion point outside the slash fraction (but still under the square root sign) and type +.

16. Insert another slash fraction and repeat steps 12 through 14, using b as a subscript instead of a.

Figure 45.7 shows the completed equation.

FIGURE 45.7.

The second equation.

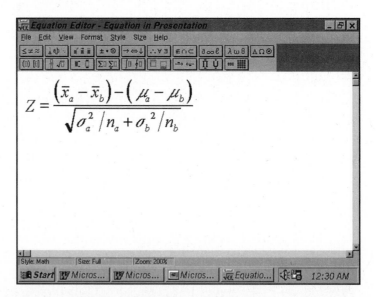

NOTE

In the equation shown in Figure 45.7, you can see the value of planning ahead, particularly with the placement of the vertical and slash fractions.

For a real challenge, try to create the formula in Figure 45.8, which comes from the world of international finance.

FIGURE 45.8.

The international finance equation.

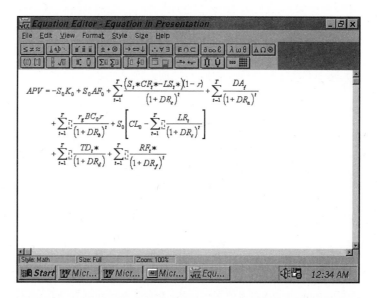

NOTE

Equation Editor doesn't make for fast typing. You no sooner get your hands back in position on the keyboard than you have to move to the mouse again to insert something from a palette. How fast, though, would brute-force typing be, anyway?

Organization Chart

With Organization Chart, you can create and format organization charts. Organization Chart automatically resizes your chart as you add and delete boxes and makes it easy to apply different formats to your chart.

TIP

You can use Organization Chart to represent other types of hierarchic information. However, you are limited to four lines of text per box, which is fine for an organization chart, but perhaps is a bit limiting for other uses.

In any of the three host Office applications—Word, PowerPoint, or Excel—you open Organization Chart by selecting Insert|Object|MS Organization Chart 2.0 from the menu bar. Organization Chart looks exactly the same in all its host Office applications. In addition, you can open Organization Chart in PowerPoint by selecting an Organization Chart slide layout, then double-clicking where indicated on the slide.

Creating an Organization Chart

When Organization Chart opens, it displays a menu bar, a toolbar, and a default organization chart in its window. (See Figure 45.9.) The default chart consists of four boxes—one superior with three subordinates. These default boxes have prompts to help you enter information in the boxes. When one of the lines is highlighted, type in the information you want to appear in the box.

FIGURE 45.9.

The Organization Chart window.

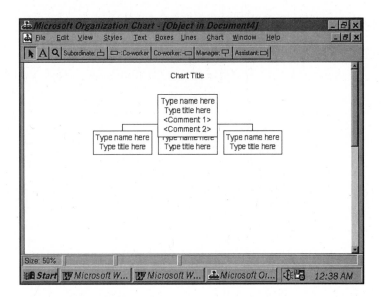

All Organization Chart boxes have room for four lines:

- Name
- Title
- Comment 1
- Comment 2

When you open an organization chart, the top-level name slot is active. Typing characters replaces the default information. Press Tab to move to the next line. If you enter fewer than four lines of information, the box shrinks to only the number of lines used; the exception is an "empty" box, which displays as a blank box of one line.

CAUTION

The default information in an organization chart remains in the chart unless you specifically overwrite or delete it. Ignoring the default information gives you an organization chart with boxes containing the text `Type name here` and `Type title here`. It's a fair guess that no one in your organization has quite these characteristics.

To place new boxes in your organization chart, select the box type desired from the toolbar; the cursor changes to a miniature of the box selected. Click on the box to which the new one relates: If you are creating a subordinate, click on the superior's box; if you're adding a co-worker, click on a co-worker's box. Organization Chart adds the box and rearranges existing boxes by doing the following:

- Adjusting the spacing for subordinates or co-workers at the same level
- Adding an assistant at right angles to the superior/subordinate line
- Adding a subordinate below a superior
- Adding a manager above a subordinate, but below the subordinate's original superior

Editing Your Organization Chart

In addition to adding and deleting boxes and editing the text in boxes, you can change styles, boxes, lines, and text.

TIP

Select Edit|Select from the menu bar to select all boxes and lines, specific groups of boxes, or other Organization Chart objects. Once you select a group of boxes or kinds of chart objects, you can then apply changes to the entire group at once.

With styles, you change the way Organization Chart presents your chart. Select Styles from the menu bar, and then click on the style you want. Within Styles you determine the following:

- How co-workers are grouped within levels
- Whether your chart has horizontal or vertical boxes
- How co-managers and assistants are shown

Select Boxes from the menu bar, and then select a box option to change your boxes' characteristics. With Boxes, you can do the following:

- Color boxes
- Add or change drop shadows and select the drop shadow style
- Select or change the box border style (including no border)
- Select or change the border color
- Select or change the border line style

You can also change the connecting lines in your chart. Select Lines from the menu bar and the desired line option:

- Thickness
- Style, to change the line from solid to dashed to dotted
- Color

When you select Text from the menu bar, you can change the characteristics of the text in your chart. The Text menu allows you to change the following:

- Font characteristics (font, style, size)
- Font color
- Text alignment (left, right, center)

TIP

As with all printed and displayed materials, be careful not to use too many fonts and colors. One or maybe two variations should get your most important information suitably emphasized. Take advantage of different sizes and styles (bold, italic) of the same font for additional emphasis.

NOTE

For text, boxes, and lines, you must have at least one of the desired objects selected before Organization Chart can make changes.

Organization Chart Example

Let's create a sample organization chart to see exactly how to put one together. From Word, PowerPoint, or Excel, select Insert|Object|MS Organization Chart 2.0 to open an organization chart.

TIP

Don't forget that you can create an organization chart slide in PowerPoint.

Let's say that we're creating the organization chart for the development section of a software firm. The top box contains details on the Systems Manager, Charles Johnson. We won't need the two comment lines for Charles.

Reporting directly to Charles are John Hailey, Manager of Applications Development; Susan Baer, Manager of System Development; Steve Harrison, Deployment Manager; and Carol Hastings, Manager of Support and Services. Because Organization Chart only provides three default subordinates, we'll need to add one for the fourth manager. To add the additional person, do one of the following:

- Click on the Subordinate button, then on Charles' box.
- Click on one of the Co-worker buttons, then on one of the other three manager's boxes.

TIP

Actual size, which is the default chart size, may be too big to work with comfortably. If you don't like the default chart size, select View from the menu bar, and then select the desired size.

The chart with the four managers is rather wide. Select Edit|Select|All from the menu bar, and then select Styles from the menu bar. Click on the top-right group arrangement.

Now add Susan's organization: David Worth, Supervisor, Network Development; Anne Baylor, Supervisor, Tools and Compilers; and Eric Dayton, Supervisor, Infrastructure, report to Susan. Reporting to David are Darrin Greene, Karen Keyes, and Bob Billings; to Anne, Harris Townson; and to Eric, Ed Bates, Sally Newsome, and Greg Jarrett.

We don't want to have boxes for the people who report to the supervisors (boxes take up a lot of room on a chart). To highlight all the supervisors' employees, select Edit|Select|Levels from the menu bar, then change the 1 to a 4. Select Boxes|Border Style from the menu bar, and then click on None. While the employees are still highlighted, select Styles from the menu bar, and then click on the vertical group arrangement.

We've added all the people for this chart, so we turn our attention to formatting the boxes. Because we've broken down Susan's group, let's emphasize those boxes. Click in Susan's box, then select Edit|Select|Branch from the menu bar to highlight her group. Add drop shadows to the group by clicking on Boxes|Shadow; click on the second box from the top on the right-hand side; then add a border of your choice (by selecting Boxes|Border Style). Figure 45.10 shows a portion of the completed organization chart.

FIGURE 45.10.

The completed organization chart.

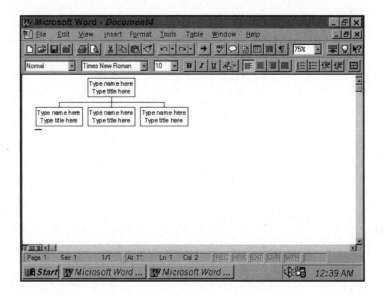

Summary

This chapter explores three more of Office's object applications: WordArt, Equation Editor, and Organization Chart. Each object functions identically whether opened in Word, PowerPoint, or Excel.

WordArt provides a tool to manipulate text. You can select shapes, shading, shadows, borders, and other text-tweaking effects. You use WordArt to create logos, special effects, and fun, attention-getting text treatments.

Equation Editor helps you create equations that meet mathematical typesetting conventions. Using a toolbar consisting of palettes of symbols and fill-in templates, you can create printed equations for many business, statistics, economics, and other needs.

With Organization Chart, you can create and edit organizational charts. Organization Chart automatically adjusts charts to readily accommodate changes in your organizational structure. The toolbar makes it easy to add managers, co-workers, subordinates, and assistants.

X

PART

Output

Printing Options and Techniques

The improved printing capabilities in Windows 95, such as faster speed and improved conflict resolution, enhance Microsoft Office printing output. Some of the changes, such as the 32-bit printer driver, make the Office suite compatible with Windows NT. This chapter covers some of the recommended techniques that make printing from the Office applications an easy and rewarding task.

Printing from Word for Windows 95

Word processing brings some unique problems that need to be resolved. Microsoft Word for Windows 95 offers many solutions as well as a vast number of options to the user.

Printing Options

From the File|Print menu, several options can be chosen. You can print pages in a range or choose odd or even pages to be printed. This is useful when you want to print both sides of the page. Printer selection can also be made from here. Other choices include the number of copies to be made and the printing range.

Other printing selections can be made from File|Print|Print What. From here, documents, summaries, annotations, styles, key assignments, and autotexts for bookmarks or fields, can be printed. Another useful printing feature found in this menu is the ability to print several files at once (see the following section).

Printing Several Files

Here's how to print several files at once:

1. In the File menu, select Open.
2. Click the name of each document to be printed while holding down the Ctrl key.
3. Click the Commands and Settings button from the File menu and then select Print. (See Figure 46.1.)

Viewing, Editing, and Printing a Large Document

It is difficult to view the general structure of a large document. For such documents, it is more convenient to display only a partial view. This can be accomplished by switching to Master view mode as follows:

1. Click the View|Master Document menu to display the pages in master document mode. *Master document* refers to a view mode that partially displays a large document. In this mode, it is possible to work from a subdocument and yet be able to view the entire document.

FIGURE 46.1.

After clicking the Commands and Settings button, select Print to print several files.

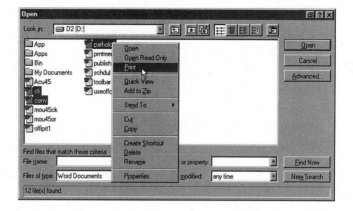

2. Expand or collapse headings to display the total area to be printed. Search Word's Answer Wizard for `collapse headings` to accomplish this.

3. Click Print from the File menu.

4. Print the document after choosing the desired printing options.

NOTE

To print the entire document, display the master document in normal view and click Print. Select printing options from this menu.

Here are some options available from the Print menu and from the Print | Options menu:

- Print document information.
- Include field codes.
- Include annotations.
- Include hidden text.
- Include drawing objects.
- Reverse print order.
- Update fields.
- Update links.
- Print a draft copy of documents.
- Toggle background printing on and off.
- Create print files. This is useful when there is not enough time to print the files straight away.

NOTE

To create print files, select File | Print | Print to File, and then enter the name and directory for the print file.

Canceling Print Jobs

To cancel a print job while the Background Printing option is turned off, just click the Cancel button in the Printing Now window. If the Background Printing option is turned on, double-click the printer icon located on the status bar.

NOTE

When you are printing a short document and the Background Printing option is turned on, the printer icon might disappear from the status bar before you can cancel the print job. In this case, the printer needs to be reset directly.

Changing the Paper Type for Part of the Document

You can change the paper type for part of a document. This is a very useful feature for some documents. Margins, paper source, paper size, and layout can be changed at any stage of the document:

1. In the File menu, select Page Setup and then select the Paper Source tab.
2. To specify a paper tray for the first page of the document, click the appropriate tray in the First Page box.
3. To specify a paper tray for other pages of the document, click the appropriate tray in the Other Pages box.

Changing the Paper Size for Part of a Document

Here are the steps to follow in order to change the paper size of part of a document:

1. Select the document section to change.
2. From the File menu, select Page Setup | Paper Size; then enter the desired paper measurements.
3. In the Apply To list, select From This Point On.

Changing the Paper Type for Part of a Document

Here are the steps to follow in order to change the paper type for part of a document:

1. In the File menu, select Page Setup, and then click the Paper Source tab.

2. To specify a paper tray for the first page of the document, click the appropriate tray in the First Page box.

3. To specify a paper tray for other pages of the document, click the appropriate tray in the Other Pages box. (See Figure 46.2.)

FIGURE 46.2.

Customizing paper size for individual pages in the Paper Source tab.

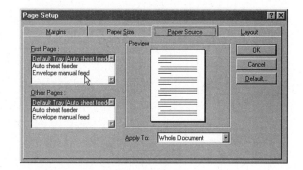

Using Automatic Feeding When Printing Envelopes

When you want your envelopes to automatically feed but Word has prompted you to feed them manually, check the Envelopes tab in the Tools | Envelopes and Labels menu. From here, click the Options | Printing Options tab. Check that the appropriate tray name has been selected in the Feed From options.

Table Gridlines in Printed Documents

Table gridlines appear onscreen only. To print vertical and horizontal lines between cells, borders need to be applied to the table. To show borders, use the Table AutoFormat command from the Table menu, which automatically applies predefined borders and shading to a table. You can also use the Borders toolbar or the Borders and Shading command from the Format menu to create custom borders and shading.

Troubleshooting Printing Problems

Printing problems can be general for most printers, or specific to the printer used. Following are some typical problems and solutions.

Solving Envelope Printing Problems

In some cases, such as when printing with HP printers, the envelope feeder is on the right side of the tray, but the printer prints the address on the left side of the tray. To solve this problem, change the Envelope Feed option. From the Tools menu, select Envelope and Labels | Envelope | Options | Feed and then change the choice of envelope feed 180 degrees from what is indicated on the printer tray. For HP printers, turn on the Clockwise Rotation option and then select the Face Down option.

When Superscripts and Subscripts Are Cut Off

Sometimes superscript characters appear to be cut off. To avoid this, increase the line spacing. In the Format | Paragraph dialog box, select the Indents and Spacing tab; then click the Line Spacing box. You can increase the point size in the At box.

If subscript characters appear to be cut off, adjust the position of the subscript. Select the subscript text, select Font from the Format menu, and then click the Character Spacing tab. Decrease the point size in the Position By box to adjust the changes.

When Printed Text Looks Different from Onscreen Text

One reason for the difference in the appearance of a font might be that Word is displaying text in draft font. From the Tools menu, select Options and then choose the View tab. From here, clear the Draft Font check box.

Another possible reason for the disparity in the font's appearance might be that the font used in the document is a printer font that is not available on your printer, so the printer substituted its own font. Changing the font in the document to a TrueType font, which will print as closely to the screen display as possible, or changing the font to one available on your printer should solve the problem.

Still another possible reason for the difference in the font's appearance might be that the font used in the document, even though it is an available printer font, doesn't have a matching screen font. To be able to display the selected font in the screen, Windows substitutes it for a TrueType font. For a better match between screen and printer fonts, change the fonts in the document to TrueType fonts.

> **NOTE**
>
> To see available printer fonts, select Font from the Format menu. In the Font box, scroll through the list for Printer and TrueType fonts.

Here is how to find out if Windows has substituted a font that was not available on your printer or if a font that was not available from Windows was replaced:

1. From the Tools menu select Options; then choose the Compatibility tab.
2. Click Font Substitution.

A message appears that informs you whether or not font substitution is being used.

> **NOTE**
>
> If the substituted font is listed as Default, Word uses the font that best matches the size and appearance of the missing font.

Changing the Font Used by Windows

The following steps show you how to change the font used by Windows:

1. Select Tools | Options | Font Substitutions. Click the Font Substitution box where the missing font name will be displayed.
2. In the Substituted Font box select the font you want.

Printing an Outline

When using the built-in heading styles to format heading paragraphs, you can regulate how much of the document is displayed and then print the displayed text. Here are the steps:

1. Select outline view to display the headings and body text to be printed. For information on how to display headings and body text, check Word's Help Wizard for the section "Display Headings to View a Document's Organization."
2. Select Heading Numbering from the Format menu and then select a numbering style for numbering the headings.
3. Click Print.

Word prints only the displayed headings. If body text is displayed, Word prints all lines of the body text, even if only the first line is displayed.

> **NOTE**
>
> If manual page breaks are visible in outline view, they will be included in the printed document. The page breaks can be temporarily removed. To do this, save the document and then delete the page breaks. After printing, the document must be closed without saving the changes.

Printing Envelopes and Labels

With Microsoft Word for Windows 95 you can print envelopes and address labels as well as add graphics and postal codes.

Printing Envelopes from Word

Word can easily print an address on an envelope. The envelope can just contain the recipient's address, or it can hold more elaborate information such as the return address with a graphic, and a bar code to simplify delivery. Depending on the printer's capabilities, Word can include two types of codes on an envelope: the POSTNET bar code and the FIM code. The POSTNET bar code is a machine-readable representation of the Zip code and the delivery address; the FIM code identifies the front of a courtesy reply envelope. Word for Windows 95 can print from one to several envelopes to different recipients as when merging an address database.

Adding an Address to an Envelope

The following steps show you how to print an envelope:

1. From the document, place the mouse cursor at the beginning of the return address.
2. From the Tools menu select Envelopes and Labels; then select the Envelopes tab.
3. Enter the address and then select the options needed.
4. Place the envelope in the printer's feed tray according to the printer's instructions and then choose Print.

NOTE

In the Preview window, options concerning the envelope size, font choice, and size for the return address are available. Other options include the position of the address in the envelope, and font selection for the recipient's address.

Printer feed tray options can be reached from the Feeder menu or from Preview Options.

TIP

If the cursor is at the beginning of the document's recipient address, Word will display the address in the envelope editor window, ready for printing.

Adding Special Text and Graphics to Envelopes

The following steps show you how to add special text and graphics to your envelopes:

1. From the Tools menu, select Envelopes and Labels; then click the Envelopes tab.
2. Check to ensure that the delivery and return addresses entries are correct.
3. Click on Add To Document.
4. From View, select Page Layout.
5. Type the special text that you want to appear on the envelope. Select Insert | Graphic to include an exciting picture on the envelope. The picture can also be created from Word's drawing tools.
6. Drag the special text or graphic to reposition as needed. Or you can use the Frame command from the Insert menu.

Printing Mail Codes on an Envelope

The following steps show you how to print mail codes on your envelopes:

1. From the Tools menu, select Envelopes and Labels; then click the Envelopes tab.
2. Select Options | Envelope Options
3. Select either the Delivery Point Bar Code or the FIM-A Courtesy Reply Mail check box. (These check boxes will be unavailable if the country installed for Windows 95 is other than the USA.) The FIM-A Courtesy Reply Mail check box places an identification mark for the post office's mail presorting.

> **NOTE**
>
> Envelope postal bar codes are applicable for United States Mail only.
>
> To print FIM-C codes, which are often used in the United States for bulk mail, use the BAR CODE field. For more information, see Word Help topics.

Creating Return Addresses for Envelopes

It is possible to create a simple return address that appears on envelopes or design a more elaborate return address that includes a logo or other graphic image.

Creating a Return Address Containing Text Only

The following steps show you how to create a return address that contains text only:

1. From the Tools menu select Options; then click the User Info tab.

2. Enter a return address in the Mailing Address box if one is not already there.

3. Select Tools | Envelopes and Labels | Envelopes.

4. Clear the Omit check box.

Creating a Return Address with a Graphic Logo

The following steps show you how to create a return address that contains a graphic logo:

1. Create the text portion of the return address as done in the previous list.

2. Choose an existing graphic or create one in Microsoft Paint or another graphics program.

3. From the Insert menu select Picture; then select the file that contains the graphic logo. Click OK to load it. Figure 46.3 illustrates how to load the selected picture.

4. Click the graphic logo onscreen.

5. From the Edit menu select AutoText.

6. In the Name box, type EnvelopeExtra1. Click Add. (See Figure 46.4.)

FIGURE 46.3.

Loading the picture to include in the return address.

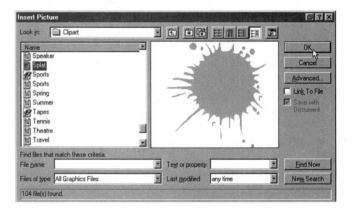

Creating a Return Address with More Complex Graphics

The following steps show you how to create a graphic logo with the return address:

1. From the Insert menu select Picture. Then, select the graphic logo and click Insert to insert it on the Word screen.

2. Select the graphic logo.

3. From the Edit menu select AutoText.

4. Type EnvelopeExtra1 in the Name box. Click Add.

5. From the Tools menu select Options; then click the User Info tab.

6. Delete all the text in the Mailing Address box and replace it with a space.

FIGURE 46.4.

If you enter
`EnvelopeExtra1` *in the
Name window and click on
Close, the picture will be
added to the return address
on the envelope.*

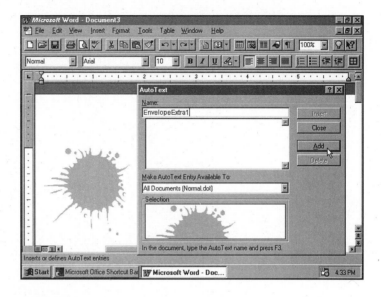

Creating Mailing Labels

In Word for Windows 95 it is possible to print anywhere from one label to several pages of labels for mass mailings.

Printing One Label

Here are the steps for printing one label:

1. Place the cursor at the beginning of the delivery address.

2. Select Tools | Envelopes and Labels; then click the Labels box.

3. Make sure the delivery and sender addresses are correct, select options as needed, and print.

> **NOTE**
>
> Some of the options available are printing a full page of the same labels, printing a page of different labels, and printing just one label.
>
> More options can be found in the Labels menu by selecting Options. From here, the label style and size, the printer type, and the printer tray options can be selected.

Printing Several Labels of the Same Address

From Tools | Envelopes and Labels, select Labels. Select the option Full Page of the Same Label. Choose any other options as needed and then print.

Merging an Address List to Mailing Labels

One of the first steps in creating a list of names and addresses for a mail merge is to decide which Office application is suited for the task. If the intended mail merge is large, a suitable list would be one created from Word, Microsoft Excel, Microsoft Access, or Schedule+. Here are some other points:

- For a small to a medium size list of names and addresses that do not require much manipulation, a data source can be created with Word Mail Merge Helper.

- A Schedule+ contact list can be used in a mail merge. For more information on this, search Word's Letter Wizard for "Using Names and Addresses from Schedule+ and Microsoft Exchange."

- Microsoft Word can be used when a numbered list is required.

- For larger lists requiring much manipulation or list number support, Microsoft Excel is indicated.

- Microsoft Access or Excel are indicated when complex data sorting and searching capabilities are required.

- Microsoft Access is the preferred choice when potent relational database capabilities and work sharing are necessary. Access is also indicated for large mailing lists.

Here are the steps for creating a mail merge:

1. Select New from the toolbar menu to start a new document.
2. From the Tools menu select Mail Merge | Create | Mailing Labels. Click Active Window to make the active document the mail merge main document.
3. Click Get Data.
4. Click Set Up Main Document.
5. Select the printer and label types. Label size can be customized.
6. From the Create labels menu, insert the merge fields for the address information. Click OK.
7. From the Mail Merge Helper dialog box, click Merge.
8. From the Merge To box, click Printer.
9. Click Merge.

Figures 46.5 and 46.6 illustrate steps 5 and 6, and Figure 46.7 shows the merged labels.

FIGURE 46.5.

Selecting the label's options.

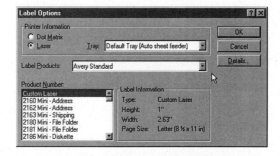

FIGURE 46.6.

Inserting the merge fields for the address information.

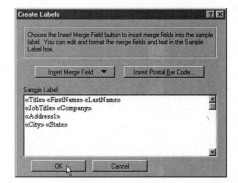

FIGURE 46.7.

The resultant merged labels.

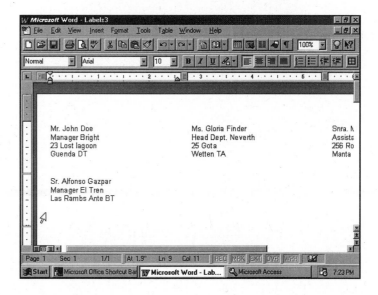

NOTE

To create a new list of names and addresses in Word, click Create Data Source; then set up the data records. For more information on how to create a data source, see the section in the Word Help Wizard titled "Create a New Data Source in Word."

It is possible to use an existing list of names and addresses, as well as existing documents, worksheets, databases, and other sources by selecting GetData|Open Data Source from the Mail Merge Helper Window.

If the addresses are from an electronic address book, click Use Address Book.

TIP

To print labels only for selected recipients, load or create a mail database from a mail merge and then select Query Options. From this menu you can specify criteria for selecting the data records.

Creating a Custom Mailing Label

If none of the listed labels match the label's dimensions, you can alter a listed label that is close to the size you need. To do this, follow these steps:

1. From the Tools menu select Envelopes and Labels|Labels|Options. From the Product Number box select a label type that is similar in size to the label size you need.

2. For laser labels, click Details to check that the label dimensions and the number of labels per sheet match the label sheet. For dot-matrix labels, check the number of columns on the label form.

3. If the dimensions and layout do not match the labels sheet, click Cancel to close the Custom Information dialog box. Select the printer type in the Product Number box. Click Details and then fill in the information for the labels.

TIP

The label size indicated by the label manufacturer might be an approximation. You should measure the sheet labels directly.

NOTE

For information on merge fields, see Word's Help Wizard or check in the Word manual.

Printing to a File

To print a file at a later time, it is possible to create a file that contains the document to be printed. To do this, follow these steps:

1. From the File menu click Print.
2. In the Name box select a printer to use.
3. Select the Print to File check box. Click OK.
4. In the File Name box, type a filename for the file.

WARNING

A document that has been printed to a file with a particular printer selection might not print correctly with another printer because page breaks and font spacing might be different.

Here are the steps for making a list of names and addresses for a mail merge or for merging an existing address list:

1. Click the New toolbar icon to start a new document.
2. From the Tools menu select Mail Merge.
3. Select Create | Mailing Labels; then click Active Window. The active document becomes the mail merge main document.
4. Click Get Data.
   - ■ To create a new list of names and addresses in Word, click Create Data Source; then set up the data records. See Word's Answer Wizard for more information on how to create a data source.
   - ■ To use an existing list of names and addresses in a Word document or in a worksheet, database, or other list, click Open Data Source.
   - ■ To use addresses from an electronic address book, click Use Address Book.
5. After designating the data source, click Set Up Main Document.
6. In the Label Options dialog box select the printer and label types to be used.
7. In the Create Labels dialog box insert the merge fields for the address information.

8. In the Mail Merge Helper dialog box click Merge.

9. In the Merge To box click Printer.

10. Click Merge.

> **NOTE**
>
> If the label type required is not listed, a custom label size can be selected.
>
> To print labels only for selected addressees, click Query Options, and then specify criteria for selecting the data records.

Printing from Excel

Excel offers some specific printing capabilities that are closely related to its worksheet format.

Setting Up an Excel Worksheet for Printing

To prepare the worksheet for printing, headers and footers can be added or manipulated from the File | Page Setup | Headers menu. Gridlines can be displayed or hidden from the File | Page Setup | Sheet menu, page orientation can be manipulated from the File | Page menu, and margins can be easily customized from the Margins menu. The Margins menu contains a page preview window. Print Preview can also be accessed from the Margins menu. See Figures 46.8 and 46.9.

FIGURE 46.8.

The Sheet tab of the Page Setup dialog box, where the worksheet can be manipulated for the final printout.

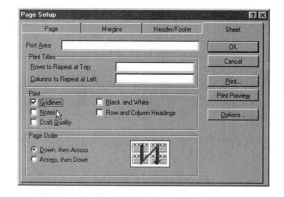

Steps to Print an Excel Report

Here are the steps to follow in order to print a report in Excel:

1. Select Report Manager from the View menu.

2. Select the report to be printed from the Reports box.

3. Click Print.

4. Enter the number of copies to be printed in the Copies box.

FIGURE 46.9.

The Margins tab of the Page Setup dialog box, where you can select several options that affect the printout.

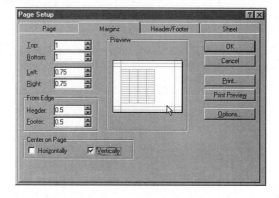

Printing a View

Here are the steps to follow in order to print a view:

1. From the View menu select View Manager.

2. In the Views box select the name of the view to be printed.

3. Click Show; then Click Print.

> **NOTE**
>
> Previously defined print areas are normally saved with the worksheet's view. If there is no print area, Excel prints the entire worksheet.

Excel Printing Options

Excel's Page Setup options—area or page to print, row and column headings, quality of print—are found in the File | Page Setup menu. The following sections provide a few examples.

Selecting a Worksheet Area to Print

To print only the worksheet area, select File | Page Setup | Print Area.

Print Order

You can print across and then down the worksheet, or down and the across the worksheet.

To have rows or columns repeat, select File | Page Setup; then enter the rows to repeat at the top or the columns to repeat at the left of the pages.

> **NOTE**
>
> To print a worksheet to a file in a readable text format, click Formatted Text in the Save As Type box (File menu | Save As command). For more information on printing, see Excel's Help Wizard.

Printing from Access

Printing from Access can be similar to printing from any other Microsoft Office Professional application. However, there are some printing commands that are unique to Access for Windows 95.

Previewing Access Forms

Access has a Print Preview button on the toolbar. Forms can be previewed while in form design view, form view, or datasheet view.

Here are the steps for previewing a form from the database window:

1. Click the Forms tab.
2. Select the form to preview.
3. Click View on the toolbar.

How Microsoft Access displays a form in the print preview depends on the view from which it is previewed. Here are some key points:

- When the form is in design view or form view mode, it is displayed in form view.
- When the form is in datasheet view mode, it is displayed as a datasheet.
- You can change the form's default views from the Design View menu. To do this, while in Form Design view, double-click the form selector to open the form's property sheet. The form's selector box is situated at the top-left corner, where the ribbons meet. The Default View property box contains Single View, Continuous Forms, and Datasheet view default options.

Zooming In and Out

There are several ways available to change the magnification of the Preview screen. Here's a list of them:

- From the Print Preview toolbar, click the arrow next to the Zoom Control box; then click or type a magnification percentage.

- From the Preview window choose Fit. Microsoft Access adjusts the magnification of the page to fit the size of the window.

- It is possible to switch between the magnification selected and 100% by clicking the magnifying glass pointer on the table, query, form, or report.

- At the bottom of the Print Preview window are some navigation buttons that can be used to move between pages. The scrollbars can be used to move around the page.

Troubleshooting Access Font Problems

Sometimes the fonts in the printed Access form look different than the screen fonts. This happens when fonts are chosen for a printed font that are not scaleable. To avoid this problem, use scaleable fonts such as TrueType.

By default, the fonts that appear in the Font box on the Formatting toolbar are screen fonts or TrueType fonts. Microsoft Access uses the screen fonts and TrueType fonts that were set up on the computer when Windows was installed.

To force Access for Windows 95 to use the printer's fonts on the toolbar, change the form's LayoutForPrint property to Yes. If the LayoutForPrint property is set to Yes, the fonts and the point sizes displayed in the Font box correspond to the fonts and sizes available on the printer specified by the File | Print command. The fonts the printer uses depend on the kind of printer used. Microsoft Access displays the screen font that is most like the printer font.

NOTE

TrueType fonts look the same onscreen and on paper.

After you have chosen a printer and designed a form, Microsoft Access uses the printer that was selected for that form. When a form is printed on a different printer, the printer might substitute fonts if it doesn't have all the fonts originally used for the form.

If superscripts and subscripts are cut off, the document was probably previously formatted with a font not available on the printer or not installed from Windows.

Creating Printing Commands

Printing in Access can be greatly simplified by creating utilities and buttons. For example, you can create command buttons that print a report, send a report to a file, and send a report to mail. Here are the steps to follow:

1. From the toolbox click on the Command button.

2. Click on the area where you want to place the command button.

3. Click on Report Operations in the Categories box; then select the type of button to create from the Actions box.

4. The rest is easy. Follow the directions in the wizard's dialog boxes to the end. Click on Finish when the desired options are completed.

Printing a Report from a Form

Printing reports can be automated by including the OpenReport and PrintOut actions in a macro or event procedure. For example, a report can be printed by clicking a button on a form, choosing a command from a custom menu, or pressing a key combination. See the Access Help Wizard for more information.

Printing from PowerPoint

Printing a presentation from PowerPoint can consist of printing slides, pictures, and special text. Here's a description of some of PowerPoint's printing features:

- Audience handouts can print a series of one, two, three, or six slides per page. The Tools | Write-Up menu provides further layout variations.

- The Tools | Meeting Minder menu can be very useful during a presentation for taking notes or for recording action items. The minutes and action items can be exported to a Word document.

- PowerPoint can add the minutes to previously created notes pages.

PowerPoint Exporting Capabilities

You can share information between Office applications by copying, moving, pasting, embedding, and storing the information in electronic binders. Power Point slides and notes can easily be exported to Word.

Exporting Slide Show Meeting Minutes to a Word Document

Follow these directions for printing slide show minutes from Word:

1. While in slide view, select the Tools | Meeting Minder menu. During the slide show, click the right mouse button, and then click Meeting Minder.

2. Click the Meeting Minutes tab; then click Export.

3. Select the check box labeled Export Meeting Minutes and Action Items To Word; then click Export Now.

Transferring Meeting Minutes to Notes Pages

Here are the steps to follow for transferring meeting minutes to notes pages:

1. From the Tools menu select Meeting Minder while in slide view.

2. Click the Meeting Minutes tab and then select Export.

3. Select the check box labeled Add Meeting Minutes to Notes Pages; then select Export again.

> **NOTE**
>
> When printing with a PostScript printer, the onscreen resolution of the display image has no effect on the printing quality of the file. This means that it doesn't matter what image format is embedded in the EPS file.
>
> With a non-PostScript printer, the printer uses the embedded file instead of the EPS image. These images are normally low resolution, so the resolution of the printed image is relatively low.
>
> If a presentation contains an EPS file without an embedded TIFF or WMF display image, or if the image is considered invalid by the converter, only the bounding box is printed on a non-PostScript printer.

Creating an Outline for Printing

While in outline view, outlines can be printed as they appear onscreen. Here are some printing variations:

- To print only the slide titles from the outlines, click the Show Titles button.

- To print all levels of text in your outline, click the Show All button.

- To print outlines with or without formatting, click the Formatting button and then choose to show or hide formatting, respectively.

- To increase or decrease the type size of outlines, click the Percent window and change the view scale.

- To show headers and footers on printed outlines, select Master | Handout Master from the View menu.

- To choose options for slides and notes and handouts, select Header And Footer from the View menu.

Setting Up the Slide Size and Orientation Prior to Printing

Here are the steps to follow in order to set up the slide size and orientation prior to printing:

1. From the File menu select Slide Setup.
2. In the Slides Sized For box select the options you need.
3. Under Slides, select either Portrait or Landscape.
4. Under Notes, Handouts, and Outline, select either Portrait or Landscape.
5. If the starting number for the slides is not 1, type the starting number in the Number Slides From box.

Here are some additional points to keep in mind:

- The slides in the presentation can have one orientation only.
- Notes, handouts, and outlines can still be printed in portrait orientation even when landscape orientation has been selected for the slides.
- To insert page numbers on a slide, select the Header And Footer command from the View menu.

Troubleshooting PowerPoint Output

Here are some points to keep in mind when troubleshooting PowerPoint output:

- If the slides are not centered on the printed page or are not the right size on the printed page, you should check the settings in the Slide Setup dialog box. From the File menu select Slide Setup; then select the correct option in the Slides Sized For box. Also check the measurements in the Width and Height boxes.
- If the display of fonts on the printed slides, notes, or handouts look different than those onscreen, the printer is probably substituting fonts. From the Format | Fonts menu change the fonts used in the presentation to TrueType fonts or use a printer font that has matching screen fonts.
- If the fonts are different when the presentation is viewed on another computer, the screen fonts are probably substitutions because the fonts used in the presentation are not installed on the computer. Switch to TrueType fonts to avoid this problem. To ensure TrueType fonts are used, save the presentation from the Save As box, and then check the Embed TrueType Fonts check box. Make sure that the TrueType fonts used in the presentation have been installed in Windows.

Printing from Schedule+

Printing from Schedule+ is very versatile. Schedule+ is compatible with 1500 different views for print schedules, contacts, to do lists, and calendar views; therefore, the application's printing needs are well covered. Here are a couple of examples of Schedule+'s printing capabilities:

- Weekly and daily views can be printed in two sizes: the Standard and Junior.
- A monthly view can be printed in a trifold graphical view that contains the daily, yearly, and to do list views.

Printing Schedules

Here is how to print schedules in Schedule+:

1. Select the File | Print menu or click the toolbar's Print button.
2. Select desired options from the Print Layout, Paper Format, Print Quality, Font Size, and Private items menus.
3. In the Schedule Range box select the date range to be printed. This is done by first selecting the starting date and then selecting the number of days, weeks, or months to print from that date.
4. Other options that can be selected are Include Blank Pages, No Shading Print to File, and Print Preview.
5. To customize margins, paper orientation, or the printer, click Setup.
6. Choose the OK button to print the selection.

> **NOTE**
>
> The date range for the to do list can only be used if no view of the to do list is currently displayed.

Schedule+ offers such a variety of layout choices and paper formats so that you can print only specific information, and in the most convenient format possible. (Tentative appointments are printed in italic fonts.)

General Troubleshooting for Printer Problems

Nothing can be more frustrating than having difficulties printing a final draft. Even the most seasoned computer user is not immune to this situation. It is possible to troubleshoot every possible clue, only to leave out the most obvious solution—checking the printer connection to the electrical source.

Steps to Printer Troubleshooting

Use the Windows Print Troubleshooter to find out if the problem originates from Windows or from Microsoft Office 95. Here are the steps:

1. From Windows | Help | Index tab, enter `print troubleshooting`.
2. Click Display and then follow the instructions in the Windows Print Troubleshooter.
3. If the Windows printer setup is correct, check the Office application's printer settings from File | Print | Options.
4. If the output is different than expected, check Page Setup from the File menu.

NOTE

Check that the selected printer matches the printer used. Select File | Print | Name box and then click the name of the printer used.

Check that the page range selected in the Print dialog box corresponds to the pages to be printed.

TIP

When troubleshooting a printing problem, try printing from Windows 95. If you are unable to print from there, try printing from DOS. If you are still unable to print, check the hardware connections and refer to the printer's manual.

Printer Options

The Printer Options menu offers flexibility of choices. For instance, to change to draft output mode, select File | Print | Print Options and then select Draft Output Mode.

To make printing changes to field codes, summaries, annotations, hidden text, and drawing objects, check the Printing | Options menu.

Print Preview

Print Preview displays a document as it will look after printing. From Print Preview it is possible to view one or more pages at a time, to make changes to the document (increasing or reducing the page size, for example), and to check and change text formatting.

FIGURE 46.10.

Select File | Print Preview, and each page of the document is displayed as it will look after printing.

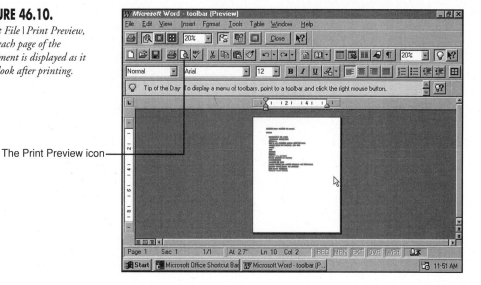

The Print Preview icon

Print Preview Views

To print from the Print Preview screen while viewing one or multiple pages, select Print from the File | Print menu, or you can press the Print Preview icon.

Editing Text from Print Preview

From the previewed page, select the beginning of the text to be edited, click the magnifier button, and then edit the text.

Adjusting Margins in Print Preview

Margins can be easily adjusted at any stage from the Print Preview menu:

1. From the Print Preview menu, display the rulers. If the rulers are not displayed, click the view ruler.

2. To move the left or right page edges, point to the edge to be shifted in the horizontal ruler and then drag the page edge as needed.

3. To move the top or bottom page margin, point to the edge to be shifted on the vertical ruler and then drag the margin edge as needed.

NOTE

Fields and linked information can also be changed from the preview window. See the application's Help Wizard for more information.

FIGURE 46.11.

The edge of a page can be shifted in the Print Preview screen.

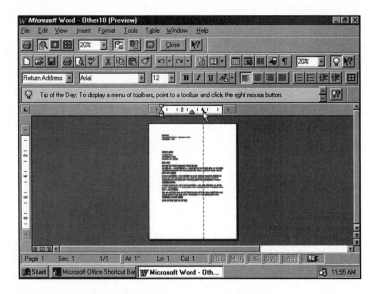

Eliminating an Almost Empty Page

Sometimes it is desirable to reduce the number of pages in a document. For instance, a document might have a page with just a line or two of text on it. From the Print Preview window, it is possible to fit the contents of the almost empty page into the rest of the document. To do this, click the Shrink To Fit Button from the Print Preview window. All the pages will be adjusted to contain more text, and the almost empty page will be removed.

Printing Multiple Documents

Microsoft Office 95 offers some common, primary printing dialog boxes for the applications in the suite; yet, each application offers some unique printing capabilities. For instance, Schedule+ offers 1000 printing options; Access printing options are often customized with macros; Excel adds some specific options to print and preview worksheets; and some of Word's basic printing options are also applicable to the other applications in the suite. Similarly, while PowerPoint offers some common printing options, options for manipulating and printing slides, graphics, and similar presentation features are also offered.

Summary

Microsoft Office 95 integrates printing between the suite applications. Each of the suite applications functions in a unified manner; yet, each application has its own ingenious way for viewing, formatting, and printing the application's output. In this chapter the dynamics of formatting, printing, and troubleshooting printing problems are discussed.

Mailing, Routing, and Faxing

by Tom Hayes

47

IN THIS CHAPTER

You'll often need to distribute your documents to co-workers, clients, and customers. When this need arises, you'll want to accomplish your task in the most efficient way possible. This chapter looks at the various ways you can distribute your documents electronically through both e-mail and fax.

First, we'll take a look at WordMail. By installing WordMail as your preferred e-mail editor, sending e-mail messages is a snap. Next, we'll explore the reasons you might want to route a document and what it takes to do so. Suppose that you've just finished the new budget proposal for next year and you want to let the other members of your project team review it. By routing your proposal, you can have others review an electronic version of your document, make revisions and comments, and automatically get it back when they're finished. The last section examines the procedures necessary to fax documents directly from your desktop. No more standing in line at the fax machine!

Using Word as an Electronic Mail Editor

With WordMail, you can use special toolbar buttons and commands to send, read, forward, and reply to electronic mail messages using Microsoft Word. You can also use Word's reviewing options (such as notes, annotations and revisions, highlighter, and so on) that make it easier for you to read comments from individuals when sending and receiving electronic mail messages.

Installing WordMail

To use Word as an electronic mail editor, you must have Microsoft Exchange, and you must have selected the option Use Word as an electronic mail editor when you installed Word. If you did not check this option when you installed Word, follow the next few steps to do so:

1. Run the Microsoft Office Setup program or the Word Setup program.
2. If you've previously installed Microsoft Office, click the Add/Remove button.
3. Select the Microsoft Word check box, and then click Change Option. (If you've previously installed Word, click Custom.)
4. In the Options box, select the WordMail check box.
5. Select OK.

> **NOTE**
>
> Once you have installed WordMail, you can switch back to the Microsoft Exchange mail editor if you wish. Simply run Microsoft Exchange and select the Compose|WordMail Options command to display the WordMail Options dialog box, shown in Figure 47.1. Clear the Enable Word as E-mail Editor check box.

FIGURE 47.1.

You can easily switch between WordMail and the Microsoft Exchange e-mail editor using the WordMail Options dialog box.

Sending a WordMail Message

Once you have WordMail installed as your preferred e-mail editor, you can send an e-mail message using WordMail exactly the same way you would using Microsoft Exchange. Simply select the File | Send command from any Microsoft Office application or the Compose | New Message command from Microsoft Exchange. Figure 47.2 shows the WordMail compose window.

FIGURE 47.2.

The WordMail compose window.

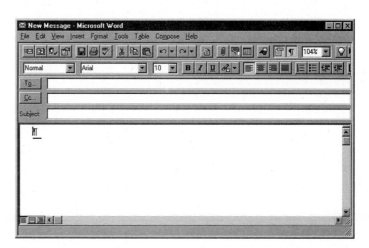

The WordMail compose window has all the features and functionality of the Microsoft Exchange editor coupled with the familiarity of Microsoft Word toolbars and commands. As you'll see later in this section, you can even attach a template to the WordMail editor so that your favorite styles and formatting features are handy.

The WordMail Properties Dialog Box

The WordMail Properties dialog box sets properties for electronic mail messages. By setting various options in this dialog box, you can control how your messages are sent, receive return receipts when messages are delivered and read, and even notify recipients of messages that are highly sensitive or confidential. Select the File | Properties command from the WordMail compose window to display the Properties dialog box and set the various options for your WordMail messages. (See Figure 47.3.)

FIGURE 47.3.

The Properties dialog box, used to set options for sending a WordMail message.

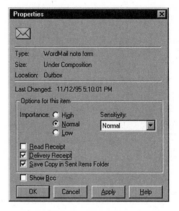

These are the options in the Properties dialog box:

- Type—Displays the type of message.
- Size—Displays the size of the message.
- Location—Displays the name of the folder in which the message is stored.
- Last Changed—Displays the date and time the message was most recently modified.
- Importance: High—Indicates a high level of importance for a message. The message will display a red exclamation point (!) in the Importance column of the recipient's inbox.
- Importance: Normal—Indicates a normal level of importance for a message.
- Importance: Low—Indicates a low level of importance for a message. The message will display a down arrow in the Importance column of the recipient's inbox.
- Sensitivity—Select a level of sensitivity from this list box. The security level and type of message will appear in the Sensitivity column of the recipient's inbox.
- Read Receipt—Activate this check box to be notified when the recipient opens the message you sent.
- Delivery Receipt—Activate this check box to be notified when the message you sent has been delivered.

■ Save Copy In Sent Items Folder—To save a copy of each message you send, activate this check box.

■ Show Bcc—When you address a message to multiple recipients, all the names appear in the From box when other recipients receive the message. Activate this check box to address a message that doesn't display all the recipients' names in the From box.

■ Apply—Select this button to apply the selected options to the message without closing the Properties dialog box.

NOTE

For additional information on how to send electronic messages, see Chapter 51, "Advanced Microsoft Exchange."

Changing How WordMail Messages Look

WordMail comes with some generic templates for writing e-mail messages. If you find yourself constantly reformatting your e-mail messages to have a greater impact, you might want to change the default template that WordMail uses. You can do this by using one of the following three methods:

■ Set the template to use one of the various templates shipped with Word.

■ Create a new template and set it as the default. For more information on how to create a Word template, see Chapter 10, "Document Patterns and Presentations."

■ Edit one of the existing templates.

WordMail Templates

The following steps show you how to change the templates used with WordMail:

1. In Microsoft Exchange, select the Compose | WordMail command to display the WordMail Options dialog box, shown in Figure 47.1.

2. In the Template box, select the template you want to use. If you want to make formatting changes to the selected template, select Edit.

3. If you want to add a template to the Template box, click the Add button. Exchange displays the Add dialog box, shown in Figure 47.4.

4. Select the Word template you want to use.

5. Select Add to return to the WordMail Options dialog box.

6. Select Close to save your changes.

FIGURE 47.4.

The Add dialog box, used to locate an e-mail template.

NOTE

If you want to use your new template as the default template, make sure you select the Set as Default Template check box in the WordMail dialog box.

Creating an Automatic Signature

Not only can you customize the templates in WordMail, but you can also create an automatic "signature" that can be appended to your electronic message. This signature can include formatted text, graphic images such as a company logo, and even a scanned image of your handwritten signature. WordMail makes adding an automatic signature a snap, as you'll see in the following procedure:

1. Open the WordMail compose window.

2. Enter and format the text as you want it to appear on your e-mail messages. If you plan on having an image included in your signature, import that graphic using the Insert | Picture command.

3. Select the text, including any graphics.

4. Select the Edit | AutoText command. Word displays the AutoText dialog box, shown in Figure 47.5.

5. Type signature in the Name edit box.

6. In the Make Auto Text Entry Available To edit box, select Documents Based on E-mail. Your signature will appear in the Selection box.

7. Select Add. You now have an automatic signature that will be appended to your e-mail messages.

FIGURE 47.5.

Use the AutoText dialog box to create an automatic signature for your e-mail messages.

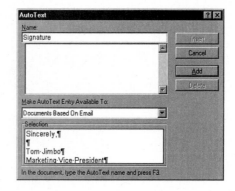

Routing Documents

You can use Office applications (that is, Excel, Word, PowerPoint, and Access) with Microsoft Exchange, or other compatible mail packages, to send an online copy of a document. The recipients can then comment on, revise, or add to the document, and it will be routed back to you via electronic mail. You may want to route a document if you have a longer review period or short list of reviewers. Figure 47.6 shows a graphical representation of how a document is routed. Some other advantages you receive by routing a document include the following:

- You automatically receive a routing status message as each recipient forwards your document.

- You ensure that each recipient is reminded to forward the document on to the next recipient.

FIGURE 47.6.

You can route a document to others and automatically receive it back when they are finished reviewing it.

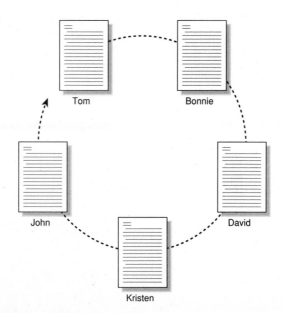

> **NOTE**
>
> Document routing might not work across electronic mail gateways. To use document routing, you need a mail system compatible with the messaging application programming interface (MAPI) or compatible with vendor independent messaging (VIM). Microsoft Exchange is a MAPI-compatible mail system and Lotus cc:Mail is an example of a VIM-compatible mail system.

Preparing Documents for Review

Before you route your Word document you may want to prepare it for review. This makes it easier to track the changes that recipients make in a document. Revision marks show where text or graphics have been added, deleted, or moved. You can also protect the document from permanent changes.

Preparing a document for review is easy, as the following procedure illustrates:

1. Open the document you want to prepare for review.
2. Select the Tools|Protect Document command.
3. If you want to let reviewers change a document and track their changes with revision marks, select the Revisions button. If you don't want reviewers to change the contents of the document but still let them insert annotations, select the Annotations button. If you want others to add only revisions and annotations without changing the contents, enter a password.

> **NOTE**
>
> If you don't protect your document with a password, anyone can unprotect the document and make undocumented revisions without your knowledge by selecting the Tools|Unprotect Document command. For more information, see Chapter 9, "Document Concepts."

4. Select OK to protect your document.

The Routing Slip

When you route a document, you specify a series of recipients on a *routing slip*. Microsoft Exchange sends the document to the first person on the routing slip. When that person is done with the document, he or she sends it, and the routing slip automatically addresses it to the next routing slip recipient. The document eventually finds its way back after each person has reviewed the document. Although you can also route other Microsoft Office documents, the following procedure shows you how to route a Microsoft Word document:

1. Open the file you want to route.

2. Select the File | Add Routing Slip command.

3. You might be asked which Exchange profile you want to use. If so, choose the profile and then select OK. The Routing Slip dialog box appears, as shown in Figure 47.7.

FIGURE 47.7.

Use the Routing Slip dialog box to select recipients and route a document.

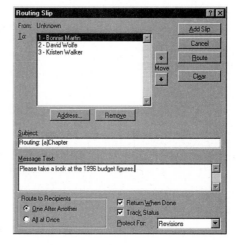

4. Select the Address button to display the Address Book.

5. In the order in which you want the workbook routed, select a recipient and then select To−>. When you're done selecting recipients, select OK to return to the Routing Slip dialog box.

> **TIP**
>
> If you want to change the order in which recipients will receive your document, highlight a recipient's name in the To box and use one of the Move arrows to change the routing order by moving the name up or down in the list.

6. Adjust the Subject text, if necessary, and enter an explanatory message in the Message Text area.

7. If you want the document returned to you after the last recipient has worked with it, keep the Return When Done check box active. If you would like to receive a message each time a recipient routes the document to the next person, leave the Track Status check box active.

8. When you're ready, select the Route button. If you want to attach a routing slip and route a document at a later time, select the Add Slip button.

> **NOTE**
>
> If you have group aliases set up in your Personal Address Book, you can select a group alias as the recipient. However, all members of the group alias are considered one recipient. To route the document to members of a group alias one after another, send it to the individual members, and not to the entire alias.

Sending a Document

Once a routing slip is attached, follow these steps to route it:

1. Select the File | Send command to display the Send dialog box, shown in Figure 47.8.

FIGURE 47.8.

The Send dialog box, used to send a routed document.

2. If you want to route the document, select the Route Document To option. If you want to send the document to an e-mail address without routing it, select the Send Copy of Document Without Using the Routing Slip option.

3. Select OK.

Opening a Routed Document

If you've just received a routed document, it will appear as an attachment to an electronic mail message. To open a routed document, follow the instructions of your electronic mail program. If you're using Microsoft Exchange, double-click the document icon to open the document attached to a mail message.

Editing a Routing Slip

If you've added a routing slip or received a routed document, the File | Add Routing Slip command changes to File | Edit Routing Slip. There will be occasions when you need to edit the routing slip. For example, one of the recipients on the list might be on vacation next week. Rather than have the document sitting in that person's mailbox until he or she gets back, you can move that person to the end of the list or delete the name from the list of recipients. The following procedure shows you how to edit a routing slip:

1. Select the File | Edit Routing Slip command to display the Routing Slip dialog box, shown earlier in Figure 47.7.

2. If you want to delete a name from the list of recipients, highlight the name in the To box and select the Remove button. To change the routing order, highlight a name in the To box and use the Move arrows to move it up or down the list. To delete the routing slip, select the Clear button.

3. Select Route if you want to send the document, or select Add Slip to save your changes and send the document at a later time.

Faxing Documents

Being able to send faxes directly from your desktop makes it easier than ever to transmit documents to others. There are two basic methods for sending a fax from your desktop directly from an application:

- Use the Send command.
- Use the Print command.

> **NOTE**
>
> Faxing documents is easier if you use the Microsoft Exchange e-mail editor rather than WordMail. To set this preference, simply run Microsoft Exchange and select the Compose|WordMail Options command to display the WordMail Options dialog box; then clear the Enable Word as E-mail Editor check box.

> **CAUTION**
>
> Faxing documents from your desktop can sometimes be a frustrating process. Performance can be hampered by the size and type of graphics in your document, the length of the document, the amount of free disk space, and the available memory. The more complex the file (that is, a long document with a lot of embedded graphics), the longer it will take the Microsoft Fax driver to render or convert the document to an acceptable fax format. Patience and a little trial and error are the keys. If you're having problems, try reducing the file size by eliminating some of the graphics.

Using the Send Command

This method is supported by most of the Microsoft products and by other page layout and drawing programs that are integrated with the Microsoft Office products. To see if you can use this method, open the document you want to fax and select the File menu to see if it contains a Send command. If it does not, skip this procedure and see the section titled "Using the Print Command."

The following procedure shows you how to fax a document using the Send command:

1. Open the document you want to send.

2. Select the File | Send command to see the Microsoft Exchange compose window.

3. Select the Tools | Fax Addressing Wizard command. Exchange displays the Fax Addressing Wizard, shown in Figure 47.9.

FIGURE 47.9.

The Fax Addressing Wizard dialog box.

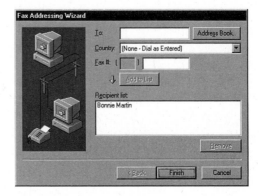

4. Select the Address Book button if the recipient is in your Personal Address Book. If not, enter the recipient's name in the To box and a fax number in the Fax # box, and then select the Add to List button. When you are done, select Finish.

5. Type the subject and any message text.

6. Select File | Send to transmit your fax.

Using the Print Command

If you don't have a Send command on the File menu, you can still fax a document from within an application. Following the next few steps makes it a snap:

1. Open the document you want to send.

2. Select the File | Print command. The Print dialog box is displayed.

3. In the Name box, select Microsoft Fax.

4. Print the document. The Fax Addressing Wizard dialog box is displayed. Fill in the necessary information; when you're done, select Finish.

TIP

You can use the Print command to fax electronic messages. Simply open your e-mail message and select the File | Print command from the Microsoft Exchange editor window. Then select Microsoft Fax as your printer.

Sending Form Letters from Word to Fax Numbers and E-mail Addresses

There may be occasions when you need to distribute a document to a large list of fax numbers or e-mail addresses. This is sometimes referred to as *broadcasting*. For example, you may want to transmit a time-critical press release to a number of local media sources, send a proposal out for bid to a list of suppliers, or send price-sensitive product information to your customers. One way to accomplish this is to send the same document to all the people on your fax or e-mail address list. An even better way is to harness the power of Word's Mail Merge feature and personalize each document with information specific to the recipient.

Before you can broadcast a document, you need to successfully create a main document and link this to a data source. For more information on how to set up a mail merge document, see Chapter 14, "Word as a Publisher." To illustrate the process of broadcasting a document, a merge document, called Price List, was created as the main document (see Figure 47.10) with the Personal Address Book as the data source.

> **TIP**
>
> To add enclosures to the main document, insert one or more INCLUDETEXT fields. When you merge the main document with the data source, Word inserts the contents of the documents specified by the INCLUDETEXT fields.

FIGURE 47.10.

A Word main document ready to be merged with a data source.

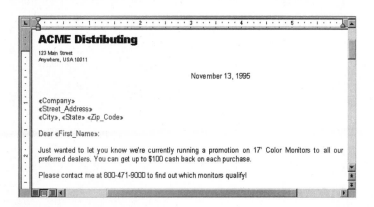

The following procedure shows you the necessary steps for merging a document to a list of fax numbers or e-mail addresses:

1. With the main document in the active window, select the Tools | Mail Merge command to display the Mail Merge Helper dialog box, shown in Figure 47.11.

FIGURE 47.11.

The Mail Merge Helper dialog box.

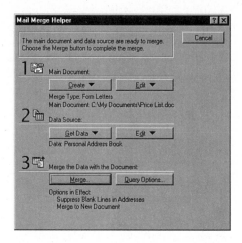

2. To avoid processing records that do not contain a fax number or e-mail address, select the Query Options button. Word displays the Query Options dialog box, shown in Figure 47.12.

FIGURE 47.12.

The Query Options dialog box, used to filter data records that do not contain a fax number or e-mail address.

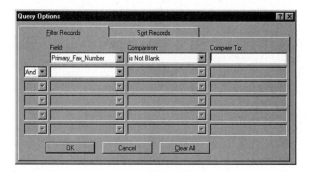

3. Select the Filter Records tab. In the Field box, select the data field that contains the fax number or e-mail address. In the example using the Personal Address Book as the data source, the field named Primary_Fax_Number contains the fax number. In the Comparison box, select Is Not Blank to filter out records that do not have a fax number or e-mail address.

4. Select OK to return to the Mail Merge Helper dialog box.

5. In the Mail Merge Helper dialog box, select Merge to display the Merge dialog box, shown in Figure 47.13.

6. In the Merge To box, select Electronic Mail if you are using Microsoft Exchange as your mail system. If you're using another mail system, select the electronic message system you want to use.

FIGURE 47.13.

The Merge dialog box, used to select an electronic message system.

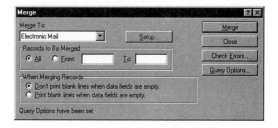

7. Select Setup to display the Merge To Setup dialog box, shown in Figure 47.14. In the box labeled Data Field with Mail/Fax Address, select the data field that contains the fax number or e-mail address. Again, the Primary_Fax_Number field is selected for this example. Select OK to return to the Merge dialog box.

> **CAUTION**
>
> To preserve the formatting of a merged document transmitted by fax or electronic mail, activate the check box labeled Send Document as an Attachment. Otherwise, Word inserts the document text in the mail message and does not retain the document formatting.

8. In the Merge dialog box, select Merge.

FIGURE 47.14.

The Merge To Setup dialog.

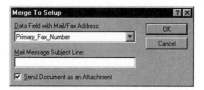

> **TIP**
>
> If the merge document will contain the recipient's name and company name, you can save money on long distance faxes by not including a cover sheet. Simply start Microsoft Exchange and select the Options menu from the Tools | Microsoft Fax Tools command to display the Microsoft Fax Properties dialog box. Select the Message tab and deactivate the check box labeled Send Cover Page.

Summary

This chapter shows you various techniques for distributing your documents electronically. You have learned how to install and use WordMail as well as how to route a document and send faxes from your desktop. Here are some related chapters to investigate:

- See Chapter 9 for tips on formatting your WordMail messages.
- To learn more about setting up a mail merge document, see Chapter 14.
- For more information about Microsoft Exchange, see Chapter 50, "Understanding and Customizing Microsoft Exchange," and Chapter 51.

IN THIS PART

The Networked Office

Office on a Network

48

by Jeff Steinmetz

By now you have seen the flexibility Microsoft Office provides to an individual. This chapter, and the remaining chapters of this section, discuss several network-related features of Microsoft Office. Many of the topics discussed in this section are intended for network administrators, although the information is presented so that it can be useful for everyone. This section touches only briefly on networking and LAN architecture as it applies to Microsoft Office. For more information, refer to the Windows 95 and Windows NT documentation.

Comparing a Peer-to-Peer Network to a Client/Server Network

Before discussing specific networking functionality within Microsoft Office, this chapter compares two methods to physically build a network. Windows 95 provides enough functionality "out of the box" to start a sophisticated peer-to-peer network system. All one needs to implement a small network within an office is a Windows 95–compatible network card and cabling. Figure 48.1 shows a typical peer-to-peer network configuration. Although this configuration works well for a small office (or even the home office), other issues should be considered before implementing a full-scale LAN (*local area network*).

> **NOTE**
>
> The network functionality referred to in Windows 95 also can be applied to Windows NT 3.51 Workstation.

FIGURE 48.1.

A typical peer-to-peer network.

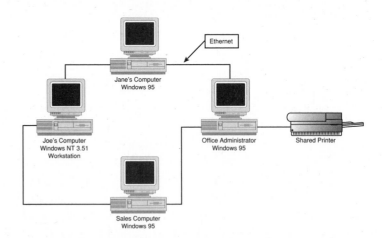

With your workstation configured for network support, you can share your folders (directories), share your printer, access other users' folders, send mail, and use Schedule+ in group-enabled mode. This same functionality is available when your LAN uses a client/server architecture.

Figure 48.2 shows a typical client/server network architecture. In this architecture, the servers handle all the network traffic for file access, mail access, and resource sharing, such as printers and CD-ROM drives. In addition, the servers provide centralized administration of security and resources.

FIGURE 48.2.

Typical client/server network architecture.

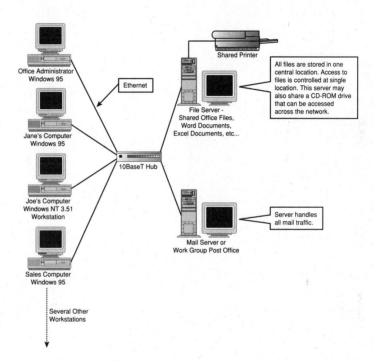

Windows NT Server provides support that complements Windows 95 and Microsoft Office, and thus is provided as a reference for the sake of comparison. Table 48.1 shows a comparison of these two network architectures, and may be used as a guideline to determine which configuration is right for your situation.

Table 48.1. Network architecture comparison.

Functionality	Peer-to-Peer	Client/Server - Windows NT Server
Set up	Very easy.	Requires some networking knowledge
Reliability	Moderate—If a user's workstation	High—Provides central location for resources.

continues

Table 48.1. continued

Functionality	Peer-to-Peer	Client/Server - Windows NT Server
	goes down, those resources will be unavailable for others.	Can be configured to perform automatic backups. Because the server is not being used as a workstation, it can provide 100 percent of its resources. Supports disk mirroring, disk striping with parity, and uninterruptible power supplies.
Security	Moderate—Sharing resources on a workstation is based on a single password. No central way to configure security.	High—Provides a single network logon that grants access to network resources, including client/server applications (such as SQL Server). This logon uses one user account and one password per user for authentication. The Windows NT file system (NTFS) provides file-level security.
Administration	Becomes more difficult as user base grows.	Provides centralized management of user accounts. A single computer can administer computers across divisions, departments, and workgroups.
Cost	Low.	Moderate to High—Because several users will be accessing the server, higher-performance hardware is suggested. Client licenses are required to access server.
Required hardware/software	Windows 95, one network card per workstation, cabling (10Base2 or 10BaseT is most common, lowest cost).	Same requirements as peer-to-peer, plus Windows NT Server (3.51 suggested), client licenses, Windows NT–compatible

Functionality	Peer-to-Peer	Client/Server - Windows NT Server
		network card. You may wish to use a 10BaseT Ethernet hub for easier network maintenance. 10BaseT is preferred over daisy-chaining 10Base2 shielded cable. 10BaseT (twisted-pair) cabling is required for each client when a HUB is used. In addition, you may wish to add Microsoft Mail Server or other Back Office products.
Extensibility/ scalability	Size should be limited to a small office. Network capabilities are limited to the operating system's functionality on each client. It can be scaled up to a client/server architecture without significant changes required on the clients.	Handles large networks. Can be scaled to a WAN (wide area network— several dispersed sites around the country or world). Support for symmetric multiprocessing systems allows your hardware to grow as your network demands grow.

Whether you implement one of the previous network architectures or use one that is already in place, you can begin to leverage the networking capabilities in Microsoft Office. The following list shows ways you can begin to use Microsoft Office on a network:

■ Provide a central location that enables clients to install Microsoft Office over the network

■ Share folders

■ Send documents via e-mail

■ Route documents via e-mail

■ Work with Schedule+ in Group-Enabled Mode

■ Provide multiuser databases

- Run network presentations with PowerPoint using the presentation conferencing feature
- Share Excel workbooks with co-workers using the shared list feature

The Mail-Enabled Network

You should consider setting up Mail on your network before proceeding with an installation of Microsoft Office at your site. By setting up Mail first, you give Microsoft Office setup the capability to query the users for specific installation options related to mail. In addition, you can use mail as a vehicle to initiate the Microsoft Office installation process (see "Installing Microsoft Office over the Network" later in this chapter). To run Schedule+ in group-enabled mode, MAPI 1.0 must be available on the client machine. In addition, the user needs a valid account on one of three mail services:

- Windows 95 workgroup postoffice
- Microsoft Mail 3.*x* server
- Microsoft Exchange server

The Windows 95 workgroup postoffice is used for examples in this chapter because Microsoft Mail Server and Exchange Server are beyond the scope of this book. The workgroup postoffice will work well for these examples because you can configure it without any additional software. Furthermore, if you don't have access to a LAN at the time you read this book, you can configure the workgroup postoffice to work from your local hard drive, and you can still follow along as mail examples are provided.

Before creating the postoffice, determine where you want to place the shared directory. This directory may grow very large, so consider this before proceeding. The location should have read/write permissions for all users who will be using mail. To set up a workgroup postoffice under Windows 95, follow these steps:

1. Open the Control Panel and select the Microsoft Mail Postoffice icon.
2. Select Create a new Workgroup Postoffice, as shown in Figure 48.3, and then click Next >.
3. In the resulting dialog box, enter the Postoffice Location in which the shared directory will reside. This can be a directory, or a network path, as shown in Figure 48.4. \\SERVER1\PUBLIC is used for this example.
4. Click Next >. You will be prompted to confirm that you want a new directory created at the location specified in Step 3 (for example, \\SERVER1\PUBLIC\wgpo0000).
5. Now you create a mail account that will be used to administer the postoffice. This account is used to create and remove users from the Workgroup Postoffice (see Step 6 for creating additional accounts). Figure 48.5 shows a sample entry for the user

account. The password should be unique to prevent others from administering the postoffice. You can use the full name of the user in the Name field. The Mailbox field is restricted to 10 characters and cannot contain spaces.

FIGURE 48.3.

Creating a new workgroup postoffice.

Click here to open the
Microsoft Workgroup
Postoffice Administration
dialog box

FIGURE 48.4.

Selecting a location for the new workgroup postoffice.

FIGURE 48.5.

Creating the administrator account on the new workgroup postoffice.

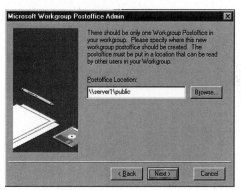

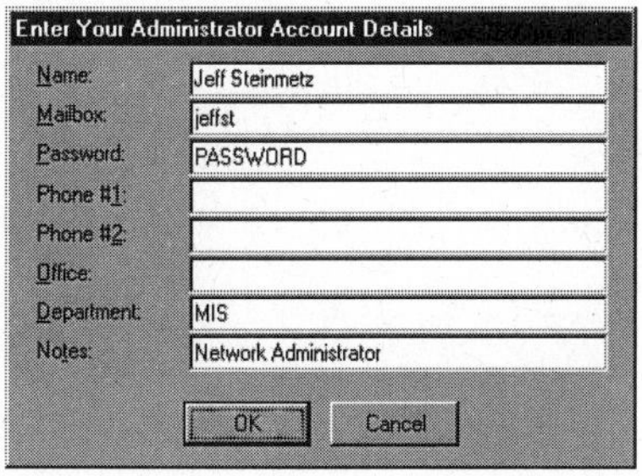

6. After you create the workgroup postoffice, you need to create accounts for everyone that will use mail. Open the Control Panel and double-click the Microsoft Mail Postoffice icon.

7. Select Administer an existing Workgroup Postoffice and click Next >.

8. You will be prompted for your administrator mailbox name and password. This is the same name and password that you created in Step 5. Select Next >.

9. The resulting dialog box, shown in Figure 48.6, enables you to modify, add, and delete users from the postoffice. In this case, select Add User.

10. Figure 48.7 shows the addition of a fictitious user, Jan Smith. You will want to leave the password as PASSWORD. Instruct the users that their temporary password is PASSWORD, and that they will need to change their password to something unique when they begin to use the account.

11. Repeat Steps 9 and 10 for each user who will access mail.

FIGURE 48.6.

Administering users on the workgroup postoffice.

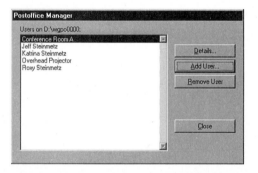

FIGURE 48.7.

Adding a new user to the workgroup postoffice.

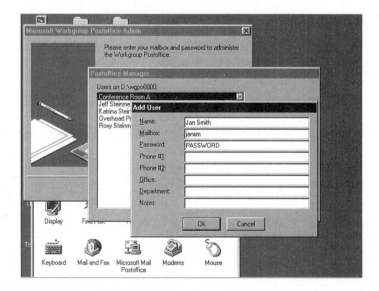

TIP

You might want to implement a standard way of supplying a mailbox name. One guideline I have used is the full first name (or at least eight characters of it), and the first two letters of the last name. You also should be aware that passwords are case sensitive: PASSWORD is different from password.

At this point, you have created a workgroup postoffice that is accessible over the network, and you have created a user account for everyone. In order to use the workgroup postoffice, you need to perform the following steps at every user's workstation:

1. Open the Control Panel and double-click the Mail and Fax icon. The MS Exchange Settings Properties dialog box appears. (See Figure 48.8.)

FIGURE 48.8.

The Microsoft Exchange Settings Properties dialog box.

Select this icon to open the Microsoft Exchange Setting Properties dialog box

2. Select Add. The Add Service To Profile dialog box appears. (See Figure 48.9.)

FIGURE 48.9.

Adding Microsoft Mail as a service on Microsoft Exchange.

3. Double-click Microsoft Mail. The property sheets that define how Microsoft Mail will function appear. When prompted to enter the path to your postoffice, enter the workgroup postoffice location you created earlier. For this example, type \\SERVER1\PUBLIC\wgpo0000.

4. Click the Logon tab. Be sure that the mailbox name is correct for the user.

5. Select OK. The user's workstation is now configured for mail!

Installing Microsoft Office over the Network

The administrative setup option provides an efficient method of rolling out Microsoft Office to your workforce. This option is a welcome alternative to administering each client's workstation individually.

> **NOTE**
>
> You still are required to have a sufficient number of licensed Microsoft Office users in order to allow everybody to perform the installation from the server.

Before starting, you must determine a directory location that will be shared across the network. When you complete this setup, this directory should be accessible by all clients requiring Microsoft Office. This example assumes that the server on which the directory will be located is called SERVER1 and a new directory called PUBLIC has been created. By creating the PUBLIC directory, you can place all required subdirectories in this location, and thus you will require only a single share. After you determine where the setup files will reside, start the Microsoft Office setup program by running the following command from the Windows NT command prompt, or from File | Run under the Program Manager:

```
x:setup /a
```

Replace *x* with the name of your CD-ROM or floppy drive that contains the Microsoft Office setup disk. The /a instructs setup that you are not installing Microsoft Office on a workstation, but are requesting that all files necessary for subsequent installations be extracted to the network drive. In addition, you will be able to determine how Microsoft Office will be set up on the client's workstation.

After you select the location, you are prompted by the Network Server Confirmation dialog box. (See Figure 48.10.) In this dialog box, you should see the server name and the location to which the shared applications will be extracted. The shared applications that will be installed to \MSAPPS are those, such as Word Art and Art Gallery. The directory \MSOffice will contain the main office components, such as Word and Excel. In the example, the final directory structure will look like the following:

```
\\SERVER1
    \PUBLIC
        \MSOffice
            \MSAPPS
```

FIGURE 48.10.

The Network Server Confirmation dialog box.

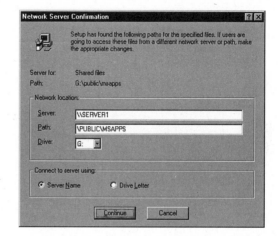

Unless you plan to have *every* client connected to \\SERVER1\PUBLIC with the same drive letter (drive G: in this example), you should use the Server Name option in the Connect to server using area. By using a *UNC* (Universal Naming Convention), you can be assured that all clients will find the directory, without the need for mapping a specific drive. Remember that you are trying to make a central installation point that makes the administrator's life easy. Select continue to advance to the next step.

The Microsoft Office 95 Setup dialog box, shown in Figure 48.11, enables you to customize the client installation even further. If you want to conserve disk space on the client's workstation, you can force shared applications to be used from the server, thus eliminating installation on the client side. The downside to this is that the network connection must always be available for this to work. If you feel that disk space is not a problem, you can select the Local Hard Drive option as the location for shared files. These first two options eliminate the user from the setup process. The final option, User's Choice, prompts users for their preference during setup.

When administrative setup is complete, provide read-only access to the installation directory (\PUBLIC in this example) and instruct the users that they may connect to that directory and install Microsoft Office. If you are familiar with logon scripts, you might even want to create a method that automatically installs Microsoft Office during a predefined upgrade period. In this example, you can run setup from a script or directly from the client as follows:

```
\\SERVER1\PUBLIC\MSOffices\setup.exe
```

FIGURE 48.11.

Select the location of shared files.

In Windows 95 you could use the Exchange client to e-mail a shortcut to this executable. Right-click on the Windows 95 desktop, and select New | Shortcut. Based on this example, when prompted for the command line, enter the following:

`\\SERVER1\PUBLIC\MSOffice\setup.exe`

Open Exchange and create a new mail message addressed to all who want to install Microsoft Office. Drag this icon from the desktop onto the mail message. After you send this message, users simply double-click the icon to start the setup process.

Under Windows NT, you can use the Object Packager to send the link. While composing your message with Microsoft Mail, select Insert | Object, and then select Package. While in the Object Packager, click Edit | Command Line and enter the full path to the setup executable. In this case, you can enter the UNC

`\\SERVER1\PUBLIC\MSOffice\setup.exe.`

To create an icon, select the Insert Icon button. Use Browse to select setup.exe on the network directory in which Microsoft Office was installed. Select Edit | Label and label the package as `MS Office 95 Setup`. Finally, select Update from the File menu so that the link will be placed into the mail message.

Customizing the Installation Even Further

When the users begin the setup process from the methods described earlier, they will be given the option of four installation types:

- ■ Typical—A predefined subset of components that include the most commonly used features of Office.
- ■ Compact—A predefined subset of components that provide the minimum necessary files to run Office.

- Custom—The user has complete control over which Office components are installed.
- Run from Network Server—The main Office application files remain on the server and will be run from the network.

The last option, Run from Network Server, has the lowest local hard drive space requirements, yet a penalty in performance will be observed because all applications must be loaded across the network.

To predefine the type of installation, you have two options. You can use the command-line setup options or create a custom setup table file (STF) with the Network Installation Wizard.

> **NOTE**
>
> The Network Installation Wizard is available in the Microsoft Office for Windows 95 Resource Kit. It is not part of the Microsoft Office for Windows 95 release.

If you see where the setup files are installed, you will notice a setup.stf file. This file determines the sequence that setup will follow. The Network Installation Wizard enables you to create custom tables that determine which installation type to use (Typical, Compact, Custom, or Network), which components are to be installed, default answers to yes/no questions, default program groups/icons, and destination folders.

If you have the Network Installation Wizard, you might want to create various setup tables based on who will be installing Microsoft Office. For example, you might want to make one setup table for users who have minimal disk space. Then create yet another installation for the users in the sales department, and another table for the accountants. The sales installation may include the entire PowerPoint arsenal of templates, whereas the accounting department receives the entire arsenal of Excel add-ins.

For example, create four setup table files:

- full.stf—For power users who need everything and have the disk space to do it
- minimum.stf—For users with minimal disk space, or those who don't need all components
- sales.stf—The sales department receives all the PowerPoint templates
- account.stf—The accounting department receives all the Excel templates and add-ins

After you create these files, you can provide installation procedures as described earlier in this chapter. The command lines would look like the following:

```
setup.exe /t sales.stf
```

or

```
setup.exe /q /t minimum.stf
```

The first example installs the components you configured for the sales staff. The second example installs the components you configured for a minimum installation. In addition, the /q option causes the setup to run in quiet mode; the user is not prompted with any dialog boxes.

If you do not have access to the Network Installation Wizard, the setup utility provides some useful command-line switches. To install Microsoft Office with typical components, for example, run the following command:

```
setup.exe /b 1
```

The /b option defines which installation type to perform: 1 = typical, 2 = compact, 3 = custom, and 4 = network installation. This option alone may be all you need to create a customized installation.

TIP

If you believe that the registry and OLE settings related to Microsoft Office have been corrupted, you can try using the setup /y command.

This performs the Microsoft Office setup without actually copying files. It carries out the standard setup sequence and re-registers the applications. This alone may solve the problem.

Summary

In this chapter you have learned about the various network architectures that will enable you to use Microsoft Office to exchange information with your co-workers. The information provided should enable you to install Mail on your network and provide a central location from which users can install Microsoft Office. In addition, this chapter discusses how to customize the Microsoft Office installation. With these customizations, you can exercise a great deal of control over how the Office applications will be deployed. The topics discussed cover some basic requirements for a network and enable you to explore the functionality in the chapters to follow.

Sharing Your Work

49

by Jeff
Steinmetz

Sharing your work no longer means just putting a file out where others can get to it. This chapter explores the ways Microsoft Office extends the capabilities of your network. This chapter also covers the use of document properties, explains how to implement methods to find files quickly, and demonstrates how to share your work through e-mail.

Sharing Your Files

The most common method of sharing work is the use of shared network directories. This may be your own directory you provide as a shared resource or a centrally shared directory on a server. Sharing files has been around since the inception of networks. The hurdle users face with this method occurs when the number of shared directories and files increases. Finding the file you want can be challenging, and was even more difficult on operating systems in which you were limited to an eight-character name with a three-character extension. Now we are not bound by these size limitations under Windows 95.

Filenames and Properties

With the use of long filenames and document properties, we are able to assign descriptive information to Microsoft Office documents. It may be beneficial to your office to implement a standard way to name files and encourage the use of file properties. File properties are accessed from the File menu in Word, Excel, PowerPoint, and Access. Figure 49.1 shows the properties for a Word document. Word is used as the basis for the following examples.

FIGURE 49.1.

Document properties.

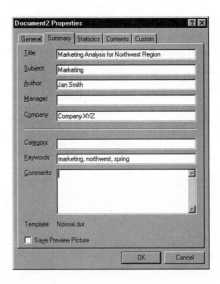

These are the default properties that Microsoft Office provides for you. Some of the fields are automatically filled in, such as the title and author. The title is based on the first line of text in your document. This may not always be what you want, but at least Microsoft Office has made an attempt to title it for you. If you do not like the title Microsoft Office has selected for you, replace it with a descriptive title of your own. The author field is based on the information provided when Microsoft Office was initially set up. If you want to change the default name, select Options from the Tools menu. In the Options dialog box that appears, you will find the User Info tab in which you can make changes.

We have filled in other information, such as subject and keywords. The more information you provide, the easier it will be to track down lost files. As mentioned earlier, you may want to make a companywide decision about how to best utilize these fields. The usefulness of properties will become more apparent when file searches and file indexes are discussed, later in this chapter.

If you don't find a property that suits your needs, you can use custom properties. Figure 49.2 shows the addition of a custom property titled Client. If you select the Name list box, you will find that Microsoft Office has predefined some custom properties for you. If one of these properties does not suit your needs, you can supply your own. You also can select the type of value to be associated with the name: Text, Date, Number, or Yes/No. For example, you can create a custom property that tracks whether the document has been approved for release. In this case, you could create a custom property named Approved, and make it a Yes/No value. This enables you to perform a search for all documents that have not been approved.

FIGURE 49.2.

Adding a custom property.

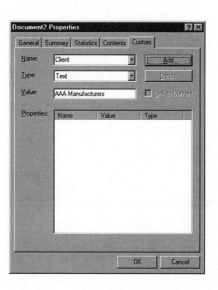

With this knowledge of document properties, you should be able to set up a standard way for users to save their work. For example, a law office might want to use a custom property named Client to help track files. A columnist might use the built-in property Category as a place to enter the type of article he or she is writing (for example, Movie Review, Variety, Editorial, and so on). It is up to you how to best implement properties.

Using the Microsoft Office Find Fast Utility

You may be unaware that the Microsoft Office Find Fast utility is running on your computer right now. The Find Fast utility is installed during the Microsoft Office setup process and runs automatically in the background, indexing all of your Office documents. If Find Fast is installed, it will be located in your StartUp folder. To access the Find Fast utility, look in your Control Panel. If you don't find the Find Fast utility, you may want to install it. To do this, run Microsoft Office setup and select Add/Remove. To add the Find Fast utility, highlight Office Tools and select the Change Option button. Figure 49.3 shows the Find Fast utility in the list of optional Office tools. Select the Find Fast Utility and continue with the setup operation.

FIGURE 49.3.

Installing the Find Fast utility.

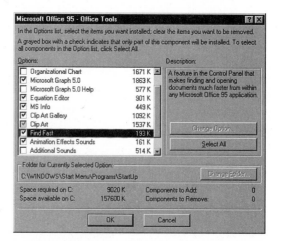

So why do you want this running all the time? Because you have put a lot of work into giving your documents descriptive names and useful properties. The indexes that Find Fast creates enable you to quickly search for documents based on any number of parameters.

> **NOTE**
>
> The file searching capabilities of the index are not related to the Find function located on the Windows 95 Start button. The indexes are used when opening a file from within Microsoft Office.

Find Fast creates hidden .ff* files in the root directories that you specify for indexing. The default is to place the index file at the root directory of each hard drive. If you run the Find Fast utility from the Control Panel, you will see the directories being indexed. Figure 49.4 shows that drives C: and D: are being indexed.

FIGURE 49.4.

The Find Fast utility displays which directories are being indexed.

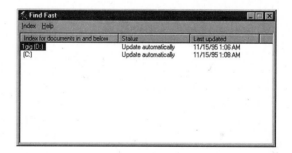

The index will cover files in and below each specified path. You can create indexes anywhere you prefer; however, keep in mind that searches will be more thorough if users can point to one main directory and search within it and all underlying directories. Alternatively, it may be inefficient to require Find Fast to search every directory when it performs its updates. If you plan to save all your Microsoft Office documents in a directory called My Documents, you can instruct Fast Find to index in and below that directory only. Within the My Documents directory you can create subdirectories to further organize your work. Be assured that Find Fast will index those as well.

> **TIP**
>
> After you create a Find Fast index, you cannot create any indexes in subdirectories. Find Fast will warn you that the index you are trying to create is in the scope of one of its parent directories. There is no need to create indexes below any parent indexes. If you want to create multiple indexes, you need to delete any indexes in parent directories.

Network drives can be indexed the same way as your local drive. Following are the ways to maintain an index on a network drive:

- If the computer that is sharing its directory has Office installed, it can maintain it just as it is maintained on a user's local drive. This would be the case in a peer-to-peer network where a user has shared one of his or her local directories and made it available for use by others.

- A user with Microsoft Office can be designated to create and keep the index updated. To create an index, use the Find Fast utility in the Control Panel and select Create Index from the Index menu. Figure 49.5 shows an index being added to the \\SERVER1\PUBLIC directory. This user should be running the Find Fast utility at all times (this is done automatically if it is in the StartUp folder, as mentioned earlier) in order to keep the index current. Only one computer needs to maintain the index. Do not allow several users to update the same index. You might want to make this an administrative activity by granting write access to the administrator only.

FIGURE 49.5.

Creating a Find Fast index on a network directory.

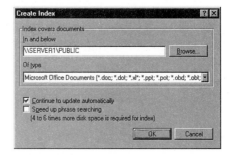

- If the directory is being accessed from Windows NT Server, you can obtain the Find Fast NT service from the Microsoft Office for Windows 95 Resource Kit. Because it runs as a service, it will run in the background without requiring a user to log on to the server. This is the most efficient way to maintain the indexing since the processing is off-loaded onto the server, thus reducing network traffic and removing the burden from a user's workstation. Remember that all users must have at least read permissions at the directory level where the index files are located. Keep in mind that the indexes are created in and below the specified path.

> **WARNING**
>
> Do not install Find Fast NT and the Find Fast single-user version shipped with Microsoft Office on the same computer. Delete the single-user version from the StartUp group to prevent it from running.

Finding Files

Now that you've done a great job setting up your network, you have convinced people to use document properties, and you have set up Find Fast indexing for quick and comprehensive searches, and users are creating documents left and right. It's time to put the file search capabilities of Microsoft Office to the test.

Using Word as an example again, select Open from the File menu. The Open dialog box, similar to the one shown in Figure 49.6, appears. The basic search criteria available in this first screen include Filename and Text or property. You can select a specific directory in which to search, or select a root directory to search in and below. One thing to be aware of is the Commands and Settings button in the upper-right corner of the dialog box. You must use this drop-down menu to select Search Subfolders.

FIGURE 49.6.

The Open dialog box.

Commands and Settings button

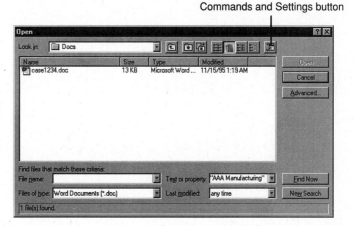

By default, subfolders are not searched. The speed of the searches performed here is due to the Find Fast indexes you created earlier. The Text or property field enables you to search for text that is in the body of the document, or one of the properties that you have defined in your document. It was mentioned earlier that a law firm might use a custom property, Client, to label its documents. In this field, one would enter the client name, and the results of the search would return documents related to a specific client. If your search text contains spaces, place quotation marks around the phrase, as in `"AAA Manufacturing"`.

Because you are not defining where you want AAA Manufacturing to appear, you might find files that contain `"AAA Manufacturing"` in the body of the text. You can narrow the search by selecting the Advanced button. Figure 49.7 shows how you have narrowed the search criteria to look for AAA Manufacturing in the Client property only.

FIGURE 49.7.
The Advanced Find dialog box enables you to build very specific search criteria.

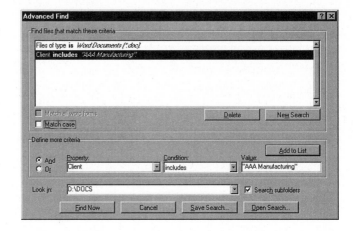

You can create precise searches by defining the property, condition, and value. Every time you define the criteria, you select Add to List. If you specify And when adding a subsequent criterion, the files found will logically satisfy both criteria. Use Or to create a search that matches either criterion.

For example, you may wish to find documents with the Client property matching AAA Manufacturing *and* documents that where authored by Jan Smith. In this case, set Property to Client, and Value to AAA Manufacturing. Select Add to List. Then, for the subsequent criteria, set the condition to And, select Author for Property, and enter Jan Smith as the value. Again, select Add to List. You have now created a logical search that will search for specific documents that match the conditions you have created.

When you select Find Now, the search will commence and return you to the original File Open dialog box. The files found that match the criteria will be presented in the list view. If you want to further modify your search, you can select the Advanced button again and make changes to your last search.

If at any time you feel you have created an advanced search that will be useful in the future, be sure to save the search for later retrieval. Select the Save Search button at the bottom of the Advanced Find dialog box. Give the search a name and select OK. You can retrieve the search any time by selecting Open Search.

Shared Lists in Excel

When files are shared over a network, you eventually will encounter a dialog box warning you that another user already has the file open. The options presented to you include opening the file in Read-Only mode, creating a copy of the file, and waiting for the user to finish with the document. None of these options is appealing when you are trying to get work done. Excel for

Windows 95 provides an alternative to hunting down the person that has the document open: *shared lists.* A shared list is a workbook that can be opened and edited by multiple users at the same time.

The term "shared list" indicates that data in Excel lists and databases are the only things that can be updated. You are allowed to insert data, insert and delete ranges, and sort the data. Be aware that formatting cells and entering formulas are not allowed; therefore, you should format your ranges and edit your formulas before designating them as a shared list. These operations are disabled since it would interfere with other users using the workbook.

After you place the workbook on a shared network resource, you can designate the workbook as a shared list by performing the following steps:

1. Select Shared Lists from the File menu. The Shared Lists dialog box appears. (See Figure 49.8.)

FIGURE 49.8.

The Shared Lists dialog box enables you to use multiuser editing.

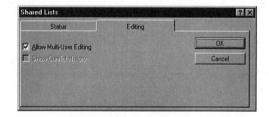

2. In the Editing tab, activate the Allow Multiuser Editing check box.
3. Select OK. At this point, Excel will require you to save the workbook.
4. If you have never used shared lists before, Excel will prompt you for your User Identification. The name you supply will be used to track the users of the notebook. Change the user name if needed and then select OK.
5. When Excel returns you to the workbook, you will notice that [Shared] is appended to the workbook's title bar.

TIP

If you receive the error message Can't access read-only document *filename.xls* when attempting to open the Shared Lists dialog box, it may be because you have opened a workbook as read-only. You either do not have read/write permission for the network directory or you explicitly opened the file as read-only. In the File Open dialog box, be sure you have not selected Open Read Only under the Commands and Settings menu.

Working with a Shared List

Now that your workbook is set up as a shared list, try opening the workbook on multiple users' machines. To see which users are accessing the file, select Shared Lists from the File menu and then select the Status tab. Figure 49.9 shows a sample list of users that currently have the workbook open.

FIGURE 49.9.

Select the Status tab to view which users are currently accessing the shared list.

If you want to update the workbook with each user's changes, select Save from the File menu. If the update includes changes made by others, Excel will inform you.

If two users have edited the same cell, the Conflict Resolution dialog box will appear. Figure 49.10 shows that you and another user have made a change to cell C3. In this example, you have entered a value of 23, and the other user has entered a value of 22.3. Select the Use my changes button to keep your work, or select Use these changes to allow the changes made by the other user. If you want to track these conflicts, select Shared Lists from the File menu. In the Editing tab, activate the Show Conflict History check box. A new sheet named Conflict History will be appended to the end of the workbook.

FIGURE 49.10.

The Conflict Resolution dialog box appears when multiple users have changed the same cell range.

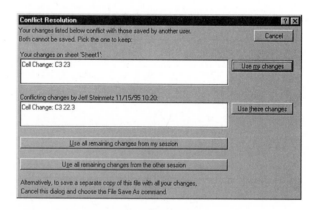

Using Mail to Share Documents

Mail provides a great vehicle to distribute documents throughout your workgroup. The two methods that are discussed are using Send to mail a document, and routing a document.

Using Send to Mail Documents

There is no need to exit the Office application you are currently using in order to send mail. Every Microsoft Office application enables you to mail the document you currently have open. With your document open, select Send from the File menu. If the Choose Profile dialog box appears, select the profile you use to send mail. Figure 49.11 shows the mail message that is created in Microsoft Exchange. Notice that the document has been inserted automatically into the body of the text. You are not limited to sending the document alone—you can add comments and additional attachments in the body of the message.

FIGURE 49.11.

The mail message created with the Send command places your document in the body of the text.

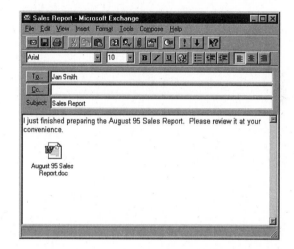

When the intended recipient receives the mail message, he or she simply double-clicks the document's icon to open the file. The recipient can store the document in one of two ways: use Save As from within the Microsoft Office application after he or she has opened the document, or move the mail message to a folder in his or her Personal Information Store.

A bit of explanation is required for Personal Information Store. Microsoft Exchange enables you to create custom folders in addition to the standard Inbox, Outbox, Sent Items, and Deleted Items. You can create your own folder, such as Saved Items. To keep the mail message for a period of time, simply drag mail messages from your Inbox to your Saved Items folder.

To create the Saved Items folder, select New Folder from the File menu of Microsoft Exchange. Name the folder and select OK. When you save items in this manner, they are located only in the scope of e-mail. No one else can access your personal information store. This is a great way to temporarily archive documents you are interested in. I say *temporarily* because you don't want to eat away at the resources your mail server (or workgroup postoffice) provides.

Routing Documents

When you use Send to mail a document, each recipient receives his or her own copy of the original. Routing a document enables you to distribute a single copy of the original. You are able to control the recipients and the order in which the document is sent. See Chapter 47, "Mailing, Routing, and Faxing," for further routing techniques.

Summary

This chapter reviews how to add properties to your Microsoft Office documents. These properties help users locate documents on shared directories. This chapter examines how file searching performance can be improved by implementing the Find Fast utility. You should have a better understanding of how the Find Fast utility works, as well as how to create and manage the Find Fast indexes. This chapter also covers the shared lists capabilities in Excel that enable multiple users to work on the same workbook. Be sure to examine Chapter 47 for other ways to share your documents with Mail.

Understanding and Customizing Microsoft Exchange

50

by Kevin Chestnut

What Is Microsoft Exchange?

Microsoft Exchange is an integrated mailbox for handling e-mail and faxes within Windows 95. This means you can use a single front-end application for all mail services. So, for example, rather than using Qualcomm's Eudora for Internet mail and Delrina's WinFax for fax mail, you can use Exchange instead. But Exchange promises to do much more than just replace mailbox applications, as you learn in this chapter.

Electronic Mail Is Evolving

Early in 1993, Bill Gates announced Microsoft's vision of a new way for computer users to work together, sharing information with "anyone, anywhere, anytime." In the future, he said, users would be able to automate routine business processes, eliminate paper forms, automatically negotiate meeting times and places, and collaborate on shared projects in entirely new ways.

The backbone of this system of universal information exchange, Gates said, would be Microsoft's next generation of electronic mail coupled with client/server computing and new operating systems. Figure 50.1 illustrates the evolution of electronic mail according to Microsoft.

FIGURE 50.1.

The evolution of electronic mail from simple file-sharing to true client/server systems promises new kinds of collaboration and information sharing between users.

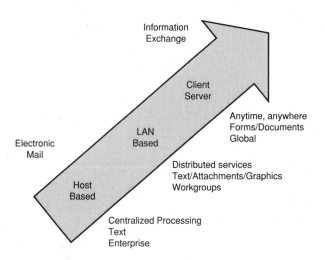

Microsoft has made some large promises. But a few years and millions of development dollars later, a major part of this vision is shipping with Windows 95 in the form of the Microsoft Exchange client. The word *client* is key here. A mail system has two major components. The first component, visible to you, is the mailbox interface you use to handle mail on your desktop. This is the mail *client*. The second component, called the mail *server*, works in the background to send, receive, and store messages.

Microsoft's Messaging API (MAPI)

Microsoft has created an entirely new messaging architecture to support Exchange and other mail applications. Called the *Messaging Application Program Interface* or *MAPI*, it provides a standard, program-level interface between client applications and mail services. The relationship between MAPI and the mail client and server components is shown in Figure 50.2.

FIGURE 50.2.

MAPI provides a standard way for the client and server components of various mail services to communicate with one another.

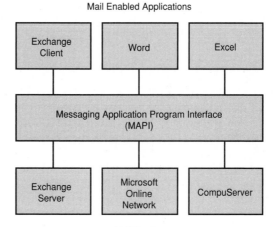

MAPI is much more than a protocol for communication between different manufacturers' mail servers; it provides a structure that gives all servers equal treatment. This makes it possible for servers to integrate within the Exchange client's user interface and other mail-enabled applications. Exchange itself is possible only because of MAPI.

Compatibility with MAPI is becoming an important measure for all messaging systems. It is designed as a long-term standard that developers can use to create new kinds of mail applications. As a result, you can install new mail applications, servers, and services without learning a new user interface or dealing with the operational details of the mail server itself.

The Quest for the Universal Mailbox

The need for a single mailbox is becoming critical. Messaging technology is clearly changing the way people communicate. A recent study revealed that 74 percent of all business phone calls reach a voice-mailbox rather than a person. On top of this, the exploding interest in the Internet is leading to an e-mail revolution. By conservative estimates, 100 million people will have e-mail access within the next four years!

E-mail and voice mail are certainly convenient, but they could be a lot more convenient! Typically, you have to check for new mail in two or more places. Different systems have different user interfaces, capabilities, and commands, and it's difficult or impossible to send mail directly from an application such as a word processor. Worse, one mail system often doesn't know about the other. You have different mailing addresses and passwords on each system, and it's usually impossible to forward a message directly between systems.

A universal mailbox would eliminate these problems by providing a single interface for all messages: text, fax, voice, and attached data files. Not only would it handle any kind of mail; it would connect to any kind of mail server or service and integrate fully with other desktop applications.

For now, Exchange handles text and fax. Out of the box, Exchange works with Microsoft Mail, Microsoft Fax, and the Microsoft Network mail service. Microsoft Plus! adds Internet mail. Support for CompuServe mail is also available. Expect to see Lotus cc:Mail and Notes as well. Novell Groupwise, America Online, and other major e-mail server and service providers are supposed to be added soon.

Beyond text and fax, several companies have announced a wide range of voice-mail products for Exchange, including integration with large, private voice-mail systems and voice-mail services provided by telephone companies. It also includes new kinds of small-office voice-mail systems based on Exchange.

Even more exciting is the integration with wireless services from AT&T, the Ardis network, and others that is on the horizon. Equipped with a wireless modem, this means that your portable or palmtop will always be in touch. Truly universal mail!

Exchange Is Two Products

Microsoft uses the name *Exchange* for two separate products: Exchange client and Exchange server. This can be confusing. The Exchange server is not yet available. It is currently scheduled for release in early 1996. The Exchange server will eventually replace Microsoft Mail, Microsoft's current mail-server product.

To add to the confusion, there are two versions of the Exchange client. During much of the beta testing for Windows 95, Microsoft shipped a single, full-featured version of the client. In fact, most early press reviews of Exchange are based on this original version.

Unfortunately, testing on the full client demonstrated that some people had trouble configuring it during Windows 95 installation. In addition, some of the features designed for users of corporate e-mail systems were unfamiliar and confusing to home and small-office users. Microsoft decided to make Exchange installation an option and ship a more modest version of the client with Windows 95. The original version of the client will be shipped with the Exchange server.

Microsoft's Exchange client and server pieces work together to form a complete mail system, but you don't need one to use the other. They are specifically designed to work independently. That is part of the promise of Exchange. The Exchange client works with other mail servers, including the latest version of Microsoft Mail. You learn about Microsoft Mail and other server components in detail in the section titled "Microsoft Mail Services" later in this chapter.

Our Focus Is on the Client

The focus of the rest of this chapter and of Chapter 51, "Advanced Microsoft Exchange," is on the Exchange client currently shipping with Windows 95. For simplicity, it is referred to as *Exchange* from here on unless a specific distinction needs to be made between the client and the server.

The rest of this chapter looks at the features Exchange offers and shows how to configure and connect it to Microsoft Mail and other servers, including remote mail services provided by the Microsoft Network, CompuServe, and others. Chapter 51 looks at the user interface in detail and shows ways to customize it to simplify e-mail and fax handling.

Exchange Features

Exchange is the first product capable of making the universal mailbox a reality. It integrates different mail formats, servers, and services in one place and automatically handles the necessary format-translation and communication chores. In addition, Exchange handles mail services for other Windows applications. All the mail features of Microsoft Office, including the mail-sending features found in Word and Excel and the meeting-making features of Schedule+, rely on Exchange. Here are some of Exchange's key features:

- Send and receive e-mail and faxes through a variety of mail services, including Microsoft Mail, Microsoft Fax, the Microsoft Network, CompuServe, and the Internet. Other systems and services will be accessible soon, including Lotus cc:Mail and Lotus Notes, Novell Groupwise, and America Online.

- Compose richly formatted e-mail (different fonts, paragraph settings, boldface, italics, and so on) using Exchange's built-in text editor or send faxes or documents including attached files or embedded OLE objects directly from Word, Excel, and other applications.

- Keep copies of any message you send or receive in a *personal message store* and organize stored messages in *folders* for easy retrieval.

- Keep important address and contact information in a *personal address book* that can be shared by other Windows 95 and Microsoft Office programs.

- Configure different Exchange *profiles* for different users or different uses. For example, you can configure Exchange to operate one way when a portable computer is connected to the office LAN and another way when it's on the road.

■ Customize the look of the Exchange toolbar and message lists.

As you might have guessed, Exchange is a rich, complex product, worthy of a book by itself. Although this book can't explore all the features, it *can* take you step by step through the installation hurdles, show you the most useful features, and help you avoid common problems.

The Components of a Mail Server

Let's look briefly at the basic components that make up a mail server. Understanding these components will help you understand the overall organization of Exchange and help make sense of the installation and configuration process. The components illustrated in Figure 50.3 provide Exchange with the support needed to send and receive mail.

FIGURE 50.3.

The basic components of any mail system enable it to transport mail to and from other servers, address messages, and store messages.

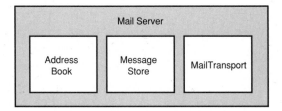

Mail Transport

The most basic job a mail server performs is physically delivering the file or files and addressing information that make up a mail message from the sender to the receiver. Microsoft calls this *mail transport* to reinforce the idea of moving message data from one server to another. Ideally, the mail-transport component understands and handles the communications between servers and services and takes care of translating address and mail formats as needed.

Address Books

The server must maintain address information for each person who has a mailbox on the system. The degree of addressing information can range from a simple name-and-mail-system address to extensive contact information such as phone numbers, a street address, and so on. Exchange maintains detailed address books that it can share with other applications. You will use Exchange's address book in Chapter 51, when you learn how to create and send mail.

In addition to individuals, the server also usually maintains distribution lists that group related people together for convenience. This enables you to address mail to "all employees," for example.

Message Stores

The server stores the files that make up a mail message in a central location that is equally accessible to everyone on the system. A central message store also makes it possible for the server to track messages as they are received and read, sending return receipts and marking messages for eventual deletion. It also enables the server to handle centralized maintenance and administrative chores such as cleaning up storage space and automatically backing up mail for safekeeping.

> **NOTE**
>
> Exchange (MAPI, really) requires an installable driver for each mail server or service. Called a *service provider*, this driver defines the specifics of what a particular server can do and provides an interface to the server's transport, address book, and message store. These service providers (or simply, *services*) are installed and configured with the Mail and Fax icon in the Windows 95 Control Panel. You have to install a particular service before you can use it with Exchange.
>
> Microsoft supplies service providers for Microsoft Mail, Microsoft Fax, and the Microsoft Network with Windows 95. Microsoft Plus! adds Internet mail. Providers are currently available from CompuServe, and will soon be available for other online services and other manufacturers' mail servers.

Installing Exchange

You can install Exchange as part of the Windows 95 setup or separately. To install Exchange with Windows 95, however, you must select the right combination of setup options; otherwise Exchange and other mail-system components won't be installed.

Installing Exchange is really a two-part process: First you install the Exchange application itself; then you install and configure the services you want to use with it. Microsoft enables you to install Exchange and the Microsoft service providers that come with it at the same time.

The Windows Setup program installs Exchange and then automatically starts the Exchange Inbox Setup Wizard to help you configure the mail services you select. Even though it seems like you are doing everything at one time, the Inbox Setup Wizard only does a minimal job. It takes some additional steps to configure the services the way you need them.

In the following steps, the combination of Windows Setup and the Inbox Setup Wizard does most of the work; then I show you how to fine-tune the various services.

> **CAUTION**
>
> The amazing features and flexibility of Exchange come at a price, of course: the application is quite resource intensive. You must have at least 8MB of RAM (the minimum recommended by Microsoft) and at least 20MB of free space on the drive that Windows uses to create its dynamic swap file.

Installing Exchange with Windows 95

If you have not yet installed Windows 95, you have two ways to install Exchange and Microsoft's service providers. Either way adds its own unique confusion:

- Typical Option—If you select Typical from the list of setup options presented by the Windows 95 Setup Wizard, Exchange is not installed automatically. However, a few screens later, the Setup Wizard asks if you want to install Microsoft Network support, Microsoft Mail, or Microsoft Fax. Each of these services requires Exchange, so selecting one or more of them installs Exchange automatically.

- Custom Option—If you select Custom instead of Typical, the Setup Wizard presents you with a list of components to choose from. Check Microsoft Exchange. If you have a fax modem installed, you can also check Microsoft Fax service at this point. If you want Microsoft Network, scroll to the end of the components list. If you want Microsoft Mail, you have to highlight Microsoft Exchange and then click the Details button. This displays a list of secondary mail components, including Microsoft Mail.

At the end of the Windows 95 setup process, the Exchange Inbox Setup Wizard is started automatically. See the section in this chapter titled "Using the Inbox Setup Wizard to Create a Profile" for details.

Installing Exchange Separately

If the Exchange Inbox icon is not on your desktop, you need your Windows 95 Installation CD-ROM or disks to add Exchange and the other mail-system components.

To install Exchange separately follow these steps:

1. Open Control Panel and double-click the Add/Remove Programs icon. Click the Windows Setup tab to see a list of previously installed and installable components similar to what is shown in Figure 50.4.

FIGURE 50.4.

Choose the Windows Setup components you want to install from the Add/ Remove Programs Properties dialog box.

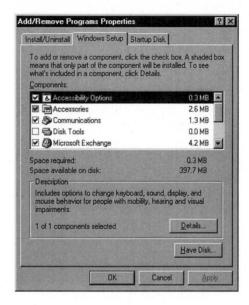

2. Check Microsoft Exchange. If you have a fax modem installed on your PC, check Microsoft Fax as well. With a modem, you might also want to install Microsoft Network access. (Scroll to the end of the list of components to see the Microsoft Network check box.)

3. If you want to install the Microsoft Mail service provider, highlight Microsoft Exchange in the components list and then click the Details button. Check Microsoft Mail on the list of additional components and then click OK to return to the main dialog box.

4. Click OK and follow the onscreen instructions to continue installation.

Using the Inbox Setup Wizard to Create a Profile

At the end of the Exchange installation process, Windows automatically starts the Exchange Inbox Setup Wizard to help you configure a profile. A *profile* identifies the services you want to use and sets the various configuration options available for each service. The Inbox Setup Wizard lists all installed services and takes you step by step through the process of creating a profile.

One Profile or Several?

When Exchange is installed, it creates a single default profile called MS Exchange Settings. If you don't need additional profiles, use the default. You will probably want additional profiles if

■ More than one person uses your computer. This separates your name, mail accounts, passwords, and preferences from those of other users.

■ You use your computer in more than one location. This identifies variations in service conditions like the numbers you dial to reach an outside line, long distance access codes, communications protocols, and so on.

■ You experience performance problems or conflicts with service providers. Some beta testers found sluggish performance with certain combinations of service providers. If you experience problems, you might need to keep a service provider in a separate profile until the supplier corrects the problem.

TIP

Profiles are great for portable computers. For example, you can create an Office profile that uses the LAN and knows to dial 9 to reach an outside line, and a separate Home profile that uses a modem for remote access and dials direct. Or, if you travel, you can create a Trip profile that knows to dial numbers in your home area code as long distance.

Starting the Inbox Setup Wizard Manually

You can also use the Inbox Setup Wizard to guide you through creating a new profile. After you have created the basic profile, you can edit the various mail services to fine-tune them.

To start the Inbox Setup Wizard manually, follow these steps:

1. Open Control Panel and double-click the Mail and Fax icon.

2. Click the Show Profiles button in the Exchange Settings Properties dialog box. The Exchange Profiles dialog box lists existing profiles, including one called MS Exchange Settings. This is the default profile that is normally created during Windows 95 installation.

NOTE

If you want to modify the default profile (MS Exchange Settings) instead of adding a new one, press Alt+F4 to close this dialog box and skip down to the section in this chapter titled "Editing an Exchange Profile."

3. Click the Add button to start the Inbox Setup Wizard.

When the Inbox Setup Wizard opens, it lists the installed services as shown in Figure 50.5.

FIGURE 50.5.

The Exchange Inbox Setup Wizard prompts you through creating a new profile and configuring basic options for the services you select.

Let the Wizard do its job. Select the Use the following information services option, check the services you want included in the new profile, and then click the Next button to continue. The questions the Wizard asks depend on the services you select. The process is simple. Follow it through to the finish. If you are not sure of a particular setting, you can change it later.

Remember, the Wizard skips over a lot of important details, but it's a great way to create a profile and complete the basic configuration steps. The details of fine-tuning each service are discussed in the section titled "Editing an Exchange Profile" later in this chapter.

Microsoft Mail Services

Microsoft provides the following mail-transport services for Exchange:

- Microsoft Mail
- Microsoft Fax
- The Microsoft Network
- Internet mail (included in Microsoft Plus!)

Microsoft also provides the following mail-support services:

- Personal Address Book
- Personal Message Store

These support services are "personal" in the sense that they are local resources under your control. With them, you are able to copy and save mail addresses and messages from server-based address books and message stores. You decide what addresses and messages to keep. (Technically, these two services are part of the overall MAPI mail system, but it's okay to think of them as part of Exchange itself.)

Microsoft Mail

Like Exchange, the name *Mail* is used for two separate Microsoft products. Windows 95 includes a workgroup version of Microsoft Mail. This is a serverless version designed for small offices running a single Windows workgroup. One computer in the workgroup must act as the mail post office, storing messages and address-book information. Mail service is interrupted when the post office computer is shut down.

Windows 95 includes a service provider for the workgroup version of Mail. You must install this service on each Windows 95 computer in the workgroup. Obviously, each Windows 95 computer must run Exchange as well. You see how to set up the workgroup version of Mail in the section titled "Editing an Exchange Profile" later in this chapter.

In addition to the workgroup version, there is a server version of Microsoft Mail that includes enhanced features and capacity. This version supports multiple workgroups and provides *gateways* to handle mail delivery through other servers and services like the Internet. This version of Mail will eventually be replaced by the new Exchange server.

Microsoft Fax

The Microsoft Fax service provider turns a fax modem into a powerful and amazing tool. With it, you can fax documents from Word, Excel, or other applications as easily as you can print them. The fax modem can be installed in your machine or shared in a Windows workgroup.

The service provider also handles "faxing" binary data files. This lets you painlessly transfer files between any two machines running Microsoft Fax. File transfer takes place directly without an intervening layer of mail services, file transfer protocols, or cost (other than the price of the phone call). A direct connection between two typical 14.4Kbps/second modems can transfer a 1MB file in about 3 minutes.

The Microsoft Network

The *Microsoft Network* (MSN) is an information service Microsoft launched to compete with CompuServe, America Online, and others. Because it's part of Windows 95, it is obviously easy to install MSN and open an account.

Incidentally, MSN includes full Internet access through a companion Microsoft application called *Internet Explorer*. Explorer is included with Microsoft Plus!; you can also download it via MSN.

You connect to MSN using a modem. Like the other services, MSN enables you to send and receive e-mail. The e-mail services connect you to other MSN subscribers, to subscribers on competing services such as CompuServe, and to anyone with an Internet e-mail address.

Through Exchange, MSN is fully integrated with Windows 95 and mail-enabled applications. Unlike the Internet and other online services, MSN transparently handles sending and receiving binary data files such as faxes, graphics files, and documents containing embedded OLE objects, so it's easy to send complex mail to another MSN subscriber. MSN also does a good job of understanding the types of files other mail services can handle and then doing the appropriate format translation or warning you of potential problems.

Internet Mail

Microsoft Plus! includes a general-purpose Internet mail-service provider. This provider connects to mail servers with either SMTP (Simple Mail Transfer Protocol) or POP3 (Post Office Protocol version 3) support. Through Exchange, the service provider also handles the details of sending text and binary files.

Internet mail requires that you have the appropriate TCP/IP communications-protocol support installed on your computer. This can either be a local area network connection or a dial-up modem connection. Fortunately, installation of the necessary TCP/IP protocol layers is handled pretty much automatically when you install Windows 95 or the Internet features of Microsoft Plus!.

Personal Address Book

The *personal address book* is a sophisticated personal information manager (PIM) application available to Exchange and other mail-enabled Windows applications. You can easily copy mailing-address information from a server address book to your personal address book, which enables you to create a subset of frequently used individual addresses and distribution lists that are stored locally on your computer. You can also create your own distribution lists within your address book.

When you copy an address, you can add a great deal of supplementary information about a person, including home, office, fax, pager, and other phone numbers; detailed street addresses; job titles; company information; and so on. You can keep notes on conversations or pending actions. With a compatible modem, you can even use the address book as an auto-dialer. The Phone Numbers tab of the Personal Address Book is shown in Figure 50.6.

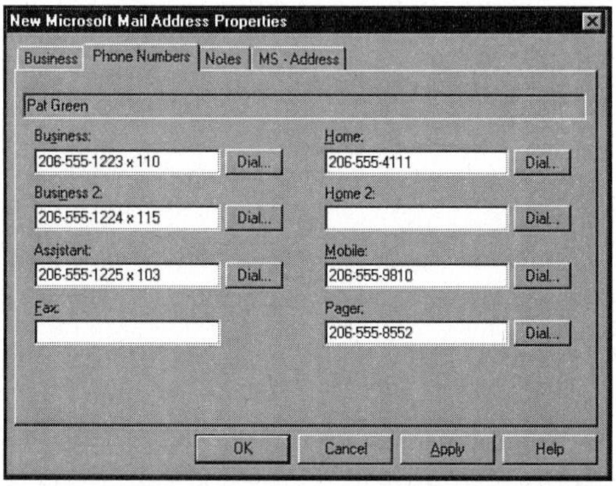

FIGURE 50.6.

You can use the personal address book to store a wealth of supplementary contact information.

The default personal address book is named Personal Address Book. The associated data file, named MAILBOX.PAB, is located in the Exchange folder. Note that all address information is stored in a single file. A profile can have only one address book associated with it. If you want to organize your addresses in different address books—perhaps one for business and another for personal use—you need to create a separate profile for each. Separate address books are also useful if several people share your computer.

TIP

Personal address books do have an annoying limitation: a person can have only one e-mail address. You can get around this limitation in one of two ways: You can create separate entries for a person, such as Pat Green/Internet, Pat Green/MSN; or you can store secondary (and presumably, less frequently used) e-mail addresses as notes. In the latter case, you'll have to remember to change to the appropriate address before you send e-mail.

Personal Message Store

The *personal message store* holds copies of any mail you send or receive. It is organized as a set of folders named Inbox, Outbox, Sent Items, and Deleted Items. Because this information is stored locally, you need to do a little maintenance from time to time, compressing or deleting old messages to reclaim storage space.

The default personal message store is named Personal Information Store. The associated data file, named MAILBOX.PST, is located in the Exchange folder. Note that all messages (from your inbox, outbox, and any folders you create) are stored in a single file. Unlike personal address books, a profile can have more than one personal message store associated with it. You can use this feature to organize messages; for example, you can have one message store for archived mail and another for current mail.

> **NOTE**
>
> Exchange also refers to the personal message store as the *personal information store* and as *personal folders*. These names are used inconsistently onscreen and in Microsoft's printed documentation. To add to the confusion, personal stores also contain *folders*.

Editing an Exchange Profile

When you install Exchange, the Inbox Setup Wizard creates a default profile based on the mail services selected. You can also use the Wizard to create a new profile. The Wizard leads you through the basic service-configuration options, making assumptions and skipping details.

Your Wizard-generated profile presents a series of tabs for each mail service it contains. These tabs give you access to a wide range of configuration options.

This section looks at configuration options for each service in detail. You observe the basic settings and see the options the Wizard skipped over.

To edit a profile, follow these steps:

1. Open Control Panel and double-click the Mail and Fax icon.
2. If you have more than one profile, select the one you want to edit from the list and click OK.

The Exchange Settings Properties dialog box for your profile should be similar to Figure 50.7.

If the Services tab is not shown, click it. This tab lists the mail services available in the profile. The default profile, MS Exchange Settings, shows at least one mail-transport service in addition to Personal Address Book (the personal address-book service) and Personal Folders (the personal message-store service). If you used the Inbox Setup Wizard to create a new profile, it shows at least one mail-transport service.

FIGURE 50.7.

The Exchange Settings Properties dialog box lists mail services available in a selected profile.

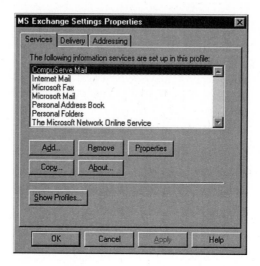

The Services tab includes several command buttons:

- Add—Adds a previously installed service provider to the current profile. If the desired service provider is not listed, it hasn't been installed.

- Remove—Removes a service provider from the current profile. This does not remove the service provider itself, however. To remove a service provider from your computer, double-click the Add/Remove Programs icon found in Control Panel.

- Properties—Accesses the service provider's specific configuration settings.

- Copy—Copies the selected service provider, including all current configuration settings, to another profile. Use this to transfer existing settings to a new profile.

- About—Displays version information about the selected service provider. Note that because mail services are installable drivers, it might be necessary to update them from time to time.

- Show Profiles—Lists available profiles. You can also click this to start a new profile.

Microsoft Mail Service

Before you configure the Microsoft Mail service provider, you need the name and directory location of the post office shared by everyone in your Windows workgroup. If you are already using Microsoft Mail, your system administrator can provide this information along with any other important details about your workgroup's post office.

If there is no post office, you can create one using the workgroup version of Microsoft Mail included in Windows 95. To do this, your computer must be connected to a LAN shared by everyone in your workgroup. You also need to decide which workgroup computer to use as the post office. The post-office computer should have ample storage space for messages, it must be on during normal working hours, and you must have rights to create directories and files. Also note that unless you purchase the server version of Microsoft Mail, everybody in your company who wants mail access has to be in the *same* workgroup.

Follow these steps to set up a Microsoft Mail post office:

1. Open Control Panel. (This should already be open on your desktop, so you can simply select it from the taskbar.)

2. Double-click the Microsoft Mail Postoffice icon (Microsoft spells *post office* as one word). If there is no icon, you have not installed Microsoft Mail. See the section titled "Installing Exchange" at the beginning of this chapter for installation instructions.

3. When the Microsoft Workgroup Postoffice Admin Wizard appears, select Create a new Workgroup Postoffice and click Next.

4. Enter a path and filename for the new post office. The default post-office name is WGPO0000, but you can pick something more memorable. Be sure to pick a path to which all members of your workgroup have access. Click Next to continue.

5. Confirm the post office path and name; then click Next to continue. Enter your administrator account details in the dialog box provided. (Because you created the post office, you are assumed to be the administrator.)

6. Click OK, and then click Finish to complete the setup process.

When you have a working post office, you can configure Mail service-provider properties. If Microsoft Mail is not listed in the current profile, click Add and select it from the list of available services. Click OK to return to the Exchange Settings Properties dialog box.

Select Microsoft Mail from the list of services in the Exchange Settings Properties dialog box. Click Properties to access the Microsoft Mail configuration options.

The Mail service provider has several pages of options. If the Connection tab is not shown, click it. (See Figure 50.8.)

Enter the post office path and name information. The Mail service provider can access a post office on the LAN or through a remote connection using a modem. Leave the default connection setting on Automatically sense LAN or Remote.

Click the Logon tab. (See Figure 50.9.)

Enter your mailbox name and password. If you are accessing an existing Mail post office (not the one you just created in the steps given previously), use the existing mailbox name and password provided by your system administrator. If this is a newly created post office, enter the name and password you used to create the administrator settings.

If you don't want to enter your password every time you log on, and you are not concerned about the possibility of others accessing your mail, you can check the When logging on, automatically enter password check box. Also note that you use this tab to change your password in the future.

FIGURE 50.8.

The Microsoft Mail Connection tab shows the location of your workgroup post office.

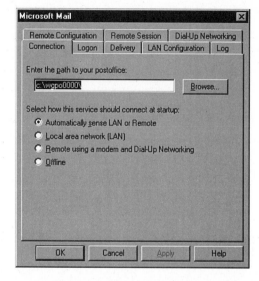

FIGURE 50.9.

Specify your mailbox name and password in the Microsoft Mail Logon tab.

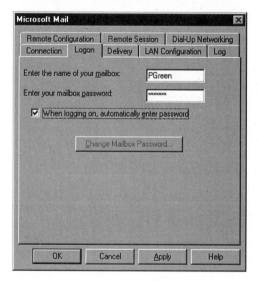

Click the Delivery tab. (See Figure 50.10.)

The defaults on this tab are usually fine. Note that the Enable incoming mail delivery check box must be checked to receive mail, and the Enable outgoing mail delivery check box must be checked to send mail.

Click the LAN Configuration tab. (See Figure 50.11.) This tab provides the following options:

- Use Remote Mail—Check this check box to limit initial message transfers to header information only. (A *message header* includes the sender's name, message subject, message priority, and other summary information.) You can then scan the headers to decide which messages you want to read and retrieve as full text using the Exchange Remote Mail feature. (See Chapter 51 for more information on Remote Mail.)

- Use local copy—Check this check box to use a local copy of the server address book rather than the copy on the server. This transfers a complete copy of the current server address book to your computer, which can improve performance in some cases. To update the local address-book copy, click the Tools menu in Microsoft Exchange, click Microsoft Mail Tools, and then click Download Address Lists.

- Use external delivery agent—This option can sometimes improve performance as well. It requires a special program to be running on the post office computer, however. Ask your system administrator for details before using this feature.

The remaining tabs control another powerful feature of Microsoft Mail called Remote Access. Let's look at this feature separately.

FIGURE 50.10.

Use the Microsoft Mail Delivery tab to control the way messages are transferred between Exchange and the Mail post office.

FIGURE 50.11.

Use the Microsoft Mail LAN Configuration tab to control the way Exchange and Mail communicate on the local area network.

Microsoft Mail Remote Access

Microsoft Mail is also accessible remotely though Windows 95 dial-up networking features. If you have a portable or you use Exchange at home, you can configure the Mail service provider for remote access.

> **TIP**
>
> You must install and configure Windows 95 Dial-Up Networking to use Microsoft Mail remotely. If you did not set this up when you installed Windows 95 (or if you don't remember), follow these steps:
>
> 1. Open Control Panel and double-click the Add/Remove Programs icon.
>
> 2. Click the Windows Setup tab, click Communications, and then click Details.
>
> 3. If Dial-Up Networking is checked, the feature is installed. Press Esc to cancel the Add/Remove Program process. (If it is not checked, check Dial-Up Networking and continue the installation process.)

Assuming Dial-Up Networking is installed, let's continue the configuration process. If the Microsoft Mail configuration dialog box is not open, select Microsoft Mail from the list of services in the Exchange Settings Properties dialog box, and then click Properties.

Click the Remote Configuration tab. (See Figure 50.12.)

The options for this tab are the same as for the LAN Configuration tab discussed previously. For best performance and minimum connect time, check Use Remote Mail and Use local copy.

FIGURE 50.12.

Use the Microsoft Mail Remote Configuration tab to control the way Exchange and Mail communicate using a dial-up connection.

Ask your system administrator before you check Use external delivery agent.

The Remote Session tab options are usually fine. If you want to dial-up Microsoft Mail as soon as you open Exchange, check the box for When this service is started. If your modem is permanently connected to a telephone line, you can choose Schedule Mail Delivery to happen automatically at specific times. Otherwise, Exchange sends any undelivered, outgoing mail whenever you connect to the Microsoft Mail server.

The Dial-Up Networking tab is a bit more complicated. You need to know how to reach the Microsoft Mail post office computer via modem. This depends upon your office LAN and modem configuration. Ask your system administrator for assistance.

Microsoft Fax Service

Microsoft Fax adds a rich and powerful set of fax-handling features for use with Exchange and other mail-enabled applications. Fax adds three accessory programs: Compose New Fax, Cover Page Editor, and Request a Fax. To access these programs, click the Windows 95 taskbar Start button, and then click Programs, Accessories, and Fax. Exchange also includes a fax viewer, which is examined in Chapter 51.

Configuring Fax options is straightforward. If Microsoft Fax is not listed in the current profile, click Add and select it from the list of available mail services. Click OK to return to the Exchange Settings Properties dialog box.

If Microsoft Fax is not in the list of available services, it is not installed. See the section titled "Installing Exchange" at the start of this chapter for installation instructions.

Select Microsoft Fax from the list of mail services in the Exchange Settings Properties dialog box. Click Properties to access the Microsoft Fax configuration options. There are several pages of options.

Start with the Message tab. (See Figure 50.13.)

FIGURE 50.13.

Set the fax format, best time to send, and default cover page to use (if any) in the Microsoft Fax Message tab.

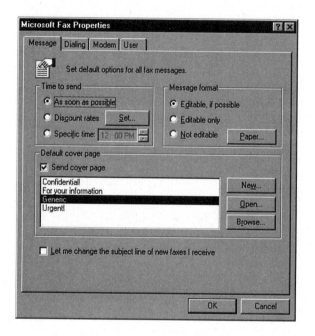

Use the Time to send selections to set the time of day for Microsoft Fax to send faxes. The As soon as possible and Specific time settings are self-explanatory. The Discount rates option enables you to specify when telephone rates for your carrier are lowest. Click Set to enter the valid starting and ending times for discount rates.

Use the Message format options to set the preferred transmission format for faxes. *Editable* means a copy of the actual file in binary format. With this format the receiver can edit the original document (assuming the application program that created the document is available as well). If the fax is not editable, it's a plain old fax—a picture of the document. Binary faxing requires a class 1 fax modem on the receiving end. *Editable, if possible* means try to send the fax as a binary file; otherwise send it as a plain fax. *Editable only* means if you can't send a binary fax, don't. *Not editable* means always send a plain fax. Click Paper to specify paper size, image orientation, or default resolution.

Use the Default cover page option to select a preferred default for your fax cover page. Click New or Open to launch the Fax Cover Page Editor.

Click the Dialing tab. (See Figure 50.14.)

FIGURE 50.14.

Use the Microsoft Fax Dialing tab to control the way outbound fax calls are dialed.

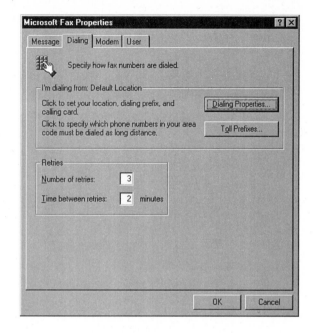

Click the Dialing Properties button to set general outbound dialing options, including your location, area code, calling card numbers, outside-line and long-distance prefixes, and so on. This tab is shared between all applications that do outbound dialing, so you have probably already set these options someplace else.

Click the Toll Prefixes button to specify the central office prefixes in your area code that must be dialed as long distance. This information is generally listed in your local white pages telephone directory.

Use the Retries options to set the number of times Microsoft Fax attempts to send a particular fax and the interval between attempts. Faxes most often fail because the fax number was busy or the machine was off, out of paper, or otherwise nonfunctional. The default settings are usually okay. If you get lots of failed attempts, try setting Time between retries to 4 or 5 minutes. If that doesn't help, the phone line connected to your fax modem might be noisy or of poor quality.

The Modem tab is another shared tab. You set these options when you configured your modem, so there's no need to discuss them here.

Click the User tab. (See Figure 50.15.)

The User tab is self-explanatory. This information is used in the variable fields on the cover pages you create with the Fax Cover Page Editor. In addition, the Fax number, Your full name, and Company field entries will appear as a single line at the top of each fax page.

FIGURE 50.15.

Fill in the Microsoft Fax User tab with the information used to prepare your fax cover sheets.

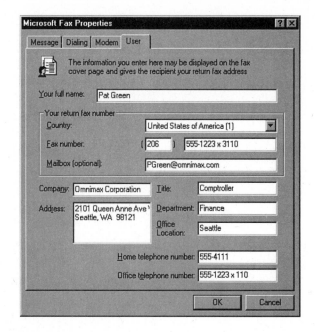

Microsoft Network Mail Service

The Microsoft Network mail-service provider controls how and when e-mail is retrieved from your remote network mailbox. If the Microsoft Network is not listed in the current profile, click Add and select it from the list of available services. Click OK to return to the Exchange Settings Properties dialog box.

If the Microsoft Network is not in the list of available services, it is not installed. Refer to the section titled "Installing Exchange" at the beginning of this chapter for installation instructions.

Select Microsoft Online Network from the list of mail services in the Exchange Settings Properties dialog box. Click Properties to access the MSN configuration options.

Click the Transport tab. (See Figure 50.16.)

Remote Mail is a special Exchange feature designed for dial-up services like MSN that makes it possible to use Exchange to read the headers of messages in a remote mailbox without downloading the message contents. A message *header* includes the sender's name, message subject, message priority, and other summary information.

You can scan the headers to decide which messages you want to read and retrieve as full text. This feature saves connection time and costs and lets you avoid downloading unimportant messages.

FIGURE 50.16.

Use the Microsoft Network Transport tab to control how and when e-mail is retrieved from your remote network mailbox.

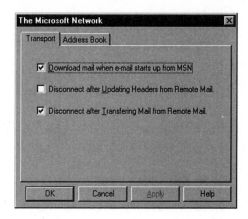

If you check the Download mail when e-mail starts up from MSN option, Exchange takes the opportunity to check your remote inbox whenever you're connected to MSN for e-mail transport—when you send a message via MSN, for example. If this option is not checked, you need to manually check your MSN box for new mail.

When you retrieve mail with the Disconnect after Updating Headers from Remote Mail option, Exchange transfers new mail headers for your MSN mailbox and then disconnects. After you scan the headers, you can use the Exchange Remote Mail feature to reconnect to MSN and retrieve the contents of selected messages.

When you retrieve mail with the Disconnect after Transferring Mail from Remote Mail option checked, Exchange transfers new mail from your MSN mailbox to your personal message store and then disconnects. This enables you to read messages offline.

Internet Mail Service

Microsoft Plus! adds several Internet features, including a service provider for Internet mail. This service provider is automatically added to Exchange when you install the Internet Jumpstart Kit from Microsoft Plus!. After you install the Plus! Internet features, you can add Internet Mail service to a profile.

The Exchange Settings Properties dialog box lists the mail services available in the current profile. To add Internet Mail services to a profile, follow these steps:

1. Click the Services tab of the Exchange Settings Properties dialog box.
2. Click Add and select Internet Mail from the list of available services. If Internet Mail is not available, follow the directions provided with Microsoft Plus! to install the Internet Jumpstart Kit.

After you add Internet Mail to a profile, select it from the list of services in the Exchange Settings Properties dialog. Click Properties to access the Internet Mail configuration options.

Click the General tab. (See Figure 50.17.) You fill in the following information:

■ Personal Information—Your name has been entered previously. Enter your Internet e-mail address in name@mycompany.com format.

■ Mailbox Information—*Internet Mail Server* is the name of your POP3 mail server. This can be a numeric IP address or a name like mail.mycompany.com. Ask your system administrator if you aren't sure. *Account name* is your e-mail name, usually as it appears before the @ sign in your Internet address. It is important that you get this right, so again, ask your system administrator.

■ Advanced Options—Your POP3 server handles incoming mail. Your SMTP server handles outgoing mail. If these servers have different names, click Advanced Options and enter the SMTP server name.

■ Message Format—This setting enables you to choose how any binary files you send are encoded. Check Use MIME when sending messages to use the newer Multipurpose Internet Mail Extension for binary encoding. Most Internet mail servers handle this encoding. If recipients complain about unreadable attachments, uncheck this box to use the older UUENCODE format.

FIGURE 50.17.

Specify mailbox and password information for your Internet mail server in the Internet Mail General tab.

> **TIP**
>
> If you use MIME encoding, set the character option to US ASCII. To do this, click the Character Set button in the Message Format dialog box. The US ASCII character set eliminates some conversion quirks that happen when MIME translates messages from the default Windows character set.

Click the Connection tab. (See Figure 50.18.)

FIGURE 50.18.

Use the Internet Mail Connection tab to specify whether you connect to the Internet through a LAN or a modem.

If you are connected to the Internet through your office LAN, select Connect using the network in the Connecting to Internet Mail group. If you connect to an Internet service provider using a dial-up SLIP or PPP connection, select Connect using the modem. This is another good example of useful configuration differences between an office profile and a home profile you might use with a portable computer.

If your dial-up Internet service provider has more than one connection phone number, the Dial using the following connection field enables you to select which connection to use. Alternate connections are created and maintained with Add Entry and Edit Entry. You can also add alternate connections if you have access to more than one modem.

Check the Transferring Internet Mail box to limit initial message transfers to header information only. A message header includes the sender's name, message subject, message priority, and other summary information. You can then scan the headers to decide which messages you want to read and retrieve as full text using the Exchange Remote Mail feature. (See Chapter 51 for more information on Remote Mail.)

Click the Login As button to enter the user name and password for access to your dial-up Internet service provider.

If you are not using Exchange's Remote Mail feature, click the Schedule button. This feature enables you to set the number of minutes to wait between new mail checks.

Personal Address Book Service

A personal address book lets you store information about the people to whom you send mail. Personal address books are stored locally on your computer. They hold a wealth of detail, making them truly useful.

If you use the Exchange defaults, the default profile (MS Exchange Settings) includes the default address book, called Personal Address Book, with an associated data file named MAILBOX.PAB. This might be all you need.

However, if you share your computer with other people or you want to organize address books by use (one for personal use and another for business, for example), you can create additional personal address book files. Note that a profile can have only one associated personal address book.

> **CAUTION**
>
> If you add a profile, it doesn't automatically include the personal address book. Even though the personal address book feature is a service, it's not listed by the Inbox Setup Wizard. You need to add this service manually after you add the new profile.

To add a new personal address book to a profile, follow these steps:

1. Open Control Panel and double-click the Mail and Fax icon. If you have more than one profile, a list of profiles is shown. Select the profile you want to modify.
2. Click the Settings tab of the Exchange Settings Properties dialog box.
3. Click Add. Select Personal Address Book from the list of available services and then click OK. This opens the Personal Address Book configuration-settings dialog box. (See Figure 50.19.)
4. Enter a name for the new personal address book. Pick something meaningful (John's Addresses, Sue's List, or Business, for example).
5. Enter a path and name for the address book data file. The filename can be anything meaningful, but you must use the .PAB extension. Click OK to complete the process.

FIGURE 50.19.

Enter a name for an address book and specify the path and name of the associated data file in the Personal Address Book tab.

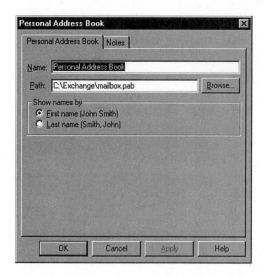

To change the personal address book associated with a profile, follow these steps:

1. Open Control Panel and double-click the Mail and Fax icon. If you have more than one profile, a list of profiles is shown. Select the profile you want to modify.

2. Click the Settings tab of the Exchange Settings Properties dialog box.

3. Select the current personal address book service. Click Remove and confirm that you want to remove this service from the current profile. (This does not delete the personal address book data file.)

4. Click Add. Select Personal Address Book from the list of available services and then click OK.

5. If you want to create a new address book for this profile, enter the new name. Next, enter a path and name for the address book data file, plus the required .PAB extension.

6. If you want to use an existing address book, enter the path and data filename or click Browse to choose from a list.

7. Click OK to complete the process.

Personal Message Store Service

A personal message store holds copies of any mail you send or receive. This information is stored locally on your computer.

If you use the Exchange defaults, the default profile, MS Exchange Settings, includes the default message store called Personal Information Store with an associated data file named MAILBOX.PST. This might be all you need.

However, if you share your computer with other people, you probably want to create a separate message store for each person. Also, unlike address books, a profile can have more than one personal message store associated with it. This is useful if you want to organize messages by category. For example, you could have one message store for archived messages and one for current messages.

To add a new personal message store to a profile, follow these steps:

1. Open Control Panel and double-click the Mail and Fax icon. If you have more than one profile, a list of profiles is shown. Select the profile you want to modify.

2. Click the Settings tab of the Exchange Settings Properties dialog box.

3. Click Add. Select Personal Folders from the list of available services and then click OK.

4. If you are adding an existing personal message store, use the File Open dialog box to select it by filename.

5. If you want to create a new message store, use the File Open dialog box to enter a path and name for the new message store data file. The filename can be anything meaningful, but the extension .PST is required.

6. Click OK to continue. This opens the Personal Folders configuration-settings dialog box. (See Figure 50.20.)

FIGURE 50.20.

Enter a name for a personal message store and specify the path and name of the associated data file in the Personal Folders dialog box.

This dialog box enables you to change the descriptive name of the message store, set a password, or compress data to save space.

CompuServe Mail Service

You can use CompuServe mail with Exchange by installing a mail-transport service provider. After the service provider is installed, you can use the CompuServe network to send and receive mail. Note that you don't have to use Exchange for CompuServe mail; you can continue to use the mail features of WinCIM, CompuServe's proprietary Windows application.

After you begin using Exchange, however, you will probably find you like it better than WinCIM for mail. In any event, you have to install the service provider if you want to use the CompuServe network as a mail transport for Exchange. CompuServe mail handles faxes and a wide range of e-mail types. CompuServe has access to many large, private, corporate mail networks; you can even access the Telex network!

The CompuServe mail service provider was originally supposed to be included in Microsoft Plus!. This did not happen, however, so you must obtain the service provider directly from CompuServe. If you already have a CompuServe account, it is easy to do.

To download and install the CompuServe service provider, follow these steps:

1. Log on to CompuServe using WinCIM.
2. Click Find and enter Exchange as the search keyword.
3. Select CS Exchange Service Provider from the list returned by the keyword search.
4. Follow the online instructions to download the file CSMAIL.EXE to your computer.
5. Log out of CompuServe and close WinCIM.
6. Copy CSMAIL.EXE to an empty working directory and launch it. This will extract the service-provider installation files from the CSMAIL.EXE archive program.
7. Open Control Panel and double-click the Mail and Fax icon. If you have more than one profile, a list of profiles is shown. Select the profile you want to use for CompuServe.
8. Click the Settings tab of the Exchange Settings Properties dialog box.
9. Click Add and then click Have Disk. Enter the path to the working directory you used in step 6. Follow the onscreen instructions to complete installation of the CompuServe service provider.

After it is installed, CompuServe appears in the list of mail services for the current profile. Select it and click Properties to see the configuration options available for the service. You already entered information for the General and Connection tabs during installation.

Click the Default Send Options tab. (See Figure 50.21.)

FIGURE 50.21.

*Use the Default Send
Options tab to control
delivery dates, set the
lifetime of unread mail,
and specify who pays for
mail-transport charges.*

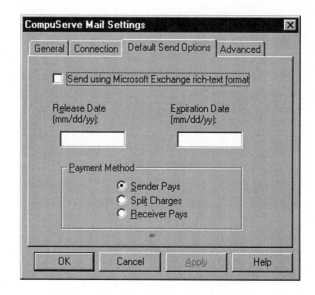

Check the Send using Microsoft Exchange rich-text format box if you send mail to other Windows users and you want to preserve text-formatting information. Note that rich-text format requires that the recipient run a compatible mail application—otherwise your message could be unreadable.

The Release Date and Expiration Date are best set when you send a specific message. Leave them blank here. If you specify a release date, a message won't be sent until that date. If you specify an expiration date, an unread message is automatically deleted from the recipient's CompuServe mailbox after that date.

The Payment Method option specifies who pays the CompuServe charge for sending a message. Unless you have prior arrangements with the recipient, leave this set to Sender Pays. Note that if you select Receiver Pays, the recipient can decline to receive your mail.

Click the Advanced tab to set advanced options. (See Figure 50.22.)

The settings on this tab apply only if you are not using the Exchange Remote Mail feature with CompuServe. The fields are self-explanatory. Note that you set Schedule Connect Times if you want to limit mail operations to specific times.

The Remote Mail feature enables you to limit initial message transfers from CompuServe to header information only. A message header includes the sender's name, message subject, message priority, and other summary information. The actual message text is not retrieved until you request it. This reduces connect time and costs, and enables you to skip unimportant messages. (See Chapter 51 for more information on Remote Mail.)

FIGURE 50.22.

Use the Advanced tab to control settings related to bulk-mail handling.

Other Exchange Settings

You have looked in detail at the individual options tabs for various mail services that you access from the Settings tab of the Exchange Settings Properties dialog box. There are two additional tabs in this dialog box that control how the various mail services in a particular profile work together: the Delivery tab and the Addressing tab.

Profile Delivery Settings

You use the Delivery tab of the Exchange Settings Properties dialog box to control which folder receives incoming mail and which transport-service priority to use when sending outgoing mail.

Click the Delivery tab. (See Figure 50.23.) Following is an explanation of how to handle the various options on this tab:

- Deliver new mail to the following location control—Use this drop-down list to set the mailbox folder that you want to receive incoming mail. Usually, incoming mail is delivered to a server-based mailbox like the one provided by Microsoft Mail. This mailbox is named Mailbox - (your name). If you want mail delivered to your personal message store instead, select Personal Folders.

- Recipient addresses are processed by these information services in the following order—This field lists the transport services available in the current profile and the priority to use when sending outgoing mail. Use this control when you have two or more transport services that can handle a particular type of mail. For example, both the Microsoft Network and the Internet Mail service providers can send Internet mail. If you want your Internet mail server to have priority when you send Internet mail, use the arrow buttons to move Internet Mail service to the top of the list.

FIGURE 50.23.

Use the Delivery tab to set which folder receives incoming mail and which transport-service priority to use when sending outgoing mail.

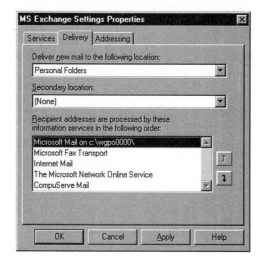

Profile Addressing Settings

You use the Addressing tab of the Exchange Settings Properties dialog box to specify how your personal address book and server address books are displayed and used.

Click the Addressing tab. (See Figure 50.24.) You can specify preferences for the following options:

- Show this address list first—Use this drop-down list to select the address book you want to open as the default.

- Keep personal addresses in—Use this to select the address book you want as the default when you add new names. Typically this is the personal address book associated with the profile.

- When sending mail, check names using these address lists in the following order— This field lists the address books available in the current profile and the priority to use when verifying an address. Before a message is sent, recipient names are checked against the various available address books to make sure the message is deliverable. Typically, you want Exchange to check a personal address book first. Setting a priority can speed up the process of verifying names. Note that you can add and remove address books here as well.

Chapter 50

FIGURE 50.24.

Use the Addressing tab to control how address books are displayed and used.

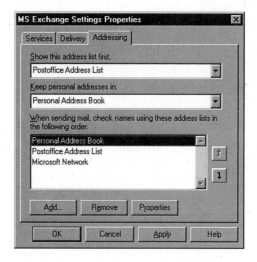

Summary

In this chapter you installed Exchange and configured one or more mail service providers. The sheer number of options makes this daunting at first. After the first one however, it really does become easier. Most mail services offer similar options and features. Also keep in mind that you haven't made any irrevocable decisions—you can always add new profiles or modify settings later. Many of the available options will make more sense once you begin to use Exchange. In Chapter 51 you will put your Exchange profile into action, sending and receiving mail. Once you've done this, you can fine-tune your profile.

Advanced Microsoft Exchange

51

by Kevin Chestnut

In Chapter 50, "Understanding and Customizing Microsoft Exchange," you learned how to configure and customize the various mail services that use the Microsoft Exchange mailbox. Using the Windows Control Panel Mail and Fax applet, you created a profile specifying your mail service preferences.

This chapter focuses on the features of the Exchange mailbox itself. After a lengthy discussion about configuring service providers, it's easy to forget that Exchange is really about sending and receiving mail quickly and easily. In this chapter, I will show you just that: how to create and send mail, how to read and respond to the mail you receive, and how to customize the look and feel of the Exchange user interface. You can judge for yourself just how close Microsoft has come to creating the true universal mailbox.

> **NOTE**
>
> Technically, the Control Panel Mail and Fax features are provided by the MAPI mail subsystem, not Exchange itself. The Mail and Fax applet is designed to configure mail services usable by *any* mail client. However, don't worry too much about confusing MAPI and Exchange at this level—Microsoft is guilty of this, too. The two products are intimately connected. Just remember that, in theory at least, the mail subsystem will support any MAPI-compatible mailbox.

The Mailbox Window

You open Exchange by double-clicking the Inbox icon on the Windows desktop or by selecting Exchange from the task bar Start button. Mail-enabled applications also open Exchange automatically, as needed. For example, Exchange opens automatically if you select the E-Mail option from the Microsoft Network opening screen.

Figure 51.1 shows the Exchange mailbox window as it appears after default installation.

The Exchange mailbox interface is similar to the Windows Explorer interface. Folders are shown in the left pane and the contents of the currently open folder are shown in the right pane. As in Explorer, items can be moved from one folder to another simply by dragging and dropping them. You can also change the size of the folder and contents panes by clicking and dragging the dividing bar between them.

Default installation includes a welcome message from Microsoft and an offer from SprintFAX. These messages are found in the Inbox folder of your Personal Folders, which by default is organized into Deleted Items, Inbox, Outbox, and Sent Items subfolders. *Personal Folders* is the default name for the personal message store created during initial installation. (You'll also see this called the *personal information store* in Microsoft documentation.) You can have more than one personal message store, and you can add other subfolders to a store. I will show you how in the section titled "Customizing Your Mailbox" later in the chapter.

FIGURE 51.1.

The Exchange mailbox interface is similar to Windows Explorer, with folders on the left and the contents of the open folder on the right.

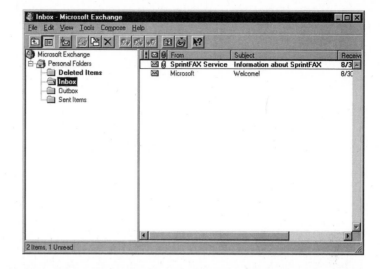

TIP

Exchange uses boldface type to show unread (unopened) mail. Unread messages and folders containing unread messages are listed in bold. Once you open a message, it is listed in regular weight type. For example, in Figure 51.1, the Welcome message has been opened, while the SprintFAX message has not. The Inbox folder is also listed in bold because it contains at least one unread message. Also note that the Deleted Items folder is in bold. This indicates that it contains one or more messages that were *deleted* without being read.

Receiving and Reading Mail

How and when Exchange receives your incoming mail depends on the types of mail services you use and the specific features supported by the service provider. There are many options:

■ Dial-up services such as the Microsoft Network or CompuServe usually check for incoming mail at the same time you connect to them to send outgoing mail. This is the default action, but you can disable it in the service provider settings. In this case, you must connect to the dial-up service and specifically check for new mail.

■ Some dial-up service providers can be set to automatically check for new mail at a scheduled time of day or at a specified interval. In this case, Exchange dials the service automatically. The CompuServe service provider supports this feature, for example. (To access this, choose Services from the Tools menu, select CompuServe, and then click the Schedule Connect Times button on the Advanced Settings tab.)

■ Locally connected services such as Microsoft Mail usually check for mail continually. However, this feature requires network support and may be disabled on your system. Alternatively, you can set the service provider to check for new mail at a specified interval. This is usually small—every 10 or 15 minutes—so it is nearly as effective as continuous checking. On the other hand, if you get a lot of mail, you might find this feature distracting. In this case, you can set a longer interval.

■ Fax services behave entirely differently because incoming fax mail is initiated by an incoming phone call from the sender. There is no checking *per se*—Exchange is aware that a new fax has arrived as soon as the transmission is successfully completed.

■ Most services, whether they are dial-up or local, can be configured to use Exchange's Remote Mail feature. Remote Mail lets you preview message headers. A message header includes the sender's name, subject, and other identifying information, but not the contents of the message itself. After reviewing the header, you decide whether or not to retrieve the entire message from the service. Remote Mail is explained in detail later in this chapter.

To review the incoming mail options available with each service, choose Services from the Exchange Tools menu. Obviously, if you have access to several mail services, the range of options can quickly become complex. The best settings for you are based on the volume and source of your incoming mail and the amount of time that is acceptable between when a message is sent and when you actually receive it.

New Mail Notification

Exchange can notify you that you have new mail waiting in several ways. To set notification options, choose Options from the Tools menu and then click the General tab. (See Figure 51.2.)

FIGURE 51.2.

The General tab of the Options dialog box lets you choose how Exchange notifies you when you receive new mail.

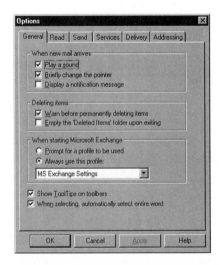

The default options are Play a sound and Briefly change the pointer. If you want to make sure that you don't miss new messages because you were away from your desktop, check the option labeled Display a notification message. Exchange will display a pop-up dialog box that you must acknowledge in order to clear it from the screen.

Checking for New Mail Immediately

To bypass service provider settings and check for new mail immediately, choose Deliver Now Using from the Tools menu. From here, you can choose All Mail Services or pick the particular service you want to use. Even though you don't have any outgoing mail to deliver (send), the menu item forces Exchange to check for incoming mail.

By default, new mail is received in the Personal Folders Inbox. You might want to specify a different Inbox if you have more than one personal message store or if you have a server-based mailbox like the one provided by Microsoft Mail. To change to a different Inbox, choose Options from the Tools menu and then click the Delivery tab. (See Figure 51.3.)

FIGURE 51.3.

The Delivery tab of the Options dialog box lets you choose which folder or folders receive incoming mail.

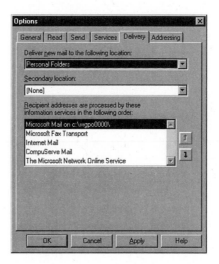

If you have more than one personal message store, choose the one to receive incoming mail from the drop-down list. With certain service providers, you might also see your server-based (remote) mailbox listed here. If you set a secondary location, the Inbox associated with the message store or service will receive copies of new mail as well.

Using the Remote Mail Feature

The Remote Mail feature of Exchange simplifies working with dial-up mail services such as the Microsoft Network or CompuServe. Remote Mail is also useful if you work out of the office with a portable computer but have a LAN-based server such as Microsoft Mail. Remote Mail allows you to work offline, reading and responding to any mail you've received. Then, when you reconnect to the server, Exchange sends accumulated outgoing mail and checks for new incoming mail, synchronizing your portable with your server-based mailbox.

With the Remote Mail feature, you connect to a dial-up service or remote mail server and preview the headers of your messages. Header preview is the key feature of Remote Mail. A message has two basic parts: the header and the message body. The header shows information about the message: who sent it, who received it, a subject line, and so on. The body of a message is its content and any attached files.

Because message headers are small, they download quickly. This saves connect time and cost. You can manage mail better by focusing on important messages and skipping or deleting the less important ones. Headers also show the size of a message and any attached files. This is a big help when you are checking messages over a relatively slow dial-up connection.

TIP

To use Exchange's Remote Mail feature, you must have previously enabled remote mail support in the desired service provider. If remote mail support is not enabled in the service provider, you won't see the mail service listed in the Remote Mail menu. Remote mail support is enabled by default for the Microsoft Network and CompuServe. Microsoft Mail also supports remote mail, but it is disabled by default. See Chapter 50 for details on configuring remote mail in each of these service providers.

To access Remote Mail, choose it from the Tools menu. Then, from the Remote Mail submenu, choose the service provider you want to access remotely. Remote Mail is managed in a separate window and each service provider has its own remote window. Figure 51.4 shows the Microsoft Network Remote Mail window.

To connect to your remote mailbox and get (or update) a list of message headers, choose Connect and Update Headers from the Tools menu. Headers are listed in the Remote Mail window.

From the list of headers, you then decide which messages to ignore, delete, or transfer into your local Inbox. Here are the steps to do this:

1. Select one or more headers and then specify the actions you want to take:

   To delete a selected message without reading it, choose Mark to Delete from the Edit menu.

FIGURE 51.4.

The Remote Mail window lets you manage dial-up mail services.

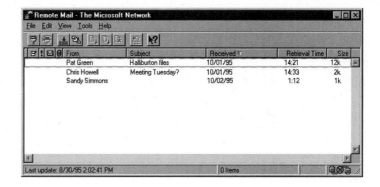

To transfer a selected message to your local Inbox and simultaneously delete it from your remote mailbox, choose Mark to Retrieve from the Edit menu.

To copy a selected message to your local Inbox and keep the original in your remote mailbox, choose Mark to Retrieve a Copy from the Edit menu.

2. Once you have marked messages for the action desired, choose Connect and Transfer Mail from the Tools menu.

3. Retrieved messages will be placed in your Inbox folder.

Unmarked headers will be ignored. If you have pending outgoing mail, it will be sent automatically when you connect to retrieve messages.

Getting the headers and retrieving the messages can be completed in a single call or two separate calls, depending on the way you configure the service provider. Service provider configuration settings are available on the Services tab of the Options dialog box. The location and wording of the setting varies among the providers, but it is generally worded this way: Automatically disconnect after getting headers. If this is set, Exchange will make separate calls to get headers and retrieve messages.

NOTE

Even though I've talked about remote mail in terms of dial-up services, certain service providers offer this feature for local connections, as well. For example, Microsoft Mail allows you to enable remote mail support with a LAN connection. This can improve performance with slow local connections or high network traffic.

Opening a Message and Attachments

To read a message, simply double-click it. This opens the message in a separate window that provides access to additional controls. Figure 51.5 shows the opened message from SprintFAX.

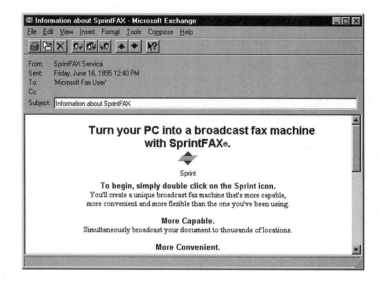

Exchange supports conventional attached files as well as embedded OLE objects. Attached files are handled by most mail servers. The content of the attached file (text, graphic, binary data, and so on) is usually identified by the filename (often by just the three-letter DOS file extension). In Exchange, you can view most common types of attached files simply by double-clicking the attached file icon.

OLE objects contain additional information about the application that created them. Messages with embedded OLE objects are generally useful only when the recipient is also running Exchange in a Windows environment. However, some service providers (the Microsoft Network is one example) automatically convert simple embedded OLE objects to attached files as needed.

Simple OLE objects are a single file containing an image, a sound, a single document from another application such as Microsoft Word, and so on. OLE objects can be considerably more complex. They can contain groups of related files including packaged executable programs. You activate an OLE object by double-clicking it. For example, the Sprint logo in Figure 51.5 is a link to an OLE object package. Double-clicking the logo executes a program that calls the SprintFAX network, steps you through opening an account, and installs the SprintFAX service provider for Exchange. This is a small example of the combined power of OLE and Exchange.

Replying to a Message

To reply to the sender of a message, choose Reply to Sender from the Compose menu (Ctrl+R is the shortcut) or click the corresponding toolbar button. To reply to all message recipients (the sender plus everyone included in the CC address field), choose Reply to All instead. Exchange addresses your reply automatically.

TIP

You can see what a toolbar button does by moving the cursor over it and pausing for a second or two. This pops up a brief description called a *ToolTip*. For a more detailed description, click and hold the button without releasing it. This displays additional information in the status bar at the bottom of the window. Move the cursor off the toolbar button before you release the mouse button to avoid activating the command itself. If the pop-up ToolTips don't appear, be sure to check the option labeled Show ToolTips on toolbars, which is found on the General tab of the Options dialog box. (Refer to Figure 51.2.)

Reply commands are found on both the message form and the main Exchange window. If you want to reply to a message without opening it, highlight the message listing in the contents pane and then choose Reply.

Forwarding a Message

To forward a message to one or more people, choose Forward from the Compose menu (Ctrl+F is the shortcut) or click the corresponding toolbar button. Exchange copies the existing message and attachments to a new message form and positions you in the To address field.

The Read tab of the Options menu controls how Exchange prepares a message for you to forward or reply to. To set these options, choose Options from the Tools menu and then click the Read tab. (See Figure 51.6.)

If you want the recipient to receive the original message, check the option labeled Include the original text when replying. If this option is checked, you probably also want to check the option labeled Close the original item. You won't need to refer to the original because Exchange will have copied it into the body of your outgoing message. To help differentiate your reply or forwarding comments from the original message, check the option labeled Indent the original text when replying. You can also click Font to specify a different typeface for your text.

FIGURE 51.6.

The Read tab of the Options menu controls how Exchange prepares a message for you to forward or reply to.

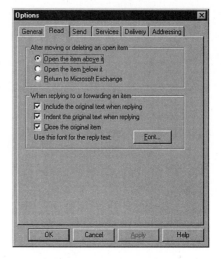

Deleting Messages

To delete an open message, choose Delete from the File menu (Ctrl+D is the shortcut) or click the corresponding toolbar button. To delete messages listed in the folder contents pane, highlight the message or messages and press the Delete key (the other methods work, too, but the Delete key is easiest to remember).

Deleted messages are not discarded immediately. Instead, they are moved to the Deleted Items subfolder of the message store. You can recover a deleted message by dragging it out of this folder. To delete a message permanently, highlight the listing in the Deleted Items folder and press the Delete key again.

Messages in the Deleted Items folder are handled according to the preferences you set in the General tab of the Options dialog box. (Refer to Figure 51.2.) If you want deleted messages to remain until you delete them manually, be certain *not* to check the option labeled Empty 'Deleted Items' folder upon exiting. In general, it's a good idea to check the option labeled Warn before permanently deleting items. Remember, a permanently deleted message is *not* recoverable.

Creating and Sending Mail

Exchange makes it easy to create and send mail without worrying about the underlying mail services or their capabilities. To create a new message, choose New Message from the Compose menu (Ctrl+N is the shortcut) or click the corresponding toolbar button. This opens a New Message form. (See Figure 51.7.)

FIGURE 51.7.

Exchange's default New Message form lets you compose e-mail for many different service providers.

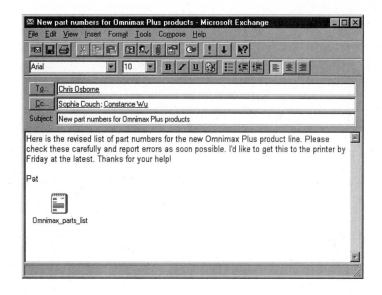

The New Message Form

Exchange's New Message form lets you compose e-mail for many different service providers. The form is effectively a mini word processor that provides sophisticated text formatting and layout control. From here, you can attach files and embed OLE objects. In addition, the form provides extended addressing features including access to your personal address book and service provider address books.

> **NOTE**
>
> The default New Message form is designed for text messages with attached data files. This is appropriate for Microsoft Mail, CompuServe mail, and other text-based services. But what about mail in a nontext format such as fax, voice, or video?
>
> Exchange's designers thought of this, too! A service provider can supply alternate forms for composing and reading messages. These alternate forms are associated with the message formats the service handles. Therefore, a voice mail service supplies a form better suited for recording voice messages and a future video mail service can provide an appropriate video form.
>
> If you installed the Microsoft Fax service provider, you will see this feature applied to fax messages. The Compose menu lists New Fax along with New Message. This opens the Create New Fax application provided with Microsoft Fax. Incoming faxes are automatically associated with the Fax Viewer application, as well.

Addressing a Message

When the New Message form opens, you are positioned in the To address field automatically. If you know the recipient's address, you can type it directly. More often, you will click the To button to access address books and extended addressing information. (See Figure 51.8.)

FIGURE 51.8.

The Address Book dialog box provides access to address books and extended addressing information.

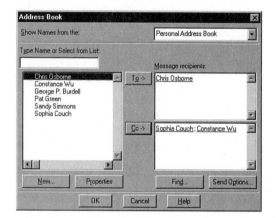

Show Names From is a drop-down list of all available address books. The Address Book dialog box opens the default address book specified in the Addressing tab of the Options dialog box (available from the Tools menu). A message can be addressed to recipients selected from several different address books. You can type a recipient's name in the space provided or select from the list. If you're not sure, click Find to search the current list.

Click New to add an address book entry for a new recipient. To edit the address book entry for an existing recipient, right-click the person's name and select Properties from the pop-up menu. Here are some other handy features:

- Click Properties to access the service provider configuration settings of the current address book.

- If the service provider supports it, you can click Send Options to set special delivery conditions (mark a message as urgent, for example).

- Once you have typed or selected a recipient's name, click To or CC to add it to the appropriate list.

- To remove a name from To or CC, highlight the name and press the Delete key.

NOTE

Some service providers support BCC (blind carbon copy) addressing in addition to CC (carbon copy). Unlike with CC, recipients of a BCC message won't see the names of the other people who received a copy of the message. If BCC is supported, the Address Book dialog box will have three list boxes instead of two.

Personal Distribution Lists

The Personal Address Book service provider supports personal distribution lists. This simplifies the routine job of sending the same message to a group of people.

Here's how you create a distribution list while addressing a message:

1. Click the New button on the Address Book dialog box.

2. Select Personal Distribution List from the listing of available address types.

3. Enter an identifying name for the list in the field provided on the New Personal Distribution List Properties dialog box. (See Figure 51.9.)

4. Use the To and CC buttons to add recipient names to the list.

5. Click OK when you are done. In the future, select the list by name to automatically address a new message to the entire group of recipients.

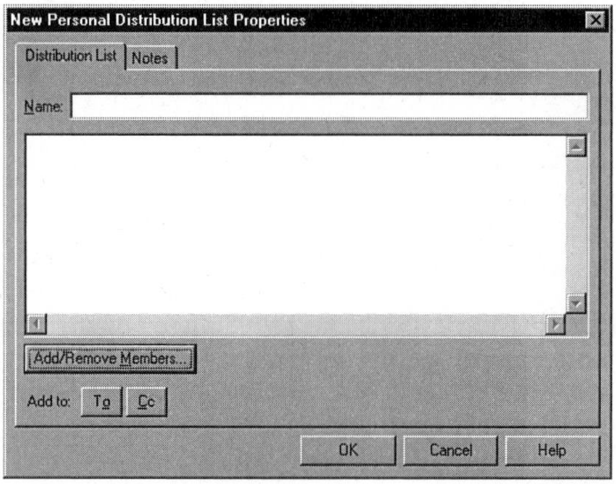

FIGURE 51.9.

The Personal Address Book also supports personal distribution lists.

Formatting a Message

Exchange supports rich text format (RTF) files. This is a common text format originally designed to preserve layout information in files swapped between different word processing systems. The New Message form is a mini text editor with familiar controls for paragraph formatting (flush left, center, and flush right), changing fonts and font attributes (bold, italic, and underline), indenting paragraphs, and creating bulleted lists. The interface is similar to Microsoft Word and other word processing programs.

This is an amazing change from the traditional e-mail world of plain text and monospaced fonts. If you've ever tried to create a bulleted list using hard returns and spacing tricks, you'll love the addition of these simple format controls. This new-found richness is both good and bad, however:

- Formatting is only meaningful if the recipient's e-mail viewer also handles RTF files. For all practical purposes, this means another Exchange user. While it's possible for someone without Exchange to open a message using an RTF-compatible word processor, it's certainly not convenient! This situation will change as other vendors release next-generation mail products.

- Just because you can apply fancy formatting, it doesn't mean you should. If modest formatting makes your message easier to read or understand, use it. On the other hand, a heavy mix of font changes, boldface, underlining, and italics will guarantee pain for the reader. E-mail is about quick, concise communication. In this case, less is definitely more.

Attaching Files to a Message

Exchange supports conventional file attachments to an e-mail message. Attached files are handled by most mail servers. The contents of the attached file can be text, graphic, binary data, and so on. In attaching files to a message, you're making the assumption that the recipient can handle the files as needed. Typically, you might explain what an attached file contains in the body of your message.

Here's how to attach a file to a message:

1. Position the cursor in your message at the point where you want the file placed.
2. Choose File from the New Message form Insert menu.
3. Type the name of the file you want or choose it from the dialog box.
4. If the file contains text, and you want the text inserted at the current cursor location, select the option labeled Insert as text only. (The default option is Insert as an attachment.)

5. If you want the message to link to the original file, check the option labeled Link attachment to original item.

6. Click OK.

If you choose the Attachment option, Exchange will add an icon to the body of your message. If the file type is one Windows understands, the icon will correspond to the file contents or the application that created it. Figure 51.10 shows a message with a variety of attached files.

FIGURE 51.10.

A message can contain attached files, messages, or folders. These attachments are represented by icons that indicate the file type or the application that created the file.

You can also attach another message or message folder. To do this, choose Message from the Insert menu, and then select the desired message or folder from your mailbox. If you want the message text inserted, select the option labeled Insert as text only. If you want the message to link to the original file, check the option labeled Link attachment to original item.

CAUTION

Linking a file or message is useful when the message recipient has network access to the original itself. Your message will contain a pointer to the original file or message rather than an attached copy. This reduces the size of your message and requires fewer server resources. The savings can be significant if a message containing attachments is being sent to a large list of people.

Linked files are useless, however, to recipients who can't access the original file. This means anyone who has an account on a different mail system or anyone without permission to access the files you attach. Unless you're sure a recipient has the same level of network access to a file that you do, don't link it.

Service providers perform any translation needed to handle attached files. For example, the Microsoft Plus! Internet Mail service provider can UUENCODE or MIME (standard Internet encoding methods) attached files automatically.

Embedding Objects in a Message

As a Windows application, Exchange is fully OLE compatible. OLE allows applications to share information in the form of objects. An object can be a picture, a spreadsheet, a Word document, or any other item created by an application. Unlike file attachments, OLE objects contain additional information about the application that created them and the type of information they contain. The recipient can activate an embedded object to view it, hear it, or modify it, with any application program that understands how to handle the object type(s) involved.

All this might sound a bit vague, and it is. OLE is abstract, complex, and powerful. It is designed to separate what an application can do from the application itself. This lets people share results—not files and applications. Couple this with Exchange's promise to make it easy to share information anytime, anywhere, and any place, and you can see the potential.

The reality for now, though, is that messages with embedded OLE objects are generally only useful when the recipient is also running Exchange in a Windows environment. In general, attached files are more likely to be usable.

Note that some service providers (the Microsoft Network is one example) automatically convert certain types of OLE objects to attached files as needed. This means that, in some cases, you can use OLE with less concern for your message recipients' capabilities.

Here's how to embed an OLE object:

1. Position the cursor in your message at the point where you want the object placed.
2. Choose Object from the New Message form Insert menu.
3. If you want to create a new object, select Create New; otherwise, select Create From File.
4. Select an object type from the list. For example, the object type can be Bitmapped Graphic, Media Clip, and so on. The list of object types available depends on the OLE-compatible applications you have installed on your system.
5. If you want the object to appear as an icon, check the option labeled Display as icon; otherwise, the actual object will appear in the body of your message (when possible).
6. Click OK.

If you are creating a new object, the system may start an OLE application for you to use, or it may add the necessary controls within the New Message form. When you are finished creating the object, close the application or controls. If you are asked to update the object, choose Yes. Figure 51.11 shows the Insert Object dialog box.

FIGURE 51.11.

Exchange is fully OLE compatible. You can use the Insert Object dialog box to embed OLE objects directly in a message.

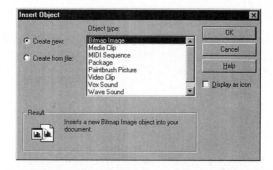

TIP

You can also use the system Clipboard to paste objects created in another application into a message. To do this, start the application and use it to create an object (or open a file that contains a previously created object). Choose Copy from the application File menu and then close the application. If you're asked whether or not you want the Clipboard contents made available to other programs, answer Yes. Return to Exchange and choose Paste or Paste Special from the New Message form Edit menu.

The Paste command is available when the Clipboard object is a common type understood by Windows (text, sound, a bitmapped graphic, and so on). The Paste Special command is available when the Clipboard object was created by an OLE application. Paste Special includes commands to let you embed the object or convert it to a common type (when possible).

Sending a Message

After you have addressed and composed a message and have attached any companion files or objects, it's time to send the message:

1. When your new message is complete, choose Send from the New Message form File menu. This transfers the message to your Outbox. What happens next depends on the mail services you use:

   - If you are using Microsoft Mail or another mail server with a LAN connection and you are not using remote mail with the LAN, messages in your Outbox will be transferred to the mail server for delivery. This is automatic, but it might take a few minutes, depending on the configuration and capabilities of the server. If this is the case, skip to Step 4.

   - If you are using remote mail (or a dial-up service), the Send command doesn't really send your message. Instead, it queues it for sending the next time you connect to the remote service. Continue with Step 2.

2. Open the Outbox subfolder. This lists all outgoing messages pending delivery.

3. If you want your messages sent immediately, choose Deliver Now Using from the Tools menu. If all the messages are to be delivered using the same service, you can choose the service by name from the submenu. If several services are involved or if you're not sure, choose All Services from the submenu; otherwise, messages will remain in your Outbox until the next time Exchange is connected to the remote service.

4. After your messages are copied to the mail server (or remote service) for delivery, they will be moved from the Outbox to the Sent Items subfolder. You can leave sent messages here, drag them to another folder for filing, or delete them. Note that this is the default behavior. If you don't want Exchange to save your outgoing messages in the Sent Items folder, deselect the option labeled Save a copy of the item in the Sent Items folder. This option is found in the Send tab of the Options dialog box.

If a message is undeliverable for some reason (usually because of a bad mailing address), Exchange will send a message notifying you of the problem. In this case, the undelivered outgoing message will remain in the Outbox. Correct the problem and send message again.

Finding Messages

Exchange makes it easy for you to keep and organize your mail. As a result, you'll eventually accumulate a lot of it. No matter how well organized your foldering scheme is, you are bound to misplace something important. The Find command gives you a powerful alternative to scanning messages and subject lines. Choose Find from the Tools menu to open the Find dialog box. (See Figure 51.12.)

FIGURE 51.12.

The Find dialog box, which lets you search for messages based on addressing information, subject, or contents.

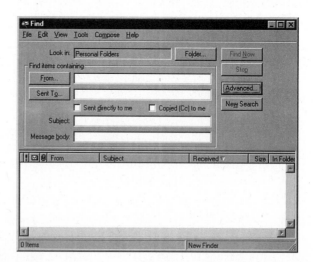

The Find dialog box is self-explanatory. Click Folder to specify a subfolder (such as Inbox) or an entire personal message store (and all its subfolders). The Stop button lets you end a search that is currently in progress. If you need to search more using complex criteria, click Advanced. (See Figure 51.13.) This adds searching based on message size, dates, and various message properties (read, unread, urgent, and so on).

FIGURE 51.13.

The Advanced dialog box, which lets you search based on size, dates, and other message conditions.

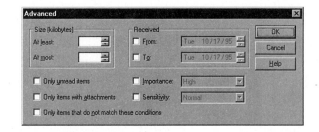

Customizing Your Mailbox

Exchange's user interface includes options available in many other Windows 95 programs, including Windows Explorer. You can customize the look of the mailbox window and the toolbar, list messages in a preferred order, and add new subfolders to help organize your personal folders (or any other personal message store).

> **NOTE**
>
> Microsoft designed Exchange with the goal of supporting as many different mail services as possible—including services that aren't available yet, such as video mail. As part of this support, service providers can extend the Exchange user interface itself.
>
> I've already mentioned that service providers can supply alternate forms for composing and reading messages (Microsoft Fax, for example). In addition, providers can add menu items, toolbar buttons, and tabs to the Options dialog box, the Find dialog box, and others.
>
> As a result, your Exchange mailbox interface might appear somewhat different from the examples given in this chapter. Generally, service provider extensions are logical and easy to understand. If you're not sure how to use a particular feature, check online help—service providers can extend the Exchange help system, as well.

The Message Folders List

I've already mentioned that you can resize the folder list and folder contents panes by clicking and dragging the divider bar between the panes. To hide the folder list altogether, unselect Folders in the View menu.

To add new subfolders to a personal message store, choose New Folder from the File menu. To delete an existing subfolder as well as any messages it contains, select the subfolder and then press the Delete key.

You can rename any subfolder you create. To do this, choose Rename from the File menu. Note that you cannot rename or delete the Deleted Items, Inbox, Outbox, or Sent Items subfolders. These are required by Exchange.

The Folder Contents List

The folder contents window shows column details about any messages it contains. By default, these columns are Importance (abbreviated as an exclamation point), Item Type (an envelope or other icon), Attachment (a paper clip), From, Subject, Date Received, and Size.

To change the width of any column, click the left edge and drag it in or out. To change the order of the columns (or to add or remove columns), choose Columns from the View menu. The Columns dialog box includes a wide range of options. (See Figure 51.14.)

FIGURE 51.14.

The Columns dialog box lets you change the size, order, and type of columns shown in the folder contents window.

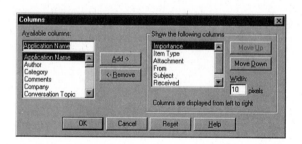

You can sort messages by any particular column attribute as well. To do this, simply click the column heading. For example, if you click the From column, messages are listed in alphabetical order by sender's name. To sort in reverse order, right-click the column and choose Descending from the pop-up list. A small arrow in the column heading shows sorting up (ascending) or down (descending).

Sorting options are available from the View menu as well. But clicking the column headings is faster and easier.

The Toolbar

To hide the toolbar, deselect Toolbar on the View menu. To change the order of the toolbar buttons (or to add or remove buttons), choose Customize Toolbar from the Tools menu. (See Figure 51.15.)

FIGURE 51.15.

The Customize Toolbar dialog box lets you change the order and grouping of buttons, or add or remove buttons, as needed.

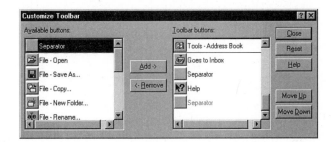

The Separator "button" adds a space so that you can create groups of buttons. You can have as many separators as you want.

> **TIP**
>
> Service providers can add to the list of available buttons. After you install a new service provider, check the Customize Toolbar dialog box. You might just find a handy shortcut or two for the new service that you can add to your toolbar.

The Options Dialog Box

We've looked at the Tools menu Options dialog box a number of times already. You should be familiar with most of the tabs. (Refer to Figure 51.2.)

It's a good idea to click through the tabs to review your options. We discussed the General and Read tabs earlier in this chapter. The Services, Delivery, and Addressing tabs are the same ones found in the Windows Control Panel Mail and Fax applet. These are discussed in detail in Chapter 50. The Services tab settings are also accessible separately under Services on the Tools menu.

TIP

The General tab (shown in Figure 51.2) includes a critical setting if you use more than one Exchange profile. Be sure to select the option labeled Prompt for a profile to be used, which appears in the section titled When starting Microsoft Exchange. Otherwise, Exchange will start with the profile shown under the option labeled Always use this profile.

If you share your computer with another user or have different profiles for local and remote use, this is potentially confusing because it's not obvious which profile you are using. Once you start Exchange with the wrong profile, you'll have to change profiles here, and then close and restart the program.

The only remaining tab we haven't discussed is Send. (See Figure 51.16.) This tab controls default return receipt, message priority, and message sensitivity settings

To specify a return receipt for your message, choose the option labeled The item has been read. This will notify you when the recipient has opened the message. To be notified when a message makes it to a recipient's mailbox, choose the option labeled The item has been delivered.

The options in the Set Sensitivity list identify the nature of your message. Normal, Personal, and Confidential are informational. Private actually prohibits changes to your original message if it is forwarded or included in a reply.

FIGURE 51.16.

The Send tab controls default return receipt, message priority, and message sensitivity settings.

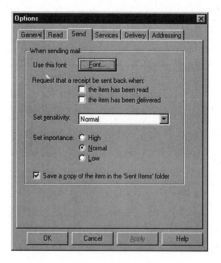

The Set Importance options identify the priority of your message: High, Normal, or Low.

> **NOTE**
>
> Service providers can add tabs to the Options dialog box. If you see tabs in addition to those shown here, be sure to investigate them. If you have questions about settings on a tab, click Help. Service providers add information to Exchange's help system, as well.

Summary

You've now seen most of the cool features available with Exchange and the current service providers. Along the way, I've shown you all the potential pitfalls, as well. You're on your own now. Please explore.

Exchange is a powerful product that will continue to improve and expand. Microsoft is hard at work on products that will make Exchange the foundation of a new generation of software for collaboration and simplified work flow. In addition, many other companies have announced exciting new products based on Exchange. If you're like most busy professionals, you've probably wondered how in the world you ever got along before e-mail. In time, I can guarantee that you'll wonder how you got along without Exchange.

Schedule+ on a Network

52

by Jeff Steinmetz

If you have ever tried to coordinate the scheduling of a conference room, or been sent in circles trying to determine which meeting times are best for everyone, then you will appreciate the use of Schedule+ in group-enabled mode.

Think about how you currently schedule a meeting in your organization. First, you have to determine when the conference room is available. Then, if you need the overhead projector, you have to determine whether it is available at the same time. What if three people can make it at that time, but two others can't? In that case, it is back to the drawing board to reschedule the conference room and overhead projector. Then you have to reconfirm the availability of the attendees. Round and round it goes, where it stops Schedule+ knows.

Setting Up Schedule+ in Group-Enabled Mode

In order to use Schedule+ to coordinate meetings, schedule resources, and track the availability of co-workers, your organization should make a conscious decision that everyone will use Schedule+. Technically speaking, you need to run Schedule+ in *group-enabled* mode. Each user needs MAPI 1.0 installed (this is done automatically under Windows 95 when you set up Microsoft Exchange) and a valid mail account on one of the following three supported mail services:

- Windows 95 Workgroup Post Office
- Microsoft Mail 3.*x* server
- Microsoft Exchange server

For details on how to set up mail on your network, refer to Chapter 48, "Office on a Network."

After the preceding conditions are met, you can configure Schedule+ at each user's workstation to work in group-enabled mode. When you first start Schedule+, the user will be queried with the Group Enabling dialog box. (See Figure 52.1.) Select the Yes, work in group-enabled mode option. You will be presented with this dialog box each time Schedule+ is started, unless you enable the check box next to Don't ask me this question again.

These choices are presented for users who want to use Schedule+ in standalone mode, even though they are networked to a mail service.

TIP

After you select to work in standalone mode and disable the Group Enabling dialog box shown in Figure 52.1, you will not be able to work in group-enabled mode, even if your station is properly configured for mail. The network administrator can re-enable this dialog box by updating the following registry entries:

```
HKEY_CURRENT_USER\Software\Microsoft\Schedule+\Application
```

The entry `MailDisabled` should be changed to 0:

```
HKEY_LOCAL_MACHINE\SOFTWARE\Microsoft\Schedule+\Application
```

The entry `MAPIPresent` should be changed to 0.

FIGURE 52.1.

The Group Enabling dialog box enables you to determine whether you want to work in group-enabled mode or standalone mode.

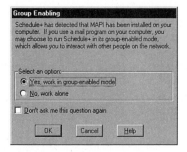

Creating and Configuring Accounts for Users and Resources

Schedule+ is tightly integrated with your mail account. If mail has not been started yet, you will be prompted for your mailbox name and password. The account name you enter here has been assigned by the administrator who set up your mail account. The mailbox account will be slightly different from your full name because it is limited to 10 characters, and does not allow spaces. In Chapter 48 you created a mail account for a fictitious user, Jan Smith. In this case, *jansm* was used for the mailbox ID.

> **NOTE**
>
> When your mailbox account was created, your full name was supplied. The only time you will see this cryptic mailbox id is when you first log on to mail or Schedule+. All correspondence through mail will show your full name. In addition, when you invite participants to a meeting, you can use their full names or browse the address book, which also lists full names.

Configuring Options for Your Account

After you log onto your Schedule+ account for the first time, you will want to verify your options as follows:

1. Select Options from the Tools menu.

2. Select the General tab. You will be presented with the options shown in Figure 52.2:

Calendar name—By default, the calendar name will be your full name. Change this if required.

Week starts on—Verify that this option is set to Monday if your office works Monday through Friday. Otherwise, set it accordingly.

Day starts at/Day ends at—Set the start and end times to match the hours you are in the office. After you begin to use the Meeting Wizard, you will see why setting the correct range for the work week and business hours is important.

FIGURE 52.2.

Use the General tab in the Options dialog box to set your scheduling preferences.

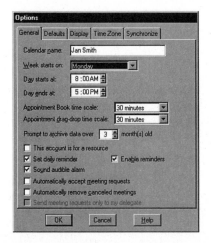

NOTE

Skip to the final three options at the bottom of the dialog box. The others are not directly related to this discussion at this point.

Automatically accept meeting requests/Automatically remove canceled meetings— Each time you are invited to a meeting, or a meeting is canceled, you will be sent mail that enables you to confirm the changes to your schedule. If you enable these options, you will not receive any notifications via mail. If you decide to go this route, you will need to check your schedule frequently, as the organizer of the meeting will assume that you will be attending. In most cases, you will want to leave these settings disabled.

Send meeting requests only to my delegate—If you want a delegate (previously Schedule+ 1.0 called this an *assistant*) to receive meeting requests, select this option. A delegate will be responsible for accepting and declining meetings on your behalf. Before you can use this option, a delegate must be assigned to your Schedule+ account (this is discussed later in the section "Setting Access Permissions and Creating Delegates for Your Schedule").

3. Select the Synchronize tab. You will be presented the options shown in Figure 52.3:

Synchronize interval in minutes—This option enables you to specify how often your current schedule will be updated to your mail account. Scheduling decisions by others are based on the most up-to-date information found on the mail server. Keep this interval frequent to avoid scheduling conflicts.

Always synchronize upon exit—This synchronizes your schedule every time you exit Schedule+. In most cases, you will want to leave this option enabled.

Work primarily from local file—The schedule you maintain is stored over the network in your mail account. If you are running Schedule+ from a laptop, you may want to have access to your schedule if you are not connected to your network. Select this option to create a local schedule file to store offline information. Keep in mind that scheduling conflicts will occur unless you keep your local file synchronized with your mail account on the network. You can use the Synchronize Now button to force the schedule stored on your hard drive to be updated to the mail server.

4. Select OK to accept the changes.

FIGURE 52.3.

The Synchronize tab of the Options dialog box enables you to determine when to synchronize your schedule with your mail server.

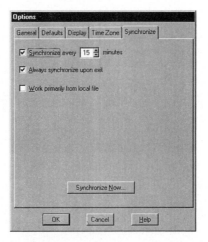

Setting Access Permissions and Creating Delegates for Your Schedule

Schedule+ enables you to configure how your schedule can be accessed. In addition, you may create a delegate for your account. By default, only you can open your schedule file. These permissions should be viewed as functionality above and beyond what is needed by Schedule+ to perform its standard appointment scheduling. In other words, there are no access permission settings that will interfere with the Meeting Wizard's capability to query your schedule for your availability, or for others to request meetings with you. The access permissions options are intended to control access to your schedule file for direct manipulation and for assigning a delegate to your account. The following steps are an example of how you might set up access permissions and create a delegate:

1. Select Set Access Permissions from the Tools menu. The Set Access Permissions dialog box appears. (See Figure 52.4.)

2. Select the Users tab.

3. This dialog box enables you to set up access permissions to your schedule information. The Default user controls how your schedule can be accessed. For example, to give everyone the capability to open your schedule for reading only, set the User role in the Permission Details area to Read.

FIGURE 52.4.

You use the Permissions dialog box to control how others can access your schedule.

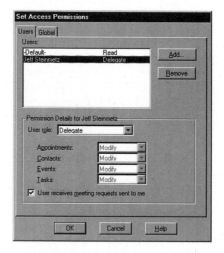

4. If you want a delegate to receive and approve meeting request on your behalf, select the Add... button to display the postoffice address book. Select the delegate. In the Permission Details area, select Delegate as this user's role. Notice that this enables the option for the user to receive meeting requests: Leave this selected.

5. You may continue to give other specific users one of several access permissions, such as

    None—Provides no permissions to the selected user.

    Read—The selected user receives read-only access, except for items marked Private.

    Create—The selected user can read existing items and create new items, but not items marked Private.

    Modify—The selected user can read and modify existing items, but not items marked Private.

    Delegate—The selected user can read existing items and modify them in the area to which this permission is assigned, including items marked Private.

Owner—The selected user can modify your entire schedule. Owners can view and modify private items in your schedule and can change users' access permissions for your schedule. This provides full control to your schedule, as if you were accessing it yourself.

Delegate Owner—This is the same as Owner, but adds the ability to send and receive meeting messages on your behalf.

Custom—This enables you to specify access rights to the individual sections of your schedule: Appointments, Contacts, Events, and Tasks.

Creating an Account for a Resource

If you create accounts for resources such as conference rooms, A/V equipment, or technicians, Schedule+ will aid in scheduling their availability just as is done for users. The following steps used to create an account for a resource are similar to creating one for a user:

1. Create a new mail account—Have the administrator of the postoffice create a new account. For example, create an account with the name *Conference Room A.* The administrator of the account might want to make the password unique in order to restrict access to the resources schedule information. See Chapter 48 for more information on creating mail accounts.

2. Log on to Schedule+ as the resource—When you start Schedule+, log on using the mailbox name assigned to the resource in step 1.

3. Set Options/General—Select Options from the Tools menu. Verify that the calendar name matches the name of the resource. Enable the check box next to This account is for a resource. If you want the resource to maintain its schedule unattended, enable the checkmarks next to Automatically accept meeting requests and Automatically remove canceled meetings.

4. Assign a delegate—This step is optional. For example, if a technician or a member of the building support staff is required to make arrangements for A/V equipment or a conference room, you will want to make them the delegates for the resource. In this case, follow the steps outlined in the previous section, which covered setting access permissions and delegates.

Scheduling Meetings

At this point, all your users and resources should be set up and ready to accept appointments. Now you can begin to put Schedule+ to use. You will use the Meeting Wizard to quickly create appointments that work for everyone. You also will schedule meetings at times you specify, without using the Meeting Wizard. After you schedule the meetings, you will learn how meetings are accepted or declined via mail. Finally, you will learn how to cancel a meeting and automatically inform all attendees of the cancellation.

Using the Meeting Wizard

The Meeting Wizard is used to automatically search for blocks of time that accommodate every person and resource you invite. In this example, you will require the attendance of a few people, schedule a location, and request a resource:

1. By default, the Meeting Wizard will scan for blocks of time, starting from the current date and time. If you want to start the scan from a different location, switch to the Planner tab and highlight an area to begin the search.

2. Click the Meeting Wizard icon on the toolbar, or select Make Meeting from the Tools menu.

3. When the Meeting Wizard starts, the first Meeting Wizard dialog box appears. (See Figure 52.5.) Select the types of attendees to be scheduled for your meeting. In this example, select required attendees, a location, and a resource. Select Next.

FIGURE 52.5.

The Meeting Wizard enables you to select who and what you want to schedule for a meeting.

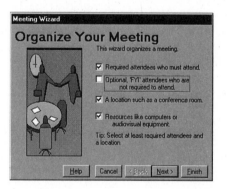

4. The Meeting Wizard will prompt you for the required attendees. (See Figure 52.6.) You have the option of typing in each name, separated by semicolons (;), or selecting Pick Attendees to open the postoffice address list. After you choose the attendees, select Next.

5. Because a meeting location was requested, the next dialog box requests that you enter the location you want to use. Figure 52.7 shows Conference Room A as the location. Remember, Conference Room A was set up ahead of time as a resource. Select Next.

6. You should enter any required resources in this next dialog box. (See Figure 52.8.) Just as the conference room was previously selected as a location, Overhead Projector is the selected resource. Select Next.

FIGURE 52.6.

Select the attendees required for your meeting.

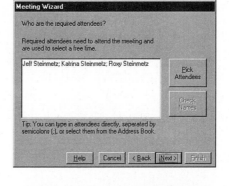

FIGURE 52.7.

Select the location in which you want to hold the meeting.

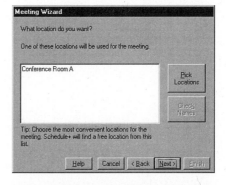

FIGURE 52.8.

Select the Overhead Projector as a required resource.

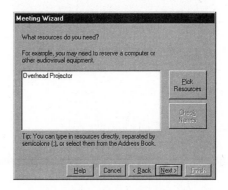

7. At this point, you need to determine how long the meeting is going to run and how long it takes people to get to the meeting. These parameters determine the block of time that the Meeting Wizard will search for, in order to accommodate all of the required attendees and resources. For this example, request a 2-hour meeting. (See Figure 52.9.) Because the office and the conference room are located in the same building, select 1 minute as the travel time to and from the meeting. Select Next.

FIGURE 52.9.

To help the Meeting Wizard find a block of time, enter the meeting length and travel time to and from the meeting.

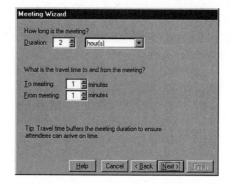

8. The next dialog box enables you to restrict the meeting to a range of time and particular days of the week. (See Figure 52.10.) By default, these are the values you entered as options when you configured your workday and work week. For this example, you want to find a block of time anywhere between 9:00AM and 5:00PM, during any weekday. Select Next.

FIGURE 52.10.

Use this dialog box to narrow down the time and date of your meeting.

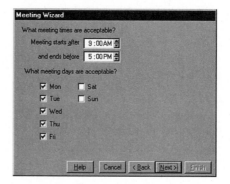

9. At this point, the Meeting Wizard will search the schedules of all those invited, including resources. It will then display an available time that satisfies all the available criteria supplied by you up to this point. Figure 52.11 shows that the Meeting Wizard has found a block of time on November 22, from 1:00PM to 3:00PM. It also provides a summarized version of the planner, enabling you to view the times before and after the proposed meeting. Color-coded bars show up in the planner to signify busy times that correspond to the required attendees, optional attendees, resources, and yourself. If you don't like the time that the Meeting Wizard has selected for you, continue to select the Pick Next Time button until you are satisfied with the results. Select Next.

FIGURE 52.11.

The Meeting Wizard displays its suggestions for the meeting time.

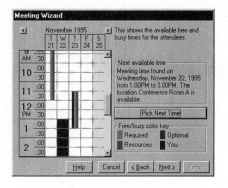

10. When you are ready to request the meeting select the Finish button. A mail message will be created that requests attendance to your meeting. The conference room and the overhead projector will be reserved for you. Figure 52.12 shows that you have added a subject to your mail message, and you have supplied an agenda in the text of your message. The information you place in the body of a message is preserved as part of the meeting information. This information shows up on the Notes tab when you double-click the appointment from within Schedule+.

FIGURE 52.12.

The Meeting Wizard creates a mail message with the requested appointment.

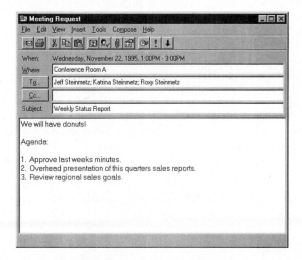

11. Select Send from the File menu, or click the Send icon on the toolbar to mail the meeting request. You have successfully created an appointment for all to attend.

Using the Planner to Schedule Meetings

You can schedule the same meeting manually from within the planner. Here's how:

1. Select the Planner tab on your schedule.
2. Click the Invite button and select the required attendees, optional attendees, and a resource, such as Conference Room A. Figure 52.13 shows the selections made for this example. Select OK.

FIGURE 52.13.

Invite attendees to your meeting.

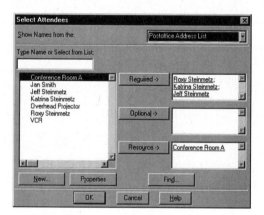

3. After the attendees are invited, your planner will be marked with color-coded bars, reflecting the free/busy status of everyone, including yourself. Figure 52.14 shows a sample calendar with these markings. Highlight an area on the calendar for your meeting, avoiding areas that signify an invited attendee as busy.
4. A mail message will be created requesting attendance of your meeting. Select Send from the File menu, or click the Send icon on the toolbar. Your meeting has been scheduled.

Chapter 52

FIGURE 52.14.

The Planner tab shows the availability of invited attendees.

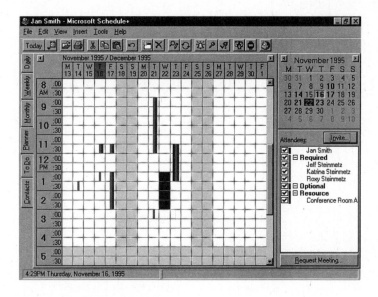

Accepting and Declining Appointments

Unless you enable automatic acceptance of meetings, you should review your mail frequently for meeting requests. Figure 52.15 shows a typical meeting request opened from your in box.

FIGURE 52.15.

A Schedule+ mail message requesting attendance of a meeting. You may accept or decline the request.

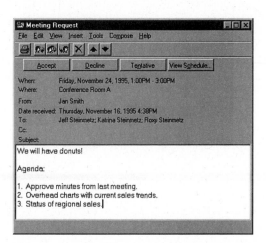

The buttons across the top of the Meeting Request dialog box enable you to accept the request, decline the request, tentatively schedule the request, or view your schedule before making the decision. The decision you make is mailed back to the originator of the message. (See Figure 52.16.) Use the body of the message to add any additional text to the response.

FIGURE 52.16.

Accepting a meeting request.

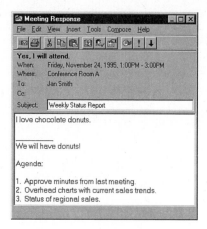

Reviewing Your Schedule, Canceling a Meeting

You can at any time double-click on an appointment in your schedule to review or edit its information. Figure 52.17 shows the information for the appointment you just accepted. If you need to cancel the appointment, select the Delete button. Use this procedure if you created the original appointment. After you delete an appointment, you will be presented with the option to send a cancellation notice to everyone.

FIGURE 52.17.

Reviewing appointment information.

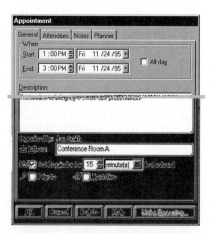

WARNING

When you select Delete you will *not* be given an opportunity to cancel your actions. Schedule+ does not confirm the deletion the way to which you are accustomed (that is, displaying a message box that asks Are you sure you want to delete this item, Yes/No?).

Summary

This chapter walks you through the requirements for using Schedule+ in group-enabled mode. With Schedule+ group-enabled, you are able to create appointments that conformed to the schedule of several attendees. At the same time, you reserve resources for the meeting such as a conference room or A/V equipment. The Meeting Wizard helps you find a block of time that meets the requirements you set forth for the appointment. The chapter finishes with a look at how users receive the appointment requests through mail. The recipients are able to accept or decline a meeting request right from the mail message.

PART

Extending Office

Getting Started with VBA

by Paul
McFedries and
David Medinets

53

IN THIS CHAPTER

Access and Excel support Microsoft's Visual Basic for Applications programming language (which is referred to as *VBA*). Excel was the first program to include VBA, but now other Microsoft applications feature VBA as well. It's also possible that Microsoft will license the technology to other vendors so that they can incorporate VBA into their applications. At the very least, you're likely to see other applications and programming languages that are "VBA compatible."

This chapter introduces you to VBA and shows you how to use this powerful tool to create simple programs that help automate routine or not-so-routine tasks.

To get the most out of VBA, you will need to do some programming. This chapter gets you started by showing you how to use variables, constants, operators, and language constructs to write VBA procedures.

What Is VBA?

VBA is a programming language designed specifically for application control that includes high-level programming constructs (such as loops and branches) as well as a large number of pre-defined functions. It also has powerful debugging tools.

These features make the power of VBA very clear, but its biggest advantage might be that it's integrated into the Office applications. This means that you can attach your functions and procedures to menus, keyboard combinations, and events inside the applications to form a seamless environment for yourself or your users. You also can create dialog boxes simply by drawing the appropriate controls. Other visual tools enable you to customize menus and toolbars as well, so you have everything you need to create simple applications.

What Is a Macro?

A *macro* is a small program that contains a list of instructions (VBA statements) that you want an application to perform. Like DOS batch files, macros combine several operations into a single procedure that you can invoke quickly.

Macros are typically used for simple, everyday tasks and don't take long to create. An example of a macro might be to select, format, and print a range of spreadsheet cells in Excel. Or you might need to change paragraph styles in Word.

In Access, macros have a slightly different tone. Access macros are created using only a set of predefined functions with a controlled list of parameters. More information can be found in Chapter 32, "Creating Access Macros."

What Is a Module?

A *module* contains the VBA code that you want to attach to your spreadsheet or database. You can think of modules as borders around VBA code—if VBA code and variables are marked *private*, programs outside the module won't be able to see or access them.

Figure 53.1 displays a new module page in Access. This is a blank slate for you where you can create any type of program code you want.

FIGURE 53.1.

A blank module page in Access.

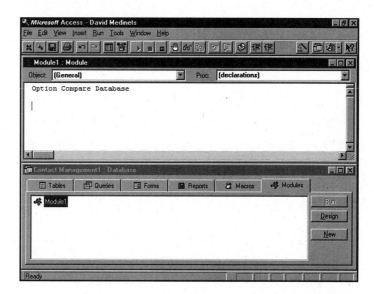

There are only three things you can place on a module page: variables, constants, and procedures. Variables are discussed in the "Working with Variables" section later in this chapter. Constants are discussed in the "Working with Constants" section later in the chapter.

There are two types of procedures:

- Function procedures—These are user-defined groups of VBA code that work just like an application's built-in functions. Their distinguishing characteristic is that they accept arguments, manipulate those arguments, and then return a result.

  A properly designed function macro should have no effect on the current environment. The section "The Function Procedure" shows you how to create your own functions.

- Sub procedures—These are procedures that contain VBA statements that are the equivalent of menu options and other application commands in addition to looping and branching statements.

One distinguishing feature of Sub procedures is that they have an effect on their surroundings (a menu, an Excel worksheet, an Access Table, and so on). Whether the procedure is formatting a range, printing a report, or creating custom menus, it *changes* things. The section "The Sub procedure" shows you how to create sub procedures.

An Introduction to VBA Programming

Most of the time you will only need to use a few lines of code to accomplish your task. However, no matter how small the procedure or macro you need, you will still need to know VBA programming fundamentals. This section introduces you to procedures, declarations, and control structures.

> **NOTE**
>
> While you actually create VBA modules and macros differently in each application, the basic concepts and definitions are the same. Therefore, this introduction to VBA programming is applicable to all Office applications.

Working with Procedures

The basic unit of VBA programming is the *procedure,* which is a block of code in a module. Earlier in this chapter you learned about the two most common types of procedures: Function and Sub procedures. Now you will see how to define them.

The Function Procedure

You might already be familiar with functions. A function can be used to calculate the radius of a circle or the area of a square. A function's distinguishing characteristic is that it returns a value.

A function's defining characteristic is that it returns a result. A function can perform any number of calculations on numbers, text, logical values, and so on, but it's not allowed to affect its surroundings. It can't move the active cell, format a range, or change a database setting. In fact, anything you can access using the menus is off limits in a user-defined function.

So, what *can* you put in a user-defined function? All of Access's or Excel's built-in functions are fair game, and you can use any VBA function that isn't the equivalent of a menu command or desktop action.

Access and Excel already have hundreds of built-in functions. However, even with this vast collection, you will still find that plenty of applications are not covered. For example, you might need to calculate the area of a circle of a given radius or the gravitational force between two objects. You could, of course, easily calculate these things on a worksheet, but if you need them frequently or in more than one application, it makes sense to define your own functions that you can use anytime.

Following is the basic structure of a function procedure:

```
Function ProcedureName (argument1, argument2, …)
    [VBA statements]
    ProcedureName = returnValue
End Function
```

Note the third line, which says

```
ProcedureName = returnValue
```

This is the line that sets the return value. Every function must have at least one of these lines.

For example, Listing 53.1 is a Function procedure that sums two ranges, stores the results in variables named totalSales and totalExpenses (see the section "Working with Variables" later in this chapter), and then uses these values and the fixedCosts argument to calculate the net margin.

Listing 53.1. A sample Function procedure.

```
Function CalcNetMargin(fixedCosts)
    totalSales = Application.Sum(Range("Sales"))
    totalExpenses = Application.Sum(Range("Expenses"))

    CalcNetMargin = (totalSales-totalExpenses-fixedCosts)/totalSales
End Function
```

Following is a summary of the various parts of a function:

- The Function statement—This keyword identifies the procedure as a user-defined function.

- The function name—This is a unique name for the function. Names must begin with an alphabetic character, they can't include a space or a period, and they can't be any longer than 255 characters.

- The function arguments—Just as many of the built-in functions accept arguments, so do user-defined functions. Arguments are typically one or more values that the function uses as the raw materials for its calculations. You always enter arguments between parentheses after the function name, and you separate multiple arguments with commas.

- The VBA statements—This is the code that actually performs the calculations. Each expression is a combination of values, operators, variables, and VBA or Excel functions that produce a result.

■ The return value—User-defined functions must return a value. To do this, include a statement where you set the function name equal to an expression. For example, in the CalcNetMargin function, the following statement defines the return value:

```
CalcNetMargin = (totalSales-totalExpenses-fixedCosts)/totalSales
```

■ The End Function keywords—These keywords indicate the end of the function procedure.

All your user-defined functions will have this basic structure, so you need to keep three things in mind when designing these types of macros:

■ What arguments will the macro take?

■ What formulas will you use within the macro?

■ What value or values will be returned?

The *Sub* Procedure

The Sub procedure enables you to modify the environment to your heart's content. Its limitation is that it can't return a value. In a way, the two types of procedures are direct opposites of each other.

Following is the basic structure of a Sub procedure:

```
Sub procedureName (argument1, argument2, …)
    [VBA statements]
End Sub
```

Listing 53.2 shows an example, using Excel, of a Sub procedure that enters some values for a loan in various ranges and then adds a formula to calculate the loan payment.

Listing 53.2. A sample Sub procedure.

```
Sub EnterLoanData()
    Range("IntRate").Value = .08
    Range("Term").Value = 10
    Range("Principal").Value = 10000
    Range("Payment").Formula = "=PMT(IntRate/12, Term*12, Principal)"
End Sub
```

Procedure Scope

All procedures have a *scope*. The scope of a procedure simply indicates which modules, worksheets, or databases can use it. Anything outside of the scope will not be able to access the procedure.

Some procedures are used only inside their own modules and shouldn't be called from another module or from a worksheet. To ensure this, you can declare the procedure to be *private*. This means that no other module or worksheet can access the procedure. To declare a procedure as private, include the keyword `Private` before either `Sub` or `Function`. For example, the following statement declares the `SupportCode` procedure as private:

```
Private Sub SupportCode()
```

Using a Procedure

After you write a procedure, you can use it in several different places: in another procedure, in a worksheet or database formula, or in a cell. This is known as *calling* the procedure.

The basic method of calling a procedure is simply to use it, supplying any parameters that may be needed. For example, you call the `CalcNetMargin` function from a worksheet cell by entering a formula such as the following:

```
=CalcNetMargin(1340000)
```

Similarly, you can use the function inside another procedure. For example, the following VBA statement sets a variable named `marginDiff` equal to the expected net margin minus the calculated net margin:

```
marginDiff = expectedMargin - CalcNetMargin(1340000)
```

While each procedure in a module must have a unique name, you can have multiple modules in a workbook and sometimes procedure names can be repeated. Additionally, you might use some procedures that another person has written and they might have chosen the same procedure names as you.

Using a Procedure from a Different Module

If you have an environment with two or more procedures that have the same name, you can differentiate between them by calling each procedure with the following general format:

```
ModuleName.ProcedureName
```

For example, to call a procedure named `NetMargin` in a module named `Financial`, you would use the following form:

```
Financial.NetMargin
```

If the module name contains more than one word, enclose the name in square brackets, as in the following:

```
[Financial Functions].NetMargin
```

Using a Procedure from a Different Workbook or Database

If you have a VBA statement that needs to call a procedure in another database or workbook, you first need to set up a *reference*. Doing this gives you access to all the procedures in the referenced database or workbook. The following procedure shows you what to do:

1. Activate the module containing the procedure that must access the other database or workbook.
2. While editing a module, select References from the Tools menu. The References dialog box appears, as shown in Figure 53.2.

FIGURE 53.2.

Use the References dialog box to set up a reference between VBA and a workbook.

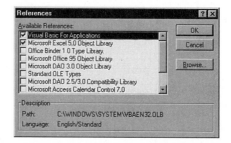

3. If the database or workbook is open, it will appear in the Available References list. Highlight the workbook and activate the check box. If the workbook isn't open, click the Browse button, choose the workbook you want from the Browse dialog box that appears, and then select OK to return to the References dialog box.
4. Select OK to return to the module.

After you establish the reference, you call the procedure the same way you call the procedures in the current workbook. If the two workbooks have procedures with the same names, you need to add the reference name and module name to the call, as in the following:

`[ReferenceName].ModuleName.ProcedureName`

For example, the following statement calls the `CalcNetMargin` procedure in the `Financial` module of the Budget.xls workbook:

`[Budget.xls].Financial.CalcNetMargin`

Again, if the module name uses multiple words, enclose it in square brackets.

> **TIP**
>
> In the same way that you can make an individual procedure private, you also can make an entire module private. This prevents any other module or workbook from accessing

the module's procedures. To declare a module as private, include the following statement near the top of the module (that is, before you define any procedures):

```
Option Private Module
```

Exiting Procedures

If you want to exit a procedure before reaching the End Sub or End Function statement, use either the Exit Sub or Exit Function statement.

Listing 53.3. Exiting from a Sub procedure.

```
Sub EnterLoanData()
    Range("IntRate").Value = .08
    Range("Term").Value = 10

    If testValue = 0 Then Exit Sub

    Range("Principal").Value = 10000
    Range("Payment").Formula = "=PMT(IntRate/12, Term*12, Principal)"
End Sub
```

> **NOTE**
>
> The If statement is discussed later in this chapter in the section "The If...Then Statement."

Working with Variables

In addition to procedures, your module may also need to store temporary values. For example, you might want to store values for total sales and total expenses to use in a gross margin calculation.

In VBA temporary values are stored in *variables*. This section explains this important topic and shows you how to use variables in your VBA procedures.

Declaring Variables

Declaring a variable tells VBA the name of the variable you're going to use. You declare variables by including Dim statements (Dim is short for *dimension*) at the beginning of each Function, Sub, or module.

The basic `Dim` statement has the following syntax:

```
Dim variableName
```

where *variableName* is the name of the variable. The name must begin with an alphabetic character, it can't be longer than 255 characters, it can't be a VBA keyword, and it can't contain a space or any of the following characters:

```
. ! # $ % & @
```

For example, the following statement declares a variable named `totalSales`:

```
Dim totalSales
```

> **NOTE**
>
> To avoid confusing variables with the names of objects, properties, or methods, many macro programmers begin their variable names with a lowercase letter. This is the style used in this chapter.

Most programmers set up a declarations section at the beginning of each procedure and use it to hold all their `Dim` statements. Then, after the variables have been declared, you can use them throughout the procedure. Listing 53.4 shows a `Function` procedure that declares two variables—`totalSales` and `totalExpenses`—and then uses Excel's `Sum` function to store a range sum in each variable. Finally, the `CalcGrossMargin` calculation uses each variable to return the function result.

Listing 53.4. An example of the `Dim` statement.

```
Function CalcGrossMargin

' Variable Declarations

Dim totalSales

Dim totalExpenses


' VBA Code

With Worksheets("1995 Budget")

totalSales = Application.Sum(.Range("Sales"))
```

```
totalExpenses = Application.Sum(.Range("Expenses"))

End With


CalcGrossMargin = (totalSales - totalExpenses) / totalSales

End Function
```

Notice that in the `CalcGrossMargin` function you store a value in a variable with a simple assignment statement of the following form:

```
variableName = value
```

> **TIP**
>
> To conserve space you can declare multiple variables on a single line. In the `CalcGrossMargin` function, for example, you could declare `totalSales` and `totalExpenses` using the following statement:
>
> ```
> Dim totalSales, totalExpenses
> ```

Avoiding Variable Errors

One of the most common errors in VBA procedures is to declare a variable and then later misspell the name. For example, suppose that I had entered the following statement in the `CalcGrossMargin` procedure from the preceding section:

```
totlExpenses = Application.Sum(.Range("Expenses"))
```

VBA supports *implicit declarations,* which means that if it sees a name it doesn't recognize, it assumes that the name belongs to a new variable. In this case, VBA would assume that `totlExpenses` is a new variable, proceed normally, and calculate the wrong answer for the function.

To avoid this problem, you can tell VBA to generate an error whenever it comes across a name that hasn't been declared explicitly with a `Dim` statement. You can do this in the following two ways:

■ For an individual module, enter the following statement before the first procedure:

```
Option Explicit
```

■ To do it for all your modules, select Options from the Tools menu, select the Module General tab, and activate the Require Variable Declaration check box.

> **NOTE**
>
> Activating the Require Variable Declaration check box forces VBA to add the Option Explicit statement at the beginning of each new module. However, it *doesn't* add this statement to any existing modules; you need to do that manually.

Variable Datatypes

The *datatype* of a variable determines the type of data the variable can hold. Table 53.1 lists all the VBA datatypes.

Table 53.1. The VBA datatypes.

Datatype	Description	Storage Size	Type-Declaration Character
Array	A set of variables where each element in the set is referenced by an index number.	Depends on the size of the array.	
Boolean	Takes one of two logical values: TRUE or FALSE.	2 bytes	
Currency	Used for monetary or fixed-decimal calculations where accuracy is important. The value range is from −922,337,203,685,477.5808 to 922,337,203,685,477.5807.	8 bytes	@
Date	Used for holding date data. The range is from January 1, 0100, to December 31, 9999.	8 bytes	
Double	Double-precision floating point. Negative numbers range from −1.79769313486232E308 to −4.94065645841247E−324. Positive numbers range from 4.94065645841247E−324 to 1.79769313486232E308.	8 bytes	#
Integer	Small integer values only. The range is from −32,768 to 32,767.	2 bytes	%

Datatype	Description	Storage Size	Type-Declaration Character
Long	Large integer values. The range is from –2,147,483,648 to 2,147,483,647.	4 bytes	&
Object	Refers to objects only.	4 bytes	
Single	Single-precision floating point. Negative numbers range from –3.402823E38 to –1.401298E–45. Positive numbers range from 1.401298E–45 to 3.402823E38.	4 bytes	!
String	Holds string values. The strings can be up to 64KB.	1 byte per character	$
Variant	Can take any type of data.		

NOTE

There is one additional variable type: Object. An object is something in an application, such as a cell, a worksheet, a database table, or a report. Objects are a very important part of VBA. You can find additional information about Excel objects in Chapter 25, "Understanding Objects."

You specify a datatype by including the As keyword in a Dim statement. Following is the general syntax:

Dim *variableName* As *DataType*

variableName is the name of the variable and *DataType* is one of the datatypes from Table 53.1.

For example, the following statement declares a variable named textString to be of type String:

Dim textString As String

The following are a few notes to keep in mind when using datatypes:

■ If you don't include a datatype when declaring a variable, VBA assigns the Variant datatype. This enables you to store any type of data in the variable.

- If you declare a variable to be one datatype and then try to store a value of a different datatype in the variable, VBA displays an error. To avoid this, many programmers like to use the *type-declaration characters*. (Refer to Table 53.1.) By appending one of these characters to the end of a variable name, you automatically declare the variable to be of the type represented by the character. For example, $ is the type-declaration character for a string, so the variable textString$ is automatically a String datatype variable. Having the $ at the end of the variable name also reminds you of the datatype, so you'll be less likely to store the wrong type of data.

> **NOTE**
>
> The Option Explicit statement discussed in the "Avoiding Variable Errors" section will prevent you from using type-declaration characters. However, because every variable will be declared, Visual Basic will still generate errors if you try to assign the wrong datatype to a variable.

- To specify the datatype of a procedure argument, use the As keyword in the argument list. For example, the following Function statement declares variables x and y to be Single:

```
Function HypotenuseLength(x As Single, y As Single)
```

- To specify the datatype of the return value in a Function procedure, use the As keyword at the end of the Function statement:

```
Function HypotenuseLength(x, y) As Single
```

Variable Scope

All variables have a *scope*. The scope of a variable simply indicates which procedures can use it. Any procedure outside the scope will not be able to access the variable. If Option Explicit is being used, VBA will generate an error indicating that the variable is undefined.

If a variable is defined inside a procedure, then only that procedure can use it. When the procedure is done, the variable essentially disappears. The next time the procedure is run, the variable starts with a value of 0.

If you want to use a variable in all the procedures in a module, place the declaration at the top of the module before your first procedure.

Using Array Variables

In VBA an array is a group of variables of the same datatype. Why would you need to use an array? Well, suppose that you wanted to store 20 employee names in variables to use in a procedure. One way to do this would be to create 20 variable names, such as employee1, employee2, and so on. It's much more efficient to create a single `employee` array variable that can hold up to 20 names, as in the following:

```
Dim employee(19) As String
```

As you can see, this declaration is very similar to one you would use for a regular variable. The difference is the 19 enclosed in parentheses. The parentheses tell VBA that you're declaring an array, and the number tells VBA how many elements you'll need in the array.

Why 19 instead of 20? Each element in the array is assigned a *subscript*, where the first element's subscript is 0, the second is 1, and so on, up to, in this case, 19. So the total number of elements in this array is 20.

You use the subscripts to refer to any element simply by enclosing its index number in the parentheses, as in the following:

```
employee(0) = "Ponsonby"
```

By default, the subscripts of VBA arrays start at 0 (this is called the *lower bound* of the array) and run up to the number you specify in the `Dim` statement (this is called the *upper bound* of the array). If you prefer your array index numbers to start at 1, include the following statement at the top of the module (that is, before declaring your first array and before your first procedure):

```
Option Base 1
```

> **NOTE**
>
> If you do decide to use the `Option Base` statement, make sure that you add comments detailing exactly why you are doing so. If you come back to your code in a year or so, you'll need the reminder.

Another way to specify a specific lower bound is to add the `To` keyword to your array declaration, as in the following:

```
Dim arrayName(LowerBound To UpperBound) As DataType
```

arrayName is the name of the array variable.

LowerBound is a long integer specifying the lower bound of the array.

UpperBound is a long integer specifying the upper bound of the array.

DataType is one of the datatypes from Table 53.1.

For example, the following is a declaration that creates an array variable with subscripts running from 50 to 100:

```
Dim myArray(50 To 100) As Currency
```

Dynamic Arrays

What do you do if you're not sure how many subscripts you'll need in an array? You could guess at the correct number, but that might leave you with one of the following problems:

- If you guess too low and try to access a subscript higher than the array's upper bound, VBA will generate an error message.
- If you guess too high, VBA will still allocate memory to the unused portions of the array, so you'll waste precious system resources.

To avoid both of these problems, you can declare a *dynamic* array by leaving the parentheses blank in the Dim statement:

```
Dim myArray() As Double
```

Then, when you know the number of elements you need, you can use a ReDim statement to allocate the correct number of subscripts (notice that you don't specify a datatype in the ReDim statement):

```
ReDim myArray(52)
```

A partial listing of a procedure named PerformCalculations follows. The procedure declares calcValues as a dynamic array and totalValues as an integer. Later in the procedure, totalValues is set to the result of a function procedure named GetTotalValues. The ReDim statement then uses totalValues to allocate the appropriate number of subscripts to the calcValues array.

```
Sub PerformCalculations()
    Dim calcValues() As Double, totalValues as Integer
    .
    .
    .
    totalValues = GetTotalValues()
    ReDim calcValues(totalValues)
    .
    .
    .
End Sub
```

Multidimensional Arrays

If you enter a single number between the parentheses in an array's Dim statement, VBA creates a *one-dimensional* array. But you also can create arrays with 2 or more dimensions (60 is the maximum). Suppose that you wanted to store both a first name and a last name in your employees array. To store two sets of data with each element, you would declare a two-dimensional array, as in the following:

```
Dim employees(19,1) As String
```

The subscripts for the second number work like the subscripts you've seen already. That is, they begin at 0 and run up to the number you specify. So this Dim statement sets up a table (or a *matrix*, as it's usually called) with 20 rows (1 for each employee) and 2 columns (1 for the first name and 1 for the last name). Following are two statements that initialize the data for the first employee:

```
employees(0,0) = "Biff"
employees(0,1) = "Ponsonby"
```

Working with Constants

Constants are values that don't change. They can be numbers, strings, or other values, but, unlike variables, they keep the same value throughout your code. VBA recognizes two types of constants: built in and user defined.

Using Built-in Constants

Many properties and methods have their own predefined constants. For VBA objects, the constants begin with vb. For Excel objects, these constants begin with the letters xl. For Access objects, the constants begin with ac.

For example, the window object's WindowState property recognizes three built-in constants: xlNormal (to set a window in its normal state), xlMaximized (to maximize a window), and xlMinimized (to minimize a window). To maximize the active window, for example, you would use the following statement:

```
ActiveWindow.WindowState = xlMaximized
```

You can see a list of the built-in constants by following these steps:

1. Select Object Browser from the View command from either Access or Excel to display the Object Browser dialog box.

2. In the Libraries/Workbooks list, select the library you want to look at (try VBA for now).

3. In the Objects/Modules list, select Constants. A list of built-in constants appears in the Methods/Properties list, as shown in Figure 53.3.

FIGURE 53.3.

You can use the object browser to display a list of the Excel and VBA built-in constants.

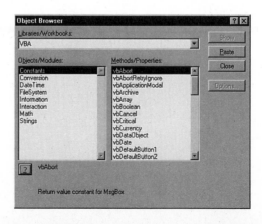

4. If you want to use the constant in your code, highlight it and then click the Paste button. Otherwise, select Close to return to the module.

Creating User-Defined Constants

To create your own constants, use the `Const` statement:

```
Const CONSTANTNAME = expression
```

CONSTANTNAME is the name of the constant. Most programmers use all-uppercase names for constants.

expression is the value (or a formula that returns a value) that you want to use for the constant.

For example, the following statement creates a constant named `DISCOUNT` and assigns to it the value `0.13`:

```
Const DISCOUNT = 0.13
```

Constants are very useful when you're trying to create readable and maintainable code. The constant name can be self-documenting. If you look at a piece of VBA code six months after you wrote it, and see the number 0.13 you probably won't remember what the number represents. By making it into a constant, you have a better chance to remember.

In addition, by consistently using the constant rather than the number, changing the value in the future is simple. Just go to the top of the module and make the change. You don't need to hunt through your code and find all the occurrences.

Working with Operators

Just as you use operators, such as addition (+) and multiplication (*), to build formulas in Access fields and Excel worksheets, so too do you use operators to combine functions, variables, and values in a VBA statement. VBA operators fall into four general categories: arithmetic, comparison, logical, and miscellaneous.

Arithmetic Operators

VBA's arithmetic operators are similar to those you've been using in your worksheets. Table 53.2 lists each of the arithmetic operators you can use in your VBA statements.

Table 53.2. The VBA arithmetic operators.

Operator	Name	Example	Result
+	Addition	10+5	15
–	Subtraction	10–5	5

Operator	Name	Example	Result
–	Negation	–10	–10
*	Multiplication	10*5	50
/	Division	10/5	2
%	Percentage	10%	0.1
^	Exponentiation	10^5	100000
Mod	Modulus	10 Mod 5	0

The Mod operator works like Excel's MOD() worksheet function. That is, it divides one number by another and returns the remainder. Here's the general form to use:

```
result = dividend Mod divisor
```

dividend is the number being divided.

divisor is the number being divided into *dividend*.

result is the remainder of the division.

For example, 16 Mod 5 returns 1 because 5 goes into 16 three times with a remainder of 1.

Comparison Operators

You use the *comparison* operators in a statement that compares two or more numbers, text strings, cell contents, or function results. If the statement is true, the result of the formula is given the logical value True (which is equivalent to any nonzero value). If the statement is false, the formula returns the logical value False (which is equivalent to 0). Table 53.3 summarizes VBA's comparison operators.

Table 53.3. The VBA comparison operators.

Operator	Name	Example	Result
=	Equal to	=10=5	False
>	Greater than	=10>5	True
<	Less than	=10<5	False
>=	Greater than or equal to	="a">="b"	False
<=	Less than or equal to	="a"<="b"	True
<>	Not equal to	="a"<>"b"	True

Logical Operators

You use the logical operators to combine or modify `True/False` expressions. Table 53.4 summarizes VBA's logical operators.

Table 53.4. The VBA logical operators.

Operator	General Form	What It Returns
And	*Expr1* And *Expr2*	True if both *Expr1* and *Expr2* are True; False otherwise.
Eqv	*Expr1* Eqv *Expr2*	True if both *Expr1* and *Expr2* are True or if both *Expr1* and *Expr2* are False; False otherwise.
Imp	*Expr1* Imp *Expr2*	False if *Expr1* is True and *Expr2* is False; True otherwise.
Or	*Expr1* Or *Expr2*	True if at least one of *Expr1* and *Expr2* are True; False otherwise.
Xor	*Expr1* Xor *Expr2*	False if both *Expr1* and *Expr2* are True or if both *Expr1* and *Expr2* are False; True otherwise.
Not	Not *Expr*	True if *Expr* is False; False if *Expr* is True.

Miscellaneous Operators

Besides the operators just mentioned, VBA also recognizes three other operators: concatenation (&), similarity (`Like`), and equivalence (`Is`).

You use VBA's concatenation operator (&) to combine strings, spreadsheet cell contents, string variables, or the results of string functions. For example, the following listing shows a simple `Function` procedure that accepts two strings as arguments and returns the two strings combined, separated by a space:

```
Function Concatenate(firstWord as String, secondWord as String) As String

    Concatenate = firstWord & " " & secondWord

End Function
```

The similarity operator (`Like`) compares two strings using the following syntax:

```
result = string Like pattern
```

string is a string, string variable, cell value, or string function result.

pattern is the string or pattern that you want to compare with *string*. You can use a string, string variable, cell value, or string function result. If you use a string, you can include the following wildcard characters:

Character	What It Matches
?	Any single character
*	A group of characters
#	A single digit
[*charlist*]	Any single character in *charlist*
[!*charlist*]	Any single character not in *charlist*

result is True if *pattern* is contained in *string*; it is False otherwise.

Table 53.5 lists a few examples of the Like operator in action.

Table 53.5. An example of using the Like operator.

Expression	Result
"Reed" Like "Reid"	False
"Reed" Like "R*d"	True
"1234.95" Like "1234.9#"	True
"Reed" Like "Re[aei]d"	True
"Reed" Like "Re[!ae]d"	False

NOTE

VBA string comparisons are case sensitive by default. If you prefer to use case-insensitive comparisons, add the following statement to the top of the module:

```
Option Compare Text
```

You use the equivalence operator (Is) to see whether two object variables refer to the same object, as in the following syntax:

result = *object1* Is *object2*

object1 is an object variable.

object2 is an object variable.

result is True if both *object1* and *object2* refer to the same object; it is False otherwise.

Working with Decision Statements

One of the advantages of writing your own VBA procedures is that you can create procedures that make decisions based on certain conditions and that can perform *loops*—running several statements repeatedly. The statements that handle this kind of processing—*control structures*—are the subject of this section.

A smart procedure performs tests on its environment and then decides what to do next based on the results of each test. For example, suppose that you have written a Function procedure that uses one of its arguments as a divisor in a formula. You should test the argument before using it in the formula to make sure that it isn't 0 (to avoid producing a Division by zero error). If it is, you could then display a message that alerts the user of the illegal argument.

The *If...Then* Statement

Simple True/False decisions are handled by the If…Then statement. You can use either the single-line syntax:

```
If condition Then statement
```

or the *block* syntax:

```
If condition Then
    [statements]
End If
```

With *condition* you can use either a logical expression that returns True or False or you can use any expression that returns a numeric value. In the latter case, a return value of 0 is functionally equivalent to False, and any nonzero value is equivalent to True.

statement(s) is the VBA statement or statements to run if *condition* returns True. If *condition* returns False, VBA skips over the *statements*.

Whether you use the single-line or block syntax depends on the statements you want to run if the *condition* returns a True result. If you have only one statement, you can use either syntax. If you have multiple statements, you must use the block syntax.

Listing 53.5 shows a revised version of the CalcGrossMargin procedure from Listing 53.4. This version—called CalcGrossMargin2—uses If…Then to check the totalSales variable. The procedure calculates the gross margin only if totalSales is not 0.

Listing 53.5. An *If*…Then **example.**

```
Function CalcGrossMargin2()


' Variable Declarations
```

```
Dim totalSales

Dim totalExpenses

' VBA Code

With Worksheets("1995 Budget")

totalSales = Application.Sum(.Range("Sales"))

totalExpenses = Application.Sum(.Range("Expenses"))

End With

' Setup a default value in case totalSales is zero.

CalcGrossMargin2 = 0

If totalSales <> 0 Then

CalcGrossMargin2 = (totalSales - totalExpenses) / totalSales

End If

End Function
```

TIP

You can make the If…Then statement in the CalcGrossMargin2 procedure slightly more efficient by taking advantage of the fact that in the condition, 0 is equivalent to False and any other number is equivalent to True. This means that you don't have to explicitly test the totalSales variable to see whether it is 0. Instead, you can use the following statements:

```
If totalSales Then
    GrossMargin = (totalSales-totalExpenses)/totalSales
End If
```

On the other hand, many programmers feel that including the explicit test for a nonzero value (totalSales <> 0) makes the procedure easier to read and more intuitive. Because in this case the efficiency gained is only minor, you're probably better off leaving in the full expression.

The *If...Then...Else* Statement

Using the If...Then statement to make decisions adds a powerful new weapon to your VBA arsenal. However, this technique suffers from an important drawback: A False result only avoids one or more statements; it doesn't execute any of its own. This is fine in many cases, but there will be times when you need to run one group of statements if the condition returns True and a different group if the result is False. To handle this, you need to use an If...Then...Else statement:

```
If condition Then
    [TrueStatements]
Else
    [FalseStatements]
End If
```

condition is the test that returns True or False.

TrueStatements is the statement to run if condition returns True.

FalseStatements is the statement to run if condition returns False.

If condition returns True, VBA runs the group of statements between If...Then and Else. If it returns False, VBA runs the group of statements between the Else and the End If.

Look at an example. Suppose that you want to calculate the future value of a series of regular deposits, but you want to differentiate between monthly deposits and quarterly deposits. Listing 53.6 shows a Function procedure called FutureValue that does the job.

Listing 53.6. A procedure that uses *If...Then...Else.*

```
Function FutureValue(Rate, Nper, Pmt, Frequency)

    If Frequency = "Monthly" Then
        FutureValue = Application.Fv(Rate / 12, Nper * 12, Pmt / 12)
    Else
        FutureValue = Application.Fv(Rate / 4, Nper * 4, Pmt / 4)
    End If

End Function
```

The first three arguments—Rate, Nper, and Pmt—are, respectively, the annual interest rate, the number of years in the term of the investment, and the total deposit available annually. The fourth argument—Frequency—is either "Monthly" or "Quarterly". The idea is to adjust the first three arguments based on the Frequency. For example, if Frequency is "Monthly", you need to divide the interest rate by 12, multiply the term by 12, and divide the annual deposit by 12.

The If...Then...Else statement runs a test on the Frequency argument:

```
If Frequency = "Monthly" Then
```

If this is True, the function adjusts Rate, Nper, and Pmt accordingly and returns the future value. Otherwise, a quarterly calculation is assumed, and different adjustments are made to the arguments.

> **TIP**
>
> If...Then...Else statements are much easier to read when you indent the expressions between If...Then, Else, and End If, as done in Listing 53.6. This enables you to easily identify which group of statements will be run if there is a True result and which group will be run if the result is False. Pressing the Tab key once at the beginning of each line does the job.

> **NOTE**
>
> Notice that Listing 53.6 uses a built-in Excel function by preceding the function name with the Application object (for example, Application.Fv).

The *Select Case* Structure

One problem with If...Then...Else statements is that you can make only a single decision. The statement calculates a single logical result and performs one of two actions. But there are plenty of situations that require you to choose from multiple alternatives before you can decide which action to take.

One solution is to use the And and Or operators to evaluate a series of logical tests. For example, the FutureValue procedure probably should test the Frequency argument to make sure it's either "Monthly" or "Quarterly" and not something else. The following If...Then statement uses the Or operator to accomplish this:

```
If Frequency = "Monthly" Or Frequency = "Quarterly" Then

[Perform some calculations]
Else

[Handle the error condition]
End If
```

If `Frequency` doesn't equal either of these values, the entire condition returns `False` and the procedure can return a error message to the user.

This approach works, but you're really only performing multiple logical tests; in the end, you're still making a single decision. A better approach is to use VBA's `Select Case` statement:

```
Select Case TestExpression
   Case FirstExpressionList
        [FirstStatements]
    Case SecondExpressionList
        [SecondStatements]…
    Case Else
        [ElseStatements]
End Select
```

`TestExpression` is evaluated at the beginning of the structure.

`ExpressionList` is a list of one or more expressions in which each expression is separated by a comma. VBA examines each element in the list to see whether one matches the `TestExpression`. These expressions can take any one of the following forms:

> `Expression`
>
> `Expression To Expression`
>
> `Is LogicalOperator Expression`
>
> The `To` keyword defines a range of values (for example, `1 To 10`). The `Is` keyword defines an open-ended range of values (for example, `Is >= 100`).

`Statements` are the statements VBA runs if any part of the associated `ExpressionList` matches the `TestExpression`. VBA runs the optional `ElseStatements` if no `ExpressionList` matches the `TestExpression`. This is typically where errors are trapped when unexpected values are encountered.

NOTE

If more than one `ExpressionList` contains an element that matches the `TestExpression`, VBA runs only the statements associated with the `ExpressionList` that appears first in the `Select Case` structure.

Suppose that you want to write a procedure that converts a raw score into a letter grade according to the following chart:

Raw Score	Letter Grade
80 and over	A
70 to 80	B
60 to 69	C
50 to 59	D
Less than 50	F

Listing 53.7 shows the LetterGrade procedure, which uses a Select Case statement to make the conversion.

Listing 53.7. A procedure that makes multiple decisions using a Select Case statement.

```
Function LetterGrade(rawScore)

    Select Case rawScore
        Case Is < 50
            LetterGrade = "F"
        Case Is < 60
            LetterGrade = "D"
        Case Is < 70
            LetterGrade = "C"
        Case Is < 80
            LetterGrade = "B"
        Case Else
            LetterGrade = "A"
    End Select

End Function
```

> **NOTE**
>
> The preceding Select Case statement is very position dependent; if you move one of the Case statements above another, the result would not be what you want. To avoid this problem, make each case independent of the others. Here's an example:
>
> ```
> Case 60 to 69:
> ```
>
> or
>
> ```
> Case Is >= 60 And <= 69:
> ```

Working with Looping Statements

If your procedure needs to repeat a section of code, you can set up a loop that tells VBA how many times to run through the code. The next few sections look at VBA's three different types of loops.

The *Do...Loop* Statement

What do you do when you need to loop but you don't know in advance how many times to repeat the loop? This could happen if, for example, you want to loop only until a certain condition is met, such as encountering a blank cell. The solution is to use a Do…Loop.

The Do...Loop has four different syntaxes:

- Do While *condition* [*statements*] Loop checks *condition* before entering the loop and executes the *statements* only while *condition* is True.

- Do [*statements*] Loop While *condition* checks *condition* after running through the loop once and then executes the *statements* only while *condition* is True. Use this form when you want the loop to be processed at least one time.

- Do Until *condition* [*statements*] Loop checks *condition* before entering the loop and executes the *statements* only while *condition* is False.

- Do [*statements*] Loop Until *condition* checks *condition* after running through the loop once and then executes the *statements* only while *condition* is False. Again, use this form when you want the loop to be processed at least one time.

Listing 53.8 shows a procedure called BigNumbers that runs down a worksheet column and changes the font color to magenta whenever a cell contains a number greater than or equal to 1000.

Listing 53.8. A procedure that uses a Do...Loop to process cells until it encounters a blank cell.

```
Sub BigNumbers()

    Dim rowNum As Integer, colNum As Integer, currCell As Range

    rowNum = ActiveCell.Row                          'Init row #
    colNum = ActiveCell.Column                       'Init col #
    Set currCell = ActiveSheet.Cells(rowNum, colNum) 'Get first cell

    Do While currCell.Value <> ""                    'Do while not empty

        If IsNumeric(currCell.Value) Then            'If it's a number,
            If currCell.Value >= 1000 Then           'and a big one,
                currCell.Font.Color = RGB(255, 0, 255) 'chg to magenta
            End If
        End If
        rowNum = rowNum + 1                          'Increment row #
        Set currCell = ActiveSheet.Cells(rowNum, colNum) 'Get next cell

    Loop

End Sub
```

The idea is to loop until the procedure encounters a blank cell. This is controlled by the following Do While statement:

```
Do While currCell.Value <> ""
```

currCell is an object variable that is set using the Cells method (which is described in Chapter 54, "Advanced VBA Programming"). Next, the first If...Then uses the IsNumeric function to check whether the cell contains a number, and the second If…Then checks to see whether the number is greater than or equal to 1000. If both conditions are True, the font color is set to magenta—RGB(255,0,255).

NOTE

Use the RGB(red,green,blue) VBA function any time you need to specify a color for a property. Each of the three named arguments (red, green, and blue) are integers between 0 and 255 that determine how much of each component color is mixed into the final color. In the red component, for example, 0 means no red is present and 255 means that pure red is present. Following are some sample values for each component that produce common colors:

red	green	blue	Result
0	0	0	Black
0	0	255	Blue
0	255	0	Green
0	255	255	Cyan
255	0	0	Red
255	0	255	Magenta
255	255	0	Yellow
255	255	255	White

The *For…Next* Statement

The most common type of loop is probably the For…Next loop. Use this loop when you know exactly how many times you want to repeat a group of statements. The structure of a For…Next loop looks like the following:

```
For counter = start To end [Step increment]
    [statements]
Next [counter]
```

counter is a numeric variable used as a *loop counter*. The loop counter is a number that counts how many times the procedure has gone through the loop.

start is the initial value of *counter*. This is usually 1, but you can enter any value.

end is the final value of *counter*.

increment is an optional value that defines an increment for the loop counter. If you leave this out, the default value is 1. Use a negative value to decrement *counter*.

statements are the statements to execute each time through the loop.

The basic idea is simple. When Excel encounters the For…Next statement, it follows this five-step process:

1. Set *counter* equal to *start*.

2. Test *counter*. If it's greater than *end*, exit the loop (that is, process the first statement after the Next statement). Otherwise, continue. If *increment* is negative, VBA checks to see whether *counter* is less than *end*.

3. Execute each statement between the For and Next statements.

4. Add *increment* to *counter*. Add 1 to *counter* if *increment* is not specified.

5. Repeat steps 2 through 4 until done.

Listing 53.9 shows a simple Sub procedure—LoopTest—that uses a For…Next statement. Each time through the loop, the procedure uses the StatusBar property to display the value of Counter (the loop counter) in the status bar. When you run this procedure, Counter is incremented by one each time through the loop, and the new value gets displayed in the status line.

Listing 53.9. A simple For…Next loop in an Excel procedure.

```
Sub LoopTest()

    Dim counter

    For counter = 1 To 10
    'Display the message
        Application.StatusBar = "Counter value: " & counter
    ' Wait for 1 second
        Application.Wait Now + TimeValue("00:00:01")
    Next counter

    Application.StatusBar = False

End Sub
```

NOTE

The LoopTest procedure also uses the Wait method to slow things down a bit. The argument Now + TimeValue("00:00:01") pauses the procedure for one second before continuing.

Following are some notes on For…Next loops:

■ If you use a positive number for *increment* (or if you omit *increment*), *end* must be greater than or equal to *start*. If you use a negative number for *increment*, *end* must be less than or equal to *start*.

- If *start* equals *end,* the loop will execute once.

- As with If…Then…Else structures, indent the statements inside a For…Next loop for increased readability.

- To keep the number of variables defined in a procedure to a minimum, always try to use the same name for all your For…Next loop counters. The letters *i* through *n* traditionally are used for counters in programming. For greater clarity, you might want to use names such as counter.

- If you need to break out of a For…Next loop before the defined number of repetitions is completed, use the Exit For statement, described in the section "Exiting Your Loops."

The *For Each…Next* Statement

A useful variation of the For…Next loop is the For Each…Next loop, which operates on a collection of objects. You don't need a loop counter because VBA just loops through the individual elements in the collection and performs on each element whatever operations are inside the loop. Following is the structure of the basic For Each…Next loop:

```
For Each element In group
    [statements]
Next [element]
```

element is a variable used to hold the name of each element in the collection.

group is the name of the collection.

statements are the statements to be executed for each element in the collection.

As an example, create an Excel procedure that converts a range of text into proper case (that is, the first letter of each word is capitalized). This function can come in handy if you import mainframe text into your worksheets, because mainframe reports usually appear entirely in uppercase. This process involves three steps:

1. Loop through the selected range with For Each…Next.
2. Convert each cell's text to proper case. Use Excel's PROPER() function to handle this:

    ```
    PROPER(text)
    ```

    text is the text to convert to proper case.

3. Enter the converted text into the selected cell. This is the job of the range object's Formula method:

    ```
    Object.Formula = Expression
    ```

    Object is the range object in which you want to enter *Expression*.

    Expression is the data you want to enter into *Object*.

Listing 53.10 shows the resulting procedure, `ConvertToProper`. Note that this procedure uses the `Selection` object to represent the currently selected range.

Listing 53.10. An Excel `Sub` procedure that uses `For Each…Next` to loop through a selection and convert each cell to proper case.

```
Sub ConvertToProper()

    Dim cellObject As Object

    For Each cellObject In Selection
        cellObject.Formula = Application.Proper(cellObject)
    Next

End Sub
```

Exiting Your Loops

Most loops run their natural course and then the procedure moves on. There might be times, however, when you want to exit a loop prematurely. For example, you might come across a certain type of cell, or an error might occur, or the user might enter an unexpected value. To exit a `For…Next` loop or a `For Each…Next` loop, use the `Exit For` statement. To exit a `Do…Loop`, use the `Exit Do` statement.

Listing 53.11 shows a revised version of the `BigNumbers` procedure, which exits the `Do…Loop` if it comes across a cell that isn't a number.

Listing 53.11. In this version of the `BigNumbers` procedure, the `Do…Loop` is terminated with the `Exit Do` statement if the current cell isn't a number.

```
Sub BigNumbers2()

    Dim rowNum As Integer, colNum As Integer, currCell As Range

    rowNum = ActiveCell.Row                          'Init row #
    colNum = ActiveCell.Column                       'Init col #
    Set currCell = ActiveSheet.Cells(rowNum, colNum) 'Get first cell

    Do While currCell.Value <> ""                    'Do while not empty

        If IsNumeric(currCell.Value) Then            'If it's a number,
            If currCell.Value >= 1000 Then           'and a big one,
                currCell.Font.Color = RGB(255, 0, 255) 'cng tomagenta
            End If
        Else                                         'If it's not,
            Exit Do                                  'exit the loop
        End If
        rowNum = rowNum + 1                          'Increment row #
        Set currCell = ActiveSheet.Cells(rowNum, colNum) 'Get next cell
```

```
    Loop

End Sub
```

Optimizing Your Loops

One of the cornerstones of efficient programming is loop optimization. Because a procedure might run the code inside a loop hundreds or even thousands of times, a minor improvement in loop efficiency can result in considerably reduced execution times.

Two of VBA's slowest methods are `Activate` and `Select`, so they should be used sparingly. One `Select` method is slow; a thousand will drive you crazy.

Also, weed out from your loops any statements that return the same value each time. For example, consider the following fragment from an Excel procedure:

```
For i = 1 To 5000
    Application.StatusBar = "The value is " & Worksheets("Sheet1").[A1].Value
Next i
```

The idea of this somewhat useless code is to loop 5000 times, each time displaying in the status bar the contents of cell A1 in the Sheet1 worksheet. The value in cell A1 never changes, but it takes time for Excel to get the value, slowing the loop considerably. A better approach would be the following:

```
currCell = Worksheets("Sheet1").[A1].Value
For i = 1 To 5000
    Application.StatusBar = "The value is: " & currCell
Next I
```

Transferring the unchanging `CurCell` calculation outside the loop and assigning it to a variable means that the procedure has to call the function only once.

To test the difference, Listing 53.12 shows the `TimingTest` procedure. This procedure uses the `Timer` function (which returns the number of seconds since midnight) to time two For…Next loops. The first loop is unoptimized and the second loop is optimized. When run, the optimized loop should take a little less than half the time of the unoptimized loop to run.

Listing 53.12. A procedure that tests the difference between an optimized and an unoptimized loop.

```
Sub TimingTest()

    Dim i As Integer, currCell As Variant
    Dim start1 As Long, finish1 As Long
    Dim start2 As Long, finish2 As Long
```

Listing 53.12. continued

```
    ' Start timing the unoptimized loop
    start1 = Timer
    For i = 1 To 5000
        Application.StatusBar = "The value is " _
& Worksheets("Sheet1").[A1].Value
    Next i
    finish1 = Timer

    ' Start timing the optimized loop
    start2 = Timer
    currCell = Worksheets("Sheet1").[A1].Value
    For i = 1 To 5000
        Application.StatusBar = "The value is " & currCell
    Next i
    finish2 = Timer

    MsgBox "The first loop took " & finish1 - start1 & " seconds." & _
            Chr(13) & _
            "The second loop took " & finish2 - start2 & " seconds."

    Application.StatusBar = False

End Sub
```

Summary

This chapter discusses VBA—a programming language used to automate tasks in the Microsoft Office suite of applications.

You have learned how Function and Sub procedures are created and how to use variables and constants. In addition, the basic VBA decision and looping statements are covered.

One of the most important aspects of VBA is its capability to reach into the heart of an application and directly manipulate its objects. More information about the objects available in Excel can be found in Chapter 25. The Access objects can be found in Chapter 33, "Using OLE and OLE Automation."

Advanced VBA Programming

54

by Paul McFedries and David Medinets

IN THIS CHAPTER

Chapter 53, "Getting Started with VBA," is all about the VBA language itself. Little mention is made of things that you can accomplish using it. This chapter will partially remedy that.

Access and Excel implement the VBA language in different ways. This makes sense to a certain extent. For example, Access has no need to know about worksheets and cells. Likewise, Excel has no need to know about tables and queries.

This chapter discusses the following advanced aspects of VBA that the two applications have in common:

- Interacting with the user through message boxes and beeps
- Using the data access objects (if you ever need to automate database activities, read this section)
- Debugging your procedures
- Adding add-in programs

Before discussing the hard stuff (data access and debugging), look at some easier things first.

Keeping the User Involved

A well-designed application or set of procedures not only makes intelligent decisions and streamlines code with loops, but also keeps the user involved. The application or procedure should display messages at appropriate times and ask the user for input. When interacting with the application, the user feels that he or she is a part of the process and has some control over what the program does, which means that the user won't lose interest in the program and will be less likely to make careless mistakes.

Displaying information is one of the best (and easiest) ways to keep your users involved. If an operation is going to take a long time, keep the user informed of the operation's time and progress. If a user makes an error (for example, enters the wrong argument in a user-defined function), he should be gently admonished so that he will be less likely to repeat the error.

In the next few sections, you will see how to display information, get user input, and make some noise.

Displaying Information

Every application needs to be able to display information to let the user know what is going on or to simply display error messages. MsgBox, discussed in the next section, is one of the easiest ways to communicate with the user.

Using the *MsgBox* Function

The problem with using the StatusBar property to display messages is that often it is a bit too subtle. Unless the user knows to look in the status bar, he or she might miss your messages altogether. When the user really needs to see a message, you can use the MsgBox function:

```
MsgBox(prompt,buttons,title,helpFile,context)
```

prompt is the message you want to display in the dialog box

buttons is a number or constant that specifies, among other things, the command buttons that appear in the dialog box (see the following section for more information). The default value is 0.

title is the text that appears in the dialog box title bar. If you omit the title, VBA uses Microsoft Excel.

helpFile is the text that specifies the Help file that contains the custom help topic. If you enter helpFile, you also have to include context. If you include helpFile, a Help button appears in the dialog box.

context is a number that identifies the help topic in *helpFile*.

The following statement, for example, displays the message dialog box shown in Figure 54.1:

```
MsgBox "You must enter a number between 1 and 100",,"Warning"
```

FIGURE 54.1.

A simple message dialog box produced by the MsgBox *function.*

NOTE

The MsgBox function, like all VBA functions, needs parentheses around its arguments only when you use the function's return value. See the section "Getting the MsgBox Return Value."

TIP

For long messages, VBA wraps the text inside the dialog box. To create your own line breaks, use VBA's Chr function and the carriage-return character (ASCII 13) between each line, as in the following example:

```
MsgBox "First line" & Chr(13) & "Second line"
```

Setting the *MsgBox* Style

The default message dialog box displays only an OK button. You can include other buttons and icons in the dialog box by using different values for the *buttons* parameter. Table 54.1 lists the available options.

Table 54.1. The MsgBox buttons parameter options.

Constant	Value	Description
	Buttons	
vbOKOnly	0	Displays only an OK button (the default).
vbOKCancel	1	Displays the OK and Cancel buttons.
vbAbortRetryIgnore	2	Displays the Abort, Retry, and Ignore buttons.
vbYesNoCancel	3	Displays the Yes, No, and Cancel buttons.
vbYesNo	4	Displays the Yes and No buttons.
vbRetryCancel	5	Displays the Retry and Cancel buttons.
	Icons	
vbCritical	16	Displays the Critical Message icon.
vbQuestion	32	Displays the Warning Query icon.
vbExclamation	48	Displays the Warning Message icon.
vbInformation	64	Displays the Information Message icon.
	Defaults	
vbDefaultButton1	0	The first button is the default.
vbDefaultButton2	256	The second button is the default.
vbDefaultButton3	512	The third button is the default.
	Modality	
vbApplicationModal	0	The user must respond to the message box before continuing work in the current application.
vbSystemModal	4096	All applications are suspended until the user responds to the message box.

You derive the *buttons* argument in one of two ways:

- By adding up the values for each option
- By using the VBA constants separated by plus signs (+)

For example, Listing 54.1 shows a procedure named `ButtonTest`, and Figure 54.2 shows the resulting dialog box. Here, three variables—*msgPrompt*, *msgButtons*, and *msgTitle*—store the values for the `MsgBox` function's *prompt*, *buttons*, and *title* arguments. In particular, the following statement derives the *buttons* argument:

```
msgButtons = vbYesNoCancel + vbQuestion + vbDefaultButton2
```

You also could derive the *buttons* argument by adding the values that these constants represent (3, 32, and 256, respectively), although the procedure becomes less readable that way.

Listing 54.1. A procedure that creates a message dialog box.

```
Sub ButtonTest()

    Dim msgPrompt As String, msgTitle As String
    Dim msgButtons As Integer, msgResult As Integer

    msgPrompt = "Are you sure you want to copy" & Chr(13) & _
                "the selected files to drive A?"
    msgButtons = vbYesNoCancel + vbQuestion + vbDefaultButton2
    msgTitle = "Copy Files"

    msgResult = MsgBox(msgPrompt, msgButtons, msgTitle)

End Sub
```

> **TIP**
>
> VBA's automatic syntax checking is a real time saver. To make sure this option is turned on, activate the Display Syntax Errors check box in the Module tab of the Options dialog box.

FIGURE 54.2.

The dialog box that is displayed when you run the code shown in Listing 54.1.

Getting the *MsgBox* Return Value

A message dialog box that displays only an OK button is straightforward. The user either clicks OK or presses Enter to remove the dialog box from the screen. The multibutton styles are a little different, however; the user has a choice of buttons to select, and your procedure should have a way to find out what the user chose.

You do this by storing the `MsgBox` function's return value in a variable. Table 54.2 lists the seven possibilities.

Table 54.2. The MsgBox function's return values.

Constant	Value	Button Selected
vbOK	1	OK
vbCancel	2	Cancel
vbAbort	3	Abort
vbRetry	4	Retry
vbIgnore	5	Ignore
vbYes	6	Yes
vbNo	7	No

To process the return value, you can use an If...Then...Else or Select Case structure to test for the appropriate values. For example, the ButtonTest procedure shown earlier used a variable called *msgResult* to store the return value of the MsgBox function. Listing 23.11 shows a revised version of ButtonTest that uses a Select Case statement to test for the three possible return values. (Note that the vbYes case runs a procedure named CopyFiles. The ButtonTest procedure assumes that the CopyFiles procedure already exists elsewhere in the module.)

Listing 54.2. This example uses Select Case to test the return values of the MsgBox function.

```
Sub ButtonTest2()

    Dim msgPrompt As String, msgTitle As String
    Dim msgButtons As Integer, msgResult As Integer

    msgPrompt = "Are you sure you want to copy" & Chr(13) & _
                "the selected files to drive A?"
    msgButtons = vbYesNoCancel + vbQuestion + vbDefaultButton2
    msgTitle = "Copy Files"

    msgResult = MsgBox(msgPrompt, msgButtons, msgTitle)

    Select Case msgResult
        Case vbYes
            CopyFiles
        Case vbNo
            Exit Sub
        Case vbCancel
            Application.Quit
    End Select

End Sub
```

Using Dialog Boxes

Many VBA methods are known as *dialog box equivalents* because they enable you to select the same options that are available in Access's or Excel's built-in dialog boxes. Using dialog box equivalents works well if your procedure knows which options to select, but there are times when you might want the user to specify some of the dialog box options.

For example, if your procedure will print a document (using the `PrintOut` method), you might need to know how many copies the user wants or how many pages to print. You could use the `InputBox` method to get this data, but it's usually easier just to display the Print dialog box.

The built-in dialog boxes are `Dialog` objects, and `Dialog`s are a collection of over 200 built-in dialog boxes. To reference a particular dialog box, use one of the predefined constants. Remember that you can look in the Object Browser for all the constant names.

Table 54.3 lists a few of the more common dialog box constants.

Table 54.3. Some of Excel's built-in dialog box constants.

Constant	Dialog Box
xlDialogChartWizard	ChartWizard
xlDialogColumnWidth	Column Width
xlDialogDefineName	Define Name
xlDialogFindFile	Find File
xlDialogFont	Font
xlDialogFormatAuto	AutoFormat
xlDialogFormulaFind	Find
xlDialogFormulaGoto	Go To
xlDialogFormulaReplace	Replace
xlDialogFunctionWizard	FunctionWizard
xlDialogGoalSeek	Goal Seek
xlDialogNew	New
xlDialogNote	Cell Note
xlDialogOpen	Open
xlDialogOptionsCalculation	Options (Calculation tab)
xlDialogOptionsEdit	Options (Edit tab)
xlDialogOptionsGeneral	Options (General tab)
xlDialogOptionsView	Options (View tab)
xlDialogPageSetup	Page Setup

continues

Table 54.3. continued

Constant	Dialog Box
xlDialogPasteSpecial	Paste Special
xlDialogPivotTableWizard	PivotTable Wizard
xlDialogPrint	Print
xlDialogPrinterSetup	Printer Setup
xlDialogPrintPreview	Print Preview
xlDialogRowHeight	Row Height
xlDialogSaveAs	Save As
xlDialogSort	Sort

NOTE

To see a complete list of constants for Excel's built-in dialog boxes, select the Object Browser from the View menu from any module. In the Object Browser dialog box, select Excel from the Libraries/Workbooks list and then choose Constants in the Objects/Modules list. You'll find the dialog constants in the Methods/Properties list. (They all begin with xlDialog.)

To display any of these dialog boxes, use the Dialog object's Show method. For example, the following statement displays the Print dialog box:

```
Application.Dialogs(xlDialogPrint).Show
```

NOTE

The Dialogs method may fail your if procedure is run in an invalid context. For example, to display the Format Data Labels dialog box using

```
Application.Dialogs(xlDialogDataLabel).Show
```

the active sheet must be a chart; otherwise, the method fails.

If the user selects Cancel to exit the dialog box, the Show method returns False. This means you can use Show inside an If statement to determine what the user did, as in the following:

```
If Not Application.Dialogs(xlDialogPrint).Show Then
    MsgBox "File was not printed"
End If
```

Making Sounds

The simple act of making noise come out of the computer will spice up your application or procedure tremendously. Even if you just beep at the user occasionally, it will wake them up and they be more involved in their tasks.

Beeping the Speaker

The most rudimentary form of sound is the simple, attention-getting beep. It's VBA's way of saying "Ahem!" or "Excuse me!" and it's handled, appropriately enough, by the Beep statement.

For example, Listing 54.3 shows the RecalcAll procedure that does some work recalculating all the open workbooks and then sounds two beeps to mark the end of the process.

Listing 54.3. A procedure that recalculates something and then sounds two beeps.

```
Option Explicit

Sub RecalcAll()
    ' [Recalculate something]
    Beep
    Pause 2
    Beep
End Sub

Sub Pause(numSeconds As Single)
    Dim startTimer As Single

        startTimer = Timer    ' Set start time.
        Do While Timer < startTimer + 1
            DoEvents    ' Yield to other processes.
        Loop
End Sub
```

The Pause procedure was added so that VBA would wait 2 seconds before sounding the second beep. Otherwise, the beeps would merge and sound like one.

> **WARNING**
>
> Avoid overusing the Beep statement. You need to get the user's attention, but constant beeping only defeats that purpose; most users get annoyed at any program that barks at them incessantly. Good uses for the Beep statement are signaling an error and signaling the end of a long operation.

Working with Data Access Objects

Data access objects (DAOs) enable you to query external databases from within VBA procedures. This section takes you through the basics of using DAO to access and work with external databases.

About Data Access Objects

DAO is a separate library of objects and their associated properties and methods. These objects expose the full functionality of the Microsoft Jet database engine—the engine used in Access, which is Microsoft's relational database system.

Setting Up a Reference to the DAO Library

To make the DAO library available to your VBA applications, you need to set up a reference to the library in the module that contains your code. The following steps show you how it's done:

1. Activate or create the module you'll be using to access external databases.

2. Select References from the Tools menu to display the References dialog box.

3. In the Available References list, activate Microsoft DAO 3.0 Object Library, shown in Figure 54.3.

FIGURE 54.3

To use data access objects in the current workbook, you need to establish a reference to the DAO library.

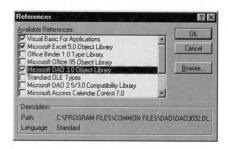

4. Select OK. The reference is set up and you are returned to the module.

The Data Access Objects Hierarchy

After you set up a reference to the DAO library, the full DAO hierarchy becomes available to your VBA code. Figure 54.4 shows a simplified version of the DAO hierarchy.

FIGURE 54.4.

A simplified version of the DAO hierarchy.

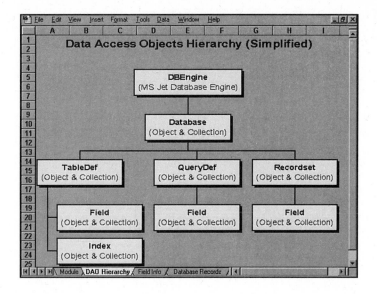

The following is a rundown of the various objects in this hierarchy:

- DBEngine—This top-level object represents the Microsoft Jet database engine as a whole. A particular session of the DBEngine object is called a Workspace, but you'll rarely have to deal with a Workspace object directly.

- Database—A Database object represents an open database (such as an Access MDB database or a FoxPro DBF file). The Databases collection refers to all the open Database objects.

- TableDef—A TableDef object represents the definition of a table in a Database object. A TableDef is a container for the table's Field and Index objects. The TableDefs collection refers to all the table definitions in a Database object.

NOTE

DAO distinguishes between two kinds of tables: a *base table* and an *attached table*. A base table is a table in a Microsoft Jet (MDB) database. Attached tables are tables from another database that are linked to a Microsoft Jet database. (This is why attached tables are also called *linked tables*.) As you'll see a bit later, the most efficient way to work with a non-Jet database (such as a FoxPro or dBASE file) is to link it to an existing Jet database.

- QueryDef—A QueryDef object represents the definition of a query in a Database object. A QueryDef is a container for the query's Field objects. The QueryDefs collection refers to all the query definitions in a Database object.

■ Recordset—A Recordset object represents either the records in a base table from a Database object or the records that result from a query. Most of your DAO labors will involve manipulating Recordset objects in one way or another. The Recordsets collection refers to all the open Recordset objects in a Database object.

■ Field—A Field object represents a column of data. For a TableDef or QueryDef object, a Field object contains the specifications for a field used in a table or query. For a Recordset object, a Field object represents the value in a particular field for the current record. The Fields collection refers to all the fields in a TableDef, QueryDef, or Recordset object.

■ Index—An Index object specifies an order for the records in a TableDef object. The Indexes collection refers to all the Index objects stored in a TableDef object. Note that each Index object has an associated Fields collection that contains the fields used for the index.

Now turn your attention to using these objects to connect to external databases.

Accessing Data in an External Database

Accessing the data contained in an external database from a VBA procedure takes three or four steps, depending on the type of database:

1. Declare variables for the objects you'll be using (you usually will need variables for at least a Database and a Recordset object).

2. Open the database. If you're using a non-Jet external database (such as a FoxPro, Paradox, dBASE, or SQL Server database), open a Jet database to use for attaching the external database.

3. For a non-Jet external database, attach the database to the open Jet database.

4. Open the recordset for the table with which you want to work.

The next two sections supply the details for these steps.

Connecting to a Jet Database

As you might expect, the Jet database engine has the easiest time connecting to databases in its native Jet format (the MDB files, such as those created with Access). Listing 54.4 shows an example.

Listing 54.4. A procedure that connects to a Jet database.

```
Sub JetConnection()

    Dim db As Database
    Dim rs As Recordset
```

```
' Open the Jet database
Set db = OpenDatabase("C:\MSOffice\Access\Samples\NWind.MDB")

' Open the Recordset
Set rs = db.OpenRecordset("Customers", dbOpenTable)

' Display confirmation message
MsgBox "Opened " & db.Name & " Successfully!" & _
       Chr(13) & Chr(13) & _
       "The open Recordset is " & rs.Name

' Close the database
db.Close

End Sub
```

First, the Database and Recordset object variables are declared (db and rs, respectively). Then the OpenDatabase method is invoked to open the database. OpenDatabase is a method of the Workspace object (which, you'll recall, is an instance of the DBEngine object). Following is the syntax:

`object.OpenDatabase(dbname,exclusive,read-only,source)`

object is the Workspace object in which you want to open the database. If you omit *object*, VBA uses the current workspace.

dbname is the full pathname (including the drive and directory) of the database file (for a Jet database). For a non-Jet database, use an ODBC source name or a directory name (such as a directory of FoxPro files).

exclusive opens the database with exclusive access when set to True. The default value is False.

read-only opens the database with read-only access when set to True. The default value is False.

source is a string that specifies extra parameters for opening the database (see the next section for details).

After the database is open, the procedure then opens a Recordset object using the Database object's OpenRecordset method:

`object.OpenRecordset(source,type,options)`

object is the Database object that contains the *source* to use for the Recordset. (You can also use a TableDef or QueryDef object.)

source is a string specifying the source for the Recordset. You can use a table name, a query name, or a SQL statement.

type is the type of Recordset you want to create. Use dbOpenTable (the default) for a table Recordset; use dbOpenDynaset for a dynaset Recordset; use dbOpenSnapshot for a snapshot

Recordset. (For an explanation of each type of Recordset, see the section "Understanding the Recordset Types," later in this chapter.)

options is one or more (integer) constants that specify the characteristics of the new Recordset:

- dbAppendOnly—You can append only new records. (Used only with dynaset types.)
- dbForwardOnly—A forward-scrolling snapshot. Use this option for faster performance if you're making just a single pass through the records.
- dbSQLPassThrough—Enables you to pass SQL statements through to an ODBC database. See the section "Client/Server Query Considerations," later in this chapter.
- dbSeeChanges—Generates an error if another user changes a record you're editing.
- dbDenyWrite—Prevents others from editing and adding records.
- dbDenyRead—Prevents others from viewing records. (Used only with table types.)
- dbReadOnly—You can't make changes to the records.
- dbInconsistent—You can update all fields in a multiple-table query Recordset. (Used only with dynaset types.)
- dbConsistent—You can make changes only to a field in a multiple-table query Recordset that keep the records consistent with each other. (Used only with dynaset types.)

Finally, a MsgBox statement displays the name of the open database (using the Database object's Name property) and the name of the open Recordset (using the Recordset object's Name property).

Connecting to a Non-Jet Database

If the data you want to work with exists in a non-Jet database, you need to attach the data source to an existing Jet database as a new TableDef object. (It's possible to run the OpenDatabase method directly on a non-Jet database, but it's more efficient—and your Recordset operations will perform faster—if you link the database to a Jet database.)

> **NOTE**
>
> What do you do if you don't have access to a Jet database? The answer is easy: Create your own using the CreateDatabase method. For example, the following statement creates a Jet database named MyJetDB.mdb and assigns it to a Database object variable (the dbLangGeneral argument specifies the collating order used for string comparisons):
> ```
> Dim db As Database
> Set db = CreateDatabase("MyJetDB.mdb", dbLangGeneral)
> ```

Listing 54.5 shows the NonJetConnection procedure that connects to a FoxPro database.

Listing 54.5. A procedure that connects to a non-Jet database.

```
Sub NonJetConnection()
    Dim db As Database
    Dim tdFox As TableDef
    Dim rs As recordset

    ' Open the Jet database
    Set db = OpenDatabase("C:\MSOffice\Access\Samples\NWind.MDB")

    ' Create TableDef and set the connection information.
    Set tdFox = db.CreateTableDef("Linked FoxPro Table")
    tdFox.Connect = "FoxPro 2.6;DATABASE=C:\Progra~1\Common~1\Msquery"
    tdFox.SourceTableName = "Customer"

    ' Append the TableDef to create the link
    db.TableDefs.Append tdFox

    ' Open the Recordset
    Set rs = db.OpenRecordset("Linked FoxPro Table", dbOpenSnapshot)

    ' Display confirmation message
    MsgBox "Opened " & db.Name & " Successfully!" & _
        Chr(13) & Chr(13) & _
        "The open Recordset is " & rs.Name & _
        Chr(13) & _
        "The source table is    " & tdFox.SourceTableName

    ' Close the database
    db.Close

End Sub
```

A `TableDef` object variable named `tdFox` is declared to hold the new `TableDef`. A Jet database is opened and then the new `TableDef` is created using the `Database` object's `CreateTableDef` method. This method has a number of arguments, but your code will be easier to read if you use the `TableDef` object's properties to set up the `TableDef`. In most cases, all you need to include in the `CreateTableDef` method is a name for the new `TableDef` (linked FoxPro table in Listing 54.5).

The next two lines set the Connect and SourceTableName properties. Here's a simplified syntax for the Connect property:

object.Connect=*databasetype*;DATABASE=*path*

object is the `TableDef` object.

databasetype is a string indicating the type of database you're attaching. The following are your choices:

dBASE III	Paradox 5.*x*	Excel 3.0
dBASE IV	Btrieve	Excel 4.0
dBASE 5	FoxPro 2.0	Excel 5.0

Paradox 3.*x*	FoxPro 2.5	Excel 7.0
Paradox 4.*x*	FoxPro 2.6	Text

path is the drive and directory (folder) containing the table you want to use (such as a FoxPro DBF file). Note that you'll usually have to specify directory names using MS-DOS eight-character names.

The SourceTableName property specifies the table you want to use. In Listing 54.5, setting this property to Customer tells DAO that you want to work with the Customer.dbf table.

When the new TableDef object is ready, you add it to the Database object's TableDefs collection by using the Append method. When that's done, you can use the TableDef as though it were a Jet table (including opening a new Recordset on the table, as done in Listing 54.5).

Connecting in a Client/Server Environment

In client/server environments, the Connect property usually requires a few more parameters. When linking to a SQL Server data source, for example, you'll need to specify not only a database but also a user name, a password, and a data source name (DSN). For these types of ODBC databases, the *databasetype* argument is ODBC; you specify the other parameters using the UID (user ID), PWD (password), and DSN (data source name) keywords. Following is the general form:

```
object.Connect = "ODBC;DATABASE=dbname;UID=userID;PWD=password;DSN=datasource"
```

For example, the following statement connects a linked TableDef object named tdSQLServer to a SQL Server data source named Publishers, specifies the database named Pubs as the default database, and also specifies a user ID and password:

```
tdSQLServer.Connect = "ODBC;DATABASE=pubs;UID=bwana;PWD=nottelling;DSN=Publishers"
```

TIP

If the Connect string is only ODBC; (for example, tdWhatever="ODBC;"), VBA displays the SQL Data Source dialog box with a list of all the defined data sources so that the user can choose (or even create) the one he or she wants. Note that if the user cancels this dialog box, a trappable runtime error number 3059 occurs.

NOTE

As mentioned earlier, it's possible to use the OpenDatabase method to connect to a non-Jet database directly. This also holds, naturally, for ODBC databases located on servers; you simply use the OpenDatabase method's *source* argument to specify the appropriate connection string (the user ID, password, and so on).

However, you'll find that your work with the resultant Recordset (and especially your queries) will be noticeably faster if, instead, you link the server data to a Jet database on the client machine. That's because the Jet database engine caches information (such as the field and index data) locally, which greatly improves performance. Note, however, that if you change any fields or indexes on the server, you need to update the cached data by running the TableDef object's RefreshLink method.

Working with *Recordsets*

As mentioned earlier, after you open a database, attach an external table (if necessary), and create a new Recordset, you'll spend most of your time manipulating the Recordset in some way. This section gives you more information about Recordsets and takes you through a few useful properties and methods.

Understanding the *Recordset* Types

As you know from the discussion of the OpenRecordset method, you can specify one of three different Recordset types. Here's a rundown of what each type of Recordset means:

- Table type—This type refers to a base table or attached table in an open Database object. Certain actions, such as sorting and indexing, can be performed only on table-type Recordsets.
- Dynaset type—This type refers to a dynamic, virtual table that is (usually) the result of a query. Dynasets can include fields from multiple tables, and they are dynamic because you can update the records by adding, editing, or deleting.
- Snapshot type—This type is similar to a dynaset, except that the records are static; you can't make changes, add records, or delete records. This is the fastest type, and it's the one you should use if you only want to view the data.

Getting Field Information

Before working with a Recordset, you might need to find out some information about the fields in the Recordset. For example, you might want to find out the names of all the fields, their sizes, whether a field requires a value, and the type of data each field uses. Each Recordset object is a container for all the Field objects in the Recordset. Therefore, you can get information on each field by running through the Fields collection. Listing 54.6 shows an Excel procedure that does this. If you are feeling adventurous you might like to add some code to automatically print the resulting worksheet. This would enable you to document the field structure of a database.

Listing 54.6. An Excel procedure that displays information on all the fields in a Recordset.

```
Sub DisplayFieldInfo()

    Dim db As Database
    Dim rs As recordset
    Dim fld As Field
    Dim i As Integer

    ' Open the Jet database
    Set db = OpenDatabase("C:\MSOffice\Access\Samples\NWind.MDB")

    ' Open the Recordset
    Set rs = db.OpenRecordset("Customers", dbOpenSnapshot)

    ' Head for Field Info to monitor the action
    Worksheets("Field Info").Activate

    With Worksheets("Field Info").[B1]
        ' Clear the current data
        .Clear
        .Offset(1).Clear
        .Offset(3, -1).CurrentRegion.Offset(0, 1).Clear

        ' Display Recordset name
        .Offset(1).Value = rs.Name

        ' Enumerate all fields in the Recordset
        For i = 0 To rs.fields.Count - 1
            Application.StatusBar = _
                "Enumerating field " & _
                i + 1 & " of " & _
                rs.fields.Count

            ' Set the Field variable and then run through the properties
            Set fld = rs.Fields(i)
            .Offset(3, i).Value = fld.Name
            .Offset(4, i).Value = fld.AllowZeroLength
            .Offset(5, i).Value = fld.Attributes
            .Offset(6, i).Value = fld.CollatingOrder
            .Offset(7, i).Value = fld.DefaultValue
            .Offset(8, i).Value = fld.OrdinalPosition
            .Offset(9, i).Value = fld.Required
            .Offset(10, i).Value = fld.Size
            .Offset(11, i).Value = fld.SourceField
            .Offset(12, i).Value = fld.SourceTable
            .Offset(13, i).Value = TypeOfField(fld.Type)
            .Offset(14, i).Value = fld.ValidationRule
            .Offset(15, i).Value = fld.ValidationText
            .Offset(1, i).EntireColumn.AutoFit
        Next i

        ' Display database name
        .Value = db.Name
    End With

    ' Close the database
    db.Close
```

```
        Application.StatusBar = False
End Sub

Function TypeOfField(fldConstant As Integer) As String
    Select Case fldConstant
        Case 1    ' dbBoolean
            TypeOfField = "Boolean"
        Case 2    ' dbByte
            TypeOfField = "Byte"
        Case 3    ' dbInteger
            TypeOfField = "Integer"
        Case 4    ' dbLong
            TypeOfField = "Long Integer"
        Case 5    ' dbCurrency
            TypeOfField = "Currency"
        Case 6    ' dbSingle
            TypeOfField = "Single"
        Case 7    ' dbDouble
            TypeOfField = "Double"
        Case 8    ' dbDate
            TypeOfField = "Date"
        Case 10   ' dbText
            TypeOfField = "Text"
        Case 11   'dbLongBinary
            TypeOfField = "OLE Object"
        Case 12   ' dbMemo
            TypeOfField = "Memo"
        Case 15   ' dbGUID
            TypeOfField = "GUID"
    End Select
End Function
```

The For…Next loop runs from 0 (the first field number) to one less than the number of fields in the Recordset rs (the number of fields is given by rs.Fields.Count). In each pass through the loop, the fld variable is set to rs.Fields(i), and then the properties of this Field object are enumerated (such as Name, AllowZeroLength, Size, and Type.) Note that the procedure doesn't return the Type property directly. Instead, the constant is translated into a string by the TypeOfField function. (You can create similar functions that translate the constants returned by the Attributes and CollatingOrder fields.)

Recordset **Properties**

Here's a look at some Recordset properties you'll use most often:

- AbsolutePosition—Returns or sets the relative record number in the Recordset. (Note that the relative position of a particular record might change each time you create the Recordset, so you can't use this property as a substitute for the xBASE RECNO() function.)

- BOF—Returns True if the current record position is before the first record.

■ Bookmark—Sets or returns a Variant value that uniquely identifies the current record. For example, the following code saves the current position to a Variant variable named CurrRecord, moves to the end of the Recordset (using the MoveLast method), and then returns to the previous position:

```
currRecord = rs.Bookmark
rs.MoveLast
rs.Bookmark = currRecord
```

■ Bookmarkable—Returns True if the Recordset supports bookmarks. You should always test your Recordset's Bookmarkable property before attempting to set a bookmark.

■ DateCreated—The date and time the Recordset was created.

■ EOF—Returns True if the current record position is after the last record.

■ Filter—Returns or sets the criteria that determines which records are included in the Recordset. For example, the following statements set the variable rsCustomers to the Customers tables and the Filter property to include only those records in which the Country field is Canada and then open a new Recordset (rsCanada) based on the filtered records:

```
Set rsCustomer = OpenRecordset("Customers")
rs.Filter = "Country = 'Canada'"
Set rsCanada = rsCustomer.OpenRecordset()
```

■ Index—Returns or sets the current Index object for a table-type Recordset. Use the TableDef's Indexes collection to find out the available indexes for a table.

■ LastModified—Returns a bookmark that identifies that most recently added or modified record.

■ LastUpdated—The date and time of the most recent change made to the Recordset.

■ NoMatch—Returns True if the Seek method or one of the Find methods failed to find the desired record. Returns False, otherwise.

■ RecordCount—The number of records in the Recordset.

NOTE

The RecordCount property works only for base tables (attached tables always return 1). To find the number of records in an attached table, you could use the following code fragment (assuming that rs represents a Recordset for an attached table):

```
rs.MoveLast
TotalRecords = rs.AbsolutePosition + 1
```

(The MoveLast method moves to the end of the Recordset, as described in the next section.) In the Chap26.xls workbook that comes on this book's CD, you'll find a TotalAttachedRecords function that uses this code to return the total number of records in an attached table. Note that this is only an approximate number in a multiuser environment (because other users might be in the process of adding or deleting records.)

- Sort—Returns or sets the sort order for a dynaset-type or snapshot-type Recordset. (Use the Index property to sort a table-type Recordset.) To set the sort order, set this property equal to a field name, followed by either Asc (the default) or Desc. Here are a couple of examples (where rs is a Recordset variable):

```
rs.Sort = "Country"
rs.Sort = "LastName Desc"
```

Recordset Methods

Following are a few methods you can use to manipulate a Recordset:

- AddNew—Adds a new record to a table-type or dynaset-type Recordset.
- CancelUpdate—Cancels any pending changes made by the AddNew or Edit methods. (Changes aren't written to the Recordset until you run the Update method.)
- Close—Closes the Recordset.
- Delete—Deletes the current record in a table-type or dynaset-type Recordset.
- Edit—Copies the current record in a table-type or dynaset-type Recordset to the copy buffer for editing. For example, the following code uses the FindFirst method to find the first record where the Country field equals Czechoslovakia. The record is opened for editing using the Edit method, the Country field is modified, and then Recordset is updated with the Update method. The FindNext method looks for more instances of Czechoslovakia. Following is the code:

```
findString = "Country = 'Czechoslovakia'"
replaceString = "Czech Republic"
rs.FindFirst findString               ' Find first occurrence
Do While rs.NoMatch                   ' Loop until no more matches
    rs.Edit                           ' Open record for editing
    rs.Fields("Country") = replaceString  ' Modify Country field
    rs.Update                         ' Update the Recordset
    rs.FindNext findString            ' Find the next match
Loop
```

- FindFirst, FindLast, FindNext, FindPrevious—Search the Recordset for the first, last, next, or previous records that meet the specified criteria. If no record matches the criteria, the NoMatch property returns True.
- GetRows—Retrieves multiple records into an array. See the section "Retrieving Data into Excel" for details on this method.

- Move—Moves the current record pointer by a specified number of records. Here's the syntax:

  object.Move(*rows,start*)

  object is the Recordset object.

  rows is a long integer specifying the number of records to move. Use a negative number to move backwards.

  start is a variable name that identifies a bookmark from which to start the move. If you omit, *start*, the move occurs from the current record.

- MoveFirst, MoveLast, MoveNext, MovePrevious—Move the current record to the first, last, next, or previous record in the Recordset. Use the BOF property to determine if MovePrevious moves the record pointer before the first record; use EOF to determine whether MoveNext moves the record pointer past the last record.

- Seek—Searches an indexed table-type Recordset for a record that meets the specified criteria. Here's the syntax for the Seek method:

  object.Seek(*comparison.key1,key2…*)

  object is the indexed table-type Recordset object.

  comparison is a comparison operator: =, >, >=, <, <=, or <>.

  key1,key2… is one or more values that correspond to the fields in the current index.

  Note that you need to set the current index for the Recordset before you use the Seek method. For example, the following code sets a Recordset's Index property and then uses Seek to find a matching record:

  ```
  Set rs = db.OpenRecordset("Customers")
  rs.Index = "Country"
  rs.Seek "=", "Czechoslovakia"
  ```

TIP

Index-based Seek searches are much faster than any of the Find methods, so you should always use Seek if an appropriate Index object is available.

- Update—Writes changes made by AddNew or Edit to a table-type or dynaset-type Recordset.

Querying a *Recordset*

In general, the Recordsets you open will contain all the records in the underlying table. If you want to filter the records, however, DAO gives you the following three choices:

- Specify the Recordset's Filter property and then run the OpenRecordset method on the filtered records. (The Filter property was described earlier in this chapter.)

- Run the OpenRecordset method and specify a SQL expression instead of a table name.
- Run the OpenRecordset method on a QueryDef object.

Opening a *Recordset* Using a SQL Expression

Listing 54.7 shows a procedure that opens a Recordset based on the Customers table in the Nwind.mdb database. However, selectStr variable holds a SELECT statement that filters the data as follows:

- Only the CompanyName, Region, and Country fields are used.
- The records are restricted to those where the Country field is Canada.
- The Recordset is ordered by the CompanyName field.

Listing 54.7. A procedure that opens a Recordset using a SQL SELECT expression.

```
Sub QueryCustomers()

    Dim db As Database
    Dim selectStr As String
    Dim rs As Recordset

    ' Open the Jet database
    Set db = OpenDatabase("C:\MSOffice\Access\Samples\NWind.MDB")

    ' Store the SELECT statement in a string variable
    selectStr = "SELECT CompanyName,Region,Country " & _
                "FROM Customers " & _
                "WHERE Country = 'Canada' " & _
                "ORDER BY CompanyName"

    ' Open the Recordset
    Set rs = db.OpenRecordset(selectStr)

    ' Display confirmation message
    MsgBox "The filtered Recordset contains " & _
            rs.RecordCount & " records."

    ' Close the database
    db.Close

End Sub
```

Opening a *Recordset* from a *QueryDef* Object

If the Database object already contains one or more queries in the form of QueryDef objects, you can open a Recordset by using the QueryDef object's OpenRecordset method. For example, Listing 54.8 opens a database, assigns the variable qd to the "Products Above Average Price" QueryDef object, and then creates the Recordset from the QueryDef.

Listing 54.8. A procedure that creates a `Recordset` from a `QueryDef` object.

```
Sub QueryDefExample()

    Dim db As Database
    Dim qd As QueryDef
    Dim rs As Recordset

    ' Open the Jet database
    Set db = OpenDatabase("C:\MSOffice\Access\Samples\NWind.MDB")

    ' Assign the QueryDef object
    qd = db.QueryDefs("Products Above Average Price")

    ' Open the Recordset
    Set rs = qd.OpenRecordset()

    ' Display confirmation message
    MsgBox "The filtered Recordset contains " & _
           rs.RecordCount & " records."

    ' Close the database
    db.Close

End Sub
```

> **NOTE**
>
> You can create new `QueryDef` objects by using the `Database` object's `CreateQueryDef`
> method. This method takes two arguments: the name of the new `QueryDef` object and
> the SQL expression that defines the query. For example, the following statement
> creates a new `QueryDef` object called `"Canadian Customers"`, based on the SQL expres-
> sion used in Listing 54.8:
>
> ```
> Dim db As Database, qd As QueryDef
> Set db = OpenDatabase("NWind.MDB")
> selectStr = "SELECT CompanyName,Region,Country " & _
>             "FROM Customers " & _
>             "WHERE Country = 'Canada' " & _
>             "ORDER BY CompanyName"
> Set qd = db.CreateQueryDef("Canadian Customers",selectStr)
> ```

Client/Server Query Considerations

For client/server applications, you have the following two choices when it comes to querying
the server:

- You can construct ordinary Jet queries based on the linked server data.
- You can construct a *pass-through* query that the Jet engine sends directly to the server
  for processing.

The type of query you use depends on the application, but there are a few general guidelines you can follow:

Use a pass-through query if...

- You would prefer to off-load some of the query processing to the server.
- You need to take advantage of some server-specific features that have no equivalent in VBA (such as stored procedures and security functionality).
- You need to use some server-specific SQL features that aren't supported by the Jet SQL standard.
- You want to create a new database or table on the server.
- You want to perform some system administrator chores (such as updating user accounts).

Use an ordinary Jet query if...

- You want to update the resultant Recordset. A pass-through query always returns a snapshot-type Recordset, which you cannot update.
- You're not sure about the exact syntax that the server database uses. By creating the query in the Jet syntax, the Jet engine will translate your query into the SQL statement that's appropriate for the server.
- You need to include a user-defined function as part of your query.

If you decide that a pass-though query is the way to go, you can execute a SQL pass-through query by specifying the dbSQLPassThrough constant as the *options* argument in the OpenRecordset method.

Retrieving Data into Excel

To get data from an external database into an Excel worksheet, you have three choices:

- Retrieve an individual field value
- Retrieve one or more entire rows
- Retrieve an entire Recordset

Retrieving an Individual Field Value

For individual field values, move to the record you want to work with and then use the Field object's Value property. For example, the following statement returns the value of the current record's Country field in the Recordset named rs and stores it in cell A1 of the active worksheet:

```
ActiveSheet.[a1] = rs.Fields("Country").Value
```

Retrieving One or More Entire Rows

To get full records, use the Recordset object's GetRows method. The GetRows(*n*) method returns *n* records in a two-dimensional array, where the first subscript is a number that represents the field (the first field is 0) and the second subscript represents the record number (where the first record is 0). Listing 54.9 shows an Excel procedure that opens a Recordset from a QueryDef and enters the first 100 rows into a worksheet named Database Records.

Listing 54.9. An Excel procedure that reads 100 rows from a Recordset into a worksheet.

```
Sub ReadDataIntoExcel()

    Dim db As Database, qd As QueryDef, rs As Recordset
    Dim selectStr As String, recArray As Variant
    Dim i As Integer, j As Integer

    ' Open the Jet database, QueryDef, and Recordset
    Set db = OpenDatabase("C:\MSOffice\Access\Samples\NWind.MDB")
    Set qd = db.QueryDefs("Canadian Customers")
    Set rs = qd.OpenRecordset()

    ' Head for Database Records and clear the sheet
    Worksheets("Database Records").Activate
    With Worksheets("Database Records").[a1]
        .CurrentRegion.Clear

        ' Read the data using GetRows
        recArray = rs.GetRows(100)
        For i = 0 To UBound(recArray, 1)
            For j = 0 To UBound(recArray, 2)
                .Offset(i + 1, j) = recArray(i, j)
            Next j
        Next i

        ' Enter the field names and format the cells
        For j = 0 To rs.fields.Count - 1
            .Offset(0, j) = rs.fields(j).Name
            .Offset(0, j).Font.Bold = True
            .Offset(0, j).EntireColumn.AutoFit
        Next j

    End With

    ' Close the database
    db.Close

End Sub
```

Retrieving an Entire *Recordset*

If you need to retrieve an entire `Recordset` into a worksheet, you can do so easily with the `Range` object's `CopyFromRecordset` method:

object.`CopyFromRecordset(`*data,maxRows,maxColumns*`)`

object is a `Range` object that specifies the upper-left corner of the destination range.

data is the `Recordset` containing the data you want to retrieve.

maxRows is the maximum number of records to retrieve. If you omit *maxRows*, Excel copies every record.

maxColumns is the maximum number of fields to retrieve. If you omit *maxColumns*, Excel copies every field.

Following are a few notes to bear in mind when working with `CopyFromRecordset`:

- ■ Excel begins the copying from the current record. If you want to retrieve every record, make sure you run the `MoveFirst` method to move to the first record.

- ■ When the `CopyFromRecordset` method is done, the `Recordset` object's EOF property is True.

- ■ `CopyFromRecordset` will choke if the `Recordset` object has a field that contains OLE objects.

Listing 54.10 shows the `RetrieveCategories` procedure that uses the `CopyFromRecordset` method.

Listing 54.10. A procedure that filters out OLE object fields before retrieving a Recordset.

```
Sub RetrieveCategories()

    Dim db As Database, rs As Recordset, fld As Field
    Dim selectStr As String, i As Integer

    ' Open the Jet database
    Set db = OpenDatabase("C:\MSoffice\Access\Samples\NWind.MDB")

    ' Open the full Categories table
    Set rs = db.OpenRecordset("Categories")

    ' The selectStr variable will hold the SQL SELECT statement
    ' that filters the Recordset to remove OLE Object fields
    selectStr = "SELECT "

    ' Run through the Recordset fields
    For Each fld In rs.fields
        ' Check for OLE Object fields
        If fld.Type <> dbLongBinary Then
            ' If it's not an OLE Object field, add it to the SELECT statement
```

continues

Listing 54.10. continued

```
            selectStr = selectStr & fld.Name & ","
      End If
Next fld

' Remove the trailing comma
selectStr = Left(selectStr, Len(selectStr) - 1)

' Add the FROM clause
selectStr = selectStr & " FROM Categories"

' Open the filtered Recordset
Set rs = db.OpenRecordset(selectStr)

' Retrieve the records
Worksheets("Database Records").Activate
With Worksheets("Database Records").[a1]
    .CurrentRegion.Clear

    ' Retrieve the records
    .Offset(1).CopyFromRecordset rs

    ' Enter the field names and format the cells
    For i = 0 To rs.fields.Count - 1
        .Offset(0, i) = rs.fields(i).Name
        .Offset(0, i).Font.Bold = True
        .Offset(0, i).EntireColumn.AutoFit
    Next i

End With

' Close the database
db.Close

End Sub
```

RetrieveCategories connects to a Jet database and opens the Categories table as the rs Recordset variable. You want to make sure that you don't try to copy any OLE Object fields, so the procedure constructs a SQL SELECT statement that excludes any fields that contain OLE objects. The selectStr variable will hold the SELECT statement; therefore, it's initialized to "SELECT ". Then a For…Next loop runs through each field in rs and looks for OLE Object fields (where the Type property is dbLongBinary; see the DAO Help listing for the constants that correspond to the other field types). If a field isn't an OLE object type, its name (and a comma separator) is appended to the SELECT statement.

Next, the trailing comma is removed and the FROM clause is concatenated to the SELECT statement. A new Recordset is opened based on selectStr, and then the CopyFromRecordset method retrieves the records.

Working with Errors

Properly designed procedures don't leave the user out in the cold if an error occurs. Instead, they designate an *error handling routine* to process errors and (usually) report back to the user.

To trap errors, use the On Error GoTo *line* statement, where *line* is a label that indicates the start of your error handling code. (A *label* is a text string—without spaces or periods—followed by a colon.)

Listing 54.11 shows an example. The TestDir procedure is designed to see if a directory exists. If a directory like a:\test is checked and the disk drive is empty, the error handler will be invoked.

Listing 54.11. A procedure with an error-handling routine.

```
Sub TestDir(dirName as string)

    ' Define the error handling code
    On Error GoTo ErrorHandler

    Dir (dirName)

Exit Sub     ' Bypass the error handling code

ErrorHandler:    ' Code branches here if an error occurs
    msg = "The following error has occurred:" & Chr(13) & _
        "   Error number:  " & Err & Chr(13) & _
        "   Error message: " & Error(Err) & Chr(13) & Chr(13) & _
        "Select Abort to bail out, Retry to re-enter the drive" & Chr(13) & _
        "letter, or Ignore to attempt the backup again."
    result = MsgBox(msg, vbExclamation + vbAbortRetryIgnore)
    Select Case result
        Case vbAbort
            Exit Sub
        Case vbRetry
            done = False
            Resume Next
        Case vbIgnore
            Resume
    End Select

End Sub
```

The error routine is set up with the following statement:

```
On Error GoTo ErrorHandler
```

The ErrorHandler argument refers to the ErrorHandler: label. If an error occurs, the procedure jumps to this label and runs the code between the label and the End Sub statement. In this case, a message is displayed that includes the error number (as given by the Err function) and an error message (as given by the Error(Err) function).

The error handler's `MsgBox` gives the user three choices, which get processed by the subsequent `Select Case` statement:

- ■ `Abort`—Selecting this option (`Case vbAbort`) bails out of the procedure altogether by running the `Exit Sub` statement.

- ■ `Retry`—Selecting this option (`Case vbRetry`) means the user wants to re-enter the drive letter. The `done` variable is set to `False` (`done` controls the `While...Wend` loop) and then the `Resume .Next` statement is run. `Resume Next` tells VBA to continue running the procedure from the statement *after* the statement that caused the error. In this case, the next statement is `Wend`, so the procedure just loops back (since we set `done` to `False`) and runs the `InputBox` function again.

- ■ `Ignore`—Selecting this option (`Case vbIgnore`) means that the user wants to attempt the backup again. For example, if the user forgot to insert a disk in the drive, or if the drive door wasn't closed, the user would fix the problem and then select this option. In this case, the error handler runs the `Resume` statement, which tells VBA to continue the procedure from the statement that caused the error.

> **NOTE**
>
> For more sophisticated error handling, use the `Err` function in conjunction with `Select Case` to test for different errors and process the result accordingly. For a list of error codes, load the VBA Help file and use the Index tab to look for the `trappable errors` topic.

Working with the Debugger

It's usually easy to get short `Sub` and `Function` procedures up and running. However, as your code grows larger and more complex, errors will inevitably creep in. Many will be simple syntax problems you can fix easily, but others will be more subtle and harder to find. For the latter—whether the errors are incorrect values being returned or problems in the overall logic of a procedure—you'll need to be able to look "inside" your code to scope out what's wrong. The good news is that VBA provides you with several reasonably sophisticated debugging tools that can remove some of the burden of program problem solving. This chapter looks at these tools and shows you how to use them to help recover from most programming errors.

> **NOTE**
>
> A *bug* is a logical or syntactical error in a computer program. The term descends from the earliest days of room-size computers, when problems occasionally were traced to insects actually getting stuck between vacuum tubes!

Debugging, like most computer skills, involves no great secrets. In fact, all debugging is usually a matter of taking a good, hard, dispassionate look at your code. Although there are no set-in-stone techniques for solving programming problems, you can formulate a basic strategy that will get you started.

When a problem occurs, the first thing you need to determine is what type of error you're dealing with. There are four basic types:

- Syntax errors—These errors arise from misspelled or missing keywords and incorrect punctuation. VBA catches most (but not all) of these errors when you enter your statements.

- Compile errors—When you try to run a procedure, VBA takes a quick look at the code to make sure things look right. If it sees a problem (such as an If…Then statement without a corresponding End If), it highlights the statement where the problem has occurred and displays an error message.

- Runtime errors—These errors occur during the execution of a procedure. They generally mean that VBA has stumbled on a statement that it can't figure out. It might be a formula attempting to divide by zero or using a property or method with the wrong object.

- Logic errors—If your code zigs instead of zags, the cause is usually a flaw in the logic of your procedure. It might be a loop that never ends or a Select Case that doesn't select.

After you determine the species of error that has occurred, you need to decide how to deal with it. Syntax errors are flagged right away by VBA, which means that you just have to read the error message and then clean up the offending statement. Unfortunately, not all of VBA's error messages are helpful. For example, one common syntax error is to forget to include a closing quotation mark in a string. When this happens, VBA reports the following unhelpful message:

```
Expected: To or list separator or )
```

Fixing compile errors also is usually straightforward. Read the error message and see where VBA has highlighted the code. Doing so almost always gives you enough information to fix the problem.

Runtime errors produce a dialog box, such as the one shown in Figure 54.5. These error messages usually are a little more vague than the ones you see for syntax and compile errors. It often helps to see the statement where the offense has occurred. You can do this by selecting the Goto button. This activates the module and places the insertion point on the line where the error has occurred. If you still can't see the problem, you need to rerun the procedure and pause at or near the point in which the error occurs. This enables you to examine the state of the program when it tries to execute the statement. These techniques are explained in the "Setting a Breakpoint" section later in this chapter.

FIGURE 54.5.

A typical runtime error message.

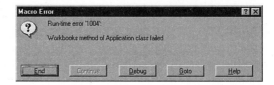

Logic errors are the toughest to pin down because you don't get any error messages to give you clues about what went wrong and where. To help, VBA enables you to trace through a procedure one statement at a time. This enables you to watch the flow of the procedure and to see whether the code does what you want it to do. You also can keep an eye on the values of individual variables and properties to make sure they're behaving as expected.

Pausing a Procedure

Pausing a procedure in midstream enables you to see certain elements, such as the current values of variables and properties. It also enables you to execute program code one statement at a time so you can monitor the flow of a procedure.

When you pause a procedure, VBA enters *break mode* and displays the Debug window, shown in Figure 54.6. The Debug window is divided into two parts:

- Watch pane—This area enables you to monitor the values of procedure variables, properties, or expressions. See the section "Monitoring Procedure Values."

- Code pane—This area shows a section of the currently running procedure. The current statement (that is, the one that VBA will execute next) is surrounded by a box. See the section "Stepping into a Procedure."

FIGURE 54.6.

VBA displays the Debug window when you enter break mode.

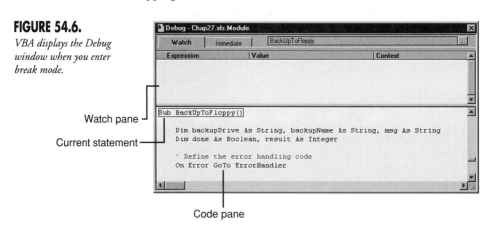

Watch pane

Current statement

Code pane

Entering Break Mode

VBA gives you no fewer than five ways to enter break mode:

- From a runtime error dialog box
- At the beginning of a procedure
- By pressing Esc or Ctrl+Break while a procedure is running
- By setting breakpoints
- By using a Stop statement

Entering Break Mode from an Error Dialog Box

As mentioned earlier, when a runtime error occurs, you should first try clicking the Goto button in the dialog box. This takes you to the statement causing the problem and, in many cases, enables you to fix the error right away.

For more obscure problems, you'll need to enter break mode and take a look around. You can do this by selecting the Debug button from the error message dialog box.

Entering Break Mode at the Beginning of a Procedure

If you're not sure where to look for the cause of an error, you can start the procedure in break mode. Place the insertion point inside the procedure and select the Run | Step Into command or click the Step Into button on the Visual Basic toolbar. VBA displays the Debug window and highlights the Sub statement.

> **TIP**
>
> You also can press F8 to start a procedure in break mode.

Entering Break Mode by Pressing the Esc Key

If your procedure isn't producing an error but appears to be behaving strangely, you can enter break mode by pressing Esc (or Ctrl+Break) or by clicking the Step Macro button on the Visual Basic toolbar while the procedure is running. VBA pauses on whatever statement it was about to execute.

Setting a Breakpoint

If you know approximately where an error or logic flaw is occurring, you can enter break mode at a specific statement in the procedure by setting up a *breakpoint*. The following procedure shows you what to do:

1. Activate the module containing the procedure you want to run.
2. Place the insertion point on the statement where you want to enter break mode. VBA will run every line of code up to, but not including, this statement.
3. Select Toggle Breakpoint from the Run menu or click the Toggle Breakpoint button on the Visual Basic toolbar. VBA highlights the entire line in red, as shown in Figure 54.7.

FIGURE 54.7.

When you set a breakpoint, VBA highlights the entire line in red.

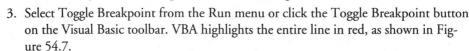

```
' Check to see if OK was selected
If backupDrive <> "" Then
    ' Make sure the backup drive contains a colon (:)
    If InStr(backupDrive, ":") = 0 Then
        backupDrive = Left(backupDrive, 1) & ":"
    End If
    ' First save the file
    ActiveWorkbook.Save
    ' Assume the backup will be successful and
    ' so set done to True to exit the loop
    done = True
    ' Concatenate drive letter and workbook name
    backupName = backupDrive & ActiveWorkbook.Name
    ' Make a copy on the specified drive
    ActiveWorkbook.SaveCopyAs filename:=backupName
Else
    Exit Sub
End If
```

Breakpoint →

4. Repeat Steps 2 and 3 to set other breakpoints.

Entering Break Mode Using a *Stop* Statement

When developing your applications, you'll often test the robustness of a procedure by sending it various test values or by trying it out under different conditions. In many cases, you'll want to enter break mode to make sure things look okay. You could set breakpoints at specific statements, but you lose them if you close the file. For something a little more permanent, you can include a `Stop` statement in a procedure. VBA automatically enters break mode whenever it encounters a `Stop` statement.

Listing 54.12 shows the `TestDir` procedure with a `Stop` statement inserted just before the statement that runs the `Dir` method, which might generate an error.

Listing 54.12. You can insert `Stop` statements to enter break mode at specific procedure locations.

```
Sub TestDir(dirName As String)

    ' Define the error handling code
    On Error GoTo ErrorHandler

    Stop     ' HERE IS THE STOP!

    Dir (dirName)

Exit Sub     ' Bypass the error handling code
```

Exiting Break Mode

To exit break mode, you can use either of the following methods:

- Resume normal program execution by selecting Continue from the Run menu, by clicking the Resume Macro button on the Visual Basic toolbar, or by pressing F5.

- End the procedure by selecting End from the Run menu or by clicking the Visual Basic toolbar's Stop Macro button.

Stepping Through a Procedure

One of the most common (and most useful) debugging techniques is to step through the code one statement at a time. This enables you to get a feel for the program flow to make sure that things such as loops and procedure calls are executing properly. You can either step *into* procedures or step *over* them.

Stepping into a Procedure

Stepping into a procedure means that you execute one line at a time. To step into a procedure, first enter break mode as described earlier in this chapter. The Debug window appears, and VBA places a box around the current statement. Now select Step Into from the Run menu or click the Step Into button on the Visual Basic toolbar. VBA executes the current statement and displays the box around the next statement. Keep stepping through until the procedure ends or until you're ready to resume normal execution.

Stepping Over a Procedure

Some statements call other procedures. If you're not interested in stepping through a called procedure, you can step *over* it. This means that VBA executes the procedure normally and then resumes break mode at the next statement *after* the procedure call. To step over a procedure, follow these steps:

1. Enter break mode as described earlier in this chapter. The Debug window appears, and VBA displays a box around the current statement.

2. Step into the procedure until you come to a procedure call you want to step over.

3. Select Step Over from the Run menu or click the Visual Basic toolbar's Step Over button. VBA executes the procedure and then places the box around the next statement.

4. Repeat Steps 2 and 3 until the procedure ends or until you're ready to resume normal execution.

Monitoring Procedure Values

Many runtime and logic errors are the result of (or, in some cases, can result in) variables or properties assuming unexpected values. If your procedure uses or changes these elements in several places, you'll need to enter break mode and monitor the values of these elements to see where things go awry. VBA enables you to set up *watch expressions* to do just that. These watch expressions appear in the Watch pane of the Debug window.

Adding a Watch Expression

To add a watch expression, you use the Add Watch dialog box, shown in Figure 54.8. This dialog box contains the following elements:

- Expression—The watch expression. You can enter a variable name, property, user-defined function name, or any other valid VBA expression.

- Context—Specifies the context of the variable (that is, where the variable is used). You enter the procedure and the module.

- Watch Type—Specifies how VBA watches the expression. The Watch Expression option displays the expression in the Watch pane when you enter break mode. Break When Value is True tells VBA to automatically enter break mode when the expression value becomes True (or nonzero). Break When Value Changes automatically enters break mode whenever the value of the expression changes.

FIGURE 54.8.

Use the Add Watch dialog box to add watch expressions.

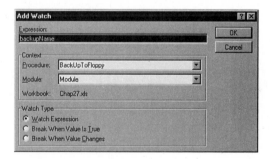

Follow these steps to add a watch expression:

1. If the expressions exists inside the procedure (for example, a variable name), select the expression as follows:

   For single-word expressions, place the insert point anywhere inside the word.

   For more complex expressions, highlight the entire expression.

2. Select Add Watch from the Tools menu to display the Add Watch dialog box.

3. If necessary, enter the expression you want to watch in the Expression text box and select the Context options.

4. Select a Watch Type option.

5. Select OK.

After you add a watch expression, you monitor it by entering break mode and selecting the Watch tab in the Debug window. Figure 54.9 shows an example of this.

FIGURE 54.9.

The Debug window with a watch expression.

Watch expression   Current value   Expression context

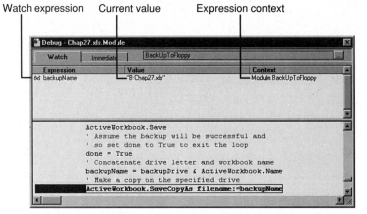

> **TIP**
>
> The Add Watch command from the Tools menu is available when the Debug window is active. Therefore, you can add watch expressions while in break mode.

Editing a Watch Expression

You can make changes to a watch expression while in break mode. The following procedure takes you through the necessary steps:

1. Select the Watch pane by clicking it or by pressing Ctrl+F6.
2. Highlight the watch expression you want to edit.
3. Select Edit Watch from the Tools menu. VBA displays the Edit Watch dialog box.

> **TIP**
>
> You also can display the Edit Watch dialog box by double-clicking the watch expression.

---

4. Make your changes to the watch expression.
5. Select OK to return to the Debug window.

Deleting a Watch Expression

To delete a watch expression you no longer need to monitor, follow these steps:

1. Select the Watch pane by clicking it or by pressing Ctrl+F6.

2. Highlight the watch expression you want to delete.

3. Select Edit Watch from the Tools menu. VBA displays the Edit Watch dialog box.

4. Select the Delete button. VBA deletes the expression and returns you to the Debug window.

> **TIP**
>
> You can quickly delete a watch expression by highlighting it in the Watch pane and pressing Delete.

Displaying an Instant Watch

Many variables and properties are set once, and they don't change for the rest of the procedure. To avoid cluttering the Watch pane with these expressions, you can use an Instant Watch to quickly check the expressions' values. To do this, follow these steps:

1. In the Debug window's Code pane, place the insertion point inside the expression you want to display.

2. Select Instant Watch from the Tools menu or click the Instant Watch button on the Visual Basic toolbar. VBA displays the Instant Watch dialog box, shown in Figure 54.10.

FIGURE 54.10.

Use the Instant Watch dialog box to quickly display the value of an expression.

> **TIP**
>
> You also can display the Instant Watch dialog box by pressing Shift+F9.

3. If you want to add an expression to the Watch pane, select the Add button. To return to the Debug window without adding the expression, select Cancel.

Using the Immediate Pane

The Watch pane tells you the current value of an expression, but often you will need more information than this. You also might want to plug in different values for an expression while in break mode. You can perform these tasks with the Debug window's Immediate pane (which you can display by selecting the Immediate tab in the Debug window).

Printing Data in the Immediate Pane

Using the special `Debug` object, you can use its `Print` method to print text and expression values in the Immediate pane. Following are the two ways to do this:

- By running the `Print` method from the procedure
- By entering the `Print` method directly into the Immediate pane

The `Print` method uses the following syntax:

```
Debug.Print outputList
```

outputList is an expression or list of expressions to print in the Immediate pane. Separate multiple expressions with semicolons. If you omit *outputList*, a blank line is printed.

Running the Print Method from a Procedure

If you know that a variable or expression changes at a certain place in your code, enter a `Debug.Print` statement at that spot. When you enter break mode, the *outputList* expressions appear in the Immediate pane. For example, Figure 54.11 shows a procedure in break mode. The information displayed in the Immediate pane was generated by the following statement:

```
Debug.Print "The backup filename is "; backupName
```

FIGURE 54.11.

Use `Debug.Print` *in your code to display information in the Immediate pane.*

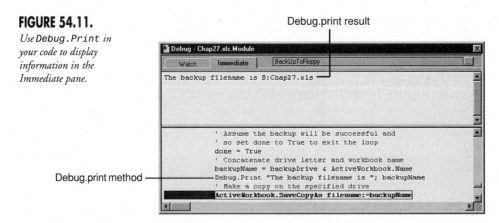

Running the Print Method in the Immediate Pane

You also can use the `Print` method directly in the Immediate pane to display information. Because you're already in the Debug window, you don't need to specify the `Debug` object.

Figure 54.12 shows a couple examples. In the first line, print backupDrive was entered. VBA responded with B:. In the second example, ? backupName (? is the short form for the Print method) was entered, and VBA responded with B:Chap27.xls.

FIGURE 54.12.

You can enter Print *statements directly in the Immediate pane. Note the use of the question mark (?) as a short form for the* Print *method.*

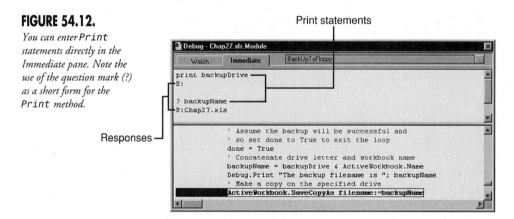

Executing Statements in the Immediate Pane

Perhaps the most effective use of the Immediate pane, however, is to execute statements. There are many uses for this feature:

- To try some experimental statements to see their effect on the procedure.
- To change the value of a variable or property. For example, if you see that a variable with a value of 0 is about to be used as a divisor, you could change the variable to a nonzero value to avoid crashing the procedure.
- To run other procedures or user-defined functions to see if they operate properly under the current conditions.

You enter statements in the Immediate pane just as you do in the module itself. For example, entering the following statement in the Immediate pane changes the value of the backupName variable:

```
backupName = "A:Chap27.xls"
```

Debugging Tips

Debugging your procedures can be a frustrating job—even during the best of times. The following sections include a few tips to keep in mind when tracking down programming problems.

Indent Your Code for Readability

VBA code is immeasurably more readable when you indent your control structures. Readable code is that much easier to trace and decipher, so your debugging efforts have one fewer hurdle to negotiate. Indenting code is a simple matter of pressing Tab an appropriate number of times at the beginning of a statement.

It helps if VBA's automatic indentation feature is enabled. To check this, select Options from the Tools menu, select the Module tab, and activate the Auto Indent check box.

> **NOTE**
>
> By default, VBA moves the insertion point four spaces to the right when you press the Tab key. You can change the default by entering a new value in the Tab Width spinner in the Module tab of the Options dialog box.

Require Variable Declarations

To avoid errors caused by using variables improperly, you should always declare your procedure variables. To make VBA display an error if you don't declare a variable, add the following statement to the top of the module:

```
Option Explicit
```

> **TIP**
>
> To have VBA include the Option Explicit statement in every new module, activate the Require Variable Declarations check box in the Module tab of the Options dialog box.

Break Down Complex Procedures

Don't try to solve all your problems at once. If you have a large procedure that isn't working right, test it in small chunks to try to narrow down the problem. To test a piece of a procedure, add an Exit Sub statement after the last line of the code you want to test.

Enter VBA Keywords in Lowercase

If you always enter keywords in lowercase letters, you can easily detect a problem when you see that VBA doesn't change the word to its normal case when you enter the line.

When a Procedure Refuses to Run

If your procedure refuses to run, check the following:

■ Make sure the workbook containing the module is open.

■ If you're trying to run the procedure by pressing a shortcut key, make sure the shortcut key has been defined.

■ Check to see whether another procedure has the same shortcut key. If one does and it appears earlier in the Macro dialog box list, your procedure won't run. You'll need to change the shortcut key for one of the procedures.

■ Make sure that another open module doesn't have a procedure with the same name.

Comment Out Problem Statements

If a particular statement is giving you problems, you can temporarily deactivate it by placing an apostrophe at the beginning of the line. This tells VBA to treat the line as a comment.

Break Up Long Statements

One of the most complicated aspects of procedure debugging is making sense out of long statements (especially formulas). The Immediate pane can help (you can use it to print parts of the statement), but it's usually best to keep your statements as short as you can. After you get things working properly, you often can recombine statements for more efficient code.

Use Range Names Whenever Possible in Excel

In Excel, procedures are much easier to read and debug if you use range names in place of cell references. Not only is a name such as Expenses!Summary more comprehensible than Expenses!A1:F10, but it's also safer. If you add rows or columns to the Summary range, the name's reference changes as well. With cell addresses, you have to adjust the references yourself.

Take Advantage of User-Defined Constants

If your procedure uses constant values in several different statements, you can give yourself one fewer debugging chore by creating a user-defined constant for the value. This gives you the following three important advantages:

■ It ensures that you don't enter the wrong value in a statement.

■ It's easier to change the value because you have to change only the constant declaration.

■ Your procedures will be easier to understand.

Working with Add-Ins

If you've used any add-in applications, you know they're handy because they add extra functions and commands and look as though they were built right into the program. For your own applications, you can convert your procedures to add-ins and gain the following advantages:

- Your Function procedures appear in the Function Wizard dialog box in the User Defined category.

- Your Sub procedures do *not* appear in the Macro dialog box. This means users must access your add-in procedures entirely by shortcut keys, menu commands, toolbar buttons, or other indirect means (such as the event handlers).

- Add-ins execute faster than normal files.

- The code is compiled into a compressed format that no one else can read or modify.

It's important to keep in mind that add-in applications are *demand loaded.* This means that when you install your application, it gets read into memory in two stages:

1. The application's shortcut keys are enabled, its menus and menu commands are added to the appropriate menu bar, and its toolbars are displayed. And in Excel, the functions are added to the Function Wizard.

2. The rest of the application is loaded into memory when the user either chooses one of the add-in functions, presses an add-in shortcut key, selects an add-in menu item, or clicks an add-in toolbar button.

The exception to this is when the add-in file contains an Auto_Open procedure. In this case, the entire add-in is loaded at the start.

Creating an Add-In

When you've fully debugged and tested your code and are ready to distribute the application to your users, you can create an add-in file of your own.

Only Excel has the capability to create add-in files, although both Access and Excel can use them.

Follow these steps to create the add-in:

1. Activate the Excel module you want to save as an add-in.

2. Select Make Add-In from the Tools menu to display the Make Add-In dialog box.

3. Enter a new name, drive, and folder (if required) for the file.

4. Make sure that Microsoft Excel Add-In is selected in the Save File as Type drop-down list.

5. Select OK.

Be sure to fill in both the Title and Comments boxes on the Summary tab of the Utilities Properties dialog box (select Properties from the File menu; see Figure 54.13) before converting the workbook to an add-in. The Title text will be the name of the add-in and the comments will appear at the bottom of the Add-Ins dialog box when you highlight your add-in.

FIGURE 54.13.

Use the Summary tab of the Utilities Properties dialog box to describe the file before converting it to an add-in.

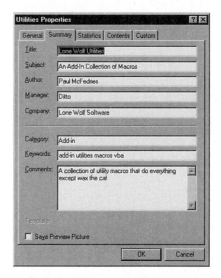

Don't save the add-in using the same name as the original workbook. You can't edit an add-in file, so if you lose the original, the add-in can never be changed.

Controlling Add-Ins with VBA

VBA provides you with several methods and properties that enable you to control add-in applications at the procedural level. From a VBA point of view, an AddIn object is an individual add-in application, and AddIns is the collection of all the add-in applications available to Excel. The AddIns collection is identical to the list of add-ins you see when you display the Add-Ins dialog box (by selecting Add-Ins from the Tools menu).

To refer to an AddIn object, use the AddIns method:

```
AddIns(index)
```

The *index* argument can be any one of the following:

- A number representing the add-in you want to use, where 1 signifies the first add-in that appears in the Add-Ins dialog box, 2 is the second add-in that appears, and so on.
- The name, as text, of the add-in you want to use. For the add-ins that come with Excel, the name of the add-in is the name that appears in the Add-Ins dialog box. For your own add-ins, the name is either the file name (minus the extension) or the text you entered into the Title edit box of the Summary Info dialog.
- An array of numbers or names.

For example, the following statement refers to the Solver add-in application:

```
AddIns("Solver Add-In")
```

Before you can work with your own add-ins, you need to add them to the AddIns collection. VBA provides the Add method to do just that, as in the following:

```
Addins.Add(fileName, copyFile)
```

fileName is a string containing the full pathname of the add-in file.

copyFile is an optional logical argument to use when the add-in file is stored on a floppy disk, CD-ROM, or network drive. If *copyFile* is True, the application copies the add-in file to your hard disk. If it's False, the application leaves the file where it is. If you omit *copyFile*, the application displays a dialog box that asks what you want to do. The *copyFile* argument is ignored if *fileName* references a file on your hard disk.

The Add method's only purpose in life is to tell the application that the add-in is available. To actually use the file (in order to make its commands and functions available to the user), you need to install it by setting its Installed property to True. (This is the equivalent of activating the add-in's check box in the Add-Ins dialog box.) This does the following two things:

- It performs the first part of the demand-loading sequence (in other words, the add-in's functions, shortcut keys, menus, and toolbars become available).
- The add-in's Auto_Add procedure (if it has one) is executed. This is another of the automatic procedures discussed earlier. It's useful for things such as initializing the add-in and telling the user that the add-in is loaded.

Listing 54.13 shows you how to work with add-ins from a VBA procedure.

Listing 54.13. Working with add-in applications.

```
Sub InstallBudgetTools()

    AddIns.Add FileName:="C:\Budget\Tools.xla"
    With AddIns("Budget Tools")
```

```
        .Installed = True
        MsgBox "The " & .Title & _
            " add-in is now installed.", _
            vbInformation
    End With

End Sub
```

The `InstallBudgetTools` procedure adds and installs an add-in named `"Budget Tools"`. First, the `Add` method makes the add-in available to the application. Then a `With` statement takes the `Budget Tools` add-in and installs it and then displays a message telling the user the add-in has been installed.

Note, in particular, the use of the Title property in the `MsgBox` statement. `AddIn` objects share many of the same properties found in Access and Excel objects. These properties include Author, Comments, FullName, Name, Path, Subject, and Title.

When you no longer need to work with an add-in, you can remove it by setting its Installed property to `False`.

Summary

This chapter covers several important things. Debugging is, of course, one of the most important things to learn. It might save endless hours searching in vain for some little variable that was misspelled or used in the wrong module.

The data access objects are very important if you need to access or manipulate databases. Even creating database tables using the DAOs can be useful. For one thing, it's self-documenting and if the database becomes corrupted, you can be guaranteed a way to reconstruct the basic tables in exactly the same way.

Where should you go for more information? You could try the following:

- Chapter 25, "Understanding Objects," discusses the objects that Excel exposes via OLE automation.
- Chapter 26, "Working with Other Applications," mentions working with OLE automation and VBA.
- Chapter 32, "Creating Access Macros," will give you more information about the actions that Access enables you to use. All the macro action can be used in VBA procedures.
- Additional programming information can be found in Part XIII, "Office Solutions Kits."

PART

Office Solutions Kits

Analysis and Design for Microsoft Office Products

55

by Dan Silkworth

IN THIS CHAPTER

This is the first of three chapters that describe case studies of real-world business problems that were solved by using Microsoft Office products. This chapter reviews analysis and design techniques used to reliably produce successful business solutions. These chapters do not attempt to teach the nuances of these techniques, but serve as an introduction with references to more complete treatments. Chapter 56, "Case Study 1: Project Management Information Integrator," and Chapter 57, "Case Study 2: Paperless Office—Business Infrastructure Automation," are devoted to product case studies, which include a project-management information integrator and business infrastructure automation application. These case studies are implemented using Visual Basic as the glue to integrate various components of the Microsoft Office suite.

Why Analyze?

Software analysis is the process of capturing the business requirements and environment in which a software system will function. Any system that will use multiple Office products to produce an integrated solution to a business problem is sufficiently complex to necessitate doing some analysis. One of the most common pitfalls of software developers is getting caught up in the technology and failing to understand the problem they are trying to solve. The purpose of analysis is to understand the problem exclusively in terms of the business. Business experts (and clients) will find it much easier to validate a solution if it is described in terms they are familiar with. Deferring technology issues until the design phase also results in a specification of the problem and its proposed solution(s), which is independent of any particular software or hardware system. This independence allows various software/hardware solutions to be evaluated against meaningful criteria. A technology-independent specification is also much more likely to facilitate reuse by separating essential business objects from their presentation or storage forms.

The Purpose of Design

Software design can be defined as the process of mapping the analysis (business) model onto an appropriate technology. Design is therefore necessary to the creation of any software system. Any technology has its own model, although this model may not be formally recognized. The Visual Basic model, which is made up of the controls one places on a form and internal storage structures, is an example of a technology model. The process of design is finding a way of using the technology model to implement the analysis model. For large, complex systems it is sometimes necessary to create a logical design model and a technology-specific design model. This can aid in evaluating specific technologies and make the resulting system more portable should the chosen technology need to change over time.

Some Popular Methods

The choice of a particular method is more a matter of personal preference than any particular strength of one method over another. Because the modeling language and graphical symbols differ slightly from one method to another, it is important to be consistent within a development project and organization. If your organization has already adopted or adapted a particular method, by all means use that method. Consistent use of a method across a development organization will simplify communication between developers. For those of you who have not been exposed to formal methods before the following object-oriented methodologies will be of interest:

- James Rumbaugh's *Object Modeling and Design*
- Grady Booch's *Object-Oriented Design with Applications*
- James Martin and James J. Odell's *Object-Oriented Analysis and Design*

All the examples in this chapter and Chapters 56 and 57 use the Rumbaugh object modeling approach to analysis and design. A brief introduction to the graphical object model notation is presented in Figure 55.1.

FIGURE 55.1.

The Rumbaugh object model notation used in this section.

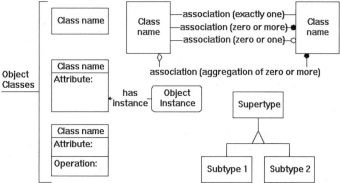

In a nutshell, the basic approach of analysis is to collect requirements from the system's users and formulate these requirements into a model of the system in which the software will operate. In Rumbaugh's method, an object model is used to describe the system in terms of object classes, associations between object classes, and attributes of object classes. The related terms can be defined as follows:

- Object class—A type of person, place, or thing that is essential to the system being described. Instances of this type will share the same attributes, associations, and behaviors.
- Object instance—An occurrence of a object class; a specific person, place, or thing.
- Attribute—A characteristic that describes all instances of an object class. Attributes should have well-defined domains (for example, an integer, an enumerated set of values, a string of length 50).
- Method—A behavior that can be exhibited by all instances of a class.

- Association—A relationship that may exist between instances of two object classes. Associations can be mandatory or optional for each participating class. Either single or multiple occurrences of an association may be allowed.

- Aggregation—A special type of association in which a collection of component parts make up a whole.

- Generalization—A special type of association between a superclass and one or more subclasses in which the subclasses inherit the attributes, methods, and association of the superclass.

- Subclass—Generally a class that inherits attributes, associations, and methods from its superclass.

- Superclass—Generally a class that defines attributes, associations, and methods to be inherited by one or more subclasses.

A simple way to think of the object classes is as types of *persons, places, or things* (nouns) of interest to the system. Attributes are the type of adjectives we wish to use to describe these things in the system. Associations are verb phrases used to relate the objects to each other in terms of the system. For instance, in Microsoft Word, a Paragraph Style definition is an object class that can be contained (an association) with a font size (an attribute) in a document template (another object class). The models in this section are simplified versions of the models that would be developed for a commercial project. (See Figure 55.2.) It is beyond the scope of this chapter to teach the intricacies of modeling. These models serve as an illustration of how requirements can be formalized and are used to guide the design and implementation of software projects. The reader who wishes to gain a deeper understanding of modeling techniques is recommended to the books listed previously.

FIGURE 55.2.

Database design diagram notation.

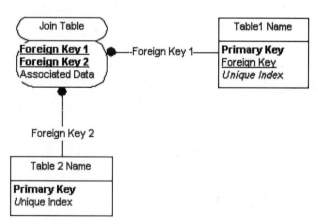

Tools for Automating Analysis

A large number of tools are available for assisting the analyst in developing a specification. These range from multipurpose, off-the-shelf graphical editors to elaborate computer-aided software engineering (CASE) products. In general, for small- to medium-size systems with only a few developers involved, a highly usable analysis specification can be put together using Microsoft Word with embedded graphics and tables. As systems become larger, the investment in CASE tools may become justifiable in order to keep track of large numbers of objects and to facilitate communication between project team members. The models in this chapter and Chapters 56 and 57 were created using Visio and the Visio Advanced Software Diagram shapes.

Summary

Analysis and design are essential for the successful completion of any complex software system. Analysis produces an abstract model of the system and its environment to be automated by the software. Software design is the process of selecting suitable technologies with which to implement the software and mapping these technologies to the analysis model. Chapters 56 and 57 present real-world examples of applying analysis and design to business problems with the Microsoft Office products.

Case Study 1: Project Management Information Integrator

56

by Dan Silkworth

IN THIS CHAPTER

The Business Problem

A construction company is looking for a way to leverage its data on the results of past projects to improve its ability to make quick, accurate bids on future jobs. (See Figure 56.1.) A large collection of template project plans are available, tailored for various types of construction jobs. These templates provide the following:

- A detailed breakdown of the project into individual steps
- The steps that must be completed before a given step can be started
- The personnel roles necessary to perform these steps
- The necessary materials to complete the steps
- The resultant product of the steps
- The costs associated with each task based on the personnel and material involved
- The safety standards that must be met for each step

FIGURE 56.1.

The project management information integrator environment.

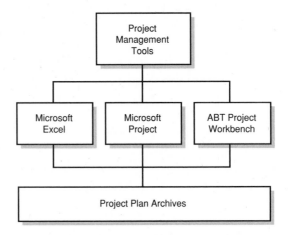

A salesperson preparing a bid on a job needs to perform the following tasks:

- Select the appropriate template plan(s) for the job
- Customize the structure of the plan based on job requirements of the client
- Prepare PERT charts showing precedence dependencies between steps
- Review/adjust the personnel roles assigned to the various tasks to account for availability of personnel and materials
- Summarize the plan for management and accounting
- Generate an estimate of time and costs for the bid
- Verify that all necessary standards are met by the plan
- Generate an initial project plan for use during the project

While developing the bid, the salesperson might have to reiterate some or all of these steps until an acceptable bid is created.

The Technology Problem

The company uses IBM-compatible PCs and laptops, running Window for Workgroups 3.11, for its sales force. All PCs have Microsoft Office installed on them. The company does not have any specific standards for project management software. Some salespeople use Microsoft Project or Excel while other salespeople use other project management software. The company does not want to force its sales force to use any particular software package. The template project plans are stored on Excel spreadsheets and contain some data that is not exportable to the project management software. However, the company does use ShapeWare's Visio as a standard for preparing graphics.

The Management Problem

As usual, there are very limited time and resources available for solving these problems. A staged development plan has therefore been adopted for this project: A complete analysis model and database design has been developed to fully explore the context of the problem and evaluate proposed solutions. The design and implementation is broken into several stages according to priorities established by the end users. The first priority is to provide an automated way for preparing PERT charts for the sales force.

The Analysis Model

The analysis phase of the project consists of interviewing the users of current project-planning templates to determine their requirements for the product. The resultant analysis model is presented in Figure 56.2.

The Project Plan template class is the primary object class in the model. It has attributes for a name, type of building, whether or not the plan is a customized plan, and a description of the plan. The methods for the Project Plan template include open, new, delete, save, compute cost, and add component. The Project Plan template is an aggregation of zero or more organizational components. An *organizational component* is an arbitrary collection of steps (or other organizational components). The organizational unit is used to break large projects into smaller groups of related steps. The only necessary attribute for an organizational unit is its name and an order attribute to determine its order of appearance relative to other components at the same level. The operations that an organizational component must support are display components, hide components, compute cost, and add and remove components.

The lowest-level aggregation of the Project Plan template is a step that has name, order, and estimated duration attributes. Steps have preceding steps and following steps, which indicate what steps must be completed before a step can be performed and what steps cannot begin until after a step is completed. Steps are associated with the materials they consume, the products they produce, and the personnel roles necessary to perform them. Note that because this product is primarily used by salespeople preparing project bids, actual dates have been left for the project management software, which this product will populate.

FIGURE 56.2.

The project management information integrator analysis model.

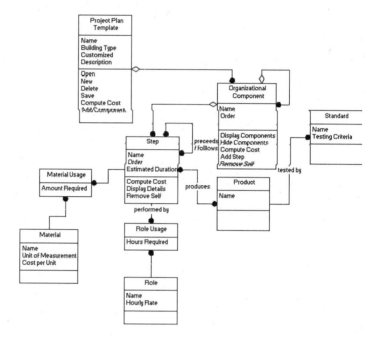

The amount of material required by a particular step is captured as an attribute of the material usage class. The amount cannot be attributed to the step or the material because different steps might use differing amounts of the same material, and vice versa. Materials have name, unit of measurement, and cost per unit attributes. The number of person hours required of a given role to perform a step is specified as an attribute of the role usage class. Again, the hours cannot be attributed to the step or the role because different steps might require different hours of the same role, and vice versa. Roles have a name and an hourly rate. Steps produce products that are components of the complete project. Some products might require several steps before their construction is completed. A given step can contribute to the completion of more than one product. Products are identified by their names. Some products must be tested against government standards with defined testing criteria. Each standard has a name, a description of the testing criteria, and an estimate of how much time will be required for testing (testing duration).

The instance model presented in Figure 56.3 gives some concrete examples of each class in the analysis model shown in Figure 56.2. In Figure 56.3, the class type is separated from the name (or attribute value) of the instance with a colon.

FIGURE 56.3.
The project management information integrator instance model.

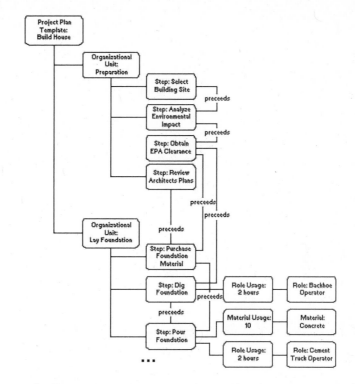

The Design Model

A database design that covers the entire analysis model is presented in this section. The design of the methods needed to implement the PERT Chart Generator is also presented.

The Database Design

Due to its presence on all target machines, Microsoft Access was chosen as the database engine. To chose a relational DBMS requires a refinement of the original object model into a database design suitable for a relational implementation. Database design has been the subject of innumerable books; the database design titles mentioned in Chapter 55, "Analysis and Design," are highly recommended.

In any case, the primary goal of database design is to define a schema for storing all persistent data with a minimum of redundancy, without unduly sacrificing performance. Redundancy of data is to be avoided because duplicate data requires multiple updates, which is both inefficient and a common source of error in many systems. *Normalization* is a technique that is very effective in reducing data redundancy and is used in this database design. For more information on normalization, refer to any of the database design titles mentioned in Chapter 55. A diagram of the database design is presented in Figure 56.4.

FIGURE 56.4.

*The project management
database design.*

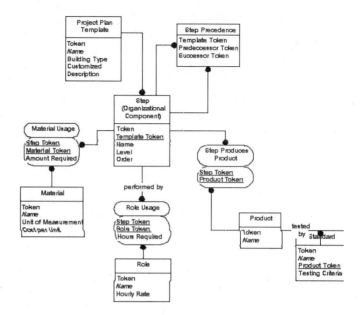

Deriving Relational Tables from Object Classes

Each object class is implemented as a single table in a Microsoft Access database. Each row in a table represents a persistent instance of an object class. It should be noted that tables in a relational database can never fully represent an object class because they do not capture the class methods or its inheritance hierarchy. Only an object-oriented development environment can directly implement an object model.

An additional table (Step Produces Product) is created to deal with the many-to-many relationship between the step and product object classes (see the section "Deriving Join Tables" later in this chapter). Every table created from an object class has a *token* column, with the exception of the join tables. By using the counter data type in Access, this token will have a unique value for all rows of the table; therefore, it can be used as the primary key. The token column is also indexed with unique values to speed up searches based on the token value. The advantage of using the token column instead of an identifying attribute known to the user (for example, *name*) is that the value of a name column can be changed without having to change all references to this row (object instance) in any other tables, provided that the name column is not the primary key. This approach maintains a parallel construction between object classes and tables as well as object instances and rows of a table. The token field serves as an identifier for the object within the database.

Deriving Relational Table Columns from Object Classes, Attributes, and Associations

The remaining columns in each table are derived from the attributes of the corresponding object class. Columns representing values that uniquely identify an instance of an object class to the end user should be uniquely indexed because they are likely to be used as search criteria in queries. Additional columns, called *foreign keys* (underlined in Figure 56.4), are created in a table whenever the object class that the table represents has a many-to-many association with another object class. These foreign key columns will contain the value of the token column in the row of the table whose instance they are related to. For example, if a step is part of a particular template, that step will have the value of the token field of that template in its template token column. Foreign keys serve as pointers to rows in other tables by referencing the primary key of the other table.

Implementing Aggregation Associations

The aggregation associations in the object model between the Project Plan template, the organizational component, and the step have been implemented in a single table. During the development of the object model, the question of whether the same step or organizational unit can be used in multiple project templates was left unspecified. The design process almost always uncovers some questions like this that were not addressed during the analysis. Of course, at this point the appropriate thing for the designer to do is to discuss this question with the analyst and end user. The database design as presented in Figure 56.4 supports unique organizational components and steps in each project plan. In other words, even though a step has the same *name* in two different project templates, it is actually a separate instance of step by virtue of the fact that it is in a separate template (or position). This is accomplished by making the foreign key project template token part of a unique index of the Step table.

> **NOTE**
>
> Microsoft Access only allows one unique index consisting of multiple columns—the primary key. Therefore, a compound primary key consisting of template token and name has been made the primary key of the Step table instead of token. A unique index should be placed on the token column so that it can be used as a foreign key for the other tables. This effectively creates two unique keys for the Step table. The token field of the Step table can be used as a foreign key in other tables that need to refer to it.

The step and organizational components of the object class have been implemented in a single table by introducing the level attribute. The *level attribute* is an integer that determines at which level in the hierarchy of organizational components a particular row of the Step table is located. Combined with the *order attribute*, which keeps track of the order in which components and steps occur in the template, a unique hierarchy can be determined. It is left to the software that updates this table to ensure that a sensible hierarchy is maintained. This structure lends itself well to outline controls available in Visual Basic or Excel.

Deriving Join Tables

A *join table* is a table used to implement a many-to-many association or an associative object class. An *associative object class* represents an object instance that cannot exist without the objects it is associated with. There are two associative objects in Figure 56.2 that result in the two join tables—Material Usage and Role Usage—of Figure 56.4. The primary key of a join table is created from the primary keys of the tables it is joining. In other words, the primary key of a join table is made up of foreign keys pointing to the tables it is joining. Join tables, therefore, always have multicolumn primary keys. Additional columns of a join table, if any, are derived from the attributes of the associative object class they implement. A join table is also used to implement a many-to-many association, because attempting to add a column to either table would result in redundant storage of information. A step can produce multiple products, but a product can be produced by more than one step. If you have a foreign key column for products in the Step table, you would have to replicate the data in the other columns whenever a step produces more than one product, and vice versa. It is not possible to store the fact that a step produces a product in either the Step or Product table without replicating data in some of the fields. To get around this problem, a join table is created containing only columns for the primary key fields of the tables related by the many-to-many association.

The PERT Chart Generator Design

A PERT chart is a network of nodes representing steps and links, showing the precedence of one step over another. An arrowed line connecting Step A to Step B indicates that Step A must be completed before Step B is begun. The step precedence instances shown in Figure 56.3 are represented in the PERT chart in Figure 56.5. ShapeWare's Visio product has been chosen as the graphical drawing tool for this implementation because of its effective integration with Visual Basic and Word. Because Visual Basic does not support object-oriented programming beyond the manipulation of user interface controls, a more traditional approach to the design of the PERT chart generator has been adopted. The design is expressed by using Yourdon-style structure charts and pseudo code.

FIGURE 56.5.
The sample PERT chart.

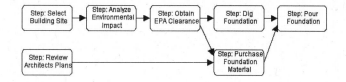

Design Limitations

The problem of drawing a network in a two-dimensional space without crossing lines is difficult to solve computationally, even though this is a relatively trivial task for people. No attempt has been made to produce a PERT chart without crossing lines. It is a simple matter to manually rearrange the nodes of the PERT chart through the Visio interface. For large projects, the size of the PERT chart will exceed a single page. No provision has been made in this design to split a large PERT chart over multiple pages. Again, this can easily be performed by the user in Visio.

User Interface Design

The user interface requirements are minimal for this simple project:

- Present the user with an alphabetical list of project templates from which to choose.
- After the user selects a template, allow him or her to generate one or more PERT charts.

These requirements can be met by producing a single window form like the one shown in Figure 56.6. The assumption is made that all project template data will be contained in a single database that will be distributed with this application. This assumption makes a File Open dialog box for opening the database unnecessary. The `Form_Load` procedure of the main window extracts the project template names and tokens from the database and loads them into a combo box control from which the user can choose an item in the list. Simultaneous to loading the combo box list with template names, the `ItemData` array (associated with all Visual Basic list controls) is used to store the corresponding project template's token. The value of the project template token is used to identify the template in the software. In its initial state, the Generate button on the form is enabled. When the user selects a template, the `ProjPlan_Click` method is invoked; in turn, it enables the Generate button. The design of the `Generate_Click` method is discussed in the section "PERT Chart Generation Functional Design." When the user selects the Generate button, the `Generate_Click` method executes, creating a Visio diagram containing the PERT chart for the diagram. The Exit button executes the `Exit_Click` method, which shuts down the Visio application if it is running and then ends the program.

FIGURE 56.6.

The PERT Chart Generator user interface design.

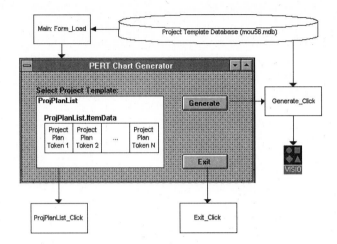

PERT Chart Generation Functional Design

The essential problem in generating a PERT chart from the information in the database design presented in the previous section is mapping the precedes/follows association from the structure of the Step Precedence table onto a two-dimensional drawing surface. Imagine dividing the two-dimensional surface into cells that contain steps. (See Figure 56.7.) The position of a step on the two-dimensional surface can be represented by its position in a two-dimensional array of step tokens. Using similar logic, the links can be represented in an array of Cartesian coordinates. The presence of a link can be indicated by placing the successor's step coordinates in the predecessor's cell position. However, a three-dimensional array is necessary for the links because one step can have multiple successors. The resultant `PertChart` and `PertChartLinks` arrays serve as internal representations of the PERT chart, which can be manipulated in memory before it is committed to the drawing surface. This provides flexibility for enhancements such as splitting large charts across multiple pages or introducing anti–line-crossing heuristics to the implementation. These enhancements can be applied to the completed arrays without needing to redesign existing parts of the implementation.

FIGURE 56.7.

Overlaying a two-dimensional array on the drawing surface.

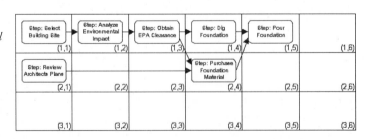

The process of generating the PERT chart can be broken into three subprocedures: getInitialSteps, chartSuccessors, and generateVisioDiagram, as shown in Figure 56.8. The getInitialSteps subprocedure extracts the steps in the project that can be started at the beginning of a project. This is accomplished by selecting the steps in the project, based on the project template token provided through the user interface, that do not have any predecessors. In the sample database these initial steps have a precedence token value of zero. These initial steps are placed in column 1 (y value=1) on separate rows (x values) of the PertChart array by the chartSuccessors function. The chartSuccessors function fills out the array with the remaining successor steps and precedence links, as described in the section "Chart Successors Functional Design." The generateVisioDiagram function uses the PertChart and PertChartLinks arrays to draw the chart on a Visio page, as described in the section "generateVisiodiagram Functional Design."

FIGURE 56.8.

The Generate PERT Chart functional design.

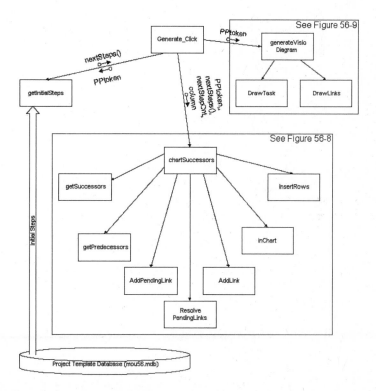

The *chartSuccessors* Functional Design

The chartSuccessors subroutine populates the PertChart and PertChartLinks arrays with the steps and links as they are drawn on the Visio diagram. (See Figure 56.9.) It accomplishes this by recursively examining a set of steps (the initial step for the first recursion) to select the successors of the steps that should appear in the current column. A successor may not be placed in the current column if it has a predecessor that has yet to be placed in the chart. For instance, even though Purchase Foundation Material is an immediate successor of Review Architects Plans, it cannot be placed in column 2 because it is also a successor of Obtain EPA clearance, which does not appear until column 3. (Refer to Figure 56.5.) Those successors that cannot be placed yet are held in the `pendingLinks` array. Steps that have multiple predecessors are detected as successors to multiple steps. Check to see that a step is not already in the chart before adding it. Steps with multiple successors require new rows to be inserted, and all arrays must be updated accordingly. Finally, the `chartSuccessors` subroutine is recursively called with the steps in the new column. When no more steps are left to be added, the recursive call is not made and the recursion ends.

FIGURE 56.9.

The `chartSuccessors` *functional design.*

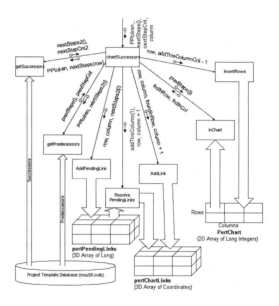

The following pseudo code segment expresses a more detailed design of the `chartSuccessors` subprocedure. The `chartSuccessors` subroutine is called recursively, once for each column needed in the PERT chart. A third array, called `pendingLinks`, is required by `chartSuccessors` to hold successors steps that should not be placed in the current column because there are also successors to one or more steps that have not yet been placed in the `PertChart` array. This algorithm assumes that there are no cycles in the graph. That is, no step can be a successor of itself, either immediately or through other steps. Comments are enclosed in parentheses. Here's the pseudo code segment:

```
Inputs: PPtoken (Project Template Database Token)
        NextSteps (Array of Step Tokens)
        NextStepsCnt (Integer number of steps in NextSteps)
        column (Current column number)

FOREACH Step in NextSteps
   INCREMENT row
   CALL getSuccessors with Step
   FOREACH Successor of Step
      CALL getPredecessors with Successor Step
      FOREACH Predecessor of SuccessorStep
         (Check for Predecessors of the Successors which have not been placed in
         the array yet)
         IF SuccessorStep NOT EQUAL TO Step THEN
            IF PredecessorStep Not In Array PertChart THEN
               CALL addPendingLink with Step, row, column
            ENDIF
         ENDIF
      ENDFOREACH
      IF ALL PredecessorSteps Are In Array PertChart
         THEN (It is ok to add the successor in the column)
         IF SuccessorStep Is In Array PertChart THEN
            ADD SuccessortStep to AddInThisColumn Array
         ELSE (This successor has already been placed, just add the link)
            CALL AddLink with Row, Column, Row SuccessorStep found in, Column+1
         ENDIF
      ENDIF
   ENDFOREACH
   IF only one successor need be added to this row, column
      THEN (Do not need to add a row)
      PertChart(Row, Column) = AddInThisColumn(1)
      CALL AddLink with Row, Column, Row, Column+1
      CALL ResolvePendingLinks with AddInThisColumn(1), row, column+1
   ELSEIF more than one successor  must be added THEN
      CALL InsertRows with row, (Size of AddInThisColumn)-1
      FOREACH SuccessorStep to be added
         PertChart(Row, Column) = AddInThisColumn(row)
         CALL AddLink with Row, Column, Row, Column+1
         CALL ResolvePendingLinks with AddInThisColumn(1), row, column+1
         INCREMENT row
      ENDFOREACH
   ENDIF
ENDFOREACH
INCREMENT column
ERASE nextSteps Array
FOREACH row in PertChart
   IF PertChart(Row, Column) contains step THEN
      ADD PertChart(Row, Column) to nextSteps Array
   ENDIF
ENDFOREACH
IF nextSteps Not Empty THEN
   CALL chartSuccessors with PPtoken, nextSteps Array,
      count of nextSteps Array, column
ENDIF
```

The *generateVisioDiagram* Function Design

Generating the Visio diagram is simply a matter of translating the PertChart array onto a Visio diagram page. (See Figure 56.10.) The Visio product is sold with a number of standard stencils from which master shapes can be dragged onto a page, either by the user or though Visual Basic code. For this application the standard Flowchart stencil is used. The *process* master shape is used to represent steps and the *next* master shape is used to represent task precedence. The generation of the PERT chart is broken into two subroutines: DrawTask and DrawLinks. The generateVisioDiagram function calls the DrawTask subroutine once for each task in the PertChart array with the template token, step token, row position, column position, and the master shape. The DrawTask subroutine extracts the name of the step from the database, drags an instance of the master shape to the appropriate position on the page, and then sets the text of the dropped shape to the name of the step. As the step shapes are created, they are placed in a two-dimensional array of shapes so they can be referred to easily by the DrawLinks function. The generateVisioDiagram function then calls the DrawLinks subroutine once for each link in the PertChartLinks array, with the origin shape, the destination shape's coordinates, and the next master shape. The subroutine DrawLinks drags an instance of the next master shape onto the page and connects its beginning point to the right side of the predecessor shape and the endpoint to the left side of the successor shape.

FIGURE 56.10.

The
generateVisioDiagram
function design.

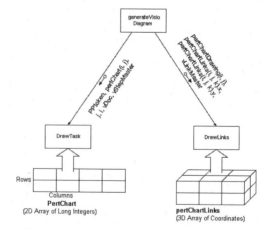

The Implementation

The solution has been implemented using Microsoft's Visual Basic 3, Access 2, and ShapeWare's Visio 2.

NOTE

Use of Access 95 with Visual Basic 3 requires installation of Microsoft's VB 3/Access 2 compatibility layer. The compatibility layer installation software can be downloaded from the library files on the Access or Visual Basic forums on CompuServe.

Database Implementations

Only three tables are used by the PERT Chart Generator: Project Plans, Steps, and Step Precedence. The definition of the tables, based on the design shown in Figure 56.4, is shown in Figure 56.11. The composite primary key in the Step Precedence table ensures that no duplicate predecessor/successor links can exist within a project template. The composite primary key in the Steps table ensures that step names are unique within a project template. The token field, with data type counter, of the Steps table is actually used as the primary key in the source code. The token field in the Steps table is uniquely indexed to speed up retrieval of step names by their token.

NOTE

The data type for all fields that serve as foreign keys is set to Long Integer. This is necessary to ensure join compatibility between the foreign keys and the token fields, which have the data type counter, in tables to which they point.

FIGURE 56.11.

Table implementation for PERT chart generation.

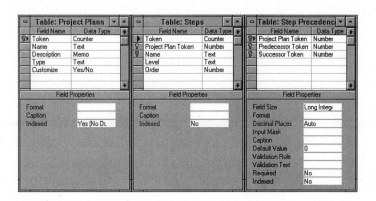

Visual Basic Project Files

Only five files are required to implement the solution in Visual Basic, and three of these are provided with Visual Basic and Visio. (See Figure 56.12.) The file CONSTANT.TXT contains standard Visual Basic global constants and should be included in every Visual Basic project.

The file VISCONST.BAS contains global constants used when interfacing with Visio. The file VISREG.BAS contains subroutines and functions used to start or find a running Visio application. The file CONSTANT.TXT can be found in the VB directory. The files VISREG.BAS and VISCONST.BAS are found in the VISIO\ADD-ONS\LIBRARY directory. The file GLOBAL.BAS contains user-defined type definitions and global constants, as described in the following section, "Global Declarations." The file MAIN.FRM contains the form layout and all the remaining source code.

FIGURE 56.12.

The Visual Basic project file for the PERT Chart Generator.

Global Declarations

The global declarations are contained in the file GLOBAL.BAS. A separate file is necessary because type declarations cannot be defined in the declarations section of a form module. The user-defined type *coordinates* are used as the data type for the pertChartLinks array. The pertChartLinks array is used to store the destination (successor) of a link. The x and y values of the coordinates type are used to store the position of the successor in the two-dimensional array PertChart. The global constant gDBname is used to store the name of the Access database file. The gDB global variable is used to hold the database object so that it can be accessed as needed in the source code:

```
Type Coordinates
    x As Integer
    y As Integer
End Type

Global Const gDBname = "MOU56.MDB" ' Name of database file name
Global gDB As database ' Database containing project templates
```

Form Declarations

These form declarations and all remaining source code are found in the MAIN.FRM file. The form constant maxRows is used to define the maximum size of the arrays. This limits the size of any PERT chart to a grid of 10 by 10 steps. The three arrays are declared but not dimensioned at this time. The arrays are not dimensioned because they will be redimensioned as needed during the execution of the program, reducing the amount of memory required by the program while generating small PERT charts. The form variables curMaxRow and curMaxCol are used to hold the actual size of the arrays during execution. Finally, the pertChartDrawing array of objects is declared to hold the Visio shape objects as they are placed on the page. This array of shape objects is used to identify the shapes when the links are being dropped on the page:

```
Const maxRows = 10
Rem declare a 2 dimensional array of step tokens representing the Pert chart
Dim pertChart() As Long
Dim pertChartLinks() As Coordinates
Dim pendingLinks() As Long
Dim curMaxRow As Integer
Dim curMaxCol As Integer
Dim pertChartDrawing() As Object
```

The Method of the Main Form

The `Form_Load` method of the main form opens the Access database and populates the ProjPlanList combo box with the template project names. A simple SQL statement is used to populate a snapshot object with the contents of the Project Plans table, ordered by the Name field. The `while` loop then executes once for each template name in the table and adds the name to the ProjPlanList combo box and the token for the project template to the `ItemData` array of the ProjPlanList combo box.

> **NOTE**
>
> The use of the path property of the application object (`App.Path`) in the `OpenDatabase` statement allows the software to find the database no matter where it is installed in the user's directory structure, provided that the executable and database files are kept in the same directory. `App.Path` returns the drive and directory path from which the application was invoked.

> **NOTE**
>
> If you are not familiar with SQL syntax, you can use the Access Query Designer to "write" your SQL for you. The Access query definition for the SQL statement used in `Form_Load` is shown in Figure 56.13.

In order to produce an equivalent SQL statement, just switch to the Designer's SQL mode by selecting SQL from the View menu. The SQL statements (see Figure 56.14) can then be copied directly from the Access window to the Clipboard and then to the VB code window:

```
Sub Form_Load ()

Dim sql As String ' used to hold SQL statements
Dim dbProjPlans As snapshot ' of Project Plans table
Dim visioLoaded As Integer
```

```
Rem Open Database
Set gDB = OpenDatabase(App.Path & "\" & gDBname)

Rem get project plans
sql = "Select * From [Project Plans] Order by Name"
Set dbProjPlans = gDB.CreateSnapshot(sql)

Rem Load project plan names into combo list
Do While Not dbProjPlans.EOF
    ProjPlanList.AddItem dbProjPlans!Name
    ProjPlanList.ItemData(ProjPlanList.NewIndex) = dbProjPlans!Token
    dbProjPlans.MoveNext
Loop
End Sub
```

FIGURE 56.13.

Select project templates.

FIGURE 56.14.

Select project template SQL statements, as generated by Access.

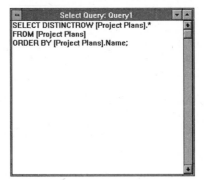

The *ProjPlanList_Click* Method

The purpose of the code in ProjPlanList_Click method is to enable the Generate button, allowing the user to generate a PERT chart. This button is initially disabled to prevent the user from pressing it before he or she selects a project template from the list. If the ListIndex property of the ProjPlanList is zero or greater, the user has selected a template:

```
Sub ProjPlanList_Click ()
```

```
If ProjPlanList.ListIndex > -1 Then
   Generate.Enabled = True
Else
   Generate.Enabled = False
End If

End Sub
```

The *Exit_Click* Method

The `Exit_Click` method checks to see if there is a copy of Visio running and, if so, attempts to shut it down. The variable `g_appVisio` is a global variable declared in VISREG.BAS to hold the Visio application object. The `If` statement tests to see if this variable has been instantiated and sends the `quit` command if it is instantiated. If there are any generated PERT charts that have not been saved, Visio will prompt the user to save them before quitting. The `End` statement terminates the VB application:

```
Sub Exit_Click ()
   If Not (g_appVisio Is Nothing) Then g_appVisio.quit
   End
End Sub
```

The *Generate_Click* Method

The `Generate_Click` method contains the bulk of the code. The first step is to erase and redimension the arrays. This gets rid of any leftover data from a previous generation. The token of the Project Plan template is extracted from the `ItemData` array of the ProjPlanList combo box. The function `getInitialSteps` retrieves the steps that have no predecessors. These initial steps are used to populate the first column of the `PertChart` array and set the initial number of rows. The subroutine `chartSuccessors` is called to populate the `pertChart` array with the remaining steps. Finally, `generateVisioDiagram` is called to construct the Visio diagram of the PERT chart:

```
Sub Generate_Click ()

Dim PPtoken As Long ' Project Plan Token
Dim nextSteps() As Long ' array to hold successors of a step
Dim nextStepCnt As Integer ' number of successors found
Dim i As Integer ' counter for for loop
Dim row As Integer, column As Integer ' indices into the pertChart array

Rem declare 2D array of positions ((x, y) where x and y are coordinates)
Rem for steps on chart
Erase pertChart
ReDim pertChart(maxRows, 1) As Long
curMaxRow = 0

Erase pertChartLinks
ReDim pertChartLinks(maxRows, maxRows, 1) As Coordinates

Erase pendingLinks
ReDim pendingLinks(maxRows, maxRows, 1) As Long
```

```
Rem the current Project Plan Token, as selected by the user, is in the
Rem ItemData array of the ProjPlanList indexed by the ProjPlanList.ListIndex
PPtoken = ProjPlanList.ItemData(ProjPlanList.ListIndex)

Rem 1st get the inital steps, which have no predecessors
nextStepCnt = getInitialSteps(PPtoken, nextSteps())

Rem Populate the first logical column of the Pert chart
column = 1
For row = 1 To nextStepCnt
   curMaxRow = curMaxRow + 1
   pertChart(row, column) = nextSteps(row)
Next row

Call chartSuccessors(PPtoken, nextSteps(), nextStepCnt, column)

Call generateVisioDiagram(PPtoken)

End Sub
```

> **NOTE**
>
> Since only the last dimension of an array can be changed with the `Redim Preserve`
> statement, the first dimension of `pertChart` and `pertChartLinks` is set to the form
> constant `maxRows`. The form variable `curMaxRow` is reset to zero, indicating the actual
> number of rows.

The *getInitialSteps* Function

The function `getInitialSteps` returns the number of steps in the project plan that have no
predecessors. The array `InitialSteps` is populated with the token values of these steps.

> **NOTE**
>
> If you are not familiar with SQL syntax, you can use the Access Query Designer to
> "write" your SQL syntax for you. The Access query definition for the SQL syntax used
> in the function `getInitialSteps` is shown in Figure 56.15.

In order to produce an equivalent SQL statement, just switch to the Designer's SQL mode by
selecting SQL from the View menu. The SQL statements (see Figure 56.16) can then be copied directly from the Access window to the Clipboard and then to the VB code window:

```
Function getInitialSteps (ProjPlanToken As Long, InitialSteps() As Long)
   As Integer

Dim sql As String, dbInitialSteps As snapshot, stepCnt As Integer
```

```
sql = "Select * from [Step Precedence] "
sql = sql & "Where [Project Plan Token]=" & ProjPlanToken
sql = sql & " and [Predecessor Token]=0" ' 0 indicates step has no precedessor
Set dbInitialSteps = gDB.CreateSnapshot(sql)
stepCnt = 0
Do While Not dbInitialSteps.EOF
   stepCnt = stepCnt + 1
   ReDim Preserve InitialSteps(stepCnt)
   InitialSteps(stepCnt) = dbInitialSteps![Successor Token]
   dbInitialSteps.MoveNext
Loop
getInitialSteps = stepCnt

End Function
```

FIGURE 56.15.

The query definition for the
getInitialSteps
function.

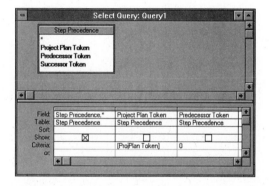

FIGURE 56.16.

The SQL statement for the
getInitialSteps
function.

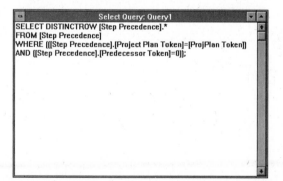

NOTE

The experienced user might ask, Why not define the query in Access and use it as a `QueryDef` in Visual Basic to execute the query. In my experience, it is more efficient to define the SQL statement in the source code without the overhead of declaring and instantiating the query definition. It also keeps the definition of the query with the function using it. This function can also be moved from the MAIN.FRM file and placed in another basic (BAS) file for reuse by other VB programs.

The *chartSuccessors* Subroutine

The subroutine `chartSuccessors` adds a column to the PERT chart and then determines what steps belong in that column. The input array `nextSteps` contains the steps from the previous column. The successors of each of these steps are examined to see if they can be placed in the current column. Only steps that have all of their predecessor steps already placed in the `pertChart` array can be placed in the current column. Steps that do not have all of their predecessors in the `pertChart` array are held in the `pendingLinks` array, which is maintained by the `AddPendingLinks` and `ResolvePendingLinks` subroutines. A step can have multiple predecessors, which means it will be discovered once for each predecessor in this subroutine. Therefore, it is necessary to make sure that a step is not already in the PERT chart (via the `inChart` function) before a step is added to the `pertChart` array. If the step has already been added to the array only, the link is added to the `pertChartLinks` array. If the step is not yet in the array, it is added to the `addThisColumn` array. After all successors of a step have been checked, each step in the `addThisColumn` is placed in the `pertChart` array. If more than one step has to be added, additional rows are inserted in the arrays to handle the additional steps. After a step has been added, the `ResolvePendingLinks` subroutine is called to update the `pertChartLinks` tables with any links that are waiting for the placement of this step. The `nextSteps` array is then repopulated with the current column; the column number is incremented; and `chartSuccessors` is called recursively to process the remaining steps. If no steps have been placed in this column, the `pertChart` array is complete and the recursion ceases:

```
Sub chartSuccessors (PPtoken As Long, nextSteps() As Long, nextStepCnt As Integer,
                     column As Integer)

Dim nextSteps2() As Long ' array to hold successors of a nextSteps
Dim prevSteps() As Long ' array to hold predecessors of a step
Dim row As Integer, i As Integer, j As Integer ' counters for for loops
Dim nextStepCnt2 As Integer ' number of successors
Dim prevStepCnt As Integer ' number of predecessors
Dim foundInRow As Integer ' row of chart a predecessor was found in
Dim fndInRow As Integer, fndInCol As Integer
Dim addThisColumn() As Long, addThisColumnCnt As Integer
Dim startRow As Integer ' row number before insertion of rows
Dim fndOtherPredsNotOnChart As Integer, uPL1 As Integer, uPL2 As Integer
Dim addThisColumnCnt2 As Integer, emptyColumn As Integer
Dim nextColumn() As Long, nextColCnt As Integer

curMaxCol = column
ReDim Preserve pertChart(maxRows, UBound(pertChart, 2) + 1) As Long
For row = 1 To nextStepCnt
   Rem 1st get the successors
   nextStepCnt2 = getSuccessors(PPtoken, nextSteps(row), nextSteps2())
   If nextStepCnt2 > 0 Then
      addThisColumnCnt = 0
   End If

   For i = 1 To nextStepCnt2 ' For each successor do ...
      Rem First get predecessors
      prevStepCnt = getPredecessors(PPtoken, nextSteps2(i), prevSteps())
      fndOtherPredsNotOnChart = False
```

```
    For j = 1 To prevStepCnt
        If prevSteps(j) <> nextSteps(row)
            Then ' ignore, we are looking for other predecessers
            Rem We have found a predecessor other than the current Step Token
            Rem If it is we need to arrange the rows to avoid crossing lines
            foundInRow = inChart(prevSteps(j), fndInRow, fndInCol)
            If foundInRow <= 0 Then
                Rem we want to delay placing the successor because not all of its
                Rem predecessors have been put in the chart yet.
                fndOtherPredsNotOnChart = True
                Call AddPendingLink(row, column, nextSteps2(i))
            End If
        End If
    Next j

    If Not fndOtherPredsNotOnChart Then
        Rem it is ok to place this step on the chart - but where?
        foundInRow = inChart(nextSteps2(i), fndInRow, fndInCol)
        If foundInRow <= 0 Then
            addThisColumnCnt = addThisColumnCnt + 1
            ReDim Preserve addThisColumn(addThisColumnCnt)
            addThisColumn(addThisColumnCnt) = nextSteps2(i)
        Else
            Call AddLink(row, column, foundInRow, column + 1)
        End If
    End If
    Next i

    Rem Now the addThisColumn array contains all steps to added in this column
    Rem for this row

    If addThisColumnCnt = 1 Then ' we don't need to create any new rows
        pertChart(row, column + 1) = addThisColumn(1)
        Call AddLink(row, column, row, column + 1)
        Call ResolvePendingLinks(addThisColumn(1), row, column + 1)
    ElseIf addThisColumnCnt <> 0 Then
        startRow = row
        Call insertRows(row, addThisColumnCnt - 1)
        row = row + (addThisColumnCnt - 1)
        addThisColumnCnt2 = 0
        For i = startRow To startRow + (addThisColumnCnt - 1)
            addThisColumnCnt2 = addThisColumnCnt2 + 1
            pertChart(i, column + 1) = addThisColumn(addThisColumnCnt2)
            Call AddLink(startRow + (addThisColumnCnt - 1), column, i, column + 1)
            Call ResolvePendingLinks(addThisColumn(addThisColumnCnt2),
                                     i, column + 1)
        Next i
    End If
Next row
column = column + 1

nextColCnt = 0
For i = 1 To curMaxRow ' For each successor do ...
    If pertChart(i, column) > 0 Then
        nextColCnt = nextColCnt + 1
        ReDim Preserve nextColumn(nextColCnt)
        nextColumn(nextColCnt) = pertChart(i, column)
    End If
Next i
```

```
If nextColCnt > 0 Then
    Call chartSuccessors(PPtoken, nextColumn(), nextColCnt, column)
End If

End Sub
```

The *getSuccessors* Function

The function getSuccessors returns the number of successors a step has, as identified by the value of ProjPlanToken and PredToken. The array SuccSteps is populated with the token values of these steps.

> **NOTE**
>
> If you are not familiar with SQL syntax, you can use the Access Query Designer to "write" your SQL syntax for you. The Access query definition for the SQL syntax used in the function getSuccessors is shown in Figure 56.17.

FIGURE 56.17.

The query definition for the getSuccessors function.

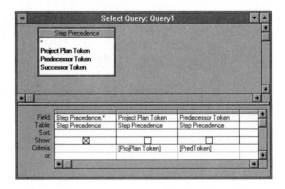

In order to produce an equivalent SQL statement, just switch to the Designer's SQL mode by selecting SQL from the View menu. The SQL statements (see Figure 56.18) can then be copied directly from the Access window to the Clipboard and then to the VB code window:

```
Function getSuccessors (ProjPlanToken As Long, PredToken As Long,
                        SuccSteps() As Long) As Integer

Dim sql As String, dbSuccessors As snapshot, stepCnt As Integer

sql = "Select * from [Step Precedence] "
sql = sql & "Where [Project Plan Token]=" & ProjPlanToken
sql = sql & " and [Predecessor Token]=" & PredToken
Set dbSuccessors = gDB.CreateSnapshot(sql)
stepCnt = 0
Do While Not dbSuccessors.EOF
    stepCnt = stepCnt + 1
    ReDim Preserve SuccSteps(stepCnt)
```

```
    SuccSteps(stepCnt) = dbSuccessors![Successor Token]
    dbSuccessors.MoveNext
Loop
getSuccessors = stepCnt

End Function
```

FIGURE 56.18.

The SQL statement for the getSuccessors *function.*

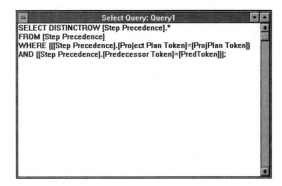

The *getPredecessors* Function

The function getPredecessors returns the number of predecessors a step has, as identified by the value of ProjPlanToken and SuccToken. The array PredSteps is populated with the token values of these steps.

> **NOTE**
>
> If you are not familiar with SQL syntax, you can use the Access Query Designer to "write" your SQL syntax for you. The Access query definition for the SQL syntax used in the function getPredecessors is shown in Figure 56.19.

FIGURE 56.19.

The query definition for the getPredecessors *function.*

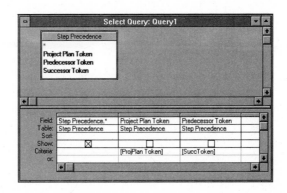

In order to produce an equivalent SQL statement, just switch to the Designer's SQL mode by selecting SQL from the View menu. The SQL statements (see Figure 56.20) can then be copied directly from the Access window to the Clipboard and then to the VB code window:

```
Function getPredecessors (ProjPlanToken As Long, SuccToken As Long,
                          PredSteps() As Long) As Integer

Dim sql As String, dbPredecessors As snapshot, stepCnt As Integer

sql = "Select * from [Step Precedence] "
sql = sql & "Where [Project Plan Token]=" & ProjPlanToken
sql = sql & " and [Successor Token]=" & SuccToken
Set dbPredecessors = gDB.CreateSnapshot(sql)
stepCnt = 0
Do While Not dbPredecessors.EOF
    stepCnt = stepCnt + 1
    ReDim Preserve PredSteps(stepCnt)
    PredSteps(stepCnt) = dbPredecessors![Predecessor Token]
    dbPredecessors.MoveNext
Loop
getPredecessors = stepCnt


End Function
```

FIGURE 56.20.

The SQL statement for getPredecessors *function.*

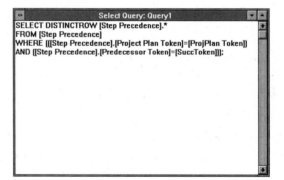

```
Select Query: Query1
SELECT DISTINCTROW [Step Precedence].*
FROM [Step Precedence]
WHERE [[[Step Precedence].[Project Plan Token]=[ProjPlan Token]]
AND [[Step Precedence].[Predecessor Token]=[SuccToken]]];
```

The *inChart* Function

The function inChart accepts a step's token as input and returns the row number if the step is in the pertChart array; otherwise, it returns zero (False) if the step is not found in the pertChart array. This function also sets the row and col values to the row and column in which the step was found. The value of curMaxRow is used instead of the Ubound function—which would always return the upper bound of the first dimension of the array (10)—in order to speed up the search. The Ubound function can be used on the second dimension of the array because the second dimension is dynamically sized:

```
Function inChart (stepToken As Long, row As Integer, col As Integer)

Rem This function returns the row of a step in the Pertchart array or false(0)
Rem if it is not in the chart array

Dim i As Integer ' row index
Dim j As Integer ' col index

inChart = False
For i = 1 To curMaxRow
   For j = 1 To UBound(pertChart, 2)
      If pertChart(i, j) = stepToken Then
         inChart = i
         row = i
         col = j
         Exit For
      End If
   Next j
   If j < UBound(pertChart, 2) Then
      If pertChart(i, j) = stepToken Then
         Exit For
      End If
   End If
Next i

End Function
```

The *AddLink* Subroutine

The subroutine AddLink adds a link between two positions in both the pertChart array and the pertChartLinks array. It accepts as input the x1 and y1 coordinates of the predecessor in the pertChart array and the x2 and y2 coordinates of the successor step in the pertChart array. The x1 and x2 parameters serve as indexes to the pertChartLinks array. The x2 and y2 parameters are assigned as values of pertChartLinks (x1, x2). Remember, pertChartLinks is an array of coordinates (see the "Global Declarations" section of this chapter). If a successor link has already been recorded for the step coordinate (x1, y1), the pertChartLinks array might need to be redimensioned to accommodate the new link:

```
Sub AddLink (x1, y1, x2, y2)

Dim i As Integer

For i = 1 To UBound(pertChartLinks, 3)
   If pertChartLinks(x1, y1, i).x = 0 Then
      Exit For
   End If
Next i
If i > UBound(pertChartLinks, 3) Then
   ReDim Preserve pertChartLinks(maxRows, maxRows, i) As Coordinates
End If
pertChartLinks(x1, y1, i).x = x2
pertChartLinks(x1, y1, i).y = y2

End Sub
```

The *ResolvePendingLinks* Subroutine

The subroutine ResolvePendingLinks accepts stepToken (row and column) as inputs and checks the pendingLinks array to add any links awaiting placement of the step represented by stepToken by using the AddLinks subroutine. This is accomplished by iterating though the cells of the pendingLinks array until a value matching the value of stepToken is found. The AddLink subroutine is then called with the indexes of the pendingLinks array, representing the predecessor and the parameters row and col, which represent the coordinates of the successor step:

```
Sub ResolvePendingLinks (stepToken As Long, row As Integer, col As Integer)

Dim i As Integer, j As Integer, k As Integer

For i = 1 To curMaxRow
   For j = 1 To curMaxCol
      For k = 1 To UBound(pendingLinks, 3)
         If pendingLinks(i, j, k) = stepToken Then
            Call AddLink(i, j, row, col)
         End If
      Next k
   Next j
Next i

End Sub
```

The *insertRows* Subroutine

The subroutine insertRows adds rows to the pertChart, pertChartLinks, and pendingLinks arrays using the input parameters rows, representing the row before which the insertion should occur, and NumRows, indicating the number of rows to insert. The insertion is accomplished by adding numRows to the global variable curMaxRow. Starting with the last original row, each row, down to the row number indicated by the parameter row, is copied to the NumRows higher in the array. At the same time the row values in pertChartLinks are also updated to reflect the inserted rows. Finally, the newly inserted rows are initialized to represent empty rows:

```
Sub insertRows (row As Integer, NumRows As Integer)

Dim rowBnd As Integer, i As Integer, j As Integer, k As Integer

Rem add rows to end of array
curMaxRow = curMaxRow + NumRows

Rem move rows up
For i = curMaxRow To row + NumRows Step -1
   For j = 1 To curMaxCol
      pertChart(i, j) = pertChart(i - NumRows, j)
      For k = 1 To UBound(pertChartLinks, 3)
         If j <= curMaxCol Then
            pertChartLinks(i, j, k).x = pertChartLinks(i - NumRows, j, k).x
            pertChartLinks(i, j, k).y = pertChartLinks(i - NumRows, j, k).y
            If (pertChartLinks(i, j, k).x >= row) Then
               pertChartLinks(i, j, k).x = pertChartLinks(i, j, k).x + row
```

```
            End If
        End If
    Next k
    For k = 1 To UBound(pendingLinks, 3)
        If j <= curMaxCol Then
            pendingLinks(i, j, k) = pendingLinks(i - NumRows, j, k)
            pendingLinks(i, j, k) = pendingLinks(i - NumRows, j, k)
        End If
    Next k
  Next j
Next i

Rem initialize new rows
For i = row To (row + NumRows) - 1
  For j = 1 To curMaxCol
    pertChart(i, j) = 0
    For k = 1 To UBound(pertChartLinks, 3)
        If j <= curMaxCol Then
            pertChartLinks(i, j, k).x = 0
            pertChartLinks(i, j, k).y = 0
        End If
    Next k
    For k = 1 To UBound(pendingLinks, 3)
        If j <= curMaxCol Then
            pendingLinks(i, j, k) = 0
            pendingLinks(i, j, k) = 0
        End If
    Next k
  Next j
Next i

End Sub
```

The *generateVisioDiagram* Subroutine

The subroutine generateVisioDiagram creates a Visio diagram and draws the PERT chart on it. It accepts PPtoken, representing the token of the Project template, as input. It draws the chart by first drawing the steps as boxes and then adds the links using connecting arrowhead shapes. First, the array pertChartDrawing, an array to hold Visio shape objects, is dimensioned to correspond with the dimensions of the pertChart array. Next, the Visio application is started (or found) by using the function vaoGetObject, provided by ShapeWare in the file VISREG.BAS. The standard Visio stencil file, FLOWCHRT.VSS, is used to provide master shapes that will be dragged onto the drawing to represent the steps and links. A new document file is opened on which to draw the chart. For each step found in the pertChart array, the subroutine DrawTask is called with the template token, step token, position (j, i), Visio document object, and master shape. After all the steps are placed, the subroutine DrawLinks is called for each link found in the pertChartLinks array:

```
Sub generateVisioDiagram (PPtoken As Long)

Const stencil = "FLOWCHRT.VSS"
```

```
Dim vDocs As Object, vDoc As Object, i As Integer, j As Integer
DimvisioLoaded As Integer
Dim vMasters As Object, vMaster As Object, vStepMaster As Object
Dim vLinkMaster As Object
Dim k As Integer

ReDim pertChartDrawing(curMaxRow, UBound(pertChart, 2))
visioLoaded = vaoGetObject()
If visioLoaded = visOK Then
    Set vDocs = g_appVisio.Documents
    Rem Open a new document with the flowchart stencil
    Set vDoc = vDocs.Add("FLOWCHRT.VSS")
    Set vMasters = vDoc.Masters
    For i = 1 To vMasters.Count
        Set vMaster = vMasters.Item(i)
        If vMaster.Name = "Process" Then
            Set vStepMaster = vMaster
        End If
        If vMaster.Name = "Next" Then
            Set vLinkMaster = vMaster
        End If
    Next i
    Set vDoc = vDocs.Add("")
    For i = 1 To curMaxRow
        For j = 1 To UBound(pertChart, 2)
            If pertChart(i, j) > 0 Then
                Call DrawTask(PPtoken, pertChart(i, j), j, i, vDoc, vStepMaster)
            End If
        Next j
    Next i
    For i = 1 To curMaxRow
        For j = 1 To curMaxCol
            For k = 1 To UBound(pertChartLinks, 3)
                If pertChartLinks(i, j, k).x > 0 Then
                    Call DrawLinks(pertChartDrawing(i, j),
                                   pertChartLinks(i, j, k).x,
                                   pertChartLinks(i, j, k).y,
                                   vLinkMaster)
                End If
            Next k
        Next j
    Next i
Else ' Visio has not been invoked
    MsgBox "Unable to start Visio. Aborting PERT chart generation."
    End
End If
Erase pertChartDrawing

End Sub
```

The *DrawTask* Subroutine

The subroutine DrawTask looks up the step name in the Steps table using the PPtoken and
stepToken parameters. Provided that the step exists, the position of the step on the page is calculated and an instance of the vMaster shape is dropped at the position x1, y1 on the Visio
page. The resultant shape object is placed in the pertChartDrawing array. The height and width

of the shape are proportioned so that the step name will appear without undo line breaks. Finally, the name of the text property of the shape is set to the step name:

```
Sub DrawTask (PPtoken As Long, stepToken As Long, x As Integer,
              y As Integer, vDoc As Object, vMaster As Object)

Const xWidth = .9, yHeight = .6
Dim dbSteps As snapshot, sql As String, taskShape As Object
Dim x1 As Single, y1 As Single
Dim vHeight As Object, vWidth As Object

Set dbSteps = gDB.CreateSnapshot("Steps")
dbSteps.FindFirst "[Project Plan Token]=" & PPtoken & " AND Token=" & stepToken
If Not dbSteps.NoMatch Then
    x1 = (1.4 * x)
    y1 = 9 - y + 1
Set pertChartDrawing(y, x) = g_appVisio.ActivePage.Drop(vMaster, x1, y1)
    Set vWidth = pertChartDrawing(y, x).Cells("Width")
    vWidth.Result(visNumber) = vWidth.Result(visNumber) * .5
    Set vHeight = pertChartDrawing(y, x).Cells("Height")
    vHeight.Result(visNumber) = vHeight.Result(visNumber) * .5
    pertChartDrawing(y, x).Text = dbSteps!Name
End If

End Sub
```

NOTE

For more information on manipulating Visio shapes from Visual Basic, see the Visio Programming Language Reference help file (progref.hlp) distributed with Visio.

The *DrawLinks* Subroutine

The subroutine DrawLinks places the links representing the predecessor/successor associations on the Visio drawing page. The originStep parameter is the Visio shape that represents the predecessor. The parameters destX and destY represent the position of the successor in the pertChartDrawing array. The vLinkMaster parameter is the master shape to be dropped onto the page to represent the predecessor/successor association. The drawing of the links is accomplished only if both the successor and predecessor shapes exist. First, the link shape is dropped on the surface of the page. Second, the Begin point of the link shape is attached to the Connection point on the right side of the predecessor (origin) shape. Then the end point of the link's shape is attached to the left side of the successor's (destination) shape:

```
Sub DrawLinks (originStep As Object, destX As Integer, destY As Integer,
               vLinkMaster As Object)

Dim vLink As Object, vCell As Object, vOriginCell As Object
Dim vDestCell As Object, vDestShape As Object
```

```
If Not (originStep Is Nothing) Then
    If Not (pertChartDrawing(destX, destY) Is Nothing) Then
        Set vDestShape = pertChartDrawing(destX, destY)
        Set vLink = g_appVisio.ActivePage.Drop(vLinkMaster, destX, destY)
        Set vOriginCell = originStep.CellsSRC(visSectionExport, 2, 1)
        Set vCell = vLink.Cells("BeginX")
        vCell.GlueTo vOriginCell
        Set vDestCell = vDestShape.CellsSRC(visSectionExport, 1, 2)
        Set vCell = vLink.Cells("EndX")
        vCell.GlueTo vDestCell
    Else
        MsgBox "Internal Error: pertChartDrawing(" & destX & "," & destY & ")
                is point to nothing.)"
    End If
Else
    MsgBox "Internal Error: originStep is nothing in draw link.)"
End If

End Sub
```

Summary

Although the implementation described in this chapter is a useful first step, several issues need to be addressed before it can be put into use:

- Improving exception handling
- Detecting and avoiding cycles in the predecessor/successor graph
- Splitting large charts over multiple Visio pages
- Handling PERT charts larger then 10 by 10
- Developing a setup program and disk for the generator application for users who do not have VB installed on their machines
- Allowing portions of a project template to be charted

The implementation should handle exceptions and invalid data with appropriate messages to the end user. The generateVisioDiagram routine should be enhanced to detect when a chart exceeds a single page and to map the pertChart array onto as many Visio pages as are required. Larger PERT charts can be handled with the existing arrays by increasing the value of the global constant maxRows. A setup kit is provided by Microsoft with the Professional Edition of Visual Basic that allows the user to create setup programs and disks for distributing Visual Basic applications. Finally, the user interface could be extended to allow the user to produce a chart based on one or more organizational units within a project. This requires modifying the getInitialSteps, getPredecessors, and getSuccessors functions to consider in which organizational unit a step is contained.

Case Study 2: Paperless Office— Business Infrastructure Automation

57

by Dan Silkworth

IN THIS CHAPTER

This case study is organized into a statement of the problem, including business requirements, technology issues, and management concerns. An analysis model that formalizes the understanding of the problem is presented. A design that addresses specific database and algorithmic needs is presented. Finally, one implementation that satisfies the problem is presented.

The Business Problem

A small, but rapidly growing, business (ABC, Inc.) is trying to minimize administrative overhead while improving conformance to operational policies and procedures. The process of creating and administering corporate policies is illustrated in Figure 57.1. A solution is being sought that meets the following goals:

- Ensure that all employees have access to relevant policies and procedures.
- Minimize the need for generating paper reports and forms.
- Facilitate electronic distribution and processing of operational data for the following:

  New policies and procedures
  Expense reports
  Approved travel agents
  Corporate travel discounts
  Supply requisitions
  Vacation requests
  Personnel backgrounds and short biographies
  Expense approval levels and authority

- Facilitate training of new employees regarding operational policies.

FIGURE 57.1.

Corporate policy administration.

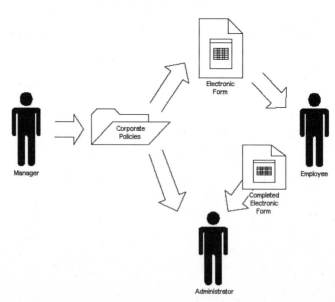

A policy manual is currently being maintained using Microsoft Word. This policy manual organizes the policies into four general categories: General, Administrative, Reporting, Computer Hardware and Software, and Internal Controls. The following information is recorded for each policy:

- The date the policy became active
- The person who originally approved the policy
- The department responsible for administering the policy
- The position which handles inquiries about the policy
- A statement of the purpose of the policy
- A statement of who is responsible for enforcing the policy
- A description of the policy

Policies can also be composed of subpolicies. The administration of some of the policies of ABC, Inc., have been partially automated using existing Microsoft Office products. Examples include a standardized Excel spreadsheet for expense reporting and a personnel database implemented in Microsoft Access.

The Technology Problem

The company uses IBM-compatible laptops, running Window 3.1. All PCs have Microsoft Office installed on them. A local area network is available at the home office, using Windows for Workgroups 3.11. The research department has identified hypertext technology as being an effective tool for the electronic distribution of textual data. The Window Help Viewer is a hypertext viewer available on all company machines.

The Management Problem

As a proof of concept, a prototype of a tool, which allows managers to define policies, tracks the data in these policies and generates an electronic hypertext policy manual. The electronic policy manual should describe each policy and, where possible, integrate with applications in the Microsoft Office suite, which automates the administration of these policies.

The Analysis Model

The major business objects discovered during analysis are personnel, position, organizational unit, policy, application, electronic form template, electronic form instance, and form action. (See Figure 57.2.) The policy object is the central object of the model and is attributed with a name, effective date, purpose, responsibility, description, and type. Policies are the responsibility of an organizational unit, which may administer multiple policies. A particular position, usually the position of the person approving the policy, within the organization is identified to handle inquiries regarding the policy. The person who originally approved the policy must be retained even if the person changes positions in the organization.

Each position is filled by a person, but some employees may fill multiple positions. Each organizational unit (department) is managed by a particular employee. Some employees may manage multiple departments. A position reports to some other position, unless the position is the company president. Organizational units are contained in some other organizational unit, except for the corporation. The position reporting hierarchy and the organizational unit hierarchy are not necessarily mirror images.

Policies can be supported by one or more electronic form templates. These templates are supported by an application that has a name, a working directory, and a command line. Electronic form templates may be used to produce one or more instances of an electronic form. The system may track examples of completed electronic forms for personnel training purposes. An electronic form can have one or more actions performed against it by some employee. Certain form actions may be restricted to specific positions within the organization (for example, expense report approval).

FIGURE 57.2.

Business Infrastructure Automation Analysis model.

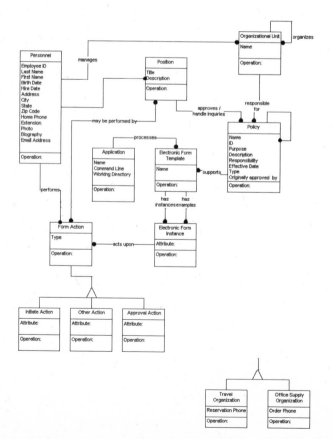

Using an expense reporting policy as an example, Figure 57.3 presents a instance diagram based on the model shown in Figure 57.2. Expense reporting is the responsibility of the accounting department, which is managed by Jane Doe, the chief accountant. An Excel spreadsheet has been developed to standardize the reporting of expenses. Joe Smith has submitted an expense report for the week ending 10/21/95 that must be approved by his sales manager, Frank Worth.

FIGURE 57.3.

The Business Infrastructure Automation Instance model.

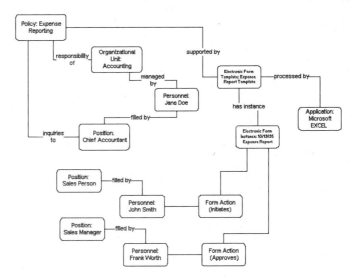

The Design Model

A database design that covers the entire analysis model, except for the electronic form action object, is presented in the following section. The design of the methods necessary to implement the policy administrator can be organized into three logical modules: policy authoring module, hypertext generation module, and an application dispatching module.

The Database Design

The database design (see Figure 57.4) is derived from the analysis object model using the same techniques illustrated in Chapter 56, "Case Study 1: Project Management Information Integrator." Primary keys appear in boldface, uniquely indexed columns are italicized, and foreign keys are underlined. The lines connecting the tables are labeled with the foreign keys they represent.

For the first prototype, only the Policy, Personnel, Position, and Organizational Unit objects have been implemented in the database design. Three tables—Files, Paths, and File Locations—have been included in the design to keep track of the electronic form template files and the textual components of the hypertext manual. These files are stored externally from the database, rather than as OLE objects, to reduce the size of the database. All filenames are stored in the Files table, and all paths used to store files are stored in the Paths table. The File Location table has a unique path token and file token, which determine a unique location for each file. This approach allows for both reuse and multiple versions of the textual object instances stored in these files. The object class Application is represented by the application type column of the Policy table.

The electronic form template files are stored in the native format of the Microsoft Office application with which they are associated. The textual components of the policy manual (purpose, responsibility, and description columns of the policies table) are stored in rich text format (RTF), which is the only format accepted by the help compiler.

FIGURE 57.4.

Policy Administration database design.

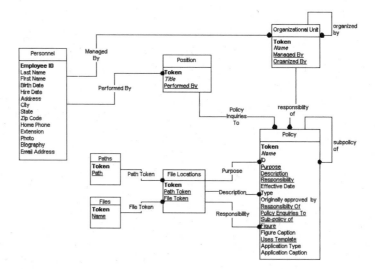

The Policy Administration Application Design

The Policy Administration application has two main components. The first component is a user interface component that allows the policymakers to update the database for the following reasons:

- Creating new policies
- Assigning policy attributes
- Editing the textual attributes of the policy
- Deleting policies
- Associating template files with policies and applications
- Including graphics with the policies

The second component is a help file generator that produces an RTF file suitable for processing by the help compiler. The help file generator performs the following functions:

- Creates hotspotted lists for each type of policy
- Creates a help topic for each policy
- Inserts appropriate context string, browse sequence, and title footnotes for each topic
- Inserts a hotspot jump between subpolicies and their parent policy
- Inserts hotspot jumps for any graphic files to be displayed
- Inserts hotspot macros to execute any MS Office applications with appropriate template files

User Interface Design

The user interface for the policy administration applications consists of three forms: Policy Outliner, Create Policy, and Policy Editor. Figure 57.5 specifies how the Policy Outliner and Create Policy forms behave. The Policy Outliner is the first form that appears when the application is invoked. It uses an outline control to display the table of contents of the policy manual. At the first level of the outline only the five policy types—General, Administrative, Reporting, Computer Hardware and Software, and Internal Controls—are displayed. At the second level of the outline the actual policy names of each type appear in the order in which they will be placed in the hypertext title. The `Form_Load` procedure of the Policy Outliner form extracts the policies' names from the database and places them in the outline control through a subprocedure called `LoadOutline`. There is no technical reason why the subpolicies could not be shown in the outline except that the designer chose to limit the list to two levels.

Activation of the Add Policy command button control causes the appearance of the Create Policy form. This form allows the user to type in a new policy name and type. This form is application modal, which means that the form must be unloaded before any other form is activated. Application modal forms should be used on dialog controls when the user must complete or cancel an action before proceeding. The Cancel command button unloads the form without any action being taken. The OK command button adds the new policy name to the database before unloading the form. The Delete button control deletes the active policy from the database and refreshes the Outline control.

> **NOTE**
>
> When designing a user interface, you should make a control inactive if it is not appropriate for the current state of the interface. For example, the Delete button on the Policy Outliner form is disabled until the user selects a policy, because a user cannot delete a policy without selecting one first. The OK button on the Add Policy form is disabled until a name is entered and a type selected.

FIGURE 57.5.

The Policy Outliner and Add Policy forms.

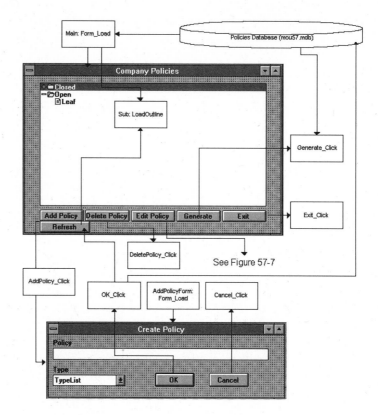

The Edit Policy control button causes the appearance of the Policy Editor form. (See Figure 57.6.) The various text fields of the policy table (Name, Figure Caption, Originally Approved By, Application Caption) are represented as text box controls in the Policy Editor form. The foreign key fields (Policy Inquiries To and Responsibility Of) are represented by combo box controls, which are populated with the names from the table to which the foreign key points.

The Application Type field is represented by the radio buttons found in the Application and Template 3-D frame control. The Hot Text Label and Browse controls are not enabled unless an application type other than None is selected. The Browse button uses a common dialog control to get the file specification and set the value of a Template File control. The Template File control itself is never enabled. The Mail to on completion control has not been implemented.

FIGURE 57.6.

The Policy Editor form in property view.

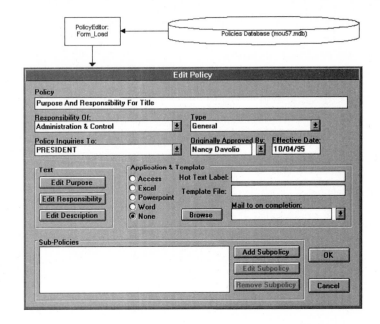

The subpolicy list box displays the current subpolicies, if any. The Add Subpolicy, Edit Subpolicy, and Delete Subpolicy controls work in the same manner as the Add Subpolicy, Edit Subpolicy, and Delete Subpolicy buttons on the Policy Outliner form, except that they only affect the subpolicies of the current policy.

The OK button control commits changes to the current policy to the database and closes the form. The Cancel button control ignores any changes to the policy and closes the form.

The three buttons in the Text frame are used to edit the text associated with the policy. These buttons actually change the appearance of the form by making the WordOLE, EmbedFigPanel, and WordOLEbuttons controls visible. (See Figure 57.7.) The WordOLE panel contains an embedded OLE control for Word 6. This control is populated with the appropriate RTF file for the policy. This allows the user to use a subset of Word 6 to perform word processing activities on the textual components of the policy manual. The policy administration's applications maintain control over the location and name of each of the RTF files. The Browse button control on the EmbedFigPanel allows the user to select a graphics file through a common dialog control, which is to be displayed as part of the policy. The OK and Cancel controls on the WordOLEbuttons panel allow the user to confirm or cancel changes to the RTF text. The OK and Cancel controls also restore the form to its original appearance by making the WordOLE, EmbedFigPanel, and WordOLEbuttons controls invisible.

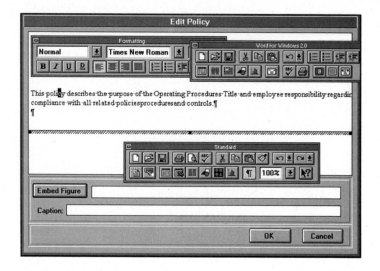

Help File Generator Design

In order to understand the design of the generator, it is necessary to have a rudimentary understanding of how the Windows help compiler works. The current design makes a number of assumptions about the development environment detailed in the following section. The design makes use of the similarities between a hypertext document and a relational database. A jump in a hypertext document is analogous to the occurrence of a foreign key in a relational database. The design uses this fact and the guaranteed uniqueness of primary keys to simplify the generation of the RTF file.

The Windows Help Compiler

The purpose of the help file generator is to take the information from the database and reformat it into input that is accepted by the Windows help compiler. The Windows help compiler builds a hypertext document with embedded graphics from a set of rich text format (RTF) files and bitmap files. The help compiler uses footnotes, underlining, and hidden text to indicate hyperjumps. Double-underlined text followed by a hidden context string indicates a jump to the point in the document where there is a pound sign (#) footnote with the same context string as the footnote's value. The jumps normally go to the start of a help topic. A topic is delimited by a manual page break. If there are one or more paragraphs that have the Keep With Next property at the start of a topic, then these paragraphs appear in a nonscrolling region at the top of the topic help window. All subsequent paragraphs appear in a scrolling region comprising the rest of the window. It is also possible to have jumps to *secondary windows*, which may contain hot graphics. *Hot graphics* are also hyperjumps. In addition to jumps to other topics, hot text or graphics can result in the execution of a macro or even an external program. A project (HPJ) file is used to tell the help compiler what files to use when compiling, and it allows the specification of a number of other variables. Complete documentation for the help compiler is available from Microsoft in the form of the *Help Compiler Guide* (Document No. DB50618-0293), which is distributed with Visual Basic.

Help File Generator Assumptions

The help file generator designed here assumes that a standard shell is used to build the RTF file. This shell is included in the source material for this chapter and consists of the following files: INTRO.RTF, INTRO.SHG, MAINBKG.SHG, LOGO.BMP, and ORG1.SHG. The project file POLICY.HPJ is also included against which to run the help compiler. The file INTRO.RTF is expected to be in a subdirectory PRDCTN under the application directory. The graphics files are expected to be in the subdirectory PRDCTN\GFX. The POLICY.HPJ file must be updated to indicate the correct paths. The sample help file, POLICY.HLP, has been compiled using the Microsoft Help Compiler Version 3.10.505 (extended). It is also known as HCP.EXE. The RTF source file used is PM111695.RTF, which is found in the PRDCTN directory.

The Design

A structure chart illustrating the calling structure of the design is shown in Figure 57.8. The subroutine GenerateHelpFile creates an OLE object for Word 6 Basic. This object allows the manipulation of Word by using Word Basic commands from Visual Basic. Using the wordBasic object, the file INTRO.RTF is opened and saved to a new filename based on the current date. For each type of policy a topic is created with # footnotes and $ (title) footnotes. The # footnotes have the values TOC1, TOC2,...TOC5 to match the jumps already coded in INTRO.RTF. The subroutine FormatPolicies is then called for each type of policy.

The subroutine FormatPolicies creates a list of hyperlinks for each policy of the type it is processing. The context strings for these hyperlinks are derived from the primary key of the policy. After the list of hyperlinks is created, a topic is created for each policy by calling the subroutine InsertPolicyTopic. One topic is created for each member of the hyperlink in the list.

The subroutine InsertPolicyTopic first inserts a context string (#), title footnotes ($), and browse sequence footnotes (+). The nonscrolling region of the topic is then built using the company logo (LOGO.BMP) name of the policy, the name of the person who originally approved the policy, where to query about the policy, and the effective date of the policy. If the policy is a subpolicy of some other policy, then a hot jump to the parent policy is included in the nonscrolling region. After the nonscrolling region, the files containing the text for the policies' purposes, responsibilities, and descriptions are included. The purpose and responsibility text properties are only included for primary policies (not subpolicies). If the policy is associated with a template file, a hotspot is generated that invokes the appropriate Microsoft Office product with the template file. This is accomplished by calling the executable 57MOU.EXE (the Application Dispatcher described in the following section) by using an ExecProgram macro call. If a graphic has been provided for the policy, a hotspot is created to display the graphic in a secondary window. A topic containing the reference to the graphic file must also be added after the current topic. Finally, the subroutine `FormatPolicies` is recursively called to process any subpolicies.

FIGURE 57.8.

The Generate Help File functional design.

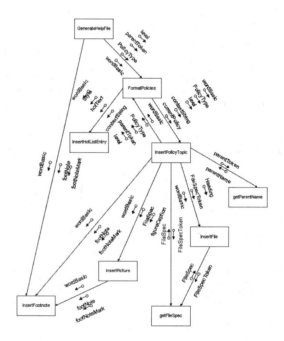

Application Dispatcher Design

The purpose of the Application Dispatcher is to invoke the current version of a Microsoft Office product with the template file provided. The question is Where are the office products installed? The user may have installed them in a nonstandard subdirectory, on a partitioned drive, or even on a network drive. The answer is the little-known Windows registration database.

The WinSDK Help file provided with Visual Basic states, "The registration database is a systemwide source of information about applications. This information is used to support the integration of applications with Windows File Manager and is used by applications that support object linking and embedding (OLE)." The structure of the registration database is hierarchical. It is navigated by finding successive keys. The subkey shell/open/command below the application's primary key (for example, EXCEL.SHEET) provides the command line, with an absolute path, for opening the application. The sole purpose of the Application Dispatcher is to get the absolute paths by which to invoke the applications. This is accomplished by using routines in the Windows 3.1 API.

The Implementation

The solution has been implemented using Microsoft's Visual Basic 3, Access 2, and Word 6.0.

> **NOTE**
>
> Use of Access 2 with Visual Basic 3 requires installation of Microsoft's VB 3/Access 2 compatibility layer. The compatibility layer installation software can be downloaded from the library files on the Access or Visual Basic forums on CompuServe.

Database Implementation

The database implementation, based on the design shown in Figure 57.4, requires seven tables, as shown in Figures 57.9 and 57.10. The template files, and the text for the description, responsibility, and purpose properties are not stored directly in the database. Instead, this data is stored in external files whose location is captured in the files, paths, and file locations tables. This reduces the size of the database and eliminates the need to store OLE objects in the database. It is a simplified version of object linking for Access database and VB, bypassing the overhead of OLE.

> **NOTE**
>
> The data type for all fields that serve as foreign keys is long integer. This is necessary to ensure join compatibility between the foreign keys and the token fields, with data type counter, in the tables to which they point.

FIGURE 57.9.

The table implementation for Policy Administrator— Organization Units, Personnel, and Positions.

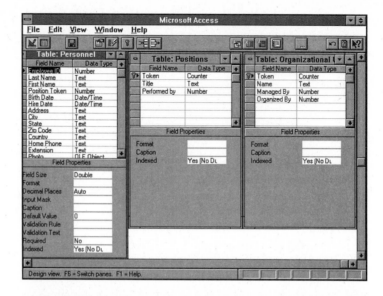

FIGURE 57.10.

The table implementation for Policy Administrator— Policies, Files, Paths, and File Locations.

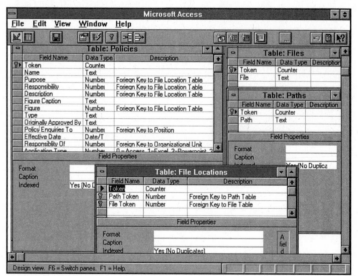

Visual Basic Project File

Ten files are required to implement the solution in Visual Basic, and six of these are provided with Visual Basic. (See Figure 57.11.) The file CONSTANT.TXT contains standard Visual Basic global constants and should be included in every Visual Basic project. The file CONSTANT.TXT can be found in the VB directory. The file GLOBAL.BAS contains user-defined type definitions, global constants, and global functions, as described in the following section. The files ADDPOLICY.FRM, PLCYEDIT.FRM, and POLICIES.FRM contain the form layouts and all the remaining source code. The VBX files are standard Visual Basic controls, available in VB 3.

FIGURE 57.11.

A Visual Basic project file.

The global declarations are contained in the file GLOBAL.BAS. A separate file is necessary because these variable are shared over multiple forms. The global constant is the name of the Access database for policy administration. The constant gAppTitle is the name of the application to be used for any message dialog controls. The global variables gPolicyToken and gFileSpec are used for communication between forms:

```
Global Const gDBname = "57mou.mdb"
Global Const gAppTitle = "Policy Manager"
Global gPolicyToken As Long
Global gFileSpec As String
```

getFileSpec

The global function getFileSpec returns a file specification given a LocToken value, which exists in the table File Locations:

```
Function getFileSpec (LocToken As Long) As String

Dim gDB As database, dbFileLocs As Snapshot, sql As String, spec As String

Set gDB = OpenDatabase(App.Path & "\" & gDBname)
sql = "SELECT DISTINCTROW Paths.Path, Files.File "
sql = sql & "FROM ([File Locations] "
sql = sql & "INNER JOIN Files ON [File Locations].[File Token] = Files.Token) "
sql = sql & "INNER JOIN Paths ON [File Locations].[Path Token] = Paths.Token "
sql = sql & "WHERE [File Locations].Token=" & LocToken
Debug.Print sql
Set dbFileLocs = gDB.CreateSnapshot(sql)
If Not dbFileLocs.EOF Then
   getFileSpec = dbFileLocs!Path & "\" & dbFileLocs!File
Else
   getFileSpec = ""
End If

End Function
```

deleteChildren

The deleteChildren subroutine is a recursive subroutine that deletes all the children of the policy whose token is the input parameter parentToken:

```
Sub deleteChildren (parentToken As Long)

Dim DB As database, dbPolicies As dynaset, newParentToken As Long

Set DB = OpenDatabase(App.Path & "\" & gDBname)
Set dbPolicies = DB.CreateDynaset("Policies")
dbPolicies.FindFirst "[Sub-policy of]=" & parentToken
Do While Not dbPolicies.NoMatch
   newParentToken = dbPolicies!Token
   Call deleteChildren(newParentToken)
   dbPolicies.Delete
   dbPolicies.FindNext "[Sub-policy of]=" & parentToken
Loop

End Sub
```

PoliciesOutline Form

The PoliciesOutline form enables the user to create a policy, delete a policy, select a policy for editing, or generate the help title's source RTF file.

AddPolicy_Click

This method sets the global variable gPolicyToken to zero, indicating that the policy has no parent. It then shows the form AddPolicyForm as a application modal form:

```
Sub AddPolicy_Click ()
   gPolicyToken = 0
   AddPolicyForm.Show 1
End Sub
```

dblSlash

The function dblSlash returns a string with two backslash characters for every one backslash in the input variable snglSlash. This is necessary because the help compiler requires two backslashes in all file specifications:

```
Function dblSlash (snglSlash As String) As String

Dim i As Integer, result As String

result = ""
For i = 1 To Len(snglSlash)
   If Mid$(snglSlash, i, 1) = "\" Then
      result = result & "\"
```

```
      End If
      result = result & Mid$(snglSlash, i, 1)
   Next i
   dblSlash = result

   End Function
```

DeletePolicy_Click

The `DeletePolicy_Click` method deletes the selected policy, and all its subpolicies, from the database. It also updates the `PolicyOutline` control:

```
Sub DeletePolicy_Click ()

Dim DB As database, dbPolicies As dynaset, sql  As String, parentToken As Long

Set DB = OpenDatabase(App.Path & "\" & gDBname)
Set dbPolicies = DB.CreateDynaset("Policies")
dbPolicies.FindFirst "Token=" & PolicyOutline.ItemData(PolicyOutline.ListIndex)
If Not dbPolicies.NoMatch Then
   dbPolicies.Delete
End If
parentToken = PolicyOutline.ItemData(PolicyOutline.ListIndex)
Call deleteChildren(parentToken)

PolicyOutline.RemoveItem (PolicyOutline.ListIndex)
End Sub
```

EditPolicy_Click

The `EditPolicy_Click` method sets the global parameter `gPolicyToken` to the token of the currently selected policy, which is stored in the `ItemData` array of the `PolicyOutline` control (see the `LoadOutline` subroutine). It then shows the `policyForm` application modally. The `setfocus` command ensures that this form gets the focus back when the `policyForm` is unloaded:

```
Sub EditPolicy_Click ()

Dim policyForm As New PolicyEditor

   gPolicyToken = PolicyOutline.ItemData(PolicyOutline.ListIndex)
   policyForm.Show 1
   SetFocus
End Sub
```

Exit_Click

The method `Exit_Click` terminates the application:

```
Sub Exit_Click ()
   End
End Sub
```

Form_Load

The Form_Load subroutine calls the LoadOutline subroutine to load the outline control with the policies. The Refresh_Click method also calls the LoadOutline subroutine:

```
Sub Form_Load ()

Call LoadOutline

End Sub
```

FormatPolicies

The FormatPolicies subroutine creates a hot list of each policy of a PolicyType by calling the subroutine InsertHotListEntry. It then creates topics for each policy of a PolicyType by calling the subroutine InsertPolicyTopic. Consistency in naming the context strings for the hot lists and the topics is achieved by deriving the context string from the primary key of the Policies table:

```
Sub FormatPolicies (wordBasic As Object, PolicyType As String,
     parentToken As Long, level As Integer)

Dim DB As database, dbPolicies As Snapshot, sql As String, hotText As String
Dim contextString As String, policyName As String

Set DB = OpenDatabase(App.Path & "\" & gDBname)
sql = "SELECT DISTINCTROW Policies.*, Positions.Title "
sql = sql & "FROM Policies "
sql = sql & "LEFT JOIN Positions "
sql = sql & "ON Policies.[Responsiblity Of] = Positions.Token "
sql = sql & "WHERE Policies.Type=" & Chr$(34) & PolicyType & Chr$(34)
sql = sql & "  AND Policies.[Sub-policy of]=" & parentToken
Debug.Print sql
Set dbPolicies = DB.CreateSnapshot(sql)

Rem first build hot list of the policies
If Not dbPolicies.EOF Then
    Do While Not dbPolicies.EOF
        hotText = dbPolicies!Name
        contextString = "cs" & Format$(dbPolicies!Token, "00000000")
        Call InsertHotListEntry(wordBasic, "List", hotText, contextString)
        dbPolicies.MoveNext
    Loop

    Rem Now build policy topics
    dbPolicies.MoveFirst
    Do While Not dbPolicies.EOF
        contextString = "cs" & Format$(dbPolicies!Token, "00000000")
        Call InsertPolicyTopic(wordBasic, dbPolicies, contextString,
                            level, PolicyType)
        dbPolicies.MoveNext
    Loop
End If

End Sub
```

Generate_Click

The `Generate_Click` method sets the mouse cursor to an hourglass and calls the subroutine `GenerateHelpFile`. On return from `GenerateHelpFile`, the mouse cursor is reset to the default pointer:

```
Sub Generate_Click ()

screen.MousePointer = 11  ' hourglass
Call GenerateHelpFile
screen.MousePointer = 0   ' default

End Sub
```

GenerateHelpFile

The subroutine `GenerateHelpFile` runs all the code necessary to generate the RTF file for input to the help compiler. It depends on the title shell already set up in the file INTRO.RTF. It inserts a topic for the table of contents hot list of each type for policy and calls `FormatPolicies` to generate the hot list and the policy topics. The object variable `wordBasic` is set in the routine to allow Word Basic commands to be processed by Word 6. All Word Basic commands must be preceded by a reference to the `wordBasic` object (for example, `wordBasic.fileopen`):

```
Sub GenerateHelpFile ()

Rem This routine and the routines that call it assume the file intro.rtf
Rem is using the standard MS word template manual1.dot

Const ProductionSubDir = "\prdctn"
Dim wordBasic As Object

Set wordBasic = CreateObject("Word.Basic")
REM the second argument to the file open command (0) prevents the
REM conversion dialog from appearing
wordBasic.fileopen App.Path & ProductionSubDir & "\intro.rtf", 0
wordBasic.filesaveas App.Path & ProductionSubDir &
                     "\PM" & Format(Date$, "MMDDYY") & ".rtf",
                     6' RTF format

wordBasic.endofdocument
Call InsertFootnote(wordBasic, "$", "General Policies")
Call InsertFootnote(wordBasic, "#", "TOC1")
wordBasic.Insert "General Policies"
wordBasic.Style "Heading 1"
Call FormatPolicies(wordBasic, "General", 0, 2)

wordBasic.InsertPara
wordBasic.InsertPageBreak
Call InsertFootnote(wordBasic, "$", "Administrative Policies")
Call InsertFootnote(wordBasic, "#", "TOC2")
wordBasic.Insert "Administrative Policies"
wordBasic.Style "Heading 1"
Call FormatPolicies(wordBasic, "Administrative", 0, 2)
```

```
wordBasic.InsertPara
wordBasic.InsertPageBreak
Call InsertFootnote(wordBasic, "$", "Reporting Policies")
Call InsertFootnote(wordBasic, "#", "TOC3")
wordBasic.Insert "Reporting Policies"
wordBasic.Style "Heading 1"
Call FormatPolicies(wordBasic, "Reporting", 0, 2)

wordBasic.InsertPara
wordBasic.InsertPageBreak
Call InsertFootnote(wordBasic, "$", "Computer Hardware & Software Policies")
Call InsertFootnote(wordBasic, "#", "TOC4")
wordBasic.Insert "Computer Hardware & Software Policies"
wordBasic.Style "Heading 1"
Call FormatPolicies(wordBasic, "Computer Hardware & Software", 0, 2)

wordBasic.InsertPara
wordBasic.InsertPageBreak
Call InsertFootnote(wordBasic, "$", "Internal Control Policies")
Call InsertFootnote(wordBasic, "#", "TOC5")
wordBasic.Insert "Internal Control Policies"
wordBasic.Style "Heading 1"
Call FormatPolicies(wordBasic, "Internal Controls", 0, 2)

wordBasic.filesaveas App.Path & ProductionSubDir & _
                     "\PM" & Format(Date$, "MMDDYY") & ".rtf", _
                     6' RTF format
wordBasic.filecloseall

End Sub
```

getParentName

The getParentName function returns the name of a policy given its token—parentToken:

```
Function getParentName (parentToken As Long) As String

Dim DB As database, dbPolicies As Snapshot, sql As String
Set DB = OpenDatabase(App.Path & "\" & gDBname)
sql = "SELECT DISTINCTROW Name FROM Policies "
sql = sql & "WHERE Token = " & parentToken
Set dbPolicies = DB.CreateSnapshot(sql)
If dbPolicies.EOF Then
   getParentName = ""
Else
   getParentName = dbPolicies!Name
End If

End Function
```

InsertFile

The InsertFile subroutine inserts a file into the Word document. It uses the function getFileSpec to retrieve the file specification from the database based on a file location token. This is how the descriptions and other text properties of a policy get placed in the RTF file:

```
Sub InsertFile (wordBasic As Object, FileSpecToken As Long, Heading As String)

Dim FileSpec As String

FileSpec = getFileSpec(FileSpecToken)
If FileSpec <> "" Then
   wordBasic.InsertPara
   wordBasic.FormatFont , , , , , , , , , , , , , , , , 1
   wordBasic.Insert Heading
   wordBasic.FormatFont , , , , , , , , , , , , , , , , 0
   wordBasic.InsertPara
   wordBasic.Style "Body Text"
   wordBasic.InsertFile FileSpec, , 0, 0
End If

End Sub
```

InsertFootnote

The InsertFootnote subroutine inserts a footnote into a document using the footNoteMark as the custom mark. It is important to close the footnote area (wordBasic.ViewFootnoteArea False) before proceeding. This prevents subsequent insertions from being placed in the footnote window:

```
Sub InsertFootnote (wordBasic As Object,
                    footNoteMark As String,
                    footNote As String)

wordBasic.ViewFootnoteArea False
wordBasic.InsertFootnote footNoteMark
wordBasic.Insert footNote
wordBasic.ViewFootnoteArea False

End Sub
```

InsertHotListEntry

The subroutine InsertHotListEntry creates a single hot paragraph in a list. The hot text is double underlined, indicating a jump. (Single underlining results in a pop-up topic.) The context string immediately follows the hotText (no spaces) and must be hidden:

```
Sub InsertHotListEntry (wordBasic As Object,
                        Style As String,
                        hotText As String,
                        contextString As String)

wordBasic.InsertPara
wordBasic.Style Style
wordBasic.DoubleUnderline 1
wordBasic.Insert hotText
wordBasic.DoubleUnderline 0
wordBasic.Hidden 1
```

```
wordBasic.Insert contextString
wordBasic.Hidden 0

End Sub
```

insertPicture

The subroutine `insertPicture` inserts hot text containing the figure captions that the user speci-fied. This hot text is made to jump to a secondary window (`figwin`) by appending the string `">figwin"` to the end of the context string. The window definition for `figwin` is contained in the help project (HPJ) file. It is also necessary to create a new topic (page break) with a refer-ence to the graphic file (`{bmc <FileSpec>}`). This subroutine must only be called at the end of a policy topic because it creates this new topic to display the graphic file. The static variable `figCnt` is used to ensure that unique context strings are generated:

```
Sub insertPicture (wordBasic As Object,
                   FileSpec As String,
                   figureCaption As String)

Static figCnt

figCnt = figCnt + 1
wordBasic.InsertPara
wordBasic.Style "Caption"
wordBasic.DoubleUnderline 1
wordBasic.Insert figureCaption
wordBasic.DoubleUnderline 0
wordBasic.Hidden 1
wordBasic.Insert "fig" & Format$(figCnt, "000000") & ">figwin"
wordBasic.Hidden 0
wordBasic.InsertPara
wordBasic.InsertPageBreak
Call InsertFootnote(wordBasic, "#", "fig" & Format$(figCnt, "000000"))
wordBasic.Insert "{bmc " & FileSpec & "}"

End Sub
```

InsertPolicyTopic

The subroutine `InsertPolicyTopic` performs most of the formatting of the policy topics. It sets up the nonscrolling area by making use of the header styles in the Word template manual1.dot. These styles all have the Keep with Next property activated. The necessary foot-notes for the context string, title, and browse sequences are inserted first. The reference to the logo bitmap is inserted next. The header fields including Policy Name, Originally Approved By, Policy Inquiries To, Effective Date, and Subpolicy Of are inserted as necessary. The text files containing the purpose, responsibility, and description text are inserted next. A hotspot, using the application caption, is generated if this policy is associated with an application. A hotspot, using the figure caption, is generated if this policy is associated with a graphic file. Finally, a hot list that jumps to the subpolicies, if any, is generated with a recursive call to `FormatPolicies`:

```
Sub InsertPolicyTopic (wordBasic As Object,
                       currentPolicy As Snapshot,
                       contextString As String,
                       level As Integer,
                       PolicyType As String)

Static seqNum As Integer
Dim policyName As String, parentToken As Long, FileSpecToken As Long
Dim BrowsSeqence As String, parentName As String, childToken As Long
Dim FileSpec As String, Caption  As String

seqNum = seqNum + 1
BrowsSeqence = "browse:" & Format$(seqNum * 10, "00000000")
policyName = currentPolicy!Name
wordBasic.InsertPara
wordBasic.InsertPageBreak
wordBasic.Style "Heading " & level
Call InsertFootnote(wordBasic, "$", policyName)
Call InsertFootnote(wordBasic, "#", contextString)
Call InsertFootnote(wordBasic, "+", BrowsSeqence)
wordBasic.Insert "{bml logo.bmp}"
wordBasic.Insert "Policy: " & policyName
If level = 2 Then
    wordBasic.FormatFont wordBasic.Fontsize() - 4
    If Not IsNull(currentPolicy![Originally Approved By]) Then
        wordBasic.InsertBreak 6 ' line break
        wordBasic.Insert "Approved by:" & currentPolicy![Originally Approved By]
    End If
    If Not IsNull(currentPolicy!Title) Then
        wordBasic.InsertBreak 6 ' line break
        wordBasic.Insert "Policy Inquiries to: " & currentPolicy!Title
    End If
    If Not IsNull(currentPolicy![Effective Date]) Then
        wordBasic.InsertBreak 6 ' line break
        wordBasic.Insert "Effective Date:" & currentPolicy![Effective Date]
    End If
End If
If currentPolicy![Sub-policy of] > 0 Then
    wordBasic.InsertBreak 6 ' line break
    parentToken = currentPolicy![Sub-policy of]
    parentName = getParentName(parentToken)
    wordBasic.DoubleUnderline 1
    wordBasic.Insert "Subpolicy of:" & parentName
    wordBasic.DoubleUnderline 1
    wordBasic.Hidden 1
    wordBasic.Insert "cs" & Format$(parentToken, "00000000")
    wordBasic.Hidden 0
End If

If level = 2 Then
    If Not IsNull(currentPolicy!Purpose) Then
        FileSpecToken = currentPolicy!Purpose
        Call InsertFile(wordBasic, FileSpecToken, "Purpose")
    End If
    If Not IsNull(currentPolicy!Responsibility) Then
        FileSpecToken = currentPolicy!Responsibility
        Call InsertFile(wordBasic, FileSpecToken, "Responsibility")
    End If
```

```
End If
If Not IsNull(currentPolicy!Description) Then
   FileSpecToken = currentPolicy!Description
   Call InsertFile(wordBasic, FileSpecToken, "Description")
End If

If currentPolicy![Application Type] > 0
   And Not IsNull(currentPolicy![Application Caption]) Then
   Caption = currentPolicy![Application Caption]
   FileSpecToken = currentPolicy![Uses Template]
   FileSpec = getFileSpec(FileSpecToken)
   wordBasic.InsertPara
   wordBasic.Style "Caption"
   wordBasic.DoubleUnderline 1
   wordBasic.Insert Caption
   wordBasic.DoubleUnderline 0
   wordBasic.Hidden 1Select Case currentPolicy![Application Type]
      Case 1 ' Access
         wordBasic.Insert "!EP(" & Chr$(34)
                          & "57MOU.EXE ACCESS.DATABASE "
                          & dblSlash(FileSpec) & Chr$(34) & ",0)"
      Case 2 ' Excel
         wordBasic.Insert "!EP(" & Chr$(34)
                          & "57MOU.EXE EXCEL.SHEET "
                          & dblSlash(FileSpec) & Chr$(34) & ",0)"
      Case 3 ' Powerpoint
         wordBasic.Insert "!EP(" & Chr$(34)
                          & "57MOU.EXE POWERPOINT.SHOW "
                          & dblSlash(FileSpec) & Chr$(34) & ",0)"
      Case 4 ' Word
         wordBasic.Insert "!EP(" & Chr$(34)
                          & "57MOU.EXE WORD.DOCUMENT "
                          & dblSlash(FileSpec) & Chr$(34) & ",0)"
   End Select
   wordBasic.Hidden 0
End If

If Not IsNull(currentPolicy!Figure)
   And Not IsNull(currentPolicy![Figure Caption]) Then
   FileSpecToken = currentPolicy!Figure
   Caption = currentPolicy![Figure Caption]
   FileSpec = getFileSpec(FileSpecToken)
   Call insertPicture(wordBasic, FileSpec, Caption)
End If

parentToken = currentPolicy!Token
Call FormatPolicies(wordBasic, PolicyType, parentToken, level + 1)

End Sub
```

LoadOutline

The LoadOutline subroutine clears the existing contents of the outline control and populates it with the policies from the database. The first level of the outline control contains the five types of policies. The second level contains the primary (parentless) policies themselves. The ItemData array for the outline control is used to store the token of the policy for easy retrieval when the user selects a policy:

```
Sub LoadOutline ()

Dim DB As database, dbPolicies As Snapshot, sql  As String, index As Integer

PolicyOutline.Clear
Set DB = OpenDatabase(App.Path & "\" & gDBname)

index = 0
PolicyOutline.AddItem "Corporate Policies"
PolicyOutline.Indent(index) = 0

PolicyOutline.AddItem "General"
index = index + 1
PolicyOutline.Indent(index) = 1
sql = "SELECT Token, Name FROM Policies "
sql = sql & "WHERE [Sub-policy of]=0 "
sql = sql & "AND Type=" & Chr$(34) & "General" & Chr$(34)
Set dbPolicies = DB.CreateSnapshot(sql)
Do While Not dbPolicies.EOF
   index = index + 1
   PolicyOutline.AddItem dbPolicies!Name
   PolicyOutline.Indent(index) = 2
   PolicyOutline.ItemData(index) = dbPolicies!Token
   dbPolicies.MoveNext
Loop

PolicyOutline.AddItem "Administrative"
index = index + 1
PolicyOutline.Indent(index) = 1
sql = "SELECT Token, Name FROM Policies "
sql = sql & "WHERE [Sub-policy of]=0 "
sql = sql & "AND Type=" & Chr$(34) & "Administrative" & Chr$(34)
Set dbPolicies = DB.CreateSnapshot(sql)
Do While Not dbPolicies.EOF
   index = index + 1
   PolicyOutline.AddItem dbPolicies!Name
   PolicyOutline.Indent(index) = 2
   PolicyOutline.ItemData(index) = dbPolicies!Token
   dbPolicies.MoveNext
Loop

PolicyOutline.AddItem "Reporting"
index = index + 1
PolicyOutline.Indent(index) = 1
sql = "SELECT Token, Name FROM Policies "
sql = sql & "WHERE [Sub-policy of]=0 "
sql = sql & "AND Type=" & Chr$(34) & "Reporting" & Chr$(34)
Set dbPolicies = DB.CreateSnapshot(sql)
Do While Not dbPolicies.EOF
   index = index + 1
   PolicyOutline.AddItem dbPolicies!Name
   PolicyOutline.Indent(index) = 2
   PolicyOutline.ItemData(index) = dbPolicies!Token
   dbPolicies.MoveNext
Loop
```

```
PolicyOutline.AddItem "Computer Hardware & Software"
index = index + 1
PolicyOutline.Indent(index) = 1
sql = "SELECT Token, Name FROM Policies "
sql = sql & "WHERE [Sub-policy of]=0 "
sql = sql & "AND Type=" & Chr$(34) & "Computer Hardware & Software" & Chr$(34)
Set dbPolicies = DB.CreateSnapshot(sql)
Do While Not dbPolicies.EOF
    index = index + 1
    PolicyOutline.AddItem dbPolicies!Name
    PolicyOutline.Indent(index) = 2
    PolicyOutline.ItemData(index) = dbPolicies!Token
    dbPolicies.MoveNext
Loop

PolicyOutline.AddItem "Internal Controls"
index = index + 1
PolicyOutline.Indent(index) = 1
sql = "SELECT Token, Name FROM Policies "
sql = sql & "WHERE [Sub-policy of]=0 "
sql = sql & "AND Type=" & Chr$(34) & "Internal Controls" & Chr$(34)
Set dbPolicies = DB.CreateSnapshot(sql)
Do While Not dbPolicies.EOF
    index = index + 1
    PolicyOutline.AddItem dbPolicies!Name
    PolicyOutline.Indent(index) = 2
    PolicyOutline.ItemData(index) = dbPolicies!Token
    dbPolicies.MoveNext
Loop

End Sub
```

PolicyOutline_Click

The PolicyOutline_Click method is used to enable those controls (for example, DeletePolicy and EditPolicy) that should function only when a policy is selected. The AddPolicy control should be enabled only when a policy type is selected:

```
Sub PolicyOutline_Click ()
    If PolicyOutline.Indent(PolicyOutline.ListIndex) = 1 Then
        AddPolicy.Enabled = True
    Else
        AddPolicy.Enabled = False
    End If
    If PolicyOutline.Indent(PolicyOutline.ListIndex) = 2 Then
        DeletePolicy.Enabled = True
        EditPolicy.Enabled = True
    Else
        DeletePolicy.Enabled = False
        EditPolicy.Enabled = False
    End If

End Sub
```

PolicyOutline_DblClick

The subroutine `PolicyOutline_DblClick` is used to make a double-click on the outline control equivalent to selecting a policy and activating the `EditPolicy` control:

```
Sub PolicyOutline_DblClick ()
    If EditPolicy.Enabled Then
        Call EditPolicy_Click
    End If
End Sub
```

RefreshOutline_Click

The `RefreshOutline_Click` subroutine is never activated directly by the user because the `RefreshOutline` control is not visible. This control is used by the AddPolicy form to refresh the outline control before the AddPolicy form is unloaded:

```
Sub RefreshOutline_Click ()
    Call LoadOutline
End Sub
```

The AddPolicy Form

The AddPolicy form enables the user to create a new policy or subpolicy.

Cancel_Click

The method `Cancel_Click` simply unloads the `AddPolicy` form without creating a policy:

```
Sub Cancel_Click ()
    Unload Me
End Sub
```

EnableOK

The `EnableOK` subroutine enables the OK button, provided some text has been entered for the policy name and a policy type has been selected:

```
Sub EnableOK ()

ok.Enabled = False
If Len(PolicyName.Text) > 0 Then
    If TypeList.ListIndex >= 0 Then
        ok.Enabled = True
    End If
End If

End Sub
```

Form_Load

The `Form_Load` method adds the policy types to the TypeList control so that the user can select one of them:

```
Sub Form_Load ()

TypeList.AddItem "General"
TypeList.AddItem "Administrative"
TypeList.AddItem "Reporting"
TypeList.AddItem "Computer Hardware & Software"
TypeList.AddItem "Internal Controls"

End Sub
```

OK_Click

The `OK_Click` method inserts the new policy into the Policy table with the user-selected type. It then activates the refresh button on the PolicyOutline form to refresh the outline control on that form. If a policy with the same name already exists, the creation is not performed and the user is prompted to enter a unique policy name:

```
Sub OK_Click ()

Dim db As database, dbPolicies As dynaset, sql  As String, index As Integer

Set db = OpenDatabase(APP.Path & "\" & gDBname)
Set dbPolicies = db.CreateDynaset("Policies")
dbPolicies.FindFirst "Name=" & Chr$(34) & Trim$(PolicyName.Text) & Chr$(34)
If dbPolicies.NoMatch Then
   dbPolicies.AddNew
      dbPolicies!Name = Trim$(PolicyName.Text)
      dbPolicies!Type = TypeList.List(TypeList.ListIndex)
      dbPolicies![Sub-policy of] = gPolicyToken
   dbPolicies.Update
Else
   MsgBox "A policy with the name '" & PolicyName.Text
      & "' already exists. Enter a different name."
End If
PoliciesOutline.RefreshOutline.Value = True
Unload Me

End Sub
```

PolicyName_Change and TypeList_Click

The methods `PolicyName_Change` and `TypeList_Click` call `EnableOK` to see if the OK button should be enabled:

```
Sub PolicyName_Change ()
   Call EnableOK
End Sub
```

```
Sub TypeList_Click ()
   Call EnableOK
End Sub
```

PolicyEditor Form

The PolicyEditor form displays the current properties and associations of a policy and enables the user to edit them.

ApplOptions_Click

The `ApplOptions_Click` method enables the Browse and MailTo controls if an application radio button other than *none* is selected. The none radio button has an index property value of 5:

```
Sub ApplOptions_Click (index As Integer, Value As Integer)

If index >= 0 And index <= 4 Then
   Browse.Enabled = True
   MailTo.Enabled = True
Else
   Browse.Enabled = False
   MailTo.Enabled = False
End If

End Sub
```

Browse_Click

The `Browse_Click` method uses the common dialog control, BrowseDialog, to enable users to select a template file of the appropriate type for the application they have selected:

```
Sub Browse_Click ()

Dim index As Integer

BrowseDialog.CancelError = True
For index = 0 To 3
   If ApplOptions(index).Value Then
      Exit For
   End If
Next index
Select Case index
   Case 1 ' Access
      BrowseDialog.DefaultExt = ".MDB"
      BrowseDialog.DialogTitle = "Select Access Database"
      BrowseDialog.Filter = "*.MDB"
      BrowseDialog.Filename = "*.MDB"
   Case 2' Excel
      BrowseDialog.DefaultExt = ".XLS"
      BrowseDialog.DialogTitle = "Select Excel File"
      BrowseDialog.Filter = "*.XLS"
      BrowseDialog.Filename = "*.XLS"
```

```
    Case 3 ' Powerpoint
        BrowseDialog.DefaultExt = ".PPT"
        BrowseDialog.DialogTitle = "Select Powerpoint File"
        BrowseDialog.Filter = "*.PPT"
        BrowseDialog.Filename = "*.PPT"
    Case 4 ' Word
        BrowseDialog.DefaultExt = ".DOC"
        BrowseDialog.DialogTitle = "Select Word Document"
        BrowseDialog.Filter = "*.DOC"
        BrowseDialog.Filename = "*.DOC"
End Select
BrowseDialog.InitDir = App.Path
BrowseDialog.Flags = OFN_FILEMUSTEXIST Or OFN_HIDEREADONLY Or OFN_PATHMUSTEXIST
On Error GoTo Browse_Click_Cancel
BrowseDialog.Action = 1
TemplateFile.Text = BrowseDialog.Filename
TemplateFile.Tag = BrowseDialog.Filetitle

Exit Sub

Browse_Click_Cancel:
If Err = CDERR_CANCEL Then
    Exit Sub
Else
    MsgBox Error$(Err)
End If

End Sub
```

Cancel_Click

The Cancel_Click method unloads the form without updating the policy:

```
Sub Cancel_Click ()
    Unload Me
End Sub
```

EditDescription_Click, EditPurpose_Click, and EditResponsibility_Click

The EditDescription_Click, EditPurpose_Click, and EditResponsibility_Click methods enable the user to edit the appropriate text for the policy using an embedded Word OLE control. First, the file specification for the RTF file containing the text is retrieved from the database. The subroutine getRTFfile is then called to set up the Word OLE control:

```
Sub EditDescription_Click ()

Dim i As Integer, FileSpecToken  As Long, parentToken As Long
Dim FileLocToken As Long
Dim fileSpec As String, FileNum, dbPolicy As dynaset, db As database

Set db = OpenDatabase(App.Path & "\" & gDBname)
Set dbPolicy = db.CreateDynaset("Policies")
dbPolicy.FindFirst "Token=" & Val(Me.Tag)
```

```
FileLocToken = IIf(IsNull(dbPolicy!Description), 0, dbPolicy!Description)
If FileLocToken > 0 Then
   fileSpec = getFileSpec(FileLocToken)
   If fileSpec = "" Then
      fileSpec = App.Path & "\POLCYSRC\" _
                 & "D" & Format$(dbPolicy!Token, "0000000") & ".RTF"
   End If
Else
   fileSpec = App.Path & "\POLCYSRC\" _
            & "D" & Format$(dbPolicy!Token, "0000000") & ".RTF"
   FileLocToken = setFileSpec(fileSpec)
   dbPolicy.Edit
   dbPolicy!Description = FileLocToken
   dbPolicy.Update
   dbPolicy.Close
End If

Call getRTFfile(fileSpec)

End Sub


Sub EditPurpose_Click ()
Dim FileLocToken As Long, dbPolicy As dynaset, db As database
Dim fileSpec As String

Set db = OpenDatabase(App.Path & "\" & gDBname)
Set dbPolicy = db.CreateDynaset("Policies")
dbPolicy.FindFirst "Token=" & Val(Me.Tag)

FileLocToken = IIf(IsNull(dbPolicy!Purpose), 0, dbPolicy!Purpose)
If FileLocToken > 0 Then
   fileSpec = getFileSpec(FileLocToken)
   If fileSpec = "" Then
      fileSpec = App.Path & "\POLCYSRC\" _
                 & Format$(dbPolicy!Token, "P0000000") & ".RTF"
   End If
Else
   fileSpec = App.Path & "\POLCYSRC\" _
            & Format$(dbPolicy!Token, "P0000000") & ".RTF"
   FileLocToken = setFileSpec(fileSpec)
   dbPolicy.Edit
   dbPolicy!Purpose = FileLocToken
   dbPolicy.Update
   dbPolicy.Close
End If

Call getRTFfile(fileSpec)

End Sub

Sub EditResponsibility_Click ()
Dim i As Integer, FileSpecToken  As Long
Dim parentToken As Long, FileLocToken As Long
Dim fileSpec As String, FileNum, dbPolicy As dynaset, db As database

Set db = OpenDatabase(App.Path & "\" & gDBname)
Set dbPolicy = db.CreateDynaset("Policies")
dbPolicy.FindFirst "Token=" & Val(Me.Tag)
```

```
FileLocToken = IIf(IsNull(dbPolicy!Responsibility), 0, dbPolicy!Responsibility)
If FileLocToken > 0 Then
    fileSpec = getFileSpec(FileLocToken)
    If fileSpec = "" Then
        fileSpec = App.Path & "\POLCYSRC\"
                        & Format$(dbPolicy!Token, "\R0000000") & ".RTF"
    End If
Else
    fileSpec = App.Path & "\POLCYSRC\"
                    & Format$(dbPolicy!Token, "\R0000000") & ".RTF"
    FileLocToken = setFileSpec(fileSpec)
    dbPolicy.Edit
    dbPolicy!Responsibility = FileLocToken
    dbPolicy.Update
End If

Call getRTFfile(fileSpec)

End Sub
```

FigureEmbed_Click

The `FigureEmbed_Click` method uses the common dialog control, EmbedDialog, to enable users to select a graphic file (BMP or SHG) to be included in the topic for this policy:

```
Sub FigureEmbed_Click ()

Dim index As Integer

FigureFile.Text = ""
EmbedDialog.CancelError = True
EmbedDialog.DefaultExt = ".BMP"
EmbedDialog.DialogTitle = "Select Access Database"
EmbedDialog.Filter = "*.BMP¦*.SHG"
EmbedDialog.Filename = "*.BMP"
EmbedDialog.InitDir = App.Path
EmbedDialog.Flags = OFN_FILEMUSTEXIST Or OFN_HIDEREADONLY Or OFN_PATHMUSTEXIST
On Error GoTo FigureEmbed_Click_Cancel
EmbedDialog.Action = 1
On Error GoTo 0
FigureFile.Text = EmbedDialog.Filename
FigureFile.Tag = EmbedDialog.Filetitle
CaptionText.Enabled = True

Exit Sub

FigureEmbed_Click_Cancel:
If Err = CDERR_CANCEL Then
    Exit Sub
Else
    MsgBox Error$(Err)
    Exit Sub
End If

End Sub
```

Form_Load

The Form_Load subroutine populates the various combo box controls with the appropriate data from the database and then calls the subroutine getPolicy to populate the controls with the actual values for the current policy:

```
Sub Form_Load ()

Dim dbPolicies As Snapshot, gDB As database, dbPolicyMakers As Snapshot
Dim sql As String, dbOrgUnit As Snapshot, dbPositions As Snapshot

Set gDB = OpenDatabase(App.Path & "\" & gDBname)

sql = "SELECT  Positions.Token as Token, Positions.Title,
         Personnel.[First Name], Personnel.[Last Name] "
sql = sql & "FROM Positions INNER JOIN Personnel
      ON Positions.[Performed by] = Personnel.[Employee ID] "
Debug.Print sql
Set dbPolicyMakers = gDB.CreateSnapshot(sql)
Do While Not dbPolicyMakers.EOF
   AuthorizedBy.AddItem dbPolicyMakers![First Name]
                        & " " & dbPolicyMakers![Last Name]
   AuthorizedBy.ItemData(AuthorizedBy.NewIndex) = dbPolicyMakers!Token
   PolicyInquiry.AddItem dbPolicyMakers!Title
   PolicyInquiry.ItemData(PolicyInquiry.NewIndex) = dbPolicyMakers!Token
   dbPolicyMakers.MoveNext
Loop

Set dbOrgUnit = gDB.CreateSnapshot("Organizational Units")
Do While Not dbOrgUnit.EOF
   ResponsibilityOf.AddItem dbOrgUnit!Name
   ResponsibilityOf.ItemData(ResponsibilityOf.NewIndex) = dbOrgUnit!Token
   dbOrgUnit.MoveNext
Loop

sql = "SELECT  Positions.Token as Token, Positions.Title,
             Personnel.[First Name], Personnel.[Last Name] "
sql = sql & "FROM Positions INNER JOIN Personnel
             ON Positions.[Performed by] = Personnel.[Employee ID] "
Set dbPositions = gDB.CreateSnapshot(sql)

Set dbPositions = gDB.CreateSnapshot(sql)
Do While Not dbPositions.EOF
   MailTo.AddItem dbPositions!Title & " "
              & dbPositions![First Name] & " " & dbPositions![Last Name]
   MailTo.ItemData(MailTo.NewIndex) = dbPositions!Token
   dbPositions.MoveNext
Loop

TypeList.AddItem "General"
TypeList.AddItem "Administrative"
TypeList.AddItem "Reporting"
TypeList.AddItem "Computer Hardware & Software"
TypeList.AddItem "Internal Controls"
```

```
Set dbPolicies = gDB.CreateSnapshot("Policies")
dbPolicies.FindFirst "Token=" & gPolicyToken
If Not dbPolicies.NoMatch Then
   Tag = dbPolicies!Token
   Call getPolicy(dbPolicies)
   PolicyName.Text = dbPolicies!Name
End If

End Sub
```

getPolicy

The getPolicy subroutine sets the controls to display the correct values for the current policy:

```
Sub getPolicy (dbPolicy As Snapshot)
'
Dim i As Integer, FileSpecToken  As Long
Dim  parentToken As Long, FileLocToken As Long
Dim fileSpec As String, FileNum, dbPolicy2 As dynaset, db As database

For i = 0 To TypeList.ListCount - 1
   If TypeList.List(i) = dbPolicy!Type Then
      TypeList.ListIndex = i
      Exit For
   End If
Next i
If i = TypeList.ListCount Then
   TypeList.ListIndex = -1
End If

EffectiveDate.Text = Format$(IIf(IsNull(dbPolicy![Effective Date]),
                     "__/__/__",
                        dbPolicy![Effective Date]), "mm/dd/yy")

AuthorizedBy.Text = IIf(IsNull(dbPolicy![Originally Approved By]),
                   "", dbPolicy![Originally Approved By])

For i = 0 To PolicyInquiry.ListCount - 1
   If PolicyInquiry.ItemData(i) = dbPolicy![Policy Enquiries To] Then
      PolicyInquiry.ListIndex = i
      Exit For
   End If
Next i
If i = PolicyInquiry.ListCount Then
   PolicyInquiry.ListIndex = -1
End If

For i = 0 To ResponsibilityOf.ListCount - 1
   If ResponsibilityOf.ItemData(i) = dbPolicy![Responsiblity Of] Then
      ResponsibilityOf.ListIndex = i
      Exit For
   End If
Next i
If i = ResponsibilityOf.ListCount Then
   ResponsibilityOf.ListIndex = -1
End If
```

```
If dbPolicy![Application Type] >= 1 Then
   If dbPolicy![Application Type] <= 4 Then
      ApplOptions(dbPolicy![Application Type]) = True
      FileSpecToken = dbPolicy![Uses Template]
      TemplateFile.Text = getFileSpec(FileSpecToken)
      For i = 0 To MailTo.ListCount - 1
      If MailTo.ItemData(i) = dbPolicy![Processed By] Then
         MailTo.ListIndex = i
         Exit For
      End If
      Next i
      If i = MailTo.ListCount Then
      MailTo.ListIndex = -1
      End If
   Else
      ApplOptions(0) = True
      TemplateFile.Text = ""
      MailTo.ListIndex = -1
   End If
Else
   ApplOptions(0) = True
   TemplateFile.Text = ""
   MailTo.ListIndex = -1
End If

parentToken = dbPolicy!Token
Call refreshSubPolicies(parentToken)

CaptionText.Text = IIf(IsNull(dbPolicy![Figure Caption]),
                       "", dbPolicy![Figure Caption])
If Not IsNull(dbPolicy![Figure Caption]) Then
   CaptionText.Enabled = True
Else
   CaptionText.Enabled = False
End If
FileLocToken = IIf(IsNull(dbPolicy!Figure), -1, dbPolicy!Figure)
FigureFile.Text = getFileSpec(FileLocToken)

End Sub
```

getRTFfile

The subroutine getRTFfile retrieves an RTF file and displays it in the Word OLE control. First, the WordOLE and its associated controls are made visible to the user and are moved in front of, and thereby effectively hiding, the existing controls. The RTF file is then opened and read sequentially into an array. This array is used to build a string that is passed to the OLE control through the DataText property after the Format of the OLE control is set to Rich Text Format. This allows the embedded OLE control to display the contents of the file for editing:

```
Sub getRTFfile (fileSpec As String)

Dim Fnum As Integer, i As Integer, RTFtext() As String, RTF As String
WordOLE.Visible = True
WordOLE.ZOrder
WordOLEbuttons.Visible = True
```

```
WordOLEbuttons.ZOrder
EmbedFigPanel.Visible = True
EmbedFigPanel.ZOrder

If Dir$(fileSpec) = "" Then ' file does not exist
    FileCopy App.Path & "\POLCYSRC\" & "EMPTY.RTF", fileSpec
End If

Fnum = FreeFile
Open fileSpec For Input As Fnum
i = 0
Do While Not EOF(Fnum)
    i = i + 1
    ReDim Preserve RTFtext(i)
    Input #Fnum, RTFtext(i)
Loop
Close #Fnum

WordOLE.Verb = -1
WordOLE.Action = 7 ' activate

WordOLE.Format = "Rich Text Format"
WordOLE.Tag = fileSpec

RTF = ""
For i = 1 To UBound(RTFtext)
    RTF = RTF & RTFtext(i)
Next i
WordOLE.DataText = RTF
WordOLE.Action = 6 ' update

End Sub
```

OK_Click

The OK_Click method calls the subroutine setPolicy to update the database and then unload the form:

```
Sub OK_Click ()
  Call setPolicy
  Unload Me
End Sub
```

refreshSubPolicies

The refreshSubPolicies subroutine clears the list of subpolicies and repopulates it from the database. This routine is used to refresh the subpolicies list after a subpolicy is added:

```
Sub refreshSubPolicies (parentToken As Long)

Dim db As database, sql As String, dbSubPolicies As Snapshot

Set db = OpenDatabase(App.Path & "\" & gDBname)
```

```
SubPolicies.Clear
sql = "SELECT DISTINCTROW Name, Token FROM Policies "
sql = sql & "WHERE [Sub-policy of]=" & parentToken
Set dbSubPolicies = db.CreateSnapshot(sql)
Do While Not dbSubPolicies.EOF
   SubPolicies.AddItem dbSubPolicies!Name
   SubPolicies.ItemData(SubPolicies.NewIndex) = dbSubPolicies!Token
   dbSubPolicies.MoveNext
Loop

End Sub
```

setFileSpec

The setFileSpec function creates entries in the File Locations, Paths, and Files tables for a file specification (if these entries are necessary). It returns the token from the File Locations table that it has created or found:

```
Function setFileSpec (fileSpec As String) As Long

Dim gDB As database, dbFiles As dynaset, dbPaths As dynaset, dbLocs As dynaset
Dim Path As String, Filename As String, i As Integer

   For i = Len(fileSpec) To 1 Step -1
      If Mid$(fileSpec, i, 1) = "\" Then
      Exit For
      End If
   Next i
   Path = Left$(fileSpec, i - 1)
   Filename = Right$(fileSpec, Len(fileSpec) - i)
   Set gDB = OpenDatabase(App.Path & "\" & gDBname)
   Set dbFiles = gDB.CreateDynaset("Files")
   dbFiles.FindFirst "File=" & Chr$(34) & Filename & Chr$(34)
   If dbFiles.NoMatch Then
      dbFiles.AddNew
      dbFiles!File = Filename
      dbFiles.Update
      dbFiles.FindFirst "File=" & Chr$(34) & Filename & Chr$(34)
   End If
   Set dbPaths = gDB.CreateDynaset("Paths")
   dbPaths.FindFirst "Path=" & Chr$(34) & Path & Chr$(34)
   If dbPaths.NoMatch Then
      dbPaths.AddNew
      dbPaths!Path = Path
      dbPaths.Update
      dbPaths.FindFirst "Path=" & Chr$(34) & Path & Chr$(34)
   End If
   Set dbLocs = gDB.CreateDynaset("File Locations")
   dbLocs.FindFirst "[Path Token]=" & dbPaths!Token
                    & " AND [File Token]=" & dbFiles!Token
   If dbLocs.NoMatch Then
      dbLocs.AddNew
      dbLocs![Path Token] = dbPaths!Token
      dbLocs![File Token] = dbFiles!Token
      dbLocs.Update
```

```
            dbLocs.FindFirst "[Path Token]=" & dbPaths!Token
                            & " AND [File Token]=" & dbFiles!Token
        End If
        setFileSpec = dbLocs!Token

End Function
```

setPolicy

The setPolicy subroutine updates the database with any changes that the user has made to the policy:

```
Sub setPolicy ()

Dim i As Integer, fileSpec As String, gDB As database, dbPolicy As dynaset
Dim FileNum, FileLocToken As Long

Set gDB = OpenDatabase(App.Path & "\" & gDBname)
Set dbPolicy = gDB.CreateDynaset("Policies")
dbPolicy.FindFirst "Token=" & Val(Tag)
If Not dbPolicy.NoMatch Then
    dbPolicy.Edit
        dbPolicy!Name = Trim$(PolicyName.Text)

        If TypeList.ListIndex >= 0 Then
        dbPolicy!Type = TypeList.List(TypeList.ListIndex)
        Else
        dbPolicy!Type = ""
        End If

        If Len(EffectiveDate.Text) > 0 Then
        dbPolicy![Effective Date] = IIf(Format$(EffectiveDate, "mm/dd/yy")
                                    = "__/__/__",
                                 "",
                                    Format$(EffectiveDate, "mm/dd/yy"))
        Else
        dbPolicy![Effective Date] = ""
        End If

        dbPolicy![Originally Approved By] = Trim$(AuthorizedBy.Text)

        If PolicyInquiry.ListIndex >= 0 Then
        dbPolicy![Policy Enquiries To] =
            PolicyInquiry.ItemData(PolicyInquiry.ListIndex)
        Else
        dbPolicy![Policy Enquiries To] = 0
        End If

        If ResponsibilityOf.ListIndex >= 0 Then
        dbPolicy![Responsiblity Of] =
            ResponsibilityOf.ItemData(ResponsibilityOf.ListIndex)
        Else
        dbPolicy![Responsiblity Of] = 0
        End If
```

```
      If MailTo.ListIndex >= 0 Then
      dbPolicy![Processed By] = MailTo.ItemData(MailTo.ListIndex)
      Else
      dbPolicy![Processed By] = 0
      End If

      For i = 1 To 4
      If ApplOptions(i) Then
         Exit For
      End If
      Next i
      If i > 4 Then
      dbPolicy![Application Type] = 0
      dbPolicy![Processed By] = 0
      dbPolicy![Uses Template] = 0
      Else
      dbPolicy![Application Type] = i
      If MailTo.ListIndex >= 0 Then
         dbPolicy![Processed By] = MailTo.ItemData(MailTo.ListIndex)
      Else
         dbPolicy![Processed By] = 0
      End If
      dbPolicy![Application Caption] = ApplHotSpot.Text
      fileSpec = TemplateFile.Text
      dbPolicy![Uses Template] = setFileSpec(fileSpec)
      End If
   dbPolicy.Update
End If

End Sub
```

SubPolicies_Click

The `SubPolicies_Click` method enables the SubpolicyEdit and SubpolicyRemove controls if a subpolicy has been selected; otherwise, it disables them:

```
Sub SubPolicies_Click ()

If SubPolicies.ListIndex >= 0 Then
   SubpolicyEdit.Enabled = True
   SubpolicyRemove.Enabled = True
Else
   SubpolicyEdit.Enabled = False
   SubpolicyRemove.Enabled = False
End If

End Sub
```

SubpolicyAdd_Click

The `SubpolicyAdd_Click` method sets `gPolicyToken` to the current `Policy` token, saved in the Tag property for the form, and modally shows the AddPolicyForm form. Upon returning from the AddPolicyForm form, the `subPolicy` list is refreshed by calling the subroutine `refreshSubPolicies`:

```
Sub SubpolicyAdd_Click ()
    gPolicyToken = Val(Tag)
    AddPolicyForm.Show 1
    Call refreshSubPolicies(Val(Tag))
End Sub
```

SubpolicyEdit_Click

The `SubpolicyEdit_Click` method recursively calls `subPolicyForm` to edit subpolicies:

```
Sub SubpolicyEdit_Click ()

Dim subPolicyForm As New PolicyEditor

gPolicyToken = SubPolicies.ItemData(SubPolicies.ListIndex)
subPolicyForm.Show 1

End Sub
```

SubpolicyRemove_Click

The `SubpolicyRemove_Click` method removes the selected subpolicy and its children:

```
Sub SubpolicyRemove_Click ()

Dim db As database, dbPolicies As dynaset, parentToken As Long

Set db = OpenDatabase(App.Path & "\" & gDBname)
Set dbPolicies = db.CreateDynaset("Policies")
dbPolicies.FindFirst "Token=" & SubPolicies.ItemData(SubPolicies.ListIndex)
If Not dbPolicies.NoMatch Then
    dbPolicies.Delete
End If
parentToken = SubPolicies.ItemData(SubPolicies.ListIndex)
Call deleteChildren(parentToken)

SubPolicies.RemoveItem (SubPolicies.ListIndex)

End Sub
```

WordOLEcancel_Click

The `WordOLEcancel_Click` method restores the original policy-editing view of the form without updating the RTF file:

```
Sub WordOLEcancel_Click ()

WordOLE.Action = 9
WordOLE.Visible = False
WordOLEbuttons.Visible = False
EmbedFigPanel.Visible = False

End Sub
```

WordOLEok_Click

The WordOLEok_Click method restores the original policy-editing view of the form after updating the RTF file. The RTF file is updated by deleting the old file, retrieving the DataText property from the Word OLE object, and performing a binary write of this data to a new RTF file. If a figure has been specified for this policy, the database is updated with the figure caption and file location token:

```
Sub WordOLEok_Click ()

Dim Fnum As Integer, RTF As String, gDB As database, dbPolicy As dynaset
Dim fileSpec As String

If Dir$(WordOLE.Tag) <> "" Then ' file does  exist
    Kill WordOLE.Tag
End If

Fnum = FreeFile
Open WordOLE.Tag For Binary As Fnum
WordOLE.Action = 6 ' update
RTF = WordOLE.DataText
Put #Fnum, , RTF
Close #Fnum

If FigureFile.Text <> "" Then
    Set gDB = OpenDatabase(App.Path & "\" & gDBname)
    Set dbPolicy = gDB.CreateDynaset("Policies")
    dbPolicy.FindFirst "Token=" & gPolicyToken
    If Not dbPolicy.NoMatch Then
        dbPolicy.Edit
        dbPolicy![Figure Caption] = Trim$(CaptionText.Text)
        fileSpec = FigureFile.Text
        dbPolicy!Figure = setFileSpec(fileSpec)
        dbPolicy.Update
    End If
End If

WordOLE.Action = 9
WordOLE.Visible = False
WordOLEbuttons.Visible = False
EmbedFigPanel.Visible = False

End Sub
```

Application Dispatcher

The Application Dispatcher is contained in the project file 57MOU.MAK, which includes a single file 57MOU.BAS. This program executes a Microsoft Office product with a file provided as an argument on the command line.

Module Declarations

The following function declarations allow the Windows 3.1 API calls to be made from Visual Basic. The global constants represent values that are returned or sent to these functions. The global variable is used to hold the arguments passed to this program:

```
Declare Function RegOpenKey& Lib "SHELL.DLL"
   (ByVal hKey&, ByVal lpszSubKey$, lphKey&)
Declare Function RegCreateKey& Lib "SHELL.DLL"
   (ByVal hKey&, ByVal lpszSubKey$, lphKey&)
Declare Function RegQueryValue& Lib "SHELL.DLL"
   (ByVal hKey&, ByVal lpszSubKey$, ByVal lpszValue$, nSize&)
Declare Function RegEnumKey& Lib "SHELL.DLL"
   (ByVal hKey&, ByVal iSubKey&, ByVal lpReturnedString$, ByVal nSize&)
Declare Function RegSetValue& Lib "SHELL.DLL"
   (ByVal hKey&, ByVal lpszSubKey$, ByVal fdwType&,
    ByVal lpszValue$, ByVal dwLength&)
Declare Function RegDeleteKey& Lib "SHELL.DLL" (ByVal hKey&, ByVal lpszSubKey$)
Declare Function RegCloseKey& Lib "SHELL.DLL" (ByVal hKey&)
Declare Function lstrcpy Lib "Kernel"
   (ByVal lpString1 As Any, ByVal lpString2 As Any) As Long

Global Const HKEY_CLASSES_ROOT = 1
Global Const MAX_PATH = 256
Global Const REG_SZ = 1

' return codes from Registration functions
Global Const ERROR_SUCCESS = 0&
Global Const ERROR_BADDB = 1&
Global Const ERROR_BADKEY = 2&
Global Const ERROR_CANTOPEN = 3&
Global Const ERROR_CANTREAD = 4&
Global Const ERROR_CANTWRITE = 5&
Global Const ERROR_OUTOFMEMORY = 6&
Global Const ERROR_INVALID_PARAMETER = 7&
Global Const ERROR_ACCESS_DENIED = 8&
Global CommandLine As String
```

GetProgramPath

The function `GetProgramPath` queries the registration database for the shell/open/command key for the parameter `programKey`. It returns the fully qualified path of the executable program or a null string if it was not found. The function `RegQueryValue` must be called twice to get the proper return value:

```
Function GetProgramPath (programKey As String) As String

    Dim sSubKey As String * MAX_PATH, temp As String
    Dim sValue As String * MAX_PATH, ret As Long
    Dim BuffLen As Long, BuffLen2 As Long, hkSFE As Long, server As String
    Dim i As Integer

GetProgramPath = ""
BuffLen& = CLng(MAX_PATH)
```

```
sSubKey = String(MAX_PATH, " ")
sValue = String(MAX_PATH, " ")
If RegOpenKey(HKEY_CLASSES_ROOT, programKey, hkSFE&) = 0 Then
    If RegQueryValue(hkSFE&, "CurVer", sSubKey, BuffLen&) = 0 Then
        server = Left$(sSubKey, BuffLen& - 1)
        If RegOpenKey(HKEY_CLASSES_ROOT, server, hkSFE&) = 0 Then
            If RegQueryValue(hkSFE&, "shell\open\command",
                                sValue, BuffLen2&) = 0 Then
                ret& = RegQueryValue(hkSFE&, "shell\open\command",
                                    sValue, BuffLen2&)
                GetProgramPath = Left$(sValue, InStr(sValue, " ") - 1)
            End If
        End If
    End If
End If

End Function
```

Main

The Main subroutine parses the command string to separate the registration database key from the template filename. The function GetProgramPath is then called to retrieve the correct path for the executable. Finally, the shell command is used to launch the application with the template file:

```
Sub Main ()

Dim programKey As String, args As String, spacePtr As Integer
Dim exe As String, x

spacePtr = InStr(Command, " ")
If spacePtr > 0 Then
    programKey = Trim$(Left$(Command, spacePtr - 1))
    args = Trim$(Right$(Command, Len(Command) - spacePtr))
    Select Case LCase(programKey)
        Case "access.database"
            exe = GetProgramPath(programKey)
        Case "excel.sheet"
            exe = GetProgramPath(programKey)
        Case "powerpoint.show"
            exe = GetProgramPath(programKey)
        Case "word.document"
            exe = GetProgramPath(programKey)
    End Select
    x = Shell(Trim$(exe & " " & args), 1)
End If

End Sub
```

Summary

The design and implementation presented in this chapter represent one possible solution to the business problem: automating business infrastructures. Other solutions are possible using the same or different products in the Office tool suite. The implementation described in this chapter has several limitations that could be improved. They include the following items:

- Automatic updating of the help project file with the correct source RTF filename
- Automatic generation of the actual help file, not just the help source file
- Increased user control in the formatting of the policy topics (at the risk of a more complex user interface)
- Improved exception handling
- A setup disk and program developed for distribution of the generator to users who do not have VB installed on their machines

INDEX

SYMBOLS

Graph 1177

Index

Graph

1178

UNLEASHED

X-Y-Z

Add to Your Sams Library Today with the Best Books for Programming, Operating Systems, and New Technologies

The easiest way to order is to pick up the phone and call

1-800-428-5331

between 9:00 a.m. and 5:00 p.m. EST.
For faster service please have your credit card available.

ISBN	Quantity	Description of Item	Unit Cost	Total Cost
0-672-30474-0		Windows 95 Unleashed (book/CD-ROM)	$39.99	
0-672-30531-3		Teach Yourself Windows 95 Programming in 21 Days, Second Edition	$35.00	
0-672-30706-5		Programming Microsoft Office (book/CD-ROM)	$49.99	
0-672-30647-6		Microsoft Office Developer's Guide (book/disk)	$45.00	
0-672-30596-8		Develop a Professional Visual Basic Application in 21 Days (book/CD-ROM)	$35.00	
0-672-30620-4		Teach Yourself Visual Basic 4 in 21 Days, Third Edition	$35.00	
0-672-30771-5		Essential Visual Basic 4	$25.00	
0-672-30869-X		Essential Access 95	$25.00	
0-672-30792-8		Teach Yourself Access 95 in 14 Days, 3E	$25.00	
0-672-30752-9		Electronic Publishing Unleashed (book/CD-ROM)	$49.99	
0-672-30612-3		The Magic of Computer Graphics (book/CD-ROM)	$45.00	
0-672-30865-7		Virtual Reality Madness! 1996 (book/3 CD-ROMs)	$49.99	
0-672-30456-2		The Magic of Interactive Entertainment (book/CD-ROM)	$39.95	
0-672-30785-5		Access 95 Unleashed (book/CD-ROM)	$39.99	
0-672-30739-1		Excel for Windows 95 Unleashed (book/CD-ROM)	$39.99	
0-672-30855-X		Teach Yourself SQL in 14 Days	$29.99	
❑ 3 ½" Disk		Shipping and Handling: See information below.		
❑ 5 ¼" Disk		TOTAL		

Shipping and Handling: $4.00 for the first book, and $1.75 for each additional book. Floppy disk: add $1.75 for shipping and handling. If you need to have it NOW, we can ship product to you in 24 hours for an additional charge of approximately $18.00, and you will receive your item overnight or in two days. Overseas shipping and handling adds $2.00 per book and $8.00 for up to three disks. Prices subject to change. Call for availability and pricing information on latest editions.

201 W. 103rd Street, Indianapolis, Indiana 46290

1-800-428-5331 — Orders   1-800-835-3202 — FAX   1-800-858-7674 — Customer Service

Book ISBN 0-672-30819-3

Installing the CD ROM

The companion CD-ROM contains sample documents, spreadsheets, and databases developed by the authors, plus an assortment of third-party tools and product demos. The disc is designed to be explored using a browser program. Using Sams' Guide to the CD-ROM browser, you can view information regarding products and companies, and install programs with a single click of the mouse. To install the browser, here's what you do:

Windows 3.1 Installation Instructions:

1. Insert the CD-ROM disc into your CD-ROM drive.

2. From File Manager or Program Manager, choose Run from the File menu.

3. Type `<drive>\setup` and press Enter, where `<drive>` corresponds to the drive letter of your CD-ROM. For example, if your CD-ROM is drive D:, type `D:\SETUP` and press Enter.

4. The installation creates a program manager group named Microsoft Office Unleashed. To browse the CD-ROM, double-click the Guide to the CD-ROM icon inside this Program Manager group.

Windows 95 Installation Instructions:

1. Insert the CD-ROM disc into your CD-ROM drive. If the AutoPlay feature of your Windows 95 system is enabled, the setup program will start automatically.

2. If the setup program does not start automatically, double-click the My Computer icon.

3. Double-click the icon representing your CD-ROM drive.

4. Double-click the icon titled Setup.exe to run the installation program. Follow the onscreen instructions that appear. When setup ends, the Guide to the CD-ROM program starts up, so that you can begin browsing immediately.

Following installation, you can restart the Guide to the CD-ROM program by pressing the Start button, selecting Programs, then Microsoft Office Unleashed and Guide to the CD-ROM.

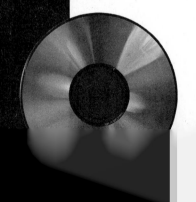

> **NOTE**
>
> The Guide to the CD-ROM program requires at least 256 colors. For best results, set your monitor to display between 256 and 64,000 colors. A screen resolution of 640 × 480 pixels is also recommended. If necessary, adjust your monitor settings before using the CD-ROM.